Home Networking Bible

2nd Edition

Home Networking Bible

2nd Edition

Sue Plumley

WILEY

Wiley Publishing, Inc.

Home Networking Bible, 2nd Edition

Published by
Wiley Publishing, Inc.
10475 Crosspoint Boulevard
Indianapolis, IN 46256
www.wiley.com

Copyright © 2004 by Wiley Publishing, Inc., Indianapolis, Indiana

Published simultaneously in Canada

ISBN: 0-7645-4416-0

Manufactured in the United States of America

10 9 8 7 6 5 4 3 2

2O/QT/QS/QU/IN

For general information on our other products and services or to obtain technical support, please contact our Customer Care Department within the U.S. at (800) 762-2974, outside the U.S. at (317) 572-3993 or fax (317) 572-4002.

Wiley also publishes its books in a variety of electronic formats. Some content that appears in print may not be available in electronic books.

Library of Congress Cataloging-in-Publication Data: 2004100649

WILEY

About the Author

Sue Plumley has owned and operated her own business, Humble Opinions Company, Inc., since 1988. Humble Opinions specializes in network installation, configuration, maintenance, and troubleshooting for a variety of small businesses and corporations. Sue also has taught networking and the use of various software applications at the College of West Virginia and Glenville College in West Virginia. In addition, Sue has written and contributed to more than 75 books about networking and computer software for various publishers.

Credits

Acquisitions Editor
Katie Feltman

Development Editor
Kevin Kent

Production Editor
Angela Smith

Technical Editor
Tom Brays

Copy Editor
Joanne Slike

Editorial Manager
Mary Beth Wakefield

Vice President & Executive Group Publisher
Richard Swadley

Vice President and Executive Publisher
Robert Ipsen

Vice President and Publisher
Joseph B. Wikert

Executive Editorial Director
Mary Bednarek

Project Coordinator
April Farling

Permissions Editor
Carmen Krikorian

Graphics and Production Specialists
Karl Brandt, Lauren Goddard,
Jennifer Heleine, Michael Kruzil,
Kristin McMullan, Lynsey Osborn,
Mary Gillot Virgin

Quality Control Technicians
Andy Hollandbeck, Carl William Pierce,
Dwight Ramsey, Kathy Simpson

Proofreading and Indexing
TECHBOOKS Production Services

I'd like to dedicate this book to Morgan Darrow and Zack Kessler, the newest generation of computer experts!

Preface

Most homes today have at least one PC for accessing the Internet, playing games, or keeping the family finances. Many homes have more than one PC, or the families are considering purchasing another computer for use by a spouse, teenager, and even younger children. If you have two or more PCs in your home, you can network them together to double and even triple the advantages you get from computing.

Home networking can be easy and fun. You can learn about the technologies while setting up your network, and after that, if you like, you can continue to explore the possibilities. Add to your network to make it more useful to you and your family. You can even extend the network to automate one room or your entire home. And it doesn't have to be expensive, either.

Why You Need This Book

If you are considering setting up your own home network, you can use *Home Networking Bible, 2nd Edition,* to guide you through the process. This book helps you plan and prepare for your network, purchase the appropriate equipment and software, install the networking equipment, and make it work with Windows, Macintosh, and even Linux.

From start to finish, you learn everything you need to complete the job without depending on multiple references, vendors, magazine articles, or other sources. Everything you need to know is contained in *Home Networking Bible.*

In addition to terminology and information, you will find helpful advice about choosing the appropriate hardware for your situation, tips on saving money, and more. Included in the text are the names of many manufacturers of home networking products and suggested retail prices for the equipment.

Whether you want to set up a simple network between two computers or you want to run e-mail over your network and attach your network to the Internet, you'll find suggestions on how best to complete the task in *Home Networking Bible.*

If you run your own home-based business, or even a small business office, *Home Networking Bible* helps by giving small business tips to make your venture more useful, efficient, and prosperous.

Who Should Read This Book?

Anyone who owns two or more PCs can use this book to learn how to connect them and get the most from the resulting network. If you want to work on your laptop while your young children run educational software on another computer, this book is for you. If you and your spouse have computer work and are always competing for the printer, this book is for you. If you're a teenager trying to bring your parents into the twenty-first century, *Home Networking Bible* is for you.

You might want to learn how to create Web pages so that you can start your own home business. *Home Networking Bible* shows you how to set up your own home Internet (called an intranet) that you can use for experimentation and learning.

If you own a small business and you want to make it easier for your employees to print and share files, *Home Networking Bible* offers advice on how best to accomplish this goal and more.

You might have both a PC running Windows and a Macintosh and wonder if you can network them. *Home Networking Bible* explains how to do it.

Maybe you want to learn more about the Internet, but your spouse is always online. You can learn how to share an Internet connection, use chat programs over the Internet, and more, by reading *Home Networking Bible*.

If you are a home user or a small business owner looking for information about setting up a small network, *Home Networking Bible* is for you.

What Is the Audience Level for This Book?

Home Networking Bible is written for beginning to intermediate users. You should understand how to use Windows, the Mac, and/or your Linux distribution, as well as basic applications, such as word processing programs, games (if you might use them on your network), or perhaps Internet Explorer. You don't have to be an expert in Windows, however. *Home Networking Bible* explains the steps you follow to install and operate any networking software. It also shows you how to connect the other computers and printers on the network — and then how to use them after you connect them.

In addition, you don't need to be familiar with networking hardware or software. *Home Networking Bible* explains networking terms, technologies, hardware, and software. It also gives you advice on how to purchase, install, and use networking hardware and software.

Beginning users should start at the beginning of the book to get the most out of it. The book builds on previous knowledge, so if you skip the earlier chapters, you might need to go back to read about terms, processes, or procedures.

Intermediate users can use the book as a reference. If you're familiar with networking basics but want to set up e-mail or your own intranet, for example, you can go directly to the relevant chapters to find out how.

What's in This Book?

Home Networking Bible is organized such that simple topics are presented first, with the subjects becoming increasingly complex as you progress through the book. The first parts of the book explain various network types and methods of preparing for setting up your network. The latter parts cover more specific and complex networking topics. Following is a brief description of each part.

+ **Part I, "Making Basic Network Choices,"** helps you decide what type of network you need. It deals with questions such as what programs you want to use, how much money you want to spend, and others to help you plan your network. Part I also includes descriptions of the two network types and discusses their advantages and disadvantages, basic requirements, and other information about them.

✦ **Part II, "Planning and Setting Up Networking—Hardware and Software,"** first discusses topics you need to consider before setting up your network. Next, you learn about various methods of connecting (wiring) your computers together. Part II describes each method and its advantages and disadvantages, gives suggestions for purchasing and installing the wiring, and more. You are introduced to networking terminology and learn about specific products that make setting up the wiring easier. Also included in Part II is information about purchasing and installing other networking hardware necessary for setting up your network. You learn about installing the necessary software and configuring the programs, too. Finally, Part II describes methods of adding non-Windows computers to your network, such as Macintoshes, Linux boxes, and portable computers.

✦ **Part III, "Working with Networked Computers,"** explains how to use Windows, Macs, and Linux boxes over the network. It explains features that enable you to share your files, use printers on networked computers, log on to the network, find other computers on the network, and more. You also learn about managing printing over the network and protecting your files.

✦ **Part IV, "Adding the Internet, E-Mail, and an Intranet,"** explains how to expand your network. It shows how to use one Internet connection for multiple computers and explains the available Internet services. Part IV shows you how to set up e-mail for the Internet and discusses common and popular e-mail applications for the various operating systems. Also included in Part IV is information about setting up your own private Internet, called an intranet, and a discussion of how to approach the technologies that go into making up a Web page.

✦ **Part V, "Working with Files, Folders, and Applications,"** explains how to install and use network applications as well as how to work with files over the network. You learn about various networked applications, such as games and communications programs. Part V also covers backing up files and securing your files from accidents or malicious sabotage.

✦ **Part VI, "Managing the Network,"** covers Windows management tools you can use to make the network more efficient and effective. Windows includes network tools that can help you locate network problems and optimize the network. You can also use third-party applications to help manage your network.

✦ **Part VII, "Adding to Your Home Network,"** describes multimedia devices and intelligent homes. This part explains various multimedia devices, applications, and more. It gives you advice on buying sound and video cards, digital cameras and scanners, Web TV systems, and so on. You also learn about managing the multimedia in Windows. In addition, Part VII offers information about wiring your entire home with computers and devices to make your life easier and more fun.

The book concludes with a troubleshooting appendix to help you with network and connection problems, an appendix about using the TCP/IP protocol, an appendix about telecommuting and remote access, and a glossary of technical terms.

What Conventions Are Used in this Book?

Step-by-step instructions include a pathway to folders and programs, as in the following example:

Choose Start ⇨ Settings ⇨ Control Panel.

This instruction describes clicking the Start menu button, selecting the Settings command, and then selecting Control Panel from the resulting menu.

 A note offers additional information that might be useful to you.

 A tip offers advice or shortcuts.

 If some process or procedure holds some risk, this icon warns you of it.

 A cross-reference lists other chapters in the book that have additional information on the topic.

 Small business tips give you advice about the topic in an office situation, as opposed to a home networking situation.

Acknowledgments

I would like to thank the many people who helped with this book. I'm grateful to Katie Feltman for the support and consideration she showed me. Kevin Kent has been a helpful and energetic editor. Thanks, Kevin. I'd also like to thank the many vendors who gave me information about their products, as well as the many who sent me samples of their products so that I could try them before writing about them. Thanks, too, to Angela Smith for handling the editorial tasks as the book moved into production, Tom Brays for his excellent technical review of the book, and the production staff for making this book a reality.

Contents at a Glance

Contents

• •

Part I: Making Basic Network Choices   1

Part IV: Adding the Internet, E-Mail, and an Intranet 353

Chapter 16: Accessing the Internet 355

Chapter 17: Using E-Mail 383

Making Basic Network Choices

Part I introduces some fundamental definitions and explanations of networking. The Chapter 1 Quick Start gives you an overview of the process of building a network. Chapter 1 also points to certain procedures explained in the book, just in case you've already started a network and need some help with specific choices or processes.

Chapter 2 covers the advantages and disadvantages of networking and describes the different types of networks available. Chapters 3 and 4 explain two networking structures: workgroup and client/server. Use these chapters to decide which network structure you will use in your home.

Quick Start – Sharing on a Network

✦   ✦   ✦   ✦

In This Chapter

Overview of the process

Finding the help
you need

✦   ✦   ✦   ✦

Where are you in planning and installing your network? Do you already have computers that you want to connect? Do you have one printer that everyone in the house would like to share? Is having only one Internet connection a problem? You can share computers, printers, Internet connections, and more by installing a network in your home.

Do you need help choosing and buying the necessary networking equipment? Perhaps the equipment is already installed, but you're unfamiliar with networking with Windows 98 or Windows XP. You might have your network up and running but want to add an intranet and e-mail technologies. You find instructions for each of these tasks, in addition to hundreds more, in *Home Networking Bible*.

Home Networking Bible, 2nd Edition, covers new information on some of the technologies introduced in the first edition, such as wireless networking breakthroughs, Wireless-g protocol, power line networking enhancements, universal serial bus (USB) hubs and adapters, and the future of networking. In this second edition, you'll also find greater detail on how to lay cabling, place wireless access points, configure computers (include Linux and Macs), share Internet connections, and more.

Chapter 1 presents an overview of the steps you need to plan your network. This chapter gives you an idea of the decisions and assessments ahead of you. You'll need to consider what you already have, what equipment and hardware you want to share among your family or your small-business network, and what type of network benefits your situation. This chapter also presents a roadmap that helps you target the area in the book that will help you the most.

Overview of the Process

When you decide to connect your home computers to form a network, you have to ask yourself many questions.

✦ What type of network will you use?

✦ What operating systems do you have?

✦ Which operating systems do you want to add?

✦ How much money do you want to spend?

✦ What type of hardware and software is best for what you want to do?

The list goes on and on. *Home Networking Bible* can help you make these decisions and more.

Home Networking Bible presents information, definitions, possibilities, and advice about setting up and running your home network. You may want to set up a quick and inexpensive network to enable file sharing between your desktop and laptop computers. You may want to build a more complex network that includes a server, six workstations, multiple printers, and other shared resources. In either case, you'll find the information you need in this book.

As you read *Home Networking Bible*, you'll run across topics such as cabling, installing networking hardware and software, and adding applications to your system. You'll learn about choosing cabling, network cards, and other equipment. You'll even find out how to share your Internet account with everyone else on the network.

You probably have the beginnings of a network already: computers, a printer or two, and perhaps other resources. In addition, one of the most important reasons to have a network is to share resources, such as hard drive space, a printer, a CD-RW, and so on. Taking an inventory of your current equipment can help you make wise choices about what to purchase and what to share on your new network.

An important decision you must make before you begin putting together your network is whether to build a network using a server. There are advantages and disadvantages of both types of networking. Just so you'll understand what you're getting yourself into, the following sections present abbreviated steps for setting up a network. The order of these steps generally reflects the order of the material as organized by chapters in this book. You can, of course, approach the text in a different order to better suit your network needs.

Taking inventory

Your first step to planning a network is to take inventory of the equipment and software already in your home. You want to make use of all available resources. Computers, printers, a scanner or camera — any and all of these may be put to use in your network.

Perhaps, for example, you use your computer to keep your checkbook and to surf the Internet. Your son also has a computer he uses for homework and games. Your spouse uses a notebook computer primarily for work and must often bring it home to complete daily work. Any of these computers, with minor alterations, can probably work on a network. After networking the computers, everyone can print to one printer, check on the homework, surf the Internet, and more.

Note   You also want to be reasonable in your expectations of these resources. If one of your computers is old and operates slowly, placing it on a network isn't going to make the computer better. It might even slow the network down. You can always check to see if you can upgrade a computer's memory, processor speed, or operating system; but compare the cost of an upgrade against the cost of a new computer before making any decisions.

Begin your inventory with a list of your computers. For each computer, write down the following. You can always check your original invoice for the computer to find out the information for each item.

✦ Processor and memory

✦ Hard drive space

✦ Operating system (Windows 98, Windows XP, Mac OS 9, Linux, and so on)

✦ Attached hardware (CD-ROM, CD-RW, DVD, Zip drive, network card, modem, and such)

✦ External hardware and peripherals (camera, printer, scanner, and so on)

After your inventory, consider whether you need to replace or upgrade any of your hardware. If, for example, a computer has an operating system below Windows 95, such as DOS or Windows 3.11, consider purchasing a new computer. If the computer uses Windows 95, find out what it takes to upgrade the computer or replace it. Once you have your computers and other hardware in order, you're ready to consider the network.

Looking at resources to share

You can share printers, CD and DVD drives, flash cards, modems, some applications, and more on a network. You can also add resources as you build your network. Using a network to share resources offers many advantages and a few disadvantages that you'll want to consider before you build your network together.

Sharing a printer, for example, means you need only one printer for three or four computers. However, if everyone prints often, they may have to stand around waiting for their print jobs. Sharing a hard drive with other family members means all of those free gigabytes of space may fill more quickly than originally planned, but everyone has backups of their data.

With your inventory in hand, discuss with your family the pros and cons of sharing one printer, one large hard drive, one modem, or any of the other available resources. Then, consider which resources you want to share and which resources may need to be purchased. As previously mentioned, you can add resources as you build your network and as you see a need for them.

Listing steps for a workgroup network

A *workgroup* or *peer-to-peer network* is one in which all computers on the network can pool their resources together. Each individual computer usually retains its control over files, folders, and applications; however, every computer on the network can use another's printer, scanner, CD drive, and so on. Workgroup networks contain a small number of computers. Workgroups can be made up of 2, 5, or even 10 computers. It is important to note that the more computers in the workgroup, the slower the network may run.

Note
Peer-to-peer is the actual name for a network in which all users share all resources, as previously described. Microsoft Windows calls peer-to-peer *workgroup*, so if you're used to Windows, you'll recognize that term. Peer-to-peer and workgroup mean the same thing. In this book, I mostly use the term workgroup, however.

If you choose to use a workgroup network, you should perform the following steps. Many steps are optional, depending on your networking choices, whether or not you want Internet access, and so on.

Cross-Reference For more information about workgroup networks, see Chapter 3. For definitions of terms, see the Glossary toward the end of this book.

1. Learn the advantages and disadvantages of networking and decide exactly what it is that you want from your network.

2. Consider some guidelines about the network that you will present to your family.

3. Define your networking goals: budget, computer placement, computer contents, applications issues, and so on.

4. Decide what speed the network will be, considering your family needs and equipment limitations.

5. Choose the network topology and technology.

6. Choose cabling: traditional, wireless, power, or phone lines.

7. Buy the networking hardware. Depending on the choices you make, you could purchase a kit containing everything you need, or you may purchase individual pieces of hardware and cabling.

8. Install network cards.

9. Install networking hardware: cabling, hubs, or other hardware as needed.

10. Configure the networking software — protocol, clients, services, and adapters — on each computer.

11. Attach any non-Windows computer or portables to the network.

12. Set shares in each computer. Test the shares.

13. Access the network, test IDs, passwords, and so on.

14. Learn to find other computers on the network.

15. Set up printers and test connections.

16. Set up Internet access, if you want.

17. Set up e-mail, if you want.

18. Create an intranet, if you want.

19. Install and configure applications.

20. Work with files and folders.

21. Understand how to manage the network.

22. Add other elements to the network, such as multimedia equipment or chat applications.

Listing steps to add a server

Client/server networking is a setup in which files, applications, and resources are centralized on one high-speed, powerful computer called a *server*. Other computers, called *clients*, then attach to the server and use the resources as they need them. Client/server networks are faster than workgroup networks, and a server supports more clients, or *users*, than a workgroup network. For example, a client/server network may have from 10 to 2,000 users attached to a server.

If you choose to add a server to your network, you need to perform some additional steps. For more information about adding a server to your network, see Chapter 4. In brief, you'll need to do the following, in addition to the preceding set of steps:

1. Determine the type of network operating system you want to use.

2. Purchase a server and configure the server's operating system by setting up user accounts and permissions, setting up rights on files and folders, setting up a print server, installing and configuring applications, setting up permissions, and so on. See Chapter 12 for information about securing your computer and files.

3. Configure the clients to see and use the server, and perhaps create login scripts and other security measures.

4. Check all client/server connections.

Small Business Tip

If you're creating your network for a small business, either in your home or in an office, you may want to use client/server networking instead of workgroup. There are certain advantages to the client/server configuration in a business network. In a client/server environment, the network is easy to expand to include more client computers, network operations in a larger group are faster, you can provide more services to everyone on the network, and security is tighter.

Finding the Help You Need

You may already be familiar with networking types. You may already have a network set up in your home. Perhaps you purchased *Home Networking Bible* to learn more about sharing Internet access or setting up printer sharing. You may want more information on managing your network or want to learn about Transmission Control Protocol/Internet Protocol (TCP/IP).

If you're in one of the stages of building your network and just want some assistance getting through that stage, this section can help. Following are some common networking scenarios and suggestions as to which chapter to read to help you solve your networking problems.

Planning your network

As you might know, you go through several stages to plan a network. You must decide what type of network you want, which speed to use, what kind of cabling and hardware is best for your situation, and so on. You'll find all of the information you need to plan your network in *Home Networking Bible*. Consider the following scenarios.

Budget considerations

You want a home network, but your budget is limited. You have only about $150 to spend on all of the equipment you need to connect two computers. You want to know if you really have to spend more money than this for such a simple task.

Now, you can connect two computers for as little as $20. Additionally, you can use any number of kits to connect two computers now, and add computers later when you're ready. For information about various kits and networking solutions, see Chapter 8.

In contrast, say you're building a home and you have no limit to the amount of money you spend on your network. In fact, you want to cable the home to perform more than just computer networking: You want to include climate and environment controls, security lights and cameras, and video and stereo equipment on your network.

Chapter 26 explains the possibilities of wiring a "smart" home, or SmartHome, and also suggests manufacturers of systems and estimated costs.

Server issues

You've heard that the kid next door has a server in his basement, so you want a server too. However, you don't want to use a server like the one at work or in larger offices, which uses the NetWare or NT Server operating system. You want something that's simple to operate and maintain and easy for everyone to access for storing their files, printing, and so on. What do you do? Consider using a powerful computer with Windows XP as the operating system. For information about setting up a Windows server like this, see Chapter 4.

You want to back up all of your data to another computer, but you wonder if it has to be a server computer. Must a tape drive or Zip drive be connected to a server? Do you have to use a server's software to back up files? You can back up files to any other computer on the network. You can also attach a tape, CD drive, or Zip drive to any computer on the network and save to those drives. For more information, see Chapter 21.

Network cabling

You have no idea what networking cabling is available or what it means. Network speed depends on the type of cabling and hardware you use, but you're not sure what network speed is or how much you'll need. Chapter 6 explains the various cabling schemes and how each cable type affects speed. It also explains why you might need faster speeds and when you can get by on slower cabling and networking hardware.

In addition, Chapter 7 explains the various wireless technologies and standards, wireless performance, and wireless configuration. Make your choice about networking cabling after checking both of these chapters.

You have Ethernet 10/100 network cards already installed in your computers. You need to know what type of cable you can use with these cards, what the difference between 10 and 100 is, and if there's any other hardware you need to set up your computers. Chapter 6 explains network cabling for the Ethernet 10/100 network card. Additionally, Chapter 9 defines types of network interface cards.

Networking software

You want to connect to the Internet, so you want to know if you have to use the TCP/IP protocol on your network. This is a common misunderstanding. TCP/IP is the protocol of the Internet, but you can use a separate protocol for your network, even if you're attaching to the Internet. Chapter 10 explains.

In planning your network, you realize that everyone in the house uses a PC except for your youngest son. He uses an iMac. Is there any way you can attach his computer to the network, or will you have to purchase him a printer of his own? You can attach Macintoshes to a PC network and enable them to share printers and files by using special networking software. For more information about this software, see Chapter 11.

You've always wanted to know about TCP/IP and how it works. See Appendix B for more information.

Using the network

If you have already set up your network — installed cabling and hardware — but you're having trouble getting computers to see each other or locate resources on the network, you can quickly find the help you need in this section. Consider these scenarios.

Connecting computers

Ever since you set up your network, you have one computer that just won't see the other computers in the Network Neighborhood. You've tried everything you can think of, but you're ready to throw the computer out the window. What do you do? Appendix A defines various procedures to check connections and to solve network access problems. For more information about the Network Neighborhood, see Chapter 14.

You recently changed the network card on your computer and now you can't get that computer to attach to the network. Is there anything you can try that you haven't already? You should take a look at Chapter 10. You might need to update or reinstall your adapter driver or reconfigure your protocol configuration.

Your husband uses a Linux computer, and he doesn't want to change the operating system. Is there any way you can attach his computer to the network? Yes. Chapter 11 explains how.

Your daughter can't remember her network password. Is there any way you can help her get onto the network again? Yes, there is. See Chapter 13, which discusses network IDs and passwords.

Your office has a computer network, and you would like to connect your home computer to your work computer. If you could make a connection, you could work on multiple files from home, print to the printer at work while at home, and so on. For information, see Appendix C.

Using network printers and other resources

Your printer is set up and ready to go; however, no one on the network can see the printer in his or her computer. You know there's something else you must do, but you're not sure what it is. You'll want to make sure that you've installed the appropriate network printer driver to each computer. See Chapter 15 for more information.

Only one computer on the network contains a Zip drive, but you want everyone on the system to have access to it. How do you set up access? See Chapter 12 for information about sharing drives.

Finding computers, files, printers, and such on the network

Now that you're connected to the network, how do you find another computer's resources? Windows includes many tools for viewing computers and resources; you can use the Network Neighborhood, the My Computer window, or the Windows Explorer. Chapter 14 explains how to accomplish this task. In addition, Chapter 14 includes information for finding computers on Macs and Linux machines.

Your hard disk is nearly full, and you really don't want to delete any of your files. Short of saving to a floppy disk, where can you store your files? The handy thing about using a network is that you can store files on the hard drives of other computers. Chapter 21 covers this topic.

Using the Internet, e-mail, and intranets

One of the most popular reasons for people to have computers in their homes is for Internet access. If you have an Internet account, *Home Networking Bible* can make your life easier in many ways. Additionally, home-based e-mail accounts and intranets make your network fun and educational. An *intranet* is a private network that works similarly to the Internet; you use a Web browser to view documents that you and your family create in a special format.

Small Business Tip

A business, in particular, can use an intranet to publish business and financial reports, sales figures, employee handbooks, specials, calendars, and much more. See Chapter 19 for more information.

Internet

Everyone loves the Internet—using it for Web browsing, sending e-mail, joining newsgroups, and so on—but multiple Internet accounts are expensive. You have one Internet account in your home, but there are three people who want to use the Net, usually at the same time. Is there any way you can share the one Internet account and modem over the network? Yes, there are several software programs and hardware that enable you to share an Internet account. See Chapter 16 for more information.

You would like to use some sort of chat program to have a conversation over the Internet with your cousin in Florida. You've heard about programs that let you talk to others who are connected, but you would like to know more. Chapter 18 explains how Internet chats work and tells you about the most popular chat applications. Chapter 18 also discusses instant messaging programs.

E-mail

Some say you're silly to want e-mail for your home network, but you know that your kids would love sending messages to each other and that it's safer than allowing them to use Internet e-mail at this point in their experience. If you want to set up e-mail for your network, see Chapter 17.

Small Business Tip

E-mail within your business network is extremely important in a small business, to keep communications open, for transferring files quickly, for sharing schedules and ideas, and more.

Intranet

You have an intranet at work, and you enjoy the way you can share documents, pass around files, and so on. You also want to give the kids experience at designing Web pages, and it seems like a good idea to start them out on a private intranet instead of on the Internet. You can find out more by looking at Chapter 19.

An intranet is the perfect forum for a small business. You can share forms, an employee handbook, customer information, ordering and invoicing data, and so on so that every member of the network has quick and easy access to the documents they need to do their work.

Managing the network

If your network contains only two computers, you might not need to manage the resources. However, anytime you have multiple users on a network, problems can occur. The network can slow down so much that you think you'd be better off without it. Anyone can accidentally delete information from the Registry. You'll want to know more about managing a network so you can prevent, or at least assist, when something does go wrong.

Management tools

Now that your network is up and running, you want to be able to see which files are being shared, to see which users are online, and sometimes even to disconnect a user. The network seems unbearably slow, and you want to figure out why. Windows's System Monitor enables you to look at how things are being used. Chapter 22 offers help for the System Monitor, PGP for the Mac, and other suggestions for optimizing your system.

Every time your daughter turns on the computer, she complains that her brother has changed her desktop colors, screen savers, and game settings. You wish you could find a way to keep him from toying with her computer's settings. You can. See Chapter 23.

Registry

Your spouse decided to try to edit the Registry but made a mess of the computer's settings. Was there anything you could have done to protect the computer from these changes? Yes, you could have made backups of all Registry files on all computers, just in case the original file becomes corrupted. See Chapter 24 for more information.

Summary

In this chapter, you've learned about what it takes to build a network and about how this book can help you with many different networking problems. Specifically, you learned about the following:

✦ Building a workgroup network

✦ Building a client/server network

✦ Finding specific help in this book

In the next chapter, you learn the fundamentals of networking, such as the advantages and disadvantages of networking, the definition of a network, and how to get your family ready for a network.

✦　　✦　　✦

Understanding Network Basics

All networks use some basic hardware and software, but different configurations of this equipment define the type and uses of the network. For example, you may want to network two computers in the same room. The equipment you use to achieve this network can be different from the hardware you use to network two computers in different rooms or even in different buildings. Similarly, the hardware you use to enable two computers to use one Internet connection is different than the software you use for two computers sharing a printer. Understanding network uses and network types helps you plan your network.

Because networking your home or office is often involved and time-consuming, you need to understand the advantages and disadvantages of networking before planning your network. Understanding the pros and cons of networking helps you plan the exact network that's right for you and your family. In addition, before you can plan your network, buy the hardware and software, and teach your family to use your network, you need to understand some basic networking terms and technologies.

Understanding Networks

Networking the computers in your home enables your family to share the hardware and software on one or more of your computers. For example, your kids can surf the Internet on their computer while you shop the Net on your computer. Your spouse can attach a notebook to the network and print to your printer. Your son can print his homework to that same printer. Meanwhile, you and your spouse can make entries in your online investment accounts, get your e-mail, and check your to-do lists on separate computers.

If you have two or more PCs in your home, you can save everyone in your family time, energy, and money by networking your computers to share files, printers, and Internet access.

Note There are many names for networks, often related to their size. *Local area network* (LAN) is perhaps the most common name for a network. A LAN contains two or more computers and is generally housed in one building. Home networks, however, are starting to be called by other names. TAN stands for *tiny area network*. Then there's HAN, which stands for *home area network*.

Figure 2-1 illustrates a home equipped with three computers. Dad's notebook computer travels to work with him and home again every day. The family laser printer is also set up in Dad's den. Mom uses her computer for e-mailing the family, Internet research, and designing Web sites in her home office. The teenager has a desktop computer in his room that he uses for homework, listening to music, surfing the Net, and for playing games.

As it stands now, Mom and the teenager have to copy files to a CD-R and then take the disk to Dad's den to print anything. If a network connected these computers, everyone could print from his or her own room. Additionally, they could share files, folders, CD-ROM drives, printers, Internet connections, and other network resources.

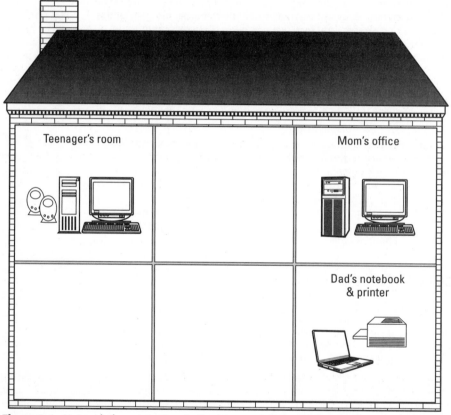

Figure 2-1: Network the computers in the house so that everyone can use the same printer.

No matter how you use your PC — writing letters, balancing your checkbook, playing games, or surfing the Internet — you can benefit from networking your home computers. A network is a system that connects two or more computers so that they can communicate and share resources with each other. When you're a member of a network, you have access to more disk space, applications, files, and useful equipment. You can communicate with other users on the network without leaving your desk. You can share files without carrying a floppy disk or CD back and forth from computer to computer. You can even share an expensive piece of equipment with everyone else in the house.

Sharing expensive equipment is particularly important for small businesses. Everyone on the network can print to the appropriate printer for their business needs — forms to a dot-matrix printer, reports to a laser printer, or charts to a color inkjet printer, for example.

Planning your network

As you read this book, consider the equipment you already have and the ways you can make the most of your hardware and software. For example, in the previous figure, the printer was located in Dad's den. Since Dad uses the notebook away from the house at work, no one can use the printer while he's gone. A better placement of the printer would be upstairs with Mom's or the son's computer. However, in that case, Dad has to walk upstairs every time he prints something. So placement of resources and convenience factor into your network plan.

Think about the resources you have available and how you can best use them. The computer with the most disk space may be the computer everyone uses to save files and folders. That computer should probably be left on all the time so files are always available. In this case, you want to place the computer in a room that is safer from lightening, such as a room with all inside walls, and attach a surge protector to the computer. Might that also be the computer to which the printer is connected? As you plan your network, try to consider what is easiest and most efficient.

Introducing network equipment

A network includes two or more computers. Those computers may be desktop PCs (IBM-compatible personal computers), but they can also be notebooks or laptops, handheld computers, Macintoshes, Linux boxes, or others. The instructions in this book mainly deal with IBM-compatible personal computers. The products, configuration, and steps described in this book target the Windows 98 and Windows XP operating systems; however, Macintoshes and Linux boxes are also discussed. The network equipment is similar for any type of operating system you use.

You certainly can use other computers in your network, such as a laptop from work or your child's Macintosh. Chapter 11 describes using such types of computers on your network. In addition, other operating systems are mentioned in chapters when appropriate.

Networked computers are attached to each other with cables or wires, and it is across those wires that the shared information passes. There are also some wireless methods of attaching computers, such as with radio frequencies or infrared. Chapter 6 describes common network wiring methods. Chapter 7 explains wireless standards and technology.

Some cabling methods better suit an office than a home, depending on the number of computers, network type, and office space. You'll likely want to use more traditional cabling for a small-business office.

There are even some alternatives to traditional cabling for your home network. You can use your phone lines, for example, or the electrical wires running through your home. Chapter 8 explains some of these options.

In addition to the actual cables, there are other pieces of networking hardware you'll need. The hardware varies, depending on the methods you use, the speed you want, and the type of files and data you'll be transferring. For instance, you'll almost always need to install a network adapter card for each computer on the network. The cards enable the computers to communicate with each other. You can find out more about networking equipment in Chapter 9.

As part of your network, you'll want to attach printers, scanners, digital cameras, and other peripherals. All the users on the network can share this equipment. Sharing equipment is accomplished through the hardware and the software in your network.

Introducing networking software

A network requires software as well as hardware. Luckily, most computers already contain the basic networking software you'll need. Windows, Macintosh, and Linux are usually ready to network out of the box. Most computers come with network cards built in, or you can easily add the card and the software that goes with it.

But you'll still have to make some decisions. A vital component of networking software is the language that the computers use to communicate, called a *protocol*. A protocol is a standard procedure for relating data transmission between computers and other network resources. Many, many protocols exist, but generally, you choose from three protocols. Each protocol has certain advantages and disadvantages. You can use the IPX/SPX, NetBIOS Extended User Interface (NetBEUI), or Transmission Control Protocol/Internet Protocol (TCP/IP) with your network. TCP/IP is the most common and most efficient, and it is the one you'll probably use for your network. These protocols are discussed in more detail throughout the book.

You'll also need to install software, called a *driver*, which enables your network card to work within the network. Some computers have more than 60 drivers. A driver is a software program written specifically for a piece of hardware, such as a modem, network card, CD drive, printer, and so on. The driver enables the hardware to work with other parts of the computer and with your applications.

You'll also have to configure the software that enables you to share your files and folders with others. Chapter 10 explains all of these components in detail.

For the most part, all of the networking software you'll need is included with the operating system installed to your computer, or you can install it with program discs that come with the operating system. Some software is available for free download from manufacturers' sites, and you can also purchase supplementary software to enhance your network. For example, you may want to share an Internet connection with the other computers on the network. You can sometimes use the operating system software, third-party software, or even a hardware device to accomplish this goal.

Similarly, you may need to purchase additional networking software if you plan to use an alternative method of wiring your network, or if you want to play a networked game with your spouse or child. You'll find suggestions for this type of software throughout the book.

Looking at the Advantages and Disadvantages of a Network

For the most part, you'll find that networking your computers benefits everyone in the house or office. Sharing resources makes your computer more efficient and effective, and gives you more equipment with which to work.

No matter what you do, however, there are always some disadvantages. The cost may be too much, for example, or security issues may bother you. Fortunately, there are enough options and solutions to your problems with networking to make the good outweigh the bad.

Considering the advantages

If you were installing a network for a corporation with hundreds of computers, you could expect a huge and difficult job. Installing a home network, however, is much easier. If you're planning to connect two to ten computers in your home, you can do it with little hassle and with great success.

Small Business Tip

You can connect two to ten computers in a small office as well as in your home, but you may want to connect more than ten computers in the office. If that is the case, you may want to use a network that involves one large server computer and multiple smaller workstations, or client computers. See Chapter 4 for more information.

Many Windows, Macintosh, and Linux computers include the networking software you need; you can purchase the networking hardware and install it all yourself. Alternatively, kits are available that include all the hardware you need to put together a home network. You can choose the features that are important to you, whether you desire speed, shared Internet access, security, or all these features. If you're hesitating about installing a home network, consider the following advantages.

Sharing files

Share files with everyone on the network. You can write a letter and let your partner take a look at it before you send it. Take some digital photographs and share them with your family. Your son or daughter can complete a homework assignment, and you can check it over before he or she takes it to school. If you have a personal accounting program, you and your spouse can access the records for bills, checks, and investments.

Figure 2-2 shows Sue's computer on the network with a set of digital photographs in the Windows Explorer. Molly can take a look at the pictures and see which one she wants to use for this year's Christmas cards.

The computer

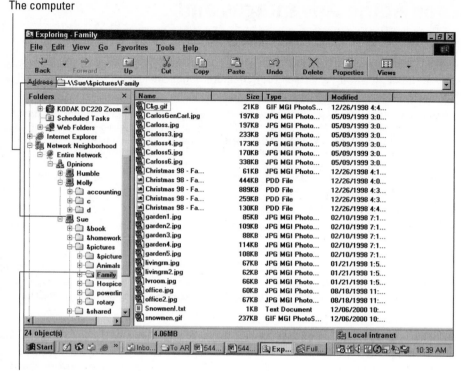

Family pictures

Figure 2-2: Share files of all kinds over the network.

It's quicker to transfer files across the network than saving them to a disc and copying them from that disc onto another computer. You might want to copy a large file, such as an application file, to your hard drive. You can copy it over the network instantly. Copying files is also an excellent method of backing up files; you can save extra copies of pictures, letters, and other valuable files on another computer on the network.

Sharing disk space

Disk space is always at a premium. With graphic and image files, music files, large application files, and data files taking up your hard disk space, you can take advantage of a network and save files to any hard disk on the network. If you do not need your 60 gigabytes (GB) of hard disk space, you can share it with your spouse for saving pictures of the family or for storing music files.

In addition to sharing hard disks, you can share file storage drives, such as tape drives, Zip drives, CD burners, and even floppy disk drives. Sharing a Zip disk that holds 100 or 250 megabytes (MB) of data means you can save your data files on one or two disks and access them whenever you want, even if they are on another computer in the house. Imagine sharing a CD burner — that's over 600MB of space. Share your DVD burner for over 4.5GB of space for each disc.

Creating backups

Backing up your data files is important. You should always keep an extra copy of important files in case your hard disk goes bad, a file becomes corrupted, or someone accidentally deletes your work. You can back up all of your data quickly and easily over the network—on either a storage disk or on another hard disk. Restoring that data would also be quick and easy over the network.

Figure 2-3 shows a backup drive—designated drive M—on Sue's computer. Sue partitioned (or divided) her large 40GB hard disk into smaller drives so that others could use the smaller partitions for backups. Molly backs up important folders and applications in case her hard disk fails or someone accidentally deletes her files or folders.

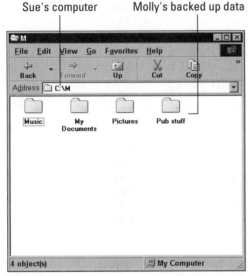

Figure 2-3: Keep backups of your important data on another computer's hard disks for safety.

Small Business Tip

Backups are even more important in a small-business office, because accounts receivable and payable data, customer information, inventory, and other critical data can result in lost business if your hard disk crashes or becomes corrupted.

Sharing peripherals

Expensive peripherals—such as a color inkjet or laser printer—are more affordable if everyone in the house can use them. If a printer isn't networked, only one person has continual use of that piece of equipment. Naturally, others can move to the computer to which it's attached, but that may not always be convenient or appropriate. If the peripheral is attached to the network, however, everyone can make use of it. You'll save money and time, and do more with less.

Working with applications

Multiplayer games—such as Xconq or CittaTron—have gained popularity over the last year. Many games are available for two or more players to participate in concurrently. Networking computers means your children (and you) can connect and share a game for wholesome family fun.

Suppose that you want to install a program from CD-ROM, but the CD-ROM drive attached to your computer is only a 2× speed. Your spouse, however, has an 8× CD-ROM drive. Using the network, you can install the application from the 8× drive much more quickly.

Figure 2-4 illustrates shared drives on Sue's computer in the Network Neighborhood. Note that the CD-ROM drive is also shared.

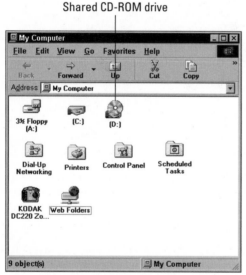

Figure 2-4: Share fast CD-ROM drives with others on the network.

Accessing the Internet

Sharing Internet access is ideal for many families. If you have one Internet service provider (ISP) account but you have two, three, or more people who want to connect to the Internet, you can achieve that with a network without constraint, separate telephone lines, and separate Internet accounts. Using the right software or hardware, you can configure your modem—including telephone modem, Digital Subscriber Line (DSL), or cable modem—to connect to the Internet and simultaneously share that connection with other users. One person can collect e-mail, another can surf the Web, and a third can read newsgroups, all at the same time.

Figure 2-5 shows a Web site in the Windows Internet Explorer. You can view travel agents' sites and plan your vacation while your spouse sends e-mail to friends and family.

Figure 2-5: Share Internet access to save money.

In addition to using the Internet for Web browsing, you can send and receive e-mail over the Internet. Similarly, you can set up your own e-mail system in your home. Send a memo to your kid about a family gathering this weekend; send notes to your spouse about bills that are due or appointments to keep. Sending and receiving e-mail is one of the most popular computer pastimes in the world today, and you can set up your own mail system on your network or e-mail over the Internet, if you prefer.

Expanding your network

As you begin using your network, you may decide to expand the network. You could, for example, attach to a network at work, via an extranet or a virtual private network (VPN). You may also want to develop your network to control more than just your computers.

If your job is one in which you can work from home, either part-time or full-time, you can not only network your home computers, but also attach to a work computer. E-mail your coworkers, print documents, send and receive files, and more, all from the comfort of your home.

Using your computer to control your heat and air conditioning, telephones, security systems, TV and video, and your PC network are not dreams of the future; they are available now. Networking your home can be as simple as sharing a printer or as complex as home automation.

Considering the disadvantages

Now that the advantages are clear to you, it's time to consider the disadvantages. Planning and installing a network is a scary proposition. You'll need to invest time and money. You'll have to learn about various networking hardware and software products. Sharing equipment and files poses problems as well.

As you read *Home Networking Bible*, you'll notice that various methods of networking are described. Within the coverage of networking methods are comments on the problems they may cause and possible solutions to those problems. Following are some of the disadvantages to setting up and using a network.

Investing time and money

There are always some disadvantages to taking on a new project — even setting up your own home or business network. Obviously, you'll have to invest time. When you learn something new, it takes time to understand all its intricacies. Installing hardware and software also takes some time. Teaching the procedures to the rest of the family will take time as well.

Money is another consideration. You may not want to invest a lot of money in your computer system — you just want to use it to play some games or share a printer. You may have already spent your technology budget just buying the computers. On the other hand, you might have the means to install a model network, with all the bells and whistles you've ever wanted.

Small Business Tip

You can create a simple network using three to five computers, a hub, and some cabling that is very inexpensive. No need to start your small-business network with a server and several workstations. Use what you already have and add a little at a time, so you can see if a network works for your business. If, after 6 months or a year, you find the network is growing and you're using it more and more, then you can think about adding a server, a switch, routers, and other devices that cost more and do more for you.

It all comes down to priorities. If computers are a hobby for which you have little time, you'll spend less money and less time. If your work depends on a computer, if your children use computers at school and can benefit by having one at home, or if you're interested in new and interesting technologies, you might want to spend a bit more time and money on a network.

Fortunately, you can choose from multiple levels of networking. You can purchase a kit, for example, for less than $100 that enables you to set up a small and simple network between two computers and a printer. Now, that network isn't the fastest or the most efficient network, but it does provide simple file sharing and printer sharing with the investment of just a little time and money.

If you want to install a higher level of networking for sharing the Internet, working with multimedia files, or sharing equipment such as scanners and printers and cameras, for example, you can install a faster, more efficient network. The expense and time spent will be a bit more than a simple network, but so will the benefits to everyone in the family.

Finally, if you want to put more time and money into your home network, you can. Smart Homes enable you to control your heat and air conditioning, telephones and TVs, security lights and cameras, and your computers from one central area. You can wire your home and control all these components from one central computer or from multiple controls throughout the house. You choose the level of networking and the amount of money and time with which you're comfortable. For every problem you may have with installing a network in your home, there are possible solutions. Following are more disadvantages to home networking and some solutions you should consider.

Considering the level of difficulty

Setting up a network can be difficult. You first must decide just what you need to make a network possible. After purchasing the appropriate equipment, you must install the hardware, configure software, connect it all, and then make sure all network components are working. Depending on the equipment you buy, it can take days to set up a working network — or it can take an hour or two.

Figure 2-6 illustrates the TCP/IP Properties dialog box. Looking at the options and tabs in this dialog box could keep you from even thinking about networking your computers.

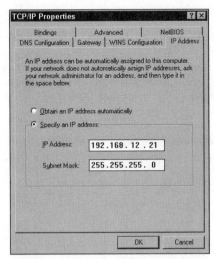

Figure 2-6: Networking protocols can be intimidating, if you don't understand them.

Consider these points, however:

✦ *Home Networking Bible* explains how to set up the hardware and software to run a network, including TCP/IP (see Chapters 9 and 10).

✦ TCP/IP is only one of three protocols you can use in Windows. The other two — Internetwork Packet Exchange (IPX) and NetBEUI — are simpler to use.

Note

NetBEUI stands for NetBIOS Extended User Interface, and NetBIOS stands for Network Basic Input/Output System. These acronyms sound complicated and awesome, but they really aren't. They are simply a way of describing how two computers communicate with each other; NetBEUI is just another computer language.

✦ Some methods of networking discussed in this book don't use these protocols and don't require extensive software configuration.

The network equipment you buy depends on several things: how much you are willing to spend, how simple you want it to be, and your goals for the network. Fortunately, *Home Networking Bible* helps you figure these things out. Chapter 5 guides you in determining your network goals and planning the type of network you'll need.

Other chapters in this book help you decide on which equipment to buy and which method of installation to use. For example, Chapter 6 explains various methods of cabling and gives you instructions and advice about wiring your home. Chapter 7 covers wireless technologies and standards you can consider.

Home Networking Bible covers the hardware and software you'll need to purchase in order to build the type of network you want. So even though planning and installing a network seem like intimidating tasks, this book will help you through it.

Maintaining and troubleshooting the network

Maintaining the network includes keeping reliable connections between the computers and peripherals, troubleshooting problems between computers, and providing the available services (like e-mail or networked games) to all computers on the network. The more equipment you connect to the network or the more services you offer, the more difficult maintaining the network will be.

Problems with a network range from the simplest error to the most complex issues. A loose network wire can be as much trouble as being kicked off the Internet every 10 minutes. You'll gain experience with networking problems as you work more with your system. Until you gain that experience, you can use *Home Networking Bible* to help you. See Appendix A for more information.

Solving security problems

Another disadvantage to being a member of a network is system security. You don't want a child to accidentally delete or modify data in an accounting file, for example. You may not want your teenager changing the settings on your printer.

Figure 2-7 shows the hard disk of a computer available to the entire network. Imagine the damage a child could do if he or she started deleting, copying, and moving files and folders on your computer. It's scary.

Fortunately, Windows, Macintosh, and Linux offer the option of setting access limits on files, folders, printers, and other resources. You can choose not to share any of your resources with others on the network. You can also set certain limits on those resources to protect them from only certain network users. See Chapter 12 for more information.

Sharing equipment and files

When you're sharing your equipment (such as a printer or Zip drive) over a network, you take the chance that the equipment won't be readily available when you need it. Say your spouse just sent a 24-page color document to a networked inkjet printer. You'll have to wait your turn to print, and that could take awhile, depending on the network setup, printer speed, and so on.

Figure 2-8 shows a network print queue. A queue lists all jobs waiting to be printed. If someone on the network just sent several print jobs to the printer, you'll have to wait your turn. Sharing resources can often be frustrating.

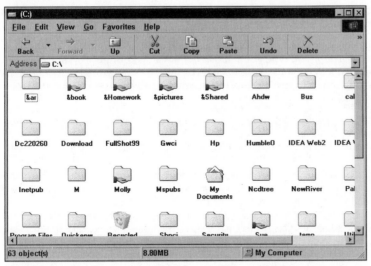

Figure 2-7: If you're not careful with your files and folders, someone on the network could delete them.

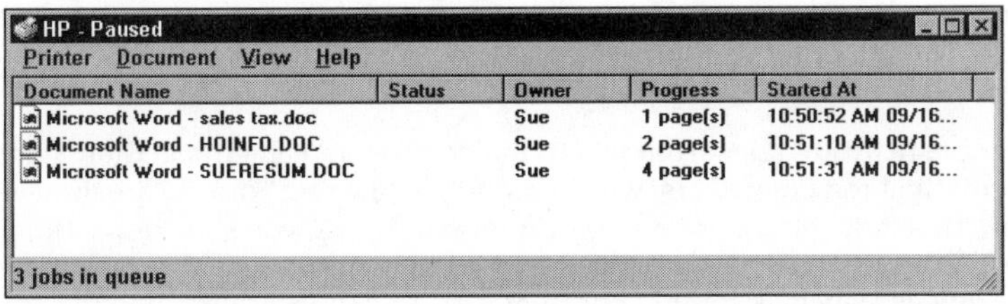

Document Name	Status	Owner	Progress	Started At
Microsoft Word - sales tax.doc		Sue	1 page(s)	10:50:52 AM 09/16...
Microsoft Word - HOINFO.DOC		Sue	2 page(s)	10:51:10 AM 09/16...
Microsoft Word - SUERESUM.DOC		Sue	4 page(s)	10:51:31 AM 09/16...

3 jobs in queue

Figure 2-8: If your document is last in a line of print jobs, you could be in for a long wait.

There are some solutions to these problems: You can speed up your network so that printing and other processes don't take as long. As another example, you may be able to change the order of the documents being printed in order to rush your job to the front of the line. *Home Networking Bible* offers advice in the appropriate chapters to help you successfully share your equipment.

Additionally, sharing files and applications can cause problems if two people want to use a file at the same time. Some applications are built for more than one user to use program files at the same time; others are not. This book explains how to tell whether you can use files simultaneously — see Chapter 20.

Considering network traffic

One final disadvantage you may notice when working on a network is a general slowing down of all applications and processes. Depending on the type of network equipment you use, the types of applications, and your uses for the network, connecting your home computers can slow down your work considerably. Some methods of networking are built for speed; others are built for simple sharing at a rather slow pace.

Understanding Network Types

There are two types of networks from which you can choose for your home network: client/server or workgroup. The type you choose depends on your networking goals, the equipment you want to install, your experience level, and the time you plan to invest. Each method of networking provides distinct advantages and disadvantages.

If this is your first network or if you want only a small and simple network, you will most likely set up a workgroup network to start. A workgroup network is simpler to operate and less expensive than a client/server network. After you gain experience, however, you may want to switch over to a client/server network, using your workgroup setup as a foundation.

Cross-Reference

This section provides an overview of these network types so that you can begin thinking about your own network. Each networking type is discussed in more detail elsewhere. See Chapters 3 and 4 for more information. For the most part, this book discusses workgroup networking solutions. Workgroup networking is the most simple and inexpensive network to set up. Network administration is easy, as well, with workgroup networking. Client/server networking, the alternative to workgroup networking, creates more work, more expense, and more administration time.

Using a workgroup network

In a workgroup network, all computers share their resources—including files, folders, drives, printers, and so on—with all others on the network. Each PC still runs its own local applications and programs.

A workgroup network usually contains from two to ten computers cabled together. You could possibly include more than ten computers, with the right hardware and software; however, when you have more than ten computers on a workgroup network, you slow down the performance of every computer on the network, as well as limit network speed, security, and efficiency. You can use devices, such as routers and switches, to connect more than ten computers efficiently; however, remember that the more computers on your network, the more management, time, and money it will involve.

Figure 2-9 illustrates one example of a workgroup network. Although these computers appear to be beside each other, each one could be located in a different room in a house. The Windows computers, the notebook computer, and the laser printer are all connected; the computers share all resources equally.

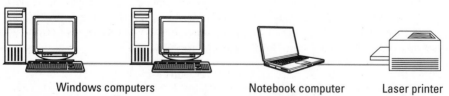

Windows computers   Notebook computer   Laser printer

Figure 2-9: Each computer shares its resources with the others.

Figure 2-10 shows another example of a workgroup network. Once again, these computers wouldn't necessarily appear side by side in the home. Each computer has a peripheral attached — a laser printer, an external DVD burner, and a color inkjet printer — and each computer can use any peripheral in the network.

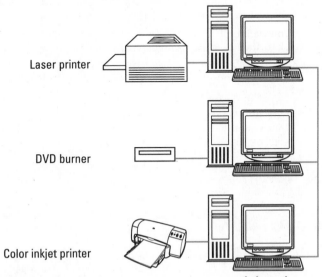

Laser printer

DVD burner

Color inkjet printer

Figure 2-10: It's easy to connect computers and share the resources.

Workgroup networks do present some disadvantages. Obviously, using a workgroup computer means the users must trust each other — to be careful of files and programs, to use printers and other equipment responsibly, and to make their computer available to everyone else dependably. You can use a network to teach your children trust and responsibility to other members of your family.

Security of your files can be a slight problem on a workgroup network. You do, however, have the option of not sharing all your files and folders. You can choose only those folders to which you want to grant access and share them. See Chapter 12 for more information.

Small Business Tip

Security issues are more serious in a business environment than in your home network. Sensitive files and data (salaries, for example) must be private from the general population. There are several ways to deal with security issues; however, using the client/server network may be the best way to make sure confidential files remain private.

Another disadvantage is backing up the computer. With workgroup networking, each computer user is responsible for his or her own backups. Perhaps not every user will need a backup of the data on his or her computer; however, each user should understand the importance of backups and understand how to create a backup. See Chapter 21 for more information about backing up your system.

Windows as a Workgroup Operating System

A computer's operating system (OS) allocates the system resources — such as memory, disk space, processor time, and the use of printers and other peripherals. An OS also enables applications to gain access to the resources when they need them, so that your word processor, spreadsheet program, and games can work properly. The computer loads the operating system first, as the computer boots, and the OS remains in memory as long as the computer remains on.

Some operating systems also provide the data and software a computer needs to become a part of a network. That networking software includes a protocol or computer language, a client that can make use of certain services or shared resources, and other programs that help the computer communicate over the network.

Windows 98, 2000, and XP Professional are perfect operating systems for workgroup networks. Windows XP Home Edition and Windows Me will work with workgroup networks, but each has its limitations; for example, Windows XP Home and Windows Me limit the number of users you can efficiently work with on your network. For more information about Windows XP Home Edition, see Chapter 3. Windows includes the networking software you need to communicate and share information with other Windows computers. All you have to do is set some options. Chapter 10 explains what this software is and how to configure it.

After you install and configure the software that enables your computer to transmit data to another computer, Windows also provides methods of viewing and using the resources from other machines. You're probably familiar with the Windows Explorer and the My Computer window. You can use either of these to display the resources belonging to another computer. Windows also includes Network Neighborhood and My Network Places windows designed specifically for viewing networked computers and resources. You can find more information about these applications in Chapter 14.

Windows contains other applets (or mini-programs) that help you access and manage the network. You can find computers by their names or by network path. You can manage your printing. You can also monitor the network and discover who else is sharing your resources, how the system is working, and so on.

Finally, Windows includes e-mail and Web browser applets that enable you to attach to a network much larger than your own home network: the Internet. You can surf the Web, send and receive messages, download files, and more. Plus, if you acquire a third-party program, you can share your Internet account with others on your network. See Chapter 16 for more information.

There are other workgroup operating systems you may have heard of or even used at work. Novell's Personal NetWare and Artisoft's LANtastic are two common operating systems for workgroup networks.

Using a client/server network

A client/server network is different from a workgroup network in that only one computer — called the server — shares its resources with all other computers — called clients. The computers in a workgroup network could also be called clients; a client is a device that makes use of the available services. In a client/server network, the clients only use the server's services.

Note   You might also hear the term workstation used when referring to client computers on a network. A *workstation* refers to any computer other than a server that is attached to a network.

A server generally stores all data files, many applications, and control over peripherals and
resources. Some networks contain one server, and others may contain multiple servers. The
number of servers depends on the number of clients and the number of services offered.

Figure 2-11 shows a simple client/server network. The server controls all files, folders, printers, and other resources. The client computers must request a service and be approved
before they can access a resource. Note that cables connect all devices to a small box, called
a *hub*. Most networks need a hub to help modify transmission signals, and to extend the network past two workstations. For more information about hubs, see Chapter 9.

A client/server network, depending on the hardware, services offered, and the network operating system, can serve anywhere from 10 to 150 or so clients. As in a workgroup network, the
more clients attached to the network, the busier the network traffic and perhaps the slower
the transmissions. Some larger networks have multiple servers to provide a wide variety of
services to the clients.

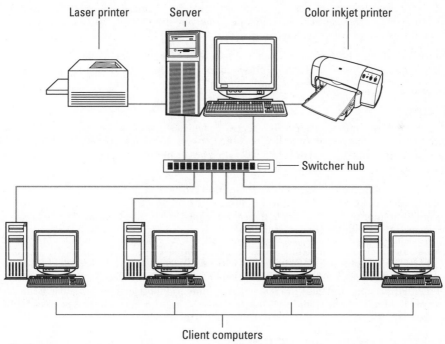

Figure 2-11: A simple client/server network has just one server and multiple clients and
peripherals.

Server types

If a network uses only one server, the server provides all services to the clients. Some services include file storage, application management, printer and other peripheral management, backup and restoration services, Internet access, and so on. If not many clients are attached to the network and the server is a powerful machine, one server can easily provide all of these services.

If, however, many clients are on a network and they all need a variety of services, it's often a good idea to add one or more additional servers. With a second, third, and fourth server added, network efficiency improves.

Small Business Tip

In a home, you're not likely to need more than one server; in a business environment, however, using multiple servers may be necessary. You can use one server, for example, as a file and print server, and another as a backup server, Web server, database server, or other type of server, depending on the type of business you run and the amount and type of information you use in that business.

When more servers are added to a network, each server usually specializes in certain jobs to help improve productivity. For example, one server might contain all the data files and folders for all clients, one server might provide e-mail and Internet access, and another server might furnish shared applications.

Figure 2-12 illustrates a network using multiple servers. Each client computer in the figure represents ten clients. The services provided to these clients are divided among the three servers so network traffic is faster and wait time is shorter.

Security

One of the most important services a server provides is *authentication*, or checking to make sure that a user has permission to access the network. In a small network, one server might perform authentication and other services. In a larger network with multiple servers, an authentication server might perform the job.

Similar to Windows checking your username and password, an authentication server does not allow a user access to the network unless he or she types in the exact information called for and that information appears in the server's master list. The list contains usernames, passwords, and user account information.

User account information includes a list of permissions, or rights, for a specific user on the network. These rights specify whether the user can access certain files, folders, and services. If a user wants to print, for example, the client computer sends a request to the server, which then either accepts or denies the request according to that user's permissions. If the server accepts the request, the print job is then sent to the appropriate printer. The network administrator sets the rights and permissions for each user of the network.

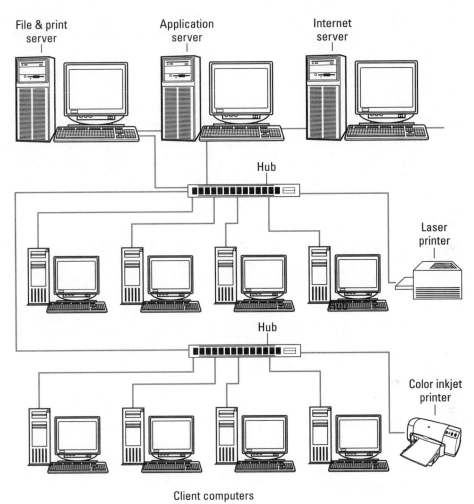

Figure 2-12: A larger client/server network uses more servers to provide services.

Client/Server Operating Systems

Both client and server computers have an operating system that enables them to be a part of the network. Client operating systems vary, but Windows 98, 2000, and XP Professional are standard because of the built-in networking software they contain. You can set Windows to act either as a client on a workgroup network or as a client on a client/server network.

In addition, Macintoshes and Linux machines have networking software included with the operating system that make either computer a good addition as a client to nearly any network.

Servers, however, are a different matter altogether. Servers use a *network operating system* (NOS) that enables the server computer to manage users and resources. Authentication, for example, is a specialized service that not any operating system can perform. Similarly, many network management programs provide particular services, such as logging user activity, redirecting data between clients and servers, file tracking and locking, and so on.

Popular network operating systems include Novell NetWare and Microsoft 2000 Server. Linux has quickly become a popular network operating system as well. All of these NOSs fit perfectly into a client/server network. Other network operating systems, such as Unix, are targeted to mainframe or minicomputers, as opposed to PCs.

In addition to a network operating system, many servers contain other software meant for client/server computing. A Web server is one example of client/server software. The server software manages the Web site with all of the Web pages that appear on the Internet. The software may also take orders from people online, send confirmations, and collect information from Web visitors. The client software for a Web server is an Internet browser.

Other server software includes databases, accounting programs, e-mail programs, and so on.

Deciding between client/server and workgroup

The type of network you choose depends on your network goals. Think about how much money, time, and effort you want to spend on your network. Client/server networks require more than workgroup networks — more time, more money, and more effort. Client/server networking, however, may provide you with the services and benefits you need and want.

Consider these questions when deciding between workgroup and client/server:

✦ **How many computers will you attach to the network?** If you plan to connect more than 10 computers, you should use client/server networking. Client/server networks can provide better data throughput (a measure of the rate data transfers over the network), more efficient use of resources, and more effective use of your computers. You can also use client/server networking with fewer than 10 computers. A server can serve two or three or four client computers just as well as, if not better than, 50 or 100 client computers.

✦ **Is strict security a problem for your data and files?** Generally, security is a problem when a user tries to hack into a system and uncover confidential files. A client/server network can track and prevent such hacks to the system. A workgroup network can only prevent access to files; if a cracker (someone who maliciously invades your system) wants to get into a file that's not readily available, he or she most likely can. Security risks like this are not usually a big problem in the home.

✦ **How much control do you want over the network?** Strict control over all files, directories, and resources on the network is a function of client/server networking. Although you can control your computer in a workgroup environment, that's not the real plus to that type of networking. Sharing and trust go better with workgroup networking.

✦ **How much time do you want to put into your network?** A workgroup network is easier to manage and takes less time than a client/server network. With client/server, you must provide users' accounts, set permissions on files and folders, manage applications on the server, manage resources and connections, and maintain and troubleshoot problems. You'll also be troubleshooting connections and problems with a workgroup network; however, much less can go wrong when you're not supporting a server.

✦ **Do you plan to use an application, such as an accounting or database program, that supplies client/server components?** You may need to use a client/server program at home. If you have a home-based business, for example, and you need two or more people to access a program at the same time, you may need a client/server network. Check your applications carefully before choosing the type of network you'll be using.

Unless you have a specific reason for starting with a client/server network, such as one of the preceding situations, then you would be better off to start with a workgroup network. You can connect your computers, share files and resources, and see how that works before continuing on a more expensive and work-intensive path.

You can also purchase hardware that will lend itself to both workgroup and client/server networking, in case you later want to upgrade. Investing a little more initially if you think you might change network types makes good sense in the long run.

 Note   You can use a computer running Windows 98 or XP Professional as a server of sorts. For more information, see Chapter 4.

Converting workgroup to client/server

As previously mentioned, you might want to set up a workgroup network while keeping your options open for a client/server later. It makes sense to begin your networking experience with a workgroup network: become familiar with networking hardware and software, try various configurations of computers and resources, practice networking shares and permissions, and so on.

You can always add a server to your network when you outgrow your workgroup or conditions change to merit adding a server. For instance, you might form a business in your home, need to protect certain information from visitors, or just want to try a server to learn more for your work situation. Adding a server to your network means you'll only need to change permissions and access to files, folders, and resources. For more information about these topics, see Chapter 4.

Getting Your Family Ready for a Network

You may think all you have to do to get your family ready for the network is to sit them down in front of the computer and say, "Go to it." If you do that, you'll have a lot of problems before the first day is through. If, however, you can prepare everyone for what is to come, you will all definitely have a more successful networking experience.

You'll want to explain to the family the concept of networking and sharing resources. You may want to implement a few guidelines to help everyone adjust to the new way of working and to thrive in the networking environment. Naturally, you'll want to teach everyone how to use the network. In this matter, it might be best if you teach the adults in your family first, and then each of you can take turns teaching the children.

Small Business Tip

You'll also need to consider your employees if you plan to set up a network in your business. Teaching coworkers or staff to use the network is most important in a business situation, because mistakes and ignorance can bring the entire network down, thus costing the company time and money.

Setting limits

Following are some suggestions for preparing the family. You can add your own ideas as you read through these.

Start with the hardware portion of the network. Explain that the cables should not be pulled, tugged, or snapped around. Vacuum cleaners, animals, and some toys can damage a network cable and render the connection useless, so everyone should be careful whenever they come near a cable. Also, make sure that they know the cable connects to a card in the computer. The card can easily be damaged if someone pulls or jerks the cable.

Next, make sure that your family understands the danger of viruses. You already may have discussed with your kids the risks of bringing disks home from school, but now the risk will be to the entire network, not just to one computer. You also want to warn of the dangers of opening files attached to e-mail messages and those downloaded from the Internet, if your network will be attached to the Net. Any executable (EXE) file can contain a virus. All machines on the network should have an antivirus program installed on it and used daily.

One of the first things computer users should understand is the probability of computer crashes when the computer's configuration is changed. Teenagers (and sometimes adults) are notorious for messing with the Control Panel icons just to see what will happen. Some changes are harmless and will not endanger the network. You should stress to the users, however, not to change network configurations in any way. After the network is set up, changing configurations will most likely disconnect that computer from the network and, unfortunately, it may be difficult to trace the changes and reconfigure them correctly.

Another important issue to stress is that changing the configuration, in any way, of another computer on the network is banned. No one should have to boot his or her computer and discover that all the settings have been changed.

You might want to ask your children, and especially your teenagers, to come to you when they have a problem with the network—such as connecting, sharing a file, opening a folder, and so on—instead of trying to fix the problem themselves. You may save yourself some headaches this way.

Find a central location to store documentation, application disks, computer books, boot disks, and so on. You could store all documentation in one place or assign certain locations for each item or program. Emphasize the importance of CDs and boot disks. Without them, you have no backup of your computer's settings and data if the hard disk fails.

Talk to the family about changing configurations and settings on printers and other equipment that is shared on the network. Changing ports, defaults, and especially drivers can cause trouble for everyone.

If your network is connected to the Internet, consider discussing the download of large files. Files you download from the Internet, such as graphics, games, and other programs, can take up a lot of disk space. Consider assigning everyone some extra hard disk space to which they can store and download files.

Ask that each person in your family keep their hard disks clean. Removing temporary files (TMP) and Internet temporary files periodically can really save space on a computer. Also, everyone should explore their hard drives once a month or so and remove any extraneous files. Remember, if your kid's hard drive is full, he or she may start saving files to your hard drive, and soon, your drive will be full too.

Note   To remove TMP files from your computer, open the Windows Explorer and go to the Windows\TEMP folder. Select and then delete all files ending in a TMP extension. For information about using the Windows Explorer, see Chapter 14.

Discuss whether to leave computers and printers on when finished with them. To print to a printer attached to a computer, that computer must be left on. To use a scanner or CD-ROM drive, the computer must be left on.

Emphasize to the users that no one should turn off their computer without first warning everyone on the network. Even if the computer has locked up, someone else could still be accessing files or applications from the locked up computer. Turning that computer off could damage the open files or program.

No one should ever rename, delete, move, or otherwise change the file system of someone else's computer. If there's a need to change a file, suggest that they copy the file instead.

Make sure that everyone understands what program files are and the importance of the Program Files folder, the Windows folder, and any folders containing drivers. Changes to the files in these folders, or in the location of these files, can crash applications or even the operating system of the computer.

Tip   You can place some controls on computers and their use on the network with an applet that comes with Windows. For more information, see Chapter 23.

Setting guidelines

You can easily set some guidelines for using the network. You might list which files and folders are off-limits on their own and others' computers and then share the list with everyone on the network. Following are some other guidelines you might consider:

✦ Guidelines for the use of the individual computer. Perhaps some family members are familiar with computer usage, but a refresher never hurts.

✦ Rules for the use of the network, including saving files, restarting the computer, leaving the computer and resources on, and so on.

✦ Rules for using printers and other peripherals.

✦ Guidelines for using the Internet.

✦ A description of appropriate file storage and backup guidelines.

✦ Game usage, especially when it comes to inviting friends over to play on the network.

Using naming conventions

You can create a naming convention that helps the people who use the network to easily organize and find files and folders. Consistent use of names on the network makes it easier for your family to find their way around on the network. You need to consistently name both files and folders.

As an example, certain file types—DOC, JPEG, WAV, and so on—should be stored in their own folders. You can create a Document folder, Picture folder, and a Music folder. You may also want to create a folder or directory for Applications, another for Drivers, and yet another for Shared files. You can create a file folder for each member of the family on the largest computer on the network, such as Sue, Molly, Carlos, and Willa. Each family member then stores important documents in that folder as well as on their own machine.

When naming files, consider keeping the names short, if possible. Even though Windows allows for long filenames, long filenames are often hard to organize and keep in any order. You might want to name files by date, or by the initials of the creator of the file plus a numbering scheme. SP0503.doc represents a file created by Sue Plumley on May of 2003, for example. Another idea for naming files that the family will share is by topic or subject. Fototexas and Fotobeach are examples of photo files of various places, or Hwmath01 and Hwsocstu10 are examples of homework files for various subjects.

However you choose to name your files and folders, make sure everyone understands the strategy and that everyone agrees to keep within the naming conventions.

Understanding rights and permissions

When you're a member of a network, you have certain responsibilities to respect the others on the network. This is an important concept to teach your kids and even your spouse. If you feel you can trust everyone on the network, and if you don't have any confidential information, then you needn't worry about rights and permissions. However, if you do have some things that should remain private, you can easily set rights on the files or folders so that no one but you can see them.

A client/server network gives you more control over rights and permissions—authorization to use specific resources. Most NOSs let you, the administrator, define a user's permission to use each resource. See Chapter 4 for more information.

Workgroup networking enables you to control rights and permissions simply by placing passwords on specific files and folders. See your operating system documentation for more information.

Teaching the use of the network

Before you can expect everyone to use the network without any problems, you'll have to teach them the finer points of network usage. You may want to sit down with the entire family or go over it with each individual. It's a good policy to show the adults in the house how to use the network first, and then let them help you teach the kids.

You don't have to teach everyone the intricacies of the network; you just need to show them how to get what they need and go where they must go. The less you tell kids, as a matter of fact, the better off you'll be in the beginning. As teenagers work with the network more and more, you can begin to show them the details of how it works.

Consider the following issues to teach the kids:

✦ Browsing the network

✦ Directory structures

✦ Opening folders on other computers

✦ Copying folders and files from others' computers

✦ Creating folders on others' computers

✦ Backing up to a specific drive or folder

✦ Finding the printer or other peripherals

✦ Choosing the default printer (if you have more than one printer)

Tip

For very young children, you can map drives and folders to make it easier for them to find their way to another computer's files. Mapping drives cuts through the directory structure and represents a folder as only a drive letter. For more information about mapping drives, see Chapter 13.

In teaching anyone about the network, perhaps the best way is to allow that person to use the network in everyday tasks. If you're teaching your spouse, ask him or her to open a program, save some files, back up some files, print, and otherwise perform normal tasks by using the network drives, folders, and printers. When teaching a child, have the child open games or other programs and play them. Use their tasks in teaching the lesson.

Protecting a Computer from Its Owner

If you're concerned that a child is perhaps too young to use a computer or that your teenager may change configurations just to spite you, you can install a program, Fortres 101, that limits the changes a person can make to his or her own computer.

Fortres is a program that enables you to block and control access to the computer. It's an invisible guard that examines each user command and compares it to a list of restrictions you have prescribed. You can choose which applications are executable, which files are accessible, and which configurations in the Control Panel and elsewhere can be changed.

Fortres protects the boot process, the desktop settings, and the file system arrangement of the computer. It enables you to control access to local drives, files, and directories. This program works with both standalone and networked machines.

You install Fortres and configure it for each computer. It uses a central control module that enables you to control configuration on the network remotely. You can execute any program on any machine, reboot, log off, and shut down any computer on the network as well. Fortres works with Windows 98, 2000, and XP computers.

Summary

In this chapter, you learned about network basics. You learned the definition of a network and how to understand some common network components. Additionally, you learned the following:

✦ Advantages to networking

✦ Disadvantages to networking

✦ The difference between a client/server network and a workgroup network

✦ How to prepare your family for using a network

In the next chapter, you learn about workgroup networking requirements, division of labor among your computers, and limitations of workgroup networking.

✦   ✦   ✦

Understanding Workgroup Networking

When planning and setting up your network, you may want to go the easiest and least expensive route. Workgroup (also called peer-to-peer) networking is the answer. Workgroup networking provides file and printer sharing, some network security, and bonuses such as e-mail, shared Internet connections, and flexibility in the use of the other computers on the network. If you're new to networking, workgroup is the best way to start. Even if you're a network authority, workgroup is probably the best choice for a home network.

Understanding Workgroup Requirements

Workgroup networks connect up to 10 computers for the purpose of sharing files, folders, printers, and other peripheral equipment. Technically, you can connect more than 10 computers (up to 25); however, the more computers you connect to a workgroup network, the more the performance of each computer becomes impaired.

A workgroup network is easy to maintain and set up. It's also cost-effective, especially for home network use. A wide range of cabling and networking solutions are available for your home network. Some solutions provide fast and powerful networking; others offer slower connections yet reliable service.

Cross-Reference For a complete discussion of the advantages and disadvantages of a workgroup network, see Chapter 2.

Boosting computer performance

A workgroup network can be efficient for many networking duties. When only two or three people are using the network, the network traffic should not hamper any one computer's performance. Network traffic encompasses any data sent from one computer to another computer or to a printer or other resource connected to the network.

Figure 3-1 illustrates a simple home network. Mom has a laptop and desktop computer in her office; the laser printer is connected to Dad's computer in his den; and the teenager uses another computer in his room. All computers can access the laser printer, as well as the resources on other machines in the house.

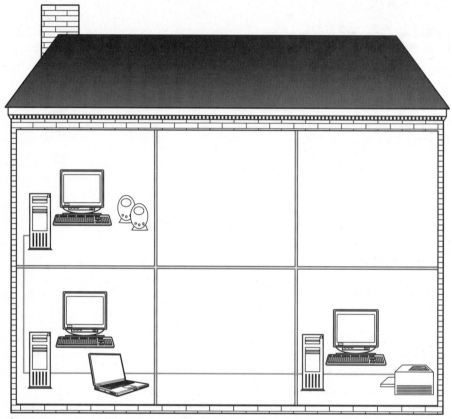

Figure 3-1: A typical home network is perfect for workgroup networking.

When more people access resources on the network and traffic increases, however, or when the network tasks become increasingly more complex, individual machine performance may suffer. Computers with minimal power, memory, and disk space not only exhibit slow performance for the user, but can also slow down the entire network if its resources are used by multiple people.

Figure 3-2 shows a more complex home network. More peripherals and computers make additional network traffic. With more computers accessing each other and the attached resources, the individual computers also take a performance hit.

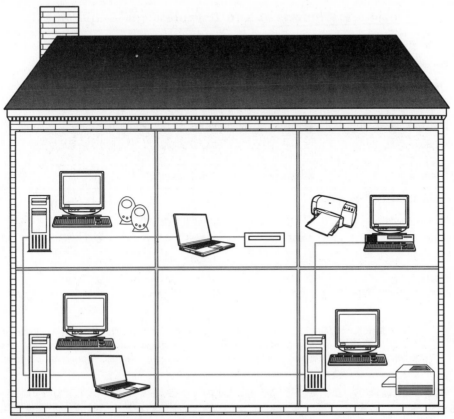

Figure 3-2: When you add more computers and peripherals to a network, you need more networking and computer power.

Small Business Tip

You might want to use a workgroup network in your small business. It can be efficient if you keep the network small—ten or fewer computers. In an office situation, people will access the computers and the network more than in a home situation; therefore, network traffic is likely to be higher than in the home as well. Consider building a workgroup network with an eye toward upgrading to a client/server network in the near future, especially if you'll be adding more computers to the network.

The best way to avoid problems with network traffic is, first, to begin building your network with computers that are capable of operating efficiently as standalone computers. Most computers—Windows and Macintosh, for example—have minimal and recommended requirements. If you can afford a computer that meets the optimal requirements or better, you'll see much better network performance as well as general computer performance. You can add memory, hard disk space, and processor speed at a minimal cost when purchasing a computer.

Table 3-1 describes the minimal, recommended, and optimal requirements for Windows 98 and XP Professional.

Table 3-1: Windows 98 and XP Professional Requirements

Component	Minimal	Recommended	Optimal
Windows 98			
Processor	166 MHz	Pentium/Celeron	Pentium 166 or higher
RAM	24MB	32MB	64MB
Hard disk space	295MB	1GB	8GB
Display	VGA	24-bit SVGA	24-bit SVGA
Component	Minimal	Recommended	Optimal
Windows XP Professional			
Processor	233 MHz	Pentium/Celeron	Pentium 300 or higher
RAM	64MB	128MB	32MB or more
Hard disk space	1.5GB	1.5GB	8GB
Display	SVGA	24-bit SVGA	24-bit SVGA

Note   For the Windows operating system, you will also need a 3.5-inch high-density floppy disk drive or a CD-ROM drive, depending on the media, a mouse, an audio card and speakers, a modem, a network card, and other hardware, depending on the tasks you want to perform.

Bytes, Megabytes, and Gigabytes

Hard disk space and random access memory (RAM) are measured in megabytes and gigabytes. First, you need to understand the basic unit in this numbering scheme—the bit. A *bit* is the basic unit of information in the binary numbering system, representing either 0 (for off) or 1 (for on). Computers read binary numbers, or strings of 0s and 1s.

Bits are grouped to form larger storage units, the most common of which is a *byte*. Bytes are made up of 7 and 8 bits, which, collectively, are also known as an *octet*. The word byte is a contraction of BinarY digiT Eight. The most important thing to remember here is that a byte usually holds one character—such as a number, letter, or symbol.

Bytes represent very small amounts of storage, so they are usually grouped in larger quantities. A *kilobyte* (KB) contains 1,024 bytes. You'll see your file sizes in the Windows Explorer, for example, listed in kilobytes if the files are small. The prefix *kilo* indicates 1,000 in the metric system.

A *megabyte* (MB) contains 1,048,576 bytes. The prefix *mega* represents 1 million in the metric system and is used for file size, as well as for computer memory and hard disk capacity.

A *gigabyte* (GB) contains 1,073,741,824 bytes. The prefix *giga* represents 1 billion in the metric system. You generally see gigabytes when talking about hard disk capacity. Large gigabyte hard drives now are the norm; you can purchase 40GB drives with no problem in a computer these days.

Windows XP Home Edition versus XP Professional

Windows XP comes in two different forms: Home Edition and Professional. The operating system you choose depends on your uses for the computer. Both XPs network well; both have features for sharing resources, Internet connections, e-mail, and more. So how do you choose which XP is right for you? XP Professional is generally known as a better operating system for networking, even though the XP Home Edition is advertised as a home networking OS.

XP Professional is more powerful for "power users." One definition of power user is someone who knows how to use the system — computers, programs, peripherals, and so on. Another definition for power user is a user who is denoted the highest level of rights and permissions on a network. If you're a power user, XP Professional would be a better choice for you. With XP Professional, you can use advanced networking, host and manage personal Web sites, use multiple processors, and use multiple languages.

You might also choose XP Professional if you plan to connect your computer to a larger network, say, when you take your notebook to work, for instance. XP Professional offers more security and is able to join a larger domain. You can access your home computer from your work computer as well. XP Professional provides more security to protect sensitive data by using encryption of files and folders and restricted file access.

XP Professional provides more protection from disk failure and corruption than Windows XP Home Edition provides. XP Professional gives you more options for backing up and restoring data.

Note　A common misunderstanding exists concerning the distinction between hard disk space and computer memory. *Hard disk space* is the amount of storage area on the hard disk. Disk storage might be 20GB, 40GB, and so on. Contrast this measurement with *computer memory* (or RAM), which might be 32, 64, or 128MB, for example. Computer memory is not the same as storage; memory is what the computer uses to perform tasks. Although the same measurements are used — megabytes — the definitions of disk space and memory are very different.

Boosting network performance

The network equipment you use when setting up your home network defines the speed and efficiency of your network. You may need only an intermittent connection for file or printer sharing, or you might want to connect to another computer to use the Internet or to play a game. You first must decide how you'll be using each computer on the network and how the resources will be shared, and then you choose your networking hardware.

The requirements of a workgroup network include the following:

✦ Two or more computers

✦ A network interface card for each computer

✦ Cabling or alternative equipment that enables the computers to communicate, plus networking hardware, when applicable

✦ A compatible (workgroup) operating system

✦ Optionally, a printer and other peripherals for sharing

The type of networking equipment you use dictates the performance of your network. You can start out with an efficient network, or you can upgrade as necessary. The type of cabling, network cards, and other networking hardware you use will dictate the speed of the network.

You can use a direct cable between your laptop and a desktop computer, for example, and copy files back and forth between the two computers (as shown in Figure 3-3) without the addition of network cards. The copy process will be slow, but it will get the job done. The direct cable plugs in between USB ports, serial ports, or even parallel ports. Using a direct cable is a great way to move files from one computer to the other and to keep computers in sync. A direct cable will cost you $25 to $35.

Note   A program named FastLynx is available for fast and easy transfer of files, folders, entire MP3, or digital video files. The program also lets you transfer files between Linux and Windows and between various Windows platforms. FastLynx costs around $70. For more information about FastLynx, go to www.fastlynx.info.

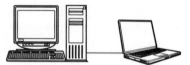

Figure 3-3: Connect two computers using only a cable, and no network cards.

Small Business Tip   If you're building a network in your office, you should probably choose the traditional Ethernet wiring and networking equipment. Trying to build an efficient network for office work with anything less will cost you more in time and frustration. Wireless technologies may work for you, too, depending on the type of work you plan to do on the network. For example, bookkeeping, billing, invoicing, and other accounting programs don't often work well over wireless because the program must access the processor continuously, and wireless sometimes drops the connection, even if it is for only a second or two.

You can use phone lines or your house electrical wiring to connect your computers and to share files, folders, and printers. Using a phone or electrical wiring network, you can connect more than two computers and you can offer more resources to all the computers on the network. The connection is still quite slow, but the cost of connecting two computers can be as low as $100. You can then add more computers to the network as you want.

Finally, you can connect two or more computers by using traditional wiring, called *Ethernet*, and other networking equipment. Ethernet provides a fast connection: ten times faster than a network using phone or power lines. The networking equipment includes cabling, network cards, and a hub. Naturally, the price for the technology is more, perhaps as much as $200 for two computers.

Figure 3-4 illustrates a small Ethernet network. Each of the computers contains a network card. Cables run from each computer to the hub. Using Ethernet cabling, network cards, and a hub means the network runs fast and efficiently.

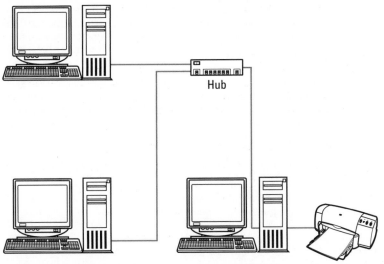

Figure 3-4: Traditional cabling using Ethernet networking equipment means fast connections between computers.

Cross-Reference For information about direct cabling and using telephone or power lines as network wiring, see Chapter 8. For information about optimizing your networking hardware, see Chapter 6.

Dividing Computer Duties and Resources

As you plan your workgroup network, you should think about which computers will perform certain tasks in the network. Some tasks include file storage, Internet access, backing up data files, and resource usage. Use the best computer for each job so that the entire network will run efficiently and economically.

The first thing you should consider is which computers will be on and available most of the time. Before anyone can use a computer and its resources, of course, that computer must be turned on. This should help you decide computer and resource placement. After all, you may not want to run upstairs to turn on a computer every time you want to use its CD-ROM drive or printer. When you're finished, you have to run back upstairs to turn off the computer again.

Other items to consider include computer memory, disk space, and specialty hardware for use with resources. In addition to using computers that operate efficiently, you may need to add hardware to computers that will perform special network tasks.

Assigning computer duties

Depending on the computers you plan to connect to the network, you'll want to decide which computers perform certain tasks on the network. You may want each computer to store its own files, for example, or you may have one exceptionally large hard drive that can hold everyone's extra files.

Figure 3-5 illustrates a home network with multiple options for file storage and backups. The computer with the Zip drive might be used for saving graphic files, for example. The computer with the tape drive can back up everyone's data files. And the computer with the large-capacity hard disk can contain folders in which each user can store his or her files, as well as folders for storing applications, Internet files, and other shared files.

First, determine the duties you expect from your computers. A computer can store files—word processing, database, graphics, application, data, and other files—for any or all of the users on the network. A computer also can store backup files for any or all of the computers on the network.

The difference between normal file storage and backup file storage not only determines the amount of hard disk space used but also influences network traffic. If you store your data files on your spouse's computer, for example, you will have to access your spouse's computer when you need the files. Each time you open or save a file, you create network traffic and use your spouse's computer resources, even if it is for only a moment or two. In addition, your spouse's computer will need to be turned on whenever you need files.

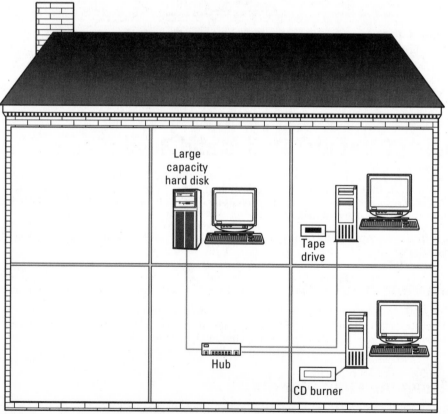

Figure 3-5: Determine which computers work best for file storage, file sharing, and backups.

On the other hand, when you back up your files to your spouse's computer, you probably will not need to access the files at all. Generally, you need to access a backup only if something happens to your original files — corruption, disk failure, and the like. The process of backing up, however, takes longer than just saving one file to another computer. Also, because you should back up your files frequently, you will need to access your spouse's computer every time you back up. For more information about performing backups, see Chapter 21.

Small Business Tip

You must be sure to arrange for backups in an office setting. You may want to include two sets of backups, using different computers or even mass storage devices, such as a tape drive. You have to weigh the inconvenience and expense of backing up against the inconvenience and expense of re-creating your accounting, payroll, and customer information.

Disk space

You need to consider each computer's hard disk space before deciding which computer to use for file storage and backups. A computer with only 2 to 5GB of disk space cannot reasonably store many graphics files or music files, for example. However, a 2 to 5GB drive could comfortably store word processing and spreadsheet documents, in addition to several applications. Most new computers come with much larger hard drives now. It's not unusual to see drives that offer 40, 60, 80, or more gigabytes of space.

Depending on your computer's hard disk space, you might want to divide the file storage duties. You could back up all files to one computer, or back up your files to your spouse's machine, your spouse's files to your son's machine, and your son's files to your machine. Plan ahead, depending on the hard disk sizes of your computers.

Computer power and memory

Consider, too, the power and memory of each computer on the network. A very slow machine, such as a 300 MHz, might not be the appropriate choice for containing files that need to be accessed often. Such a computer slows down the rest of the network when accessed frequently.

Similarly, computers with less memory react more slowly than those with more memory. Reserve the Windows 98 computer with only 64MB of RAM and a Pentium II processor for network jobs that aren't processor- and memory-intensive. Use the Windows XP Professional computer with 256MB of RAM and a Pentium IV processor for backing up files quickly and effectively.

Dividing resources

The members of a workgroup network act as both the client and the server. As a server, each computer shares its files and resources; as the client, each computer partakes of the others' resources. You must consider the resources you'll be using on the network.

You can assign resources — such as printers, scanners, storage devices, and so on — to certain computers in your network so that everyone has access but no one computer is burdened by the load.

Figure 3-6 shows one solution to resource placement. The laser printer is located on the first floor of the house because there are two computers downstairs and only one upstairs. The scanner, on the other hand, is upstairs because the teenager uses it the most and that computer has the appropriate hardware to run the scanner. The other two computers are on the network, however, so they can access scanned images anytime from the teenager's computer.

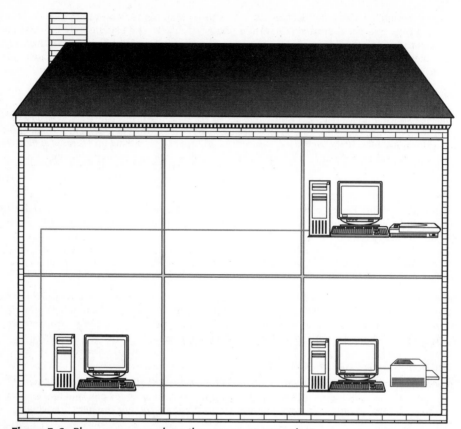

Figure 3-6: Place resources where they are most convenient.

Note

Typically, all computers on the network share all their resources with the others. It is possible, however, to limit which folders, files, and such can be shared by whom. For example, Windows computers use a sharing system to limit the access others can have to the machine. If you want to share files, you can make them available to everyone, or you can make them available only to those who have the appropriate password. Alternatively, you can choose not to share a resource at all. See Chapter 12 for more information.

For each resource you add to the network, you must determine which computer best suits that resource's requirements. Consider the requirements for scanners, printers, CD-ROM drives, modems, and others. Remember, too, that when you share a resource, the computer attached to that resource will take a performance hit whenever the resource is being used.

Small Business Tip

If your business uses several different printers, scanners, or other special devices that you plan to share over the network, consider using a client/server network for more efficient delegation of services.

When you install a scanner on a computer, you also need to install an adapter card and scanner software. That means the computer on which you install the hardware must have a free slot for the adapter card and room enough for the scanning program. Scanned images create large files, so you'll need plenty of storage space. Additionally, scanning requires substantial memory and processor speed.

The computer to which you install a modem and with which you connect to the Internet also must have considerable memory and processor speed for quick and easy access. The software for sharing an Internet account has special requirements; alternatively, you can use a piece of hardware (called a *router*) to share Internet connections. See Chapter 12 for more information.

Temporary Internet files and cookies take up a lot of disk space as well. Cookies are identifiers saved on your hard disk during your visits to various Web pages. Software on the Web sends the cookie to collect information—such as your name, e-mail address, site password, and so on—and then logs that information on your hard disk. The next time you visit that particular site, software from the site recalls the cookie so that it knows who you are. Most cookies are harmless.

Figure 3-7 shows the C:\Windows\Cookies folder with several cookies listed in the folder. Note that these are very small text files. You can delete them periodically to make more room on your computer; when you delete a cookie for an Internet site you visit often, however, you also may be deleting a saved password and username that makes it easier for you to get onto that site.

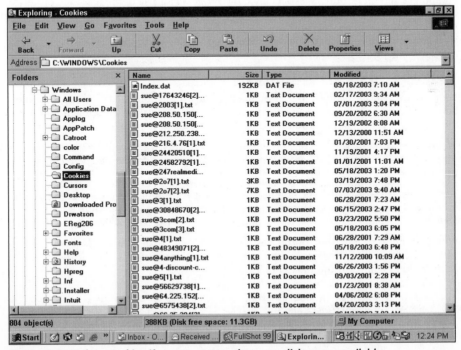

Figure 3-7: Delete cookies if you want to make more disk space available.

Small Business Tip

If you use a Web connection on your small-business network, you should certainly employ some sort of security. It's common for crackers to break into local networks from the Internet and pilfer business records, confidential files, payroll information, and more. The cracker could be your competition, a disgruntled employee, or even a kid experimenting with applications built for cracking systems. Consider using software such as a firewall or a proxy server. For more information, see Chapter 16.

You may prefer to back up files or store files on a CD drive, Zip drive, or other mass storage device. When deciding whether to attach the storage device to a computer, check compatibility as well as requirements. Tape drives are often difficult to install on some computers, for example. CD drives are easy to use, inexpensive, and popular for storing and backing up files.

Understanding the Limits of Workgroup Networking

Workgroup networks offer many advantages for the home network. You can share resources and files with other users, read each other's schedules, learn about e-mail, and share an Internet access account, for example. You also can experience some real problems with a workgroup network.

As mentioned earlier in the chapter, workgroup networking can place a strain on individual computers and on resources, especially if the requests for use of the resource or network traffic is high. Also, workgroup networking offers little security for your files and data, and it limits the number of people you can attach to the network. Understanding the limits of a workgroup network will help you determine some solutions to the problems.

Considering performance

Your network performance depends on many issues. You should make sure that you have sufficient computer power, and you need to consider the networking equipment you'll use. The most positive aspect of performance is that you can always upgrade your equipment.

In home networking, you can begin building your network with even the most minimal computer and networking equipment. After you use the network for a while, you can decide if the performance is adequate for your needs.

For this plan to work, however, you need to be sure your initial purchases are upgradable. For example, if you purchase a computer, check to see if you can add additional hard disks, if you have plenty of slots for adapter cards, and if the memory is easy to find and upgradable.

With your network hardware purchases, you also should plan ahead. When you buy network cards, buy cards that fit several different cabling types and speeds, if possible. When you buy cabling, don't limit your upgrade choices.

Cross-Reference

For more information about network cards, see Chapter 9. For more information about cabling, see Chapters 6, 7, and 8.

Thinking about security issues

You probably won't need to worry too much about security issues in your home network. You most likely trust your spouse and your children with any information on the network. There are, however, a few issues to consider.

✦ First, accidents happen. Someone could access your hard disk accidentally and delete a few files, a folder or two, or your entire hard disk's contents. This kind of potential problem is a security issue.

✦ Second, a child could always bring home a friend who fancies him- or herself a hacker. It's not too unlikely that such a kid could access and then alter, delete, or just read your private files.

✦ Third, if you have an Internet connection, the possibility always exists that someone could crack your system and compromise your data.

Most operating systems provide some safety measures that can protect your files from access by others on the network. You can choose which files to share and which remain private. Also, applications are available that enable you to control other computers on the network so that files, settings, and configurations are not accessible by anyone without a password. Finally, you can add software to your network to help protect it from intruders via the Internet.

Cross-Reference
For more information about limiting access to your files and your computer, see Chapter 12. For more information about Internet security, see Chapter 16.

As you plan your network, remember the possible problems and solutions and build them into your plan.

Limiting the number of users

As you know by now, a workgroup network limits the number of users you can add to your network. Ten users are the most you can connect before you start to see a major deficit in performance. Even if you have fewer than ten users, you can experience performance problems. Three or four users who use network resources heavily can slow down performance and hinder everyone's computer and network operation.

If you have any idea at all that you'll be adding more users or heavy-usage users to your network, consider using high-performance networking equipment, such as Ethernet or Fast Ethernet. You also should consider using a client/server network.

Ethernet and Fast Ethernet are networking technologies that provide speed and superior performance. For more information, see Chapter 6. A client/server network may better serve your needs by using a dedicated server and specialized software. See Chapter 4 for more information.

Troubleshooting Workgroup Networks

Troubleshooting a workgroup network is fairly easy. First, a workgroup network has only a few users and computers to check when something goes wrong. Second, after the initial setup, only a few things can go wrong to make the network stop working. As far as administering a workgroup network is concerned, your job will be easy.

Solving workgroup networking problems depends on the hardware you use to build your network. Unless someone changed the configurations, the problem isn't likely to be in the networking software. When a connection or access problem occurs, you should check all connections to the network: A cable or network card could be the problem. Replacing these networking items is quick and easy.

Each chapter of this book includes some troubleshooting tips. Additionally, check Appendix A for information on specific problems.

Summary

In this chapter, you learned about workgroup networking. Specifically, you learned about the following:

✦ Understanding workgroup requirements

✦ Dividing up computer duties and resources

✦ Understanding the limits of workgroup networking

In the next chapter, you learn about client/server networking.

✦   ✦   ✦

Understanding Client/Server Networking

A client/server network might work for you if you have special circumstances that require a server, such as a database program that must run on a server. You may want to work with a server for the knowledge and experience of setting up and managing a more complicated network. Although the client/server type of network is more expensive and takes more administrative time than workgroup, there is a definite place for its use in networking today.

Understanding Client/ Server Requirements

A client/server network consists of two or more client, or user, computers and at least one server computer. In a true client/server situation, the client computers do not use each other's resources, only those of the server. The server computer controls all files, folders, printers, and other resources on the network.

Note   A small network might use one server for 2 or 100 clients. As networks expand and the need for services increases, you can add multiple servers to a network. Very large networks might use 10 or 20 servers, for example, that serve hundreds or thousands of clients.

Client/server networking lightens the load for the client PCs. Clients can use the server to store files and to perform some processes, such as monitoring print jobs and running certain applications. The server's load, on the other hand, increases, especially as more and more clients request services.

Figure 4-1 illustrates a simple client/server network. The server is a powerful computer that authenticates users and supplies files, folders, and resources to the users. The server also controls the network printer. Client computers must send a request to print, access a file, and so on, to the server first. Note that the hub is the central connection for all cables.

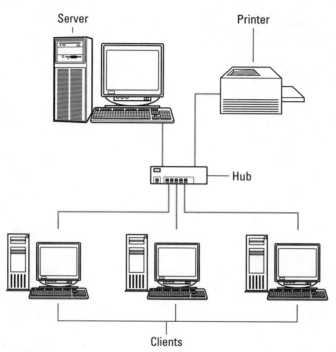

Figure 4-1: A simple client/server network using traditional cabling methods

Servers generally use faster processors and have more memory (RAM) and disk space to perform the management of the network. Servers perform multiple duties, including the following:

✦ Authenticating users

✦ Allowing access to resources — files, folders, printers, and so on

✦ Providing Web access

✦ Tracking resource usage

✦ Logging security breaches

✦ Distributing e-mail

✦ Providing application access and data

Note   The client/server network has many advantages and disadvantages. You can read more about these in Chapter 2.

Considering network requirements

The requirements for the clients on a client/server network are similar to those of a workgroup network. Usually, a client/server network uses two or more client computers attached to a server computer. Although having only one client and one server in a client/server network is possible, you may not need a server in this situation. See Chapter 2 for more information on deciding whether to use a workgroup network or a client/server network.

For each computer on the network, you need a network adapter card. Compatible cabling is also necessary, as well as any other networking hardware, such as a hub, switch, or phone jacks. See Chapters 6, 7, and 8 for more information.

You can add printers and other resources to your network as well. When you add resources, you choose whether to attach them to a local computer or to the server computer. For example, you might have a laser printer you attach to the server and let everyone share. On the other hand, you also might have a color inkjet or an old dot-matrix printer that you attach to just one machine for use by that one person.

Figure 4-2 illustrates a small client/server network in which the users share the laser printer attached to the network. The inkjet printer and the scanner, however, are attached to individual computers and can be used only locally. A network operating system doesn't share resources attached to the clients, only resources attached to the network or to the server.

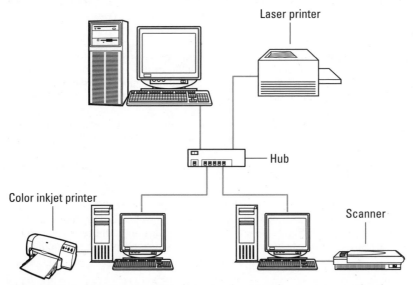

Figure 4-2: A client/server network uses only network resources, not local resources.

Tip

If you want to set up the network in Figure 4-2 to share the inkjet printer and the scanner, you can, depending on the network operating system you use and how you configure your network.

In addition to the client and networking hardware, you need to obtain and set up a server computer.

Tip   You always should use an uninterruptible power supply (UPS) on the server so that you can shut down the server properly before the power outage affects it. A UPS is a battery backup that keeps your computer running long enough during a power outage for you to save your work and shut down properly. A UPS does not, however, enable you to continue to work after a power outage. Most UPSs last only for 5 minutes or so, just long enough to shut the computer down.

Considering server requirements

A server computer must have sufficient processor speed, RAM, and disk space to provide various services to the clients. The server's hardware configuration depends on the type of services it will offer and the number of clients on the network.

In addition to hardware, the server needs a compatible operating system. You can use a network operating system, or you can use Windows 98 or XP as a server of sorts. (Microsoft has phased out Windows 2000 Professional — a client computer — but they still make a specific network operating system called Windows 2000 Server.) A network operating system supplies more management, security, and other features and tools that make operating the network efficient. Windows 98 or XP as a server operating system limits the services, but might work for your network. See the section in this chapter titled "Looking at Available Network Operating Systems."

Note   Windows 2000 Server (and Professional) requires special hardware to run. You cannot upgrade a Windows 98 computer, for example, with just the operating system. If you purchase Windows 2000, it is best to buy a server computer with the operating system installed, so you'll be sure you have enough power, memory, and other hardware to run the program.

The hardware you choose for your server, first and foremost, must be compatible with the operating system. You first should choose the OS you will use and then purchase the server computer. Each OS requires specific amounts of memory and disk space and perhaps certain types of drives — such as Small Computer System Interface (SCSI) or Integrated Drive Electronics (IDE) — and other such requirements.

Note   *IDE* is a popular hard disk interface standard that provides only medium to fast data transfer rates. IDE isn't always a good interface for server applications because it's slow and has other limitations in functionality that hamper a server's operations. You can use an IDE interface in some server circumstances, however, depending on the network operating system (NOS).

SCSI, on the other hand, is a high-speed parallel interface. In addition to being fast and extremely practical for server use, you can use SCSI devices to connect a personal computer to as many as seven peripheral devices at a time — using just one port. A *port* is a socket into which you plug a card, cable, or other device. SCSI devices include hard disks, tape drives, CD-ROM drives, other mass media storage devices, scanners, and printers.

You can purchase server computers, complete with operating system, that are built specifically for the job. These computers have all the hardware compatible with the chosen operating system. You might be able to afford a supercomputer, which is a computer that has massive amounts of RAM, caching (temporary memory for speeding up computer processing), and disk space. However, you might need only a computer with extra memory and disk space for storing files and accessing the Internet.

The choice you make depends on your budget, the number and type of services you want to offer, and the number of client computers.

Small Business Tip

If you decide you need a server in your business, you also should consider a backup server. It doesn't take long for a server to become indispensable to a company, and the data stored there is often irreplaceable. A backup server, running a NOS, keeps up-to-date replications of all data on the other server. If the original server crashes or becomes inoperable for some reason, the backup server can take over without a loss of time, money, or data.

Considering client requirements

Client computers can be almost any brand, any operating system, and have few or many bells and whistles. As long as a client computer is relatively new (2 to 3 years old) and you install a network interface card and networking software, you can use that computer as a client. Naturally, the client computer will work more efficiently on the network if it's a newer and more powerful computer; but even older computers and operating systems will likely work.

The first thing you need to do is check the operating system. If your computer uses Windows 3.1, DOS, Macintosh OS 7 or below, for example, it's probably too old to try to upgrade and attach to a network. It's not impossible, but it won't be efficient and will be difficult. If your computer has a more modern operating system, such as Windows 98 or higher (Windows 95 might work in some cases) or Macintosh OS 8 or higher, then you can use it on a network.

The next thing you need to check is the hardware. Does the computer already have a network card? If not, does it have a slot for a network card? For more information about network cards, see Chapter 9. After you confirm your operating system and get a network card, you're ready to connect the computer as a client. For more information, read Chapter 10.

Considering Network Operating Systems

A network operating system is one designed specifically for a server. A NOS offers many features and tools that help you manage the network, clients, applications, security, and other facets of the network. A network operating system is also difficult to install, configure, and maintain.

As I have already mentioned, you can purchase a server computer, complete with a NOS installed. Nevertheless, you still need to configure the users, shares (permissions for others to use your files, folders, and so on), and other elements of the system in order to reap the full benefit of the server.

Choosing a network operating system

You already may be familiar with a network operating system from your job or some other experience. You may want to use a NOS for any of a variety of reasons. Perhaps you have specific networking needs — security problems, home business, Web business, and so on.

Another reason to choose a particular network operating system is that you're using an application that requires it. For example, Internet Information Server (a Web server) works best with the Windows 2000 network operating system. Some vertical (specially built) applications, such as a program for selling and listing real estate or managing an insurance business, might require a specific NOS.

Finally, you may have a server computer with an operating system already installed. Perhaps you bought a used server from work, or someone gave you equipment compatible with a specific network operating system.

If you have no preferences for a NOS, you should research the alternatives and find one that suits your needs. If, for example, you like Windows and you're comfortable with Windows, you might want to try Windows 2000 Server, or try using Windows XP as a server. If you're a big Linux fan, consider using a Linux server.

Realize, however, that a network operating system is not as easy to install, configure, and maintain as Linux or Windows on a standalone machine. A NOS takes a lot of time and effort to run successfully.

Considering network operating system essentials

When looking for a NOS, decide what is important to you in your network. Obviously, easy maintenance should be a priority in a home network. You also must consider your budget. Any network operating system should include certain essentials, however, and some features you simply might want in a NOS. Consider the following:

✦ All network operating systems include a tool for naming the users of the network and limiting their access to certain resources. Through user accounts, you can choose which files and folders a user may access, as well as which resources he or she can use, and you can limit access to other computers or servers as well.

✦ A good network operating system should include some sort of printer management tool. This tool helps you direct print jobs to the appropriate printer, cancel and delete jobs, and otherwise control printing on the network.

✦ Most network operating systems include diagnostic tools for examining the network components, such as protocols and connections. When something goes wrong with a connection, these tools make it easier to find the problem.

✦ Tools and utilities for gathering and analyzing network data might be important to you. Some NOSs log application errors and security breaches, for example. Others use optimization utilities to help you figure out where the network connections are slow.

✦ Some NOSs include Web utilities and support for browsers. You might want to create your own Web server, for example, for displaying home pages over the Internet.

Small Business Tip

If you own a small business, a network operating system with a Web server is an excellent idea for selling products over the Internet, advertising your business, or contacting customers. Microsoft 2000 Server, for example, includes a program for creating Web sites (FrontPage) and the Internet Information Server (IIS) for posting Web pages to the Internet. For information about security on a workgroup network, see Chapter 12.

Looking at Available Network Operating Systems

Network operating systems are complicated to install and operate. If you plan to use a NOS, you'll be investing considerable time and energy in learning the program and managing the network. Before you purchase a network operating system, find out about the features, requirements, and compatibilities of the system first. Make sure that the system meets your networking needs before you purchase it.

Following is a list of the most popular network operating systems:

✦ Microsoft Windows 2000 Server

✦ Novell NetWare/IntranetWare

✦ Mac OS eSoft Server

✦ Linux

As an alternative to using a network operating system in your home network, you can use a machine with Windows 98 or XP Professional as a server, of sorts. Windows includes many management tools to help you manage the network, but it doesn't include nearly all the features a NOS does.

Cross-Reference   See Part VI of this book for information about Windows management tools. Part VI includes chapters about Net Watcher, System Monitor, the System Policy Editor, and the Registry.

In general, a server should be able to maintain various levels of service, including the following:

✦ Serving clients who run their own applications but request data from the server, such as a spreadsheet or database program.

✦ Running programs on the server to share information between network users, such as e-mail.

✦ Running programs on the server that maintain a smaller version of that program running on the client. The server application supplies the processing and data; the client version makes requests for the data from the server, as in the case of a database application.

✦ Authenticating users and supplying each user with limited access to resources.

✦ Possessing the tools to diagnose network problems, log errors and events, and otherwise help in the management and organization of the network.

Windows 98 cannot meet all of these requirements for a network operating system. Windows XP comes closer to meeting many of these requirements. Both Windows operating systems can meet some of the qualifications for a server, however, and in your home network, one may be the best choice for your server's operating system.

Running a true NOS is difficult. You constantly must administer, manage, troubleshoot, and cope with a network operating system. It takes a great deal of time and study to install, configure, and maintain a client/server network. But using Windows 98 or XP for your server may be exactly what you need on your network.

You can use a Windows 98 or XP computer as a server in a small office, using many of the techniques and features described here. If you think your network may grow at all, however, you should consider using a true client/server operating system. A business has more files that need protection and more resources that need to be delegated, and as the network grows, new problems arise that can only be handled with a network operating system.

Using Windows 2000 Server

Windows 2000 Server is a 32-bit operating system that supports multitasking, which is the simultaneous execution of two or more programs, just as other Windows operating systems do.

2000 Server works well with Windows 98 and XP clients, as well as with Macintosh and Linux. You also can use computers running Windows 2000 Professional (although, as mentioned earlier in the chapter, Microsoft is phasing this operating system out) as clients for 2000 Server.

2000 Server provides security features that enable you to limit access to the server, printer, files, folders, and other resources on the network. You also can incorporate a logging and tracking feature that enables you to follow any application or system errors, so you can easily troubleshoot network problems.

Additionally, 2000 Server provides tracking and logging for security breaches. If someone tries to gain access to the network but doesn't have the appropriate permissions, for example, 2000 Server records the event in a log so that you can see the time, username, and other information. You might not need this feature in your home network; however, if your teenager brings his friends home to work on the computer, you may be glad you have 2000 Server security.

Windows 2000 Server also provides the following features:

✦ **Support for remote access** — You can dial up your home server from work to copy or transfer files, to print, and to perform other tasks remotely.

✦ **Manageable print services** — You can install network printers and share them; you can even choose which print jobs are first in line or cancel a job from the server.

✦ **Special backup services** — 2000 Server includes a replication feature that enables you to create a copy of the server drive on another computer, for complete backups of the NOS, configurations, applications, and data.

Windows 2000 Server supports all Microsoft BackOffice applications, including Internet Information Server, SQL Server (a database management program), Exchange Server, and so on. If you're running a small business, you can use a 2000 server with BackOffice to supply your users with every service they need. For more information about database management programs, see Chapter 20.

Using Novell NetWare

Novell NetWare is a 32-bit operating system that runs on Pentium processors. NetWare works with a variety of client computers, including Windows 98, Windows XP, and Linux.

NetWare is considerably more difficult to manage than a Windows NOS. You must learn cryptic DOS commands in order to accomplish anything. With NetWare, you cannot use the server computer as a workstation. You cannot even access the server files and such from the server; you must go to a workstation and log in to the server as an administrator to do anything on the server. This requirement means you must use a dedicated server computer with a workstation handy to log in to the server.

NetWare provides security features to limit access to drives, folders, and files on the server. It also provides tracking and logging features. You can use multiple utilities to manage the network, users, and resources.

Looking at Mac OS X Server

Apple has a server operating system that replaces AppleShare IP and Rhapsody-based OS Server. Mac OS X Server offers cross-platform file and printer sharing as well as Internet services. Cross-platform services enable Macs, Windows, and Linux machines to share files and to print within the network. You can manage these services for each user or for groups, controlling who may access which resources through permissions.

Note | If you use the cross-platform features of Mac OS X Server, you'll find there are some problems with client support. To enable Windows clients to attach to the server, you have to use special security passwords, which in turn means Mac operating systems below Mac OS X 10.2 (such as OS 8) are not able to attach to the server. Previous Mac OSs can upgrade to 10.2, however. There are other problems with Windows file services and connections, such as file compatibility between PC and Mac and file transfers.

Like Windows, Mac OS X Server enables multitasking and multiprocessing; the server software also offers networking support and security standards. Security standards are especially important in business settings; however, you may want to use the common security in your home and especially on the Internet. Internet services also include e-mail and Web hosting.

Mac OS X Server also offers management software, remote management, server monitors, and a user directory that makes administering the network easier than previous versions of the server software.

Considering Linux

There are many brands (called distributions or distros) of Linux, some of the most popular being Red Hat, Mandrake, Debian, Slackware, Gentoo, and SuSE. To make a Linux workstation into a server, you must install extra applications (called packages, in Linux). Some of the services (daemons, in Linux) you install for a server include FTP, HTTP, and SSH:

✦ **File Transfer Protocol (FTP)** enables you to transfer files between computers, whether over a network or over the Internet.

✦ **Hypertext Transfer Protocol (HTTP)** lets you transfer information across the World Wide Web.

✦ **Secure Shell (SSH)** is a program for opening programs on a remote computer.

Linux distros use permissions for files, directories (folders), and other resources. Linux permissions are similar to those in Unix. Unix is an operating system made up of cryptic commands and programs.

X is a graphical user interface (GUI) that lets you view the program with icons and menus, more like Windows. You can use it in the server; but you don't have to use it. You could, instead, use a desktop environment like K Desktop Environment (KDE) and GNU Network Object Model Environment (GNOME) that adds functions to the GUI to make it more like Windows. Linux uses an interface, called Samba, to control sharing of files and printers with Windows computers. Although difficult to set up, Samba is necessary if you use the Linux server with Windows clients.

Looking at a Windows 98 or XP Professional server

For your home network, you may not need all of the security, error logging, authentication, and other services you can get from a network operating system. If you need only a centralized computer for storing your files, managing your printers and resources, and accessing the Internet, then you can use a Windows 98 or XP Professional computer as a server.

Using a Windows 98 or XP computer as a server saves other computers on the network from performance problems. Computers do not need to access each other, only the server computer. Naturally, it also means that you'll have to equip the server computer with plenty of hard disk space, RAM, and any hardware and software necessary to run the extra peripherals.

Using resources

A Windows server can store everyone's files in folders and mark those files as shared, as appropriate. You can share all files with everyone or limit access to any folder or file on the computer. You also can use a Windows server as backup storage for individual computers on the network and as a repository for any applications to be copied to or installed on the client machines.

Figure 4-3 illustrates the Windows Explorer on a client computer. The server selected in the left window (Humble) displays shared folders to which the client has access in the right window. The server enables the client to view files and folders on the server for which he or she has share rights.

You can attach printers, tape drives, and other peripherals to a Windows server so that everyone uses that one computer for those resources. Placing the server in a central location makes it easy to retrieve printed materials or to insert CD-ROMs.

Windows provides a sharing feature that enables you to choose which files and resources are shared and to limit access to resources. Figure 4-4 illustrates the Properties dialog box for a shared drive on the server. Giving everyone full access means that each user can back up his or her data files to this drive. For more information about sharing drives, folders, and files, see Chapter 12.

Windows also includes some network management tools for viewing the network connections and for managing some network features.

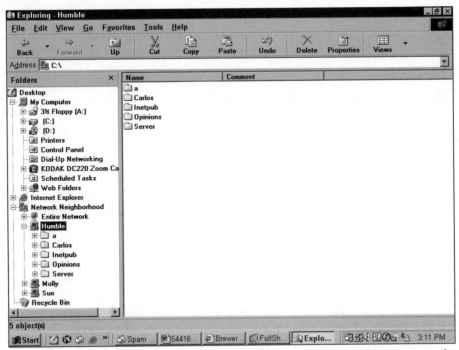

Figure 4-3: Only certain folders on the server computer are shared with everyone on the network.

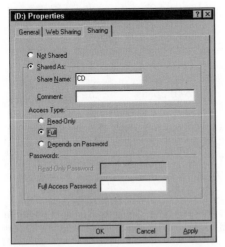

Figure 4-4: Control which server drives you share.

Using the Internet and e-mail

You can create a post office on the Windows 98 or XP server to distribute and collect e-mail within the home network. Using a server for e-mail means no one client computer gets bogged down with e-mail distribution.

Attach a modem and phone line, a cable modem, or a Digital Subscriber Line (DSL) modem to a Windows computer, install Internet access software, and you can easily share an Internet account with all members of the network.

Implementing Windows 98 or XP as a server

If you want to use a Windows 98 or XP computer as a server, you need to make a few decisions about the use of the computer, its placement, and the status of resource sharing.

Note   Windows XP is another operating system that requires specific hardware for the operating system to run efficiently. For example, you cannot upgrade a Windows 95 computer, or probably a Windows 98, to XP without upgrading the hardware as well.

Basically, the Windows server is another member of the workgroup network; it just has more power, memory, and disk space than the other computers. You can use the server as a dedicated machine. As a dedicated server, no one actually works on the computer; its function is to grant users' requests.

Alternatively, you can use the server as another workstation. When someone uses the server as a workstation, however, he or she may notice a performance hit, because others are requesting services. Also, those requesting services might notice slow performance because someone is using the computer for everyday work.

Considering server hardware

First, you need to make sure that you purchase or build a powerful computer to use as a server machine. In addition to a fast processor, hard disk space, and plenty of RAM, you'll want to install any software for peripherals attached to the server computer. If you're using XP as a server computer, make sure you have drivers specified for XP for all hardware (printers, modems, network cards, and so on).

Consider whether you'll use the computer as a dedicated server or as a server/workstation. Then add additional memory and processor power to compensate for the extra applications and the types of services you add.

Cabling and networking hardware for a Windows 98 or XP server are the same as for another network. You might want to use traditional (Ethernet) cabling, cards, and hubs to make the connections to the server as fast and efficient as possible. See Chapter 6 for more information. You may prefer wireless networking. If so, see Chapter 7.

Locating resources

Place the server computer in a central location. Attach all resources to the server computer that you want to be available to everyone on the network. You also need to create folders on the server in which users can store their data files, as well as folders for shared files and folders for backups. Because the computer will function as a server, you must turn it on whenever anyone wants to use a shared file or resource.

The Windows server is attached to a workgroup network, so users also can share their files and any resources attached to their machines, if they want. Figure 4-5 illustrates such a situation. The server computer shares the laser printer with all other computers on the network. See Chapter 15 for more information.

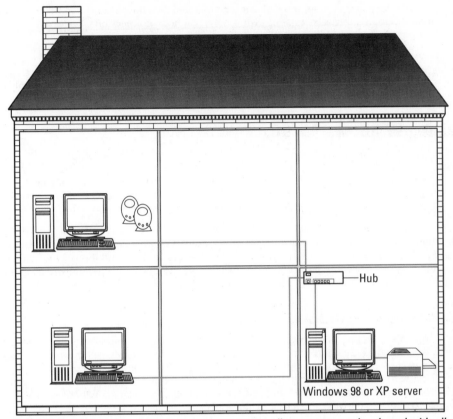

Figure 4-5: When using a Windows 98 or XP server, all resources can be shared with all users.

Looking at Client Operating Systems

When you use a server and server software, you naturally add client computers to take advantage of the services. Client computers can be any of the computers you have in your house now, such as a Windows 98 computer or an iMac. All you need to make a computer into a client is networking software, a network card, and a connection to the server.

Networking software comes with most operating systems. Windows, Macintosh, and Linux all have built-in networking software. Networking software includes a protocol (or language) the computers use to communicate with each other, a client program that prepares the computer to receive and make use of services offered by other computers, and network adapter drivers that enable the computer to send and receive communications over the network. See Chapter 10 for more information on configuring network software.

A network card is a piece of hardware you add to the computer if it didn't come with the system. Many types of cards exist, so you'll need to learn about them and then find out which type of card your computer takes. In addition, you'll need to make sure your computer has room (or a slot) for the network card. See Chapter 9 for more information.

To connect the client computer to the server, you must also have traditional wiring, wireless technology, or an alternative type of wiring, such as phone connections. See Chapters 6, 7, and 8 for more information.

However, first you need to consider your computer's operating system. You know which operating system you have and what it does for you. You obviously have reasons to use that system and understand how it works with general tasks. The following descriptions simply cover networking with various operating systems, no more. The choice is up to you.

Using Windows 95/98

Windows 95 and Windows 98 are perfect for client operating systems, although a Windows 95 computer might be a bit old and slow to work efficiently on the network. These operating systems have all of the necessary software for connecting to the network. Configuring Windows 95/98 is easy if you go step-by-step; unlike many of the newer operating systems, network configuration is not automatic. The steps are outlined in this book, however.

After connecting to a server, Windows 95 and 98 enable you to easily connect to a workgroup or client/server network. You can use any of the built-in protocols for networking, such as NetBEUI or TCP/IP. TCP/IP is also known as the Internet Protocol, and it provides high speed on any network. For more information about TCP/IP, see Appendix B. Windows also supports a wide variety of networking types, logon configurations, user profiles, and more.

Looking at Windows Me

Windows Me is an operating system built especially for home use and home networking. Windows Me does not enable you to attach to a server. Windows Me is, however, a great operating system for workgroup computing. When you attach a Windows Me computer (which has a network card) to other computers in a network, it automatically locates other computers, installs the software needed, and sets up communication for you. Windows Me is an easy-to-use workgroup networking operating system.

Considering Windows XP Home Edition

XP Home Edition is another operating system that does not work well with a server. XP Home Edition is built for home networking in workgroups. As with Windows Me, the operating system is built to recognize a network and communicate easily within a workgroup. When you connect XP to a network, the Windows XP Network Setup Wizard takes you through the configuration, step-by-step, to share computers and resources.

 Note   Using XP Home Edition is also beneficial in a workgroup setting because it enables you to share an Internet connection with the other computers in the workgroup. Also, XP includes the Internet Connection Firewall that helps keep the connection safe and secure. For more information about the Internet and firewalls, see Chapter 16.

Looking at Windows XP Professional Edition

XP Professional was built to use on networks, either workgroup or client/server. XP Professional can take advantage of a server's services, such as file sharing, printer, and other resource access. You can set up users on XP to assign permissions for use of the computer, and you can set up permissions for network users on each individual computer.

Like XP Home Edition, XP Professional lets you use the Network Setup Wizard to connect with other computers on the network, share an Internet connection, and use the Internet Connection Firewall. The Internet Connection Firewall is a security system that protects your computer, and other computers on your network sharing the Internet connection, from hackers and other intruders.

Windows XP Professional also enables you to connect many types of network adapters, such as phone line, Ethernet, wireless, and so on. XP uses a network bridge to simplify the configuration and enable access.

Using Windows 2000 Professional

Windows 2000 Professional is the client version of Windows 2000 Server, even though you can use a variety of clients with 2000 Server. 2000 Professional is based on NT technology; NT is an early Microsoft operating system for both servers and clients that developed increased speed, multiprocessing, resource sharing, and other networking enhancements. NT was so successful, Windows 2000 Server and Professional were built on that technology and improved upon.

Note   One problem with the newer Windows operating systems, including Windows 2000, is many companies have not yet produced drivers and applications that work with the operating system. Drivers for universal serial bus (USB) devices and peripherals, CD and DVD drives, sound adapters, network adapter cards, video adapters, mass storage controllers, removable storage devices, and input devices such as mice and tablets must be compatible with the operating system. Applications and drivers are abundant for Windows 2000 Server; however, Windows 2000 Professional has not taken off the way Microsoft had hoped. So drivers and applications might be difficult to find.

Adding Windows 2000 as a client brings some extra difficulties into the configuration. One thing you'll need to do is add the Windows 2000 computer to the network. Another thing you must do is create user accounts and profiles (describing permissions and rights plus other definitions for each user of the computer) for both the computer and the network. Using Windows 2000 Professional is difficult and involved. If you're new to networking and to Windows 2000 Professional, I suggest you use another operating system to begin your adventure. However, if you do succeed in properly setting up Windows 2000, you can expect increased speed and better performance on the network.

Tip   If you're currently using Microsoft HomeClick Networking with Windows 95 or 98, upgrading to Windows 2000 means your upgraded computer will not connect to the HomeClick Network. Currently there are no drivers for 2000 to work with HomeClick Networking. (HomeClick Networking was simple networking software Microsoft and 3Com put out to connect Windows 95 and Windows 98 computers.)

Using Mac operating systems

Using a Macintosh operating system as a client is similar to using a Windows operating system. You can share files and printers between Macs and between a Mac and a server or other Windows computer. You set up networking information and software in the Network pane of System Preferences on a Mac.

There are problems with Macs and networking, as there are with all operating systems. For example, sharing between different versions of Macs is often difficult. Mac OS X 10.2 and later include printer sharing, but when you connect a printer to the computer, it allows only other Mac OS X computers to use the printer; Mac OS 9 computers cannot use it. There is a workaround, however; you can make the printer work with Mac OS 9 computers by using the USB Printer Sharing service.

You can transfer and share files by setting up the Web sharing feature in the Web Sharing control panel of the Mac. Any computer, not just Windows and Mac, can share files using this method and a standard HTTP connection.

You can alternatively enable Apple File Protocol (AFP) on the Mac to enable it to see a Windows NT or 2000 server. You use the AppleShare icon in the Chooser to look at the resources on the 2000 Server.

If you plan to use a Mac with a Windows 98 "server," you need to install Server Message Block (SMB), a Windows file sharing protocol, to the Mac. Windows 98 doesn't offer AFP. You'll need a third-party program to install SMB to the Mac; for example, MochaSoft makes Mocha SMB or Connectix makes DoubleTalk, which you can use to create connections between a Mac and Windows computers. SMB is particularly beneficial when your computers are mostly Windows 95 or 98.

Note   Mac OS X versions 10.0 to 10.0.4 can connect to AppleShare only over TCP/IP. Mac OS 8.6 and earlier offer AppleShare only over the AppleTalk protocol. You'll need to upgrade to Mac OS 9 or Mac OS 10.1 or higher to achieve true bidirectional sharing. AppleShare is the Macintosh networking software, of which there are many versions.

Using various Linux flavors

Linux is a free operating system that is Unix-based. Because Linux is free, developers around the world add to the development of various flavors of the program. The operating system is developed under the GNU General Public License, meaning the source code is freely available to everyone and anyone can modify the source code.

As I indicated earlier in the chapter, many brands of Linux, called distributions, or distros, exist. Some distros are more user-friendly and customizable than others.

To use a Linux box for a client on a client/server network, you need the Windows GUI (usually X), a window manager, and analogs of the Windows applications.

Tip   In Linux, X is the GUI, but it also needs a separate program called a *windows manager* to handle windows, title bars, and the desktop.

Samba is a program that handles Windows' networking tasks, such as file sharing and print sharing. Linux clients are very customizable and versatile, especially in a networking environment.

Summary

In this chapter, you learned about setting up a client/server network for your home. Specifically, you looked at the following:

✦ Understanding client/server requirements

✦ Understanding network operating systems

✦ Reviewing network operating systems

✦ Reviewing client operating systems

In the next chapter, you learn about planning and preparing for your network.

✦   ✦   ✦

Planning and Setting Up Networking – Hardware and Software

Part II explains the information you need to connect your computers. After planning your network, you're ready to decide on the type of cabling and networking hardware you want to use. Chapter 5 gives you some tips on planning your goals for the network. Chapters 6, 7, and 8 explain various types of cabling and connections, methods of installing cable, and speeds to expect from the various options.

In addition to cabling, you must consider the networking hardware you'll install, including network cards and, perhaps, hubs. Chapter 9 covers in detail purchasing and installing networking hardware. After your hardware is installed, you must configure Windows to connect over the network. Chapter 10 explains how to configure protocols, clients, services, and adapters. Finally, Chapter 11 covers accessing the network with various operating systems.

Preparing for a Network

Before you begin planning your network, you must make some basic decisions. You need to look at a number of issues, such as the type of programs you might use, your budget for the project, and what you might add to the network in the future. Consider the requirements for the type of network you choose and the placement of the equipment in your home. Planning ahead gives you a basis for making decisions about the hardware and software you use in your network.

Defining Network Goals

You set network goals to help determine the networking hardware and software you'll use to build your system. You must consider equipment expense, network speed, the layout of the network, uses of the network, and so on. You also want to consider the needs of the family—what are their expectations and desires, as far as a network is concerned?

Consider which applications each person needs to run. Think about the resources you already have and what equipment you want to add to the network. Discuss not only near-term uses of the network but also future uses.

Cross-Reference

See Chapter 20 for information about licensing and using applications over a network. *Licensing* refers to the number of computers on which an application may be installed. Manufacturers use licensing to control the illegal use of their products.

Small Business Tip

Consider how your business might grow. You may need to add more employees, for example, and computer services such as accounting, payroll, inventory, customer services, Internet access, and so on. Try to consider all the possibilities for the next 1 to 5 years.

Determine the functions your network will perform—sharing files and printers, sharing other peripherals, providing Internet access, and so on. Understanding your networking goals helps you determine the hardware and software you'll need.

Looking at family needs

Before you decide on your network type and before you purchase networking equipment, you should sit down with your family and find out what everyone wants and needs. Make a list of your needs, and then question each family member about his or her needs. See where software and peripherals overlap and make a note of them. Decide which of the requests are the most important and concentrate on those first; add other programs and equipment as you become able to afford them.

Tip   Ask your family members to be thinking about their own username and password, which each of them will use on the network. Decide if you want to know everyone's password or not. It's a good idea for one person in the house, at least, to know everyone's password, in case someone forgets it.

Your first consideration should be operating systems. Does everyone have similar computers? Most Windows and Macs have built-in networking software. You can save money by using these operating systems because they contain built-in e-mail, a Web browser, a file management system, network management applets, and more. Of course, you can integrate other operating systems into your network, such as Linux, but networking is so much easier if everyone uses the same operating system. Think about upgrading your computers, if at all possible.

Note   Consider, too, if you plan to use a server. See Chapter 4 for more information about planning for and setting up a server in your home network.

Figure 5-1 shows the variety of computers and operating systems you can connect to a workgroup network. Each computer type uses different software to enable it to communicate with the other computers on the network.

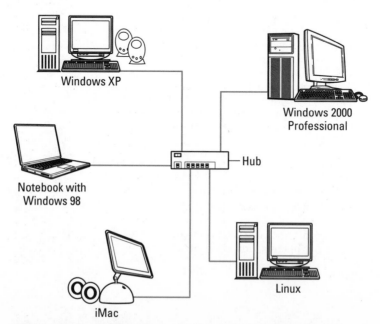

Figure 5-1: Attach all your computers to your workgroup network.

Next, you want to discuss applications. Which applications do you already have? Which ones do you and your family want in the near future? Don't forget to consider long-range application plans.

Are there any applications you want to share over the network? You might want to purchase multiuser network games. Scheduling and calendar programs are useful if you like to keep a schedule for everyone in the house. Sharing it over the network means everyone can input his or her own schedule and everyone else can view it. See Chapter 20 for more information.

Accounting or personal checking programs are another example. You share the data from these programs. If you've networked a personal checking program, the application locks the data while you're using it so that no one else can share the file until you're finished. That way the data is up-to-date when you use it and there's no chance it will become corrupted.

Figure 5-2 illustrates the shared folders for a personal checking program and the files it contains. You can share the data if the program is networked, so you and your spouse, for example, can use it.

You should also take an inventory of your current peripheral equipment: printers, scanners, CD or DVD burners, Zip drives, modems, and so on. Is the printer you now own old, or can it stand up to multiple users? Perhaps you all used the printer before installing a network, but consider that the ease of network printing places more load and stress on the printer. You may need to buy a new printer for network use.

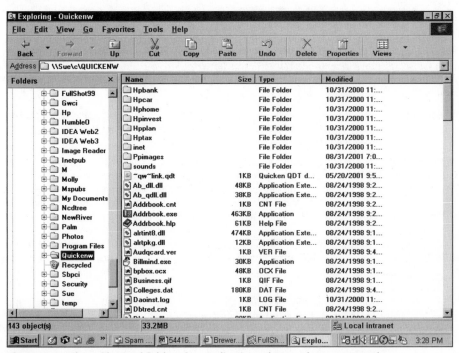

Figure 5-2: Share files and folders for applications that work on a network.

Tip   You can still make use of the older printer by letting one person use it exclusively or by sharing it with everyone. In the latter case, the older printer can pick up the slack when the new
one is busy, but it won't have to carry the entire load by itself.

Also, if you plan to use a CD or DVD burner extensively over the network, you might want to
invest in one drive that is faster to save time loading programs. If you have one or more stu-
dents in your home, reference books and other applications you run from a CD or DVD might
be used frequently. A faster drive helps the student, is available for all users, and saves on
network traffic.

If you don't have one computer with a large hard drive — for saving everyone's downloaded
files and backups, for example — you might want to invest in a Zip drive or CD-R/RW drive. A
Zip drive acts as another shareable drive on a computer. It uses cartridges — similar to floppy
disks but larger — that hold 250MB of data. Zip disks are perfect for backing up a lot of information. CD burners are also perfect for backing up information. Most CDs hold at least 700MB
of data now, and CDs are less expensive than Zip disks.

Finally, think about your future plans for the network. Will you be adding a computer for
another child soon? Are you thinking about telecommuting or working out of your home? Are
there any plans to take up a new hobby, attach to the Internet, or add a digital camera to your
life? Make a list of the things you might to add in the future so that you can consider these
issues when you're planning your network.

Considering your budget

With all of the networking equipment and software available, you can spend anywhere
between $25 and $15,000 (or even more), if you want, on your home network. You can connect two computers in a simple but effective network, or you can wire your entire house not
only for a computer network but also for environmental controls, security, and multimedia
systems.

The amount of money you need to spend on the network depends on several things: How
important is the network in your family's life? How much will you use the network each day?
What results do you want from the network?

Think about how fast, convenient, and useful you want the network to be. If you don't plan to
use the network a great deal — say, every day for several hours — then you can make due
with a slower network connection, which costs less money than a faster connection. If two or
more people use the network every day, you might want to invest a bit more money to make
the connections quicker and the equipment more reliable.

**Small
Business
Tip**   If you have a home office and the network is a part of your work — say, you have an in-home
business or you work part-time at home — you may be able to use the network as a tax
deduction. Check with your accountant.

Right now, you don't have to list the amount of money you can spend on each piece of networking hardware or on each computer. All you need to do at this point is estimate a total
amount of money you're willing to spend on the entire network. It might be $100 or less, $500
or less, or $1,500.

Note Keep your budget in mind as you read about hardware and software solutions in the next chapters; for the most part, approximate costs are listed throughout this book, along with Web addresses, when available. Make sure, however, that you check with the manufacturers or various Web sites for current prices.

Considering security

One thing everyone is nervous about is network security. Many reasons to worry exist, even in your home network; but then safeguards against these security problems do exist. One security problem with a home network is the Internet, another may be your children's friends, and finally, you always need to worry about accidents.

The Internet is alive with people from all walks of life, of all ages, and at all levels of computer savvy. Some people make a living from hacking into computers to steal identities, financial information, and other confidential information that could mean trouble for you. Other problems with the Internet are viruses, worms, and the like. Viruses come in through e-mail; true, if you don't open the virus (or EXE file), you won't likely be infected. Worms, on the other hand, often ride the backs of e-mails or come from Web pages right into your computer with nothing stopping them, except a good antivirus program.

Luckily, many ways to protect yourself from viruses and hackers exist. First, an antivirus program, such as Symantec's Norton AntiVirus or McAfee's VirusScan, is an important investment. Yes, you can get freeware or shareware antivirus programs; however, these often do not have automatic and frequent updates of virus definitions. Without updates, any new virus or worm can attack your computer and wreak havoc. So invest in your computer's safety, if you plan to use the Internet and e-mail.

In addition, there are steps you can take to protect your network from hackers. Some software programs, such as BlackICE (www.blackice.iss.net), block hackers and prevent destructive applications. Also, some hardware solutions, such as Linksys EtherFast Cable/DSL Router (www.linksys.com), enable multiple users to connect to the Internet while protecting your connection with a firewall.

Note A router is a hardware device you can add to your network. The router receives information from the network, analyzes it, and then directs it to the appropriate destination. The destination might be another network, such as the Internet, or another section of your private network, such as in a large company or corporation.

Cross-Reference For more information on security with the Internet, see Chapters 16 and 17. These chapters discuss security options, how to set up a firewall, and other information that will help with Internet security.

Another security problem comes with friends and visitors to your home. You might think you know everyone who comes to your house and, therefore, your network is safe, but consider the following scenarios. Your babysitter's boyfriend comes by while you're out. He discovers the computer network and decides it would be fun to look into your personal checking account, your confidential financial reports, and other information you thought was safe. How about your teenager's friends? They come over and hang with your daughter, check out the network, and print information that you thought was secure. What if you use a wireless network?

No one knows who might access your files and such when you're not home. So what can you do about it? There are several solutions. Most operating systems enable you to place a password on individual files. In addition, in a network, you can choose which folders you'll share. Therefore, the folders in which you store your financial reports and accounts are not shared to the network. If you want to share those folders with just your spouse, you can. If you want to, you can even hide the folders so no one sees them; anyone who wants to look at the folders then must know the name of the folder before he or she can open it.

For information about securing your files and folders, see Chapter 21.

Another problem you must consider when you have a network is accidents. Every now and then, especially when the network is new to the members of your family, someone will accidentally delete, overwrite, or lose something. The best way to take care of this type of problem is to make sure everything that is important to you is backed up. Backups are the only way to make sure you have copies of files, folders, and other files you want to keep. You can back up to a Zip drive, a CD, a tape drive, or to another drive over the network; but you must back up and back up often.

For information about backing up your computer data, see Chapter 21.

Thinking about other network issues

In addition to budget and family needs, you should start thinking about how much you'll require from the network. Do you need to connect two, three, or four computers, or more? Is everyone likely to be on the network at the same time? Will printer use be heavy most of the time or just occasionally? Will there be an Internet connection? How many applications will you share over the network?

Figure 5-3 illustrates three computers on a network. Each computer has some sort of peripheral connected to it: a scanner, a color inkjet printer, a laser printer, and two CD burners. Connecting the three computers gives everyone the use of various peripherals.

The preceding questions go toward helping you answer two larger questions:

✦ How much network traffic will there be?

✦ And, as a result, what speed requirements will your network need to meet?

The more you work on the network, or the more people who work on the network, the more network speed you'll need.

Also, think about how the network will be laid out in your home. Where will you place the fastest computers? Where will the printers be located? Who needs the printer the most? Do you have multiple floors in your home? Can two or more computers be placed in the same room?

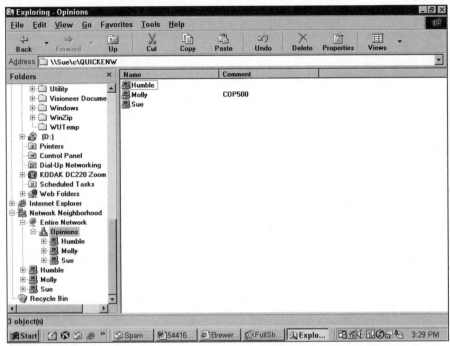

Figure 5-3: Consider how useful each computer would be on the network.

Small Business Tip

When planning computer and resource placement, consider not only the most convenient locations for printers and computers, but also think about the safest locations. For example, if you have an expensive server computer, color laser printer, scanner, or other such equipment, you might want to place them somewhere away from the general population. You don't want employees or customers playing with your expensive equipment.

How reliable does the network need to be? If you buy cheaper equipment, the network will not be as dependable as it would be if you used more expensive, brand-name hardware. Suppose that a network card fails; that computer will be off the network until you purchase a new network card. Will that be a problem?

Answering these questions helps you later when you must decide on wiring options, network hardware, and other particulars about the network.

Planning the Network

As you plan your network, you'll come up with a lot of questions about hardware, software, and networking. You'll need more knowledge before you can make any firm decisions; this book covers the information you need to make the best choices for your networking goals. As you're discovering this information, you should keep a few things in mind.

As previously mentioned, plan all your computer upgrades first—operating system, memory, hard disks, and so on. Make sure that each individual computer is in good shape before putting it on the network. Next, delegate your resources. Decide where each computer and peripheral will be located before continuing to plan your network. If you have an idea of where in the house each piece of equipment will be, you can draw a network map to help you plan wiring and networking hardware placement.

You also might want to keep a summary sheet, or a needs list, of hardware and software. As you decide on the type of networking hardware and software you'll be using, keep a list of what you will need. Check each computer to make sure that it meets the minimum hardware and software requirements for each application or networking extra you add.

Figure 5-4 shows a needs list in Word. Keeping the list in a word processor makes it easy to add to and modify the list.

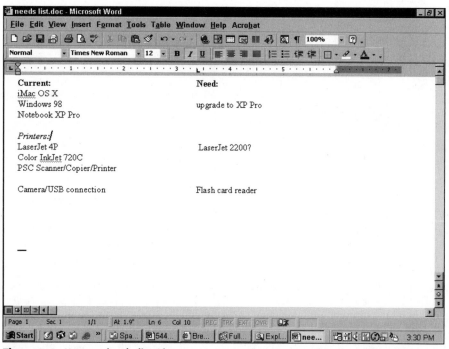

Figure 5-4: Keep a simple list of your current equipment, possible upgrades, needs, and wants.

Drawing a network map

Network maps describe how a network is put together. Not only does the map show where the computers and peripherals are located, but it also tracks important information about wiring, networking hardware, and even software used throughout your system. When you thoroughly document your system as you build it, you can use the map as a reference later, when you want to add to the network, make repairs, or troubleshoot problems.

Figure 5-5 illustrates a sample network map. It shows the rooms in which each computer and peripheral are to be located. This is the start of the map; you'll add to it as you add network cabling and hardware. You can use a drawing and a summary sheet to document all of your computer equipment, if you want.

As you continue through this book, you'll find sample network maps where appropriate. Use these examples to build your own map. You can sketch out your network on a piece of paper or use a drawing program to create the map. You can list your computer and network information on a note pad or enter it in a word processing program. Use the most convenient method for you. It's important that mapping be easy, so you'll keep your map up-to-date.

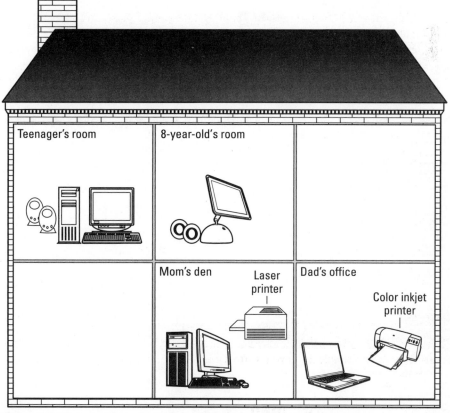

Figure 5-5: Draw out your computer and peripheral placement.

Following are a few of the things you might want to include in your network map and accompanying documentation:

✦ Computer information

✦ Peripheral information

✦ Applications

✦ Networking hardware and software

✦ Cabling information

✦ Networking applications in use

✦ Any special configurations on machines

✦ ISP and Internet settings

Small Business Tip

You should keep information about each computer in your business so that when you upgrade or purchase new equipment, you don't spend so much time searching for configuration information, applications, and other equipment. You might ask each employee to keep a record of his or her own computer, plus logs about problems, crashes, and other items that could help in troubleshooting.

Figure 5-6 illustrates a different type of network map. Using drawings and a list keeps all the information together and makes it easy to see how the equipment is divided.

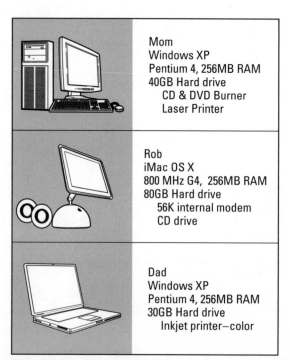

Mom
Windows XP
Pentium 4, 256MB RAM
40GB Hard drive
    CD & DVD Burner
    Laser Printer

Rob
iMac OS X
800 MHz G4, 256MB RAM
80GB Hard drive
    56K internal modem
    CD drive

Dad
Windows XP
Pentium 4, 256MB RAM
30GB Hard drive
    Inkjet printer—color

Figure 5-6: Map your network in a way that is easy to read and easy to update.

You can add to either map as you continue adding to your network. Keep the map (or maps) in a safe and convenient place. You should keep a copy of your map and information on paper, just in case there's a problem with your computer.

Understanding network requirements

In addition to your computers and peripherals, you need to acquire certain networking equipment. The type of equipment you get depends on your preferences, your needs, and your budget. In general, however, you need network cards, cabling, and perhaps other hardware, such as a hub or phone jacks.

You can choose to connect your computers with networking cable, or you can use wireless connections. You can use your phone line instead of installing cable, or you can use the electrical wiring already in place in your home. You might even want to rewire your entire home to control more than just a computer network. Speed is the main factor in making this decision, although other points factor in, such as convenience and cost.

Chapters 6, 7, and 8 cover the many available cabling options.

You might want to design your network from scratch — choosing your own cabling and hardware. You might want to use a networking kit — which includes all you need to connect two or three computers, plus easy-to-follow instructions.

Chapter 9 details the types of hardware available.

You also need to know what to plan for when choosing between a workgroup and a client/server network.

Chapters 3 and 4 explain these network types in more detail.

Workgroup

As with any network, you need to decide upon cabling to create a workgroup, or peer-to-peer, network. You also need network cards and perhaps a hub, depending on the cabling you choose. After that, you need only the peripherals and any extra networking equipment you want to add.

For example, you might want to add a modem and Internet access. To do that, you need a phone line or another type of Internet connection, as well as software or hardware for sharing the Internet account. You can add this type of networking extra to your system at any time, and it isn't a requirement of a workgroup network. You should make a list and draw a map of the locations of your equipment. Later, you can add cabling and networking hardware to your map.

Figure 5-7 shows a workgroup network with printers, a hub, and Internet access. Each printer is connected to a computer and then shared with the rest of the network. The hub connects the computers. The cable/DSL router connects to the hub and to the cable modem; thus providing Internet access to everyone on the network. See Chapter 16 for more information.

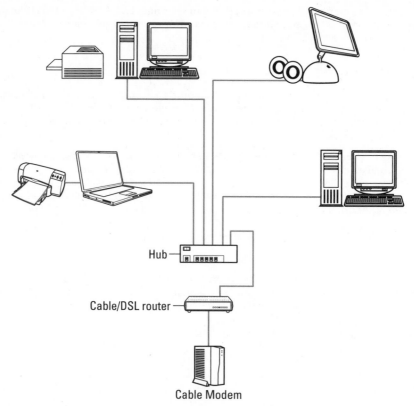

Figure 5-7: Share Internet access in a workgroup network.

You might want to connect a computer that's not running Windows or Mac OS. If you want to attach a handheld computer, for example, you need a cradle and cable, plus some additional software. Again, these items are not necessary to create the initial network, and you can add them at any time. To attach a Macintosh, Linux, or other computer to the network, you might need some additional software, but no special hardware is required, other than a network card.

A workgroup network requires little extra in the way of setting up the system. A client/server network, however, requires more hardware and more work.

Client/Server

If you plan to set up a client/server network, the first thing you need to obtain is a server computer. You can use a computer that runs Windows 98 or XP for a simple client/server network, or you can use a server that is a more powerful computer with a network operating system. The computer requirements depend, of course, on the type of network operating system you use.

Figure 5-8 shows a client/server network. The server uses the Windows 2000 Server network operating system, which provides file and printing sharing and Internet access to the clients. The cable/DSL router is also connected to the hub, and then it connects to a DSL line for

Internet access. The clients use the Windows XP and Windows 98 operating systems. One client uses her own printer, even though all clients can use the printers attached to the server.

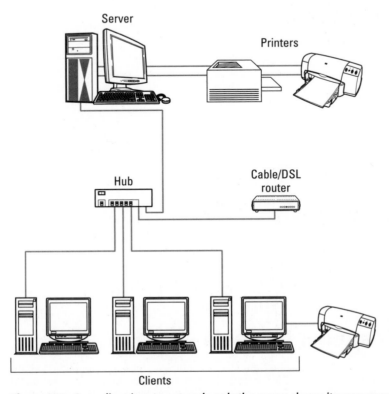

Figure 5-8: On a client/server network, only the server shares its resources.

The server is the main difference in hardware between client/server and workgroup networks. In addition to the server, you need everything previously mentioned for a workgroup network.

If you choose to use a Windows 98 or XP computer as your server, you need to make sure that the machine has sufficient RAM, hard disk space, and perhaps a UPS. If you take a Windows 98 or XP computer normally used as a standalone computer or as a workstation on the network, you should add enough RAM to it to have at least 128MB, and as much as 256MB RAM would be better. You also should have at least 20GB of disk space for file storage, backups, and other uses.

Figure 5-9 shows an example of a client/server network set up with Windows 98 as the server. The server computer shares its printer, files, and Internet account. All computers attach to the server. Only the server shares its resources; however, you could set up this network to enable the clients to share as well.

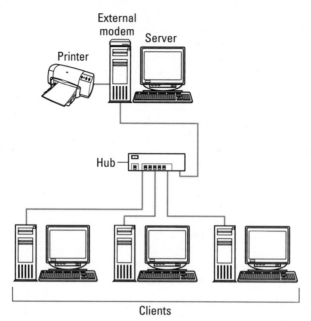

Figure 5-9: If you use a Windows 98 machine as a server, make sure that you install additional RAM and perhaps a larger hard disk.

Planning Computer Contents

An easier task you can begin tackling right away is your plan for each computer's contents. In other words, you should plan a folder structure for each computer. Although certain folders already exist on each computer, you can add folders to the structure that represent specific files, users, and so on.

You also might want to plan for sharing folders and files. If you set some sharing guidelines where folder and file use are concerned, you'll lose fewer files and make everyone's networking experience easier.

Managing folders

Folders that already exist — Windows, Program Files, folders that hold drivers or other applications, and so on — should remain exactly as they are. Never change the name or location of these folders. If you change the name of the Windows folder, for example, the operating system no longer works. Special codes within the Windows Registry point to folder locations and names. Changing anything to do with these folders throws the whole system off.

Figure 5-10 shows the folders on a normal Windows 98 computer. Following are the folders you should not share, move, or rename: Ahdw, Bus, Gwci, cabs, Dc220260, Download, Program Files, psfonts, Windows, and so on. These folders contain programs, configurations, and other files necessary to run Windows, your applications, and miscellaneous hardware, such as the CD-ROM drive, Zip drive, and other devices. Some folder names will vary, depending on your network setup. For example, you won't have the Ethernet folder if you're not using an Ethernet network.

Caution   The folders listed in Figure 5-10 will be different from the folders on your machine, whether you're using Windows 98, Mac OS 9, or Linux. You should not delete or share any folder of which you are unsure. Deleting a folder could make a program stop working; sharing an inappropriate folder could make accidental deletions easier.

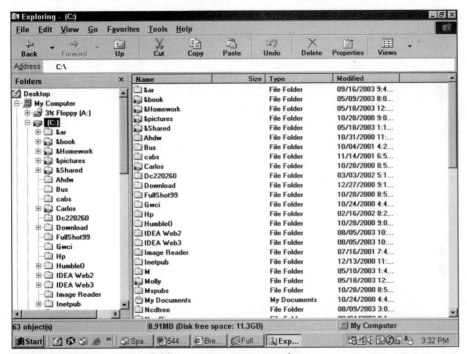

Figure 5-10: Leave certain folders on your computer alone.

You can, however, create any number of folders to hold your own data, games, backup files, and so on. When creating your own folders, or those on other computers in the network, make sure to name the folders so that they are easy to recognize. Notice in Figure 5-10, some folders — &pictures, Carlos, and Molly, for example — are shared for use on the network. The symbol of a shared resource in Windows is a hand holding the resource.

Cross-Reference   See Chapter 12 for more information about shared folders and printers.

Also, don't bury a folder within a folder within a folder if you want to use that folder often. For example, don't create a folder for saving documents in the C:\Program Files\Office\All Documents\Correspondence\Papers folder. Each time you move to that folder, you'll have to wade through folder after folder.

Instead, create a folder structure that makes sense to you or to the computer's user. Figure 5-11 shows three folders the user created — &book, &Homework, and &pictures. Each folder can contain additional folders to help in organizing the material. Note that the three folders' names begin with an ampersand to make the folders appear at the top of the list.

Your next step is to decide which folders will be shared and which will not be shared. Make a list of shared folders for each computer and keep it handy.

Managing shares

When you're sharing folders and files, you should come up with naming conventions that make the files and folders easier to find. If you must search through a list of shared folders for the one you want, you waste time and build frustration. The same is true for files, printers, and other peripherals. Using a consistent naming scheme helps everyone find the resource they want and keeps them from bothering you with file or printer searches.

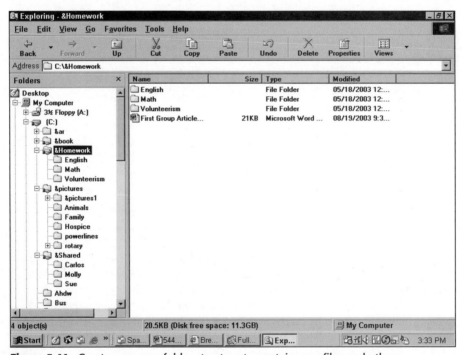

Figure 5-11: Create your own folder structure to contain your files and others.

If you use a server for your network, all shared files, folders, and peripherals appear on the server. If you use a workgroup network, shared resources appear on each computer. Naturally, the naming conventions each individual uses is up to that individual; when shared resources are involved, however, naming them in certain ways is a courtesy to the other users.

Tip   You may have only a few shared folders, files, and peripherals to begin with, but you might be surprised at how quickly the list grows as people work on the network more and more. Plan ahead.

Folders in Windows

Folder naming in Windows follows certain rules. You can use long filenames and spaces in your folder name, for example. Linux and Macintosh computers can read long filenames, as well. However, just because you can use long filenames doesn't mean you should always do that. You can use just one- or two-word folder names describing what the folder stores. When the names become too long, they are difficult to read on the screen and often difficult to locate.

Small Business Tip   It's especially important in your business to use file- and folder-naming conventions for all shared files. Employees who cannot find a file they need to complete their work might become frustrated and can waste a lot of time searching for data on the network.

Other rules govern the way folders are listed in Windows file and folder management windows. Following is a list of these rules:

✦ Folder names are listed alphabetically.

✦ Folder names beginning with a number are listed before the alphabetized folder names.

✦ Folder names beginning with a symbol are listed before numbered folder names, in this order: #, $, %, &, and @.

✦ You can use uppercase and lowercase letters in a folder's name, which doesn't affect the order in which the folder is displayed.

✦ Really long folder names are difficult to read, and you often lose half of the name when viewing them in certain windows or in the detail view, such as in the Find Files and Folders dialog box.

Figure 5-12 illustrates how the preceding rules work with folder names. Note that the folder names beginning with a symbol are listed first, folder names beginning with numbers are next, and those beginning with the alphabet are listed last.

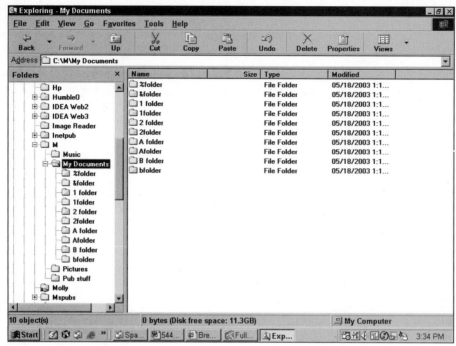

Figure 5-12: Consider the naming rules before you name folders you'll be sharing.

Figure 5-13 shows how to put the naming rules to work for you when creating folders for sharing. The ampersands place all the shared folders at the top of the list in the Windows Explorer. This technique makes it easier for the user of this computer to find the folders quickly.

The folder that contains documents everyone uses on the network, titled &Shared, contains folders for each user, and within each user's folder are more folders to hold their documents.

Folders in Macs

Macintosh naming conventions work similarly to Windows naming conventions. However, you should avoid using the characters % & * ( ) < > in file or folder names. In general, stick with the alphanumeric characters: a to z and 0 to 9. You should always use lowercase file and folder names, if possible.

Folders in Linux

Linux identifies folders as directories, and a directory in Linux is much like any other. There are naming conventions for files and directories in Linux. Each directory must have a unique name. The directory cannot consist of more than 256 alphanumeric characters, and no reserved metacharacters exist.

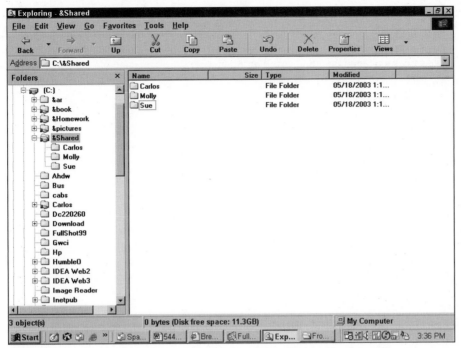

Figure 5-13: Name your folders so that they're easy to find on the network.

Files

Just as you plan your shared folder-naming conventions, so should you also plan your file-naming conventions. This approach might be a bit more difficult for everyone to adhere to, but if they do, everyone will find it easier to locate their files in a mixed group.

The rules for naming files are similar to those for naming folders. Files are listed in alphabetical order, filenames beginning with a number precede those beginning with a letter, and filenames beginning with a symbol precede numbered names.

With filenames, you have the added luxury of extensions, if you show extensions in the window in which you're viewing filenames. File extensions make it easier to sort filenames and to find the file you want. Using a file-naming convention, however, is the most helpful method of organizing files.

Windows file and folder names make use of the three-letter extension. Macintosh uses the Type and Creator codes to take the place of that extension. For example, a Word document on the Mac uses the W6BN type and the MSWD creator. You should stay away from naming folders with extensions, however, just to keep the listing clean and easy to read.

Tip   You can display filename extensions in the Windows Explorer window by choosing View ➪ Folder Options ➪ View Tab. Remove the check mark from the option Hide File Extensions for Known File Types.

You can use any method of naming that works for you and your family. You might want to name files by using a numbering scheme — say, the day and month. This method might be difficult for young users to follow, though, so you could add the first and second initials of the creator of the file. For example, the filename SJ08-12.doc in a folder titled Letters identifies a word processing document Sue wrote on August 12. Here's an example of how this file-naming convention might work:

C:\Letters:

CO08-14.doc

CO09-20.doc

HF10-22.doc

HF10-23.doc

SJ08-14.doc

SJ09-21.doc

Alternatively, you could use the first name of each family member within his or her filenames. All names won't be the same length, however, so you could cut the names to the first three letters. You then can add other descriptors to help identify the file, as follows:

C:\Documents

CAR music.doc

CAR invoice list.doc

CAR report01.doc

HUG camping.doc

HUG friends.doc

HUG scout letter.doc

SUE books.doc

SUE recipes.doc

SUE certification.doc

It's very likely that all your files will not fit into one file-naming convention. Figure 5-14 shows another method of naming files. In the &Shared folder, you see a folder for each family member. In addition, the folder contains files that everyone will need access to at one time or another. The filenames represent various types of files; for example, the 03 03 list and 04 03 list filenames represent files containing lists of purchases family members desire to make during the months of March and April. The Network Needs file represents a wish list for network equipment or software. You can use any method of organizing your files, as long as it makes sense to you and your family.

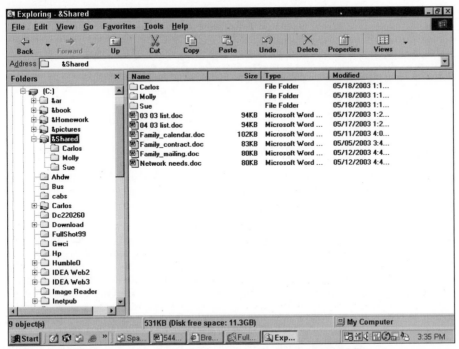

Figure 5-14: Use your own naming conventions to organize shared files.

You also can place files in folders named after individual users, or specific document types (letters, reports, and so on), or you can nest user folders inside of other folders. *Nesting* means to create a group of folders, each contained within the first. An example of nested folders is C:\Documents\Sue and C:\Documents\Hugh. Sue and Hugh are folders nested within the Documents folder. Just be careful not to nest your folders too deeply; it can be frustrating to open folder after folder.

Tip

Windows XP uses the Documents and Settings folder in which to store each user's My Documents folder. If someone with an XP computer wants to share a file, that person should use the Shared folder instead of the My Documents folder, to make the file easier for others to find.

Peripherals

As with other resources, you need to consider how you name your peripherals. If you have only one or two printers, they might be easy to recognize without making any changes. However, if you have several printers, a scanner, and other add-ons, you might benefit from a naming convention.

For example, you might name your printers in the following way:

Printer-laser

Printer-color

Printer-inkjet

Printer-dot matrix

These printers show up in a list close together, so they are easier to pick.

Considering applications

When planning the applications for your computers and network, think about the requirements for the program and its licensing. When working on a workgroup network, you install an application on each computer. The users of the application then can open the application at any time and use it.

The users also can share the data created from that program. No two users can open the same file at the same time, however. If a file — word processing, spreadsheet, accounting, or other type — is being used by one person and someone else tries to open that same file, a warning dialog box appears. The dialog box states the file is already in use and asks if the user wants to make a copy of the file. If you open a copy of the file, you can modify it, but you must save the copy under a different name. The two files cannot be merged; you end up with two copies of the file. This protection means the data in the file cannot be compromised.

Small Business Tip

Make sure that you purchase and install networkable applications, especially for your accounts, payroll, and other record-keeping programs. *Networkable* refers to applications built for a network and licensed for multiple-computer use. You need the safeguards built into the program to keep data from being corrupted or lost over the network.

Certain networkable applications — games, for example — enable two or more people to open the executable game file in order to play the game at the same time. Other networkable applications — such as databases and accounting programs — protect the open files but in a different way. These types of programs enable two or more people to open the same file, but any record one person is working on is locked from changes by the other person.

For example, if you're working on a record in a file and someone else tries to open that record, the program notifies the other person that the record is in use but that he or she can view it, if desired. This type of protection enables work to continue without corrupting or confusing the data.

Cross-Reference

For more information about various networking applications, see Chapter 20.

Licensing

Word processors, spreadsheets, drawing programs, and many games are licensed for one user only. You install these applications on your computer, and only you are licensed to use them. The manufacturer issues licensing agreements that state the legal uses of programs.

Small Business Tip

Following the licensing agreement is important in any situation; in business, however, it's even more important. If your employees think they don't have to follow the licensing terms of any program, they will feel free to bring in programs from home and install them, as well as to borrow your programs to take home to install. Also, disgruntled employees might call in the licensing violations to the manufacturers, distributors, or software police.

Some manufacturers produce network versions of their applications. You can install these programs on multiple machines, depending on the number of licenses you own. Network versions of applications have built-in features that make them efficient and effective over a network. They also contain features that protect data when it's in use by more than one person.

For example, you might network a calendar or scheduling program. You also might network an accounting program, a database, or multiuser games. When purchasing an application, make sure that you check to see if it's a network version, and find out about the licensing as well.

Application and data locations

If you plan to install network applications on a workgroup network, you'll want to install the data accordingly. Make sure that you use the most powerful computer you have (processor speed, most RAM, and so on) to contain the data to help handle the network traffic efficiently. You also want to choose a computer that stays on most of the time, because people need access to the computer to run the program. Applications that share the data should be installed on each computer on a workgroup network.

If you're using a server in your network, you can install certain applications on the server, called server software. Some special networking applications contain both client software and server software. The server software manages the data as well as the users. Install the client software on each client computer to request data and program usage.

A database program is a good example of this type of application. The server software runs on the server and keeps all the files and records. The client software runs on each individual client computer and enables the user to access the files and records on the server.

Note

Pay close attention to a network application's requirements. You want to make sure that the computer on which you're installing the program has enough memory and disk space, as well as meets all other requirements — before purchasing and installing the software.

Summary

In this chapter, you've learned how to plan for your network. You must consider the needs of everyone in the family, take inventory of your current hardware and software, and then form a strategy with that information. In this chapter, you've learned to do the following:

✦ Define network goals

✦ Plan for your family's needs

✦ Plan the computer's contents

✦ Consider the applications you'll use on the network

In the next chapter, you learn about cables and laying cable for your network.

✦　　✦　　✦

Understanding and Installing Traditional Cabling

You can network your home by using various types of cabling and networking hardware. Some cabling types are more expensive than others and more difficult to install, such as traditional cabling. Traditional cabling, however, also offers the most speed and reliability for your network. The cabling method you choose should be the one that best satisfies your need for speed, your budget, and your networking needs.

Understanding Methods of Network Cabling

Network cabling is a method of connecting two or more computers so that they can communicate and share data, programs, and peripherals. Whether you're cabling a small or a large network, you can use traditional cabling methods, which consist of various wiring and hardware techniques. With the continuing popularity of home networking, many manufacturers are producing networking kits that make cabling faster and easier. Additionally, techniques of using home phone lines and electrical housewiring (or power lines) are changing the scope of home networking altogether. Wireless connections are another popular option. Often various methods of networking cabling are combined.

The type of cabling you use in your network depends on a number of elements. You should consider network cost, the speed of the network connections, available resources, and so on. This chapter and the next two explain the various methods you can use to connect your computers as a network.

This chapter explains the traditional methods of cabling, defines cabling terms, discusses methods of wiring, and gives other technical information you should know about networking. Chapter 7 discusses various wireless standards, security, and combining traditional wiring with wireless networking. Chapter 8 covers methods of cabling that are less traditional or easier to use than the traditional methods. You should read all three chapters so that you have a better understanding of the terminology and can make more informed decisions.

Tip You also should read Chapter 9 before making decisions on cabling. Chapter 9 describes the hardware necessities for creating a network—a network card and a hubs, switches, and routers.

The two main hardware devices you need for your network are the *network interface card* (also called a *network card* or *network adapter*) and a *hub*. The network card is installed in your computer, uses specific software drivers to work with your computer, and attaches to the network by means of a network cable. A hub is a device that modifies network transmission signals and enables multiple computers to be attached to the network. You might choose to use a *switch* or *router* instead of a hub. Switches and routers are more "intelligent" devices than hubs but perform similar services.

The hub and card are dependent on the cabling, and cabling is dependent on the hub and card. The network interface card must be the appropriate type and speed for your cabling, which also must match the hub you use. You need to read Chapters 6, 7, 8, and 9 before making any decisions regarding this networking hardware.

Considering Networking Topologies and Technologies

You must lay certain foundations when building a network. In addition to choosing whether the network will be of the workgroup (or peer-to-peer) or client/server type, you should choose which topology and technology you will use for the network.

The *topology* of the network refers to how you arrange the cables, the networking hardware, and the computers. *Technology* refers to the type of wiring and hardware you use and to the general speed of the network. *Network speed* refers to how fast the data is transferred between two or more computers.

Choosing a topology

The topology is the method of arranging and connecting computers, peripherals, and other equipment on the network. Topology also refers to how the computers and hardware devices are connected and how each interacts with the other. When choosing topology, you consider the number of people on the network, the number of rooms or buildings to be networked, and changes you might make in the future.

Basically, four topologies are possible:

- ✦ Bus
- ✦ Spanning tree (or star)
- ✦ Ring
- ✦ Mesh

For your home network, you should use the spanning tree topology. Just to give you an idea of how each topology works, the following sections present brief descriptions of each.

Network Packets

Before you delve into topologies and technologies, you should understand how a network transfers data between computers. Data is sent over a network in *packets*, or *blocks*. Each packet not only contains a part of the data you want to send, but also the name of the sender and the receiver and some error-control information to help make sure that the packet makes it to its destination in one piece.

Packets can be a fixed length or of variable length. Each packet contains only a portion of the data you're sending. Your networking software disassembles the data, places it into packets, and sends it across the network. When the packets get to the designated computer, the packets are reassembled to form the data you sent. Naturally, this process is completed in split seconds.

The number of packets traveling over the network makes up the network traffic. If, for example, a packet is lost or becomes corrupted in its journey, the receiving computer notifies the sending computer, and then the packets must be re-sent to complete the data. Different topologies and technologies send different types of packets, and they provide various error correction and control methods to make sure that the packets are complete when they reach their destination.

Bus

You could use a bus topology on your home network. This topology connects each computer along a single length of cable, in a line, as shown in Figure 6-1. You can connect up to 30 users on this simple network, installation is simple, and the network is relatively inexpensive.

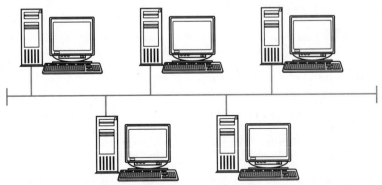

Figure 6-1: One network cable connects all users on a bus network.

One problem with the bus topology is that it results in a slow network. This topology can send only one network packet at a time. Also, when there is a problem within the network— say, a cable connecting two computers goes bad — the problem cable can be difficult to locate, and the entire network goes down until the cable is fixed. One final problem with the bus topology is that if you want to expand it in the future, it is difficult to add additional equipment because of the way the network is set up. Instead of adding a computer somewhere in the middle, you must add computers only to the end of the bus line. In addition, bus topologies require the use of terminators and adding terminators is a long and arduous task.

Two reasons you might want to use bus topology are as follows:

✦ You can connect long segments (such as 85 meters) between hubs.

✦ You already have coaxial cable in place (so you're maintaining or adding to an existing network).

If you plan to start your network from scratch, you don't want to use the bus topology.

The bus topology might work in a home network; however, you shouldn't use it in a business setting. The topology is too slow and causes great delays when a network element—such as the cabling, network card, or hub—goes bad.

Spanning tree, or star

The spanning tree topology is the one you are most likely to choose for your network, because it is versatile and easy to expand; it also uses common networking technology— Ethernet (see the "Choosing a network technology" section later in the chapter for more on Ethernet). With a spanning tree topology, all computers connect through a central hub or switch; all packets of data must pass through the hub as well. The hub is a box that contains ports into which you plug networking cables; each computer plugs into the hub with a separate cable.

Spanning tree is the perfect topology for small-business offices. You can start with three to seven computers, for example, and keep adding hubs to expand the network as needed. Additionally, spanning tree is the perfect solution for a client/server network; you can add clients and servers on various segments of the network whenever you hire new employees or add to your networking hardware.

When the hub receives a signal from a computer on the network, it modifies and then distributes the signal to all other computers on the network. In the spanning tree topology, the hub is the center of the network. You can choose from different designs and sizes of hubs. You can even connect hubs to other hubs for easy expansion of the network. See Chapter 9 for more information.

Figure 6-2 illustrates a spanning tree topology in a network. Note the use of a second hub. In this case, the first hub, a four-port hub, connects three computers plus one hub. The second hub, also a four-port hub, connects three computers and has one open port for another computer or hub. Adding hubs and computers to the network is similar to a branching tree.

The spanning tree topology is more expensive than the bus topology mainly because of the hubs. The cost of hubs, however, is dropping considerably. Also, many networking kits are available for home networks, as is described later in this chapter.

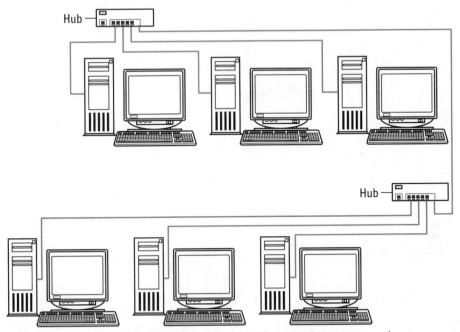

Figure 6-2: You can add multiple hubs to expand the spanning tree network.

Ring

The ring topology passes packets from one computer to the next, in only one direction, around a circle (ring). When one computer wants to send data to another, it must first capture a token, which passes around the ring, waiting for someone to transmit information. The token picks up the destination address and the message and then travels around the ring until the destination computer picks it up.

Ring networks are usually large, because the technology can cover great distances. One problem with a ring network is that if a cable or card fails, no data can pass around the network until the problem is corrected.

Figure 6-3 illustrates a ring network using a server. Each computer is attached to two other computers, which forms the ring.

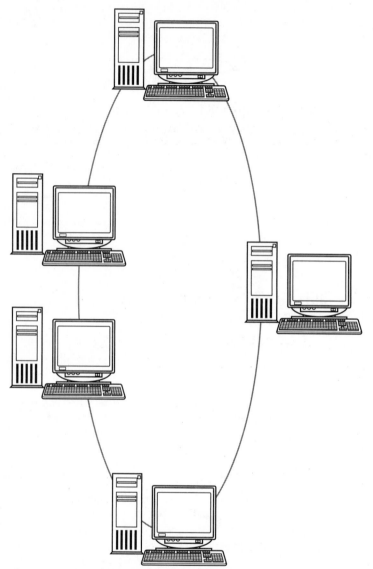

Figure 6-3: Ring networks usually cover multiple buildings, cities, and even states.

Mesh

Mesh topology represents a wide area network (WAN) used in large corporations, universities, and government agencies. The mesh topology uses multiple paths to connect multiple sites, or buildings. This topology requires more networking hardware and much more planning.

Many of the connections in a mesh topology are redundant, just in case another connection fails. Therefore, mesh networks are extremely reliable yet expensive. Mesh networks can include up to 25 or so sites, but problems are easy to manage.

Figure 6-4 illustrates a mesh network. You can see why it is so expensive and comprehensive: Each computer connects to every other computer on the network.

Choosing a network technology

Network technology refers to the architecture and protocols used on certain networks; Ethernet and Token Ring are two common technologies. The technology you choose governs the speed of the network, the type of cabling you use, and the network cards you install in your computers. Additionally, you must use special hubs and other networking hardware to match the technology you choose.

Tip   For the home network using standard network cabling, you should choose the Ethernet or Fast Ethernet protocol and architecture, unless you want to try a wireless or an alternative wiring option, as described in the next chapters.

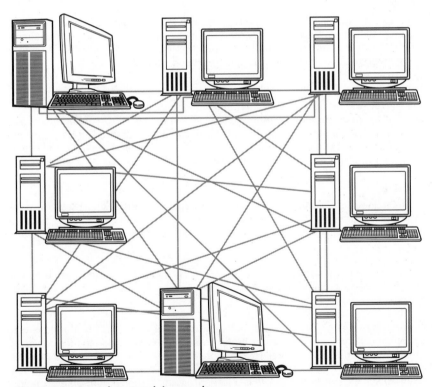

Figure 6-4: A mesh network is complex.

Speed Rates

Network speeds are measured in megabits but also can be measured in gigabits. A *megabit* (Mbit) equals 1,048,576 binary digits, or bits, of data. In general, a megabit is the equivalent of 1 million bits. A *gigabit* (Gbit) represents 1 billion bits.

A *bit* is a contraction of BInary digiT, the basic unit of information in the binary numbering system, in which 0 represents off and 1 represents on. Bits are grouped to form larger storage units, such as the 7- or 8-bit byte. A *megabyte* (MB) represents computer memory (RAM) or hard disk capacity.

Megabits per second (Mbps) measures the amount of information moving across a network or communications link in 1 second. Just to give you a reference point, Ethernet cables, network cards, and hubs move data on a network at 10 and 100 (some even go to 1000) Mbps; wireless moves data at 11 or 54 Mbps; phone line kits for networking your home move data at speeds of around 1 Mbps.

Token Ring

The token ring protocol uses the ring topology and can transmit data at 16 megabits per second (Mbps) and 100 Mbps. *Megabits per second* is a measure of network speed equaling one million bits (or 1,000 kilobits) per second. The ring topology is usually used for larger networks. The networking hardware and wiring is expensive and complicated.

Ethernet

Ethernet is a protocol and cabling scheme that transfers data at the rate of 10 Mbps. Ethernet can use the bus or the spanning tree topology connected with various cabling types, as described later in this chapter. Ethernet packets are of variable length, and they consist of a destination address, source address, data, and an error-checking mode called *cyclic redundancy check* (CRC). CRC confirms the accuracy of the data after it's received at its destination.

Fast Ethernet

Ethernet also includes Fast Ethernet and Gigabit Ethernet. Fast Ethernet's rates are 100 Mbps; Gigabit Ethernet operates at 1,000 Mbps. Both of these technologies use cabling, network cards, hubs, and other networking equipment to match their speed. Both work well with the spanning tree topology.

Note   Gigabit Ethernet is often used as the backbone for large networks. A *backbone* is the high-speed cabling that manages the bulk of the network traffic. It can connect to several different locations or buildings.

Fast Ethernet is a viable choice for your home or small office network. You should consider Fast Ethernet especially if you plan to use large graphics or audio or video files consistently, or if you plan to upgrade your network to add more clients, a server or two, and more services. Fast Ethernet provides more bandwidth for your network to accommodate these larger, processor-intensive file types. *Bandwidth* is a measurement of the amount of information or data that can pass through any given point on the network: cabling, hub, network cards, and so on. The wider the bandwidth, the more data can pass through the network.

Tip You can start your network with Ethernet and easily upgrade to Fast Ethernet if necessary; however, the prices for Ethernet and Fast Ethernet are so near to each other, you may as well get Fast Ethernet. See Chapter 9 for information about purchasing network cards and hubs that work with either a 10 Mbps or a 100 Mbps network (called 10/100).

Understanding Cabling

The cabling is a fundamental part of networking. Cabling provides the physical connection between computers; cabling is used for transmitting and receiving information over the network. You can connect your network with any of various types of cabling, or wires. You can use phone lines, power lines, or traditional cabling. You can even "connect" the network by using radio signals, infrared, or microwaves.

Note When preparing to cable your home or small-office network, you should check with your city for any applicable building codes. Some apartment, condominium, and even housing codes prohibit laying cable without specific permits and permissions.

The cable you choose must be suited for the distance between your computers. Some cables work better with short distances; others reach farther between machines. You also choose the type of cabling to match the network cards and other networking hardware. For example, if you choose the Ethernet protocol with a spanning tree, or star, topology, you also must use Ethernet network interface cards, Ethernet cabling, and Ethernet hubs. Matching all of your networking hardware is not only necessary, but it also provides a fast, efficient, and beneficial network.

Tip Distances between computers are also important to wireless connections. See Chapter 7 for more information.

Deciding on the type of cable

You have many choices of cable types. Your decision depends on the speed you want for your network. You also must consider how difficult or easy the cable is to install, how expensive the cabling solution is, the distance between computers, and security issues. Following is a brief overview; the rest of this chapter and the next two chapters explain each cabling type in detail.

Traditional cabling — coaxial, twisted-pair, and fiber-optic, for example — supplies more speed in your network connection than other choices. It costs more than some other options, however, because of the cable and the other networking hardware. Traditional cabling also offers a secure connection.

Small Business Tip For the most consistent and reliable networking, you should use Fast Ethernet traditional cabling for a small business. Phone lines and housewiring are okay for home networking, but are too slow for a business. Wireless connections might also work in a business; however, you'll want to combine traditional wiring and wireless. Combining wiring and wireless gives you more flexibility with your access points and more distance coverage; plus, you must use some wiring to connect access points.

Using your phone lines or housewiring as networking cable provides less speed but also costs less and is easier to use. If speed isn't a primary concern, this may be the solution for you. See Chapter 8 for more information.

Wireless connections used to be more expensive and less secure, but the prices have come down and the security matters have been addressed. Wireless might also be better suited because of the structure of your home. If, for example, your home is difficult to cable because of cinder blocks or other obstructions, wireless connections may be the solution. In addition, you might want to connect to another building, say, to a garage apartment or to a neighbor's house. Wireless is perfect for those situations. See Chapter 7 for more information.

Figure 6-5 illustrates a coaxial cable and a twisted-pair cable. These are the two most common cabling types used in small networks today; however, coaxial is nearly outdated. Note that both cables are cut so you can see the inside.

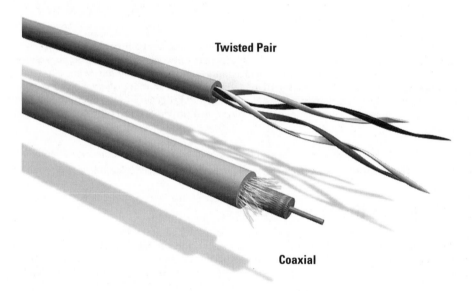

Twisted Pair

Coaxial

Figure 6-5: Coaxial cable looks like the cable from your television to the VCR; twisted-pair looks similar to phone wire.

Defining coaxial

Coaxial, or coax, cable is inexpensive to use on a network. Coaxial cable is used less frequently today because it is not upgradable. It might be an option for you, however, if you plan to use only two computers, positioned closely together, with no need for adding more computers to your network. You might want to use coax if cables are already installed. In addition, coax is often used in conjunction with wireless network equipment. See Chapter 7 for more information.

Defining Terms

The many terms that identify cabling types and cabling hardware can be confusing. Following are some explanations to help you wade through the jargon.

Each cabling type uses specific pieces of hardware to terminate the ends or connect two pieces of cabling together. These *connectors* make it possible for the network cables to transmit data efficiently throughout the network.

Coaxial cable uses BNC and T-connectors. A T-connector attaches two coaxial, or thin, Ethernet cables and provides a third connection for the network interface card. A BNC connector is an end piece that connects two or three cables together.

Twisted-pair cable uses a different connector. RJ-45 connectors consist of an eight-wire connection jack that is used to join the four pairs of networking cable in twisted-pair cable.

The Ethernet standard defines the cable type, the connectors, the rate of speed, and the distance the cables can stretch and still operate efficiently. Examples of these standards are 10Base-2, 10Base-T, and 100Base-T. Many others exist, but these are the only ones you might use with your home or small-office network.

The 10Base-2 Ethernet standard is specifically for use with coaxial cabling. The data transfer rate is 10 Mbps, and the cabling type uses BNC and T-connectors.

The 10Base-T standard refers to Ethernet standards used in twisted-pair cable. 10BaseT also transfers data at the rate of 10 Mbps. 100Base-T refers to Fast Ethernet, also used in twisted-pair cable. 100Base-T transfers data at a rate of 100 Mbps.

Coaxial cable looks like the cable that runs between your VCR and television set. Coax cable consists of a plastic jacket surrounding a braided copper shield, plastic insulation, and a solid inner conductor. The cabling is secure and generally free from external interference.

Coaxial cabling is also called ThinNet, or Thin Ethernet, cabling, and it's used with 10Base-2. 10Base-2 is an implementation of an Ethernet standard for coaxial cabling. The data transfer rate, or network speed, for 10Base-2 is 10 Mbps over 185 meters. The 185 meters (around 600 feet) describes the maximum cable-segment length.

Thin Ethernet doesn't require a hub, because you can use special connectors for joining two or more computers. You can use T-connectors to attach the thin coaxial cable to a BNC connector on the Ethernet network interface card. See the section "Looking at Cable Connectors" later in this chapter for information about BNC and T-connectors.

Thin coax works well with Ethernet; however, it cannot work with Fast Ethernet (100 Mbps). If you choose to upgrade your Ethernet to Fast Ethernet later, you'll have to throw out all of your 10Base-2 cabling and hardware and start from the beginning to build a faster network.

Small Business Tip

Whereas coaxial cabling might work for a home network, you shouldn't use it in your small business. Coaxial cabling isn't upgradable, so you don't want to limit your business possibilities by using it. Use twisted-pair cabling instead.

Defining twisted-pair (Ethernet)

Twisted-pair cabling is similar to common phone wire, but twisted-pair is a higher grade of cabling that enables high-speed data to travel over it. The majority of networks today use twisted-pair because it's relatively inexpensive (about 20 cents per foot for a high-grade wire) and it does offer high rates of transfer.

Twisted-pair cable consists of two or more pairs of insulated wires twisted together. In each twisted-pair, one wire carries the signal and the other wire is grounded. The cable can be either unshielded twisted-pair (UTP) or shielded twisted-pair (STP).

Shielded twisted-pair cable has a foil shield and copper braid surrounding the pairs of wires. STP provides high-speed transmission for long distances. Unshielded twisted-pair cable also contains two or more pairs of twisted copper wires; however, UTP is easier to install, costs less, limits signal speeds, and has a shorter maximum cable-segment length than STP. UTP is generally used in most home and business networks.

Twisted-pair uses 10Base-T standards over UTP wiring and RJ-45 connectors. 10Base-T provides data transfers at 10 Mbps. You use the star topology with twisted-pair, and each connected computer also connects to a central hub. The maximum cable-segment length for twisted-pair is 100 meters, or about 330 feet.

If you use the 10Base-T cabling scheme, then you have to buy network cards that accept 10Base-T, or twisted-pair, cabling. You also need to buy a 10Base-T hub, one with jacks for twisted-pair plugs.

There are categories, or levels, of twisted-pair cabling. Each level describes the performance characteristics of wiring standards. Of the levels of twisted-pair cabling, Category 3 (CAT 3) and Category 5 (CAT 5) are the most common.

✦ CAT 3 is less expensive than CAT 5, and its transfer rate isn't as fast; in fact, you can hardly find CAT 3 in use anymore.

✦ CAT 5 is the best cable for any network—business or home. CAT 5 works equally well with 10Base-T or with 100Base-T. You might want to start your network with CAT 5 cabling and 10Base-T hardware—10 Mbps network cards and hub—and then when you're ready, upgrade to 100Base-T hardware. 100Base provides transfer rates of 100 Mbps.

Tip   You can purchase network cards—called 10/100 cards—that operate at both 10 Mbps and 100 Mbps. Use these cards and CAT 5 cabling for a network speed of 10 Mbps, and then when you're ready, you can upgrade with only the purchase of a 100 Mbps hub. See more about 10/100 network interface cards in Chapter 9.

Understanding 10Base-T, 100Base-T, and 1000Base-T

Ethernet is a protocol (language) that provides Carrier Sense Multiple Access/Collision Detection (CSMA/CD). CSMA/CD defines how the network equipment responds when two devices try to use the same data channel at the same time. CSMA/CD provides rules about the collision of data and how long a device should wait if a collision occurs. CSMA/CD means that the Ethernet protocol is efficient and reliable in handling network traffic.

10Base-T, also called Ethernet, is a standard that defines the speed the CSMA/CD Ethernet works on CAT 3 or CAT 5 cabling. 10Base-T moves at a speed of 10 Mbps. 10Base-T is also known as an 802 standard. The 802 standards were set by IEEE for networking on local area networks. IEEE is the Institute of Electrical and Electronic Engineers (pronounced "eye triple-E"). The IEEE is an association of people who help global prosperity by promoting, developing, integrating, and sharing networking knowledge.

Fast Ethernet is also called 100Base-T (or 802.3u). 100Base-T is a protocol that connects computers on a LAN at rates of 100 million bits per second. 100Base-T works over CAT 5 twisted-pair wiring. Two standards of 100Base-T exist:

✦ 100Base-T utilizes CSMA/CD and 100VG-AnyLAN (or 802.12).

✦ 100VG-AnyLAN uses a different type of Ethernet frame to send data. (A *frame* is a block of data that uses a header and a trailer to indicate the beginning and end of the data.)

Now, there are three types of 100Base-T wiring:

✦ The first is 100Base-T4, which uses four pairs of twisted wire that is telephone-grade, or low quality, but still on a 100 Mbps network.

✦ The second is 100Base-TX, or 100Base-X, which uses two wire data grade twisted-pair wire for better communications and quality.

✦ The third is 100Base-FX that uses two strands of fiber cable. Fiber is made up of hollow cables that send data by pulses of light for a much faster method of data transmission.

Finally, there is 1000Base-T (or 802.3z/802.3ab). 1000Base-T is also called Gigabit Ethernet and transfers data at 1,000 million bits per second.

Note Fiber-optic cabling is another cable type; however, you wouldn't generally use fiber-optic cable in your home. Fiber-optic cable uses light rather than electrical pulses to carry the network signals. Because of its signal strength and immunity to electrical interference, fiber-optic cable is perfect for signals traveling over long distances at very fast speeds. It's also extremely expensive to buy, install, and maintain.

Choosing the Right Cabling Type

If you're confused about which cable type to choose, here's a little helpful hint:

Choose coaxial cabling if all the following apply to your situation:

✦ You have fewer than four PCs.

✦ You don't have any portable computers (laptops, notebooks) on the network.

✦ You plan to never expand the network or are never going to use large graphic files, streaming audio, or video.

Choose 10Base-T cabling with a hub if all the following apply to your situation:

✦ You have fewer than 10 PCs.

✦ The PCs are within 330 feet or so of each other.

✦ You have portable computers to connect to the network.

✦ You might, at some point, need to add computers to the network.

Choose 100Base-TX (Fast Ethernet) cabling with a hub if the following applies:

✦ You plan to use large graphic files, streaming audio, or video.

✦ You want a fast network for data exchange and gaming.

✦ You have portable computers.

✦ You plan to add more computers in the future.

Looking at Cable Connectors

In addition to cables, you need certain hardware to attach the cables to the network cards and hubs, and some other gear to complete connections and to make the cabling safer and nicer looking. Some of this equipment is essential; some is useful but not necessarily required.

For information about network cards and hubs, see Chapter 9.

Depending on the type of cabling you use, you need to buy appropriate connectors and terminators. Cable connectors are necessary for attaching the cable to certain pieces of computer hardware, such as the network card, hubs, switches, and so on. Some connectors attach two segments of cabling as well. You also might need to attach terminators, depending on the topology and cabling of your network; terminators are end pieces you attach to the cables. If you don't attach terminators, the network signals try to continue their journey; terminators stop the signal and clear the path for other signals.

Other cable connectors are necessary for twisted-pair cabling. Twisted-pair looks like phone cord and uses jacks similar to, but not the same as, those used with phone wiring. Additionally, you can use a wall plate for connecting to the cable, or a patch panel for safely connecting multiple cables at a central location. A patch panel is a strip of 8, 12, 24, or more jacks that make it easy to connect the cables to one device. After you connect the cables to the patch panel, you can attach the panel to a wall for easy access and safe and effective network wiring.

Also, you might (or might not) need a special tool called a punch to install the connectors. See the section "Using Networking Tools."

Tip   Many networking kits come with connectors already attached to the cabling. You also can purchase premade cabling from computer stores or electronics stores and over the Internet. Premade cabling ranges from 1 foot long to 100 feet long, and the connectors are already attached. These cables are also called *patch cables*.

Using coaxial cable connectors

Coaxial cables use a different type of connector than twisted-pair uses. Coaxial cables look like the cables you attach to your VCR for television cable service.

For coaxial cabling, you use BNC connectors. BNC connectors come in both male and female varieties, so you must fit the connector with the male end to the female jack on the network card or the hub. A T-connector is also used with coaxial cable. T-connectors attach two thin Ethernet cables and provide a third connection for the network interface card.

You only use a terminating resistor (or terminator) in a 10Base-2 network using a bus topology. Bus topology consists of one cable that connects each client; the ends of the cable are open and therefore must be terminated. Coax cable is rated at 50 ohms. (An *ohm* is a unit of electrical resistance.) You also must use a 50-ohm terminator. Figure 6-6 illustrates a BNC connector, a T-connector, and a terminating resistor. You need these connectors if you use coax cabling.

Figure 6-6: Use these types of connectors with coaxial cabling.

Using twisted-pair cable connectors

Twisted-pair cabling uses different connectors than coaxial cabling uses. In twisted-pair, you use one connector to plug into the network card or hub. You can use a second connector to plug into a wall panel, called a *jack*, or patch panel to help keep the cables safe from kinking and to look nicer in your home.

Connecting to the network card or hub

Twisted-pair cabling uses a specific connector for attaching the cable to the network card and hub. Twisted-pair uses an RJ-45 plug, or connector. An RJ-45 connector is an eight-pin plug used for data transmission over UTP cabling.

An RJ-45 connector looks similar to an RJ-11 connector, which is the modular telephone connector you've seen around your house. You use an RJ-11 connector, for example, to plug into your modem. An RJ-11 connector has four to six pins and is used for voice communications and data transfers (when used with the modem). An RJ-45 has eight pins, making it a larger connector, and it is used for data transfers only.

Figure 6-7 shows an RJ-45 and an RJ-11 connector. Both connectors are male parts that fit into the female part on the network card or hub.

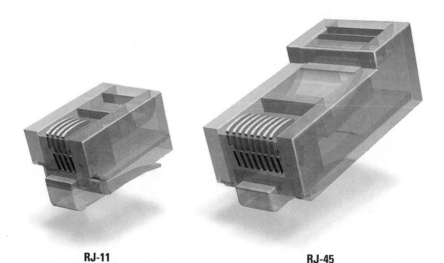

RJ-11   **RJ-45**

Figure 6-7: RJ-45 connectors are necessary for twisted-pair cabling; RJ-11 connectors are for phone wires.

Using jacks and patch cables

The twisted-pair cabling you use for networking can be either a solid or a stranded cable. Solid cabling is used for the majority of the cabling because it distributes the data quickly and efficiently. It's not a good idea, however, to attach the solid cabling directly to your network card or hub. If the solid cabling is moved around very much, the cable can become twisted or kinked. Kinking the cable can make your network connection irregular or stop the connection altogether.

Figure 6-8 illustrates a jack, a faceplate, and a patch cable. The patch cable is more flexible than a solid cable and therefore provides a better network connection if the cable should get a kink or twist in it.

Normally, you use the solid cabling for room-to-room connections and switch to the stranded cable, also called patch cable, to connect to the computer or hub. The stranded cable is much more flexible than the solid cable, so you don't have to be as careful when moving the cable, computer, or hub. You might bring the solid cabling through the wall, for example, attach a jack to the cabling, and cover it with a faceplate. From the wall outlet, you attach a patch, or stranded, cable that then plugs into the network card or hub. Patch cables are short, typically 3 to 5 feet, and flexible enough that you can move your computer or the hub around without damaging the cable and the connection.

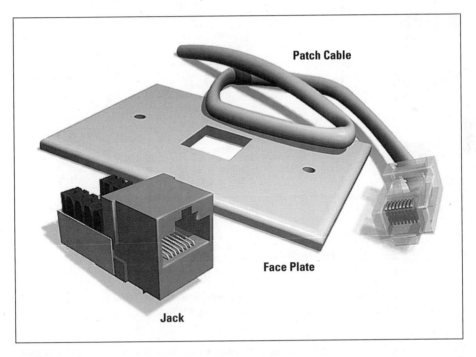

Patch Cable

Face Plate

Jack

Figure 6-8: Use jacks, faceplates, and patch cables to make the cabling more secure and neater looking.

Figure 6-9 illustrates the three methods of attaching CAT 5 twisted-pair cabling between your computer and a hub. The top example shows the easiest method, even if it's not the most secure method. The CAT 5 cable is attached directly to the hub and the computer with RJ-45 connectors. The middle example shows a safer method of connecting the computer, using a patch cable from the computer to the wall jack and an RJ-45 connector to the hub. The third example is the safest method. A patch cable connects the computer to the wall jack, the CAT 5 cable connects the wall jack to a patch panel, and a second patch cable runs from the patch panel to the hub.

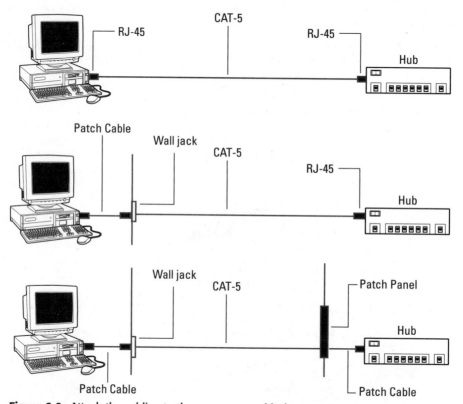

Figure 6-9: Attach the cabling to the computer and hub.

 Tip   Using a faceplate, jack, and patch cable not only protects your cabling and your network connections, but it also makes the wiring job look neater.

You can do without the faceplate, jack, and patch cable in your home network, even though this doesn't meet wiring specifications. You aren't likely to move your computers around as much as you would in a business and therefore might not damage the solid cable and your connection.

You definitely should use patch cables in a small-business office. You'll be moving computers, hubs, and users around, and any stress at all on the solid cable can cause network transfer interruptions. Also, wiring specifications require the use of patch cables and jacks.

You might want to use a device called a patch panel in your office network. Patch panels contain 8, 12, or 24 jacks within a strip for easy connection to solid cables. You can attach the patch panel to the wall, insert the solid cables, and then insert the patch cables on the other side leading to your hub, for safe and effective wiring of your network.

As I indicated earlier in the chapter, if you use jacks and patch cables, you might need a special punch to terminate the cabling and attach the jacks. You might want to hire out this part of the cabling. Call the telephone or telecommunications services in your area to find help installing the twisted-pair cabling. Alternatively, many networking kits come with the connectors and jacks attached to cables, ready for you to plug into your network.

Using Networking Tools

If you plan to take care of your own cabling, you'll need to put ends on the cables. You can use special tools you for terminating cables. You can also use many tools to test the cables to make sure you've put them together correctly. You can make your own cables for either coax or twisted-pair (Ethernet). Each uses different tools.

Unless you plan to professionally lay cable for more than just your home, you're better off either buying a kit, buying premade patch cables, or having someone who knows how to create cables do the job for you. Making cables is difficult, and they don't always work the first time. More importantly, you can put a lot of money into the tools that enable you to create the cables. If you don't think you'll use the tools more than once, you should let a professional make the cables.

Working with coaxial cable tools

To work with coax cable, you'll need to purchase a crimp and compression tool. There are many types of tools for various connectors. You should purchase the ends, the connectors, and the tools to work on the cable at the same place, so you can get help and perhaps some instruction.

Crimp tools have a ratchet action that forces the wiring into the connectors. A crimp tool can cost between $20 and $120. Remember, you get what you pay for; a $5 tool probably isn't going to last long and might not compress and crimp properly. You can also buy kits that include crimp tools, cable cutter, strippers, and so on, for around $100.

You can also strip and cut cables with a good sharp knife and a good pair of scissors.

Coax cable (RG58C), in spools, comes in 100-foot, 500-foot, and 1,000-foot rolls. Costs vary, but figure about $20 per 100 feet. You'll also need crimp-type plugs; generally the cost is $4 to $5 per plug. You might want to add a BNC coax tester. For around $50, you can purchase a tester to make sure the ends and connectors are working before you lay the cable.

Tip   Take a look at www.1-com.com for an overview of coax tools before you go shopping at your local electrician's store. This site can give you a better idea of what you need.

Working with Ethernet tools

Ethernet and Fast Ethernet are the most popular wiring for home networking besides wireless. You can purchase patch cables and kits for Ethernet to make it much easier to get your network up and running. However, if you prefer to make your own cables, you can. Naturally, you'll need tools to work with the cable and to get it ready for the network.

You'll need a punch-down tool, which inserts and cuts (terminates) the wiring into the plugs and jacks. You can buy a punch-down tool for around $50. Make sure you not only get the handle but also the blades too, which are often sold separately. The punch-down tool fastens the wire into a jack (for the wall) or a patch panel (for a large network). You have to finish the other end of the wire into a plug.

You use a crimp tool to strip, cut, and crimp the wire into plugs. The plugs then fit into the jack, into patch panel, or into the back of your computer where the network card is attached. Crimp tools cost between $20 and $120. (As you can see, making your own cabling is getting expensive.)

You'll need CAT 5 RJ-45 UTP connectors, jacks, and wall plates. You can get all of these at your local electrician's store. Connectors usually come in a bag of 100 for around $20. Jacks often cost $2.50 to $3.50 each. Wall plates can cost $2 or so each.

You can buy a kit that includes a punch-down tool, crimp tool, and various jacks and plugs for around $150 to $200. Check www.starkelectronic.com for ideas before you go shopping.

You can buy CAT 5 cable in 1,000-foot spools and cut the cable to the lengths you need. A spool costs around $65.

Tip   Make sure you get the type of CAT 5 cable that has a pull wire or cord in it. A pull wire makes stripping the cable easier and faster. Some salespeople don't know about the pull wire; others will try to sell you anything.

After you make your own cables, you should probably test the cable. You can buy a cable tester with a tone generator for around $50. You place one part of the cable tester on one end of the cable, and it generates a tone on that wire. You use the other part of the cable tester on the other end; if the tone comes through, you have communication.

Considering Network Kits

You might not want to hire someone to come into your home and lay your cabling, and you might not want to tackle the job yourself, even though you can. You might prefer to use a network kit for easy equipment purchasing and fast network installation.

You can purchase kits for both Ethernet 10 Mbps and Fast Ethernet 100 Mbps. Although the Fast Ethernet is more expensive, it allows for greater bandwidth. Consider price, your need for speed, data types you'll be transferring, and so on before purchasing a kit. If you plan to transfer only word processing, spreadsheet, and other small file formats over the network, for example, 10 Mbps works fine. If, however, you plan to transfer large graphic files, multimedia files, or audio files (like music files) over the network, you should use 100 Mbps so that those files are transferred more efficiently and quickly.

Note   Although there aren't many coaxial kits, a lot of vendors sell everything you need to create coax cabling for your network: L-Com Connectivity and Proxim are two popular dealers.

Some kits provide the hardware for a 10Base-2 or 10Base-T network; this chapter explains these kits. You can use these kits for any operating system and most any computer. You'll need to check your computer for available slots before you purchase a network interface card. Kits for wireless connections are covered in Chapter 7; kits that include everything for creating a network over your phone line or housewiring are explained in Chapter 8.

Note   When purchasing a kit, pay attention to the number of ports in the hub. A four-port hub is made for four computers. If you need seven or eight computers on your network, purchase a kit with an eight-port hub. For more information about hubs, see Chapter 9.

Looking at the advantages of a kit

If you read in the previous section about the tools for making your own cables, you'll understand the advantages of purchasing a networking kit. The only tool you need with the kit is a screwdriver. You don't have to wonder if your cable is made correctly. Everything you need to network two computers is included in the kit. In addition, you can purchase other network cards and patch cables to add to the kit as you need them.

Another advantage of using a kit is the technical support. Not only do you get instructions for setting up the network, but also you usually get a toll-free number you can call if you have trouble.

Using the kit

Ethernet network kits contain all of the hardware you need to connect two computers in your home network — such as two network interface cards, a hub, cabling, and connectors already installed on the cable ends. Usually you purchase a starter kit to connect two computers.

When you purchase the network kit, pay attention to the network specifications. For example, what speed are the cards and hub — 10 Mbps or 100 Mbps? If the cards are 10/100 and the hub is 10 Mbps, make sure that any cards you buy after that are 10 Mbps. Cards must be 10 Mbps if the hub is 10 Mbps. If the hub is 100 Mbps, the cards can be 10 or 100, although 100 gives you the fastest connections.

Cross-Reference   For more information about hubs and network cards, see Chapter 9.

You also want to note the cabling type — CAT 3 or CAT 5, UTP or STP, and so on. (As mentioned, UTP is unshielded twisted-pair and STP is shielded twisted-pair.) For any additional computers you add to the network, you should buy the same cabling type as is used in the kit. You can purchase cables in premade segments — available in 6-, 10-, 15-, 25-, 50-, and 100-foot sections — including connectors.

When you're ready to add more computers to your network, you need to buy a network card and length of cable for each computer. You want to make sure that the cards are the same speed and possibly even the same brand as in the kit. If you get the same brand of card, the diagnostic and driver software for one works for all; that makes installation and use easier on you in the long run.

Looking at Ethernet network kits

Ethernet startup networking kits run at 10 Mbps. Starter kits contain the equipment you need to start a network with two computers: two network cards, cabling, and a four-port hub. You then can purchase the network cards and additional cabling for each computer you add to your network. Any kit that includes a network card automatically includes the software drivers necessary for installing the card. Many also include diagnostic software. See Chapter 9 for more information. Kits are useful because they include cabling connectors and cards and hubs that are matches in speed and compatibility.

Note   Few of the networking kits provide the software you need to share an Internet connection over the network. Check the package carefully if you're looking for this feature. See Chapter 16 for information about programs that enable you to share Internet accounts and access.

Linksys Fast Ethernet in a Box

Linksys offers a starter kit for around $75. The kit includes the following:

✦ Two EtherFast 10/100 network interface cards (NIC)

✦ One 5-port 10/100 hub

✦ Two 15-foot network cables

✦ Drivers for a variety of operating systems

✦ LanBridge, which lets two computers share a modem

The kit also has some other technical data you should look for, including AutoSensing. AutoSensing enables the network to work at either 10 or 100, depending on the speed of all parts of the network. In addition, the cards are PCI, which describes the slot you must have in the computer. The kit works with Windows, Linux, and other operating systems. Linksys also offers good warranties on the cards and hub and Linksys offers free technical support, which is always a sign of a good deal.

Hawking 10/100 Network Kit

For around $40, you can get the Hawking 10/100 networking kit, which contains similar products as the Linksys kit, including:

✦ Two 10/100 PCI network interface cards

✦ One 10 Mbps 5-port hub

✦ Two 10-foot CAT 5 cables

ADS Technologies USB to Ethernet Starter Kit

This kit costs around $150 and you get the following:

✦ Two 10 Mbps Ethernet to USB adapters

✦ One 5-port Ethernet hub

✦ Cables (one 7 feet and one 50 feet)

✦ Software on disk and CD

TE100-SK3plus

This is a starter kit that includes a 5-year warranty and serves various operating systems. It also includes the following:

✦ Two Fast Ethernet PCI cards

✦ Five-port 10/100 Mbps Switch

✦ Two 15-foot CAT 5 cables

✦ Drivers and installation guide

Installing Cable

Installing cable can be as easy or as difficult as you want to make it. You can run the cable through walls, like telephone wire, or under the carpet to hide it. You can run the cable under the house or behind bookcases and around window frames. You might want to purchase raceway, a plastic casing that covers the cable and attaches it to the wall.

Naturally, if you don't want to install the cable yourself, you can hire someone to do it. For prices, check the Yellow Pages for telecommunications or telephone services, network consultants, or network technicians.

 Small Business Tip You should check into hiring someone to install the cabling for your business office if you're unsure of building codes, AC power line placement, and standards—and especially if you're renting the office space.

Sketching a plan

The first step is to plan where you want to place the computers. You're likely to place computers in your home office, den, living room, or a particular bedroom. You might make a sketch of your house with the computers in the appropriate rooms.

Next, decide how and where you want to run the cables and consider where to put the hub. The hub should go in a central place, someplace easy to reach from the other rooms.

You can draw the house from the side, as shown in Figure 6-10. You can show general cabling from this point of view, such as the hub placement and connections to the hub.

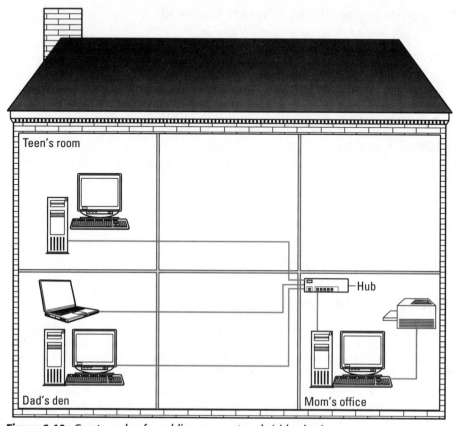

Figure 6-10: Create a plan for cabling your network (side view).

You might want to do a sketch from the top view, like a floor plan. Figure 6-11 shows a network drawn in this view. Three desktop computers appear in three separate rooms. A printer and a laptop are also connected to the network. You want to place the hub in the most convenient and central location in relation to the computers' locations.

Small Business Tip

If you hire someone to do your cabling for you, make sure that you tell him or her that you want a complete map of the cabling when he or she is finished. Question the installers to make sure you're getting the type of cabling, connectors, placement, and other things that you want from the cabling job.

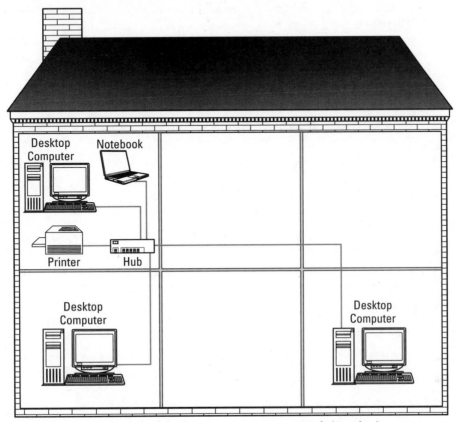

Figure 6-11: Use any method that's easy to map your network (top view).

Understanding and using the cabling rules

Standards and rules for laying cable exist, and you need to make sure to follow them. If you do not follow the rules, the network speed and connections will likely suffer. Put the cabling in the right way the first time, whether you make your own cabling or use a kit. If a professional is putting your cable in for you, keep an eye on him or her to make sure the installer is following the rules too.

Following are the rules you should follow as you install your cable:

✦ Don't kink the cable. Kinks in the cable can cause connection problems as well as ruin the cable.

✦ Don't stretch the cable when pulling it. The maximum force should be 25 pounds or less.

✦ CAT 5e cable standard is that there should no cable bends less than 5 inches.

✦ Don't use a staple gun or staples of any type to install cabling. You can nick the cable, which ruins it.

✦ Don't wrap it around a nail or other object. If you want to make cables neat and hold their place, use plastic wire tires (available in any electrician's store). Keep the ties snug but not excessively so. Don't overcinch them.

✦ If you use plastic or metal ties to hold several cables together, don't pull the ties too tightly. You might kink a cable and stop the connection.

✦ Don't install cabling so that it runs beside electrical lines of any sort. The power can interfere with the data traveling over the network cable.

✦ Don't install cabling close to fluorescent lighting (within 2 feet). Fluorescent lights interfere with the network signal.

✦ Also keep cable away from the following: copy machines, power supplies, UPS units, electric heaters, TV sets, AC power cables, welding machines, radio transmitters, radio frequency antennas or transmission lines, microwave ovens, dishwashers, telephones, fans, electric garage door openers, elevator motors, electric ovens, dryers, washing machines, shop equipment, and any magnetic surfaces.

✦ If you must cross a power line, cross it only at a right angle, which produces the least interference.

✦ Don't coil excess cabling when the cabling is in use. If, for example, you install the cable and have several feet left over, don't coil it up. Instead, lay the cable out as straight as possible. Coiling the cable can cause interference in the data transmissions.

✦ If at all possible, don't install the cable in a doorway or other heavy traffic area. Constant abuse from walking on a cable (such as one hidden under a carpet) can damage the cable and slow down data transmissions.

✦ Don't use staples or insulated metal U-shaped cable clips on the cable.

✦ Never run the cabling outside of a building. Cable attracts lightning.

Laying the cable

Twisted-pair is easy to install. If you've ever set up a new room for cable TV or run a new phone jack, you can install twisted-pair cable.

Make sure that you have the appropriate ends on the cable. If you bought a kit or patch (pre-made) cables, you have nothing to worry about. If you made your own cables and attached the connectors yourself, you should test the cabling before you begin installing it. You can use a cable tester device for that purpose.

Tip   Making your own cables is difficult, takes practice, and requires special expensive tools. Try first to go to an electrician's store and purchase patch cables. Patch cables come in many lengths and are not very expensive. A 25-foot cable costs around $18.

When you're ready to actually lay the cable, label both ends of each cable with a number or name. For example, number the first cable 1 on each end. That way, it is easier to test the cable at the hub or jack if problems occur. Leave the cables marked after you're done so you can easily find problems later as well.

Find the path of the cable. You might want to go behind walls or just along baseboards. You can go in between floors, in the ceiling, or behind desks. Make sure that if the path is out in the room, the cable is not obstructed, kinked, or bent by boxes, desks, tables, chairs, and the like. Make sure no cable is in the floor where people walk. You can attach the cable along the baseboard and up around doorways, if necessary.

If you plan to go behind walls or under the floors of your house, you should use an electrician to help you pull the wire. For one thing, you want to avoid drilling into any power lines. If you're not sure where these electrical lines are, do not drill or pull cabling until you find out where they are. You could get a nasty electrical shock, cut the power to your home, or cause some other catastrophe.

Additionally, going through walls and under floors requires some special equipment — snakes and fancy drill bits — as well as two people to pull the wire. You may need to go through cinder block walls or walls full of insulation. Make sure that you don't drill through the studs in a framed wall. Be very careful when installing network cabling in the walls of your house.

Tip   Although the process of laying cable is called "pulling wire," you don't actually pull the cable; you carefully place it and lay it in place. CAT 5 cable is very delicate. If the cable is pulled, bent, kinked, and so on, it might not work when you finally connect it.

If you use raceway along the walls to help hide the cabling and make it look neater, consider using screws to attach the raceway to the walls. If you use glue, you might not be able to get the raceway off easily when necessary.

Tip   Make sure that everyone using the network understands the difference between the RJ-11 and RJ-45 jacks in the back of the computer. RJ-11 jacks are used for connecting a modem; RJ-45 jacks are used for connecting twisted-pair networking cable. If someone plugs an RJ-11 plug into an RJ-45 jack, a telephone ring could cause damage to the network card or hub.

Splitting a Pair for an Easy Connection

Suppose you've already set up your network and everything is working well. You have a computer in your office, but you decide to add a second computer beside the first. Instead of laying new cabling to the second computer, you can use the original cable to attach the new computer to the network without pulling new wire.

CAT 5 cabling consists of four wire pairs. You use only two of those pairs to set up connections for the network. To attach another computer without adding a whole new cable, you can split the end of the wire into two sets of two pairs. One pair goes to one computer, and the other pair goes to the second computer.

You can purchase a network pair splitter, split the end of the cable, and attach two PCs using the same wire. Using a pair splitter doesn't slow down network traffic at all. You can buy network pair splitters at most computer stores or over the Internet. The directions for use accompany the hardware.

Checking the cabling

Cables are very seldom the problem when it comes to a network connection. In only a couple of situations, the cable might be bad. If you put the ends on your cable, those could be trouble spots, although it's not really the cable that is bad but the connections on the ends.

Another problem area is if the cable is coiled or kinked, or if you find a nick or cut in the cable. You should make sure that the cabling is in good shape before you lay it. You should also make sure not to lay the cabling in an area where it can become damaged with nicks or cuts easily.

Checking a cable connection is fairly easy. If the lights on the network card, the hub, or both are all lit, the cable connection is good. See Chapter 9 for information about cards and hubs.

Deciding to Use Other Networking Hardware

There are many other pieces of networking hardware you can use with your network. Some might be useful; others will not help your network at all. It's important to determine the size and the complexity of the network before you add too much hardware. As noted previously, you can use kits to start your network. You can always add onto a kit as your network grows. You don't need to buy everything at one time.

Here are some basic rules about the hardware you need to purchase for your network. For more information, see Chapter 9.

✦ You need a network interface card (NIC) for every computer on the network. These cards can be Ethernet, wireless, phoneline, or other, but you do need a network card for each computer. You'll need cabling or wireless access points (see Chapter 7 for more information). The cabling might be coax, Ethernet, phone line, or power line as well.

✦ If you're connecting two computers, you can do so by using a crossover cable and the two network cards. See Chapter 7 for more information.

✦ If you want to connect three or more computers, or if you want a nice fast connection between two computers, you need a hub with Ethernet wiring. You also need a hub when you use Ethernet with wireless. That's it. You don't need any other hardware to start your network.

Now if you want, you can add other hardware. For example:

✦ A *cable modem/Digital Subscriber Line (DSL) router* is something you can add to your network to enable the computers on the network to connect to the Internet. A router is a device that analyzes the network packets that come into it and direct the packets to the appropriate location, usually between network segments.

✦ Another piece of equipment you might want is a network *switch*. A switch is another "intelligent" device that directs packets to the appropriate computer, server, or network segment. You don't need a switch, however, if your network is small.

✦ You've seen the term patch panel in this chapter. Again, that's something you'll only need if your network is large, as it would be in a business or corporation. A *patch panel* is an area where all cables come together. They are fed into a panel full of jacks, and then shorter patch cables connect the jacks to switches or routers, or the server. You will most likely not need a patch panel in your network.

Summary

In this chapter, you've learned about topology, technology, and network cabling. Specifically, you learned about the following topics:

- ✦ Understanding the methods of network cabling
- ✦ Considering networking topologies and technologies
- ✦ Understanding cabling
- ✦ Looking at cable connectors
- ✦ Considering cabling kits
- ✦ Installing cables

In the next chapter, you learn about wireless connections, standards, products, and security.

✦   ✦   ✦

Using Wireless Network Connections

Wireless technologies were originally developed to enable workers to roam about warehouses, manufacturing plants, and other large business facilities. Wireless LANs (WLANs) are now used in many other situations, such as corporations, small businesses, colleges and universities, and home networking. WLANs often replace wired or traditionally cabled LANs and more often work as an extension to wired LANs.

What are the reasons you want to use wireless in your home network? Do you have a home in which wiring with traditional cabling would be difficult? Do you have a notebook computer you want to network yet use in different rooms of the house? Is the thought of cabling your home with traditional wiring too much? Are you curious about the technology? You can use wireless for all of these reasons and more.

Considering Wireless Methods

Wireless technology is all around you: radio, television, microwave ovens, telephones, personal pagers, remote controls for garage door openers and automotive keyless entry, security systems, and more. It only makes sense to use wireless technologies for networking computers.

Small Business Tip

And because wireless technology is all around you, interference can also affect your wireless network. Consider where your business is located, the type of building you have, and your outside environment before using wireless in your business. Power lines, heavy machinery, microwaves or satellites, and other devices can interfere with wireless network connectivity.

Four methods of wireless networking are common — infrared, radio signals, microwaves, and laser links. For home networking, the most popular wireless connections are radio signals. More and more manufacturers and software providers are supporting wireless network connections.

✦ **Infrared** works similarly to a television remote control. The connection must be line-of-sight, or point-to-point, because infrared light cannot penetrate obstacles. The narrow cone of the infrared beam enables two devices to communicate without being directly aligned. The beam itself is highly directional and ensures the infrared connection doesn't spill to other nearby devices. The transmission distance for infrared is relatively short; depending on the hardware, the distance is usually limited to around 50 feet. Unfortunately, infrared isn't as popular as its makers thought it would be, so choices are somewhat limited.

✦ **Radio frequency**, or RF, describes the number of times per second a radio wave vibrates. Two RF physical interfaces are standard: direct sequence spread spectrum and frequency hopping spread spectrum. *Direct sequence spread spectrum* can pass through light obstacles, such as thin walls and ceilings. *Frequency hopping spread spectrum* radio signals can pass through heavier walls, but the transfer rate is slow.

Radio frequency connections use 900 MHz frequencies, similar to many higher-quality cordless telephones. Spread spectrum signals are fairly secure against tampering from outside sources, such as intercepting transmissions. Additionally, spread spectrum products provide 11 to 54 Mbps data rates at a range from 50 feet to 1,000 feet, depending on the building construction, interference sources, and other factors.

✦ **Microwaves** provide wide bandwidth, but they are susceptible to external interference and eavesdropping. Microwaves require FCC licensing and approved equipment. Microwaves can use terrestrial or satellite systems. Satellite microwave can provide links to extremely remote areas, so they're useful in larger networks. Microwaves, however, aren't practical for home networking because they are extremely expensive.

✦ **Lasers** aren't practical for home networking, either, again because of the expense. A communication laser transmits a narrow beam of light that is modulated into pulses to carry the data. Laser light is also sensitive to atmospheric conditions and provides only a relatively short transmission distance, from 25 to 100 feet or so.

Using Radio Frequency for Networking

Radio signals are accessible to most users throughout the world. Radio signals penetrate light obstacles, such as walls and furniture. Popular wireless networking technologies, especially for home use, are commonly based on radio frequency principles.

Figure 7-1 illustrates the ease of placement when using wireless technologies. The notebook can travel anywhere within the house and still connect to the other computers and the printer. The printer is connected to one computer, which is connected to the wireless network. The access point (also AP or WAP for wireless access point) is the device that enables wireless network cards to connect to the network.

Wireless products usually use two basic components: a station adapter (SA) and an access point. The station adapter connects to the client computer as a network interface card (NIC), also called a network card or network adapter card. The access point connects to the LAN infrastructure and communicates with the station adapters to transfer data. If you set up a large wireless network or expect interference from the building structure or electrical noise sources, you may need several access points for complete coverage. More than likely, however, you'll need only one access point for a small home network.

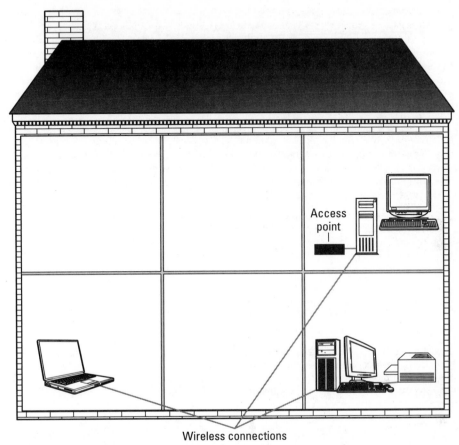

Wireless connections

Figure 7-1: RF-based wireless networks are quick and easy to set up.

Tip Access points extend the range of the network. Each access point enables 15 to 50 client devices to connect to the network. Access points generally have a finite range — 500 feet indoors and 1,000 feet outdoors.

Figure 7-2 illustrates a large corporate network that uses multiple access points. Notebooks can roam the building and access the network from anywhere. As the user "roams," the notebook switches access points to the one has the strongest signal.

Tip As a user roams, the NIC renegotiates with various access points to find the strongest connection to the network. The connection is not seamless, however; it takes a few seconds for the notebook, or other computer, to reconnect to the network.

Tip Although users of wireless local area networks are not required to have permits or licenses, the FCC does govern the equipment, such as transmitter power and methods of transmission.

About Wireless Network Topology

Any computer or other device using wireless technology needs a transceiver and an antenna, and components are either a station adapter or an access point. A *station adapter* (also called station, SA, or STA) is the client "radio." Usually the station adapter is incorporated into a wireless network card and installed into a computer. The wireless NIC can be a PC Card, Personal Computer Memory Card International Association (PCMCIA), universal serial bus (USB), or other form of radio that is integrated into the device, such as in some printers. The *access point* is the bridge between the network card and the network.

You can configure the basic wireless network with either peer-to-peer or client/server. In peer-to-peer, two or more stations talk to each other without an access point; the radio frequencies connect the computers via the wireless network cards. In client/server, multiple stations connect to an access point, which acts as a bridge to a wired network.

You can overlap basic services using access points that are connected to a wired network, in the case of a larger building or heavier construction materials, for instance. The ranges overlap to avoid interference or lapses in data transfer.

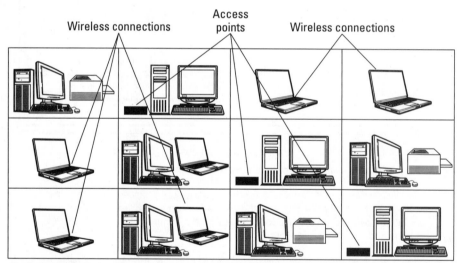

Figure 7-2: Roaming users can connect to the network via access points placed throughout the building.

Another option for wireless networking is called *wired bridging*. When using wired bridging, you connect a wireless access point to a wired Ethernet LAN. Combining wired and wireless networking gives you more control over the wireless network, faster speeds through the wired LAN, network management functions, and so on.

Cross-Reference   For more information about using wireless and wired networks together, see the section "Using Wireless in Conjunction with Cabled Networks" later in this chapter.

Advantages and Disadvantages of Wireless Technologies

Wireless LANs have become popular over the last few years with many businesses; for example, wireless technologies are used in healthcare, retail, industrial parks, trade shows, academic environments, corporate training facilities, and more. It's only natural that wireless networking move into situations for more personal uses. However, as with all things, there are advantages and disadvantages to using wireless technologies. The following discussion concentrates on the advantages and disadvantages of the use of wireless LANs in the home.

Advantages of wireless

One of the most popular uses for wireless networking is the advantage of using a roaming notebook, personal digital assistant (PDA), tablet computer, and the like. However, you might decide to install a wireless network even if you have nonroaming desktop computers. For one reason, the cost of deploying a wireless network is less than the traditional cabling, not only in the components and equipment but in the installation as well.

Another reason you might want wireless is it is very easy to install. Wireless is also easy to use and understand. If you're looking for a way to network your home computers quickly and easily, wireless is the ideal solution. In addition, you can start your network with wireless, and as you learn more about networking and as your network grows, you can add traditional cabling to the wireless.

Tip You can connect two PCs that are equipped with wireless network adapter cards to create a peer-to-peer (or workgroup) network. For example, suppose you use your notebook at home sometimes and you want to print to the printer connected to your desktop computer; all you have to do is connect the two with wireless NICs and bring the notebook in close proximity, and you're ready to network.

Wireless standards have been adopted all over the world to ensure regular improvements in new features and capabilities. Besides constant and consistent upgrades and revisions, there is widespread industry support for wireless technology. For more information about wireless standards, see the section "Considering Wireless Standards" later in this chapter.

Because of the popularity of wireless networking, wireless networking equipment is widely available. For instance, network adapter cards come in a variety of forms to fit most computers: Peripheral Component Interface (PCI), USB, PC Card, and so on. Wireless directional antennas, extension points, and other hardware are also easily obtained.

Other advantages of wireless networking include the following:

✦ Intuitive to use

✦ Convenient to install and use

✦ Economical

✦ A large number of hardware manufacturers from which to choose

What Are Hotspots?

Hotspots are all the rage now in many cities and towns. A *hotspot* is any commercial business—cafés, hotels, restaurants, bars, airports, and so on—that has a high-speed Internet connection. Many of these businesses have wired access, but even more have wireless. The business provides you with a hookup to check your mail or surf the Net while you eat, drink, or otherwise patronize the business.

The standard 802.11b is currently the most popular standard for wireless networks at hotspots (see the section "Considering Wireless Standards" later in this chapter for more information about 802.11b).

Public hotspots might be free or pay-for-use. Private hotspots also exist, located in a workplace or even a home where a private group of people create and use the hotspot. There are also community hotspots, often free and open to the public. Some community hotspots are offered by public organizations; other hotspots are affiliated with nonprofit organizations.

You can use a hotspot to access the Internet with a PDA or a notebook computer with a wireless adapter. Find hotspots in your area by checking colleges, hotels, restaurants, and such, or go to the Wi-Fi Zone at www.wi-fizone.org.

Disadvantages of wireless

What are some other questions you might ask before choosing wireless networking? Will you be sharing only files and printers, or will you be sharing applications? What type of applications will run over the WLAN? It's important to remember that wireless networking is a shared medium, not a switched medium. This means that some applications running over a wireless network do not run as efficiently or as quickly as they would over a traditionally wired network. Consider the application question before choosing wireless.

Tip   In home networking, the only applications you might share are games for the kids. Check the minimum requirements for the games you buy to see if they can run on a wireless network. Other applications you might want to run over a network include accounting programs, payroll, point of sale, and other such "business" programs.

Cross-Reference   For more information about applications and the network, see Chapter 20.

Another question you need to ask yourself is this: Will there be roaming computers on your network? If so, how far will they roam? Range is important to wireless networking, because if a roaming computer, such as a tablet or notebook, roams away from the RF range, the computer becomes disconnected from the network. Radio frequencies disperse as the distance from the transmitter increases. Also, as data rates increase, range decreases.

Question three: How fast do you want your network to transmit data? RF networks generally come in two speeds: 11 Mbps and 54 Mbps. Some manufacturers have begun to introduce 60 Mbps in recent months.

Looking at performance

As I've indicated, the most popular wireless networking hardware is radio-based technology. Because of the technology, some performance issues do exist. Some issues have solutions that are acceptable to the user; others do not.

Radio waves can be absorbed by furniture, walls, plastic, water, and other materials. For example, sometimes objects create interference with the signal, causing dead spots for the radio signal. If you find a dead spot, a spot in a room where a wireless device cannot attach to the network, you generally just move to another area. Dead spots often cover only small areas. You can, alternatively, move the wireless access points to cover the dead spots.

Wireless devices are meant to keep a reliable and consistent connection between two devices; however, connection speed varies as range and signal strength vary. Performance degrades with increased distance between devices (NIC and access point). As performance degrades, wireless technology institutes a fallback. A *fallback* is when the wireless technology slows the speed of the connection in order to maintain a more reliable connection. If, for instance, the range increases and the signal strength varies, the connection slows to make sure that transferred data is more accurate and consistent.

Radio waves grow weaker as they expand from the initial source. If, for example, your notebook computer is in the room beside the access point, it will receive data transmissions better than if the notebook is three or four rooms away from the access point.

Figure 7-3 shows an example of signal strength as it relates to range between wireless devices. Two access points, one upstairs and one downstairs, radiate waves of RF. The closer a computer — notebook, PDA, desktop, or other — is to the access point, the more reliable and stable the connections. However, a computer can roam to other rooms, and perhaps outside of the house, and still connect to the network.

Each wireless device clearly defines a range in which it works most efficiently. You can purchase wireless devices that have a range of 25, 75, 100, or 150 feet indoors. (There are some devices that offer higher ranges, such as 1,000 feet; however, these devices are quite expensive and not really for home networks.) You can also purchase signal boosters, repeaters, and a host of additional hardware to increase the signal of the wireless devices. For your home, though, you'll probably need only one or two access points.

 Tip   If you require high performance from your wireless connection, place that device closer to the access point.

Considering interference

The range of radio frequencies that wireless networking uses is known as an *unlicensed band*; the FCC does not require the use of a license for these RF ranges. Therefore, other devices also use the same frequencies, resulting in interference with RF wireless networking. Cordless telephones are a prime example of another RF device that can jam, or interfere, with RF networking. Microwave ovens are another device that can interfere with your wireless network.

The good news is that cordless telephones and microwave ovens use slightly different frequencies within the RF range; so neither is a huge threat to your wireless network, and your wireless network isn't a huge threat to your telephone or microwave system.

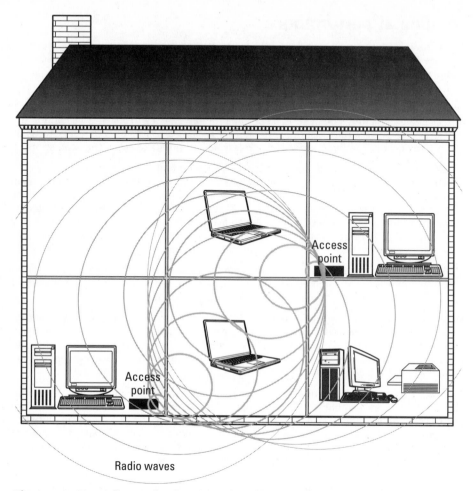

Radio waves

Figure 7-3: Depending on the size of your house, you might need two access points.

Other interference might occur with metal objects close to the access point, X10 video senders that operate in the same band (2.4 GHz), video or digital cameras, baby monitors, and so on. X10 devices are normally used in SmartHomes to automate processes and activities; for more information, see Chapter 26. Figure 7-4 shows an access point too close to metal shelves in a storeroom. Interference keeps the radio waves from reaching all computers.

Note   Interference also occurs with various construction materials. For example, wood, plaster, and glass interfere with radio waves on a low level, whereas concrete, bulletproof glass, and metal interfere on a high level. Water, bricks, and marble might also interfere with radio waves on a medium level.

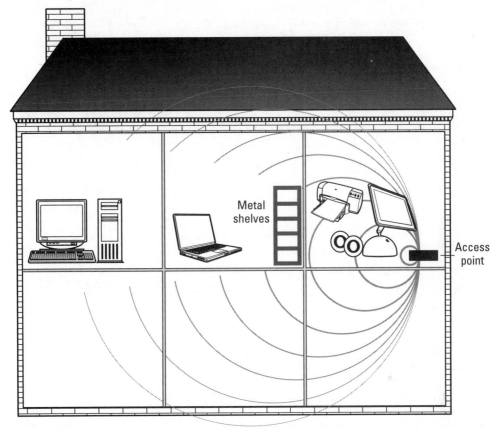

Figure 7-4: Make sure the access point is not near any metal, microwave ovens, or other materials that may cause interference.

Securing a wireless network

Hackers can easily find wireless networks and access not only information over your network but also use of your resources, such as the Internet. In fact, there are rogue ISPs that have recently been discovered in cities and small towns. People use their wireless networking to transmit signals connecting their neighbors to the Internet for free.

When using a WLAN, the data is transmitted over the air using radio waves, meaning anyone within the access point area can receive the data. Radio waves travel through walls and furniture, often even through outside walls. Without security, anyone in the area could pick up your data from your wireless network.

Small Business Tip

If you plan to use wireless networking in your small business, be especially careful about placement of the access points. Keep the points closer to the center of the building so the outside range is less. Security issues are another reason you might want to use wired networking for your small business.

Figure 7-5 illustrates an overhead view of radio waves transmitting into the street and possibly into a café across the street. The user could move the access point to the middle of the house to keep the range closer in the house.

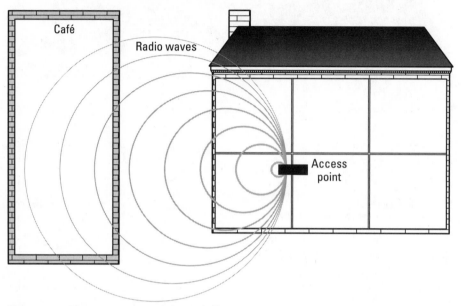

Figure 7-5: Place your access points wisely.

Most wireless networking products supply several security features. Encryption, known as Wired Equivalent Privacy (WEP), can encrypt and decrypt the transmitted data. WEP keys are vulnerable to attacks, however. You can also filter Media Access Control, or MAC, addresses, disable some broadcasts that tend to cause problems, and take other steps to protect your wireless network. To make sure your network information is safe when you are using wireless, you must use several layers of defense across the network.

If you want to make sure your home or small-business network is secure using wireless connections, you can add software that adds extra protection. Padlock, Secure.XS, and other software programs are available to secure your wireless network.

For more information about configuring your wireless network for security, see the section "Securing the Wireless Network" later in this chapter.

Since the radio signals used for wireless networking can be jammed by phones, baby monitors, and the like, look for a wireless technology that supports multiple channels, much like multichannel cordless phones.

Considering Wireless Standards

Network cabling and other networking equipment have standards that are set by the Institute of Electrical and Electronic Engineers (IEEE) to ensure interoperability of products and services from vendor to vendor. The IEEE 802 series of standards sets computing and electrical engineering standards. Following is a list of the common IEEE 802 standards defining local area network (LAN) criteria:

- ✦ **802.1** — Network management and bridging (network management has to do with devices and applications that enable an administrator to manage the network; bridging involves devices that connect one network segment to another).

- ✦ **802.2** — LAN data-link protocols (data-link protocols enable transmission of data over phone lines, cable modems, and the like, with connection to the Internet).

- ✦ **802.3** — Ethernet standards (Ethernet standards involve traditional cabling with twisted-pair, CAT 3 or CAT 5 cable).

- ✦ **802.4** — Bus topology using token passing (this describes a method of passing packets over the network through a topology — bus — and a method — token passing).

- ✦ **802.9** — Integrated data and voice networks (integrated data and voice networking includes phone line, T1, Digital Subscriber Line, and other technologies that enable both data and voice to travel on the same networking cables).

- ✦ **802.10** — LAN security (LAN security involves hardware and software such as encryption, firewalls, and other methods to prevent hackers from intruding on your private network).

- ✦ **802.11** — Wireless Ethernet (the wireless Ethernet standard covers base standards of interoperability).

The Wireless Ethernet Compatibility Alliance (WECA) is the organization that certifies 802.11 products to meet the standards. Generally, the 802.11 standard produces data rates up to 2 Mbps at 2.4 GHz. There are groups working on enhancements to the 802.11 standard, calling each enhancement *a* through *i*, as in 802.11a, 802.11b, and so on. Not all of these standards will become widely accepted. However, three are in the wireless market now and available to you for your network. These three standards are 802.11a, 802.11b, and 802.11g.

Using the 802.11b standard

802.11b was the first standard certified by WECA. Any product certified as 802.11b-compatible has a Wi-Fi logo stamped on it, and these devices are referred to as Wi-Fi devices. (The Wi-Fi Alliance is an international organization that certifies the interoperability of wireless LAN products.) Any Wi-Fi product works with any other Wi-Fi certified product, no matter the manufacturer, the cost, or the production date. Following is some additional information about the 802.11b standard:

- ✦ Since it was the first certified, it's available everywhere.

- ✦ Speed is up to 11 Mbps.

- ✦ Range is 100 to 150 feet indoors, depending on the space, setup, furniture, and construction materials.

- ✦ Of the three standards, 802.11b costs the least.

- ✦ 802.11b is in the 2.4 GHz band, which also includes cordless phones and microwave ovens.

- ✦ This standard is available in most airports, hotels, college campuses, and so on.

Using the 802.11a standard

The 802.11a standard provides data rates to 54 Mbps, thus making this wireless standard faster and more efficient than 802.11b. 802.11a is in the 5 GHz band, which means its in a relatively dispersed band; few other devices use the 5 GHz band. One problem with the 5 GHz band, however, is that more of the radio frequencies are absorbed by walls and furniture, which means more data losses. If you use the 802.11a standard, you might need to install more access points to get the higher data rates promised.

Other facts about the 802.11a standard include the following:

✦ Quite a bit more expensive than the other standards.

✦ Short range, usually 25 to 75 feet, depending on the space, setup, furniture, and construction materials.

✦ Not resident in airports, hotels, and so on.

✦ Not compatible with 802.11g; hardware is just now at the time of this writing available for compatibility with 802.11b.

Using the 802.11g standard

The 802.11g standard works on the 2.4 GHz band, as does 802.11b, so you still get interference with cordless phones, microwave ovens, and other devices on that same band. 802.11g offers data rates up to 54 Mbps, which is five times as fast as 802.11b.

This technology is compatible with 802.11b and remains compatible after upgrades and enhancements. If you set up 802.11b, for example, and find that 11 Mbps doesn't always work for you, you can add 802.11g to the network and use both standards together.

Following are some additional facts about 802.11g:

✦ It's a new technology but has become very popular, promising more use in the near future.

✦ It has rates of 54 Mbps.

✦ 802.11g is more expensive than 802.11b, but less expensive than 802.11a (unless you purchase special devices that work with 802.11a).

✦ It has ranges of 100 to 150 feet, depending on the space, setup, furniture, and construction materials.

✦ This standard works with 802.11b, and special products are just now at the time of this writing available for working with 802.11a.

Looking at HomeRF

Another wireless protocol is available yet limited in scope and practice. HomeRF Shared Wireless Access Protocol (SWAP) is designed to transmit voice and data in the home. HomeRF is a wireless network solution that carries data up to 1.6 Mbps for a distance of up to 150 feet. HomeRF is also on the 2.4 GHz band, so remember, you can and will experience some interference. You can share files and printers, plus share a dial-up connection. Also remember that 1.6 Mbps is slow, compared to speeds of 11 Mbps of 802.11b and 54 Mbps of 802.11a.

Tip Several products using HomeRF are available from Proxim and Intel AnyPoint. You can purchase kits for around $100 to $300. Similar in price to kits for 802.11g, the speed is much slower. See the section "Looking at Wireless Products" later in this chapter for more information.

Looking at Bluetooth

Bluetooth is a personal area network (PAN) and a cable-replacement technology. Mainly, the technology is used for data synchronization. Bluetooth technology is based on short-range radio links, a standard for a cheap radio chip that's plugged into printers, phones, computers, fax machines, and other digital devices. So the Bluetooth chip replaces the cable between your printer and your computer, for example.

Bluetooth supports data transmission between devices at up to 1 Mbps over 5 feet. It's also on the 2.4 GHz band. Bluetooth transmits both data and voice and does provide encryption for security.

Bluetooth was designed for wireless personal area networks (WPANs) where the network of personal electronic devices are all close to each other. Bluetooth is particularly handy to people who must have a wireless connection to devices from their notebooks, PDAs, tablet computers, and so on.

Note Hewlett-Packard is working on Bluetooth-enabled devices for mobile printing.

Choosing the Devices

Wireless networking includes many devices, but you can set up your home network using only a few. If you want to connect two computers, say, your notebook and desktop, you can use wireless network cards to enable the computers to connect, share files, and share printers. You can even connect more computers using just the network cards, if the computers are close enough and the interference is low.

Tip For home or small-business networking, stick with the 802.11g standards when possible. 802.11g gives you the most reliable, flexible, and consistent standards for your money.

If you want to connect computers that are further apart in your house, say, on separate floors or in rooms on opposite sides of the house, you can use access points to boost the connections. Access points also allow you to roam with a laptop, if you want.

Another piece of wireless equipment you might want to use is the antenna. All wireless devices have an antenna—network cards, access points, and such—but you can buy antennas that are attached to the network via antenna cables. You might want to use remote antennas to connect your wireless network across the driveway to a garage apartment, for example.

Small Business Tip You can also use antennas to connect the network between two buildings. Some antennas range for miles, and as long as you have line of sight between the buildings, you can attach two small networks together.

Figure 7-6 illustrates network adapter cards, access points, and antennas in use in a home networking environment.

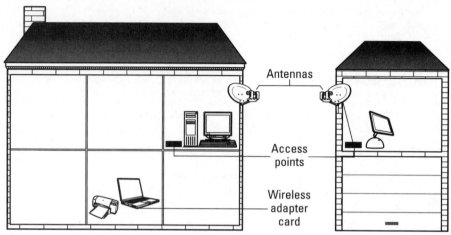

Figure labels: Antennas, Access points, Wireless adapter card

Figure 7-6: Everything is connected through wireless networking.

Tip   You can definitely use wireless with most Linux distributions (distros), but you have to install the modules that support the wireless for each particular distro. You'll have to research your system and install what's necessary to make wireless work with your Linux machine.

Using wireless network adapter cards

Wireless network adapter cards or NICs come in various standards, sizes, and for various hardware types. You can purchase 802.11a, b, or g standards for your desktop computer, your notebook computer, or your Linux, Windows, or Macintosh computers. Just make sure that all of the wireless devices you buy are compatible — all 802.11b, for instance.

You can buy PC, PCMCI, USB, and a variety of other wireless cards to use with your networks. If you make sure the standards are the same, the cards automatically communicate with each other at the highest-possible speed and data rate for the wireless technology.

Figure 7-7 shows two computers, each with wireless adapter cards. The two computers communicate, share files and folders, and share a printer.

Cards for one network share the same features. For example, all cards for a Windows network should

   ✦ Have the same speed — 11 Mbps or 54 Mbps

   ✦ If 11 Mbps, be compatible with IEEE 802.11b and 2.4 GHz-compliant equipment; if 54 Mbps, be compatible with IEEE 803.11g and 2.4 GHz-compliant equipment

   ✦ Be compatible with Windows 98, NT, Me, 2000, or XP

   ✦ Have an integrated antenna

   ✦ Have Plug and Play operations

   ✦ Work with standard Internet applications

   ✦ Have security encryption — WEP protocol

✦ Have free driver upgrades

✦ Come with at least a 1-year warranty

Similarly, if you have Macintosh on your network, you want to make sure that all Macs on the network are compatible, and/or the Macs are compatible with any Windows on the network. Macintosh uses Apple AirPort technology for wireless networking. To be compatible with the previous Windows wireless network, products for the Macintosh should

✦ Be 802.11b standard, thus, IEEE 802.11b and 2.4 GHz-compliant

✦ Be compatible with your specific Macintosh card slot and type

✦ Have an integrated antenna

✦ Work with standard Internet applications

✦ Have security encryption — WEP

✦ Come with free driver upgrades and a 1-year warranty

Note   Because card slots in Macs are so different, you need to research the type of AirPort cards and other wireless networking equipment you use with the Mac to make sure it's compatible.

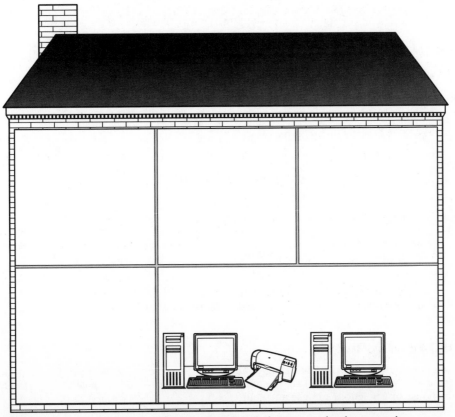

Figure 7-7: Two computers share resources via wireless network adapter cards.

Considering access points

You add an access point to your network to extend the range of the wireless network. You might want to mount the access points on the ceiling or just place them on a desk next in a central location. Access points must have power, so wherever you place an access point, make sure you have a power plug nearby.

Access points have built-in antennas that you use to help convey the radio frequencies. Most often, these antennas are pointed straight up so they can freely communicate with other wireless antennas, say, in a network adapter card.

Figure 7-8 illustrates an access point that enables the network to share resources from anywhere in a large house.

Tip   You might also want to keep the access point out of sight so curious little hands, and visitors, do not reset the point or change antenna direction. You definitely want to keep the access point out of high-traffic areas. People, coats, backpacks, and the like can create interference with the radio waves.

Make sure access points use the same IEEE standards and have the same features as the wireless network adapter cards you purchase. If your NICs use 802.11g, the access points should also use 802.11g (although you can use 802.11b with 802.11g). Check the following features as well:

✦ Transfer rate or speed (such as 11 Mbps).

✦ The number of users supported (some access points support 10 users, others 30), depending on what you need.

✦ Operating range (check indoors and outdoors ranges; those with outdoor ranges are more expensive and might not be what you need).

✦ Power management features (such as battery life and other conservative features).

✦ WEP encryption for security.

✦ Compatibility with operating systems (such as Windows 98, 2000, XP, or Macintosh).

✦ Free technical support and at least a 1-year warranty.

Note   When checking into an AirPort access point for the Mac, understand that the *base station* connects to a phone line in your home to enable the station to share a connection to the Internet. There is also a AirPort software access point that connects two or more iBook computers to a phone line. Be careful when buying wireless access points for the Mac, because many types and different compatibilities exist. Get technical help if you need it.

Tip   Signal boosters are also available in wireless devices. You can piggyback a signal booster on an access point to increase range and transfer rate and save money.

Using antennas

Antennas increase the distance, range, and gain of the radio waves in your wireless network. You use antennas when you want to connect two buildings—such as a garage apartment and the house or a neighbor's house and yours.

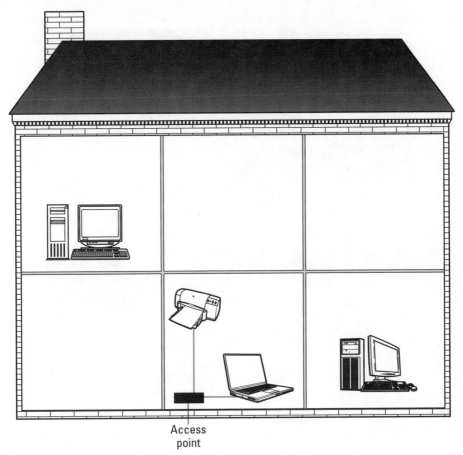

Figure 7-8: Computers share resources via an access point.

Antennas (called omnidirectional antennae) are often used for line-of-sight communications. You place the antennas facing each other, without walls, trees, or other obstructions between the two. Metal objects, in particular, between two antennas absorb the radio waves and interfere greatly with data transmissions.

Most antennas are connected to a coax cable. The coax cable is an addition to the antenna, giving it a source of power and boost in range. Antennas are also connected to an access point, which is connected to a power cord. The access point can be attached to a wired network, thus giving users even more access to data, files, and resources.

Figure 7-9 uses two antennas to connect the neighbor's teen son with your teenager's computer so they can play games. Antennas are capable of rotating after they're mounted in order to get the best range. When you use antennas, you make sure there are no other buildings, trees, or other materials in the line of sight.

When looking for antennas to connect two buildings, you can usually choose the distance you want to cover. For example, you may purchase two antennas that cover up to 300 feet; or you may look for antennas that cover up to a mile. Remember that information sent over RF can be picked up by other wireless devices, so you want higher security when transmitting data outside. Also, make sure you're using the same IEEE standard.

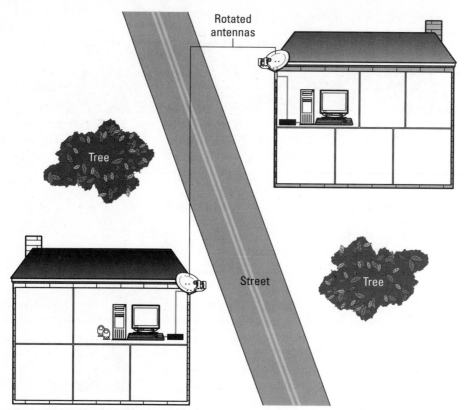

Figure 7-9: Connect with friends, family, and anyone within the line of sight of your house via wireless.

Configuring Wireless Technologies

Every wireless device or kit you purchase has instructions about installing the device. Installation is easy and fairly quick. If you have trouble with installing a network card, access point, or other device, you can normally check the Web or call a support number provided by the manufacturer of the equipment.

When configuring a wireless device, you need to understand certain terms and some common instructions that might not be clearly described, depending on the manufacturer of the device. This section describes those terms and some common instructions.

Installing a wireless network adapter card

Installing a wireless network adapter card is similar to installing an Ethernet card. The NIC comes in various sizes and types for your computer, be it a desktop with a PCI slot or a CardBus PC Card slot for a notebook. Macintoshes, so varied and innumerable, are perhaps the most difficult computers for which to purchase NICs. Check the documentation that comes with your Mac, and be sure of the type of card you need before purchasing one.

The instructions are included with the card; however, here is some general idea of how installation will go:

1. Turn the computer off.

2. If you're installing to a desktop computer, remove the case and locate the slot for the network card. Remove the slot cover and insert the card, taking care that the card is properly seated. Replace the screws and the cover.

   or

   If you're installing the card to a notebook or similar computer with a PC slot, insert the card, making sure it is properly placed and that you hear the click to verify the card is all the way in.

   or

   If you're using a USB network card adapter, follow directions to plug in the adapter.

3. Turn the computer on. When the operating system finds the card, it will ask to install the drivers. Use the CD or the diskette that came with the card to install the drivers. Follow the instructions on the disk. If you have trouble locating or installing the drivers, call the manufacturer for technical support.

4. An Ethernet MAC address is assigned to the wireless networking card. Make a note of that address (either from the card on which it is actually printed or through the installation software). You might need the address later to register with the access point.

5. During configuration, the software might ask for your security choices. You can choose between no security, 40-bit WEP, or 128-bit WEP. See the section "Securing the Wireless Network" later in this chapter for more information.

6. If told to reboot the computer, do so.

Configuring access points

When you configure one access point with settings and information, you need to repeat the configuration on each access point in your network. The access points come with a management tool that enables easy configuration. The tool is on the CD that comes with the hardware, and instructions are generally clear and easy to follow. You can manage the access point from a computer or a notebook by attaching the computer to the access point via a network cable (usually supplied with the access point). Connect the access point to its power and a wall plug as well.

Figure 7-10 shows a management tool for a Linksys Wireless G access point. You can view a user guide or click the Setup button to continue.

Tip　　You can save the configuration to your hard drive as well as to the access point. If you save it to your hard drive, you don't need the CD to change configurations. You can use your Web browser by typing in the IP address you assign the access point. The management tool then appears in HTML.

You choose a channel on which to operate. If a default exists, you can use that. Make note of the channel, though, so you can configure it in the other. You name each access point — like WAP01 and WAP02 or henry and george. Enter an administrator's password you can remember.

Depending on the brand and type of access point you buy, you might need to enable the MAC address of the wireless network cards. Follow directions that accompany the access point.

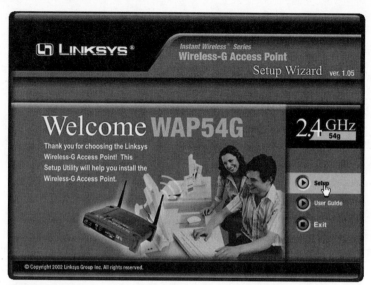

Figure 7-10: Set up the wireless access point using the CD that came with the device.
Figure courtesy of Linksys

The SSID is the *Service Set Identifier*. The SSID is a 32-character unique identifier that acts like a password whenever another wireless device tries to connect to the basic service set. It's the SSID that keeps one wireless LAN separate from another. One might be preconfigured in the access point by default, but you should create the number to help secure your network. Write the number down in case you need to duplicate it for other access points. All access points and devices attempting to connect to one WLAN must use the same SSID.

Finally, you'll have to configure security options for the wireless network. As mentioned, WEP comes in two different encryptions: 40-bit WEP and 128-bit WEP. See the section "Securing the Wireless Network" later in this chapter for more information.

Tip

Often a networking kit includes a cable modem/DSL router you can use to share Internet connections. Instructions are included, and configuration is fairly easy.

Make sure you keep the CD that comes with your wireless hardware. You can reconfigure the access points only with the use of the CD or if you save the configuration to your computer. In addition, you use the CD and the management software to upgrade firmware when necessary. Firmware is the program that controls the WAP and the management tool.

Whenever you want to check settings or change settings, you can insert the CD to a computer connected to the WAP or start up the program you have saved to your computer.

The management tool searches for wireless access points on the network; then it displays each access point with a summary of information about the configuration. Figure 7-11 shows one access point found on the network. The management tool lists the MAC address, the SSID, and the channel chosen, and it shows that the WEP is enabled.

Anytime you want to change settings for the access point, you need the password, as shown in Figure 7-12. Without the password, you can make no changes.

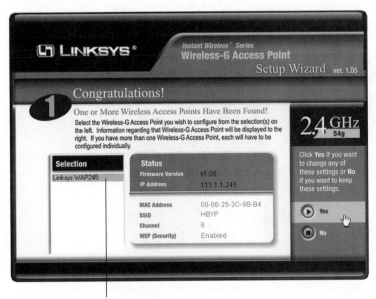

Wireless access point found

Figure 7-11: You can view or change settings for the WAP.
Figure courtesy of Linksys

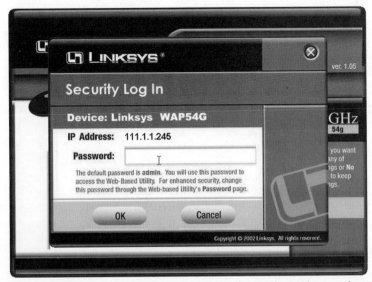

Figure 7-12: You must enter the password to change the settings on the WAP.
Figure courtesy of Linksys

After you enter the password, you can change the IP address, the subnet mask, or the access point's name. You might want to change the IP address, for example, if you add your wireless network to a wired network. You can change the name of the WAP for security purposes. IP addresses and names for each wireless access point are unique to that WAP. Figure 7-13 shows the IP Settings dialog box of the access point's management tool.

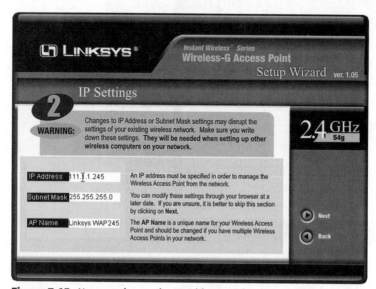

Figure 7-13: You can change the IP address or the name of the access point for security purposes.
Figure courtesy of Linksys

When you want to make sure your wireless network is secure, you can change SSID and channel numbers periodically to make sure no one can hack into your system. For more information about security, see the section "Securing the Wireless Network" that follows. Figure 7-14 illustrates the dialog box in which you change SSID and channel number. You must make sure to change these settings on all WAP on the network if you change settings on one.

Another setting you might want to set is the encryption. For more information about encryption, once again see the next section, "Securing the Wireless Network."

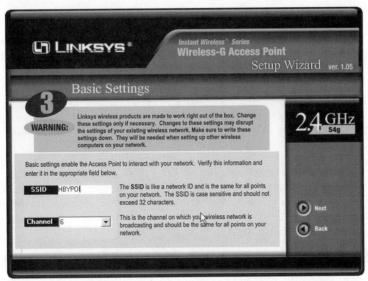

Figure 7-14: The SSID simply indicates an identification number for the WAP.
Figure courtesy of Linksys

Securing the Wireless Network

Since the wireless networking depends on radio frequencies to transmit data, it's easy to see how your data could be floating all over the neighborhood. You might not be concerned with this if your data isn't confidential or private. However, remember that other wireless devices can make use of your network. A neighbor's kid with a wireless adapter might hack into your network and use your Internet connection. Someone you don't even know might scan the neighborhood, hack into your wireless network, and do damage just for the experience of it.

Tip

Hackers know that wireless networks produce a *beacon message*, also called a *broadcast message*, announcing its availability. These messages are not encrypted and contain much network information, such as the SSID and IP addresses.

Many wireless networking devices come with a claim of working right out of the box. However, the out-of-the-box settings are well known for each brand by hackers. A hacker can get into your network by using the default password and then changing security settings as he or she sees fit.

You have to change some configuration settings and change them often to keep hackers away from your network. Fortunately, with the HTML management tool that comes with access points, it's easy to make these configuration changes.

Changing the administrator's password

Probably the easiest method of protecting your wireless network is to change the administrator's password regularly. Every wireless configuration you perform is performed in the HTML management tool (also called firmware). You can save the configuration changes to your computer or keep the changes on the original CD.

Only the administrator, with the appropriate administrator's password, can make changes to configuration and security. Change the administrator's password often and make sure the password you use is not something easy to guess, such as a pet's name, the street name, and so on.

Small Business Tip   It's especially important to use passwords that are not easy to guess in your business. So many managers or owners use a name on their license plate, or their wife's or husband's name. If the password is easy to guess, anyone, even a disgruntled employee, can access your access point and your network.

Using IP addresses and enabling MAC address filtering

Many access points let you enable MAC address filtering, which allows only those specified MAC addresses to access the network. Using MAC address filtering makes it more difficult for hackers to guess the addresses.

You can also use IP addressing to help make it more difficult for people to access your network. For more information about IP addressing, see Appendix B.

Securing the SSID

Another thing you can do to protect your wireless network is to change the SSID and change it often. SSIDs can be sniffed in plaintext if the packet doesn't contain security codes. A *packet sniffer* is a program anyone can load onto his or her computer, connect to the network, and use to read packets of data being transferred across the network. If you change the SSID often, that helps throw hackers off. SSIDs are broadcast much further than just the range of the wireless standard; anyone in a car or nearby restaurant might be able to read your broadcast. See the previous section on "Configuring access points" for more about changing the SSID.

In addition, you can disable the SSID broadcast. Broadcasting the SSID is convenient for those on your network; however, it is also convenient for hackers. If you disable the SSID broadcast, you can easily enter the SSID into other wireless devices you want to connect to the network.

Tip   Limit the range of your network by placing your access points nearer the center of your home. Radio waves can pass easily through glass, but not so easily through Sheetrock, for example. Also, if your access point enables you to set the range, check for the best range and limit it so as not to include the street and other homes in your neighborhood.

Changing WEP keys

WEP encryption was created to help secure wireless connections. Wired Equivalent Privacy suggests that encryption in wireless networks is equal to the security in wired network. Unfortunately, that's not exactly true. But you can make security better by doing the things mentioned previously in the chapter plus using the highest level of WEP offered—128-bit encryption.

Encryption is a code that enables two wireless devices to communicate. The code is established first, and if both wireless devices agree that the code is one each recognizes, then the communication can begin. WEP keys can be generated automatically or assigned to the wireless devices, but the keys must match to work.

There are two different encryption levels used with wireless: 40 bit and 128 bit. You might see 64-bit encryption advertised, but it is actually the same encryption as 40 bit, just a different name. The higher the encryption, the more time that is spent encrypting and decrypting the data sent on your network. Increasing the encryption affects network performance some, but then the network is also harder to hack. The decision is up to you, depending on the security necessary.

Note   A 64-bit key provides an encryption level, and any other point in the network must also use the same key. 40-bit is just another name for 64-bit. 40-bit uses a 40-bit secret key along with a 24-bit Initialization Vector (40 + 24 = 64). Different vendors might use either name.

Figure 7-15 illustrates the WEP key settings in the Linksys access point management tool. Choosing to disable the WEP, which is also the default setting, can be a huge mistake. You can set it 64 bit if you think you're fairly safe, but it's better to set the encryption to 128 bit if you have any doubts.

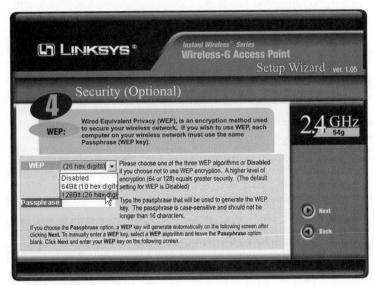

Figure 7-15: WEP helps secure your network.
Figure courtesy of Linksys

Tip   Take notice in Figure 7-15 that you can also enter a passphrase that represents the WEP key so you don't have to remember an odd assortment of letters and numbers.

In addition to setting WEP keys, you can do the following to further security in the wireless network:

✦ Use a shared key (designate the key as shared in configuring). Doing this means that only another device using the same key can communicate with your access point.

✦ Change the WEP key regularly so that even if someone guesses or hacks into your key, you change it before the person can do any damage.

✦ Use multiple WEP keys within the network so that one access point can communicate with a second and only the second can communicate with a third access point.

Using Wireless in Conjunction with Cabled Networks

Many wireless networks are used in conjunction with cabled networks. You can connect a notebook, PDA, or tablet computer to a wired network via wireless to make it easier to move around the house while working. You can attach to the network from anywhere, any room. Imagine making your shopping list on your tablet PC as you go room to room to add to the list, look up the latest prices on the Web, check your spouse's list on his or her computer, print the list, and so on.

To create a wired and wireless network, you need some sort of bridge between the networks. You can use an access point that's either hardware or software. Hardware access points have various network interfaces, such as Ethernet or token ring. A software access point enables multiple network interfaces and network types, such as Ethernet, wireless, token ring, and so on.

Figure 7-16 shows a wired network using a hub to connect multiple computers. A wireless access point connects (or bridges) the wireless LAN to the wired LAN. Each type of LAN can then communicate with the other, share resources, and so on.

You can also use wireless devices to bridge two wired networks. For example, if your neighbor and you share fundraising and other volunteer work, it's easier for you to send documents, newsletters, financial reports, fliers, and other information back and forth via a network. Perhaps you each have a network in your home. You can use wireless antennas to bridge the two networks together.

Small Business Tip   If you have only one employee located upstairs or in another, smaller office building and you need to connect that one employee to the wired network, you can use wireless networking to accomplish it.

Figure 7-17 illustrates two networked homes. The home on the left uses a hub to connect a Macintosh and a PC. A wireless access point connects the PC to the notebook. The wireless access point also connects the network to an antenna. The house across the alley, on the right, uses a hub and a totally wired network. The access point was added to connect to the antenna so the two women can send documents back and forth between their homes.

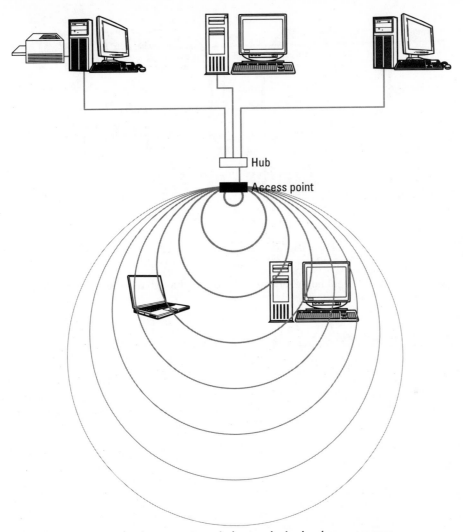

Figure 7-16: Two network segments—wireless and wired—share resources.

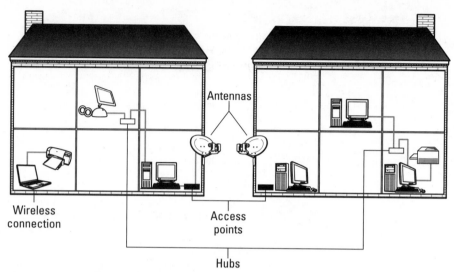

Figure 7-17: Two different home networks share data through wireless antennas acting as a bridge.

Examining Wireless Products

You can find wireless kits to buy, or you can purchase the pieces separately to form your own wireless network. You can buy all your wireless hardware from one manufacturer, or you can purchase from several manufacturers. Remember to keep within the standard you choose, and if possible, do buy the same brand of hardware. Buying different brands just because you can might cause some headaches you don't need.

Cross-Reference For information on wireless standards, see the section "Considering Wireless Standards" earlier in this chapter.

You also want to check distances in your home to make sure the technology you choose fits the distance. All kits and separate wireless devices list information about the hardware, including range for indoors and/or outdoors, standards, and so on.

Note There are differences between Macintosh and PC wireless devices, although they can usually communicate with each other. There are no differences between Linux and PC wireless hardware; but whether or not you can use wireless does depend on the modules you load with your Linux distro. Most cards, access points, and other wireless devices specify either Windows or Macintosh compatibility.

PC wireless devices

As I have indicated, some kits are available, but you can also just purchase the separate pieces of hardware for your PC. The following sections list only standards 802.11b and 802.11g, because they are the most flexible, efficient, and enduring, especially for home networking.

802.11b wireless adapters

NETGEAR produces the MA101 802.11b wireless USB adapter, which makes it easy for you to install and use without wires, without opening your PC case, and so on. Most PCs have USB ports these days, and notebooks and Gateway "Profile" computers use only PC Cards or USB cards. USB cards at NETGEAR cost around $70. The MA101 card has the following features:

✦ 11 Mbps

✦ WEP encryption — 128 and 40/64 bit

✦ Automatic speed adjustment

✦ Compatible with Windows 98, Me, and 2000

✦ 5-year limited warranty

NETGEAR Model MA401 wireless PC Card fits notebooks and profile computers. The speed is 11 Mbps because it is 802.11b standard. This card has similar features as the previous one: 128-bit WEP encryption; support for Windows 98, Me, and 2000; and a 5-year warranty. PC Cards at NETGEAR cost around $65 to $70.

SMC produces an EZ Connect Turbo wireless CardBus adapter. The speed on this notebook adapter is 11 to 22 Mbps. Cost is around $60. SMC introduces a new 256-bit encryption. Range is 1,155 feet.

3Com puts out a PCI adapter for your desktop. The speed is 11 Mbps, and it is compatible with Windows XP. It provides 128-bit encryption at 328 feet indoors, has a warranty, and costs around $110.

NETGEAR Model MA311 is a PCI adapter for installing into your desktop computer. Features are nearly the same as previous NETGEAR cards: 11 Mbps and 802.11b standards, 40/64- and 128-bit encryption; and supports Windows 98, Me, 2000, and XP. This adapter has a 3-year warranty. PCI cards cost around $75 at NETGEAR.

 Note Watch carefully when buying adapters. Some are compatible with XP and others are not, meaning they do not have XP drivers yet. You'll also need to check with your Linux distro for compatibility and drivers.

802.11g wireless adapters

NETGEAR produces the Model WG511 wireless PC Card (32-bit CardBus) using 802.11g standard; since it is the 802.11g standard, this card is also compatible with the IEEE 802.11b standard. Naturally the card's speed is 54 Mbps. This PC Card also uses 128-bit WEP encryption. Cost is around $65.

Linksys has Wireless-g PCI cards to connect at 54 Mbps and interoperates with 802.11b products as well. The standard 128-bit encryption is included. In addition, for $70, you get the following:

✦ 32-bit PCI interface

✦ Compatibly with Windows 98, Me, 2000, and XP

✦ The card, an external antenna, CD, and instructions

Linksys has created a dual-band Wireless A+G PCI adapter card that works with Wireless-a (802.11a) and Wireless-g (802.11g) networks. You still get the 54 Mbps, and because G is included, you can work with 11 Mbps Wireless-b (802.11b). Encryption with this adapter card is 152-bit. You can get the card in a PC or a PCI card. Price is around $100.

SMC produces the EZ Connect g CardBus adapter for a notebook or profile computer. The standard is 802.11g and 802.11b-compliant, so data rates are up to 54 Mbps. Operating range is 1,155 feet with 40- and 128-bit encryption. Cost is around $75.

Other good brands to use for 802.11g adapters include 3Com, Proxim, and Intel. There are many, many manufacturers of wireless adapter cards.

802.11b access points and bridges

NETGEAR makes an 802.11b wireless access point named Model ME102. Connectivity is 11 Mbps, since it uses the 802.11b standard. The WAP has both 40/64- and 128-bit encryption. It connects to either an Ethernet network or a Cable/DSL router. The WAP has a 5-year warranty. NETGEAR has several access points similar to this model; prices range from around $70 to $110.

Sony Vaio offers a wireless LAN bridge/access point that enables you to connect your wired network to a wireless network. Data transfer speed is up to 11 Mbps, because the standard is IEEE 802.11b for a range of up to 130 feet, line of sight. An additional standard is IEEE 802.11, which means there is an Ethernet interface: 10/100 Ethernet with the R-45 interface.

3Com, Intel, Hawking, Proxim, and other manufacturers also produce access points not only for 802.11b but for 802.11a as well.

802.11g access points and bridges

The NETGEAR Model WG602 is an 802.11g wireless access point. The speed is 54 Mbps, and of course, the WAP works with 802.11b standard as well. WEP standard 128-bit encryption is included. The cost is around $100.

The Linksys Wireless-g access point provides the 802.11g standard, and it is also compatible with the 802.11b standard. WEP is 40/64- to 128-bit encryption. This WAP has MAC address filtering and IP addressing; it's easy to configure and costs around $130.

Cisco, D-Link, Proxim, and other manufacturers also produce wireless access points and bridges.

Wireless antennas

You purchase antennas according to the distance between the buildings you need to link. You should also check to see if an antenna is made for inside or outside or both. You'll also come across the terms omnidirectional and directional. *Omnidirectional* means the antennas reach from point to several points. *Directional* goes from point to point. In addition, most antennas are made to work with specific wireless products; so be careful when choosing antennas. Finally, you'll need two of the same type of antennas to successfully work as a bridge between two points; the following prices are only for one antenna.

Tip   If you use outdoor antennas, check with the manufacturers of the antennas about grounding wires and such. You don't want a lightning storm to ruin your network.

NETGEAR ANT2405 omnidirectional antenna costs about $60 and works to extend coverage for existing 802.11b or 802.11g networks. This antenna configures for either omnidirectional or directional. This smaller antenna is made to work indoors on a single-floor environment to optimize range. The antenna comes with a coax cable, can be used with Wi-Fi products, and includes wall-mounting materials. This product is made to work with specific NETGEAR hardware.

Enterasys has a vehicle antenna you can use for around $70. The vehicle-mount antenna is a broadband antenna in the 2.4 GHz frequency with an omnidirectional pattern. Generally, these antennas are used on forklifts or trucks, but you might find a use for it in your home, trailer, or vehicle.

D-Link has an outdoor antenna for around $120. The antenna provides extended coverage for any existing 802.11b/g standards. It's omnidirectional and waterproof for the outdoors, and it includes a mounting kit, surge protector, and waterproof tape. The D-Link antenna supports only specific devices made by D-Link.

For around $250, the SMC wireless antenna kit achieves a range of up to 3.5 miles. The kit includes an antenna, a 24-foot cable, a desktop stand, and a lifetime warranty. This antenna penetrates trees, structures, and other obstacles because of a patent-pending technology.

Mac wireless devices

Macintosh uses the Apple AirPort software and hardware for wireless. Since the standards are the same — 802.11b, 802.11g, and so on — the products should be able communicate with other wireless devices on your network. You should test the products though and inquire before purchasing. AirPort software requires specific Mac OSs, base stations (access points), and specific versions of firmware for the wireless device. Check your Mac carefully to make sure you know versions and details before shopping for Mac wireless.

Table 7-1 shows a few of the requirements for using AirPort with various Mac OSs.

Table 7-1: AirPort Compatibility

Software	OS Required	Base Station Firmware
AirPort 2.0.2	Mac OS 9.0.4 or later	3.84/4.0.2
AirPort 2.0.5	Mac OS X 10.1.5	3.84/4.0.7
AirPort 3.0.4	Mac OS X 10.2	3.84/4.0.8/5.0.1
Firmware Update		
AirPort 4.0.7	Windows 98, 2000, XP	
Utilities for Windows		
AirPort Admin	Windows 98, 2000, XP	

AirPort adapter cards

AirPort's Extreme card costs around $100 and supplies speeds of up to 54 Mbps. AirPort Extreme cards are only for AirPort Extreme-ready systems. AirPort Extreme is a newer wireless specification, and it uses the standard 802.11g. This standard is compatible with 802.11b and Wi-Fi-certified products. The range of AirPort Extreme base station (access point) is up to 50 feet at 54 Mbps and up to 150 feet at 11 Mbps.

Note   Some AirPort cards require the use of an AirPort Card Adapter kit to work with some iMac models. If your iMac is a G3-based, slot-loading, AirPort-ready iMac, it does require the adapter kit. Check your iMac documentation. The iBook, PowerMac, and PowerBook do not require the adapter kit.

Apple has a PC Card for iBooks that enables 11 Mbps at a distance of up to 150 feet. You need a base station with the card to create a wireless network. The card costs around $80.

AirPort Base Station

The AirPort Base Station supports wireless connections between Mac systems with AirPort and AirPort Extreme cards. You can also use the base station in conjunction with an Ethernet connection. The base station also supports USB and Ethernet wireless printer sharing. Up to 50 users can work simultaneously up to 150 feet away from an Ethernet connection. AirPort and AirPort Extreme also support 128-bit encryption.

AirPort Base Stations come in omnidirectional or directional to extend the range of the network. Base stations also come in two configurations: one includes a 10/100Base-T Ethernet LAN and wide area network (WAN) port and a USB port; the second configuration includes the previous ports plus a built-in v.90 modem with a phone jack and an external antenna port.

The AirPort Extreme Base Station with a modem and antenna port costs $250. It provides speeds of up to 54 Mbps. The AirPort Extreme Base Station without modem and antenna port costs $200. Speeds are still up to 54 Mbps.

Summary

In this chapter, you've learned about using wireless networking in the home. Specifically, you've learned about the following:

✦ Using wireless standards

✦ Configuring wireless access points

✦ Setting up a wireless workgroup

✦ Using wireless networking with cabled networking

In the next chapter, you learn about using alternative cabling methods, such as phone line networking and using the house wiring for networking computers.

✦   ✦   ✦

Using Alternative Cabling Methods

If speed isn't a main concern in your home network, you can use various other methods of connecting your computers. Each of these methods is useful for file and printer sharing. Some tasks, however — such as exchanging large files, playing network games, and so on — might not work when you use alternative cabling methods. On the positive side, these alternatives are easier to set up than Ethernet cabling and many kits are available for both phone line networks and electrical wiring networks.

Connecting Two Computers or Two Users

You might have need for file sharing in your home but no interest in putting a lot of time, money, and effort in setting up a network. You'll be happy to know that you can share resources between two computers — two desktop PCs, for example, or a desktop and notebook PC — for less than $25.

If you want to connect two computers for sharing files, you can accomplish that easily and inexpensively. You use a cable that directly connects the two computers without the use of network cards, hubs, or other hardware equipment.

Alternatively, you might have only one powerful computer but two people who want to use it at the same time. You can share applications, files, printers, and so on using the same computer central processing unit (CPU) but with separate mice, keyboards, and monitors.

Using a direct cable

You can use a feature in Windows called Direct Cable Connection (DCC) to share resources between two computers over just a cable. The connection is slow, but it's also inexpensive. All you have to do is pay for the cable and attach the two computers to it. This approach works with Windows 95, 98, Me, NT, and 2000 computers. The DDC software is not available in Windows XP.

You can use DCC networking at your office to connect your laptop to a desktop computer. Also, if your desktop computer is connected to a network, such as Ethernet, you can transfer files from the laptop to the desktop, to a server, or to another computer on the network and back again. Extending the network to your laptop in this way can save time, money, and networking headaches in many situations.

The direct cabling method of networking is great for transferring or copying files — say, from a laptop to a desktop — or for installing software on a laptop with no CD-ROM drive.

Another benefit of direct cabling is evident if one of your computers is attached to a network: The computer that is directly cabled to the network also can access network files.

Naturally, the DCC method has limitations. As previously mentioned, the connection is slow. Also, when using the DCC method, you cannot share a printer; you can, however, transfer a file from one computer to the other and then print from the computer attached to the printer.

One other hindrance with DCC is that the two computers must be close together — at least in the same room and perhaps on the same desk or table. The cable itself imposes this limit. IEEE standards specify that direct cables should be no longer than 6 feet; however, some manufacturers make direct cables up to 50 feet long.

Physically connecting the computers

You can connect two computers by using a cable or a wireless connection. Both methods are relatively inexpensive to use. Each method has its advantages and disadvantages.

Cable

To connect the two computers with cable, you can use a parallel file-transfer cable, also called a high-speed direct parallel cable. The cable costs $25 to $30, and it connects to the parallel port (LPT port) on each computer. Alternatively, you can use a serial cable, which costs only about $10 but transfers data at a slower rate (10 Kbps) than a parallel cable (60 to 80 Kbps). You can use a USB cable as well.

You can use any of the following cables for a direct connection:

✦ **A standard RS-232 cable (the RS is short for Recommended Standard).** This cable transmits data at about a 20 Kbps. A serial cable generally used for connecting a computer to a peripheral device, the RS-232 has a maximum cable limit of 15 meters, or about 50 feet.

✦ **A null modem cable, or RS-232-C cable.** This cable connects two computers so that they can communicate without the use of a modem. A null modem cable connects the serial ports. Speeds with a null modem cable usually average around 20 Kbps.

✦ **A standard 4-bit cable, such as LapLink or InterLink cables.** These cables were available before 1992. Four-bit cables are parallel cables; speeds are often up to 60 Kbps.

✦ **An Extended Capabilities Port (ECP) cable.** Use this cable with an ECP-enabled parallel port; it enables data to transfer more quickly (60 to 80 Kbps) than standard cables. The ECP must be enabled in the basic input/output system (BIOS). The BIOS is a set of instructions that enables the computer's hardware and operating system to communicate with peripheral devices.

✦ **A universal cable module (UCM) cable.** A parallel cable, the UCM supports connecting different types of parallel ports.

✦ **A universal serial bus (USB) cable.** A USB cable transfers data up to 500 Kbps. You need to purchase a special cable for transfers between computers; specify you want a USB connection cable to enable PC-to-PC file transfer.

The *parallel port* is an input/output port that manages information 8 bits at a time; parallel ports also are often used for connecting printers to a computer. You can generally find a high-speed direct parallel cable at any computer store.

A *serial port* transmits data more slowly, one bit at a time. Serial cables transmit data sequentially over only one pair of wires. Because parallel cables transmit data simultaneously over multiple lines, parallel is the faster of the two connection methods: serial and parallel.

USB ports transmit data very quickly and with the use of a USB hub, you can transfer data to multiple computers.

Wireless connection

Another alternative is to set up a Direct Cable Connection using infrared light rather than a physical cable. Infrared is a method of making wireless network connections by using high-frequency light waves to transmit the data instead of cabling. With infrared, you must have clear line of sight between the two computers because the light waves cannot penetrate obstacles. You can use infrared to connect two or more computers in a network.

Infrared does supply high bandwidths, and it's an inexpensive technology. If you don't have a fairly short transmission distance, however, interference can be a problem. You configure an infrared connection the same way you configure a Direct Cable Connection, except when you are asked about the port, you choose the infrared communications port.

Infrared connections usually are limited to 1 meter (about 3 feet), but some manufacturers offer connections of up to 3 meters (about 10 feet).

If you install infrared ports on your PCs, Windows automatically detects any other infrared device within line of sight and displays the connection. If the connection becomes broken or interrupted, Windows indicates the problem with an audible signal and automatically tries to reestablish the signal for a period of time.

Many notebook computers have infrared technology built in. Check your computer for a small dark-red glass rectangle to find out if you have an infrared port. Two computers with infrared ports can communicate with each other.

Configuring the connection in Windows

To use the Direct Cable Connection in Windows, it first must be installed on your computer. DCC may not be installed by the manufacturer, in which case you need to install it yourself. After installation, Windows provides a wizard to help you complete the configuration of the connection.

To determine whether DCC is installed on your computer, choose Start ➪ Programs ➪ Accessories ➪ Communications ➪ Direct Cable Connection. If Direct Cable Connection isn't listed on the menu, you must install it (discussed in the next section). If it is listed on the menu, skip to the section entitled "Configuring the Direct Cable Connection."

Installing the Direct Cable Connection

If you have not installed DCC, you might need your Windows CD-ROM. You need to install DCC on both of the computers. Follow these steps:

1. Choose Start ➪ Settings ➪ Control Panel.

2. Double-click Add/Remove Programs. The Add/Remove Programs Properties dialog box appears.

3. Choose the Windows Setup tab, as shown in Figure 8-1.

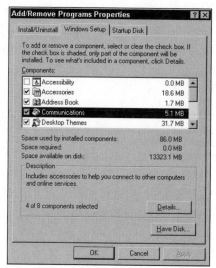

Figure 8-1: Use the Windows Setup tab of the Add/Remove Programs Properties dialog box.

4. Choose Communications, and then click the Details button.

5. Select Direct Cable Connection by clicking the check box to the left of the option, as shown in Figure 8-2.

6. If Dial-Up Networking is not installed, select it as well by clicking the check box. Dial-Up Networking contains features required by the Direct Cable Connection.

7. Click OK to return to the Add/Remove Programs Properties dialog box. Click OK again to install the feature(s). Figure 8-3 shows the components installing. Insert the Windows CD-ROM if prompted. Close the Control Panel when you are finished.

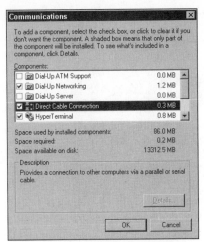

Figure 8-2: Choose to install DCC.

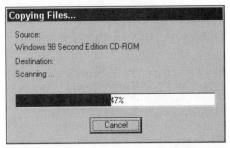

Figure 8-3: Windows installs the software.

Your next step is to configure the Direct Cable Connection.

Configuring the Direct Cable Connection

Configuring the Direct Cable Connection is simple, because Windows supplies a wizard to help. To connect the two computers, you must designate one computer as the host and one as the guest. The host computer provides the resources, similar to a server, and the guest uses the resources, similar to a client.

Note   You also can share guest's resources with the host; however, sharing is somewhat limited. Make sure that you select and indicate drives and folders on the guest as shared, and turn on file and print sharing, as outlined in the following section.

After you set up the host computer, you need to go through these steps again to set up the guest computer.

To set up DCC, follow these steps on the computer to be used as the host:

1. Choose Start ➪ Programs ➪ Accessories ➪ Communications ➪ Direct Cable Connection. The Direct Cable Connection Wizard dialog box appears, as shown in Figure 8-4.

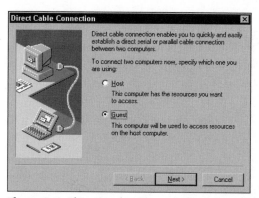

Figure 8-4: The wizard guides you through setting up the connection.

2. Click the Host button to set up the first computer as the host computer. Click the Next button.

3. The next wizard dialog box lists the available ports on the computer, as shown in Figure 8-5. Choose the port that corresponds with the direct cable you're using. Note that you must use the same port on both computers; that is, if you use a parallel port on one computer, you must use a parallel port on the other computer.

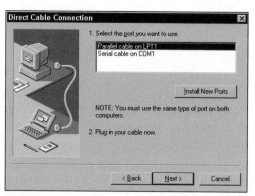

Figure 8-5: Select the port for the Direct Cable Connection.

4. Plug the cable into the ports, and then click the Next button. The last wizard box appears, telling you that the setup was successful. If you want, you can set a password for the guest computer. Setting a password means that only the user who knows the password can access your computer from the other one.

Now you can set up the guest computer. Follow the preceding set of instructions, but in Step 2, click the Guest button in the first wizard dialog box. The host computer displays a dialog box that states the connection's status, as shown in Figure 8-6. When you complete the guest setup, the two computers communicate.

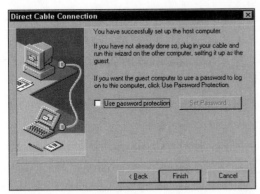

Figure 8-6: The host looks for the guest computer.

Configuring Windows to share

You need to tell Windows you want to share the files and printer on the host machine. You also need to check the name of the computers and the workgroups, check the protocols, and share the drive or folders. To share, follow these steps:

Cross-Reference

Each of the following steps is explained in more detail in the following chapters. For information about configuring protocols, see Chapter 9. For information about accessing the files, see Chapter 14.

1. Locate the Network Neighborhood on the desktop.

2. Right-click the Network Neighborhood icon and choose Properties from the quick menu. The Network dialog box appears, as shown in Figure 8-7. You might or might not have the same components listed in your computer as in the figure.

3. In the Configuration tab, click the File and Print Sharing button. The File and Print Sharing dialog box appears, as shown in Figure 8-8.

4. Check both check boxes: I Want to Be Able to Give Others Access to My Files and I Want to Be Able to Allow Others to Print to My Printer.

5. Click OK to close the dialog box.

6. Select the Identification tab, and then check your computer name and the workgroup name, as shown in Figure 8-9. Windows inserts a default name that might not be the name you want to use. The host and guest computers should have different computer names, such as Sue and Molly or Win98 and Win2000. The workgroup name should be the same. You can name your workgroup "Workgroup" or your family name, for example.

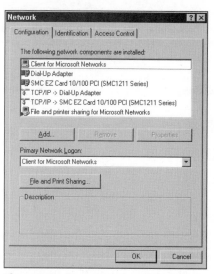

Figure 8-7: Use network settings to set up file sharing.

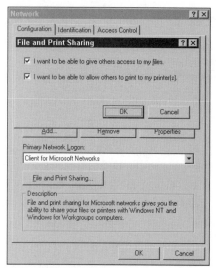

Figure 8-8: Tell Windows you want to share your files and printer.

7. Go back to the Configuration tab and check to see if a network protocol is showing, such as Transmission Control Protocol/Internet Protocol (TCP/IP) or NetBIOS Extended User Interface (NetBEUI). NetBEUI is the best choice for any Windows network if you're new to networking; it's the easiest protocol to set up and use. TCP/IP, on the other hand, offers many advantages over NetBEUI, such as speed and flexibility. Both computers must use the same protocol to be able to communicate over the network. When you install the dial-up adapter, a protocol for the adapter is installed at the same time.

You can add a protocol if one isn't listed. For more information about adding a protocol, see Chapter 10. Figure 8-10 illustrates the TCP/IP protocol as installed for the dial-up adapter. In the Network Components list, the entry that says TCP/IP ->Dial-Up Adapter is the one used for DCC.

8. Click OK to close the Network dialog box. If Windows prompts you to restart your computer, do so now.

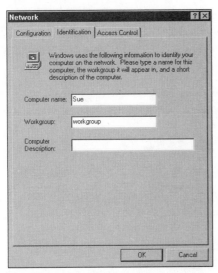

Figure 8-9: Check the computer name and workgroup name for each computer.

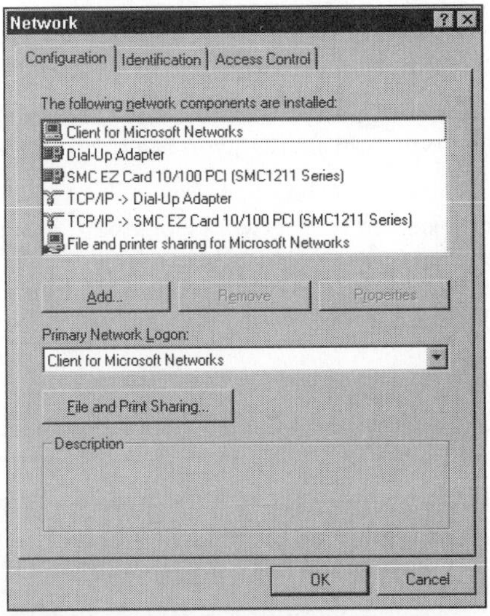

Figure 8-10: Both computers must have the same protocol installed.

Now you must share the drive or folder in the Windows Explorer or My Computer window. For information about sharing drives and folders, see Chapter 12.

Running the Direct Cable Connection

Anytime you want to connect the two computers, you first must start the host and then start the guest. You can use the Network Neighborhood to view the two computers and to share files and printers.

To establish a connection between the two computers, follow these steps:

1. On the host computer, choose Start ➪ Programs ➪ Accessories ➪ Communications ➪ Direct Cable Connection. The Direct Cable Connection dialog box appears, as shown in Figure 8-11.

Figure 8-11: Listen for the guest computer.

2. Click the Listen button. The Status dialog box appears.

3. Move to the guest computer and repeat Step 1. In the Direct Cable Connection dialog box, click the Connect button. The connection is established between the two computers.

4. Anytime you want to view the host from the guest, after he or she is connected, you can click the View Host button. When you view the host, you see the desktop of the other computer.

When you want to view files, you can open files from the Network Neighborhood, the Windows Explorer, or My Computer, just as if you were on your own computer. Figure 8-12 shows the guest and host computers in the Network Neighborhood. For information about how to use the Network Neighborhood, see Chapter 14.

Troubleshooting connections

You might find that you have some trouble with the Direct Cable Connection. Following are some common problems and their solutions:

✦ If you get the message "Unable to browse the Network" when you're in the Network Neighborhood or when you click the View Host button, it might be because the connection is slow. Give the computers a few more seconds to connect, and try again.

✦ You don't need an Ethernet network card to make DCC work. If you don't have a network card in your computer, however, you must enable the Browse Master for file and print sharing on the host computer only. To do that, open the Network properties dialog box (right-click the Network Neighborhood or My Network Places) on the desktop and choose Properties). In the Configuration tab, select File and Printer Sharing for Microsoft Networks in the list of network components. Click the Properties button. The File and Printer Sharing dialog box appears. In the Property list, select Browse Master; in the Value list, select Enabled. Click OK twice to close the dialog boxes.

✦ If you're having trouble connecting the guest to the host, make sure that the computers' names are different.

✦ If you're having trouble using TCP/IP with DCC, delete the TCP/IP protocol and use NetBEUI instead. Sometimes TCP/IP causes problems with connections between the two computers.

✦ If your shutdown for the host computer is really slow, you can speed it up by disabling LM Announce, a networking feature in Windows. To disable this feature, right-click the Network Neighborhood and choose Properties from the quick menu. In the Configuration tab of the Network dialog box, select File and Printer Sharing in the list of network components. Click the Properties button. In the File and Printer Sharing dialog box, select LM Announce in the Property list and select No in the Value list. Click OK twice to close the dialog boxes.

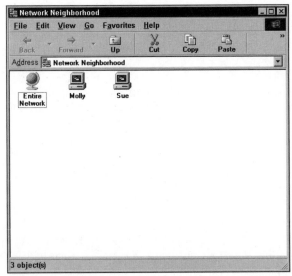

Figure 8-12: View the computers' contents in the Network Neighborhood.

Using the Buddy BeTwin to connect two users

You know two users can share Windows computers by taking turns using it. Each user can create his or her own desktop settings, screen savers, application settings, Internet Explorer and e-mail configurations, and so on by setting either share-level or user-level access control. If you're not familiar with these controls, see Chapter 10.

With today's powerful Pentium computers and Windows multitasking operating systems, one CPU can perform multiple tasks for two users at the same time. The Buddy BeTwin DualPRO kit works with a Windows computer that has a processor speed of 350 MHz or faster.

With the help of the Buddy BeTwin, a kit made by a third-party vendor, you can connect two users to the same computer at the same time. Both users have simultaneous access to one CPU and all of the files, folders, applications, and peripherals attached to that CPU. Each user, however, has his or her own mouse, keyboard, and monitor, as shown in Figure 8-13.

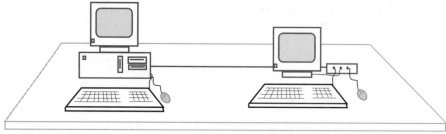

Figure 8-13: Connect two users to one computer by using Buddy BeTwin.

Small Business Tip

The Buddy BeTwin isn't appropriate for networking your small-business office, especially if the two users will be working on the computer for any amount of time. Sharing one CPU would be frustrating and waste valuable work time. You should invest in a more traditional method of networking your office computers.

You can run applications concurrently; use the Internet at the same time; send or receive e-mail or browse the Web; and share documents, a printer, a modem, a hard drive, and other peripherals connected to the computer. The price of the system is $150, excluding the price of another keyboard, mouse, and monitor, which cost around $200 if you don't already have an old computer sitting around the house.

Tip

For more information about Buddy BeTwin, see the Web site at www.getabuddy.com.

Looking at requirements

You install an internal video card on the PC, and using up to 15 feet of video and USB cabling and a USB hub, you can attach another USB keyboard, monitor, and USB mouse to use the CPU independently of the other user.

The Buddy BeTwin requires the following:

✦ Pentium 233 MHz minimum, but a 600 MHz processor is preferable.

✦ Windows 98 or Me.

✦ 128MB RAM minimum.

✦ Available Industry Standard Architecture (ISA) slot. ISA is an older, 16-bit bus design; most newer computers, however, offer one or two ISA slots. You can use an ISA slot to insert a modem, network, or other card to modify your computer.

Looking at the Buddy BeTwin

When you purchase the Buddy BeTwin, you must supply an additional monitor, keyboard, and mouse for each computer. The system does not include this hardware.

The system includes the following items:

✦ A video card to plug into your PC

✦ A 15-foot cable for video and USB usage

✦ A USB hub for attaching a second monitor, keyboard, and mouse

✦ Software for use with Windows 98 and Me (Windows 95, 2000, and XP are not currently supported)

✦ An instruction guide

Looking at the disadvantages

Naturally, a system such as this has its disadvantages. Users, for example, experience a lag time when either user is performing large file transfers, complex calculations, or other processor-intensive tasks.

When the user's computer is attached to the Buddy BeTwin, starting most applications is slower, and using applications at the same time slows down performance for both users.

Playing video clips or games might be too slow for most users. They do play on the Buddy BeTwin host, though.

Also, sharing other peripherals isn't as fast on the Buddy BeTwin station as on the first computer. Additionally, the speed of modem communications suffers from sharing the CPU.

Using network cards and crossover cable

A common method of connecting two computers is with a crossover cable. A *crossover cable* is a special cable in which the cables are "mirrored" between the ends so that you can connect two computers without a hub or switch. Make sure the cable you purchase is labeled as a crossover cable; a simple patch cable will not work.

In addition, you need a network interface card (NIC) installed to each computer. If the NICs are 10 Mbps, then that's the speed of the network; however, if both NICs are 100 Mbps, the network speed between the two is also 100 Mbps.

You can use a crossover cable and NICs between two PCs, Macs, and/or Linux computers. You must use special software to enable two different operating systems to communicate. See Chapter 10 for more information.

Using Phone Lines for Your Network

Using your phone lines to network your computers is a technology you might want to explore. You can use the telephone cabling already in place in your home without rewiring or installing traditional Ethernet cabling. You also can use the RJ-11 modular phone jacks that are already in place in your home as a port for a computer.

A phone line network enables you to share all resources on the network, including files, printers, applications, games, modems and cable/DSL modems, CD-ROM drives, and other peripherals. Most home phone line networks run at 1 Mbps, which is fast enough for general

networking. Some phone line network products claim up to 10 Mbps speeds, but it is highly doubtful you'll get that speed with phone line technology. If you want to work with multimedia, large graphic files, or complex calculations over the network, then you should consider a faster network technology.

Note You can use phone line networking with PCs, Macs, and/or Linux distributions; however, you must install the appropriate software for the computer and operating system you're using. For example, software that works for a Mac and PC might not work for Linux; software that works for a PC and Linux might not work for a Mac.

Using your phone lines for networking provides scalability — as you acquire new computers or add new users, you can add to your network without making existing devices obsolete. Using the phone lines is also secure for your network. Neighbors or others outside the home cannot access your network or computers over the network.

Small Business Tip Don't plan on using a phone line network in your small business if you work on the network for several hours or more each day. The 1 Mbps speeds are too slow for you to complete your work efficiently and effectively.

Understanding phone line networks

Phone line networks enable you to share files, printers, and other peripherals, including modems and CD-ROM drives. Figure 8-14 shows one home phone line networking solution. You can attach multiple PCs and peripherals to the network for sharing resources. Attach each peripheral to the computer by using traditional parallel or serial cables. Attach computers to the network by using telephone wires and jacks.

Standards for Phone Line Networking

The Home Phoneline Networking Alliance (HomePNA) is an incorporated, nonprofit association of industry-leading companies working together to ensure the adoption of a single, unified phone line networking industry standard for vendors and manufacturers. The HomePNA tests and reports on various networking products that use phone lines. In its testing and results on the topic, the HomePNA has set forth guidelines to guarantee home owners a successful phone line network. Following are some of the guidelines:

✦ The network must share the phone line with other devices and services so that the technology is immune to interference on the phone line. The phones, answering machines, fax machines, and other devices must not cause any electronic interference on the network.

✦ Networking across phone lines must not interrupt existing phone services.

✦ A networked phone line system must be able to allow for various wiring topologies, because the telephone wiring within each home is different and may change. A phone line network is sometimes called the *random tree topology*.

✦ The phone line network must be able to stand high levels of signal noise from appliances, heaters, and other devices in the home.

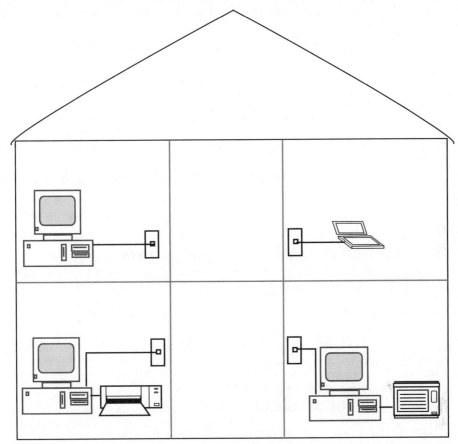

Figure 8-14: A home phone line network enables you to share files and other resources.

A phone line network uses standard telephone wire to connect your computers. The ends of the phone wire use RJ-11 jacks, just like the lines to your telephones do. All you have to do is plug the RJ-11 jacks into an extra phone jack in the wall.

The special network adapter card (different from an Ethernet card) you insert into your computer essentially divides the data traveling over the lines into separate frequencies — one for voice, one for network data, and, if applicable, one for wide-bandwidth Internet access such as Digital Subscriber Line. DSL is a technology that transmits data in both directions simultaneously over copper lines.

Tip   In addition to setting up a phone line network, you might want to use the phone line network to complement any other networking media in your home, such as Ethernet CAT 5, wireless, or power line networks.

Telephone lines are copper lines; most phone lines are now CAT 3. The phone line networking frequencies can coexist on the same telephone line without impacting the phone service. Data transfers for phone line networks run at speeds up to 1 Mbps.

With a phone line network, you don't need a hub or other networking hardware; however, you do need the following:

✦ A home phone line network adapter (certified by HomePNA) with the necessary software drivers

✦ A standard telephone wire long enough to reach from the computer to the nearest phone jack

Many of the phone line networks support Ethernet networks, so you can combine two networking technologies to build the network that's right for you. Alternatively, you might want to use a phone line network with wireless or power line network technology.

Looking at home phone line network kits and products

Kits make it easy and quick to install a home phone line network. Everything you need for networking two computers is included in most kits. All you need to do to expand the network is add a network adapter and the telephone wire to the new computer.

Linksys HomeLink Phoneline PCI Network in a Box

The Linksys HomeLink Phoneline PCI Network in a Box kit uses no switches, hubs, or other special hardware; all you need are the adapter cards, software drivers, and telephone wires to connect from 2 to 30 computers together in a network with speeds up to 1 Mbps. The operating systems HomeLink works with include Windows 95, 98, NT, and 2000.

Using the HomeLink kit, you can share files, printers, modems, and more without tying up the telephones in the house. Also, HomeLink includes software for sharing an Internet account over the network. Included with HomeLink is the Sygate Technologies Sygate Home Network Gateway software, which enables you to connect to the Internet with your home phone line network. For more information about the Internet, see Chapter 16.

HomeLink includes a CD-ROM containing software that automatically sets up the network so that all available resources can be shared. You do have control over the shares, however, and you can isolate devices that you don't want to share. Installation and setup couldn't be easier.

The HomeLink Network in a Box two-pack includes the following items, for around $75 per kit:

✦ Two phone line network adapter cards

✦ Two 15-foot phone line cables

✦ One installation CD-ROM

✦ A user guide

✦ Sygate Home Network Gateway software

Additional HomeLink Phoneline Network cards cost around $40 each.

The HomeLink Network in a Box uses 802.3 standards (10Base-T) and meets the HomePNA specifications. Also, the phone line network cards contain RJ-11 and RJ-45 ports, so you can connect the card to either a phone line network or a traditional Ethernet network.

D-Link Internal Phone Line Adapter Card

D-Link makes phone line network adapter cards you can use to share files, printers, and Internet access through the existing telephone wiring. The adapter fits into your PCI slot. You need to install a driver, supplied by D-Link, and then you can connect that computer to a standard phone jack in your home.

Installing a Phone Line Network

Just to give you an idea of how simple it is to use a phone line network, here are the steps to installing the Linksys HomeLink Phoneline Network. First, you must choose a server or host computer; this computer should be the one with the modem and Internet connection, if you plan to use the modem-sharing software. Follow these steps:

1. Turn off and unplug the PC, remove the cover, and locate an open PCI expansion slot. For more information about installing network cards, see Chapter 9.

2. Remove the strip that covers the bay, and slide the HomeLink card into the slot. To make sure that the card is properly seated, firmly snap it into the slot. Secure the card, carefully, with the screw.

3. Replace the cover on the computer, and plug the computer into the power outlet.

4. Plug one end of the telephone cable provided into the HomeLink card's telephone port, and plug the other end of the telephone cable into a wall phone jack.

5. Repeat Steps 1 through 4 for any additional PCs you want to connect to the network.

6. Turn on the server PC. Windows will recognize the HomeLink card. Insert the HomeLink CD-ROM and follow the directions on screen to complete setup. Repeat with the other PCs on the network.

HomeLink includes complete written instructions for installing the HomeLink software and for configuring the PCs on the network.

Repeat the process to connect two computers over the phone lines. This card works with Windows 98, NT, 2000, and XP. One card costs around $25; remember, you have to have two cards. You also need to purchase extra phone line wire.

2Wire PC Port

The 2Wire PC Port is a high-speed USB-to-HomePNA adapter you can use to share an Internet connection (cable, DSL, or dial-up) with multiple computers, after you set up your phone line network. You plug the PC Port into your computer's USB port and a phone jack. You must run the installation CD that comes with the PC Port, and then you're ready to share the Internet connection.

Costing around $45, the PC Port is compatible with Windows 98, 98SE, Me, NT 4, 2000, XP, and Mac OS 8.6 through 9.x. The following are included with the PC Port:

✦ Twenty-inch standard USB cable

✦ Six-foot standard telephone cable

✦ Y-adapter to provide an extra phone jack for a telephone

✦ Installation CD

Linksys HomeLink Phoneline Bridge

The Linksys HomeLink Phoneline 10M Ethernet Bridge provides a bridge between the Internet and/or your Ethernet network and your phone line network. The bridge contains a 10Base-T/ 100Base-TX RJ-45 Ethernet port, an Uplink port, and a HomeLink RJ-11 port. You can plug your cable modem or DSL modem's connection into the bridge and to a phone jack, and you can then access the Internet from your phone line network. The Linksys HomeLink Phoneline bridge is an excellent product; however, the bridge costs around $185. The bridge is compatible with any operating system, as long as the computer has an Ethernet port.

NETGEAR's Home Phoneline Adapter

NETGEAR has a home phone line PCI adapter card you can use to turn your computers into a network. The card works on the phone lines without disturbing or disrupting your phone service. NETGEAR says the technology makes it possible to have a 10 Mbps connection.

You can share your modem with this phone line network, and the card is compatible with Windows 98, NT, and 2000. It costs around $30 per card.

Linksys PC Phoneline Adapter Card

If you use a notebook on your phone line network, you can get Linksys' HomeLink Phoneline 10M Integrated PC Card. This card can connect to any 1 Mbps or 10 Mbps network. The CardBus PC Card uses two standard RJ-11 telephone ports. You can use the card to share files, printers, CD drives, and Internet access (cable modem, DSL, and/or dial-up). This card is compatible with Windows 98, 2000, and Me. The cost is around $65.

Phone line adapters for Macs and Linux

You can use many phone line network cards with a Linux machine; however, the problem is finding the correct driver for your distribution. More and more phone line NICs are becoming supported. You can find the appropriate drivers by searching the Internet under your specific distro.

Many phone line cards are available for the Macintosh, depending on your operating system and the required driver. Generally, all you need is a USB port and an adapter to connect nearly any phone line card to a Mac.

✦ For around $60, the Diamond HomeFree Phoneline External Adapter works with either a PC or a Mac. The Diamond doesn't interfere with incoming phone calls and lets you share resources, such as scanners and printers, between computers.

✦ For around $90, you can use the Farallon Home Phoneline Adapter, which will work with Windows 98 or a Mac operating system.

Xcom, D-Link, and others also make phone line NICs for Macintosh.

Using Your Home's Electrical Wiring for a Network

You can also use your power lines for your home network, if you're certain your home's electrical lines are high quality, safe, and reliable. In a power lines network, you use electrical outlets in your home to attach computers for sharing files, printers, Internet accounts, and peripherals.

Small Business Tip

Don't use a network that runs on your electrical wiring in a small-business office. The connection is slow and the heavy use of other wired products in your business will most likely interfere with data transmission; for example, a company that has fax machines, copiers, shredders, and other electrical devices drawing the power is not ideal for a power line network.

Looking at power line networking

Power line networks have solved earlier problems with interference and speed. As little as 3 years ago, you could expect speeds of only 350 Kbps with your power line networks. Now, depending on the technology you use and the specific power line network, you can expect data transmission speeds of 1 Mbps up to 12 Mbps.

However, some problems with using your power lines still exist. The noise ratio is often high, which limits not only the number of computers you can attach to the network but affects the data transfer over the network as well. However, some companies have developed new technologies to speed the transmission of data over power line networks. Linksys, for example, uses Orthogonal Frequency Division Multiplexing (OFDM). OFDM simply means that several signals of different frequencies combine to form the signal for data transmission.

When looking for a power line network, make sure the networking devices have the following:

✦ Are approved by the HomePlug Powerline Alliance. The alliance is an organization that certifies products to work in most homes — safely and efficiently.

Tip

For more information about the HomePlug Powerline Alliance, see www.homeplug.org.

✦ Uses 56-bit encryption for security.

✦ Guarantee that if power line characteristics change during a session, the product continues to provide a good network connection.

Looking at power line products

Many power line products are available for use in your home. Many of the manufacturers that produce products for Ethernet, wireless, and phone line networking also make products for power line products. Following are some of the more popular ones. If you can use an adapter for Ethernet, you can usually use it for Linux as well. The problem you'll find is in the drivers; but power line products do not always need drivers. Use bridges and USB adapters for Linux or Macs.

Caution

Power line networking data signals cannot pass through electrical transformers without being changed. Therefore, data signals become unreadable when the building connects to the regional power grid. If you're the only occupant of a building, your data is safe from people down the street. However, if you're in an office, apartment, or condo, other occupants might be on your side of the electrical transformer; so if they plug a power line networking device into their wall socket, they could read your data.

NeverWire 14 OX-201

Phonex Broadband Corporation makes a HomePlug-compliant device called NeverWire for the Macintosh or PC to use the bandwidth of standard electrical wiring. You can attach multiple computers to your power lines, share peripheral devices, play games, and share the Internet.

Since NeverWire uses no software drivers, the device supports both the Mac and Windows systems: Mac 8.6 and up including Mac OS X, TCP/IP, and AppleTalk.

Linksys' Instant PowerLine USB Adapter

Linksys makes an adapter that enables you to plug your PC or notebook into your existing USB port. The adapter then connects to the power line and enables you to share data, printers, and the Internet access of your choice. The adapter includes software that installs drivers; the adapter is also Plug and Play, so it's easy to install.

The Instant PowerLine USB Adapter enables speeds up to 12 Mbps. You can plug multiple PCs into the USB port, install the software, and network another computer easily. The adapter is compatible with Windows 98, Me, 2000, and XP. Cost is around $100.

GigaFast Ethernet's HomePlug USB Adapter Wall Mount

Similar to the Linksys USB Adapter, the GigaFast Ethernet HomePlug USB adapter enables you to create your network using your existing power lines. With speeds up to 14 Mbps over home power lines, this USB adapter uses standard encryption, has an estimated range of 900 feet in wall, and hangs on the wall to make the connection site neater and easier. Cost is around $100. Any USB adapter or bridge, such as this one, is compatible with any computer with a USB port, whether the computer is running Windows, Mac operating systems, or a Linux system.

NETGEAR's XE102 adapter

NETGEAR makes an adapter that plugs directly into the wall power socket and requires no drivers. Using this adapter, you can share an Internet connection, transfer files, and play games. Because there are no drivers, you can use the NETGEAR XE102 adapter in a PC or a Mac. You can also use the adapter with a network printer or Xbox, if you need to. You need one adapter per network device, at around $80 per adapter.

IOGEAR's HomePlug Ethernet Bridge

The HomePlug Ethernet Bridge enables you to connect your computers over the power lines and bridge your power line network to an Ethernet network. The device has a 10/100Base-T adapter, so you can connect it to a network switch or router that is connected to your Ethernet network.

Looking at Virtual Private Networks

Virtual private network (VPN) describes a network between two or more computers that communicate securely over a public network. The network is private but has limited public network access. VPNs often connect one computer to a private network, such as a client/server network at your workplace. VPNs can also connect one private LAN to another, as in server to server.

VPNs include strong authentication and encryption. They also mask information about the private network topology from hackers on the Internet. VPNs are very safe.

There are two ways to create a VPN connection: gateway to gateway and host to host. A *gateway* is a device — such as a router, switch, or even a computer — that enables the connection between two other computers. The gateway can be considered a bridge between networks. The *host* is the device — usually a computer — that has the VPN software installed. Windows 2000 and XP have the VPN host software already installed.

If you use a network at work and would like to connect to that network, ask your boss about VPN networking. For your home network, however, you have other much easier methods of networking to use.

The HomePlug Bridge enables speeds up to 14 Mbps and offers 56-bit encryption. Range is up to 900 feet, and the bridge is compatible with Windows 98, Me, 2000, and XP.

Looking at the Future of Networking Alternatives

Home networking has become increasingly popular as more and more homes add two, three, and more computers and users to the family. Traditional cabling and networking hardware might be acceptable to many home users; however, manufacturers are always looking for less expensive networking solutions.

In addition, manufacturers are looking for ways that make networking easier for home users. Laying wire, configuring software, adding drivers, management applications, and so on are all tasks manufacturers want to streamline.

Microsoft, for example, has already created operating systems — Windows 2000 and XP — that can sense the network when they are first connected, configure themselves, and join the workgroup or client/server network on their own. Other improvements and advancements are in the works, from many manufacturers.

Mobile Communications Research (also Microsoft) is working on wireless connectivity to extend and improve its effectiveness. The target of the software they are currently researching is to enable wireless devices to be both mobile-aware and location-aware. This simply means the system adapts to any interference and to changing network topology quickly so that connections are not lost; connections are not even delayed.

In addition to this wireless technology, other researchers are using Ultra-Wide Band (UWB) wireless for high-speed data communication. UWB is a digital pulse wireless technology that is able to carry huge amounts of data. UWB is currently being researched for wireless voice, land mine detection, and systems to help you see through walls; it might someday become available for networking as well.

IBM is working with Bell Atlantic to provide wiring systems to homes that provide multimedia and fast speeds. The system installs a multimedia network hub in the home, uses two coax cables, an Ethernet cable, plus other phone wiring, all connected to multimedia ports. The system can send audio/visual signals and computer data, and it supports multiple telephone lines.

Many companies are working with fiber optics and optical networking to create super high-speed data transmission. Optical networks send laser light through glass fiber. The media is more expensive than Ethernet or wireless networking, but they handle far higher capacity loads and are much faster.

Broadband is another term you're likely to hear now and in the future of networking. *Broadband* describes technology — such as cable modem, DSL, T1 lines, wireless technology, fiber optic and so on — that carries numerous voice, video, and data channels simultaneously. Broadband is a "pipeline" on which large amounts of data travel quickly, securely, and efficiently.

Summary

In this chapter, you've learned about alternative methods of connecting a computer network in the home. Specifically, you've learned about the following:

✦ Using direct cabling connections

✦ Using phone lines for a network

✦ Using electrical wiring for a network

✦ The future of networking

In the next chapter, you learn about purchasing and installing networking hardware.

✦   ✦   ✦

Purchasing and Installing Networking Hardware

In addition to the technology you use between computers — traditional cabling, wireless technology, power lines, and so on — you need to purchase and install networking hardware that enables the computers to communicate over the network. For one thing, each computer on the network needs a network interface adapter, whether it's an Ethernet NIC, a wireless PC Card, or an external USB adapter. In addition, depending on the wiring or wireless technology you choose, you must add a device that extends network signals from computer to computer, such as a hub or access point.

The wiring technology you use denotes the network hardware you choose. For example, if you use Ethernet wiring for your network, you must use Ethernet network cards, Ethernet hubs or switches, and so on. In addition, you must choose Ethernet 10Base-T or Ethernet 100Base-T, or if you're setting up a small business, you might choose Ethernet 1000Base-T. All networking hardware and cabling in that case must be Ethernet 1000Base-T.

Note　With Ethernet, you can choose to use the 10/100 technology or even the 10/100/1000 technology. For more information, see the section "Defining network interface cards" later in the chapter

The same is true with wireless: 802.11g wireless network adapter cards work best with 802.11g access points, bridges, and antennas. Power line 12 Mbps adapter cards also work best with power line 12 Mbps hubs and bridges. In most cases, power line adapters do not work with wireless network cards, which do not work with Ethernet hubs.

Understanding Networking Hardware

Depending on the type of network you choose, you'll need to add some hardware to enable the computers to communicate. In addition to cabling, you are likely to need a network interface card and a hub. This chapter covers network cards, hubs, access points, and other hardware necessary to your network. This chapter also covers some hardware you can use if you're networking your small business, such as switches and routers, which make your work network faster and more efficient.

Cross-Reference   See Chapters 6, 7, and 8 for information about various types of cabling and connections.

When it comes to networking hardware, you need to understand some terms to purchase the exact equipment you need. Within the definition for each piece of equipment—network cards, hub, access points, and so on—are multiple descriptors and identifiers you must understand to intelligently and correctly choose what you need for your network. Unless you use alternative cabling methods described in Chapter 8 to connect only two computers, you need the some of following hardware described here.

Tip   When choosing any network hardware, make sure that it is compatible with the standards for the technology. For more information, see Chapters 6, 7, and 8.

Defining Terms

In understanding the types of hardware you use with your computer, you also need to understand a couple of terms, such as bus and controller. These two terms are often used in conjunction with networking hardware but seldom explained. Following are definitions and examples that can help you when you're ready to purchase the hardware you need for your network.

A *bus* is an electronic corridor that sends signals from one part of the computer to another, such as from the processor to the memory. There are multiple types of buses in your computer:

✦ **serial** – Usually used for mice and modems, referred to as COM ports.

✦ **parallel** – Often used for printers connected on the parallel port.

✦ **USB (universal serial bus)** – A faster (12 Mbps as compared to 1 Mbps for serial and parallel), external port that transfers data for mice, keyboards, modems, printers, cameras, hubs, and other devices.

✦ **PS/2** – Used for mice and keyboards.

✦ **FireWire (IEEE 1394 standard)** – A superfast port that transfers data up to 400 Mbps, used for video recorders and the like.

✦ **Industry Standard Architecture (ISA)** – ISA is a 16-bit bus design; a slow bus used to connect expansion boards to the motherboard.

✦ **Extended Industry Standard Architecture (EISA)** – EISA is a 32-bit extension to the ISA standard bus. EISA data transfer can reach a peak of 33 megabytes per second.

NICs also use a bus to transfer information from the network card to the computer or network. Some buses used for NICs include PCMCIA and PCI. See the following section for more information.

A *controller* is an additional card, board, or other piece of equipment that receives information from the computer's processor and uses the instructions to manage additional hardware. When a device in the computer (such as a NIC) needs to connect to a device outside of the computer (Ethernet wiring, for example), the controller is the hardware that manages the flow of data between the two. Sometimes NIC drivers refer to the card as a *controller*.

Defining network interface cards

You use a network card in any computer you want to network by Ethernet, wireless, phone line, power line, or other networking technologies. A *network interface card* — also called a NIC (pronounced "nick"), network card, adapter, PC Card, or network adapter card — is a device that connects a computer to the network. The network card accommodates all the electronic components, and often any network control software used to configure the network card. The software used to control and configure the network card is called a driver. Drivers are included on a CD or floppy disk with the card when you purchase it. Many manufacturers also offer updated drivers on their Web sites as well.

Note   Many terms refer to the network card. In this book, the card is normally called a NIC or network card, unless more specific information is needed.

A network card is an expansion board, similar to a sound card or video card. Depending on the type of card, it might plug into the expansion bus slot (PCI card) on the computer's motherboard (see Figure 9-1). Alternatively, a PC Card can plug into a slot in the case of your notebook or tablet PC; the card can come built in to the motherboard of the computer (as in some Macs and PCs); or the NIC can be an adapter that plugs into a USB slot on your computer. The network card connects to the network transmission medium, such as twisted-pair or telephone wire, which in turn connects all the network interface cards to the network.

Figure 9-1: A network interface card can be a board that plugs into your computer.

The connections between the network card and cable depend on the cable type. Coaxial cable uses a BNC connector, twisted-pair cabling uses an RJ-45 connector, telephone wiring uses an RJ-11 connector, and wireless uses antennas attached to both the card and the access point with no wiring in between.

Cross-Reference   For more information about cabling, see Chapters 6, 7, and 8.

NIC software

Each network card must use control software, or a driver program, to make the card work. Usually, the driver is supplied on disk when you purchase the card. The driver is a small program the network applications use to talk to the network card. The card translates commands so that it can manage the flow of data to and from the computer.

Tip   When you purchase a network interface card, you should go to the card manufacturer's site on the Internet and download the most updated software driver for that particular card. Manufacturers are always updating the drivers to make the card work more efficiently; plus if the operating system you use is newer, such as XP, you want to get the most updated driver for that OS.

Sometimes network cards can cause problems on installation. Depending on the other devices and software on a computer, it might be difficult to get a card to work. Sometimes the problem lies in the brand of the card, and sometimes other factors are involved. See Appendix A for information about problems with network cards.

Small Business Tip   You should buy all the same types of NICs for your network, especially when you're dealing with a business network. Using the same type of NIC with the same type of network software makes installing, configuring, and troubleshooting network connections easier.

Tip   If you're using a Linux machine on your network, you can use much of the same hardware you can use with PCs and Macs; however, software drivers might be difficult to find. Often a Linux driver doesn't come out until 8 months to a year after the hardware, especially if the hardware is cutting-edge.

Types of cards

Computers use different types of network interface cards. Before you purchase a card, you need to know what type of card your computer takes. See your computer's documentation for more information. Following are the types of network cards you normally see:

✦ **Peripheral Component Interconnect (PCI) local bus** — PCI local bus enables you to plug PCI-compliant expansion cards into the computer. The most commonly used slot in today's computers, it supports speeds of 33 to 66 MHz.

✦ **Personal Computer Memory Card International Association (PCMCIA) card** — PCMCIA is a standard for portable computers. The card is usually the size of a credit card. There are several versions, or types, of PCMCIA cards; the types define the thickness and uses of the card.

✦ **Personal Computer (PC) card** — A PC Card conforms to the PCMCIA standard. PC Cards use a 68-pin connector with longer power and ground pins. Today, PC Card is synonymous with PCMCIA card.

✦ **USB Adapter card**—The USB standard is so adaptable that there are several incarnations you can use with your network. You can use an adapter to enable you to easily connect most Windows and Mac computers to an Ethernet, phone line, or power line network. The adapter plugs into the USB port on your computer, and the networking cable plugs into the other end.

Tip

You can find network cards that are a combination card, such as a modem and network card, and the deal might seem like a good one, especially if you don't have enough slots to accommodate two separate cards. If you have enough slots, however, you should purchase two separate cards. You won't have as many problems, and it is cheaper in the long run. If one card becomes damaged or quits working, for example, you'll have to replace both cards if they're on a combination card.

Tip

Linux machines cannot use USB adapters or an USB device. Linux doesn't provide for USB drivers, ports, and so on.

There are other considerations when purchasing a network card, such as network topology and cabling technology. See the section "Purchasing and Installing a Network Interface Card" later in this chapter for more information.

Defining hubs

A *hub* is a device that modifies network transmission signals, thereby enabling you to extend the network for additional workstations. There are two kinds of hubs—active and passive:

✦ An **active hub** amplifies the transmission signals to help extend cable length.

✦ A **passive hub** splits the transmission signal so that you can add another client computer.

Hubs come with a certain number of ports, or plugs, including 4, 5, 8, 16, and 24. You plug one computer into each port or plug. A hub is one of the easiest methods of connecting two or more computers together. If you purchase a network kit for Ethernet, phone line, or power line networks, a hub is one part of the kit.

When you use a hub on your network, it makes troubleshooting connection problems a bit easier. If a cable or network card goes bad, for example, only the computer with the bad card or cable stops communicating with the network. Additionally, the other computers on the network aren't hindered by one bad connection.

Small
Business
Tip

Choose a hub with more ports than you think you'll need for your business network. Consider at least doubling the number of ports you expect to need; for example, if you think you need only 4 ports, consider buying an 8- or even 12-port hub. You'll be surprised at how quickly a network can grow.

Generally, a hub is the central controlling device, although when used in a spanning tree network, it's difficult to discern one central device. Figure 9-2 illustrates a four-port hub used to connect four computers in the network. The hub is the central device in this network.

Figure 9-3 illustrates a spanning tree topology in which hubs are used to extend the network beyond the limitations of the number of hub ports. The second hub connects three additional computers to the network. It could also connect another hub, and another, to further extend the transmission signals.

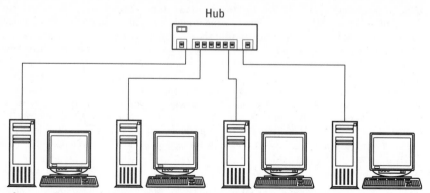

Figure 9-2: Use a hub to connect the computers to the network.

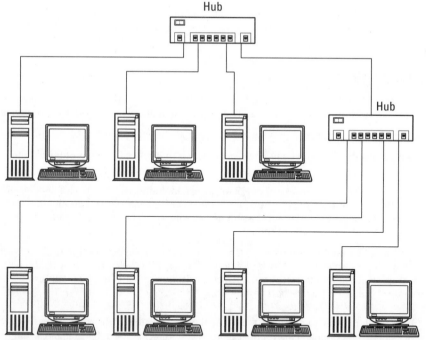

Figure 9-3: Using hubs to extend the reach of the network is also called daisy-chaining.

You must match the hub type with the type of cabling, network cards, and network technology. For example, if you use Ethernet (10Base-T or 100Base-T twisted-pair) cabling and cards, you also must use an Ethernet hub. See the section "Purchasing a hub or switch" later in this chapter.

Defining switches

In place of a hub, you could use a switch in your home network. A *switch* is a device that fil-ters the network packets and then forwards the packets through the network. A *packet* is a segment of data that's sent across the network. Many packets make up the completed data sent over the network; one packet might contain such information as the data's source, desti-nation, size, or other information helping it get to its destination.

A switch is a higher-performance device for sending packets over the network than a hub. When a computer on the network sends packets to another computer, a hub sends the pack-ets to all computers on the network; a switch determines the destination computer and sends the packets to only that computer.

A switch is particularly useful when there are four or more computers on a network, because the switch looks at the packets and sends them to right computer. You might want to use a switch instead of a hub if you're using applications that generate a lot of network traffic, for example, such as multiplayer games. You might also use a switch if you share a lot of music files, which also generates a lot of network traffic.

Tip If you're unsure whether to get a hub or switch, check prices. Generally, hubs cost a bit less, but in recent months, the price of switches has really come down. www1.dealtime.com is a good place to compare prices for various hardware.

Defining access points and base stations

You use an access point or base station as a hub for wireless connections. *Access point* is the term used for PCs, and *base station* is the term used for Macs. The two are the same basic device; the only differences are in the 802 standards used, the range, and the operating sys-tem used.

An access point or base station works as a hub or bridge in your wireless or wireless/wired LAN. A *bridge* is a device that connects two segments of a LAN or two different LANs together. A bridge simply forwards packets without analyzing or rerouting the messages. With the use of an access point or base station, you can add wireless connectivity to other wireless net-works or to an Ethernet network, for example.

Most access points and base stations come with antennas, an external connector to add a directional antenna, if you want, and like any networking hardware, you must match the standard—802.11a, b, or g—of the access point with the standard of the network cards you use. Wireless access points and base stations do come with certain security factors built in because of the technology. You can deny access to computers because of its MAC address, or you can set up WEP encryption to keep your network safe.

Cross-Reference See Chapter 7 for more information about WEP and MAC addresses with wireless networking.

Looking at routers

A *router* links a LAN to a wide area network (WAN). Routers are intelligent devices that can analyze packets and decide not only to which computer on which LAN to send the packet but the fastest way to get there. You likely will not use a router in your home network, unless of course you want to connect your home network to a larger network, such as the Internet.

A variety of routers are available for home use: cable modem/DSL routers, wireless high-speed routers, and Internet broadband routers. The list goes on and on. Most routers include encryption to ensure privacy on your network. In addition, Internet routers offer a firewall of sorts to secure against attacks from the Internet. A *firewall* is software or hardware that prevents outside network access to your private network.

When purchasing a router for Internet access at your business, it is especially important to include encryption and firewall protection. Your business information — sales, payroll, accounts payable and receivable, names and addresses of employees and customers, and other information — needs to be protected from intruders and hackers.

Broadband routers enable you to connect to the Internet quickly and efficiently. *Broadband* refers to telecommunications, such as cable modems and DSL, that enable data transmission over a variety of channels on a single wire. You can purchase a cable modem/DSL router for your home for around $65, which provides four ports into which you can plug computers. All four computers can attach to the Internet via one account.

For more information about Internet routers, see Chapter 16.

You can purchase routers that also serve as a switch or bridge between your wired and wireless networks. You can daisy-chain routers, as you can hubs or switches. Routers can be difficult to configure, but they are easier now than ever before. Only when you purchase a large router made to connect multiple large networks will you have trouble with configuration.

Purchasing and Installing a Network Interface Card

When choosing your network interface card, you first must match the card to your computer. Next you must match the card to your network cable and technology. Note that if you plan to use an Ethernet cabling scheme, you also must use an Ethernet network card. If you're setting up a wireless connection or phone line network, you must also choose the appropriate network card for that type of network.

Installing the network card is fairly easy. You must be careful not to damage the card or the computer. You can install a NIC in a matter of minutes.

Purchasing the NIC

Your first priorities when choosing a NIC are matching your computer's slots and matching the type of network you plan to use. Other things you need to consider when purchasing a network card are price, brand name, warranty, and the type of connectors on the card.

If you purchase a networking kit, the network interface card comes with the kit. You don't have to worry about the type of cabling when using a kit, but you should make sure of the type of NIC and that you have room in your computer before purchasing the kit.

You should purchase network cards that are known brands for your business network. Businesses use networks more than home users do, so the cards will get some wear and tear. Better cards hold up to the use more than cheap cards do; plus, you don't have to change the cards as often if you spend a little more for them in the beginning.

Choosing the NIC type

You can purchase a computer with a network card already installed or an onboard card built in. An onboard card has a network adapter built on to the motherboard. Either way, you'll notice a plug for the computer cable (if it's Ethernet) or perhaps an antenna if it's wireless. Make sure you check the documentation of your computer so you know whether you have a network card and what type of card it is. Otherwise, you'll need to purchase and install a NIC.

First, consider your computer's bus type or connector. As described previously in the chapter, PCI is the most common bus type. If you plan to install a card into your computer, make sure you have a PCI slot available by removing the case and checking. If you're using a notebook, tablet, or "profile" computer, you'll most likely use a PC Card.

Note　You can get PCI cards and PC Cards for Ethernet, wireless, phone line, and power line networks. Make sure you get the appropriate technology as well as the correct type of card.

Figure 9-4 shows a PCI network interface card. PCI slots in the computer are usually white, even though the pins on the card are still copper-colored.

If you're using a portable computer, you need a PCMCIA (or PC Card) card to fit the available slot in the smaller computer. Read your documentation to find out the type of card you can use with your computer. Check to see if you can use a CardBus card, for faster data transmissions; not all notebooks, tablets, and such can use CardBus cards.

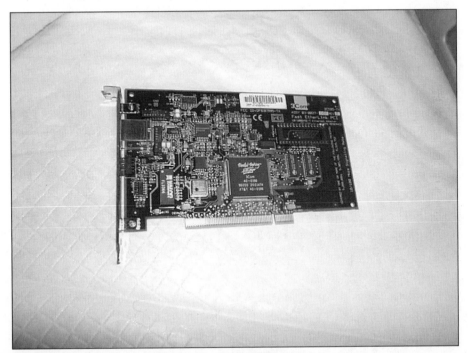

Figure 9-4: PCI cards are used in newer computers.

Next, you need to check to make sure that you have an open slot in the computer. If you already have a sound card, video card, and modem inside the computer, you may not have room for the NIC. Turn your computer off and unplug it. Most computers today keep power to the bus even though the computer is turned off; if you remove a card while there is power to it, you could short out the bus.

Tip   Make sure that if you have a low-profile computer — one of the very thin, very small computers — you get a low-profile NIC. Open the case and check the size of the card; perhaps take the card with you to purchase one. Low-profile cards are a different size than regular PCI cards.

Remove the case (you might need to look at the documentation for instructions) and set it aside. Locate the slots in your computer. Before touching the card, a slot, or a space marker with your hand or a screwdriver, touch the computer case for a ground. The case pulls any static electricity in your body so you can safely touch the insides of the computer. Keep your arm or hand on the case as long as you work inside of it to make sure no static travels from you to the motherboard. Static could cause damage to your computer.

Figure 9-5 illustrates an open computer with all PCI slots filled. You can remove one of the cards and replace it with a NIC, depending on what the other cards are.

Tip   The computer shown in Figure 9-5 has open ISA (Industry Standard Architecture) slots. Some older computers do have ISA slots, but it's difficult to find ISA network cards.

Figure 9-5: Look for the free slots in your computer.

Choosing a PCI Card

PCI cards support bus mastering, especially for use with Pentium Pro–class processors. *Bus mastering* is a process that enables advanced bus architectures to control the flow of data using a multitasking operating system that performs the transferring without constantly using the CPU. This process means the NIC receives greater system bus access and higher data transfer speeds.

Following are some other facts about PCI:

✦ PCI drivers are tuned for 32-bit performance, which matches the PCI bus architecture and the Windows operating system.

✦ PCI takes advantage of the performance and power capabilities of the Pentium-series processors. PCI is sophisticated to better suit newer computers.

✦ PCI was designed for 32-bit and 64-bit data paths, meaning faster throughput on the network.

Choosing a PC Card

A PC Card is similar to PCI in that the card is a network interface card matched to the wiring standard you have chosen — wireless, Ethernet, power line, and so on. The PC Card normally provides 16-bit data rates. However, most notebooks and tablets today use the 32-bit CardBus. A CardBus is used only on Pentium processors or better and is capable of bus speeds from 20 to 33 MHz. The PC Card slot is usually the bottom slot on your notebook, if your notebook supports it. If your notebook does not support a CardBus, you can easily find PC Cards not targeted to CardBus.

Note   *CardBus* is a trade name for an advanced PC Card. Both are primarily used in notebooks and portable computers. A CardBus card fits in the same type slot as a PC Card. The difference between the CardBus and a PC Card is that the CardBus also offers support for direct memory access, a 32-bit path for data transfer, and a faster operating speed, and a CardBus works at a lower battery voltage. CardBus is a standard for PC notebooks that is accepted by the PCMCIA as a network interface card.

The CardBus standard provides 32-bit bus speeds that can be as much as four to six times faster than previous cards. CardBus PC Cards also support hot swapping (meaning you don't have to turn the computer off to remove or insert the card) and Plug and Play capability. CardBus cards can be used only in special CardBus-capable systems with the appropriate slots. The CardBus PC Card uses a special keying system that fits only into a CardBus slot.

Choosing cabling and technology types

When choosing a network interface card, consider the speed of the cabling and card as well as the technology types. If you're using Ethernet cabling, you must use Ethernet cards. Alternatively, you might choose a phone line network, but the card must match the phone line cabling and connections.

If you're choosing Ethernet, you must match the network card and the hub with the speed — choose 10 Mbps (Ethernet) or 100 Mbps (Fast Ethernet) or 10/100. Either speed can work with CAT 5 twisted-pair cabling. Most network cards today are rated as 10/100, meaning you can use them at either speed — 10 or 100 Mbps.

If you're building an Ethernet network, definitely buy the 10/100 cards. You can use the 10 Mbps now and later upgrade to 100 Mbps, if you choose. Within a year or two, the 10 Mbps cards may become useless as the technology moves faster and faster.

Small Business Tip

Purchase 10/100 network cards with a 10 Mbps hub or switch to start your network. When you're ready, you can upgrade to a 100 Mbps hub or switch, and your cards will be ready for the change in speed.

You also must consider connectors on the network card. If your cable is coax, the card needs to have BNC connectors. If the cable is twisted-pair, make sure that the card has an RJ-45 connector. For phone line networks, the card needs an RJ-11 connector. Many cards have multiple connectors as well.

Choosing brand and quality

You also want to consider the network card's brand, price, warranty, and the technical support offered. Most network adapter cards cost about the same, with perhaps a $10 difference. You can buy cards for $35 to $65 each. You may find some cards that cost more or less. Avoid any cards that are considerably cheaper, because they might be obsolete or damaged.

Warranties range from a few months to a lifetime warranty. You should always get a card with a lifetime warranty, because there are so many cards from which to choose. You also should check for other benefits, such as cross-shipping for a replacement card. Cross-shipping is when the company sends you a new card at the same time you're sending them the old one; cross-shipping is especially important if you need to get back on the network as quickly as possible.

Use a company with a good reputation for its products and support. Following are just a few of the companies that make quality cards and offer good warranties and support.

Ethernet cards:

　　3Com

　　NETGEAR

　　SMC

　　D-Link

　　Linksys

　　Xircom (for portables)

Wireless cards:

　　Belkin

　　D-Link

　　Proxim, Inc.

　　NETGEAR

　　Xircom

Determining What You Need

Here's what you need for your network, depending on the type of cabling you're using:

Cabling or Technology	NIC	Hub or Switch
Ethernet thin coax cable	Ethernet 10 Mbps NIC	Ethernet 10 Mbps hub or switch
Ethernet twisted-pair cable (Cat 5)	Ethernet 10 Mbps NIC or Ethernet 10/100 NIC	Ethernet 10 Mbps hub or switch or Ethernet 10/100 hub or switch
Ethernet twisted-pair cable (Cat 5)	Ethernet 100 Mbps NIC or Ethernet 10/100 NIC	Ethernet 100 Mbps hub or switch or Ethernet 10/100 hub or switch
Wireless RF 802.11b	Wireless RF 802.11b NIC	No hub but access point or base station 802.11b
Wireless RF 802.11g	Wireless RF 802.11g NIC or 802.11b NIC	No hub but access point or base station 802.11g
Phone line kit	Compatible NIC	No hub
Power line kit	Compatible adapter	No hub

Phone line adapters:

> NETGEAR
>
> Linksys

Power line adapters:

> Belkin
>
> APC

Installing a network interface card

When you install a NIC, you must go through two steps. First, you physically install the card in the computer. Second, you install the network card's driver. Along with configuring the network card's driver, you need to configure the network protocol, clients, and services. Configuring the software part of the NIC and other network settings is covered in Chapter 10.

This section explains how to physically install the network card in the computer and connect it to the cabling.

Installing a card in a portable computer

If you're installing a network card in a portable computer, you do not remove the case from the computer. Portable computers have a door or slot for network cards that you can reach from the outside. Check your computer's documentation for more information.

The card slot is usually on the left- or right-hand side of the portable computer. The card fits into the slot horizontally. One side of the PC Card has a row of small pins, and the other side has a plug, jack, or antenna to connect to the network. With the computer turned off, insert the pin side gently; usually the PC Card button pops out. To remove the card again, push the button to pop the card out. Never remove or insert the card while the computer is turned on unless the card's and computer's documentation specifies that both are capable of hot swapping. Removing the card while the computer is on can result in damage to the computer and the card.

Inserting a card into a desktop computer

Before you install the network card, consult your computer's manual or documentation to see if there are any special instructions for installing the card. Next, make sure that your computer is turned off and unplugged. You also should unplug all lines, cords, and cables from the back of your computer; label each one, if necessary, so you'll know where to plug them in after you finish installing the card.

> **Tip**   Most newer computers have color-coded connections and pictures on the back of the computer to make it easy to connect mice, keyboards, monitors, printers, and network cables.

Remove the computer's case. If you have trouble removing the case, consult the computer's manual for instructions. Most cases are connected with screws or have a snap-on lock or button to press to release the case.

Inside the computer, look for a row of slots along the back edge. Some slots may have cards in them already. With a little luck, you'll have at least one open slot. PCI slots are often short and white. The longer slots are usually ISA and only in older computers.

Remove the screw that secures the cover for the slot to the frame (it's a metal strip that keeps dust out when there's no card). Keep the screw. Some slot holders use a hinged catch or key instead of screws. Be careful to not touch the gold or metallic strips on the card. Holding the card only on the edges, carefully position it over the slot and push it straight in. To seat the card, firmly push the card down into the slot.

> **Tip**   To seat the network card, push the card a little harder than you think you should.

Insert the screw to hold the card in place but be careful not to tighten the screw too tight. The screw head should be flush with the metal tab of the card, and the tab of the card should be flush to the rail of the case. Or you can snap the catch or key back into place if no screws are used.

Figure 9-6 shows the slot and network card jack from the back of the computer. Note that there are still two free slots.

Next, check to make sure that you didn't accidentally disconnect any wires or cables—such as the hard drive power cable or CD cable. Remove all tools and any extra screws from the case.

Do not touch the computer during the next step. Plug the computer in and turn it on. Watch for smoke or the smell of something burning. Also, make sure that the computer boots. If the card isn't seated properly, the computer won't boot; you won't even get video. If you detect any of these problems, turn the computer off immediately, unplug it, and reseat the card. Try again.

If you turned the computer on and everything seems okay, you can continue. Turn the computer off again and disconnect the AC power cord from the computer. Replace the case and secure it with screws, if applicable. Reattach all cables.

Figure 9-6: Use the jack on the back of the computer to plug in the network cable.

Normally, your next step would be to turn on the computer so that you can install the driver software. If the card is Plug and Play, Windows will find the new hardware and install the driver, if available, in the computer. In this case, however, you can go ahead and attach the network cables to the card and even install the hub or switch before configuring the network card. For information about configuring the network card, see Chapter 10.

Note   You should read the documentation that comes with your NIC, as well as any Read Me files on the floppy disk or CD-ROM that comes with the card. If you didn't receive a disk containing the driver software for the NIC, check the card manufacturer's Internet site for the latest driver available.

Connecting the cabling to the card

The next step is to connect the cabling to your network card. Again, the computer should be turned off for this process. To be safe, you might want to unplug the AC power line too.

The cable you purchased should have the correct connector on the end — Ethernet, BNC, phone jack, or other connector. All you have to do is plug the connector into the computer slot containing the card you just inserted. If your network is wireless, you don't even need to plug in a cable.

Note   You should use a patch cable to connect the card to a hub or wall jack if you're using Ethernet cabling. For more information, see Chapter 6.

Purchasing and Installing a Hub or Switch

A hub, also called a repeater or a concentrator, receives signals from the connected devices, and then repeats, or rebroadcasts, the signals to other devices on the network. You use a hub to extend the network. Alternatively, you can use a switch; a switch is more efficient at transferring data. See previous sections for more information.

Note   Hubs run independently of the types of computers attached to the network, so you could have a PC and a Macintosh plugged into the same hub to run on an Ethernet network. For information about using a PC and a Macintosh on the same computer, see Chapter 11.

You need a hub or switch if your network is Ethernet and connects three or more computers. You do not need a hub if you're using Direct Cable Connection. Most phone line or power line networks use a USB hub to connect multiple computers. For more information about phone line or power line networks, see Chapter 8. If you're using wireless connections on your network, you need to use an access point or base station instead of a hub or switch, unless you're connecting a wireless to a wired Ethernet network. If you've connected two computers using Ethernet technology, cabling, and network cards, you can do that without a hub; however, it would be a faster, more efficient connection if you use a hub.

Tip   A hub or switch advertised with the acronym SoHo (small office/home office) in the name or description usually refers to a 4-, 8-, or 10-port hub meant for use in the home or small-business office. SoHo simply refers to devices that are easy to set up and approved for small office or home use.

Purchasing a hub or switch

The first step to buying a hub or switch is to determine the speed of the technology you'll use. If your network cards are 10 Mbps Ethernet, for example, your hub must be 10 Mbps Ethernet. If your network cards are 100 Mbps Ethernet, your hub must also be 100 Mbps. If the hub is a 10/100 hub, it connects either 10 Mbps cards or 100 Mbps cards but not all at the same time. Only a switch determines the speed of the different network cards and adjusts speeds accordingly, at the same time. So if you have some computers with 10 Mbps cards and some with 100 Mbps cards, buy a switch to take advantage of the speed.

The next step is to determine the number of devices you need to connect to the network. List all computers, printers, servers, and such. You may want to connect your printer to a computer for print management, or connect it directly to the hub or switch. You need to choose a hub or switch with at least the number of ports required to connect all the devices you want on the network. You also want to plan for the near future, so buy a hub or switch with more ports than you currently need. It's usually less expensive to buy a hub or switch that enables your network to grow than to buy an all-new hub later.

Figure 9-7 illustrates a three-port hub made specifically for home networking. Don't buy a small hub unless you're sure your network isn't going to grow beyond that number of hubs.

Note   You can connect printers directly to the hub with the help of a network interface, such as Hewlett-Packard's JetDirect, costing anywhere from $170 to $370. See Chapter 15 for more information.

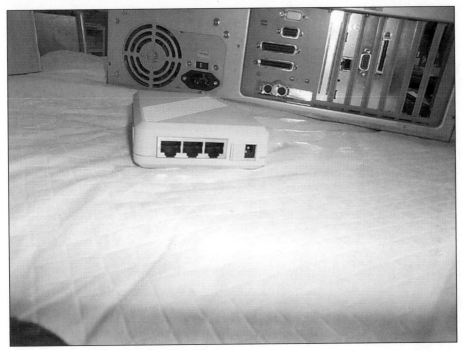

Figure 9-7: Small hubs work well in the home.

When looking for a hub or switch, search for one with a crossover, or uplink, port. The crossover port is specially designed for plugging in another hub or switch, and thus expanding the network. That way, you can build your spanning tree topology as your network grows. Hub and switch prices vary, but generally they are inexpensive. When comparison shopping, price a hub per port instead of per complete hub. Ethernet hubs should sell for less than $8 per port; switches sell for around $10 per port.

Hub and switch warranties range from a couple of months to a lifetime; you should get the lifetime warranty. Look for other benefits, such as technical support, cross-shipping of replacement parts and products, and so on.

You can start with a hub or switch with three, four, or five ports, usually one of those ports is for adding another hub. You also might want to use patch cables — short, flexible, twisted-pair cables that connect the NIC to the hub. Patch cables cut down on the twisting and kinking of the solid cabling you use to connect computers. See Chapter 6 for more information.

You might want to start with a larger hub or switch, such as an 8- or 12-port hub, depending on the number of computers and other devices you'll attach to your network. Figure 9-8 illustrates a 12-port, 100 Mbps hub. This hub is also called stackable because it's flat on the top and bottom. In larger networks, you can stack one hub on top of another to expand the network. Also note that this hub has LED lights to show when the connections are working.

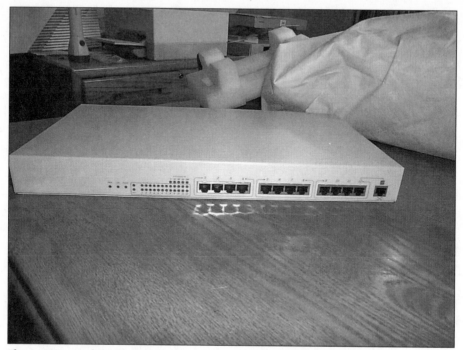

Figure 9-8: Use larger hubs or switches for your network when necessary.

Following are some more features you should look for in a hub or switch:

✦ **LED lights**—These indicate when the hub is turned on, when it's working, and collision status. Collisions are quite common with some networking technologies. A collision occurs when two or more computers try to transmit data simultaneously. Both computers stop transmitting and retransmit after a random period of time. If the LED that indicates collisions is constantly lit up, then you know there are too many collisions on the network.

✦ **IEEE 802.x specifications**—IEEE specifications mean the hub complies with a full set of processes as required by the IEEE. The processes might involve collision-handling, retransmitting packets, link tests, and other functions.

✦ **Repeater functions**—Repeater functions refer to the retransmission of network packets when a collision or timing problem takes place. Timing losses might occur when there is distortion because of cabling interference, signal loss, jitter (instability in the transmission), or some other problem. Data transmission is more reliable when a hub has repeater functions.

The price of switches has fallen considerably in the last year. Hub and switch manufacturers that make good networking hubs include Belkin, NETGEAR, 3Com, and Linksys.

Installing a hub or switch

There's really very little to installing a hub or switch. You should place the device in a central area where it will be convenient. After plugging the network cable into the network card, you can run the cable to the device and plug it into any open port.

You should label each cable on the hub or switch with a number or name so that you know where it leads, in case you have trouble with that computer's connection. You can use patch cables to make the connection stronger and more reliable.

If you plan to use the hub or switch to connect only computers, you'll have no problem. If you plan to use the hub or switch to connect another hub so that you can extend your network, you must check the device's documentation to discover how to set it for this function.

Tip   If you plan to daisy-chain hubs and switches, put the switch at the top of the daisy chain and connect only hubs into it. A better solution is to daisy-chain only hubs with hubs or only switches with switches.

For two hubs or switches to communicate with each other, the transmitter of one device must be connected to the receiver of the other device. Most hubs and switches provide an uplink or crossover port that accomplishes this task; but not all devices include this uplink port. If you do not find the uplink port on your hub or switch, you can use a crossover cable to do the same thing.

You can purchase a crossover cable for use with hubs. Crossover cables are wired differently than straight-through cables but are still made of unshielded twisted-pair cabling. Straight-through cables are your normal UTP cables for use from computer to hub.

Purchasing and Installing an Access Point or Base Station

If you choose wireless technology for your network, then depending on the range and size of your network, you'll need one or more access points and/or base stations. (As mentioned, the two devices are basically the same thing; however, Apple calls their AirPort access points base stations and uses that term in wireless discussions.)

You need an access point or base station only if the range between your computers demands a boost for data to transfer efficiently and effectively. For more information about wireless networks, see Chapter 7.

In some cases, wireless RF between adapter cards can reach 100 feet without using an access point; in other cases, 20 feet might be the limit. The range depends on interference, standards, the cards you bought, and other factors. You might want to experiment with your cards before purchasing an access point or base station. If, on the other hand, you have a large area to cover, you can go ahead and buy one access point and add others as you need them.

Purchasing an access point or base station

As with other technologies, you must make sure the access point or base station matches the standards of the adapter cards. If you purchased 802.11b cards, then purchase 802.11b access points or base stations. If you purchased 802.11g cards, then you can use 802.11g access points or base stations.

Access points for a home network cost around $90 to $100. Manufacturers of access points include NETGEAR, Linksys, and Belkin. If you're using wireless in your small business, you might want to spend a bit more on an access point so you can more efficiently and securely transmit data in your business. Again, NETGEAR, Linksys, and Belkin are manufacturers of good wireless products, but expect to pay around $500 for an access point you can use in a work environment.

Microsoft, Proxim, and other manufacturers make base stations; however, Apple's AirPort series is the official base station for Mac wireless networking. If you purchase another brand of base station, confirm that it is compatible with Macs. Prices of AirPort Base Stations vary from $175 to $275.

For either an access point or a base station, make sure to check the device for the following:

✦ Compatible with your operating system and computer

✦ Compatible with the standard: 802.11b, for example

✦ Appropriate connector types—USB, RJ-45, and so on

✦ Compatible interface—radio frequency

✦ Adequate encryption—64- and/or 128-bit WEP

✦ Check bandwidth—2.4 MHz, for example

✦ Check transfer rate—54 Mbps, for example

✦ Check range for indoors and outdoors, if applicable

✦ Compatible data link protocol—Fast Ethernet and 802.11g, for example

✦ Warranty and technical support

Installing an access point or base station

The main thing to remember about the access point is to place it in a central location in the home. You want the radio frequencies to transmit to the rooms that have your computers in them, yet you do not want your data transmitted to the street and the neighbors. See Chapter 7 for more information about access point or base station placement.

You can install an access point or base station quickly and easily. If your network is only wireless, with no wired computers, place the access point near one of your computers, plug in the power, and insert the CD with the management software. Configure the access point by following directions, and the wireless network will effortlessly connect to the adapter cards in your computers.

Chapter 7 explains the setup and installation of the software and hardware. One point to remember is if you have two or three access points, you must configure each of them with the same SSID, WEP encryption, and so on so they can communicate.

Working with a Router

In the past, most routers were used only with large, corporate networks. Routers were expensive and difficult to configure. But in recent years, routers have become useful for attaching home and small-business networks to the Internet. Routers provide a link from an Ethernet or wireless network to the Internet connection, whether the connection is via dial-up, cable modem, or DSL.

Routers are efficient and secure; they protect your network with firewalls, smart transporting of data, and superfast speeds. Some routers include a switch so you need no other device to connect your computers to each other and to the Internet.

The routers that are most popular in home and small-business networking are those that enable multiple computers to connect to one Internet connection. You can purchase SoHo routers for around $130 to serve all your home networking needs.

 Cross-Reference For more information on routers and setting them up for a shared Internet connection, see Chapter 16.

Summary

In this chapter, you learned about purchasing and installing networking hardware, including the following:

✦ Network interface cards

✦ Hubs and switches

✦ Access points and base stations

✦ Routers

In the next chapter, you learn about configuring networking software.

✦　　✦　　✦

Configuring Networking Software

Before you can attach to the network, you must install and configure several programs that enable the computers to communicate and share information. The programs include a protocol, the client for the network, and software that makes the network interface card work with the network. Some operating systems take care of most of the configuration for you; others simply supply the software for you to configure.

Networking hardware (cables, cards, and so on), when attached to your computers, cannot communicate with each other without networking software. The networking software, installed on the computer, enables the hardware to do its work.

Understanding Networking Software

In Windows, you have four different networking software components that you must add to the computer to enable networking: adapter, client, protocol, and service. You also must set your computer's identification and access control before you can begin networking.

Other operating systems, such as a Mac OS or Linux, use similar networking software. You can buy a Mac with built-in Ethernet (meaning the network card comes installed). You can change protocols, for example, and share (a service), but you don't have to set a client or adapter. In Linux, you can use a program called Samba to handle all of the Windows networking tasks — such as sharing and so on.

Note   This chapter deals more with Windows than it does with Macintosh and Linux because so many versions of operating systems for Macintosh and Linux exist; however, when appropriate, configuring software in those operating systems is covered.

Windows includes everything you need to configure the networking software for a workgroup network and most client/server networks. If you're using a client/server network, you should check the server documentation to make sure that you want to use Windows' software elements. Some network operating systems (NOSs) require specific networking software; other NOSs provide alternative software.

Note Setting up the networking software on Windows 98 is a manual task. Setting up networking software on Windows ME, 2000, or XP is a different story. You can, of course, change networking settings for these operating systems, but the easiest thing about more recent Microsoft OSs is they sense the network and configure themselves.

In Windows, you install the four networking software components in the Network dialog box, as described in the section "Installing and Configuring the Network Software" later in this chapter.

Defining adapters

Adapter is another word for a network interface card (NIC). In Windows networking, an adapter refers to the software driver that makes the card work. The adapter driver is the program that enables the network interface card to communicate with the computer and over the network.

Windows includes multiple software drivers for NICs, listed by manufacturer and network card name. You also can supply drivers from floppy disks or CD-ROMs that come with your network card; alternatively, you can download updated drivers from the Internet and install them on your Windows computer. It is important to use the right driver for your operating system; check to make sure you're installing the XP driver, for example, if you're using a Windows XP operating system.

Tip Always install the latest version of a NIC driver to ensure that the card works efficiently with Windows. It's important to note that the drivers on the manufacturer's disk that comes with your NIC are not necessarily the most recent versions. For the best solution, check the manufacturer's site on the Internet.

If you cannot find an updated version of the adapter driver, you can use one of the Windows drivers. Windows includes drivers for Adaptec, Dell, Hewlett-Packard, Belken, Intel, Linksys, 3Com, and many more.

The adapter driver you install in Windows must match the card you physically install in your computer. See Chapter 9 for more information about installing a network interface card.

Note When you first turn on your computer after installing a Plug and Play network card, Windows detects the card and prompts you to install the network driver. You can let Windows install the driver and complete the task. Later, you can add an updated driver, change the driver, or leave the adapter configured as is.

Defining the network client

The *network client* is the software that enables your computer to become a member of a network. Each network type—Windows networking, Novell NetWare, and so on—has its own specific client. You install the client software for the network type on a computer to enable the computer to communicate over the network.

Microsoft's networks, for example, include a Microsoft Windows client that works with workgroups or client/server. Microsoft supplies clients for its own networks, plus clients for other networks, such as NetWare.

Novell NetWare supplies clients for its NOS. If you set up a client/server network with NetWare, you may want to use Novell's client, because it offers more features on that particular network than the Windows NetWare client does. The Novell client, however, also offers more compatibility problems with Windows.

Tip   Always try to use one of Microsoft's clients when possible, because Microsoft's client software works best with Windows.

Defining protocols

Protocols are languages that define the procedures to follow when transmitting and receiving data. Protocols define the format, timing, sequence, and error checking used on the network.

In networking, many protocols work on many levels. Ethernet, for example, is a networking technology and a protocol, as is token ring. These are communications protocols that guarantee the synchronization and flow of data from computer to computer.

The networking protocols that must be configured, however, are transport protocols, which actually send the messages and data from one computer to another. The transport protocols include NetBIOS (Network Basic Input/Output System) Extended User Interface (NetBEUI) or NetBIOS-compatible transport protocol, Transmission Control Protocol/Internet Protocol (TCP/IP), and Internet Packet Exchange/Sequenced Packet Exchange (IPX/SPX).

You do not generally use all three of these protocols on your network; you use only one. However, you might have various operating systems and network operating systems that require you use two or even all three protocols. For example, you might use IPX/SPX if you have a Novell server or use NetWare within your network; you can use NetBEUI to communicate between your Windows computers; then you use TCP/IP to communicate between Linux or with the Internet. You can also, however, use TCP/IP for all three purposes. Windows supplies versions of the following protocols that you can install. You can use any of the three protocols with most networking topologies and technologies.

NetBEUI

NetBEUI is a Microsoft protocol you can use with any Windows operating system. NetBIOS is a programming interface for developing client/server applications; NetBIOS also works with other protocols and various network types.

It's easy to set up, it provides good performance, and it's a fast protocol. NetBEUI uses very little memory and also provides good error detection over the network. NetBEUI is sometimes used for small local area networks but cannot work with larger LANs or wide area networks. You cannot use NetBEUI with other operating systems, such as a Mac OS. NetBEUI doesn't enable packet forwarding on routed networks, so if you use a WAN, NetBEUI won't work for you.

TCP/IP

TCP/IP is the protocol of the Internet, but you also can use it on your home or office network. TCP/IP consists of many different protocols that encompass media access, file transfer, electronic mail, and more. A group of protocols is called a *protocol stack*; the stack refers to the fact that each protocol in the group builds on or acts as a foundation for another protocol. TCP/IP is versatile and fast, and it provides a wide variety of options for configuration.

At first glance, TCP/IP looks difficult to configure. You must create a numbering system for network addresses when you use TCP/IP in your home network. However, after you choose your numbering system, the rest is easy. In addition, TCP/IP works with a variety of operating systems, including Macintosh OSs, Linux, Unix, and Windows.

Cross-Reference   See Appendix B for more information and complete instructions for setting up a TCP/IP network.

TCP/IP is often used with Microsoft workgroup networks, Windows 2000 Server networks, NetWare, and others. Because TCP/IP is also used with the Internet, there is sometimes confusion about this protocol. When you install TCP/IP on your LAN, it is totally separate from using TCP/IP with your Internet dial-up connection. The addresses are different; the networks are different. For more information, see Chapter 16.

Note   For more information about network security, see *Network Security For Dummies* by Chey Cobb (Wiley Publishing, Inc. 2002). This book contains basic network security practices that apply to home and SoHo network users.

IPX/SPX

IPX/SPX is a protocol frequently used with Novell NetWare networks, although you also can use it with Microsoft networks. IPX/SPX is another protocol stack, and the protocol defines how network packets are delivered on the network.

Setting Up TCP/IP Quickly

If you want to set up a TCP/IP network, you can easily do it without going into any more detail than what is here in this sidebar. If you don't plan to connect your home or small-business network to the Internet, for creating your own Web server, you can use IP addresses that are specifically reserved for private networks. Your network will be safe from intruders, secure from the network, and even unreachable from any other network.

IP addresses need two numbers: a number for the computer (called an *IP address*) and a number for the network segment (called a *subnet*). All computers on the same segment — that is, all computers in your home or small-business network — use the same subnet. All computers use nearly the same IP address — with just one or two numbers' difference between them.

For an example, suppose you have four computers on your network. The subnet or subnet mask number is 255.255.255.0 for each computer. That number remains the same. As for the IP addresses, each one must be unique, but not too unique. So the first computer's IP address is 192.168.1.1, the second is 192.168.1.2, the third is 192.168.1.3, and the fourth is 192.168.1.4. It's as simple as that.

If you add more computers, you add to the last number: 192.168.1.6 on up to 192.168.1.255. You can have 256 (192.168.1.0 is also usable) computers on your network using this numbering scheme, and you don't have to know any more about TCP/IP than that. If you do decide to use 255 or 0 as the last number in the IP address, make sure the software and devices you're using are compatible with those numbers. Check the documentation for clarification.

IPX/SPX works with Microsoft networks. It supports many Windows features, including NetBIOS, Windows sockets (which provide an interface between Windows and TCP/IP networking), and others. Microsoft's IPX/SPX is also easy to install; however, unless you have a specific reason for using IPX/SPX, you should probably stick with TCP/IP or NetBEUI. Microsoft designed NetBEUI specifically for the Windows network, and it operates with less traffic than IPX/SPX. Also, IPX/SPX uses a NetWare file and printer sharing utility instead of Microsoft file and printer sharing.

Defining services

In networking, server machines offer *services* — such as printing, Internet access, backup and restore, authentication, and so on. In a workgroup network, services are limited. Windows offers services for file and printer sharing. You can choose to share your files and printers with others on the network, or you can limit the shares, if you want.

Windows 2000 and XP offer quality of service (QoS) and the service advertising protocol. QoS prioritizes the one type of traffic over the others when data transfers across a network so that the data transmission is more efficient. QoS is useful only on WANs that use a variety of technologies to transfer data, such as fiber, frame relay, Asynchronous Transfer Mode (ATM), and so on.

Tip QoS can be a great addition to your network if your network is a WAN or enterprise network. If you use QoS and find that some programs don't work as well as they should — for example, a scheduling program takes a long time to start — remove the QoS service to see if you notice any improvements. Sometimes QoS slows some programs down.

The Service Advertising Protocol (SAP) is another service for large networks. SAP keeps a list of servers and services on a network WAN or LAN, and it broadcasts these services to all user computers on the network. Neither of these services is useful to a home network or a small-business network.

Tip If you're using a Windows 98 or XP computer as a server on your home network and you don't want to share the other computers' resources, you can enable the file and printer sharing service on just the server. Enabling file and printer sharing makes that one computer into a server and protects the files and resources of the other computers.

Installing and Configuring the Network Software

Windows has the elements you need to network your computer from the time you install the operating system. In addition to programs such as the Network Neighborhood or My Network Places, which enable you to view other computers on the network, Windows provides the networking software you need to communicate with other computers on the network.

Cross-Reference For more information about the Network Neighborhood and My Network Places, see Chapter 14.

You can use the Windows Control Panel to install and configure the network software. The Control Panel is a program that enables you to manage settings such as passwords, date and time, your display, mouse, keyboard, and so on. The Control Panel also contains tools for adding hardware and software to your computer.

You open the Control Panel by choosing Start ⇨ Settings ⇨ Control Panel in Windows 98; choose Start ⇨ Control Panel in Windows XP. Figure 10-1 shows the Control Panel with the Network icon displayed. To open the Network dialog box, double-click the Network icon.

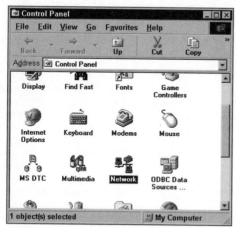

Figure 10-1: Use the Control Panel to configure your computer's settings.

Alternatively, you can right-click the Network Neighborhood or the My Network Places icon and choose Properties. Figure 10-2 shows the Network dialog box that appears in Windows 98 if you right-click the Network Neighborhood. Your Network dialog box may or may not have the same components as shown in the figure.

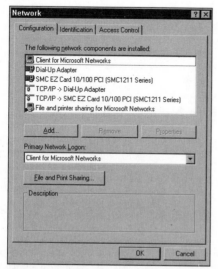

Figure 10-2: The Network dialog box enables you to add and configure your networking software.

If you right-click the My Network Places icon in Windows 2000 or XP, the Network Connections dialog box appears, as shown in Figure 10-3. Your Network Connections dialog box may look different from the one pictured.

Right-click the Local Area Connection and choose Properties. The Local Area Connection dialog box appears, as shown in Figure 10-4.

Figure 10-3: The Local Area Connection is the way to your network settings.

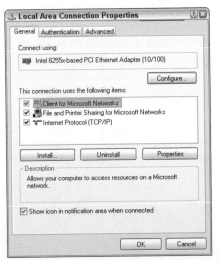

Figure 10-4: The Windows 98 and XP network dialog boxes look different, but they contain similar items.

To show you the difference between a Macintosh and a Windows computer, Figure 10-5 shows the Network dialog box in an iMac OS X. You click the Preferences icon and then the Network icon to get to the Network dialog box.

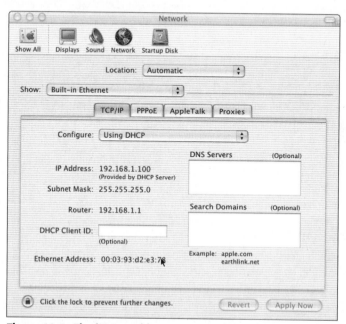

Figure 10-5: The iMac enables you to use the TCP/IP protocol, make changes and additions, and so on.

Each of the following sections describes how to install and configure the networking software.

Tip   As you install and configure the networking software, you should keep a notebook containing the settings for later reference. Enter the network interface card brand and type, any IRQ (an *interrupt request* is a setting that defines which path signals take from the processor to a specific device) or address settings, the protocol used plus configurations, and any other special preparations and provisions you use while setting up the computer. Keep a list for each computer; it will come in handy if you need to format the drive and reinstall the operating system, replace a network card, or otherwise modify your computer settings.

Adding a network adapter

If you have installed a network interface card since you last turned your computer on, and that card is a Plug and Play card, Windows detects the card and guides you through the installation of the adapter driver. If Windows doesn't find the network card, you can complete the following steps to install the driver.

Tip   If you download a driver for your network interface card from the Internet, copy the driver to a floppy disk so that you can install it easily during the steps that follow.

Installing the adapter

If Windows hasn't already recognized your network card and walked you through the installation, or if you've changed network cards, you can add the driver yourself by following these steps.

For Windows 98:

1. In the Network dialog box, click the Add button. The Select Network Component Type dialog box appears, as shown in Figure 10-6.

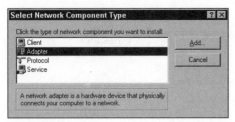

Figure 10-6: Choose the component to add to the network.

2. Choose Adapter and then click the Add button. The Select Network Adapters dialog box appears, as shown in Figure 10-7.

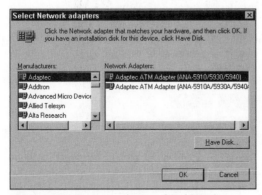

Figure 10-7: You can choose the driver from Windows or use the manufacturer's disk.

3. In the Select Network Adapters dialog box, do one of the following:

   • In the Manufacturers list, choose the manufacturer of your network card; in the Network Adapters list, choose the type of adapter. Click OK.

   • Insert the manufacturer's disk or the disk containing the updated driver in the disk drive, and then click the Have Disk button. Choose the drive and click OK.

When Windows has finished installing the network adapter, it displays the adapter in the Network dialog box, as shown in Figure 10-2. Windows also might install the Client for Microsoft Networks at this time. If it does, that's fine; if it doesn't, you can install it later.

For Windows 2000 or XP:

1. In the Local Area Connection dialog box, click the Configure button. The adapter's information dialog box appears, as shown in Figure 10-8.

Figure 10-8: You can install a new network card to your Windows XP computer.

2. Click the Driver tab. You can uninstall the current driver or update the current driver, depending on the task you want to perform, as shown in Figure 10-9. Follow the directions on-screen to complete the task.

Figure 10-9: Make changes to the existing card.

Tip If you're having trouble with your current network card, you should try updating the driver. If you've tried to update the driver and are still having trouble, try uninstalling the current driver, rebooting, and then installing a new driver. When you reboot the computer, it prompts you to install a driver if it sees a network card is present.

Configuring the adapter

You can configure the adapter at any time. In general, the configuration should be fine the way it is. The Windows operating systems handle configurations without much input from you. If there's a conflict, Windows takes care of the conflict by changing the configuration settings on its own. The Macintosh is similar in configuring network adapters. Generally, the operating systems are smart enough to handle these complex settings on their own.

However, you might need to look at the network card settings, for troubleshooting purposes, for example. You can look at the settings and even tell from the adapter's dialog box if everything is all right with the card.

Tip The first way to check to make sure a card is okay is to look at it in the back of the computer. A green or amber light (check your card's documentation) should be lit to show that the card is working and that the network is aware that the computer is on the network.

To check a Windows 98 computer's network card, follow these steps:

1. Right-click My Computer on the desktop and choose Properties from the menu.

2. Choose the Device Manager tab.

3. Click the plus sign to the left of Network adapters to display the adapter attached to your computer (see Figure 10-10). If you see a red X or a yellow exclamation point (either is called a *splat*) on the network card, you know something is wrong with the NIC.

4. Right-click your network interface card.

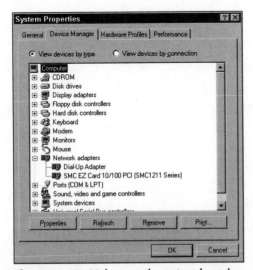

Figure 10-10: Make sure the network card is okay.

5. Choose Properties. The network card's Properties dialog box appears.

6. Check to see if the device is working properly (see Figure 10-11).

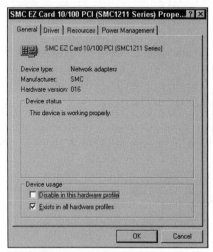

Figure 10-11: Windows lets you know if something is wrong.

7. Click OK to close the dialog box.

If something is wrong with the network card, you should first check connections (the wire connecting the card to the network). If everything is connected properly, see the following section, "Troubleshooting the network card."

For a Windows 2000 or XP computer, follow these steps:

1. Right-click the Local Area Connection in the Network Connections dialog box. Click Properties. The Local Area Connection dialog box appears.

2. Click the Configure button. The network card's dialog box appears.

3. Check the Device status, as shown in Figure 10-12.

4. If the card is working well, click OK. If the card is not working properly, see the next section.

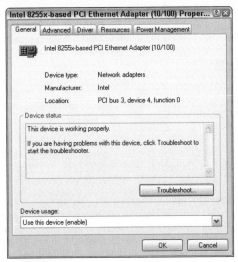

Figure 10-12: Check to make sure the card is working.

Troubleshooting the network card

Always check the connections of your network card when you're having trouble. The connection to the card on the back of your computer should be plugged in correctly, and the other end of that cable — whether to a hub, switch, or other device — should be securely connected.

Tip   Hardware problems are similar whether you're working in Windows, Macintosh, or Linux systems. Most advice in this chapter works for any computer.

You can check to see if the network card and hub or switch are working by checking the LED lights on both. Most network cards have a green light that lights up on the back of your computer when the card is working. If the card isn't working, it may display a red light or no light. The corresponding jack in the hub should also be lit up with a green light if the connection is working, or a red light or no light if it isn't.

If the network card isn't working, you should turn off the computer, remove the case, and reseat the card. This is the most common reason a network card doesn't work initially. To reseat the card, remove the card and then plug it back into the slot again. Make sure you unplug the computer first and that you touch your arm or hand to the case as you reseat the card.

You might also try plugging the network card into a different slot, if you have one open in your computer. Often switching slots will make a difference.

If the adapter has a red X through it in the Device Manager, it likely has been disabled by another application or device. You can enable the adapter by double-clicking the adapter in the list. The Device Properties dialog box appears. In the General tab, make sure that the current configuration is correct. Click OK.

Tip   If you're using Windows 2000 or XP, make sure the card and the driver are supported by the operating system. Windows operating systems built on NT technology work better with certain hardware. That hardware is listed in what Microsoft calls the Hardware Compatibility List (HCL). The HCL comes with Windows 2000 and XP, or you can go to www.microsoft.com and search for HCL for more information.

The current driver could be corrupted. You can uninstall the current driver. You'll have to reboot the computer. Windows finds the device and displays a wizard to help you reinstall it. If that doesn't work, you might want to check the manufacturer's Web site to see if there are any new, updated drivers you can install for your card and operating system.

If the problem started after you recently installed an updated driver, that could be the problem. With Windows 2000 and XP, you can open the Driver tab and click Roll Back Driver to undo the updated installation. If that works, you need a different driver to update the current one.

If the card still doesn't work, try switching the card with another one and see if the second card works. If the second card works, then the first card might be bad. You can return it to the vendor for an exchange or refund. If the second card doesn't work, then try another slot. Again, make sure that you're seating the card properly. See Chapter 9 for more information.

Adding the protocol

You can add any of the three protocols you want — TCP/IP, NetBEUI, or IPX/SPX. Stick with TCP/IP or NetBEUI if you're not using Novell's NetWare.

Note   If you select the protocol and click the Properties button, various options are available to you; it is best, however, to leave these settings as they are unless you understand the consequences of your actions. The bindings and advanced settings, if changed, can make your network nonfunctional.

You must use the same protocol for all computers on the network. You add the protocol in the Network dialog box.

Using Two Adapters in a Computer

You might want to use two NICs in a computer to attach to two different networks. Using two adapters increases security in your network. For example, you can install two NICs into the computer that attaches to the Internet. One network card is used to communicate only with the Internet; the other card is used to communicate only with your private network. Dividing tasks in this way secures the private network from hackers, viruses, worms, and other intruders through the Internet.

Another use for two adapters is to separate two private networks. You might use Novell NetWare on one network and Windows 98 on another, or Linux on one and Windows on another. Configure one network adapter to work with one operating system and the second to work with the other operating system. With this configuration, one computer can be a member of two different networks without the networks sharing information. This could be beneficial to a small business, in particular, when one network contains payroll and invoicing information and the other network contains work orders, shared documents, and so on.

For Windows 98, follow these steps:

1. Open the Network dialog box from the Control Panel.

2. In the Configuration tab, click the Add button. The Select Network Component Type dialog box appears.

3. Select Protocol in the network component list.

4. Click the Add button. The Select Network Protocol dialog box appears.

5. In the list of Manufacturers, choose Microsoft.

6. In the list of Protocols, choose the protocol, as shown in Figure 10-13.

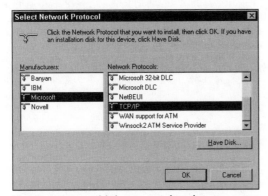

Figure 10-13: Add the protocol to the computer.

7. Click OK to add the protocol. Windows automatically adds the Client for Microsoft Networks to the list of network components, as shown in Figure 10-14.

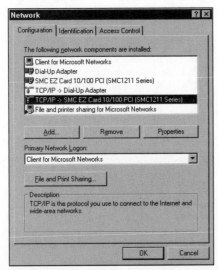

Figure 10-14: Add the protocol and client.

Protocol Properties

Each protocol has specific properties you can configure. In most cases, the Windows default for these properties is sufficient. The only property that's common to all protocols is the bindings option.

Binding is the process of assigning a protocol to the network card. Binding the protocol means the network card uses that particular language to communicate with other network cards on the network. Windows automatically binds the protocol to the card for you.

You change bindings only if you install multiple cards and protocols on your computer. Some server computers, for example, use multiple network cards to communicate with different network operating systems within the same network. A server might communicate with NetWare clients using IPX/SPX on one side of the office and with Windows 2000 or XP clients using TCP/IP on the other side of the office. You might need to change your protocol bindings in a case such as this.

Also, you can set other protocol-related items. You can change the maximum number of simultaneous connections, for example; add or remove links to other systems; and automatically assign addresses to the computer.

To add a protocol in Windows 2000, follow these steps:

1. Right-click the Local Access Connection and choose Properties.

2. In the General tab, click the Install button. The Select Network Component dialog box appears.

3. Click Protocol and click the Add button.

4. Click the protocol and click OK.

For Windows XP, the only protocols included are TCP/IP and IPX. Microsoft has discontinued the inclusion of NetBEUI with the operating system; however, you can install the protocol from the Windows XP CD. NetBEUI is the easiest protocol to configure and use. NetBEUI is in the VALUEADD folder. For information about installing features from the Windows XP CD-ROM, read your documentation or go to www.microsoft.com.

For Macintosh, you have a choice of TCP/IP or AppleTalk as your protocols. Windows file sharing protocol is Server Message Block (SMB), and SMB runs on top of the NetBIOS protocols (one of which is NetBEUI). AppleShare IP supports SMB only through TCP/IP. The implication is, then, if you have a Macintosh on your network with other PCs, you'll need to use TCP/IP. Figure 10-15 shows the Macintosh Network dialog box. The TCP/IP tab is the currently visible tab, but you could choose the AppleTalk tab to configure a Macintosh network.

Similarly, most Linux distributions (distros)—Red Hat, Mandrake, Suse, and others—come with Samba as an option during installation. If you use Samba, you can connect to Windows 2000 and XP servers and within workgroups without much trouble. You just need to create an account on the Windows computer and perform a few other tweaks to the Linux machine to map drives and share folders. You can check the Web site www.justlinux.com for more information.

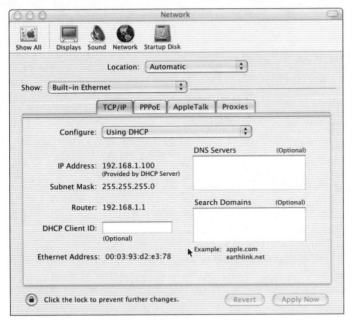

Figure 10-15: Use TCP/IP with Macs.

Note

Samba is open source, as are all Linux distributions and programs; it is also freely available under the GNU General Public License. The GNU General Public License is a project sponsored by Free Software Foundation to provide a freely distributable operating system and software as a replacement for Unix. Samba provides SMB file and print services to clients while providing a Windows-like interface.

Adding the service

In Windows, the service you can add is to enable file and printer sharing on your network. You should add this service if you're on a workgroup network. You may not want to add it on a client/server network if you're using a network operating system such as Windows 2000 Server.

The Mac OS X has a similar service just called Sharing. You can share files, printers, FTP access, and remote login, and you can enable personal Web sharing and Windows file sharing. You can also set up a firewall to prevent the sharing of specific features.

Cross-Reference

See Chapter 16 for more information about firewalls.

For Windows 98, add the service in the Network dialog box by following these steps:

1. In the Configuration tab of the Network dialog box, click the Add button. The Select Network Component Type dialog box appears.

2. Select Service.

3. Click the Add button. The Select Network Service dialog box appears, as shown in Figure 10-16.

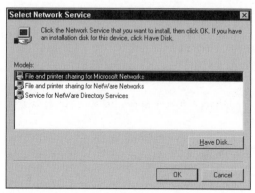

Figure 10-16: Add the Microsoft file and printer sharing service to your network configuration.

4. Click OK, and Windows adds the service to the network components window.

If you want to share your files but not your printer, or your printer but not your files, you can click the File and Print Sharing button in the Configuration tab of the Network dialog box to display the File and Print Sharing dialog box, as shown in Figure 10-17.

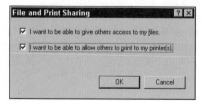

Figure 10-17: You can choose not to share printers or files.

Click the appropriate check box to clear it if you do not want to share your files or printer with others on the network. Then click OK.

Note

The Primary Network Logon drop-down box in the Configuration tab of the Network dialog box in Windows 98 is useful to you only if you're a member of two or more networks. If you're a workgroup network group member, the primary logon reads Client for Microsoft Networks.

If you choose the Windows Logon, you log on to Windows but not the network.

If, however, you belong to both a NetWare and a Windows 2000 Server network, you can use this drop-down box to choose which network you prefer to log on to first.

For information about logging on to the network, see Chapter 13.

To add the service in Windows 2000 or XP, follow these steps:

1. Right-click the Local Area Connection in the Network Connections dialog box. The Local Area Connection Properties dialog box appears.

2. In the General tab, click the Install button. The Select Network Component dialog box appears.

3. Click Service and click OK. The Select Network Service dialog box appears (see Figure 10-18).

Figure 10-18: Install file and printer sharing.

4. Click OK. Close the Local Area Connection Properties dialog box. Add the service you want.

5. Click OK to close the dialog box.

For Macintosh OS X, follow these steps:

1. Open the System Preferences dialog box.

2. Under the Internet & Network section, click Sharing, as shown in Figure 10-19. The Sharing dialog box appears.

3. In the Services tab, click the check boxes of those services you want to share, as shown in Figure 10-20. Click the Close button when you are done.

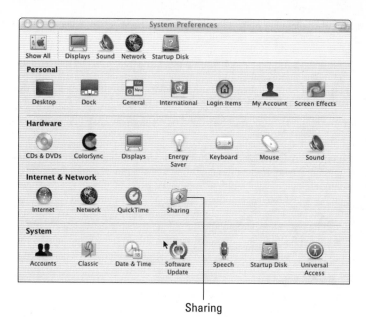

Sharing

Figure 10-19: Choose to share services on the Mac.

Figure 10-20: Share files, printers, Windows files, and other services on the Mac.

Again with Linux, you can install several sharing services, depending on the distribution and program you're installing.

Completing the installation

When you have finished adding the networking software, click OK in the Network dialog box. Windows 98 prompts you to restart Windows. You must do this in order to complete the installation of the network. Windows 2000 and XP and Macs do not usually need to be restarted. Linux sometimes does but mostly doesn't need rebooting.

After Windows 98 starts, open the Control Panel and the Network dialog box again. The dialog box now displays three tabs instead of one — the Configuration, Identification, and Access Control tabs.

You must identify your computer to the network. In the computer identification, you specify a computer name, workgroup, and (optionally) a computer description. The computer name is the name that represents this computer on the network; this name must be unique. The workgroup name is one group of computers that can share among themselves; this name must be the same for all computers in the group. Finally, the computer description is optional; you may want to list the type of computer, the processor, brand, or other information in this text box.

In Windows 2000 and XP, you identify the computer name and workgroup in the System Properties dialog box, Computer Name tab. Open the System Properties dialog box by right-clicking the My Computer icon. Figure 10-21 shows the dialog box with the Computer Name tab.

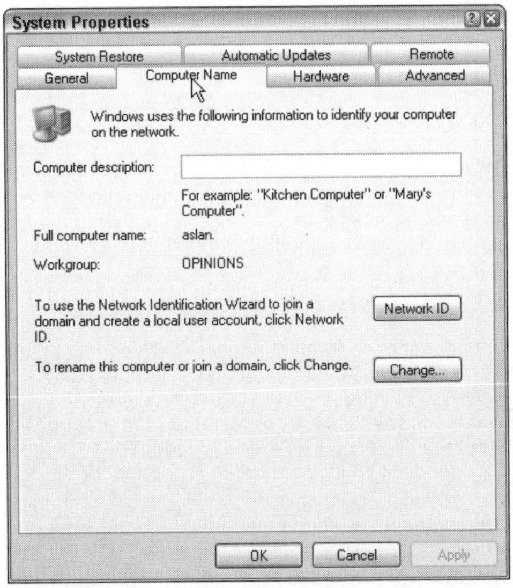

Figure 10-21: Name the computer and the workgroup.

On a Macintosh OS X computer, the computer name is found in the Sharing dialog box from the System Preferences dialog box.

Using Separate Workgroups in a Small Business

If you have several computers at work where some computers don't need to see others on the network, you can specify different workgroups for the computers. Suppose that you have three users who work with customers and billing. These users' computers share a printer, files, and other resources. You can make these computers members of the same workgroup.

In another part of the office, you have four other users who work with stock, inventory, and company forms. They have their own printers and shared folders and files. These users have no need to view or share resources with the other group of users. Put these users in their own workgroup.

Using separate workgroups cuts down on the network traffic and makes it easier for users to find what they need without wading though more files than necessary.

To identify your computer to the network in Windows 98, follow these steps:

1. In the Configuration tab of the Network dialog box, select the Identification tab, as shown in Figure 10-22.

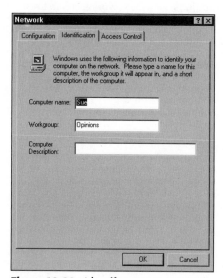

Figure 10-22: Identify your computer to the network.

2. In the Computer Name text box, enter a unique name for the computer. It could be a person's name, for example.

3. In the Workgroup text box, enter the name of your workgroup. It could be your family's last name, for example. The workgroup name must be the same on all computers on the network, unless you have multiple workgroups, as in a client/server network.

4. You can enter a computer description, if you want.

5. Click OK. You must restart your computer when Windows prompts you. Click Yes to restart the computer.

The installation is now complete. You need to repeat these steps with each computer on the network. Add the same client, protocol, and service to each computer. Add the adapter software appropriate to the network interface card installed on each computer.

Note Make sure that you use a unique computer name but the same workgroup name for all computers.

To identify your computer to the network in Windows 2000 or XP, follow these steps:

1. Open the System Properties dialog box and select the Computer Name tab.

2. Click the Change button. The Computer Name Changes dialog box appears, as shown in Figure 10-23.

Figure 10-23: Change your name or the workgroup.

3. Make any changes you want.

4. Click OK and OK again to close the dialog boxes.

When you have finished installing the networking software on all computers, your next step is to share drives, folders, files, and peripherals. For information about sharing, see Chapter 12.

Using Access Control

The Access Control tab of the Network dialog box offers two options for controlling access to shared resources: share-level and user-level. You should use share-level access for a workgroup network. User-level works best with a client/server network, such as NT Server or NetWare. The default option is share-level, so you don't have to make any changes to this tab.

Share-level access control enables you to supply a password for each shared resource. So, if you want to share a folder or printer, you can assign a password to that resource. Only people who know the password can access that resource. Also, you don't have to use passwords for sharing resources, but you have the capability if you want to use it.

User-level access control works by assigning specific users or groups of users access to resources on the computer. Client/server networks use groups for authentication and permissions purposes; thus, user-level access works better in that environment. Access control is available in Windows 98, 2000, and XP.

Summary

In this chapter, you've learned to install and configure the networking software, including the following:

✦ Network adapter software

✦ Protocols

✦ Clients

✦ Services

In the next chapter, you learn about adding various operating systems to your network.

✦   ✦   ✦

Accessing the Network with Various Operating Systems

If your computers run the Windows operating system, configuration for the network should go smoothly. However, you might be running other operating systems, or even computers other than PCs — such as Macintoshes, handheld computers, and so on. If you have a Macintosh or a Linux, for example, you can add it to your network for file and printer sharing. Working with various operating systems can make things more complex, but it is possible.

Understanding Additions to the Network

A Windows workgroup network works best with Windows 98, 2000, and XP computers. Because of the operating systems and networking software involved, these computers use the same elements. For that reason, your network connection problems are few.

Additionally, using Windows clients, or workstations, on a client/ server network makes consistent and reliable connections easy. Everything is configured similarly, equipment is similar, and your job of keeping the network up and running is fairly simple.

When you start adding various other operating systems to either network, however, you start adding possible problems. Each computer using a different operating system or different equipment can cause problems that aren't as easy to solve, because you might be unfamiliar with the network components and because compatibility is always an issue with new or different hardware and software.

You can add various operating systems and devices to your system. Sometimes you need third-party applications, special hardware, and some tweaking of the system, and sometimes the operating systems connect easily.

Small Business Tip

You are more likely to have other operating systems in a small-business setting than at home. Macs and Linux integrate well, but older computers with older operating systems add more difficulty. Although you can integrate these computers into your PC network, you should consider upgrading any older PCs and operating systems for more efficient use of your applications and the network. Upgrade as many computers and operating systems as you can to Windows XP Professional before you start adding them to the network.

Figure 11-1 illustrates some of the possibilities in your home network. You can connect a notebook, an iMac, and a Linux machine to an Ethernet network on which a Windows 98 computer is also attached to a handheld device. All computers can share files and printers in the network.

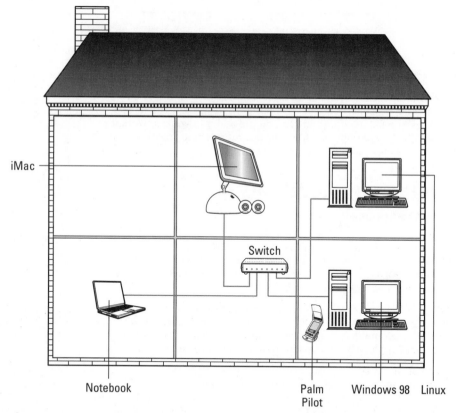

Figure 11-1: Attach a variety of computers to your home network.

Adding to a workgroup network

You are most likely to want to add an odd operating system or nonstandard equipment to a home workgroup network. After all, you might have a Linux computer your daughter uses for learning more about computers, or your spouse might be using a tablet computer for calendars, task lists, and e-mail.

Depending on how much trouble you want to tackle, you can add these and other computers to your network. You can use the following operating systems and types of computers in the same workgroup network:

✦ Windows 95/98

✦ Windows Me

✦ Windows 2000

✦ Windows XP Home or Professional

✦ Macintosh computers using System 9 or OS X

✦ Linux with Samba support

✦ Portable computers

✦ Handheld computers

✦ Tablets

You can add other operating systems, such as Macintosh System 7 or 8, but those aren't covered in this book because the older the operating system, the more difficult it is to add to a workgroup network. Also, operating systems that aren't commonly used or the newest of the technology may pose some problems as well. If you want to learn how to add a computer that's not listed here, you can search the Internet and perhaps find help there. You might look at `www.networking.ittoolbox.com` for more information.

Adding to a client/server network

If you're using a Windows 98 or XP computer as your server, you won't have much trouble connecting other operating systems to the computer. They'll act like a workgroup network in connections and data transfer; the difference is your configuration of the "server" and how much data you share.

See Chapter 12 for more information about sharing resources.

Adding various operating systems and portable computers to a client/server network is fairly easy when you use the network operating system Windows 2000 Server. Windows 2000 Server includes clients for most any Windows operating system, plus Windows 2000 Server can service Macintosh and Linux clients, as well. Following are the Windows and other operating systems Windows 2000 Server can work with:

✦ Windows 98

✦ Windows 2000 Professional

✦ Windows XP Professional

✦ Macintosh 9 and OS X

✦ Linux with Samba support

✦ Tablets

✦ Portable computers

You also might be able to find other client software with the network operating system or in third-party packages. Both NT Server and NetWare include client software for Macintosh computers. NT Server is an older operating system, but many people still use it; because of its age, you might not find a way to connect with newer clients, such as Macintosh OS X. If you're using something other than Windows 2000 Server as a network operating system (NOS), see the specific NOS documentation for more information about installing and configuring the client computers.

Small Business Tip

If you run a small business and you're using a workgroup or a client/server network, you should upgrade all computers to run compatible operating systems on the client computers. Using various operating systems on your network takes more time to administer, manage, and troubleshoot.

Adding a Windows-based computer versus a non-Windows-based computer

Naturally, adding Windows computers to a Windows network is easier than using a different operating system. Windows operating systems are similar in networking software, configuration, operation, and other processes. However, Windows operating systems can still cause problems on a network of all Windows computers.

You will find times when one Windows computer won't see another on the network, times when they won't share, and times when the computers won't print to each other's printers. And you will also have those problems when you add a different non-Windows operating system to your network. That's just the way networking is. Sometimes it works very well for months; then everything falls apart for seemingly no reason.

Cross-Reference

When that happens, and it will, take a look at Appendix A in this book for some tips and help on troubleshooting your network connections.

But don't let the fact that all your computers are not Windows 98 or Windows XP Professional keep you from trying to network them. Usually, you can connect various computers and operating systems, and being able to share files and printers makes it worthwhile.

Using Various Windows Operating Systems

Most operating systems you'll want to add to your workgroup network probably will be Windows. Computers running Windows 98, Me, 2000, and XP are all capable of existing and sharing on a network together. Configuration is similar for all Windows operating systems, with just a different look to a dialog box or different terminology. However, some Windows operating systems don't work well with client/server networks or with workgroups containing more than five users. Each Windows operating system is covered in this section.

Apple has made it easy to add Mac to Windows networks and to share files and printers with them. Older Mac operating systems, such as System 7 or 8, need help connecting by use of a third-party program. However, Mac OS X is easy to connect to the network and enables you to view other Windows computers and use their files and printers.

Linux is another matter altogether. Linux has so many different distributions that it is difficult to discuss in a book like this. If you know Linux and you understand its features, you can easily add it to a Windows network, however.

Adding Windows XP

Windows XP comes in two editions: Home and Professional. The Home Edition is not as full of features as the Professional Edition of Windows XP. As for networking, Windows XP Home Edition has built-in support for workgroup networking, but to include only five computers. In addition, you cannot connect to a server with a true NOS or a domain. (A *domain* is a way to divide large networks into smaller segments; you won't need a domain in your home or small-business office.)

Note Microsoft also has an edition of Windows XP for the tablet PC. Windows XP for the tablet is very much the same as Windows XP for a desktop or notebook, especially in networking. The few differences with the operating system have to do with inputting information. For more about the tablet PC, see the section, "Considering tablets" later in this chapter.

Small Business Tip You might not need a domain in your small-business office, but many small businesses use domains. You can use a domain to learn more about Windows 2000 Server, or you can use a domain in case you plan to expand your business, merge your business, or extend the business to remote sites in the future. If you do plan to use domains in your network, make sure you use Windows XP Professional instead of Windows XP Home Edition.

Setting Up the Network

With either the Home Edition or the Professional Edition, Windows XP detects the presence of a network card and automatically creates a connection named Local Area Connection. The network card can be of any type: wireless, Ethernet, phone line, or power line. The Local Area Connection is located in the Network Connections folder, as shown in Figure 11-2. Open the Network Connections dialog box by right-clicking the My Network Places and choosing Properties.

You open the Local Area Connection by right-clicking it and choosing Properties. The connection shows the type of card that Windows XP detected, as shown in Figure 11-3. Chapter 10 explains how to configure the card and to install the network software necessary to complete the network. See that chapter for more information.

Figure 11-2: The Local Area Connection appears when Windows XP detects a network card.

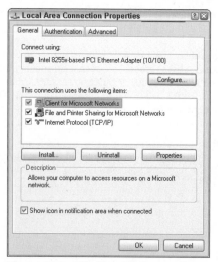

Figure 11-3: Windows XP detects the network card automatically.

When Windows XP locates the network card, it automatically installs the Client for Microsoft Networks, file and printer sharing, the QoS Packet Scheduler (which enables programs to reserve bandwidth when they need it), and the TCP/IP protocol.

Note   In Windows XP, TCP/IP is a core element of the operating system that cannot be uninstalled.

You can always make changes to the network settings or set up a network manually. For example, when you click Start ➪ Settings ➪ and Network Connections in Windows XP, under Network Tasks, you can click Create a New Connection. You have the choice of the following types of network connections:

✦ Connect to the Internet

✦ Connect to the network at your place of work or other location

✦ Connect to a home network

✦ Set up a connection for a serial, parallel, or infrared port (direct cable connection)

Using the Network Setup Wizard

Windows XP includes a Network Setup Wizard that works with Windows 98, Me, and XP computers. The Network Setup Wizard sets the XP computer on which you run it as an Internet Connection Sharing server. Internet Connection Sharing (ICS) enables other computers on the network to share the Internet connection with the ICS server. The computer with the ICS installed also has the connection to the Internet, and it serves as the ICS host. The Windows XP Network Setup Wizard doesn't run on Windows 95, NT 4, or 2000.

Note   It is important to note that your Internet service provider may have a policy against two or more people sharing a connection. Check with your ISP to be sure. For more information about ICS, see Chapter 16.

You can use the ICS if you do not have other computers, such as a Linux, Mac, or Windows 2000 computer, on your network. A version of ICS is available for use with Windows 2000 computers. ICS for Windows 2000 and Windows XP are compatible and work well together; just don't try to install ICS for Windows 2000 on an XP machine or ICS for Windows XP on a 2000 machine. There are also some limitations to ICS, such as its limit to IP addresses, limited use with a domain server, and so on; but in a home networking environment, you most likely won't have any trouble with it.

Tip   If you're adding a Windows XP computer to an existing network, don't run the ICS wizard on the other computers. You want the XP computer to conform to your network instead of the other way around.

Adding Windows 2000

Windows 2000 Professional is the client version of the former NT 4 operating system. The server versions are called Windows 2000 Server and Windows 2000 Advanced Server. The interface is similar to other Windows operating systems, but the Windows 2000 operating system is much more automated than previous versions. It also uses many wizards to help in setup and configuration.

The taskbar leads to the Start button and a set of familiar menus: Programs, Settings, Find, Help, and so on. You'll also notice that many of the Windows programs work the same way.

Setting up the network

You can easily add a Windows 2000 computer to a workgroup or client/server network. All you have to do is install a network interface card and cable, or use wireless, phone line networking, or power line networking, and connect the computer to a local area network. Windows 2000 takes care of the rest by installing the adapter driver, the protocol already in use on the network, client, and service. Networking is easier than ever.

You also can set up other network connections with the help of a wizard. You can choose the type of network from the Set Up Group Wizard as follows:

✦ Dial-up to private network

✦ Dial-up to the Internet

✦ Connect to a private network through the Internet

✦ Accept incoming connections

✦ Connect directly to another computer (as in a Direct Cable Connection)

As you continue using the wizard, you answer questions relative to the type of network to which you're attaching. When you're finished, Windows takes care of everything else and connects your computer to that network.

Configuring the network

Windows 2000 leaves little for you to configure; however, you can make changes to the client, service, protocol, and adapter settings in a Network dialog box similar to the one in Windows 98. To configure networking software, simply right-click a connection and view the Properties of that connection.

You can also use the Device Manager to set the adapter card configurations, just as you would in Windows 98 or XP.

Using Windows Me

Windows Me, or Millennium Edition, is a popular operating system used in homes because it is advertised as easy and automatic. The operating system is set up for small workgroup situations.

Small Business Tip

You cannot access a domain or server with Windows Me. If you have Windows Me in your workplace, upgrade it to Windows XP Professional before putting it on a network. Even if you use it in a workgroup situation, you're liable to have more problems than successes with it.

Networking with Windows Me is pretty automatic, but the operating system does have some problems when it comes to networking.

Tip

Make sure you download and install the Windows Me patch from Microsoft at http://support.Microsoft.com/support/kb/articles/Q272/9/91.asp. Read the article there for help with some networking problems as well.

Windows Me is an easy-to-use operating system for one computer in your home; however, Microsoft has acknowledged several problems with it and issued fixes for it when it comes to networking. Following are some of those problems. These problems do not happen all the time or on every machine, but they have occurred enough for Microsoft to add them to its database.

Caution   Many of the fixes issued by Microsoft for the following problems include editing the Registry. The Registry contains settings and extended information about Windows operating systems. You can use the Registry to control a lot of the operating system and fix a lot of issues with Windows; however, one wrong entry or deletion in the Registry can damage Windows and render it useless.

✦ You get a lot of network collisions (meaning packets of information keep each other from getting to the destination; thus, data transfers take longer or don't complete at all).

✦ My Network Places does not show the workgroup, or the entire network, or displays the error "Cannot browse the network."

✦ Protocol problems are encountered with TCP/IP.

✦ Some network cards cause the network to be slow.

✦ Printer sharing is difficult.

If you have Windows Me and plan to use it on the network, you configure it similarly to Windows 98 or XP, as explained in Chapter 10. You can install the protocol, file and printer sharing service, client, and so on and connect to the network. Make sure you install the Client for Microsoft networks instead of the Windows Family Logon so that the Windows Me computer can see and be seen by others on the network.

Using Windows 98

Although Windows 98 does not automatically configure the network settings, it is easy to set up and similar to other configurations in Windows operating systems. Chapter 10 explains the configuration of Windows 98 software: Client for Microsoft Networks, adapter cards, protocols, and file and printer sharing.

You should use Windows 98, Second Edition. Furthermore, if you're using Windows 98 on your network, make sure you install all of the following (available from Microsoft's site):

✦ Dial-up networking 1.4 upgrade

✦ The Windows 98 Customer Service Pack, which includes, among other things, the Windows 98 System update

✦ Microsoft Internet Explorer 6 upgrade

Dealing with problems between Windows computers

Windows computers can be networked together no matter the version of Windows. If you set up your network with similar settings, you should encounter few problems between the computers. However, if you do have problems, consider some standard troubleshooting steps to take as described here:

✦ If you can't see the other Windows computers in the Network Neighborhood or My Network Places, the problem may be in authentication. Because Windows 2000 and XP support computer and network security, you cannot access one over the network unless you have a valid username and password. To solve the problem, you can try several things:

  • First, make sure all systems have valid users logged in; for example, instead of hitting the Esc key when Windows 98 starts, your daughter needs to make sure to type in her username and her password.

- Second, everyone needs to enter a password. Windows 2000 and XP expect to see a password and will not authenticate unless there is a password.

- Then make sure that the users and passwords are entered into the Windows 2000 and/or XP computers. You open the Control Panel and double-click Users and Passwords. Add a new user and the password to match those the user enters on his or her own computer.

✦ Beyond authentication issues, if you still cannot see other computers in the Network Neighborhood or My Network Places, you can look for a few other things to solve that problem:

- First make sure all the computers have the same setting for Workgroup, whether it's your family name, a pet's name, or even the word *workgroup*. All computers must have the same setting.

- Second, make sure all computers have the same protocol, Client for Microsoft Networks, and the same services: file and printer sharing.

- Third, make sure each computer name is unique; you can use each family member's first name as their computer name, for example.

Tip   Windows 2000 and XP support some computer names that are not compatible with Windows 98 or Me. If your computer names are not similar in length, for example, rename the computers and try again.

✦ If you're using Windows XP's built-in Internet Connection Firewall, you have to do some tweaking to enable file sharing through the firewall. See Chapter 16 for more information.

Tip   If you are having networking problems, be sure to consider you might have a problem with a network interface card (NIC) or cable.

Using Portables on Your Network

Portable computers include tablets, notebooks, and handheld computers. If your notebook or tablet uses the Windows 98, 2000, or XP operating system, you need only install the hardware and configure the software as you would with a desktop computer. Even Macintosh notebooks (PowerBooks) connect to a network easily. If you want to add a handheld computer to your network, the process is a bit different.

Using notebooks or laptops on the network

You can attach notebooks or laptops to the network by using the same cabling types— Ethernet, phone lines, wireless connections, and so on—and you use similar networking hardware on these portable computers as well. Of course, there are some exceptions. For example, you must use a PC Card (PCMCIA) network interface card on a portable computer. Check your notebook's documentation for other changes or problems.

Note   Today, laptops and notebooks are pretty much the same thing. In past years, notebooks were smaller and lighter in weight than laptops, but the name is now used interchangeably for both.

Operating systems for notebooks

If you're using Windows 98, 2000, or XP on your laptop or notebook, you'll have no trouble configuring the networking software. You just follow the steps for installing and configuring the software on a desktop computer.

Apple also makes notebook computers that use various operating systems, including Mac OS 8, 9, and X. Connecting these to the network is very similar to connecting any Mac computer.

Cross-Reference   For information about adding the networking hardware to a notebook or laptop computer, see Chapter 9. For more about configuring software for network use, see Chapter 10.

Hardware for notebooks and laptops

When using a notebook on the network, remember that you usually insert a PC Card into the network adapter slot on the notebook. Older laptops may not have the appropriate sockets (connections) for the PC Cards. If that is the case, you need to plug a direct cable between the laptop and your desktop computer to connect them. You can purchase an adapter cable, called a *pigtail*, that plugs into the portable computer and then fits an RJ-45 or other networking connector.

Tip   You can also use a universal serial bus (USB) adapter. See Chapter 10 for more information.

Make sure you do not insert or remove a PC Card when the computer is turned on unless you use the software included with the notebook to enable you to remove the card (check your computer's documentation). You could damage the card and/or the slot.

Generally, when you install a PC Card, it will configure itself when you turn the computer on. A PC Ethernet adapter costs between $40 and $130 for a notebook computer. Be careful when buying your network card. If you buy a bargain card, you first must check to see that it's certified as compatible with your operating system. Many cheaper cards might not be XP-compatible, for example. Wireless cards are in the same cost range; Macintosh cards can be a bit more expensive.

Mac PowerBooks and iBooks generally come with wireless capability built in. Often they have slots for PC Cards as well, depending on the type of notebook you buy.

You also want to avoid the higher-end combo cards for your notebook or laptop, if possible. Combo cards include a modem and network card in a single unit, and they are notorious for compatibility nightmares.

Most notebooks and laptops use Windows-compatible or a Mac operating system that enables easy configuration of the network. Check to make sure the computer has slots for networking and/or wireless capabilities.

Looking at handheld computers

Handheld computers and pocket PCs are popular with teens, as well as with businesspeople. You can carry your handheld in your pocket and use it anytime: at work, at home, or on the road.

Handhelds enable you to schedule your time, update your address book, take memos, send and receive e-mail, complete spreadsheets, write reports, and more. You also can synchronize the information on your handheld computer with the programs on your desktop computer to make sure that you don't miss an appointment or lose an address.

Small Business Tip

If you have salespeople, customer representatives, or other employees in the field, consider supplying them with handhelds instead of notebook computers. Handhelds are much cheaper, and many programs are available for scheduling, travel expenses, and other business forms on them.

Following is a brief list of some of the things you can do with handhelds:

✦ Use the date book to view the time, schedule events, view a week or month in the date book, and add and delete dates in the schedule.

✦ Create address book entries for work and personal use, and view, modify, add, and delete entries.

✦ Create a to-do list, and then add, modify, and delete entries.

✦ Take, arrange, add, and delete memos.

✦ Use additional programs, such as the calculator or expense application.

✦ With the appropriate software and a modem, send and receive e-mail on the Internet.

✦ Create brochures, presentations, business cards, calendars, fax cover sheets, letterheads, memos, and more document types.

✦ Customize envelopes and labels, run a shipping manager program, print postage

Many handhelds also offer accessories, such as modems, full-size keyboards, cradles for synchronizing with your desktop, and more. The number of programs now available for handhelds is unbelievable.

Looking at handheld brands

Many different brands of handheld computers exist, each with its own advantages and disadvantages. Probably the most popular manufacturers are Sony, Palm, Toshiba, HP, and Compaq. Several operating systems also exist for handhelds; Palm OS, Windows CE, and Pocket PC are three of the most popular operating systems.

You can buy a handheld for $100, or you can spend $1,200. The least expensive ones have fewer features and often don't have built-in networking. Mid-range cost handhelds have some sort of networking, whether it's Bluetooth, 802.11b (Wi-Fi), or infrared. You can also buy Ethernet adapters for some handhelds.

Cross-Reference

For more information about wireless networking, see Chapter 7.

Note that there is little difference between a handheld and a PDA (personal digital assistant). Older Palms (PalmPilot) and Sony Clies were called PDAs. Sometimes newer handhelds are called PDAs as well. Just make sure that if you purchase a PDA for network use, the PDA's specifications name a network protocol or connection. Not all PDAs, or handhelds for that matter, have network capability.

Palms

Palms use the Palm OS (operating system), but include software for installing copies of the programs to Windows computers. Palms come with a cradle for synchronizing the two computers, so your schedule, task list, address book, and other information are always up-to-date. The Palm operating system is compatible with both PCs and Macintosh.

The Palm Tungsten C is one of the latest models that you can network. The Palm runs on a superfast processor and uses the latest Palm OS. This Palm uses built-in Wi-Fi technology. It also includes a wireless Web browser and infrared support. Its cost is around $500.

HP iPAQ Pocket PC

HP makes many iPAQs, but some are made to use Bluetooth technology, and others are compatible with wireless 802.11b, so be careful when purchasing an iPAQ. For around $400 to $500, you should be able to get an iPAQ that does everything you need and includes networking capabilities.

Pocket PC is the operating system in iPAQs, and you can run the same type of programs that you can with a Palm — perhaps even more programs, such as Word, Excel, and other Windows programs.

Often you'll see "Bluetooth- and IrDA-compatible" on the packaging. Bluetooth is a radio chip that communicates with other Bluetooth devices. These devices can be phones, printers, computers, and so on. The range is fairly short for Bluetooth, no more than 10 meters, and the technology is radio frequency hopping. IRDA (Infrared Data Association) cable converts computers that do not have infrared ports with an infrared connection by plugging into a USB port.

Toshiba Pocket PC

For around $600, you can get a 802.11b/IrDA wireless handheld that also has a powerful Intel processor, color LED, 96MB storage capacity, and much more. Toshiba has another handheld for around $300 with only IrDA connectivity.

NEC handhelds

NEC makes a larger handheld for $900. The MobilePro 900 weighs 1.8 pounds and has a larger footprint than the smaller handhelds. It has a PC Card slot and IrDA compatibility. It's called a handheld, but with the size, power, and such, it could be called a notebook. The MobilePro uses the HP/C 2000 operating system.

NEC also makes smaller handhelds that use Windows CE operating system or the Pocket PC. You can use IrDA, or you can get a PC Card expansion jacket to use on an Ethernet or wireless network.

You purchase your handheld for more than just the networking; you want certain features that some have and others don't. Just make sure of the connectivity and capability before purchasing if you want to use the handheld on the network.

Using handhelds on the network

Each handheld uses some sort of operating system — such as Windows CE or an OS created by the manufacturer. Most operating systems are also compatible with Windows. This compatibility enables you to attach your handheld to your desktop computer via a cradle or other means so that you can sync the data and exchange information with a copy of the software on the desktop computer.

In the past, you could use a handheld only with one computer. You could, of course, share the handheld's folder after syncing it, but you couldn't connect the handheld directly to the network. Newer models of handhelds have changed that. As you can see from the previous examples in this chapter, you can use wireless (802.11b, Bluetooth, infrared), Ethernet adapters, and other methods of connecting handhelds to your network. You can purchase pocket pack network adapters, wireless PC Cards for handhelds, an Apple connector for FireWire, USB adapters, Bluetooth adapters, and more.

Considering tablets

Tablet PCs have gained popularity and versatility over the last year. With a tablet, you can write notes with a stylus and then have the computer convert the handwriting to typed text, such as you would see in Word. Tablets are highly mobile and enable powerful computing with the Windows XP Tablet PC Edition as your operating system. Windows XP is nearly the same on a tablet as it is on a desktop or notebook computer. The differences are in orientation and input devices. Other operating systems are used with tablets, including Macintosh OSs, Windows 2000, and so on.

Networking on a tablet using Windows as the operating system is the same as networking on any other PC. You can network using a USB adapter, PC Card for Ethernet, or PC Card for wireless.

Tip   If you have trouble setting up your wireless networking encryption with a tablet PC, consider the following. The access point usually shows a passphrase or a key for encryption, and normally a PC Card or NIC enables you to use the same key so the two can communicate. If you have trouble sharing the key, try counting the alphanumeric characters in the key. For example, 64-bit encryption contains 10 characters, 128-bit encryption contains 26 characters, and 256-bit encryption contains 58 characters for the key. Sometimes when you set the encryption, the number of characters is not correctly translated; by counting them, you can be sure the number is correct. If the number is not correct, you should remove the encryption, close the configuration utility, start the utility again, and reapply the encryption key.

Compaq makes a tablet PC that uses the Windows XP Tablet PC Edition operating system. This tablet has nearly every type of networking capability you could want or need: Ethernet, Fast Ethernet, 802.11b, and many great PC features for $1,850.

Toshiba also makes tablet PCs of various price levels: $2,000 and $2,400, for example. The tablet comes with the Windows XP Tablet PC Edition, various networking capabilities, a variety of software, and many other features.

Other makers of tablets include Acer and Wyse. CalComp and Summa make accessories for tablets as well.

Adding a Macintosh to Your Network

Years ago, you couldn't add a Macintosh to a PC network or vice versa. A real division existed, not only between the users of these computers but also between the technologies. Luckily, the technologies have expanded and bridges have been built to enable both computer types to share files, printers, and other resources.

With Macintoshes, you can create a Mac-only network by stringing an AppleTalk cable between computers and setting some Share options in the System menu. Most Macintoshes come with networking software.

If you have a PC network, however, and a Macintosh on the side that you would like to connect, you can do so easily now. Both Apple and Microsoft realize the importance of interconnectivity between the Macintosh and PCs. With advanced networking technology, Macs can be integrated with PCs easily.

Networking the Macintosh

Apple advocates wireless networking with their computers as the only way to go. True, wireless is easy to set up and has many advantages. You can use all wireless, including your PCs and Macs, and your network can be exactly what you want and need. Alternatively, you might have a wired network with your PCs and want to introduce wireless Macs. That solution works well too. If you want to use wireless over your network, see Chapter 7 for information about setting it up.

You might, however, want to wire a Macintosh to your wired network. That can work too. Most Macintoshes contain a 10/100Base-T Ethernet port on the back of the computer. The built-in Ethernet support connects with twisted-pair, thin coaxial cables, fiber-optic transmission media, or other standard Ethernet cables. Connect to an Ethernet 10/100 twisted-pair by using an RJ-45 connector. You set up a Macintosh to an Ethernet network just as you set up a PC.

All Macs include built-in networking. All Macs include two types of built-in networking technologies: Ethernet and AirPort wireless. Early Macs (G3s and Power Macs) used Ethernet and LocalTalk networking. Some older Macs had infrared instead. But newer Macs have the newest Ethernet and wireless technology for adding them to your network.

Small Business Tip

You might use a Macintosh in your company's art or typesetting department. The Macintosh has excellent art, drawing, painting, and desktop publishing programs. In addition, the music programs for Macintosh are more advanced than for the PC. The capability of networking a Macintosh with PCs means more flexibility and convenience in your work.

The Mac's networking hardware

If you want to use Ethernet networking for the Mac or Macs on your network, you set them up the same as you would a PC. Ethernet cables and hubs connect the Macs in minutes. Then you configure the software. The Mac has built-in Ethernet cards. Mac notebooks have the PC Card slot; you simply add the PC Card.

Setting up the wireless networking takes a little more time, but not much. The wireless AirPort card is built into Mac desktops, servers, and notebooks. You need an access point—in Apple language, that's a *base station*. An AirPort base station has a modem and an Ethernet jack inside, so you can use it to dial your Internet service provider or a work network, or you can plug into the jack with your cable modem or DSL line for wireless Internet access. You can alternatively use the Ethernet jack to plug into your wired network at home.

Apple has two types of wireless: AirPort and AirPort Extreme. AirPort is based on 802.11b standards with speeds up to 11 Mbps. AirPort Extreme is the newer wireless technology, and the faster technology. AirPort Extreme is five times faster than AirPort; AirPort Extreme runs at 54 Mbps. AirPort Extreme is based on 802.11g wireless standards and ranges for around 150 feet. The base station sells for around $200. AirPort Extreme can work with AirPort technology as well as with Extreme technology. The AirPort cards work with either technology.

Cross-Reference

For more information on prices, ranges, and other features of AirPort cards and AirPort Extreme cards and base stations, see Chapter 7.

Bluetooth technology is also integrated into the OS X operating system and comes built into certain Mac computers, such as the PowerBook G4. If your computer or operating system does not come with Bluetooth and you want to use it, you can purchase a D-Link USB adapter.

FireWire is another built-in technology with Macs. FireWire is a high-powered bus that transfers large amounts of data quickly and over longer distances. Apple has doubled the standard of IEEE 1394b on some computers, such as the PowerBook G4 and the Power Mac G4. Use FireWire with applications such as digital video, professional audio, high-end still cameras, and home entertainment devices.

Note   IEEE 1394b FireWire is also available with Windows 2000 and XP computers.

The Mac's networking software

Whether you use wireless or wired networking, you have to set up sharing on the Mac. Adding a Mac to any network is generally easy as far as setting up protocol. Many Macs examine the network, similarly to Windows XP machines, and set up the protocol for the already wired network. You can also change the protocol settings, if necessary. Chapter 10 describes setting up networking software.

Figure 11-4 shows the Network dialog box in the Mac OS X operating system. This Mac provides built-in Ethernet with TCP/IP settings already in place; however, you can change settings, if you prefer. You can also use AppleTalk for network, say, if you're using all Macintosh computers.

Another configuration you need to complete for networking the Mac is network sharing. The Sharing folder is located in System Preference, as is the Network folder, as shown in Figure 11-5.

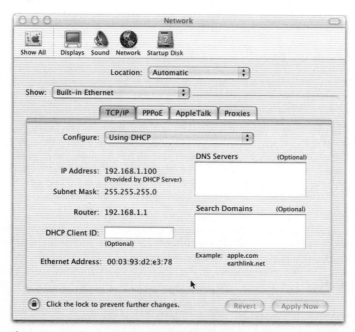

Figure 11-4: Macs contain built-in Ethernet support.

Figure 11-5: Network configurations are found in the System Preferences on the Mac.

The Sharing folder enables you to choose the services you want to share, including file and printer sharing, Windows file sharing, and so on. Figure 11-6 shows the Sharing dialog box with several services checked for sharing.

Note   For more information about sharing Windows files with your Macintosh, see the section "Accessing Windows data" later in this chapter.

Small Business Tip   If you have all Macintosh computers in your small business, consider using the AppleShare IP (ASIP) server. This is networking software that includes file sharing, Web hosting, e-mail services, Internet access, and print sharing all on one computer.

Accessing Windows data

Most popular applications—Word for Windows and other Microsoft Office applications, America Online, Quicken, and so on—are available for Macintosh now. And most of these programs give you the option of saving your files in formats for Macintosh or for Windows. Both the Mac and Windows support common file formats like DOC, XLS, PPT, JPEG, GIF, and so on.

You can share these files by e-mail, with a CD-R, with a Zip disk, and even over a network with the SMB/CIFS protocol. SMB is Server Message Block and is a common networking protocol used by Microsoft Windows. CIFS is Common Internet File System, a protocol also developed by Microsoft. CIFS runs over TCP/IP, which enables users to share files with multiple platforms.

Figure 11-6: Share files and printers, plus other services, with your Mac.

Nowadays, Windows users can browse Mac file servers and Macs can browse Windows. The difference isn't as important, as territorial, or as difficult as it used to be. The following information is focused primarily on Mac OS X and higher operating systems.

Tip Use the Mac OS X or higher for the easiest and most reliable Windows compatibility. Other Mac operating systems can share files with Windows computers, but you might need a third-party program to connect the two operating systems.

Looking at the details

Sharing a network and networking services with Windows is made easier by the industry-standard services used in today's networking. TCP/IP protocols enable the Mac and a Windows computer to use the same file server, printers, and other network services. Similarly, wireless networking products are compatible with Wi-Fi certified (802.11b) products for both Mac and Windows.

Since the Mac and Windows versions of most applications are the same—Microsoft Office applications, PDF (Portable Document Format) files, audio and video files, and so on—you can transfer files over a network, making file exchange easy and quick. No translation is necessary.

The Mac OS X v10.2 has built-in Windows file sharing based on the open source technology called Samba. Samba is a freeware software program that enables computers other than Windows, such as the Mac and Linux, to use SMB/CIFS to access files, printers, and network services.

All you have to do is click the option in the Sharing dialog box⇨ System Preferences, as shown in Figure 11-7, and you can share Windows files and networking. You don't need additional, third-party software. In addition, you can stop sharing at any time in the same dialog box.

Figure 11-7: Share the Windows network.

Looking at Windows folders and files

As with any program, Mac OS provides several ways to connect to another computer (Chapter 13 goes into accessing a network in more detail). With the Mac OS X, you can connect to another computer by choosing Go ⇨ Connect to Server. The Connect to Server dialog box appears, as shown in Figure 11-8; your dialog box may look different than the one here.

Depending on your network setup, you have the choice of a client/server, a workgroup, or a local network. You can also choose in the At box to connect to a specific computer via IP address from the drop-down list box.

When you select a computer to connect to, that computer's drive becomes available in an icon on your desktop, as shown in Figure 11-9.

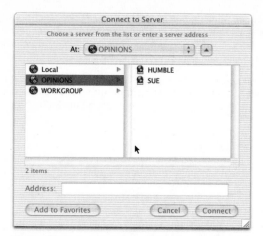

Figure 11-8: Look at the computers on the network.

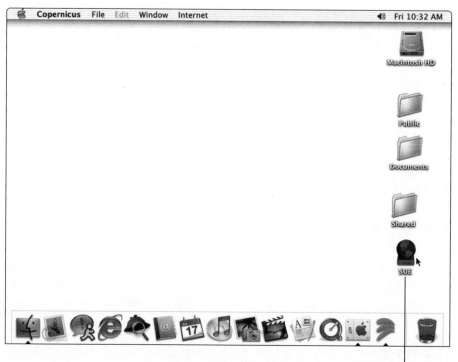

A Windows computer

Figure 11-9: Go to another computer on the network.

You can then go into any shared folders on the networked Windows PC and copy, add to, and otherwise work with the files. Figure 11-10 shows a pictures folder on a Windows computer, opened on the Mac.

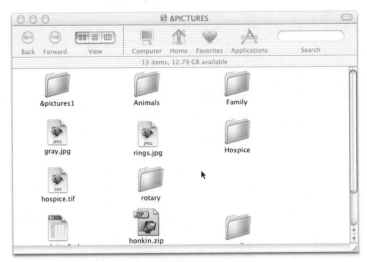

Figure 11-10: Open files on a Windows computer over the network.

Connecting through various technologies

You can network to connect a Mac to a Windows PC, including Ethernet cabling, wireless technology, virtual private networks (VPNs), USB, FireWire, and so on. For more information about each of these technologies, see Chapters 6 through 9. The following information is about how these technologies relate to networking Mac and Windows.

Ethernet attaches to both PCs and Macs using the 10/100 NIC, a hub or switch, and Ethernet cabling. TCP/IP is the only built-in protocol for Macs, so it follows that you use IP addressing to connect the two computers.

Cross-
Reference   For more information about TCP/IP and IP addressing, see Appendix B.

Wireless networking also suits both the PC and Mac. Macintosh uses the Apple AirPort Extreme wireless technologies, based on the 802.11g standard. Apple AirPort technologies are based on 802.11b standards; therefore, you can use these technologies with any wireless cards and access points you use with Windows, as long as you match the standards.

With wireless, the Mac OS X has built-in services that detect which wireless connections are available and connects automatically to the fastest and strongest signals. Plus Mac's wireless connections support 128-bit encryption with Wired Equivalent Privacy (WEP).

For more information about wireless technologies, see Chapter 7.

You can also connect to a Windows network using VPNs, perhaps to connect from home to work or from the road to home. You need a VPN client to do this and the Point-to-Point Tunneling Protocol (PPTP), which are both included in the Mac OS X. The Mac comes with USB and FireWire ports so that you can use Bluetooth devices, such as printers, scanners, storage drives, and the like, with the Mac and Windows.

Using Linux with Your Network

You might want to use a Linux computer if you have someone in your family who is an experienced Linux user or who plans to spend a great amount of time learning Linux.

You could use Linux on a slower, outdated computer, such as a Pentium or Pentium II. You could also use Linux on a desktop for a user, but Windows is a lot easier and more efficient. Another problem with Linux is that not as much hardware and software is available that's compatible with it, unlike with Windows or Mac.

If you plan to use Linux with your network, it will likely be for a server. You can use a Linux server, for example, if you have a broadband connection and you want to supply Internet services like File Transfer Protocol (FTP) or an Apache Web server. Broadband is a term describing very fast Internet connections, like Digital Subscriber Line or a cable modem.

Most families, however, won't use a Linux computer with their network. Linux has a steep learning curve, and it isn't very useful for games or most desktop applications. If you do add a Linux computer to your network, you can share files and printers with Windows computers.

Most Linux distributions can be used with Windows networks through the Samba program. Samba takes care of all of the Windows networking tasks, such as file and printer sharing. Samba configuration can be difficult, however.

Linux servers are secure and stable, although the reliability of your security depends on your ability to configure appropriate networking and operating system features. Networking services are readily available for any distribution. You choose the server depending on the distribution you're most familiar with. Linux computers are also very secure, seeing how they use a permissions system from Unix. Each file and directory has read, write, and execute access for the owner, for the group, and for the whole computer.

Note

A Linux computer has a superuser called *root*. Root overrules all permissions for every file; therefore, the root password is the most important password on the computer. Every user other than root is subject to limitations and permissions.

Ethernet and wireless work with Linux the same as with Windows. Linux has its own open-sourced tools, GUI-interfaces, and console-based tools and services for most networking technologies. If you want to learn more about networking with Linux, and more specifically your distribution, check www.justlinux.com.

Summary

In this chapter, you've learned about attaching accessing your local area network with various computers and operating systems. You've learned about connecting the following:

✦ Windows NT and 2000

✦ Windows 98, Me, and XP

✦ Notebooks and tablets

✦ Handhelds

✦ Macintoshes

✦ Linux

In the next chapter, you learn about sharing resources on the network.

✦   ✦   ✦

Working with Networked Computers

In this part, you learn about configuring your computers to work over the network, as well as how to find files and resources over the network. You first must designate your resources — files, folders, printers, and drives, for example — as shared. In sharing resources, you choose whether the resources are available to everyone or only to certain users. Chapter 12 explains sharing in detail.

Chapter 13 shows you how to log on to the network and navigate your way to various locations. In addition to navigating the network, you need to know how to find computers and other resources. Chapter 14 explains how to use Windows's popular applets to accomplish this task. And Chapter 15 covers printing on the network.

Sharing Resources

Before others can use your files, folders, or printers, you must designate those resources as shared. Sharing is a way of letting others open your files, or save files to one of your folders, or print on your printer. You can share everything on your computer or only certain things. For example, you might have files you don't want your kids to get into but a printer you want them to use; you choose what to share on your computer.

Understanding Sharing

One reason you attach your computer to a network is so you can share resources with others. The term resources refers to files, folders, drives, printers, CD or DVD drives, Zip or Jaz drives, modems, and most other components attached to your computer.

You probably want to share most resources with your spouse or with children in the house. You and your spouse might share files, for example, that contain letters, household accounting information, or genealogy data. Older children in your home might want to share their homework files so you can review them before they print the documents.

Naturally, you'll share printers, CD or DVD drives, and other hardware with everyone in the house so you can save money. Instead of buying a printer for each user, you can share expensive laser or color inkjet printers with everyone on the network.

Of course, you can limit the access to shared resources, in case you have confidential information to protect or equipment that's too expensive for children to use. You don't have to share any resource on your computer if you want to keep files or folders completely confidential or equipment away from the children.

Limiting access

You can limit the access anyone on the network has to your resources. A child, for example, could accidentally delete a folder or mix up the sums in your personal accounting program. You might not want your spouse to see your creative writing stories or your diary. You might want to limit the use of an expensive color printer as well.

For networking your small business, security may be important if you have files that list payroll amounts, sensitive customer information, and so on. Be careful about sharing folders that contain information that should remain confidential. You might consider placing these folders on an inaccessible computer or hard disk in addition to not sharing the folder; or place these files on a Windows 2000 or XP computer. Windows 2000 and XP are known for their good security.

Windows enables you to limit the access to any file, folder, drive, or other resource by assigning an access type. Following are the access types from which you can choose:

✦ **Read-only** — Read-only access enables others to open and view folders, or to open, view, and copy files; however, read-only access doesn't enable others to modify a file or delete anything. You might use this access type when you have a folder of various form letters, for example. Then anyone can open and copy a letter, use it to write another letter by customizing the contents, and then save it under a new name so as not to alter the original.

✦ **Full** — Full access enables anyone to open, change, add, or remove files and folders. Use full access for a personal checking account used by both spouses, or for word processing files you share with your spouse.

✦ **Depends on password** — You can set a password on any resource so that only the people who know the password have access to that file or folder. You can give your spouse password access, for example, but keep your children from access to a specific file or folder. Within password limits, you also can choose read-only or full access.

Mac OS X provides a folder called Home for each user to save his or her documents. Only a person who knows your name and password can open your Home folder, which contains your files and folders. When you want to share a file or folder with someone on a Mac, you place that file or folder in the Shared folder.

Linux is similar to Windows in that each file and directory has read, write, and/or execute access for the owner, the group, or the whole computer.

Understanding the rules of sharing

There are certain sharing rules that you need to understand before you share your resources. You can share everything on a Windows computer so that everyone has access to it, or you can limit access either by choosing an access type or by selecting only certain resources to designate as shared.

Figure 12-1 illustrates shared drives in the Windows 98 Explorer. The computer's C: (hard disk) drive is shared, as indicated by the outstretched hand displayed in the icon. In the list of folders and files on the right of the Explorer window, you'll notice that several folders display the sharing hand. In some cases, a user must enter a password to open a folder with read-only or full rights.

When you look at My Computer in Windows XP Professional, you see a folder called Shared Documents (see Figure 12-2). You can place files in the Shared folder so that anyone can access those files through the network, or through your computer as another user.

Windows 2000 works very similarly to XP in sharing, so when you see figures or read something about XP, you can apply it to Windows 2000 computers as well.

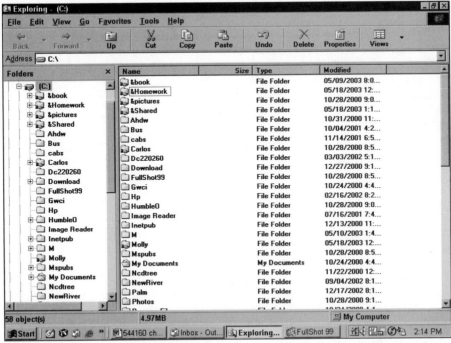

Figure 12-1: Share drives and folders on your computer with others on the network.

Figure 12-2: Use the Shared Documents folder in Windows XP to share files.

With the Mac, each person has both a Shared folder and a Public folder. The Shared folder is to share files with specific users on your computer. The Public folder is one in which you share files with others, on the network or with other users of your computer. The Public folder also contains a Drop Box folder in which others can copy files to your Drop Box but not see its contents. Figure 12-3 shows the Public folder and the Drop Box folder.

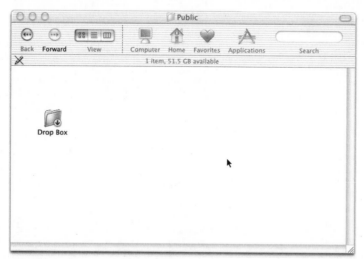

Figure 12-3: Share folders with others on the network through the Public folder.

Granting full access

If you want everyone to have full access to all your folders in Windows, share the drive on which those folders reside. When you choose to share a drive — such as your C: drive, a Zip drive, or a CD-ROM drive — you automatically share every folder and file on that drive. In Windows 2000 and XP, you can share your entire hard drive by dragging it into the Shared Documents folder.

If you have one or more folders on the C: drive that you do not want to share, then you should choose not to share the entire drive. Instead, choose only the folders you want to share on the C: drive. You cannot share the entire drive and protect certain files or folders on that drive, so be careful with your shares.

Be careful when granting everyone in the office access to everything. If an employee becomes dissatisfied with work or with you, he or she may sabotage important files.

Limiting access to folders

When you grant full access to a drive, you cannot limit access to the folders on that drive. You can limit access to folders, however, by selecting each folder and setting the limits you want, one folder at a time.

Choosing Which Folders to Share

You have a lot of folders on a Windows computer, and you don't need to share them all by any means. Sharing the entire drive would be the simplest way to set up a share; after all, you then have to create only one share, which takes only a minute. You can save yourself some headaches later, however, if you take the time to choose specific folders to share.

You don't need to share your Windows directory, for example. The Windows directory holds all the files that make Windows work, including fonts, configuration files, programming files, help files, and so on. No one has any need to access any files in your Windows folder.

Similarly, you might not want to share your Program Files folder. The Program Files folder contains multiple application folders, such as Internet Explorer, Microsoft Office, Outlook, NetMeeting, and so on. Each application folder contains the files that make a specific program run. More likely than not, the other network computers contain these applications and, therefore, don't need to share yours.

You might want to share a specific program file folder, however, if someone else needs data contained within that folder. Suppose that you use Quicken for your personal accounting program. If you store your account data in the Quicken folder (C:\Program Files\QuickenW\My Data, for example), you'll want to share the Quicken folder so that your spouse also can access the data.

Don't share any folders used to contain device drivers. Device drivers are the programs that run your CD or DVD drive, network card, tape backup, and so on. On my computer, I don't share the following folders: Plugplay, Ethernet, Iomega, Cdrom, Eapci, ATI, and so on, because these folders contain data specific to my computer. If someone were to accidentally delete any one of these folders, part of my system would stop functioning properly.

You can share folders that contain data that others might want or need, such as your My Documents folder or other folders you've created to hold your work. You also can share application folders that others can copy, such as the WinZip folder. If your spouse reformats a drive and wants to copy your WinZip32 program and install it on the new drive, copying it from your hard disk over the network is the easiest method.

When you choose to share a folder, you can assign either the read-only or the full access type to that folder. If you choose to assign a read-only limit, users can open the folder and copy any file, but they cannot make changes to a file or delete a file within that folder. This technique is a great way to protect application files from being deleted accidentally. Suppose that you want to grant access to a folder containing an application such as WinZip. Using read-only access guarantees that you won't open the folder one day and find all your files missing.

Figure 12-4 illustrates the Network Neighborhood in the Windows 98 Explorer, and the folders shared by a server computer called Humble. Naturally, you don't want to share all of the folders on the server; many folders are for the operating system and others are for applications that only the server uses. The following list is a description of each shared drive shown in Figure 12-4:

✦ **a** is a folder used for backup of important documents on each computer. It's named *a* because that places the folder at the top of the list so it's easily located.

✦ **Carlos** is a folder for the administrator of the server. He places items of interest, such as memos about when the server might be down for repair, in that folder.

✦ **Inetpub** contains files and folders for the intranet.

✦ **Opinions** contains applications any member of the network can download and then install on his or her own computer, such as shareware and freeware.

✦ **Server** describes the folder that holds all of the shared data, such as a folder for each member on the network, folders containing accounting data, music files, and so on.

Note   Shared folders from other computers on the network do not display the outstretched hand by the folder or drive icon. Only your own folders display that shared symbol.

In addition to choosing the folders you want to share, you can specify the type of access to each folder by adding a password. You can designate full access to a folder to only the persons who know the password. Use this technique when you want to share a folder with your spouse, for example, but not with your 15-year-old son.

Small Business Tip   Using a password for granting access to a folder is a good idea in a business situation. Use passwords for folders containing information that only one or two people need to access. Remember, though, that if the password gets out, then the folders might become available to all.

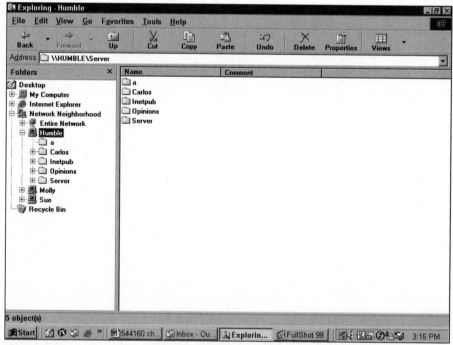

Figure 12-4: Shares on the server are limited yet sufficient for all members of the network.

You can assign different access limits to any folder. You might want to share a folder as read-only with one person and share it as full access with another. You can accomplish this goal by applying two passwords to the share, then give only the appropriate password to your 15-year-old. With a read-only password, the child can only look at the contents of a folder and copy a document; but he or she cannot make any changes to that resource.

Figure 12-5 shows the Enter Network Password dialog box, which appears when you try to open a limited-access resource. If you fill in the password correctly, you can open the folder and use it; if not, Windows displays a dialog box that states, "The password is incorrect. Try again." and denies access to the resource.

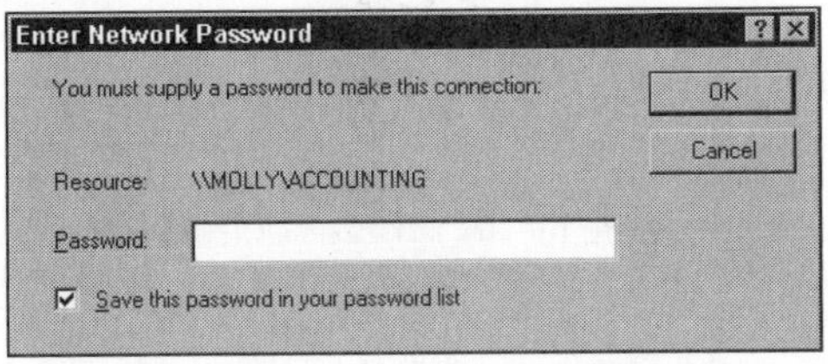

Figure 12-5: Limit access with passwords.

Windows 2000 and XP have additional sharing features that use permissions. You choose each folder you share and then specify who has permission to use that folder. Instead of using read, write, and full access, 2000 and XP often use simpler language and say something like: "Allow other users to change my files." The meaning is the same, however, as full access or read/write access. Figure 12-6 shows a folder's Properties dialog box. You can share the folder, and you can choose whether to let users change your files.

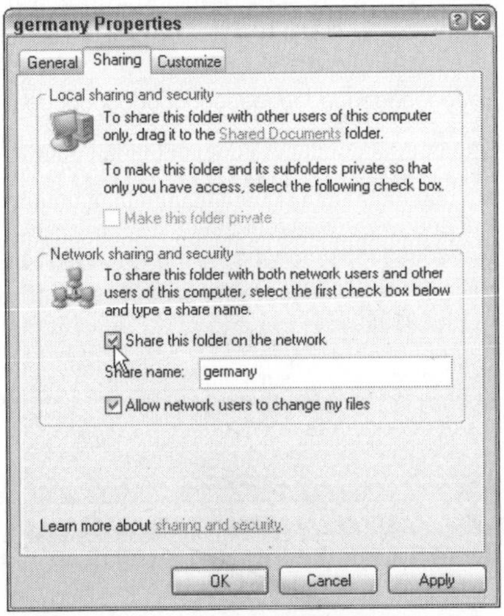

Figure 12-6: Allow users to change files.

Sharing Between Operating Systems

When you share between Windows computers, there's not much of a problem. Windows 2000 and XP have stricter sharing rules and permissions than 98 or Me, but after you get past the OS's permissions, you can share easily.

When sharing between a Mac and Windows, you use the operating system's own software to set it up if you're using Mac OS X. If you're using a version of Mac such as System 7, 8, or 9, you might have trouble connecting your Mac with a Windows network.

You can use PC MacLAN, made by Miramar, to create networking between Macs running OS System 7 or higher. You can use the software to connect over an Ethernet or wireless network. You can share files, folders, and printers using PC MacLAN quickly and easily. There are two products, PC MacLAN for Windows 95/98/Me and PC MacLAN for Windows NT, 2000, and XP. For more information, visit www.miramar.com.

Another software product you can use to help promote file and printer sharing between Macs and Windows is Thursby Software Systems DAVE 4.1. DAVE supports Mac OS 8.6 through 9.2x and 10.1.4, plus OS X v10.2.x. DAVE provides support for NTFS file format and Windows security; shares CDs, printers, folders, and such, and it features automatic workgroup detection.

Linux shares well with Windows as long as you use Samba to handle all of the Windows networking tasks.

Using Linux with Macintosh depends on the Linux distro you're using. For example, if you use the Yellow Dog Linux GUI, you can use Mac-On-Linux (MOL) to run your Mac operating system on top of Linux inside a window. Using this configuration, you can use Mac programs and files, Web browsers, and e-mail. If you use Yellow Dog Linux as a server, you can use it to set up a gateway between Macs and PCs.

Another product, GroupWise from Novell, enables you to share files between Linux and Macs as well. Use the Internet to research your distribution of Linux to see if it supports file sharing with Macs and PCs.

Sharing Folders and Drives

Microsoft networking makes sharing folders and other resources simple. You use the same steps and see the same dialog box for any resource you share. Before you can share any resource on the network, however, you first must install the networking software and hardware. When installing the networking software, you must enable file and print sharing services.

Cross-Reference   Chapters 6 through 10 explain how to set up the hardware and install networking software for your network.

After installing the appropriate software and hardware, you can designate folders and drives as shared by using the Windows Explorer or the My Computer window; both applets work similarly. Others can view shared drives, folders, and files in the Network Neighborhood, in My Network Places, or in the Go ⇨ Server window on the Mac. The Network Neighborhood and My Network Places is an icon you use to view all computers on the network. For more information about My Computer, the Windows Explorer, the Network Neighborhood, or My Network Places, see Chapter 14.

Sharing Drives

You can share any drive on your Windows computer, including hard drives, floppy drives, Zip drives, Jaz drives, MiniDisc drives, CD-ROM drives, DVD drives, or tape drives. You share drives to enable others to access the files and folders on those drives and to back up or store files. For example, you might let your teenager store her graphics and image files on your extra hard drive. You might save some business files on your spouse's Zip drive because you don't have one attached to your computer. You might use another's CD or DVD drive because it burns faster than yours. Sharing drives gives everyone on the network access to multiple devices that they might not have had otherwise.

When you share a drive, you also share everything on that drive—including all folders and files. Carefully consider sharing an entire hard drive before you do it. Some folders on that drive might be confidential. Others might be program files you don't want to lose accidentally.

If the drive you share is a secondary hard drive, however, sharing it for file storage might be a good idea. You wouldn't necessarily have any program, configuration, or operating system files on a secondary drive, so if data is lost, it can be replaced easily. You might store backup files, extra image files, document files, and other data files on a secondary drive.

Share mass storage device drives—such as tape drives, Zip and Jaz drives, and so on—for purposes of backup and file storage as well. You need to oversee the media for the drive yourself or assign someone to do it. You don't want to be unaware of when a Zip disk fills up or a tape needs to be changed. You also need to watch tape drives for when they need to be cleaned; a dirty tape drive won't back up. You can purchase a cleaning tape that you put into the drive every month or two to clean the magnetic bits of tape left over from the backup tape.

Share CD-ROM drives in order to install software quickly. Choose to share the computer with the fastest CD-ROM drive for faster and more efficient installations and downloads. Share CD or DVD burners to make it easier for everyone to create their own discs. Share only the fastest burners.

You share a drive by using the same method you use for sharing a folder. See "Designating a share" later in this chapter.

Locating a folder

You can locate and share a folder in either the Windows Explorer or the My Computer window of Windows operating systems. On the Mac, open the hard drive or use the Finder. To open the Windows 98 Explorer, choose Start ➪ Programs ➪ Windows Explorer. To open the Windows 2000 or XP Explorer, choose Start ➪ Programs ➪ Accessories ➪ Windows Explorer. To open a folder on the Mac, go to the Finder and choose Go ➪ Go to Folder.

Following is an example that shows the process of locating a folder in the My Computer window in Windows XP. To open the My Computer window, double-click the My Computer icon on the desktop (of Windows 98). For Windows XP, click Start ➪ My Computer. Figure 12-7 illustrates the My Computer window. The initial window displays all drives and selected folders.

You can select any drive in the window to designate as shared, or you can open the drive window to view folders on the drive. To open a drive in the My Computer window, double-click the drive's icon. The window changes to display the folders contained on that drive, as shown in Figure 12-8.

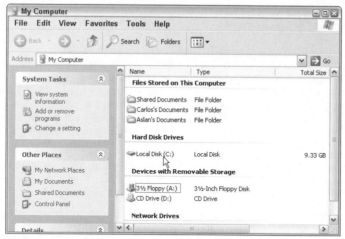

Figure 12-7: My Computer contains all drives, folders, and other resources in your computer.

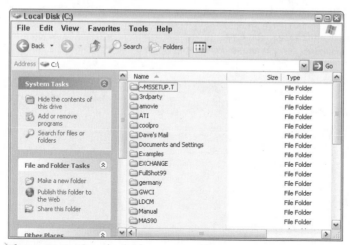

Figure 12-8: View the folders on any drive.

Designating a share

After you open the My Computer window or the Windows Explorer and locate the folder, you can designate that folder as shared. The following process also works for designating a drive as shared. In Step 1, you select the drive to be shared, and then you follow Steps 2 though 7.

To designate a folder as shared, follow these steps:

1. Select the folder.

2. Choose File ⇨ Sharing (for Windows 98 and 2000), or choose File ⇨ Sharing and Security (for Windows XP). Alternatively, you can right-click the selected folder and then choose the sharing option from the quick menu.

3. The folder's Properties dialog box appears with the Sharing tab displayed, as shown in Figure 12-9. This example is in Windows XP.

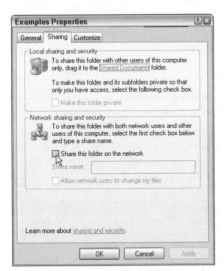

Figure 12-9: By default, the resource is not shared.

Figure 12-10 shows the Properties dialog box in Windows 98.

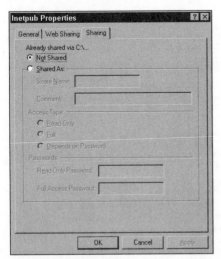

Figure 12-10: The options are somewhat different in Windows 98.

4. For Windows 2000 or XP, do the following:

    a. Click Share This Folder on the Network.

    b. Optionally, change the share name in the Share Name text box.

    c. Optionally, click Allow Network Users to Change My Files.

    d. Click OK.

For Windows 98, do the following:

    a. In the Sharing tab, choose the Shared As option. The share name becomes the same as the drive, folder, or file. The share name is the name that is displayed to other members of the network.

    b. To enter a new share name, delete the existing text in the Share Name text box and enter any text you want. If you're sharing a CD-ROM drive, for example, you can name the share CD-ROM instead of the drive letter (D: or E:, for example) so that users can recognize the drive easily.

    c. Optionally, enter any text in the Comment text box. You might want to write comments that describe the documents within a folder, for example.

    d. Click Apply to activate the share name. If you're finished with the Properties dialog box, click OK. If you want to limit access by using a password, continue with the instructions in the following section.

For the Mac, the steps depend on the operating system you're using. Generally, however, you open the hard drive and locate the folder. Copy the folder you want to share to the Shared folder in the Users folder.

Setting access limits

You can set limits on access to the shared folder by choosing an access type, by adding a password to the shared resource, or by doing both. If you choose an access type, you either limit all network users to a read-only access to the folder or you allow all users full access.

Alternatively, you can assign a password to the shared folder so that only users who know the password can access the folder. If you choose to set a password, you can give users read-only or full access with the password.

Figure 12-11 illustrates a folder that is shared using the full access type with a password. Note that the password is represented by asterisks so that no one can read it over your shoulder. This folder can be accessed only by someone who knows the password you specify.

Note   In Windows XP, you use the General tab in the Properties dialog box to set the attributes. You cannot set a password on the shared folder in Windows XP.

To set access limits in Windows 98, follow these steps:

1. Open the folder's Properties dialog box and share the folder.

2. In Access Type, choose Read-only, Full, or Depends on Password (see "Limiting access" earlier in the chapter for an explanation of these types).

3. Click OK to accept the changes and close the dialog box.

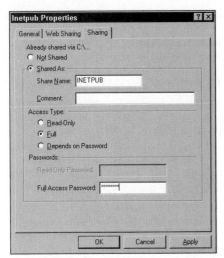

Figure 12-11: Limit access to only those who know the password.

Sharing Files

When you share a folder or drive, all files in that folder or drive are also shared. When you share files, anyone on the network can open, modify, delete, or otherwise manipulate the shared files. If you trust everyone on the network with your files, then you'll have no problem.

You really have little control over the files in a shared folder or drive. Windows does offer the options of applying a read-only or a hidden attribute to your files; however, another user can change the attributes from another machine, if he or she wants to do so. Additionally, another user can open a read-only file and then save it under a new name and make all the changes he or she wants.

The best policy is to refrain from sharing anything you don't want others to see. Then, when you leave your computer room, lock the door. Anyone who has physical access to your Windows 98 or Me computer can, just by canceling the login dialog box, view anything on your computer. Third-party applications, such as Fortres 101, are available that enable you to secure your Windows computer, drives, folders, and files. See Chapter 2 for more information.

Note   Windows NT, using the New Technology File System (NTFS), enabled you to set private security measures on individual computers. Hidden files on NT, for example, remained hidden because of the file system. Even though you cannot buy Windows NT anymore, Windows 2000 and Windows XP are based on NT technology, so they have excellent security measures. See Chapter 21 for more information.

Hiding files

In the days of DOS, you could hide a file so that no one else could use what they couldn't see. That theory is good; however, it doesn't really work for Windows. Windows includes a View option that enables you to view hidden files, even those hidden by another user on his or her own machine.

If, in Windows, you apply a hidden attribute to a file on your computer, the file becomes hidden so it no longer lists on your computer. To use the file, you must know the exact name of the file. But when another user views the shared folder containing the hidden file, he or she may be able to see your hidden file, depending on his or her computer's settings. The file appears to other users who have set their copy of Windows Explorer to show hidden files. In short, even though you think you're protecting your files by hiding them, you are not.

To hide a file, open the Windows Explorer and right-click the file. Choose Properties from the quick menu, and then choose the General tab. You can set the Hidden and Read-Only attributes on any file. Whether the hidden file remains hidden depends on each user's folder options.

Most home users won't know about hidden files or won't care enough to see what you've hidden. However, in a small business, you should use a more secure method of protecting files you want to protect.

To set the Show All Files option, follow these steps:

1. Open the Windows Explorer and choose View ➪ Folder Options. The Folder Options dialog box appears.

2. Choose the View tab.

3. In the Advanced settings list, click the Show All Files option to view all hidden files on your computer. Alternatively, click the Do Not Show Hidden or System Files option to conceal those files.

4. Click OK to close the dialog box.

Using the Read-Only attribute

The Read-Only attribute keeps others from modifying a file. Anyone can open a read-only file, but he or she cannot add to, delete, or otherwise modify the contents of the file. Read-Only doesn't keep someone from making a copy of the file by saving it under another name; however, the renamed file can be changed and modified.

Using the Read-Only attribute is a good idea for some files, such as company forms. Users can access the forms they need — such as expense forms, time sheets, order forms, and so on — save the file to their own computer, and then complete it as necessary. This way, your form bases are the same and each user fills them out as needed.

The problem with setting the Read-Only attribute is that anyone can take the attribute off as easily as you can put it on. Another user can open your shared folder in his or her Windows Explorer, open a file's Properties dialog box, and remove the Read-Only attribute.

The problems with hidden and read-only files occur only when you share a drive or folder. If you don't share a drive or folder, no one can view or modify the files.

Note Some applications enable you to assign a password to a file as you save it. Microsoft Word, for example, offers the option of applying a password to a file in order to open it or in order to modify it (choose File ⇨ Save As ⇨ Options). When a password is applied directly to the file, no one can open the file without the password.

Look for that same option in other applications. Check the Save As dialog box for a menu, tool, or button called Options. You also can check the program's documentation.

Sharing Printers and Other Peripherals

You can share many peripherals on both peer-to-peer and client/server networks. Peripherals include printers, scanners, modems, CD and DVD burners and drives, and other devices. Some peripherals require special software to make them work over a network; other peripherals require special hardware or features to make them networkable. Some peripherals require nothing but the Share designation.

Sharing peripherals over a workgroup network is different from sharing them over a client/server network. In a client/server network, the network operating system usually has tools and features that enable and manage the shared device. When you're sharing printers with Windows 2000 Server, for example, the network operating system acts as a print server. The print server distributes the various print jobs to the appropriate printers and enables the network administrator to manage the print jobs that clients send to the server.

Tip Some software, such as WordPerfect 10 and higher, provides its own print server. See WordPerfect documentation for more information.

In a workgroup network, you may not need extra tools to manage the sharing of peripherals, but if you do, you need to purchase a third-party program to enable sharing and device management.

Sharing printers

In nearly any operating system, you can easily share any printer attached to a computer on the network. Sharing a printer is similar to sharing a drive or folder. You designate the printer as shared and assign it a share name. You also can set a password on the shared device, if you want. Only someone who knows the password can use the printer. In general, however, you'll share all printers on the network with everyone else.

Tip You may want to limit sharing a printer that is especially expensive or difficult to use, such as a color laser printer. To limit sharing, either you cannot share the printer or you can share it with a password.

In addition to designating a printer as shared, other users on the network must install your printer's driver to their computers before they can access the printer. The printer's driver is a program that enables the computer to communicate with the printer.

Cross-Reference For more information about network printing, see Chapter 15.

Designating a printer as shared

Before designating your printer as shared, you must install it on your computer. You install the printer as a local printer, just as you would if you planned to use it exclusively with your computer.

Next, you designate the printer as shared by following these steps:

In Windows 98:

1. Choose Start ➪ Settings ➪ Printers. The Printers dialog box appears, as shown in Figure 12-12.

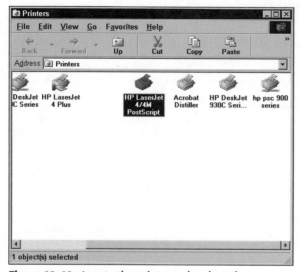

Figure 12-12: Locate the printer to be shared.

2. Right-click the printer's icon and then choose Sharing from the quick menu. The printer's Properties dialog box appears with the Sharing tab displayed.

3. Choose the Shared As option to display the share options, as shown in Figure 12-13.

4. You can either accept the suggested share name or enter a new one. The share name is the name that appears in the Network Neighborhood.

5. Optionally, you can enter a comment about the printer. The comment also appears in the Network Neighborhood.

6. If you want to control the use of the printer, enter a password in the appropriate text box.

7. Click OK to accept the changes and close the printer's Properties dialog box.

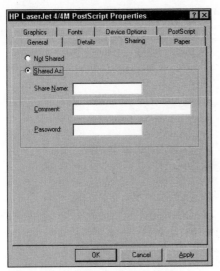

Figure 12-13: Share the printer by assigning it a share name.

You can view a printer on the network via the Network Neighborhood, the Windows Explorer, or My Computer. For information about finding a printer on the network and installing the driver, see Chapter 15.

In Windows 2000 and XP, sharing is very similar. Do the following to share a printer:

1. Click Start ⇨ Settings ⇨ Printers and Faxes (Printers in Windows 2000). The Printers and Faxes dialog box appears in XP; a list of available printers appears in Windows 2000.

2. Right-click the printer you want to share. Choose Sharing from the pop-up menu. The printer's Properties dialog box appears, as shown in Figure 12-14.

Figure 12-14: Click to share the printer in Windows XP.

3. Click the Share This Printer option and enter a share name.

4. Click OK.

In a Mac, you also have to turn on printer sharing. Mac OS X has a Print Center in which all shared printers on the network are listed. Shared printers automatically appear in the Print Center. To share a printer in a Mac, follow these steps:

1. Click the System Preferences icon. The System Preference dialog box appears.

2. Click Sharing. The Sharing dialog box appears.

3. Under the Services tab, click the Printer Sharing option, as shown in Figure 12-15.

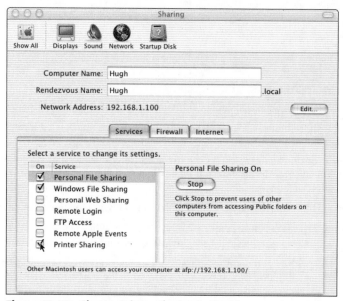

Figure 12-15: Choose Printer Sharing in the Mac.

4. Click the Close button.

In the Mac, you can view shared printers by opening the Print Center. To open the Print Center, follow these steps:

1. Double-click the Macintosh HD.

2. Double-click Applications folder.

3. Double-click Utilities folder, as shown in Figure 12-16.

Figure 12-16: Open the Print Center to view shared printers.

4. Double-click the Print Center.

You can also share printers with Linux; however, it seems that printer sharing is difficult, depending on the distribution. If you can get it to work, printing through a Linux computer is often faster than printing through Windows. You'll need to check the documentation, news-groups, and technical help for your distribution to figure out printing with Linux.

Other methods of sharing printers

When you share a printer that's directly attached to a PC, that PC must remain on for others to print to the printer. Using a device called a print server, you can save the hassle of turning the computer on and going to that printer each time you print a page.

A *print server* manages the printing for all users on a network. It receives all requests for print jobs sent by the networked PCs, places the jobs in a queue to wait their turn, and then routes the job to available printers attached to the server.

A print server is an excellent idea for small networks. If you only have one printer and not many people who need to print, you probably don't need one. If several users print most of the day, however, a print server can help divide the print load and speed the jobs along.

Several types of devices are available that you can purchase, such as a Linksys wireless print server for around $130 or HP or even Linux print servers for around the same amount. You can choose either a software or a hardware print server.

For more information about print servers, see Chapter 15.

Print Server Products

Many manufacturers offer tools and utilities for sharing peripherals over a network. Hewlett-Packard (HP), for example, offers JetDirect, which is a great print server for a small home or business network. Several different JetDirect versions are available. JetDirect is compatible with Windows 98, Me, 2000, XP, and Mac OS 8.6 and above. It also has Ethernet capability for 10/100 technology. Some JetDirects include wireless support as well.

The JetDirect print server connects to most HP LaserJets, deskjets, and multifunction devices through the USB port. One nice thing about the JetDirect is that only the PC sending the print job has to be turned on, so other users can shut their computers down without worrying about one person printing. JetDirects start at around $150.

JetLan makes a USB 10/100 print server to which you can connect two USB printers and one parallel printer. This print server does support various protocols but does not support all hardware (such as multifunction devices and certain printers), so check carefully before you buy to make sure your hardware is supported. Cost of JetLan is around $120.

Hawking makes several print servers that work well with Linux machines. You can use the TCP/IP protocol. Hawking print servers are generally less than $100.

NETGEAR makes a print server that works with wireless and Ethernet for only $50. You don't need a dedicated PC for the NETGEAR print server; some print servers do require a dedicated PC.

D-Link, another popular networking hardware manufacturer, also offers print servers. For around $200, you can purchase either a wireless or an Ethernet print server.

Sharing a modem

You probably want to share an Internet connection over your network. You also might want to share faxing capability. To share either an Internet connection or fax services, you need to share a modem. Modem-sharing software is relatively inexpensive, but you need to remember that the PC with the modem is going to take a dive in performance whenever the Internet connection is active.

Phone line modems aren't as popular for Internet connections now as they once were. Cable modems and DSL modems have taken over in many small businesses and even in homes. You can share either phone modems or cable/DSL modems. A cable modem is a device that enables you attach to the Internet through your television cable; DSL uses standard copper phone lines for fast access to the Internet as well.

Cross-Reference   See Chapter 16 for more information about cable and DSL modems, routers, and other methods of accessing the Internet.

You can share modems whether your network is of the workgroup or client/server variety. For either type of network, you can use inexpensive modem-sharing software or a hardware device called a cable/DSL modem router.

Small Business Tip   If you have sales or research people who access the Internet frequently, you probably should get separate Internet e-mail addresses within your account. If you share a phone modem for Internet access, you should look into a cable modem, DSL, T1 line, or faster connection for your company.

Internet access

The software you use for sharing an Internet account enables all the users on the network to share one account and one modem. Many software products are available for sharing an Internet account — including Avirt, Sustainable Softworks, and WinGate. Users can browse different Web sites and access e-mail at the same time. You need only one Internet service provider account and one phone modem.

Several hardware devices can enable you to share a modem. You can use a cable/DSL router and hub to connect all of your computers to one Internet connection, like one from Linksys for less than $100. You can also use just a hub made for that purpose, such as UNET II Internet Sharing Hub; cost is around $200.

Each hardware device has its advantages and disadvantages. Some have no dial-on-demand capability, for example, and others might be difficult to set up and configure.

 For more information about modem-sharing software and hardware, see Chapter 16.

Fax services

Setting up faxing services is more complex than most other shares. Configuring and successfully using a fax over one computer is difficult enough; adding a network makes the task even more complex.

 For as much trouble as faxing can be when done from computers, you probably should get a standard fax machine for your small-business office. You'll save a lot of time and effort. Configuring and maintaining electronic faxes is time-consuming and frustrating.

When you set up a fax service, you must consider what to do about incoming calls. If your faxing software is configured to accept calls, there's a chance a call will go out and come in at the same time. These calls will collide and possibly lock up the system. It might be best if you can designate one dedicated line for outgoing calls and another line for incoming calls.

On the other hand, there are fax servers (such as FAXCOMM) you can connect to your network and other hardware and software (like Lotus Notes) to help you fax. Unless you use a fax server, it's unlikely you'll be able to direct the faxes. A *fax server* is a high-powered server on a client/server network that manages incoming and outgoing faxes. The fax server routes any received faxes to an individual, department, or workgroup on the network. But in the case of your home network, that shouldn't be a problem. You also need to leave the computer with the fax server on at all times, just in case a fax comes in.

Many software programs enable you to send and receive faxes, including Mighty Fax and Just the Fax (RKS Software), Microsoft Fax, and RightFax by Captaris.

Sharing scanners

With today's multifunction printers (printer, copier, and scanner all in one machine), people are sharing more and more. All you need to do to share a multifunction printer is connect it and share it like you would a printer.

If, on the other hand, you want to share your flatbed or handheld scanner, that involves a little more work. Several programs enable you to share scanners. For example, UMAX makes Network Scan, which enables PC users to connect to a scanner attached to another computer on the network, using one PC as a host, or scan server, and another PC as the scan client. See www.umax.com for more information about prices and availability.

Stalker Software, Inc., has a utility that lets users share scanners over an AppleTalk network. For less than $100, ScanShare works with any scanner that supports the Apple Scanner interface.

Sharing CD/DVD burners

To share a CD or DVD burner, you need third-party software. Several programs available enable you to share the burners, such as NeroNET, CD Emulator, and Connectix Virtual PC.

Note   If you're using Linux, you can search the Internet to download a free Linux utility such as `cdrecord` or `koncd` for sharing your CD/DVD burner.

✦ NeroNET works across an IP intranet so that all intranet users can access all available recorders on the network. NeroNET consists of two components: NeroNET-Server and Nero, the client. NeroNET runs on one computer, and Nero runs on the other. NeroNET works only with one burner at a time; the client and server cannot run on the same PC at the same time; and NeroNET doesn't support DVD sharing at this time.

✦ You may easily share burners between like operating systems; however, you might encounter trouble between, say, a Mac and PC. Other software programs available, such as CD Emulator, are designed to help share burners between various operating systems. CD Emulator includes the server and client software to run over the network. Look for network versions.

✦ Connectix Virtual PC is a PC emulator for the Mac. You use it to run Windows on the Mac so you can access printers and other peripherals, after installing the correct Windows drivers. Using Connectix, you can share a CD burner easily between the Mac and Windows.

To share a CD burner between XP machines, enable remote desktop sharing on the machine with the burner. Then connect it using the Remote Desktop Client. This program is included with Windows 2000 and XP.

You can also share CD burners using direct cable between two computers, using a USB hub, or with wireless technology. For more information on these technologies, see Chapters 6 and 7.

Summary

In this chapter, you've learned about sharing resources over the network. Specifically, you've learned about the following:

✦ Sharing folders and drives

✦ Sharing files

✦ Sharing printers and other peripherals

In the next chapter, you learn about accessing the network by logging on, mapping drives, and logging off of the network.

✦   ✦   ✦

Accessing the Network

In This Chapter

Logging on to
the network

Mapping drives

Using network
commands

Protecting the network
from viruses

After you get your network hardware and software set up and configured, you're ready to work on your networked computer. A networked computer behaves a bit differently than a standalone computer; you have to log on (sign on) to the network, for example, and log off. You also can use shortcuts that help you find other networked computers and files. Anytime you need a resource from another computer on the network, you want to easily locate the computer and its resources.

Logging On to the Network

When you turn your computer on, you must log on (or log in). Logging on means you enter your username and password in a dialog box, and Windows, Macs, and Linux machines use that information to authenticate you (validate your logon information) on the network. A *password* is an identifier for an authorized user to gain access to the network. When you are authenticated, you gain access to the network resources for which you have access.

Depending on the type of network you're logging on to, you may need to log different information. If, for example, you log on to a Windows 2000 network, you must enter your username, a password, and the domain to which you belong. A *domain* is similar to a workgroup, except each domain includes a server that authenticates you to the network.

> **Note** If you log on to a Windows standalone computer, you enter your Windows username and password. Logging on to Windows identifies you to the operating system, which then displays your personal settings for your colors, programs, passwords to the Internet, and so on. Multiple users can access one computer, and each can customize preferences and desktop settings.

In addition to your username and password, you can set options for logging on to the network. In Windows 98, set these options in the Network dialog box. In Windows XP, you use the User Accounts dialog box. In Mac OS X, you use My Account.

If you're using a client/server network and your server software is Windows 2000, you can set up users in one of two ways: Computer Management or Active Directory. For more information about

Windows 2000 user setup and configuration, see the *Windows 2000 Server Bible* by Jeffrey R. Shapiro and Jim Boyce (Wiley Publishing, Inc. 2000) or *Windows 2000 Server Secrets* by Harry M. Brelsford (Wiley Publishing, Inc. 1999) or read the Windows 2000 Server documentation.

Setting logon preferences

In most networked computers, you can set your logon preferences. If your computer is a member of a domain, for example, you can name that domain so that the computer automatically attaches to the network when you log on. As a home network user, however, you will most likely use a workgroup instead of a domain.

Another preference you can choose is for a quick logon. A quick logon ignores any network drive connections you may have set, so you can get on the network and start working immediately. You may not have set any network drive connections (also called mapping drives — see the section on this later in this chapter). Setting a network drive connection means you create a shortcut to help you quickly connect to another network computer. You might create a shortcut to a drive or to a folder, for example. Mapping drives is particularly handy when you often connect to a folder that's buried several levels deep on another drive.

Setting logon preferences in Windows 98

To set your logon preferences in Windows 98, follow these steps:

1. Choose Start ➪ Settings ➪ Control Panel.

2. Double-click the Network icon. The Network dialog box appears.

3. In the Configuration tab, select Client for Microsoft Networks, as shown in Figure 13-1.

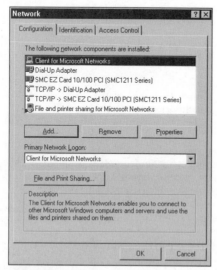

Figure 13-1: Select Client for Microsoft Networks.

4. Click the Properties button. The Client for Microsoft Networks Properties dialog box appears, as shown in Figure 13-2.

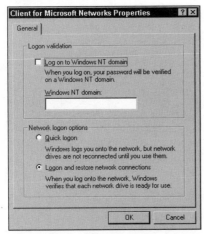

Figure 13-2: Set logon preferences in the Client for Microsoft Networks Properties dialog box.

Note   If you're a client on a Windows 2000 Server network, check the Log On to Windows NT Domain check box and enter the appropriate domain name.

5. In the Network logon options, select one of the following:

   • **Quick logon.** Windows will log on to the network quickly, without restoring network drive connections; however, you can restore these connections easily when you need them. See the section "Mapping Drives" later in the chapter for more information.

   • **Logon and restore network connections.** Windows's logon is a bit slower, but it reconnects all mapped drives so that the connections are ready when you need them.

Tip   It's best to choose quick logon if the other computers in your network are not always going to be on. If you choose to restore network connections and a network computer isn't turned on, your computer searches for a long time before asking you to cancel the connection.

6. Click OK to close the Client for Microsoft Networks Properties dialog box, and then click OK again to close the Network dialog box. Close the Control Panel.

If your Windows 98 computer is in a workgroup instead of a client/server network, you choose the Identification tab in the Network dialog box, as shown in Figure 13-3. In this dialog box, you enter the computer's name as others see it on the network, the name of the workgroup, and optionally, any comment you want others to see when it's networked.

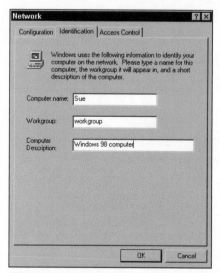

Figure 13-3: Identify your computer and the workgroup in the Network dialog box.

Setting logon preferences in Windows XP

If you're using a Windows XP computer, you can change logon information in the User Accounts dialog box. Follow these steps:

1. Click Start ➪ Control Panel. The Control Panel appears, as shown in Figure 13-4.

Figure 13-4: Set the computer logon preferences in Windows XP.

2. Click User Accounts. The User Accounts dialog box appears (see Figure 13-5).

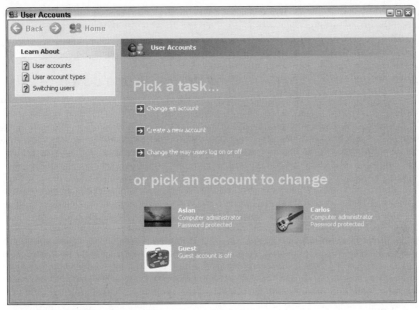

Figure 13-5: Change or create a computer user.

3. Choose an account to change, and you can change the username, password account type, and other information, as shown in Figure 13-6.

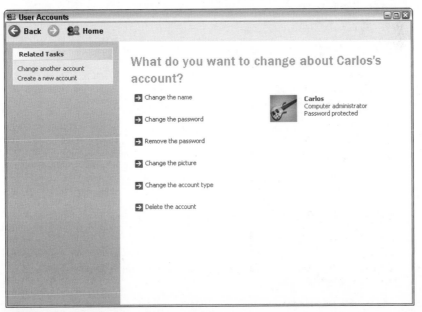

Figure 13-6: Change a user's account.

Note   The account type describes whether the user is an administrator or has limited permissions for the computer. This account type does not affect the network permissions.

4. Click the X to close the dialog boxes.

Changing user information on Windows XP in a domain

If you're using Windows XP Professional on a domain, such as in a Windows 2000 Server network, you have to configure the user(s) twice in two different places. First, you perform the steps described in the preceding section for creating or changing user accounts on the XP computer. Second, you must create or change accounts in the Computer Management dialog box to match the computer accounts. Basically, you can add finer detail to the permissions in the Computer Management dialog box.

To create or change a user in Computer Management for the domain account, follow these steps:

1. Click Start ➪ Control Panel. The Control Panel dialog box appears.

2. Click Performance ➪ Maintenance. The Performance and Maintenance dialog box appears.

3. Scroll to the bottom of the dialog box. Click Administrative Tools. The Administrative Tools dialog box appears.

4. Double-click Computer Management. The Computer Management console appears (see Figure 13-7).

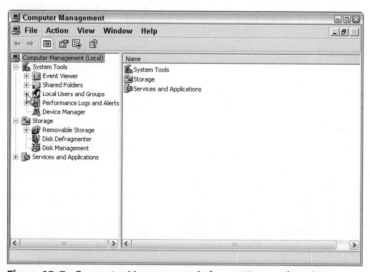

Figure 13-7: Computer Management is for an XP on a domain.

5. Expand Local Users and Groups and select Users. A list of computer users appears in the right window pane.

6. Right-click the user you want to configure, and choose Properties from the pop-up window. The user's Properties dialog box appears (see Figure 13-8).

Figure 13-8: Configuring a user for the domain in XP

Caution

The options and permissions in this dialog box refer to the domain network. Generally, only an administrator has the rights to configure users. If you do not understand the rights, then don't make any changes until you're sure of what you're doing. To learn more about Windows XP permissions, see www.microsoft.com/technet/.

Setting logon preferences in Mac OS X

To change user accounts in a Mac OS X computer, you use My Account. Follow these steps:

1. Click System Preferences. The System Preferences dialog box appears.

2. Click My Account. The My Account dialog box appears, as shown in Figure 13-9.

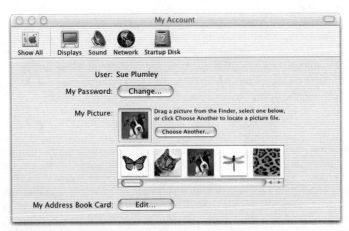

Figure 13-9: Making changes to a logon in a Mac

3. You can change the password, choose another picture for the logon, or work in your address book.

4. Click the X to close the dialog box.

Note   For information about logging on to your Linux machine, see the documentation for your specific distribution.

Understanding usernames

Your username is the name by which you're known to your computer and/or on the network. You might use your first name, a nickname, or some other identifier. You can use any combination of letters and numbers; uppercase, lowercase, or initial caps; and even spaces within the name.

Windows 98 stores each user's unique identification information in a password list (PWL) file. The name of the PWL file is the username plus the PWL extension, such as Plumlsj.pwl or Hugh.pwl. The file is stored in the C:\Windows directory.

A PWL file contains a user's passwords for various programs in Windows, including the following:

✦ Resources protected by share-level security, such as a folder on another network computer and the password you use to access that folder

✦ Internet Explorer and e-mail program passwords

✦ Any passwords for client/server networks, including NT Server and NetWare networks, but not primary logon passwords

The passwords in a PWL file are encrypted, or scrambled in a code format, so that no one can read them.

Tip   If a user on the network forgets his or her logon password, you always can delete that user's PWL file. The file is re-created when the user logs on again; however, the user also will have to enter passwords for a while until the file is totally rebuilt. Deleting the PWL file doesn't delete the user, the password, or any other important information, just the file that stores information for easy and quick access to programs.

Small Business Tip   A common problem with network users is that they automatically enter the password when their computer starts up without looking at the Username box. If someone else logged on to the network using that computer, the username will be different. Make sure that your users are accustomed to looking at the username before entering the password. If the wrong username is listed with the wrong password, access is denied to the network.

In Windows XP, there is no PWL file or even an equivalent. XP is based on NT technology, meaning it is a more secure, more closed system. It is important that if you're using XP, you create at least one user who has administrative rights and keep that user separate from all others. For example, when you first log on to XP, the default is Administrator. You should immediately set up user accounts. You might set up only one user account, but you can set up more. Whether these new accounts are administrative is up to you, but make sure you set up at least one—named ME, SuperPower, Backdoor, or some other name that you'll remember—that has administrative rights. You can make the password anything you want as well, but make sure you remember it. If you fail to set up at least one administrative account, you'll be out of luck when you want to make major changes to the operating system if your own account somehow gets locked out.

Tip

Whenever you're working with Windows, things happen that no one can explain. For example, say you turn your XP machine on one day and it won't let you log on. It doesn't recognize your username and/or your password. Why? There could be many reasons, but no on really knows exactly what happened. You can go back to the last time you were logged on and try to remember if you loaded new software or downloaded a program and perhaps got a virus. The point is that it doesn't matter how it happened as long as you have a workaround. A good workaround here is the backdoor administrator's account you created. Log on as your back door, create yourself a new user, and away you go.

Understanding passwords

You use passwords for security purposes on a client/server network. On a Windows 98 workgroup network, the password doesn't keep anyone from accessing the network, but it does help create the PWL file to store your password list. In Windows XP or on the Mac, your computer is safer than it is in Windows 98. Microsoft and Apple realized that security is a concern, even in small businesses and home networks. So in XP or the Mac, the password does work. You cannot get into an XP or a Mac without a user account and password.

On a Windows 98 workgroup network, anyone can log on to any computer at any time. One of your teenager's friends can turn on a networked computer, for example, and then enter his or her name and any password. If that person opens the Network Neighborhood, all networked computers that are currently turned on appear, giving free access to shared folders and drives.

Tip

You can protect your computer from unauthorized physical access by setting a screen saver password. This technique protects the computer only from physical entry; it doesn't keep anyone from accessing your shared folders over the network if that person successfully hacks into your system. To specify a password that's associated with the screen saver, double-click the Display icon in the Control Panel. Select the Screen Saver tab, and choose a screen saver. Click the Password Protected option, and choose Change. Enter the password, and then click OK in the dialog box.

You can change your Windows password or a network logon password anytime you want. If you're a user on a client/server network, however, you should make sure that the password is changed on the authentication server before changing it on the client computer. If the server doesn't recognize a new password, the user isn't allowed access to the network.

To change your password in Windows 98, follow these steps:

1. Choose Start ➪ Settings ➪ Control Panel.

2. Double-click the Passwords icon. The Passwords Properties dialog box appears.

3. On the Change Passwords tab, click the Change Windows Password button. The Change Windows Password dialog box appears.

4. Enter your current password in the Old Password text box.

5. Enter your new password in the New Password text box.

6. Enter the new password again in the Confirm New Password text box.

7. Click OK to close the dialog box, and then click OK again to close the Passwords Properties dialog box. Close the Control Panel.

In Windows XP, follow these steps to change your password. You can log on to the computer as an administrator to change someone else's password, or you can change your own password after you log on as yourself.

1. Click Start ⇨ Control Panel. The Control Panel appears.

2. Click User Accounts. The User Accounts dialog box appears.

3. Click the account to change. The user's account dialog box appears.

4. Click Change the password. The Change Password dialog box appears, as shown in Figure 13-10.

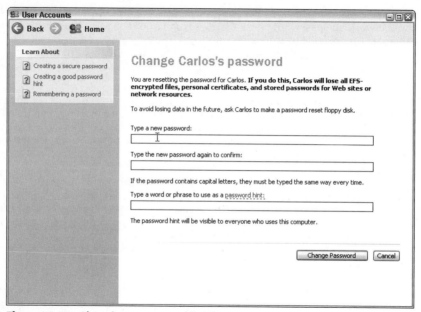

Figure 13-10: Changing a password in XP

5. Type the new password; type the password again to confirm.

6. Optionally, enter a hint.

7. Click Change Password and click X to close out of the dialog box.

To change a password on a Mac OS X computer, follow these steps. You must be logged on as yourself to change your password.

1. Click System Preferences. The System Preferences dialog box appears.

2. Click My Account. The My Account dialog box appears.

3. Beside My Password, click Change. A drop-down box appears.

4. Enter your current password. Enter the new password, and verify it by entering it a second time.

5. Optionally, enter a password hint.

6. Click OK.

7. Close the My Account dialog box.

Logging off the network

You might log off the network for several reasons. If you are on a client/server network, you might log off the network if you don't need to access any network resources or if the server is down. You also can log off if you're sharing your computer and want to give someone else time on the network.

If you're on a workgroup network, you may not have a reason to log off. However, you can log off if you want to log back on as someone else. For example, you might share your computer with someone else. You log off so the other person can log on and therefore access his or her network resources. If you don't share your computer with someone else, you don't need to log off in a workgroup situation, unless you're having trouble connecting to a resource. Sometimes logging off and then back on again cleans up connections and makes it easier to get to a resource. When you shut down your computer, you're automatically logged off and your resources are no longer available.

To log off of the network in Windows, follow these steps:

1. Save all open files and close all programs. You must follow this step before logging off so that you don't lose any data.

2. Choose Start ➪ Log Off (your username).

3. Windows displays the Log Off Windows dialog box, which asks if you're sure you want to log off.

4. Click Yes to log off or No to cancel the dialog box and return to the desktop.

5. Windows displays the Enter Network Password dialog box. You or the new user should enter a username and password to log back on to the network.

To log off a Mac, follow these steps:

1. Click the Apple menu.

2. Click Log Out. A confirmation dialog box appears.

3. Click Log Out.

Mapping Drives

Mapping drives is a method of reconnecting to a network drive and folder as a shortcut. You assign a drive letter — such as J, K, L, M, N, or some other drive not currently in use — to represent the path to the resource.

Small Business Tip

Mapping drives to frequently used folders on other computers on the network saves your users time. You should teach them how to map drives so they can create their own network connections whenever they need them.

For example, suppose that you store files on Sue's computer in the C:\Netshares folder. Each time you want to access that folder, you must double-click Sue's computer and then double-click the Netshares folder. If you map a drive to the Netshares folder and call the drive map K, for example, all you have to do is double-click K in the My Computer or Windows Explorer window and you skip directly to the Netshares folder.

Unfortunately, you can map only to one folder level. You cannot map to C:\Netshares\ Documents, for example, but you can save time by mapping to a networked computer drive and a folder.

You also can map a drive to a folder that requires a password. When you map the drive, Windows prompts for the password. After that, Windows remembers the password and fills it in for you when reconnecting to the folder.

Cross-Reference For information about using My Computer, Windows Explorer, and Network Neighborhood, see Chapter 14.

Understanding network paths

A *path* defines the complete location of a folder or file. When you enter a path for your computer, you start the path with the drive and then list the folders, such as C:\My Documents or C:\My Documents\Pictures.

When you enter a path for a network drive, the path must list the computer and then the shared folders. Also, a network path begins with two backslashes (\\) to indicate it's a network path. So, if you want to write a path to the folder C:\Netshares\Documents\Letters\ Utilities on Sue's computer, you type **\\Sue\Netshares\Documents\Letters\Utilities**. Remember though, for the purpose of mapping, you can map only to \\Sue\Netshares.

If you're ever unsure of a path, you can open the Network Neighborhood or My Network Places and find your way to the folder you want. The path then appears in the address bar of the Network Neighborhood or My Network Places window, as shown in Figure 13-11.

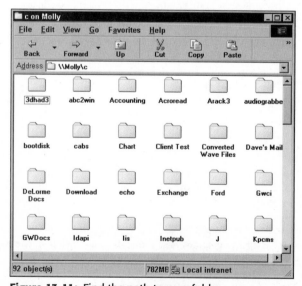

Figure 13-11: Find the path to your folder.

Mapping a drive in Windows

You can map a drive quickly and easily without opening the Network Neighborhood or My Computer window. You also can open the Network Neighborhood, My Computer, or Windows Explorer and map a drive by using the File menu.

The computer to which you are mapping must be turned on. If the computer isn't on, Windows sometimes prompts you to connect through dial-up networking. If you choose not to connect via your modem, Windows reports an error in the mapping procedure.

For quick and easy drive mapping, follow these steps. Windows 98, 2000, and XP are similar in their methods.

1. On the Windows desktop, right-click the My Computer or Network Neighborhood icon.

2. Click Map Network Drive. The Map Network Drive dialog box in Windows 98 appears, as shown in Figure 13-12.

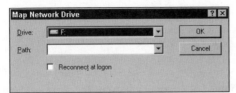

Figure 13-12: Mapping a network drive in Windows 98

Figure 13-13 shows the Map Network Drive dialog box in Windows XP Professional.

Figure 13-13: Mapping a network drive in XP

3. In the Drive drop-down list box, choose a drive letter to represent the folder you're going to map. Only available drive letters appear; you don't see drive letters already used for hard drives, CD-ROM drives, tape drives, and so on.

4. In the folder's Path text box, enter the path to the folder. Alternatively, you can click the down arrow to display a list of recently accessed computers and folders, as shown in Figure 13-14. In XP, you can also browse to the network folder to which you want to connect.

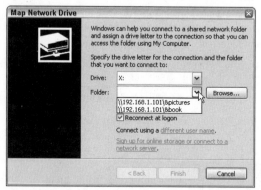

Figure 13-14: If you've recently accessed the folder, find it in the drop-down list.

5. Click the check box beside Reconnect at Logon if you want the mapped drive to connect automatically when you log on to the network. If you use quick logon, the mapped drive won't automatically be reconnected at logon, but you can easily connect when you want (see the section "Accessing and disconnecting a mapped drive," which follows shortly).

6. Click OK or Finish.

If the folder to which you are mapping a drive has a password assigned to it, the Enter Network Password dialog box appears. The first time you connect to the drive, you can save the password in your password list by clicking the Save This Password in Your Password List check box.

Mapping a drive on a Macintosh

On the Macintosh, mapping a drive is a little different on each operating system. Using Mac OS X, you follow these steps to map a drive:

1. Click Go ➪ Connect to Server. The Connect to Server dialog box appears.

2. In the At drop-down list, choose the computer's address or the server name you want to view, as shown in Figure 13-15.

3. In the window pane, double-click the computer to which you want to connect.

4. Select the folder you want to map. Click Add to Favorites.

5. Click Connect.

Figure 13-15: Locate the server containing the folder you want.

To view the mapped, or favorite, folder on the Mac, select Go ⇨ Favorites, and choose the folder you want to open.

Accessing and disconnecting a mapped drive

You easily can access a mapped drive from the My Computer window. You also can disconnect a mapped drive when you have finished using the folder, for example.

Also, if a computer to which you mapped a drive isn't turned on when you log on to the network, you can choose to reconnect the drive the next time you log on or to disconnect the mapped drive.

Accessing a mapped drive

To access a folder on a mapped drive, follow these steps:

1. On the desktop, double-click My Computer. The My Computer window appears, as shown in Figure 13-16. The figure was taken in Windows XP, but the window looks similar in Windows 98.

Tip

Alternatively, you can access the mapped drive in the Windows Explorer or Network Neighborhood. See Chapter 14 for more information about these programs.

2. Double-click the mapped drive to display the contents of the mapped folder, as shown in Figure 13-17.

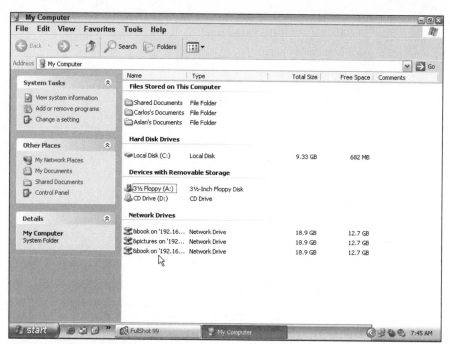

Figure 13-16: Access a mapped drive (seen in the figure under Network Drives) through the My Computer window.

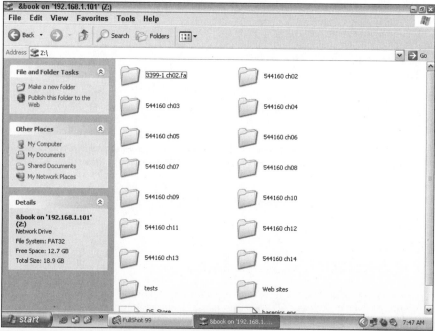

Figure 13-17: Quickly attach to the mapped folder.

Disconnecting a mapped drive

To disconnect a mapped drive and therefore lose the mapping permanently, follow these steps:

1. Right-click the My Computer icon on your desktop.

2. Choose Disconnect Network Drive from the quick menu. The Disconnect Network Drive dialog box appears, as shown in Figure 13-18. This figure is from Windows XP.

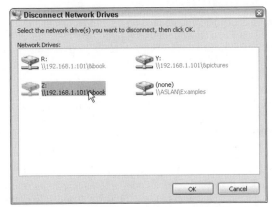

Figure 13-18: Disconnect any mapped drive you no longer use or need.

3. In the list of Drives in Windows 98 or in the dialog box in Windows XP, select the drive you want to delete.

4. Click OK to disconnect the network connection.

Reconnecting at logon

If you're using the option for reconnecting network drives upon logon (set in the Client for Microsoft Networks dialog box), Windows verifies that the computers you're mapped to are turned on. If a computer to which you are mapped is not turned on, Windows notifies you that it cannot map the drive and offers the option of reconnecting to the networked computer the next time you log on.

If someone turns on the networked computer while you're working, you always can reconnect by opening the My Computer window and double-clicking the drive mapping icon.

If you're using the quick logon option, your network drives are not automatically verified at logon. All you have to do, however, is double-click the mapped drive icon in the My Computer window to connect the drive. If the resource is available, a connection occurs immediately; if the resource is not available, a warning dialog box appears.

Using Network Commands

Windows includes several network commands you can use at the Microsoft Disk Operating System (MS-DOS) prompt. These commands enable you to view your current network connections, view any computer's shared resources, and even create permanent connections, or drive mappings. There are even help commands that you can use at the MS-DOS prompt to help you with entering network commands.

Some people are accustomed to using DOS commands from the old days; other people might be uncomfortable with the prospect if Windows is all they've ever known. These MS-DOS network commands, however, supply several options you can't get within Windows, so you might want to try them.

Understanding DOS commands

The DOS command line accepts only cryptic commands you enter at the prompt. The prompt is the C:\> or C:\Windows>, for example, that appears when you open the MS-DOS prompt window. The letter represents the drive letter, and any text after a backslash represents a directory; a directory is the same thing as a folder in Windows. To tell MS-DOS to perform a task, you type a command and then press the Enter key.

Note   To access command prompt, choose Star ➪ Programs ➪ MS-DOS Prompt in Windows 98. In Windows 2000 and XP, choose Start ➪ Programs ➪ Accessories ➪ Command Prompt. The window appears as white type on a black screen. To exit the program, type **exit** and press Enter. The window closes.

You might be familiar with typing commands at the MS-DOS prompt, such as DIR to list a directory's contents. You also might know that you can add certain text to a command to change the results. For example, typing DIR /W lists the directory in multiple columns on your screen instead of in one long, flowing column.

Commands

When you type a command in MS-DOS, you use the command name. DIR, for example, is the name of the command. DIR stands for directory. You don't have to type the command in all uppercase; in this book, however, the commands are written in uppercase so that you can distinguish them easily from ordinary text.

Some commands require parameters that identify the exact object the command is to act on. Commands also might include switches that modify the command or action. Other commands require only the command name to perform a task.

You type the command at the prompt and press the Enter key to activate it. After MS-DOS performs the command, it lists the results on the screen.

Parameters

Parameters are additional information the command needs to continue or complete the task. The parameter defines the object on which the command acts. If you type the DEL (delete) command, for example, you must tell MS-DOS what to delete. The parameter in this case, then, is the file you want to delete, as in DEL MEMO.DOC. In this example, you are telling the computer to delete the MEMO.DOC file.

Parameters can be drives, paths, files, or any specifics that provide more information for the command to act on.

Switches

A *switch* modifies the way the command performs the task. You separate a switch from the command with a space and a forward slash (/). Normally, switches are single letters or numbers that represent the modification. For example, DIR /W means to list the directory across multiple columns instead of one; W stands for wide. DIR /P means to list the directory one screen at a time, pausing (P) between screens.

Note

Another switch you can use for displaying only one screen of results at a time is |MORE. The pipe character (|), in this case, works like the forward slash to make MORE a switch. This is the only switch that uses the pipe instead of the forward slash. The pipe character is located on the backslash key; use the Shift key plus the backslash key to type the pipe character.

Some MS-DOS commands don't have any switches, and some have many. If a command has more than one switch, you can type them one after another, dividing them with spaces and forward slashes, as in DIR /W /P.

Canceling a command

Most commands are carried out quickly; however, you might be able to cancel a command after it's been entered. Press Ctrl+C to cancel a command and display the command prompt again.

Caution

Any action that took place before you canceled the command cannot be undone.

Using common MS-DOS network commands

MS-DOS includes several network commands. You don't need them all, because many are meant specifically for client/server network tasks. A few of them, however, you might use quite often, once you get the hang of them.

Viewing help

You can list the network commands, along with a brief description of each, in MS-DOS. You also can list more specific help for any MS-DOS command. You have two methods of getting general help for MS-DOS commands: NET HELP and NET /?. The question mark acts as a switch to the NET command.

Figure 13-19 shows the Command Prompt screen in XP with the NET commands listed; type NET HELP and press Enter to get the same results.

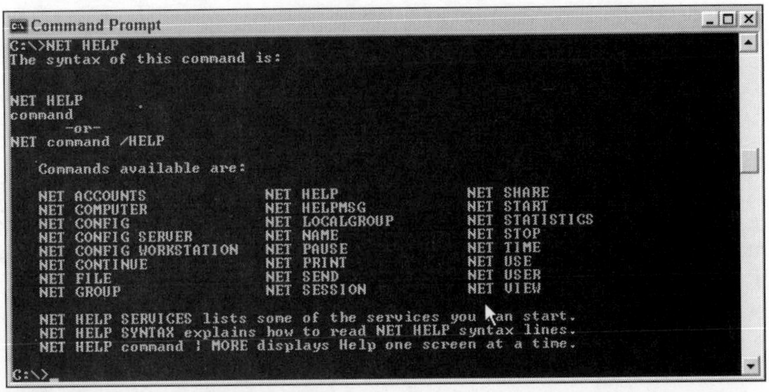

Figure 13-19: Getting NET help

Note   NET HELP works in XP, whereas NET /? does not; however, /? after any other command in 2000 and XP does work.

When you type either command, MS-DOS lists all the network MS-DOS commands, along with a brief description. Because there is more than one screen of commands, you might want display the commands one screen at a time. Using the |MORE switch or the /P switch, you can display a screen of help at a time.

If you want to display help on any one command, you can enter the command with the /? switch. For example, type NET USE /? to view a description of that command plus any parameters and switches you can use with NET USE. NET USE is a command that displays your current network connections.

Viewing connections

PING is the most common command used at a command prompt. PING sends echoes out to the IP address you specify and then lists responses back from the device. If PING doesn't work, the connection isn't working on a hardware level. For example, suppose you type the following into one computer:

    PING 192.168.11.123

The command sends the echo request to the IP address 192.168.11.123. If the network card, cable or wireless connection, hub or switch, and any other hardware in between are working, the other computer replies. If there is a problem, the PING request times out.

Cross-Reference   For more information about using PING, see Appendix B.

Viewing a computer's network settings

The NET CONFIG command, in Windows 98, enables you to view the current computer's network settings. You see the computer's name, username, workgroup name, and software (operating system) version. Following is an example of what you might see if you type NET CONFIG at the MS-DOS prompt.

    Computer Name \\Sue
    User name   PlumSJ
    Workgroup   Opinions
    Workstation Root Directory   C:\Windows
    Software Version   4.10.1999
    Redirector Version 4.00

The *redirector* is a software module on all networked computers. The redirector intercepts the requests from applications and diverts them to another computer.

Note   In Windows XP, the NET CONFIG command is of little help to you because it shows you the services you can control that are running instead of username and workgroup. Some other DOS commands you cannot use with 2000 and XP because of the security. Still, if you're in doubt, try the command. Windows will tell you what you need to know.

Viewing network shares

You can use the `NET VIEW` command to view all computers attached to the network. You also can use the command, with parameters and switches, to view the resources on any one networked computer. The resources list any shared folders, drives, printers, and so on.

The following shows a list of computers you might see if you type `NET VIEW` at the MS-DOS prompt:

```
\\Hugh
\\Molly
\\Sue
```

If you want to see the resources on one computer, type `NET VIEW \\HUGH /YES`, for example. `NET VIEW` is the command, `\\HUGH` is the computer's name, and `/YES` is a confirmation that you want to view the resources. Following is a listing of what you might see:

```
&Accounts      Disk
&Network Disk
&School    Disk
HP Color 720   Print
Zip      Disk
```

Using batch files for permanent connections

One particularly useful MS-DOS command is `NET USE`. You can use this command to set up a permanent network connection (drive mapping) for any user with Windows 98 or XP. Although you also can use Windows drive mapping to perform this task, often the user cancels the Reconnect at Logon option (if the mapped computer is turned off, for example) and loses the mapping. Then you have to create the mapping again — and again and again. To create permanent connections that the user cannot cancel, you can create a batch file in the StartUp group. A *batch file* is a text file that contains commands that are carried out automatically upon startup. The commands are entered into the system, one at a time, just as if you had typed them in yourself. Batch files use a .BAT extension to identify them as such to the operating system.

One problem with using an MS-DOS batch file for network connections is that MS-DOS cannot use long filenames or spaces in filenames. If your computer's name or any folder's name is longer than eight characters, or if you use a space within the computer's name or the folder's name, you cannot use the MS-DOS batch file for connection purposes. The path \\Sue\My Documents doesn't work with the `NET USE` command, for example, because My Documents is both more than eight characters long and contains a space.

Small Business Tip   Use a batch file for permanent connections to save your users (and yourself) time and frustration. You can create one file that lists all network connections so that the user always can find quickly the folders he or she needs.

Creating the file

`NET USE` connects to or disconnects from a shared resource. In any text editor, such as Notepad, you type the command `NET USE`. The first parameter lists the drive letter you want to assign, such as J:, K:, L:, M:, or some other drive letter. Next, type the path to the folder. You can add multiple mapped drives to the same file.

You save the file as a BAT file. You can save it anywhere, such as the Windows directory. Next, place a shortcut in the Windows StartUp folder. The next time the user starts the computer, the network connections are made automatically.

Creating a batch file is a lot easier than it sounds. Follow these steps:

1. Choose Start ⇨ Programs ⇨ Accessories ⇨ Notepad. The Notepad window appears.

2. Type the command and parameters. Following is a sample: NET USE N: \\SUE\ NETSHARE.

3. Optionally, add other drive mappings, such as NET USE N: \\SUE\NETSHARE, \\SUE\MSPUBS, and \\CARLOS\DOCS.

4. Choose File ⇨ Save As. The Save As dialog box appears.

5. In the File Name text box, enter a name; the name must be no more than eight characters long, plus the .BAT extension. Make sure that you enter the .BAT extension; otherwise, Notepad enters a .TXT extension. You might call it CONNECT.BAT, for example, or HUGH.BAT.

6. In the Save as Type box, specify that you want to save the file as a text document.

7. By default, Notepad saves files in the My Documents folder. You should not save the file here because it can be deleted easily. Save the file in the C:\Windows directory.

8. Click Save. Figure 13-20 illustrates the batch file in Notepad.

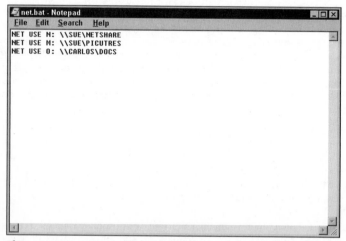

Figure 13-20: Enter multiple network connections, if you want.

9. Choose File ⇨ Exit.

Placing the file in the StartUp folder

You must place the file in the StartUp folder before it will work. Any file in the StartUp folder is executed automatically when Windows starts. When using the StartUp folder, you can use a shortcut to the file instead of the original file, so you'll have a backup for the file. (A *shortcut* is a marker that identifies the file and its location.)

You use the Windows Explorer to create the shortcut and move it to the folder. If you need help with the Windows Explorer, see Chapter 14.

To place the file's shortcut in the StartUp folder, follow these steps:

1. Choose Start ➪ Programs ➪ Windows Explorer. The Windows Explorer window appears.

2. Open the Windows folder. In the right window, scroll to the end of the folders list, where the list of files begins. Locate your file; files are listed in alphabetical order after the list of folders. Select the file.

3. Right-click the file, and from the quick menu, choose Create Shortcut. Windows creates the shortcut to your batch file and places it at the end of the file list, with the shortcut selected.

4. Right-click the selected file and choose Cut from the quick menu.

5. In the left window of the Explorer, locate the StartUp folder. It is located in C:\Windows\ Start Menu\Programs.

6. Select the StartUp folder. Choose Edit ➪ Paste. Windows pastes the shortcut to the batch file in the folder, as shown in Figure 13-21.

7. Close the Windows Explorer.

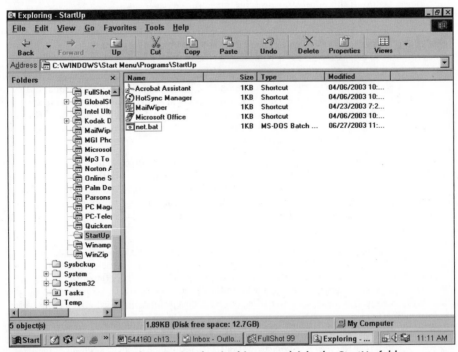

Figure 13-21: Place the shortcut (net.bat in this example) in the StartUp folder.

Using Mac network commands

Each operating system for the Mac has distinctive networking commands and features. You should use these commands or applications only if you're comfortable with the computer and you understand the consequences of your actions.

Note   Earlier versions of the Mac operating system, such as System 8 or 9, have a Network Assistant that you can use to help manage the network. Do not try to use the Network Assistant with Mac OS X, however; you could damage the operating system. Following are just a few of the incidents that could happen: The computer doesn't start, the computer starts up with a flashing question mark, or a kernel panic happens during or after startup.

Using Linux network commands

Most distributions of Linux include network commands you can install. Common commands enable you to configure the network interface, display configuration, map drives, share printers, and so on.

`IFCONFIG` is a command you can use to display the current configuration. It describes the IP address, subnet mask, and a broadcast address of the subnet. You can also use the `PING` command with Linux boxes. `NSTAT` and `NETSTAT` are two commands that result in network statistics relating to the computer on which it is typed.

Protecting the Network from Viruses

One of the first procedures any computer should perform when it boots is to check for viruses. *Viruses* are computer programs that disrupt or destroy your files, file system, software, hardware, your work, or even your network. A virus might only display a message, or it could erase or reformat your hard disk. A virus can attack one computer and then travel the network to other computers and your server. New viruses are found daily, each with its own brand of destruction and aggravation.

Your computer can catch a virus from a contaminated floppy disk, a file on the network, a file downloaded from the Internet, or a file attached to an e-mail message; a virus can even ride on the back of a worm through your Internet connection. After it's infected, your computer crashes and burns; worse yet, your infected computer could take down the entire network. Your network is only as strong as its weakest computer when it comes to fighting viruses and worms.

Because viruses can quickly spread over the network, it's important that all computers on the network are protected. Many computers come with an antivirus program installed — Symantec or Norton AntiVirus or McAfee VirusScan, depending on the computer manufacturer. Many other antivirus applications are available. You should use a virus program daily, and you should keep the program's list of viruses (called *definitions*) and cures updated.

Small Business Tip   Discuss with your employees the danger of bringing disks from home and downloading files from the Internet — especially e-mail. Also, require all users to keep an antivirus program running on their computers all the time so that it catches viruses as they appear on the computer. One virus spread to a network can cost hundreds of thousands of dollars in hardware damage and data corruption.

You can set the properties on most antivirus programs. In most cases, you can tell the program to load when you boot the computer and then scan files of various types. You also tell the program how to react to finding a virus — whether to alert you or the entire network, quarantine or delete the infected file, and so on.

Note You also must be careful with antivirus programs. Some programs can cause problems with computer or networking hardware, operating systems, and even other programs on the computer. To help guard against problems, buy only reputable brand name antivirus programs. Free antivirus programs are not usually worth the time it takes to download them. If your computer, network, or programs have problems, disable the antivirus program and see if that helps alleviate your trouble. You also might check the Internet for reported problems.

Looking closer at viruses

Computer viruses infect other programs by copying themselves into the program. They also try to hide within the program by encrypting themselves. Many viruses mutate slightly every time they replicate, so as to escape detection. Viruses can even mutate and replicate from computer to computer on a private network. You have to watch out for all sorts of attacks: viruses, worms, Trojan horses, and even hoaxes. If you have a question about a virus or you need to fix a virus your antivirus program missed, check the Symantec site: www.sarc.com.

Nuisances and viruses

One of the worst viruses to date is Klez (with variations called W32.Klez.H@mm, Klez A, Klez D, Klez E, Klez H, and anything with Klez in the name). This virus is a mass-mailing e-mail worm. Klez is difficult to remove once it gets a hold of your computer. Klez fills the hard drive with trash and garbage while destroying data and overwriting files. Then, it travels across your network easily and efficiently.

Tip If you discover a virus on any computer connected to your network, the first thing to do is unplug the cable from the network so the virus cannot travel to other computers. If you're using a wireless network, turn the infected computer off until you can verify the safety of the other computers. Unplug the access point near the infected computer before turning it back on to apply a fix.

Some viruses do more than make copies of themselves: They issue instructions that disrupt the computer's normal processes. Viruses often use the computer's clock to trigger the disruption — from displaying a message to crashing a hard disk. The Michelangelo virus is one of those that activates according to the clock: Yearly, on March 6, Michelangelo's birthday, the virus takes over your hard disk. There are other types of nuisances, and not all are classified as viruses:

✦ The Melissa virus, for example, is actually a Microsoft Word macro. Macros are mini-programs that run when a file is opened or you actually initiate the macro. Many programs use macros — Word and WordPerfect, for example — and even let you create macros that can make your work easier and help you complete tasks more quickly. However, there are macros that can activate within a program and destroy your documents. Melissa travels in a Word document and is activated only when the document is opened in Word. If you don't open the document containing the macro, the macro isn't activated. Melissa is contained in a file attached to e-mail messages.

✦ Programs that Web browsers automatically download from Web sites can modify or delete data or crash your system. Some of these hostile Java applets and ActiveX controls can even broadcast your computer data all over the Internet. If you're using the Internet Explorer, you can set the Security (View ➪ Internet Options ➪ Security tab) to block Web content that could damage your computer. Other browsers, such as Netscape Navigator, have similar options.

✦ *Trojan horses* are destructive programs that programmers sometimes hide in normal software. These programs don't necessarily copy themselves or spread from machine to machine, but they can damage or encrypt your data just the same.

✦ *Worms* are another type of virus. A worm program enters networked computers and continuously copies itself, consuming resources and hampering network operations as it goes.

✦ Hoaxes are generally sent over e-mail, and they are more a nuisance than anything dangerous. The problem with hoaxes is that they often tell you to delete a file to delete the "virus." Usually those files are files that normally exist in your Windows operating system; deleting the file can damage Windows. It's always best to check a reputable Internet site before you take any action touted in an e-mail.

Antivirus programs take care of most of the previously mentioned viruses, as long as you keep your definitions up-to-date.

Virus distribution

Most viruses spread in one of three ways: by attaching to the boot sector of the computer, by attaching to executable files, or as macros (mini-programs) in documents or spreadsheets. Worms, on the other hand, can ride into your computer on the back of e-mail, executable files, and HTML pages. Worms also ride packets across your network, infecting each computer one by one.

✦ Boot sector viruses usually come to your computer on a floppy disk that is also a boot disk. A boot disk is one you insert in the floppy drive and use to start your computer. Certain system files are present, and these files prompt the computer to start up. When you boot your system, the files copy themselves to the boot sector of your hard disk. The boot sector is the set of instructions your computer reads when it starts up.

✦ Program viruses that attach themselves to executable files load themselves into memory when you run the file. The file might have an .EXE or .COM extension, but it also might be a SYS, DLL, BIN, or other file on your system. If you double-click an infected EXE file, such as an animation file you receive from a friend, the virus is activated and spreads through your computer.

✦ A macro virus affects the NORMAL.DOT file (a Word or Excel template). When the template is infected, every document you open in that program also becomes infected.

Viruses can work on your system only if you activate them by running the program, opening the document, or booting your system with an infected disk. If you check files and documents first with an antivirus program, you can eliminate the viruses on your system — but only if you keep the program's virus definitions up-to-date.

Tip

There are mass-mailing worms that spread through file-sharing networks, such as Kazaa and IRC. These worms attempt to deactivate an antivirus program running on your computer. The best way to stop these viruses is to keep your definitions up-to-date.

Looking at antivirus programs

Many antivirus programs are on the market today. Many of them are inexpensive, reliable, and safe to use. You also can get virus upgrades for most programs over the Internet.

Before buying an antivirus program, you might want to try a demo version of the software. Usually, you can find a demo version on the Internet. Following are some of the more popular and trusted antivirus programs:

Norton AntiVirus (from Symantec Corporation) is popular and dependable. Norton AntiVirus runs in the background and checks e-mail attachments, Internet downloads, files on floppy disks, CD-ROMs, and network files. You also can retrieve new antivirus definitions from Symantec over the Internet. This program costs about $65 per computer, or you can buy a 5- or 10-pack $200 and $400, respectively. Norton is made for Windows and Macs.

Note   Symantec also makes the Symantec AntiVirus Corporate Edition for client/server networks. Install the program to the server and the client. The server schedules live updates of the virus definitions and pushes the definitions (or downloads automatically) to the clients without the users' knowledge.

McAfee VirusScan (from Network Associates) includes virus detection, removal, and support services. It scans all drives, boot sectors, file allocation and partition tables, and compressed files. McAfee costs about $50 for one computer, and Network Associates also offers multiple license packs.

Macintosh also has various antivirus programs. Norton is available for Macs, as is McAfee. Linux distributions also require virus protection. Vexira AntiVirus is one program available for Linux boxes. F-Prot Antivirus, RAV, and other programs are also available. Check your distribution, and then find a program that works best with that.

Finding and applying virus fixes

If you use an up-to-date antivirus program, you shouldn't have too much trouble with a virus getting through to your computer or your network. If, however, you miss an update or a new virus does get by your antivirus program, you can usually get a fix for the virus within a couple of days of the appearance of the virus. Again, if one computer on the network contains a virus, disconnect that computer from the network until you get the fix.

Symantec's site — www.sarc.com — offers fixes for most viruses that you can download from the site and apply to your computer. Make sure you check for the Windows or the Mac version of the fix, and do read all instructions. Many fixes involve just running the fix file you download. Other fixes involve manually removing the virus and its parts from your computer. If you must work in the Registry of Windows, for example, make sure you make a backup of the Registry before beginning.

If you think an e-mail that has been sent to you might be a hoax, make sure you check it out before sending it on to everyone in your address book. You can check the Symantec site or check this government site about hoaxes: http://hoaxbusters.ciac.org/.

Summary

In this chapter, you learned about accessing and protecting the network. Specifically, you've learned about the following:

✦ Logging on to the network

✦ Mapping drives

✦ Using batch files for permanent connections

✦ Logging off of the network

✦ Protecting the network from viruses

In the next chapter, you learn about finding and browsing computers on the network.

✦　　✦　　✦

Finding Computers on the Network

You know how to find files and folders on your own computer, but when you start looking on others' computers for specific files, you can waste a lot of time. Windows supplies several methods for finding files and folders over the network, including the Windows Explorer, Network Neighborhood, My Computer, and more. Choose the method that is most comfortable for you.

In addition, Macs and Linux computers have special methods for locating computers on the network. When you're working with various operating systems on the same network, you'll most likely run into some trouble locating all of the resources you want. This chapter covers some ideas for locating computers, even in hard-to-find places.

Using Network Paths

As you know, a path is a guide to the location of a folder or file on the computer. C:\My Documents\My Pictures, for example, leads to the My Pictures folder on the C: drive.

A *network path* is one that leads to a computer on the network and then to a folder or file on that computer. For example, \\Sue\My Documents\My Pictures leads to the My Pictures folder on Sue's computer, over the network. The double backslashes tell the operating system to locate the following over the network instead of on the local computer.

You have several methods of using the network path in Windows to get to the folder or file you want to locate. Although using the network path may not be the easiest method of getting somewhere, it works very well, as long as you know the name of the computer and the path on that computer to the folder or file. You also must have access to the resources and the resources must be shared.

Tip

Browsing the available network computers and folders may be easier for you. See the sections later in the chapter on using the Network Neighborhood, My Computer, and the Windows Explorer.

CHAPTER

14

◆   ◆   ◆   ◆

In This Chapter

Using network paths

Using Find Computer

Using My Computer

Using Windows Explorer

Using Network Neighborhood/ My Network Places

Finding computers on Macs

Finding computers on Linux

◆   ◆   ◆   ◆

Using the Run command

The Run dialog box, shown in Figure 14-1, works similarly to an MS-DOS prompt. You can enter a command, folder, or other element in the Open text box, and when you click OK, Run opens the file or folder or executes the command.

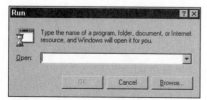

Figure 14-1: Run a program or open a file or folder in Windows 98.

To open the Run dialog box, choose Start ➪ Run. You might want to use the Run dialog box to display the contents of another computer on the network if you know the network path and you're in a hurry. Typing the path and pressing Enter or clicking OK quickly displays the networked computer.

Usually, you use the Run dialog box for starting programs. You type in the name of the program and click OK, and the program executes or runs. If you want to enter a program that's not in the root directory, you first must enter the path to that command, just as you would at the MS-DOS prompt. For example, you type the entire path plus the program's name and extension, such as **C:\FullShot99\FullShot99.exe**, to open that program.

You also can type the name of a document with its path — such as **C:\Office\Word\ referral.doc** — in the Run dialog box to open both the referral.doc document and the Microsoft Word program.

You also can type a folder name and path on the local computer or a network path. Typing a network path displays the folder's window. For example, you can enter the path in the Open text box as **\\Sue\My Documents**. Sue's computer appears in the window; you must open the folder you want yourself.

Tip   You also can click the down arrow beside the Open text box in the Run dialog box to display previously entered programs, documents, and paths. Choosing a path you've entered before is easier than typing it in again.

One last method of using the Run dialog box to access a computer on the network is to use the IP address of that computer, if you're using TCP/IP as the network protocol. Figure 14-2 shows the Run dialog box in Windows XP with an IP address of another computer on the network.

You can find an IP address by right-clicking My Network Places or Network Neighborhood and choosing Properties. In the Properties dialog box, click TCP/IP protocol and click the Properties button.

Figure 14-3 shows the resulting dialog box. The address of the networked computer is 192.168.1.101. You can tell the shared files are networked because the folder icon has a cable attached to it.

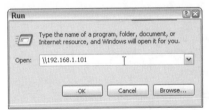

Figure 14-2: Access a computer by its IP address.

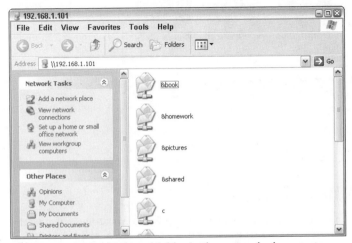

Figure 14-3: Open a shared folder in the networked computer.

 Tip

If you don't know the path, you can use the Browse button in the Run dialog box. Browsing, however, is more efficient and quick in the Network Neighborhood.

Using address bars

You also can type a network path in the address bar in the Network Neighborhood, the My Computer window, or the Windows Explorer. Typing the network path may display the folder you want more quickly than clicking through the drives and folders within the windows.

Address bars appear in Windows applets, including the Windows Explorer, Network Neighborhood, My Network Places, and My Computer. An *applet* is a mini-program included with an operating system. Figure 14-4 illustrates the address bar with a network path typed in the My Computer window. The folder displays its contents. If you had clicked folders to get to the same files, it would have taken five steps; typing the path takes only one step.

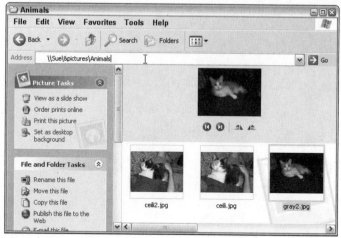

Figure 14-4: Quickly view files on a networked computer.

 Tip   If the address bar isn't showing, choose View ⇨ Toolbars ⇨ Address Bar.

Using Find Computer

You're probably familiar with the Find command in Windows 98. You commonly use the Find command to find files and folders on the local hard drive or on CD-ROM drives. In addition, you use the Find command to find computers on the network, as long as they are shared and you have access to them. In Windows XP, you use a similar method, though it's called searching instead of finding.

You can name the computer on the network, and the Find feature locates the computer, as long as it is turned on and connected. You also can type the path to a folder on a networked computer you want to locate in the Find dialog box.

After you locate the computer or folder, you can open the computer's window, create a shortcut to the computer or folder, copy a folder, and otherwise manipulate the found item.

To find the name of a Windows 98 computer, right-click the Network Neighborhood and click Properties. Click the Identification tab to see the computer's name. To display the Find dialog box, choose Start ⇨ Find ⇨ Computer. The Find dialog box appears, as shown in Figure 14-5.

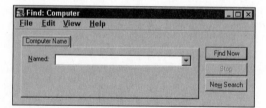

Figure 14-5: Find network computers quickly.

Type the computer's name in the Named text box, and then click Find Now. If the computer is found, the Find Computer dialog box enlarges to display the computer's name, as shown in Figure 14-6.

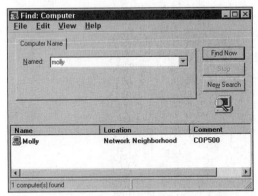

Figure 14-6: The computer has been found on the network.

Tip   You also can click the down arrow to the right of the Named text box to choose from previous computer names and paths you've entered.

Now, if all you could do was locate the computer, that wouldn't be a very useful feature. You can do much more, however: You can select the computer's name in the Find Computer dialog box and then open it, explore it, create a shortcut, and perform other procedures.

The easiest thing to do is double-click the computer's name to display the computer contents in a Window similar to the My Computer window. To display the computer's contents in the Windows Explorer, choose File ➪ Explore.

To create a shortcut on the desktop so that you can access the computer quickly, choose File ➪ Create Shortcut. Figure 14-7 illustrates the shortcut icon to the networked computer. When you double-click the icon, the window displaying the contents of the computer appears.

Tip   In addition to finding a networked computer with the Find Computer dialog box, you can find a specific folder on the computer, as long as you know the path to the folder. For example, you can type **Sue\&pictures\house**, and Find Folders locates the folder on the computer and displays it.

After you locate the folder, you can open it by double-clicking it. You also can create a shortcut, delete or rename the folder, view its properties, cut or copy it, and change the view. Use the menus in the Find Computers dialog box to perform any of these commands on the selected folder.

You also might want to use the Windows Send To feature on the selected folder. Choose File ➪ Send To in order to copy the folder to a floppy disk, Zip disk, CD-RW, or other area listed in your Send To menu.

Shortcut

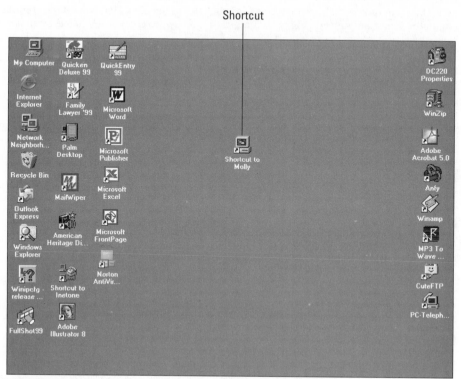

Figure 14-7: Place a shortcut to the networked computer on your desktop.

To find a networked computer in Windows XP, choose Start ➪ Search ➪ For Files or Folders. The Search Results dialog box appears. In the What Do You Want to Search For? list, select Computers or People. You can then type the name of the computer on the network that you want to find. If you have permission to use the Windows XP computer, shared computer contents appear in the window. You can then open any shared folders, open and edit files, save files to the other computer, and otherwise use the computer's resources.

Using My Computer

You're probably familiar with using the My Computer window for viewing the contents of your computer, creating shortcuts, copying and moving files and folders, and deleting folders and files.

You also can use the tools in My Computer for network folders and files. You can view networked computers and their contents, copy and move files and folders, and otherwise manipulate the contents of networked computers, as long as the computers and folders are shared and you have access to them.

The My Computer window displays the contents of your drive and any networked or mapped drives you might have. Figure 14-8 illustrates the My Computer window on a Windows XP computer when you first open it.

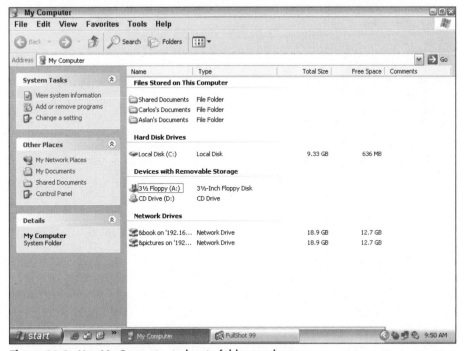

Figure 14-8: Use My Computer to locate folders and resources.

Locating the networked computers

Using the My Computer window to view networked computers may not be the most convenient method. You can use the Windows Explorer or the Network Neighborhood, of course, but you might be more comfortable with My Computer.

To get to a networked computer, you must either type the path (such as **\\Sue\&pictures**) or click the down arrow to the right of the Address text box to choose the Network Neighborhood from the list.

If you enter the path to the computer in the Address text box, you see the computer and networked folder, as shown in Figure 14-9. This view is the one you're probably most familiar with. The networked computer appears just like any other drive or folder in the My Computer window.

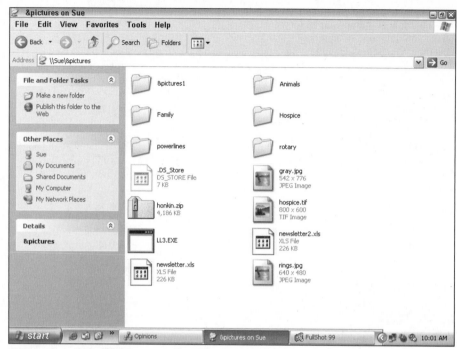

Figure 14-9: Use the My Computer window to view and access networked computers.

On the other hand, you can access the Network Neighborhood or My Network Places from the drop-down list, shown in Figure 14-10. Clicking the Network Neighborhood or My Network Places in the list displays the entire network.

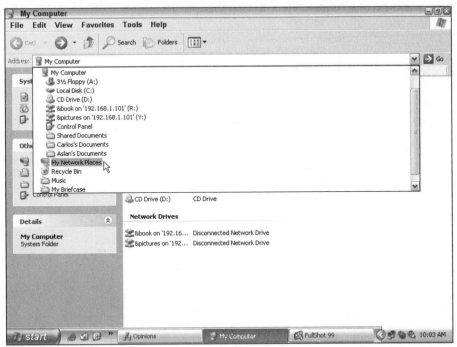

Figure 14-10: Choose the Network Neighborhood from the address bar.

When you choose the Network Neighborhood or My Network Places from the My Computer window, you're actually changing from the My Computer applet to the Network Neighborhood or My Network Places applet. All active computers appear, as shown in Figure 14-11.

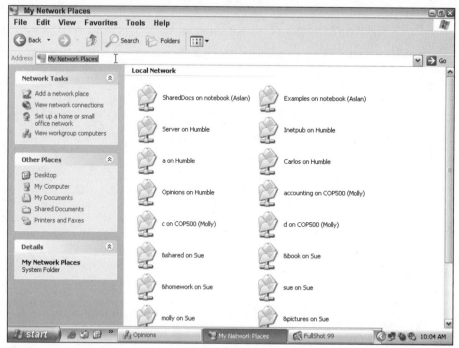

Figure 14-11: My Network Places offers a different view of the networked computers.

For more information about working in the Network Neighborhood or My Network Places, see the section "Using the Network Neighborhood or My Network Places" later in this chapter.

Working with the networked computer

When you open a networked computer in My Computer, you can perform any task on that computer's files and folders that you can on your local computer. Again, however, you must have Share access.

Opening files and folders

You might want to open and view shared folders. If you do, simply double-click the folder. You can even double-click a file to open it plus the application in which it was created. If you open a Word document from a networked computer, for example, your copy of Word opens along with the document from the other computer. The program itself doesn't open across the network. Of course, in order to open the Word document, you must have Word installed on your computer. The same is true for any file you want to open; you must have the program in which the file was created installed to your computer.

Finding files

You also can find a specific file on the networked computer by using the Find Files dialog box. In the My Computer window, first select a folder. Then choose File ➪ Find. The Find dialog box appears. Type the name of the file, text it contains, the date it was created, or other similar criteria.

In Windows XP, you choose Start ⇨ Search ⇨ For Files or Folders. In the Search Results dialog box, you choose what you want to search for: pictures, music, documents, all files and folders, and so on, as shown in Figure 14-12.

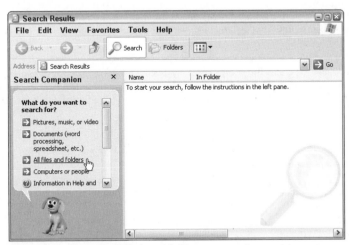

Figure 14-12: Find all files and folders on another computer.

In Windows 98, for example, you can type a filename or text that might be contained within the file. To search on another computer on the network, click the Browse button. The Browse for Folder dialog box appears, as shown in Figure 14-13. Click the computer you want to search.

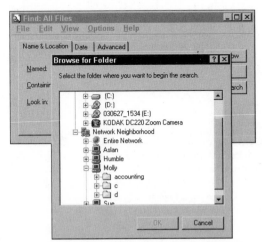

Figure 14-13: Find a file, folder, or specific text on a networked computer.

In Windows XP, you can use the Search command similarly. Click Start ➪ Search ➪ For Files or Folders. The Search Results dialog box appears. Click All Files and Folders. You can maximize the Search Results dialog box to better see the search criteria, as shown in Figure 14-14.

Type all or part of the filename and text that appears in the file, or choose other options in the Search Results dialog box. In the Look In drop-down list box, click Browse. The Browse for Folder dialog box appears. Click My Network Places and select the share in the list, as shown in Figure 14-15.

Note   With Windows 2000 and XP, check the shares carefully, because a computer doesn't show up with a computer-shaped icon, as it does in Windows 98. Computers look like folders, just as other folders do, but computer folders might be labeled something like *C on Molly*, for example, so that the entire drive is shared on Molly.

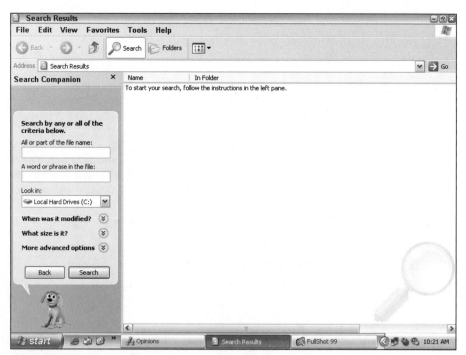

Figure 14-14: Locate a file on the network from Windows XP.

Figure 14-15: Search a share in Windows XP.

Mapping drives and creating shortcuts

In My Computer, you can create a couple of shortcuts for getting to networked files and folders quickly, and as is explained in Chapter 13, you can also map network drives. When you map a drive, you can either type the path to the networked computer or go to the folder you want to map and create the connection that way.

After you open the networked computer in the My Computer window, select the folder you want to map to and then choose Tools ➪ Map Network Drive. Figure 14-16 illustrates the resulting dialog box in Windows XP. Also, you can map to only a drive and one folder level; the command isn't available after you open a folder on the network drive in Windows 98. However, you can map subfolders in Windows 2000 and XP.

Figure 14-16: Map a drive after you locate the path and folder.

After you map the drive, the mapped icon appears in your My Computer window on the local computer.

Tip   You can create a shortcut to any folder or file on the networked computer. Simply right-click the file or folder and then choose Create Shortcut. Windows notifies you that it will place the shortcut on your desktop. The shortcut appears on the local machine. Anytime you want to connect, you simply double-click the shortcut.

Deleting and renaming

You can delete or rename files and folders on a networked computer, although you should be careful with these tasks, especially if the files belong to someone else. It could be disconcerting to try to find a file that was renamed or deleted. Make sure that you ask permission, or at least notify the owner of the files or folders, before you rename or delete files and folders.

To rename or delete a file or folder, select it in the My Computer window. Choose File and then either Delete or Rename.

Moving or copying

You can move or copy a file or folder by using the My Computer window. If you move the file or folder, make sure that you let the owner know. You move files by cutting and pasting; you copy by copying and pasting, just as you would any file or folder on your local computer.

Note   Windows 2000 and XP are more secure than Windows 98, so deleting, renaming, and moving files and folders over the network might not be as easy as you think. If you have trouble performing these tasks, talk to the computer user to see what permissions he or she has set. You might take a look at *Windows XP Annoyances* by David A. Karp (O'Reilly & Associates 2002). This is an excellent book for explaining not only Windows XP permissions but also other XP puzzles.

Using the Windows Explorer

You can perform all of the tasks with the Windows Explorer that you can with My Computer, but the Windows Explorer broadens the view of your computer and of the network. The Windows Explorer window is divided into two panes — drives and folders in the left pane, and folders, subfolders, and files in the right pane.

In addition to viewing your computer's drives and folders, you can see the entire network, as shown in Figure 14-17. In the left pane, you click either Network Neighborhood or My Network Places to view the shares on the network. In the right pane, you see the same shares, listed in a different way. Some shares are folders; others are computers. You don't know unless you're familiar with the network or you click on the share to see what it contains.

Copying and moving files

The way the Windows Explorer displays computers, drives, folders, and files makes it easier for you to copy or move files from a networked computer to your own or vice versa.

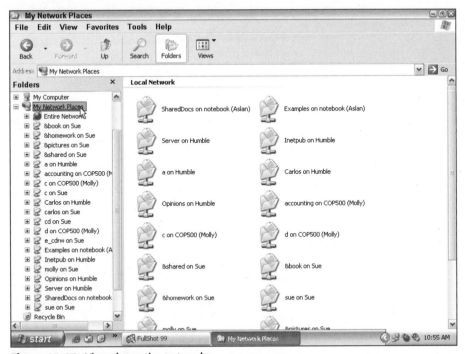

Figure 14-17: View the entire network.

Suppose that you want to move or copy a file from one computer to another. You can open both computers to display their folders in the left pane, copy or cut the file in the right pane, and then scroll the left window to locate the folder to which you want to paste the file.

Figure 14-18 shows the network path \\Molly\d\MP3 in the address bar. Its contents are on the right. In the left pane, you scroll up to My Computer and you can easily copy a file or folder on the right by dragging it to the hard drive or a folder on the left.

Performing other network tasks

You can perform other networking tasks in the Windows Explorer. In addition to deleting and renaming files and folders on your own computer or on a network computer, you can create shortcuts. You also can view file, folder, and drive properties, and you can share objects in the Windows Explorer.

Just as with My Computer, you can find files, folders, and computers quickly. You also can map and disconnect mapped network drives. The difference with the Windows Explorer is that these commands are found in the Tools menu instead of the File menu. The procedures work the same, however.

You can enter network addresses in the address bar, or you can locate computers in the left window pane of the Windows Explorer. And just as with My Computer, you can choose the Network Neighborhood from the drop-down address bar list.

Figure 14-18: Copy and move files quickly from one computer to another.

Using the Network Neighborhood or My Network Places

The Network Neighborhood and My Network Places are the Windows applets designed specifically for working with networked computers, folders, and other resources. When you first open the Network Neighborhood or My Network Places, all connected computers appear on-screen, as shown in Figure 14-19. You don't have to enter an address or double-click icons to get to the network.

The Network Neighborhood and My Network Places include all the features and tools that My Computer and the Windows Explorer include. You can create shortcuts, as well as rename and delete files and folders you view in the Network Neighborhood and My Network Places. You can cut or copy files and folders from one networked computer and paste them to another. You also can map drives, disconnect mapped drives, and find files, folders, and computers from the Network Neighborhood and My Network Places.

Because the applet is meant to work with the network, you also can perform other tasks in the Network Neighborhood and My Network Places. To open the Network Neighborhood or My Network Places, double-click the icon on the desktop.

Tip   If you right-click the Network Neighborhood icon on the desktop and choose Properties from the quick menu, the Network dialog box appears. You can install and configure networking software components — such as protocols, clients, and adapters — in the Network dialog box.

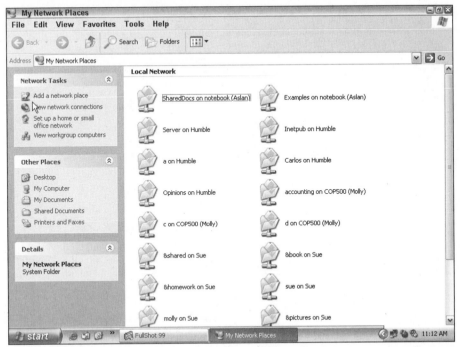

Figure 14-19: Open the Network Neighborhood or My Network Places to view all computers that are online.

Using the entire network

The Network Neighborhood and My Network Places display the computers in your workgroup plus an Entire Network icon. Your workgroup includes any computers in a workgroup network. Your workgroup also includes any Windows computers in the same domain as your computer. You find domains with client/server networks such as Novell NetWare and Windows 2000 Server.

A *domain* is a larger "workgroup" of sorts; the domain consists of a group of clients attached to a server. Those Windows computers also can see each other on their network, depending on the network configuration. A similar situation also can occur with a NetWare network: Windows 98 computers may be able to see each other in addition to the server.

That's where the Entire Network icon in the Network Neighborhood comes in for Windows 98 users. If you're a member of a workgroup and a member of a larger domain or client/server network, you can view the larger network members in the Entire Network.

Figure 14-20 shows the Opinions domain (on a Windows 2000 server) that appears after double-clicking the Entire Network. When you double-click the Opinions Domain icon, you see the computers and server that are members of that domain.

Figure 14-20: View the Entire Network.

Figure 14-21 shows the computers on the Opinions domain. Humble is the Windows 2000 server.

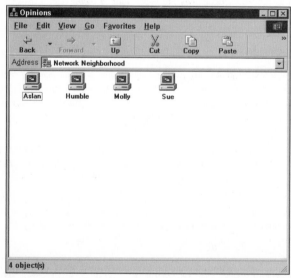

Figure 14-21: View the computers on a specific domain.

The Entire Network icon in Windows 2000 and XP is a bit different. It doesn't show up when you open My Network Places. Instead, all connections—servers, workgroup, folders, mapped drives, and any other shares—show up when you open My Network Places. You do see the Entire Network in the Windows Explorer, and when you open the icon, you see other networking services, such as the Web Client Network, Microsoft Windows Network, a Terminal Services network, if you've added one, and so on. You will not likely use or need the Entire Network icon in Windows 2000 or XP. For more information, see your Windows 2000 or XP documentation.

Finding resources in the Network Neighborhood

Windows 98 can often have problems with networking that make it difficult to include in your network. One major problem is using the Network Neighborhood to browse the network; sometimes it doesn't work. If no computer on your local area network is specified as a browse master, you can have trouble seeing your network computers in the Network Neighborhood.

You can often fix this problem by following these steps:

1. Click Start ➪ Settings ➪ Control Panel. The Control Panel opens.

2. Double-click Network. The Network dialog box appears.

3. Click File and printer sharing and then click Properties.

4. In the Property box, click Browse Master. In the Value box, click Enabled.

5. Click OK and OK again.

6. Click Yes when prompted to restart your computer.

 Note   If you have a server on your network, the server is normally the browse master. Windows 2000 automatically sets itself as browse master.

Otherwise, using the Network Neighborhood or My Network Places is very similar to using the My Computer window.

Finding Computers on Macs

The Macintosh operating systems are similar between System 7 through System 9. System 9.*x* through Mac OS X and up start changing somewhat in the way the OS deals with networking. Mac OS X makes it easy to locate computers on the network and share files and printers with them.

When you connect to the "server" in the Mac, the server isn't necessarily a server as in client/server network. The server is simply another computer with which you can share resources. Depending on how your network is set up, you'll have a domain and/or a workgroup.

To view the computers on the network with Mac OS X, follow these steps:

1. Click Go ➪ Connect to Server. The Connect to Server dialog box appears, as shown in Figure 14-22.

2. Click on the server or the workgroup you want to connect to. The list of available computers appears in the right pane, as shown in Figure 14-23.

Domain

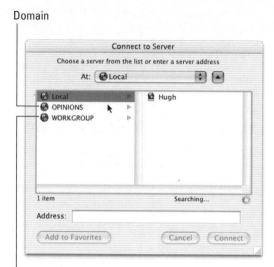

Workgroup

Figure 14-22: Finding computers on the Mac.

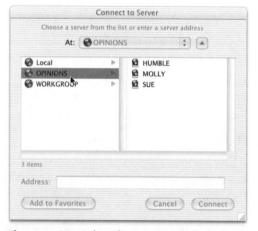

Figure 14-23: Select the computer to which you want to connect.

3. Double-click on the computer, and the SMB Mount dialog box appears (see Figure 14-24).

4. Select the share and then click OK. Depending on the network setup, the SMB/CIFS Filesystem Authentication dialog box may appear, as shown in Figure 14-25.

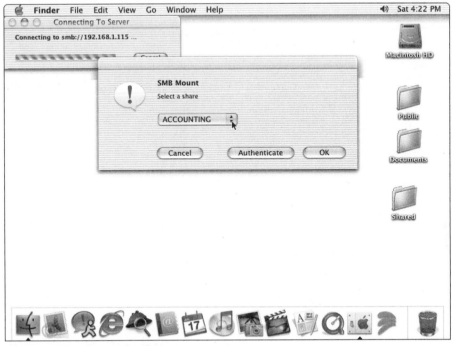

Figure 14-24: Choose the share.

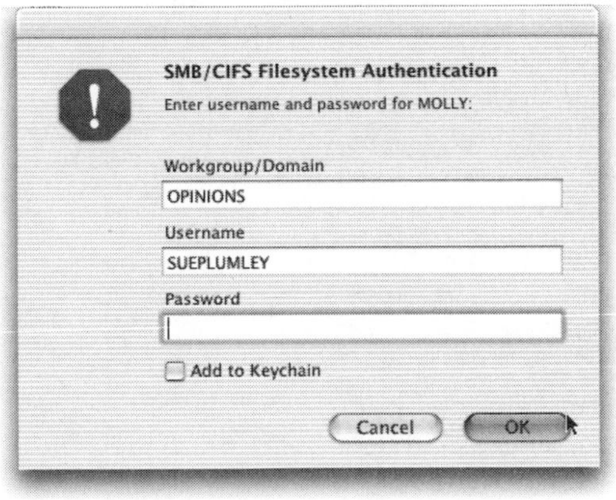

Figure 14-25: Enter a password, if necessary.

5. Type the password and click OK. The drive icon appears on the desktop, as shown in Figure 14-26.

6. Double-click the icon to open the drive on the networked computer (see Figure 14-27).

Networked drive

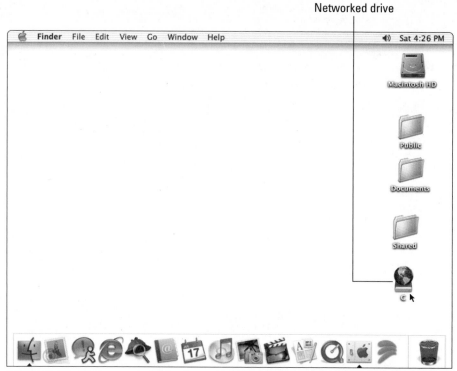

Figure 14-26: The connected drive icon appears on the desktop.

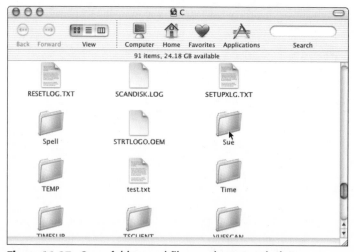

Figure 14-27: Open folders and files on the network share.

Finding Computers on Linux Machines

Most Linux distributions use Samba as a method of networking with Windows computers and/or Windows servers. Samba is a program that lets computers using Server Message Block (SMB)/Common Internet File System (CIFS) share files, printers, and other networked resources. Samba enables Linux computers to share with Windows computers on the network, and Samba enables Windows computers to see the Linux computers on the network.

Samba enables a Linux computer to share file systems, share printers, enable browsing through the Network Neighborhood, authenticate clients logging on to a Windows domain, provide name server resolution, and much more.

Generally, a Linux box needs to be the Samba server, and it provides the services to other Linux boxes on the network. If you only have one Linux box, then it can be the Samba server and client. As a Samba client, the Linux box looks and acts like a Windows computer. The GUI is the same as Windows. The Network Neighborhood works the same way as the Windows Network Neighborhood. The latest Linux distributions include an updated Samba that automatically lists local domains and/or shares when you open the program.

Summary

In this chapter, you've learned to find computers and resources on the network. Specifically, you've learned to use the following:

✦ Network paths

✦ My Computer

✦ Windows Explorer

✦ Network Neighborhood/My Network Places

Additionally, you learned to find Mac and Linux computers on the network. In the next chapter, you learn to print on the network.

✦   ✦   ✦

Printing on a Network

One of the reasons you want a network is so that your family can share expensive peripherals, a printer in particular. If three or four people can share one laser or color inkjet printer, the cost per person makes the printer costs more reasonable. Everyone can print over the network without copying a file to disk and carrying it to the computer attached to the printer.

Understanding Basic Printing

Basic printing is nearly the same whether you're printing to your local computer or to a network printer. Your local printer is attached directly to your computer with a parallel, serial, or USB cable or by means of wireless communications. Generally, a network printer is attached to another computer; you access a network printer over the network.

The main difference between printing locally and printing to a network printer is in the setup and configuration of the printer. After you install a printer on your computer, the printing procedure is the same. The only times you'll notice you're printing to a network printer are when you have to retrieve your print job, when you have to put paper in the printer, or when you clear a paper jam. At these times, you have to get up from your desk and go to the network printer's site.

Using the Print dialog box

Most of the documents you print will come from an application of some sort — Word, Excel, WordPerfect, Quicken, or some other program. When you choose to print in a program, the program displays the Print dialog box.

Figure 15-1 illustrates Word's Print dialog box. Note that the printer is a network printer, but the options are the same as with a local printer. You can choose the printer you want to use, a page range, number of copies, and other options.

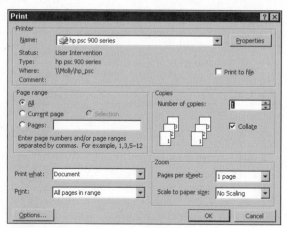

Figure 15-1: Print dialog boxes are the same whether you print locally or over the network.

The Printer area of the dialog box is where you choose the printer you want to use. In Windows 98, click the down arrow beside the printer name in the Name text box. In Windows XP, click the printer's icon in Select Printer, as shown in Figure 15-2. You install printer drivers in Windows to add printers to the list; for more information, see the section "Installing the printer" later in this chapter.

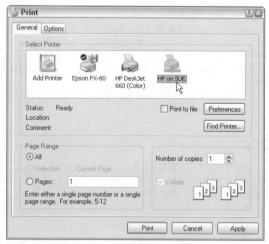

Figure 15-2: Select a printer icon.

After you choose the printer, you can set specific properties for that printer by clicking the Properties button in the Print dialog box. Properties include paper size, orientation, graphic resolution, fonts, and so on. Each printer has different properties specific to it.

In a Macintosh OS X, network printers are listed by IP addresses. Figure 15-3 shows the Print dialog box with a network printer listed in the Printer drop-down box. To change printers, click the arrow and choose another.

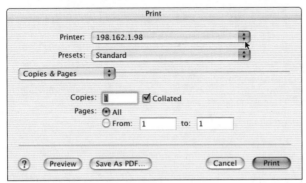

Figure 15-3: Printing in the Macintosh

 Note Naturally, even in a Mac you must indicate Printer Sharing in the Sharing dialog box before you can share a printer. In addition, to share Windows printers, you must also turn on the File and Printer sharing services in the Network dialog box. For more information about sharing, see Chapter 12.

Using drag-and-drop printing

All Windows operating systems enable you to print a document without first starting the program in which the document was created. Using an icon on your desktop, you can drag and drop a file to the icon to print it quickly.

 Small Business Tip Drag-and-drop printing might work well for small offices, because many forms, reports, documents, and spreadsheets are needed from day to day but not all need to be revised or modified. Quick printing of expense forms or time sheets, for example, can save time.

To create an icon on the desktop, you create a shortcut to the printer. This works with both local and network printers. Follow these steps:

1. Choose Start ⇨ Settings ⇨ Printers in Windows 98. Click Start ⇨ Printers and Faxes in Windows XP. The Printers window appears, as shown in Figure 15-4.

Figure 15-4: The Printers folder is where you add, remove, and control printers for your system.

2. Right-click the printer for which you want to create a shortcut, and then choose Create Shortcut from the quick menu. Windows asks if it should place the shortcut on the desktop. Click Yes.

3. Close the Printers window. Figure 15-5 shows two printer icons on the desktop; the HP LaserJet 4M is the network printer, and the Epson FX-80 is a local printer.

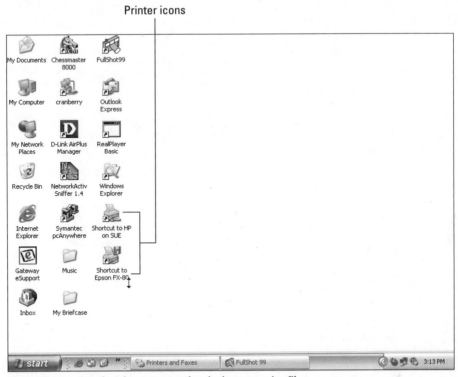

Figure 15-5: Use the shortcuts on the desktop to print files.

To print from a printer shortcut on the desktop, follow these steps:

1. Open the Windows Explorer, My Computer, or Network Neighborhood/My Network Places. Locate the file you want to print.

2. Select the document with the left mouse button, and then drag the document to the printer, as shown in Figure 15-6. Make sure the printer icon is highlighted when you "drop" the file to be printed.

Drag

Figure 15-6: Drag a file to the printer from the networked computer.

Windows associates the application with the file type—for example, a DOC is associated with Word, and a PCX file may be associated with Paint. If Windows can't associate the file with an application, it prompts you to choose an application for that purpose. You don't have to open the application; you just tell Windows which one it is. Using drag-and-drop printing, especially over the network, saves time and effort.

Tip   You can select multiple files in the Network Neighborhood/My Network Places, Windows Explorer, or My Computer and drag them all to the printer shortcut on the desktop. Windows prints all the files, one after another.

Installing and Removing a Network Printer

Before you can use a printer attached to another computer on the network, you must install the printer's software, or driver, to your computer. After you have the driver on your computer, you can use the printer like any other. You also must make sure that the printer is shared.

Cross-Reference   For information about sharing resources, see Chapter 12.

You also can delete a network printer from your computer at any time. If you choose to remove the printer from the network or replace it with another printer, you don't want extra drivers cluttering up your computer. Deleting an extra printer driver is easy and explained in this section.

Small Business Tip You should install a printer driver for every printer on the network on every user's computer. That way, if one printer is busy, the document might be such that it can be printed on another printer in the office.

Installing the printer

Windows makes it easy for you to install a network printer by using the Add Printer Wizard. When you add a network printer, Windows copies the drivers from the computer directly attached to the printer. If you were installing a local printer, you would have to choose the driver and port the printer will use. The Macintosh is a little different in setting up and installing a printer.

Tip If you're using different Windows operating systems, you must install the driver made for the operating system, such as the Windows 2000 driver or the Windows XP driver. For more information, see "Printing between Operating Systems" later in this chapter.

To install a network printer to a Windows 98 computer, follow these steps:

1. Choose Start ➪ Settings ➪ Printers. The Printers window appears. Double-click the Add Printer icon. The first wizard dialog box appears, telling you the wizard will help you install a printer.

2. Click the Next button to continue. At any time during the installation, you can click the Back button to review your choices. The second Add Printer Wizard box appears, as shown in Figure 15-7.

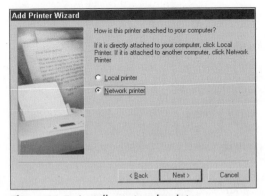

Figure 15-7: Install a network printer.

3. Choose Network printer and then click the Next button. The next wizard dialog box appears, as shown in Figure 15-8.

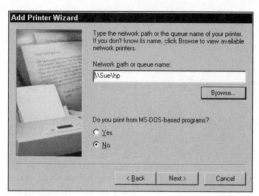

Figure 15-8: Enter the path to the network printer.

4. Type the path to the network printer; alternatively, you can use the Browse button to locate the printer. Figure 15-9 shows the Browse for Printer dialog box. Double-click the computer to which the printer is attached. Instead of the folders appearing, only the attached printers appear. Choose the printer and click OK.

Figure 15-9: Browse for available printers.

5. Choose the option for whether you print to MS-DOS-based programs. Click Next. The next wizard box appears, as shown in Figure 15-10.

6. You can enter a new name for the printer or accept the default. Also, choose whether to make the printer the default for your computer. Click Next.

7. The wizard asks if you want to print a test page. You should always test the connection. Windows copies the files, sends a test page to the printer, and asks if the page printed correctly. If the page printed, click Yes; if the page didn't print or had trouble printing, click No. If you click no, Windows displays the Print Troubleshooter to help you solve the problem.

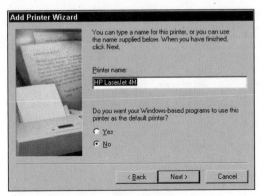

Figure 15-10: Name the printer.

After you install the printer, the printer's icon appears in the Printers window.

Tip   You also can install a network printer from the Network Neighborhood/My Network Places, Windows Explorer, or My Computer. Locate a printer on another networked computer. Right-click the printer, and choose Install from the quick menu. The Add Printer Wizard starts and guides you through the installation.

Installing a network printer in Windows 2000 or XP is similar to Windows 98. You must be sure to have the appropriate driver for the operating system. Follow these steps:

1. Click Start ➪ Printers and Faxes. The Printers and Faxes dialog box appears.

2. In Printer Tasks, click Add a Printer. The Add Printer Wizard dialog box appears.

Note   Depending on the connection—such as a USB, infrared, or FireWire port—Windows 2000 and XP automatically installs the printer for you without the wizard. However, if you're installing over the network, you will most likely need the wizard.

3. Click Next. The Add Printer Wizard displays its second dialog box (see Figure 15-11).

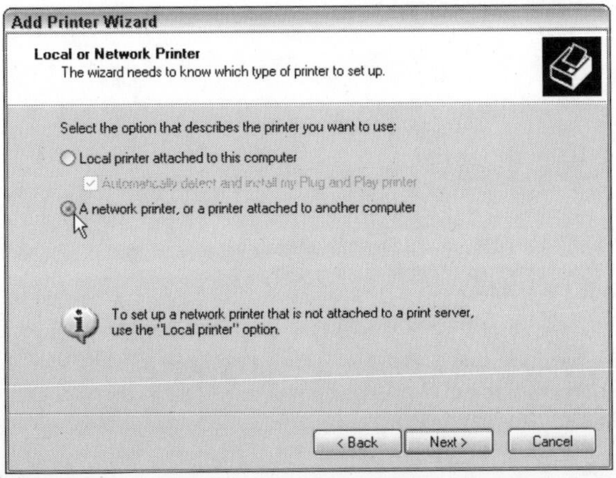

Figure 15-11: Choose to install a network printer.

4. Click the network printer option and click Next. The Specify a Printer dialog box appears, as shown in Figure 15-12.

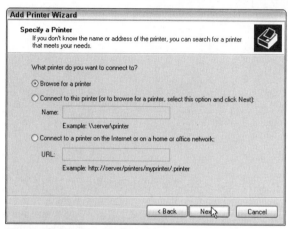

Figure 15-12: Specify the printer.

5. You can browse for the printer, enter the name and path of a printer, or enter a URL if you're printing over a virtual private network (VPN) or the Internet. Click Next.

6. If you clicked Browse, the Browse for Printer dialog box appears, as shown in Figure 15-13. Select the printer and click Next. If you clicked one of the other options, the computer looks for the printer driver.

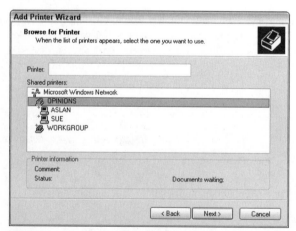

Figure 15-13: Browse for a printer.

7. If the driver is not already installed, Windows prompts you to install the proper driver. You can choose from drivers within Windows (see Figure 15-14), or you can click the Have Disk button to install the driver from a specific location, such as a folder you created when you downloaded the driver from the Net.

Figure 15-14: Install the driver.

8. Choose whether to make the printer your default printer. Click Next.

9. Click Finish to add the printer.

Cross-Reference

For information about installing printer services and printing to a Windows network from a Macintosh, see the section "Printing between Operating Systems" later in this chapter.

Note

Installing and removing printers in most newer Linux distributions is easier than in older distros. You can access many software print spoolers and managers, print servers, and line printer daemon (LPD) line printer daemons on the Internet. Research your distro for more information.

Removing the printer

If you remove the printer driver belonging to a local printer from your computer, you can no longer print on that printer. Removing a networked printer's driver doesn't affect the printer or its driver on any other computer but your own. You will no longer be able to print on the networked printer, but anyone else on the network with the installed driver can.

To remove a printer driver, open the Printers folder window. Select the printer's icon and right-click it. From the quick menu, choose Delete. Confirm the deletion. Windows may ask if you want to remove the associated files for that driver. You should answer Yes so that the files don't clutter up your drive.

Setting Options for the Printer

You can configure any network printer any way you want, and those settings apply only to that printer on your computer. Changes you make to the networked printer's properties don't affect the printer's properties on any other computer, even the one to which it is locally attached.

You can set a printer as your default printer, rename the printer, use it offline, or configure the printer's properties. You also can set the port the printer uses.

Note   Windows 2000 Server and even some XP configurations might not allow you to change some of the printer's properties.

Setting basic options

Basic options include setting the default printer, printing offline, and renaming a printer. Change these options in the Printers folder window.

Setting default printers

The most basic option you can set is whether or not the printer is your default printer. If you choose to make the printer your default printer, all applications on your computer automatically print to the default printer unless you specify a different printer with each job.

Small Business Tip   Place a printer closest to those people who use it the most, and then make that printer the default printer for that group. This saves them the time it would take to run back and forth to a printer in another office or on the other side of the building.

To set a printer as the default, right-click the printer's icon. From the quick menu, choose Set as Default. A check mark appears beside the option on the menu. When you set a printer as the default printer, that setting takes over from the last default printer you set.

Figure 15-15 shows the HP LaserJet 4M Plus as the default printer, even though it's a network printer. Note that the default printer has a check mark within a circle beside the printer icon.

Renaming a printer

You might want to rename the printer for your own purposes. Perhaps you prefer to see a shorter name or a more descriptive name in the Printers folder window. When you change the printer's name, it doesn't change on the network or the currently attached computer; the name changes only on your computer.

To rename a printer, right-click the printer and choose Rename from the quick menu. The printer name changes to a text box. Type the new name.

Using a printer offline

Using a printer offline can be done only with network printers and only through Windows 98. Windows 2000 and XP do not enable access for this feature. You print offline so that you can initiate a print job without being physically attached to the printer. If the computer attached to the printer isn't currently on, for example, you can set up your print jobs and send them to the printer later, when the computer and printer are turned on.

To use the printer offline, right-click the printer and choose Use Printer Offline from the quick menu. The printer appears grayed out, and a check mark appears beside the command on the quick menu. To use the printer online again, remove the check mark from the command by clicking Use Printer Offline on the quick menu.

Setting printer properties

Printer properties vary for each computer. Some enable you to choose graphics resolution and mode, font options, print quality, and so on. Others enable you to make choices about the network options you want to use. Windows 2000 and XP might not enable these changes, depending on how the "owner" of the printer has set up printer sharing.

Default

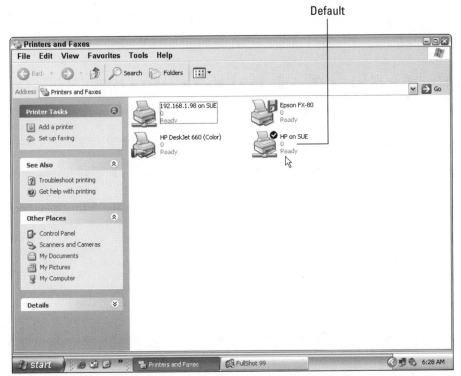

Figure 15-15: The default printer can be any printer on the network.

To set printer properties, open the Printers folder window and right-click the printer. Choose Properties from the quick menu. Each Properties dialog box will have different options. For example, a color inkjet printer might offer color management, double-sided printing, and cartridge services, whereas a laser printer offers none of these.

Capturing a printer port

Capturing a printer port is similar to mapping a drive. You assign a network path to an LPT port to fool an application. Many MS-DOS applications and some 16-bit Windows programs print only to an LPT port. You can capture a port only in Windows 98; Windows 2000 and XP no longer offer this option. These programs cannot recognize a network path as written — \\Sue\\WinHP, for example. Capturing the printer is the only way you can make the program recognize a network printer.

To capture a printer port, follow these steps:

1. In the printer's Properties dialog box, choose the Details tab.

2. Click the Capture Printer Port button. The Capture Printer Port dialog box appears.

3. In the Device drop-down list, choose the LPT port you want to assign to the capture.

4. In the Path text box, type the network path to the printer.

5. If the program is one you use often and you want to reconnect this capture each time you log on to the network, check the Reconnect at logon check box.

6. Click OK and then click OK again to close the printer's Properties dialog box.

Managing Workgroup Network Printing

When you have a local printer attached to your computer, you control the printing. You can pause the printing of all documents or pause the printing of only one document. You can re-arrange the order in which the documents print. You also can cancel the printing of a document completely.

When you print to a network printer, you cannot control any of these elements. All you can do is send your job to the printer and relinquish complete control.

To open the print queue (a temporary list of documents waiting to be printed by the network printer), open the Printers folder window and double-click the print icon. The queue appears.

Note   If you use a client/server network with Windows as your server, you can attach the printer to the server computer for complete control over the printing process. If you use a client/server network operating system, you need to read the network operating system (NOS) documentation for information about controlling the printer and print queues.

Print Servers

A print server can be the software included with a network operating system to control printers, printer drivers, and the print queue. Windows 2000 Server, for example, includes a print server applet that enables you to control the printers attached to the server. A print server also can be a device that attaches to the network. This device provides shared network access to the printers.

You attach the latter kind of print server (usually a small box with ports for plugging in printers) to the network and then attach multiple printers to the device. When a user sends a print job to the printer, the job stops first at the print server, which manages the printers attached to it so that no one printer becomes overwhelmed or overworked.

Most of the advantages to using a print server are to businesses and corporations. If you have a small business that you expect to grow, however, you might consider attaching one to your network. If you have a home network, you might use a print server to enable your Macintosh computers to print to printers attached to Windows or Linux computers. See the section "Printing between Windows and Mac computers" later in this chapter for more information.

Generally, printers attached to a print server are in a central location for easy retrieval of print jobs. Printers attached to a print server can process jobs on many different operating systems or networks. Also, print servers are easier to administer than the print server software in a network operating system.

Understanding the print queue

The *print queue* is an area in which all print jobs for a specific printer wait to be printed. The print queue holds the jobs so that you can get on with your work in Windows. As the printer becomes available to print a job, the queue sends them along, one by one.

Usually, the print queue passes documents quickly to the printer. If several jobs are waiting in the queue, or if there's a problem with the printer (out of paper, paper jam, or such), the jobs wait in the queue until they can print. You also can pause the print queue to hold jobs, such as when you want to load special paper in the printer.

Note The print queue is the list of jobs waiting to be printed, but it is the *print spooler* (simultaneous peripheral operations online) that receives, processes, and schedules the jobs in the queue. Each print job is saved in a separate file and printed in turn when the printer becomes free.

Figure 15-16 illustrates a print queue that is paused so that you can see the jobs waiting to be printed. Note that two print jobs belong to one user and two jobs belong to a second user.

Document Name	Status	Owner	Progress	Started At
http://www.google.com/		Sue	28.4KB	9:36:36 AM 07/01/...
mhtml:mid://00000021/		Sue	1 page(s)	9:37:49 AM 07/01/...
Microsoft Word - Document1		CARLOS	260 bytes	9:39:12 AM 07/01/...
Microsoft Word - Document1		CARLOS	259 bytes	9:39:18 AM 07/01/...

HP - Paused | Printer Document View Help | 4 jobs in queue

Figure 15-16: Print jobs wait in queue until the printer is ready.

Small Business Tip It's important to put responsible people in charge of the computer attached to the network printers. That person should be available for checking the printer when there's an error, keeping the printer filled with paper, and periodically checking the print queue for problems.

Controlling your own print queue

You have complete control over your own local printer's queue. You, as the printer owner, are the only one who can control the queue. You can pause all printing, for example, or pause the printing of just one document. You can change the order of the printed documents in the queue or completely purge all documents from the queue. You have control over the entire printer. You also have control over each document sent to the print queue.

Even though you have these controls over the print queue, you must remember that print jobs often go through so quickly that you don't have much time to pause, cancel, or re-arrange them.

Note You are the only person who can control the print queue of your local printer. Anyone sitting at your computer, however, can control the print queue too. In reality, whoever is sitting at the computer is the one who controls the queue of the local printer.

Controlling the printer

There are many reasons you might want to pause or delete jobs from the queue. You might want to change a toner cartridge to give the printed jobs a darker, crisper look. You might want to insert special paper. You might want to cancel all the jobs in the queue to reset the printer. You have the control over your own local printer to do the following:

✦ Pause all printing of print jobs

✦ Purge all print jobs

Pausing all jobs

To pause all print jobs, open the queue and choose Printer ➪ Pause Printing. A check mark appears beside the command, and the print jobs are held in the queue until you release them, as shown in Figure 15-16. Note the word Paused in the title bar of the print queue. To release the paused print jobs, choose Printer ➪ Pause Printing again to remove the check mark.

Purging all jobs

To purge or delete all the print jobs from the queue, open the queue. Choose Printer ➪ Purge Print Documents. All jobs are erased from the queue.

Controlling a print job

Suppose that you sent a job to the printer and another network user sent a job. The other user has an emergency meeting and needs her job immediately, but your job is first on the list. What can you do? You can rearrange the two jobs, promoting the other job in front of yours so that it will print first.

What if you want to cancel just one print job but let the others continue to print? You can do that too. You can also pause one job in the queue, if you want.

Pausing one document

To pause the printing of one document, open the queue and select the job you want to pause. Choose Document ➪ Pause Printing. A check mark appears beside that command, for just that job, and the word Paused appears in the Status area of the queue, as shown in Figure 15-17.

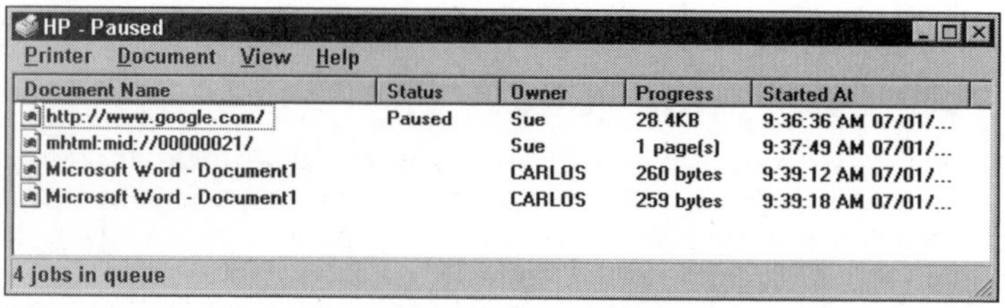

Document Name	Status	Owner	Progress	Started At
http://www.google.com/	Paused	Sue	28.4KB	9:36:36 AM 07/01/...
mhtml:mid://00000021/		Sue	1 page(s)	9:37:49 AM 07/01/...
Microsoft Word - Document1		CARLOS	260 bytes	9:39:12 AM 07/01/...
Microsoft Word - Document1		CARLOS	259 bytes	9:39:18 AM 07/01/...

HP - Paused — Printer Document View Help — 4 jobs in queue

Figure 15-17: Pause printing for just one document.

You can continue printing that document at any time by selecting the document in the Print queue and choosing Document ➪ Pause Printing to remove the check mark from the command.

Canceling one document

You can select and cancel any print job in your queue. Open the queue and select the print document you want to cancel. Choose Document ➪ Cancel Printing.

Rearranging print jobs

You also can rearrange the documents in the list of print jobs. All you have to do is select the print job you want to move and then drag it up or down. Compare Figure 15-17 with Figure 15-18. Figure 15-18 illustrates the print queue with the jobs reversed.

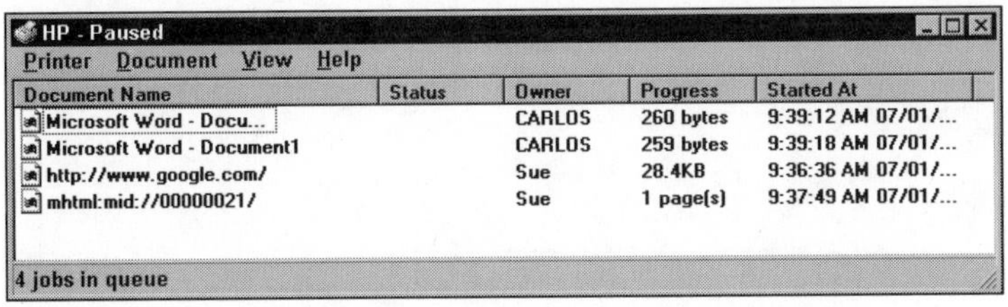

Document Name	Status	Owner	Progress	Started At
Microsoft Word - Docu...		CARLOS	260 bytes	9:39:12 AM 07/01/...
Microsoft Word - Document1		CARLOS	259 bytes	9:39:18 AM 07/01/...
http://www.google.com/		Sue	28.4KB	9:36:36 AM 07/01/...
mhtml:mid://00000021/		Sue	1 page(s)	9:37:49 AM 07/01/...

4 jobs in queue

Figure 15-18: Change the order of the jobs in the queue.

Controlling the network print queue

The print queue for a local printer on your computer is completely under your control. You have much less control over your documents when you send them across the network to another printer, and you have no control over other users' documents on a network printer that isn't attached to your computer.

Things you cannot control

In a network printer queue that is not your local printer, you cannot control any of the following:

✦ You cannot change the order of the jobs in the print queue. You cannot even change the order of your print jobs in the queue.

✦ You cannot take a printer off pause.

✦ You cannot pause a printer (see Figure 15-19).

✦ You cannot purge a printer of the jobs in the queue.

Things you can control

When you print on a network printer that is not locally attached to your computer, you can control your print jobs in a network queue—to a point. You can cancel your print job. You might be allowed to pause your print job, depending on the operating system and the permissions.

Pausing your job

To pause one of your print jobs, select the job in the queue and then choose Document ➪ Pause Printing. A check mark appears beside the command.

To start printing the job again, select it in the queue and then choose Document ➪ Pause Printing to remove the check mark from the command.

Canceling printing

To cancel one of your print jobs, select the job in the queue and then choose Document ➪ Cancel Printing.

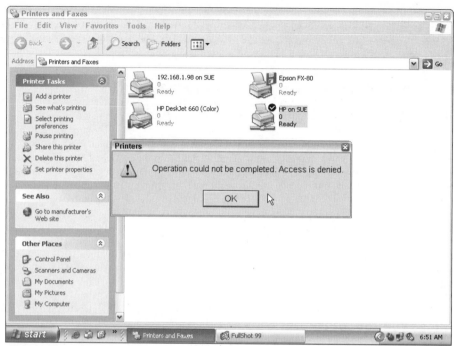

Figure 15-19: This message appears when you try to pause a network printer when you try to purge the printer of its jobs.

Optimizing Print Resources

You can do several things to optimize your printers and print services, whether the printer is a local or a network printer. Following are some things to think about:

✦ Consider the speed of the printer before you purchase it. For a home network, speed may not be a big concern; a network printer is used more, however, and a slow printer slows down the network.

✦ Make sure that you have the correct printer driver for your printer. Using a substitute driver or a similar driver may slow down your printer. Use the manufacturer's driver if you can't find the right one in Windows. Also, if you have a new printer, consider downloading an updated version of the printer driver off of the Internet.

✦ Network connections affect printing over the network. If your network is slow—1 Mbps or slower, for example—printing over the network will be slow too.

✦ Parallel port speeds are two to four times faster than serial ports. If possible, use parallel ports to attach printers to your computers.

✦ Similarly, USB ports are faster than serial ports.

✦ Keep your printer clean. Be careful when cleaning inside of the printer: Some parts are delicate. Maintain a cool and consistent temperature around the printers as well, because some printer components are sensitive to environmental changes.

✦ Watch how you store your printer paper: Damp or wrinkled paper, for example, can damage your printer as well as cause frequent paper jams. Old paper, heavier paper than your printer can manage, and cheap paper or envelopes also can cause printer problems.

Managing Client/Server Network Printing

If you're using a client/server operating system, such as Windows 2000, any printer you connect to the server can be made available to all computers on the network. You can also connect printers to individual computers on a client/server network. You can share all printers on the network. You can also use a print server if you want.

✦ Installing a printer to a server is similar to installing one to any computer. You go through the same steps of adding printer, using the appropriate driver, and then sharing the printer. You then must install that printer to the client computers, using the appropriate driver for the printer.

For example, say you install a color inkjet printer to the server and share it. First, you install it to the server, say, a Windows 2000 server, using the Windows 2000 driver. If you want to use that printer from an XP computer, then you must install that printer with an XP printer driver to the XP machine. Similarly, if you want to install that printer on a Windows 98 computer, you must use a Windows 98 printer driver. Various drivers are normally available on the CD that comes with the printers, or you can download drivers from the manufacturer's site.

✦ In addition to attaching a printer to the server for all to share, you can attach any printer to an individual computer and share it with others as well. For this situation, use the same techniques as described earlier in the chapter for workgroup printing.

✦ Finally, you can use a print server to share one or all of your printers on a client/server network. For less than $100, you can buy a print server that automatically senses the speed of the network, supports multiple protocols, and enables printers from anywhere, from any computer or application, to print.

JetLan, D-Link, Hewlett-Packard, Brother, and many more manufacturers make print servers for various needs. Make sure you purchase a print server with the appropriate technology, such as wireless, Ethernet, and so on. If you're planning on using various operating systems, such as Windows 2000, XP, Mac OS X, and Linux, make sure the print server can print from all of the OSs you plan to use.

Printing between Operating Systems

As previously noted, print servers are the easiest and most efficient methods of sharing printers between operating systems. Windows operating systems nearly always share printers with each other. Sometimes you might have to break down security and permissions; however, it can be done.

On the other hand, if you've added Macs or Linux machines to your network, you need some extra help to share printers. Both Macs and Linux computers enable sharing with Windows networks; it just takes a little work and sometimes help from a third-party company to complete the task.

Printing between Windows computers

All Windows 98 computers print easily between each other. Few restrictions (and less security) exist on the earlier Windows operating systems. When you start working with Windows 2000 and XP, however, you can find problems with sharing resources.

One of the major issues you need to remember is to install the appropriate driver for the Windows operating system you are using. If you have Windows XP Home Edition, install the driver made for the XP Home Edition. If you're using Windows Me, use the Me driver for the printer. Installing the appropriate software makes a difference to printing and to connecting to another printer on the network.

Tip

You cannot fix some problems between operating systems. Microsoft calls them *bugs* and is working on fixes for the bugs. If you have trouble with printing, and you don't see any information in this chapter about that problem, look on the Microsoft help site: www.support. microsoft.com.

Windows 2000 and XP have security issues of sharing files and printers, sharing users, and so on. One problem you might run into is when a Windows XP computer cannot print to a Windows 98 or Windows Me computer. XP issues an Unable to Print error. The reason is most likely that XP cannot verify that the other computer is a secure environment. Windows 98 and Me cannot supply a secure domain environment for Windows XP, and there's nothing much you can do about that. One solution you can try is a print server between the computers. Windows XP can print to a print server.

Another common Windows 2000/XP error you get when trying to print from a Windows 98/Me computer is an IPC$ error. If you receive an IPC$ dialog box whenever you try to access a printer's share from Windows 98 or Me, then you can make a change to the configuration of your Windows 2000 or XP computer and stop that problem. Add the exact username (that you logged on to the Windows 98/Me computer with) to the users of the Windows 2000 or XP computer. Allow the user to share the printer, and you won't receive that dialog box again.

If you find you have a problem printing between Windows 2000 and/or XP, make sure you check the Microsoft site for patches, service releases, or hot fixes. Patches can fix other problems you might be having as well.

Printing between Windows and Mac computers

You'll most likely have the most difficulty printing between any Windows operating system and your Mac, no matter which operating system you use on the Mac. The Mac OS X, for example, wants to print to an IP address. It doesn't enable you to browse the printers on the network and just print to one, like Windows OSs do. Although the Mac OS X supplies built-in support for many USB and network printers, you'll most likely need a print server or third-party software for most printing from the Mac to Windows.

Windows 2000 Server edition includes Services for Macintosh, which enables the sharing of file and printer resources. You set the Services for Macintosh up on the server. The print services feature is called MacPrint, or Print Server for Macintosh. All network computers can then send print jobs to the server, which in turn sends the jobs to the Mac. Services for Macintosh also includes many features for file sharing, volume sharing, FTP services for Macs, and so on.

Using print servers

If you're using a Mac on your workgroup network, you can use a print server to enable printer sharing between the Mac and Windows. As discussed earlier in the chapter, a print server is a device, a computer, or software that manages one or more printers on the network.

Many manufacturers make print servers. Connectix Corporation's DoubleTalk provides a Mac-in-a-PC-workgroup access to printers. Unfortunately, the PC doesn't get access to the Mac with this software.

ES Computer Company's UNICORN is software that lets you share both the Mac and Windows printers over the network. You can also share scanners, fax modems, and PDAs that are connected to a Mac modem or printer port or a Window's COM/LPT port.

Software 2000's MacJet print driver and utility package enables Macs to print to inkjet and laser printer control language (PCL) printers. MacJet supports USB, serial, parallel, AppleTalk, and Ethernet printing.

Strident's PowerPrint for Networks lets Macintosh computers print to over a thousand PC printers by connecting them to an Ethernet network.

PCMacLan is a set of utilities that lets Windows PCs use Mac printers over IP. Your Windows computer can create both network shares and printer shares. Your Mac provides the PC with various printer support, as well. The Mac can print to any PC printer, including non-PostScript printers.

Note   *Rendezvous* is a term you'll see in your Mac OS X printing dialog box. Rendezvous is a system that Apple created to make Macs more compatible with networks. Rendezvous automatically configures to Rendezvous-enabled printers, and other devices, making networking and network configuration a breeze. Being a new technology, not many printers and other devices are Rendezvous-ready now; however, Epson, Hewlett-Packard, and Lexmark are integrating Rendezvous into new printers.

Installing a printer

Installing a network printer to a Macintosh is a bit different from Windows because the dialog boxes are different. Plus, you must use an IP address instead of a printer name. Follow these steps to install a network printer to the Mac:

1. Open the hard drive. Double-click Applications. The Applications dialog box appears.

2. Scroll to the very bottom of the Applications dialog box and locate Utilities, as shown in Figure 15-20.

Figure 15-20: Locate the Utilities folder.

3. Double-click Utilities to open the folder. The Utilities dialog box appears.

4. Scroll to locate Print Center, as shown in Figure 15-21.

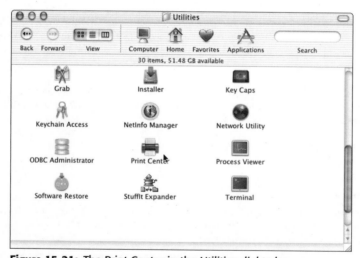

Figure 15-21: The Print Center in the Utilities dialog box

5. Double-click Print Center. The Printer List appears.

6. Click the Add button. The Printer List dialog box changes and enlarges, as shown in Figure 15-22.

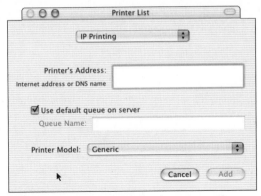

Figure 15-22: Use the dialog box to specify printing information.

7. Click the drop-down list box and choose from the types of printing available: AppleTalk, IP Printing, Rendezvous, and so on. If you're using a print server, you'll be using IP Printing.

8. In Printer's Address, type the IP address of the printer or print server.

9. Optionally, you can choose a queue name or use the default queue name that appears on the PC.

10. Choose the printer model. Check the documentation with your print server to decide which driver to use. The print model (driver) might use a generic driver, a known driver, or another type.

11. If you chose a specific model, click the model name, as shown in Figure 15-23.

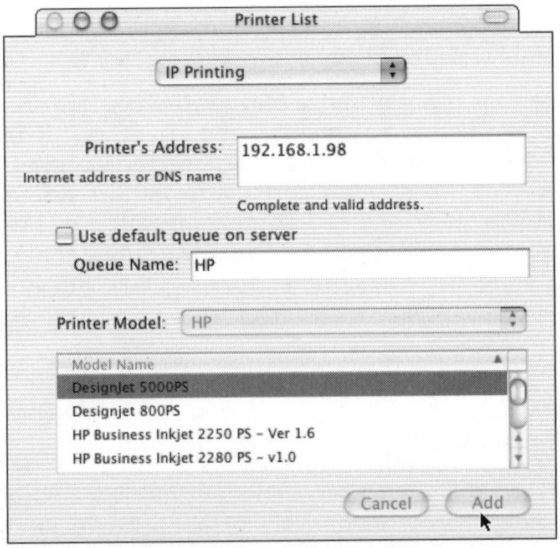

Figure 15-23: Click the Model and Model Name of the printer.

12. Click Add. The larger Printer List dialog box disappears and the smaller Printer List dialog box remains, with the added printer (see Figure 15-24).

Figure 15-24: The installed printer

Printing between Windows and Linux

You can print between Windows and Linux using the Samba application with your Linux distribution. You can use the `smbprint` script in Samba to do the printing. The script itself consists of at least 50 lines of code, depending on the distribution you're using. You can locate help on the Internet for creating or even copying the `smbprint` script for Samba and your distribution of Linux.

You can also use commands using straightforward `lpr`, if your printer knows how to talk LPD (for line printer daemon; LPD is defined at the end of this section.) `lpr` is a command that enables printing using an IP address. You can use `lpr` in Linux, Unix, Windows, or any operating system using TCP/IP; however, the command is most useful in Linux because Windows has utilities that automatically configure the command for you. Again, find these commands for your distribution on the Internet.

If you want, you can use software to help with printing from Linux to Windows and back again. A program by NeTraverse called Win4Lin is available that enables you to install Windows 98 as an application that runs on Linux. Installation is difficult; but if it works, you start Windows and it appears in a window on your desktop. You can then print, and use Windows applications, from the Linux machine to any networked Windows printer.

One of the easiest methods of printing is using a print server, as described previously in this chapter. Remote Print Manager (RPM) offers complete LPD printing software that is designed for Windows platforms over a TCP/IP network. RPM enables users to customize print jobs from host systems including Linux, UNIX, mainframes, and other Windows systems. LPD is a protocol that is used on the Internet, in Linux, and in Unix for communicating between clients and servers. When you use LPD in a command or you use the LPD printing software, you make communication between the computer and a printer possible. You can also find other solutions on the Internet. Check `www.justlinux.com` and `www.experts-exchange.com`.

Troubleshooting Printing

As you know, many things can go wrong with printing, especially printing on a network. Sometimes the answer is a simple one, and often it is complex. You should always consider the most basic printing problems and solutions before delving into the more complex ones.

Give everyone with a printer a list of basics to check in case the printer has a problem so that you don't have to do simple troubleshooting.

Checking basics first

You're probably familiar with all the common problems and solutions. Just to review, however, make sure that you check the following first when you have a printer problem:

✦ The printer is turned on and is online.

✦ The printer has paper, toner, or ink, and no printer doors are open or ajar.

✦ The paper tray is in the appropriate position.

✦ All plugs and cables are firmly and securely attached to both the printer and the computer. Make sure that all cables are connected to the appropriate ports.

✦ The printer cable is not nicked or damaged in some way.

✦ You have at least 3MB of free disk space on the computer attached to the printer. The spooler can't work without the free disk space.

✦ The appropriate printer is selected in the program's Print dialog box.

✦ The printer driver is installed and working. If any of the printer's software configuration has changed or might be corrupted, delete and then reinstall the driver in the Printers folder.

✦ Have you installed new hardware that could be conflicting with the addressing or interrupts?

✦ Have you installed new software that might have changed the printer's configuration files?

✦ Has anyone on the network made changes to the printer's configuration?

Windows 98 includes a Print Troubleshooter in Online Help that you might try. Choose Start ➪ Help. On the Contents tab, choose Troubleshooting. Windows XP also has a Print Troubleshooter in the Help feature.

Locating the problem

You can perform several tests to see if the problem is in your printer, in your cable, in your computer, or with the network. Locating the problem is the first step toward solving it. Before continuing with the following suggestions, you should switch printer cables to see if the problem is the cable.

✦ Turn the printer off and then back on, and try printing again. You might even want to turn the computer and the printer off, count to five slowly, and then turn it back on, just in case something is corrupted in memory.

✦ Next, run the printer's self test. If the test fails, the problem is inside the printer. It could be a bad part, an open door, an askew cartridge, or some other problem.

✦ Try printing locally instead of over the network. Try printing from both Windows and MS-DOS to see if the problem is related to the operating system. If you can print from MS-DOS but not Windows, it's a Windows problem.

Troubleshooting a local problem

You should try printing from another program, such as Notepad or WordPad, to see if the problem is with your program or something else. If you can print from one program but not another, the problem is with the program that doesn't print. See your software documentation for more information.

If you cannot print from any program, try removing and then reinstalling the printer driver to see if that takes care of the problem. To remove a printer driver, open the Printers folder, select the icon of the printer with the problem, and then press the Delete key. Reinstall the printer driver as explained previously in the section "Installing the printer." If all else fails, check the printer's Properties dialog box for any changes in ports or other configurations.

Troubleshooting a network problem

Check your network connection to see if your computer can communicate with the computer attached to the printer. If your computer can, then you might check the printer's shares. Next, check the remote computer's printer driver, and perhaps remove it and reload it.

If your computer cannot communicate with the computer that's attached to the printer, check your network cables and plugs. Check the logon as well; if you entered the wrong username, the computer might not communicate with the rest of the network.

Summary

In this chapter, you learned about printing on a network. You learned about the following topics:

✦ Understanding basic printing

✦ Installing and deleting a network printer

✦ Setting options for the printer

✦ Managing workgroup and client/server network printing

✦ Printing between OSs

✦ Troubleshooting printer problems

In the next chapter, you learn about accessing the Internet from a network.

✦   ✦   ✦

Adding the Internet, E-Mail, and an Intranet

In this part, you learn to expand your network to the Internet and to broaden the network's definition by adding e-mail and an intranet to your home network.

Chapter 16 shows you various ways of connecting your entire network to the Internet, including configuring your network for the Internet. Chapter 17 shows you how to work with and secure e-mail in your network. Chapter 18 shows you another method of communication over the Internet — chat programs. And Chapter 19 explains how to set up an intranet, a network within your network that enables your family to use HTML and other Internet technologies.

Accessing the Internet

The Internet might be the reason you bought a computer in the first place. The Internet opens a world of possibilities to your family — research, shopping, libraries of information, and more. You can send e-mail to friends and meet new people from other states, even other countries. You can find out about the latest movie at the theater or send greeting cards. The potential is limitless. If you have a home network, you can unlock the Internet's potential for your entire family.

Understanding Internet Access

Most homes with PCs have at least one Internet account. Kids might use the account to play games, to e-mail friends, and to gather information for school. Mom and Dad might use the Internet to e-mail family and friends, look for prices on golf carts and digital cameras, read the news, check the weather, make stock investments, bid on auctions, and more. Perhaps one or more family members want to create a Web page or subscribe to e-zines (electronic magazines).

Figure 16-1 illustrates a home page on the Internet. This site advertises entertainment links to music, games, and movie clips. You can even design your own Web pages to put on the Web.

Add to home and personal use the fact that many people work in their homes instead of in a traditional office. People working in home offices need the Internet for a variety of reasons — checking competitors, advertising with their own Web pages, e-mailing customers, sending and receiving work-related files, and perhaps even running an e-commerce site.

Figure 16-2 illustrates a business Web site that offers online help with your computer problems. You can locate a variety of products and services on the Web.

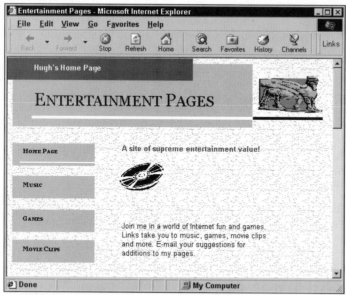

Figure 16-1: You can find anything on the Web.

Figure 16-2: Find businesses, products, and services on the Web.

Internet access is easier and cheaper than it's been in years past. Most computers come with built-in modems; or you can easily add an external modem for less than $60. There are also DSL and cable modems available in most areas of the country. All Windows versions have built-in Web browsers and e-mail programs. Most Macs also have built-in browsers and e-mail. Local and national ISPs offer deals to attract more home users.

Exploring advantages and disadvantages of Internet access

The Internet affords the possibility for anyone with a connection to access data from any other Internet connection in the world for a fraction of the cost of traditional data collection methods. Internet access and use are growing at an incredible rate. Anything so nearly infinite certainly has many disadvantages as well as advantages.

Advantages

One of the biggest advantages of Internet connections, as previously mentioned, is the availability of the technology to nearly everyone. Home users now can afford to attach to the Internet by using a standard PC that comes with a modem and the Windows operating system. The only other thing that is needed is the Internet connection. If you already have cable TV, you can add a cable modem with a faster Internet connection than dial-up for around $45 a month.

If you already have a network in your home, you have the built-in equipment for sharing an Internet connection. All you need to buy is an inexpensive piece of software or hardware that enables you to share one connection and one Internet account. You don't have to purchase additional cabling, modems, or other equipment to attach everyone in the home to the Internet.

Small Business Tip

If you have a small-business network and you're not using TCP/IP, the Internet protocol, consider changing over to IP addressing now. Using TCP/IP has many advantages, including network performance and speed and more available networking products. See Appendix B for more information.

Following are some of the advantages to using the Internet for the home user:

✦ Using the Internet promotes cooperative learning. Your kids can e-mail and share files with universities, libraries, research groups, and others. Users send links to useful Web pages to each other and sign up for informational newsletters and papers.

✦ Internet users can read about, study, and e-mail people from all over the world to share information and opinions. The Internet also increases access to experts; you can locate authors, scientists, doctors, and others easily through their Web pages or e-mail.

✦ The Internet access increases motivation. The Internet encourages exploration with a wealth of video, music, animations, and more.

Disadvantages

Naturally, having Internet access in your home also has disadvantages. Many people worry about the type of Web sites and information children access when they are not monitored. Sex, violence, and depraved individuals run rampant over the Internet community.

Also at risk is the security of your home. Depending on the information you give out on the Internet, unstable or unscrupulous intruders can invade your home through the Internet or even in person. It's a scary world, and you might be inviting it into your living room every time you access the Internet.

Other disadvantages include the following:

✦ The Internet wastes a lot of time. Surfing the Web, joining chat rooms, e-mailing list after list of people and groups — they all take time. Whether it's a child or an adult who is accessing the Internet, time and exposure should be reasonable and often limited.

✦ The expense of attaching to the Internet can increase as you discover you need more power, multimedia equipment, and other technologies that enhance the Internet experience. Upgrading hardware and software for Internet use can become addictive.

✦ Depending on your e-mail and Web access for business or personal use is a risky business. ISP connections and services are always subject to failures; you must make sure that you have an alternative when connections break down and services fail.

✦ Viruses, worms, and Trojan horses attack almost constantly over the Web and through e-mail. Your computer, data, and even networked computers can be at risk from these pests.

Looking at Internet services

If you've ever surfed the Net, you know there's a world of products and services at your fingertips. You also know that you can find information on just about anything, if you know where to look. After you locate the information, you can share it in many ways over the Net.

What's available

You can find just about any type of information you want on the Internet. Not only can you find the popular sales and service Web sites, but also you can take advantage of years of research, studies, reports, and surveys. Following are a few of the things you can explore over the Internet:

✦ Find out information about society and culture. Learn about life in foreign countries or in the United States. Study geography, religion, politics, and the people of present cultures or past ones. Examine archaeology, economics, and languages. Learn about biology, astronomy, and other sciences.

✦ Visit libraries all over the world. Find definitions and dictionaries, quotes, and anthologies. Study the biographies of famous and infamous people who are living today or who are a part of history.

✦ Read the news, check the sports, and keep an eye on the weather. Learn where the next war will break out and who is testing nuclear weapons in the world. Find out what your governor or state legislature is doing right now.

✦ Read famous works of literature, view prominent artwork, listen to a symphony. See the latest photography exhibit in Washington, DC, or visit a museum in Kansas.

✦ Research the latest movies, as well as movies of the past. Play games, read jokes, and connect with others interested in the same hobbies as you.

✦ Learn about the newest advances in medicine. Read about the medications you're taking. Find out how to keep fit and eat well.

✦ Get government forms, tax information, grant applications, stamps, and information about city, county, state, federal, and international government.

✦ Find a job. Post your resume. Inquire about openings all over the country and the world. Figure 16-3 illustrates a resume posted online. You can register your Web page with various search engines so that anyone searching for a computer book author, for example, can find your resume easily.

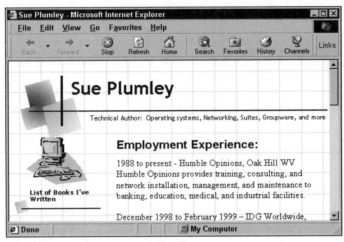

Figure 16-3: Advertise yourself online.

The Internet has something for everyone, no matter what your question or interest.

Acquiring the information

In addition to supplying enormous amounts of information, the Internet enables you to transfer the information in various ways. In addition to printing data so that you can read it at your own pace, you can transfer the information electronically.

E-mail

You can send the information you find to another user via e-mail. Attach a file or a link so that you can share any Web site with someone else. Discuss topics, pool resources, and share ideas — all with the click of a mouse. For more information about e-mail, see Chapter 17.

Figure 16-4 illustrates an e-mail message for a friend. You can send messages to friends and family all over the world with just the click of the mouse.

Small Business Tip

E-mail is a great way to give your employees the means to collaborate and share information with coworkers, vendors, manufacturers, customers, and others. Be careful, though, it's also an easy way to pass around jokes, hoaxes, stories, and viruses.

Chat programs

You also can exchange information over the Internet by using chat programs. Whereas e-mail sometimes must wait until the recipient receives and responds to your message, chat programs connect two or more people online at the same time. The conversation is held in real time. For more information about chatting over the Internet, see Chapter 18.

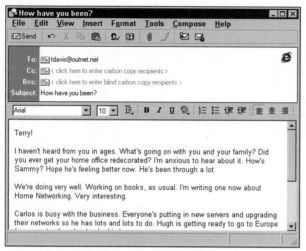

Figure 16-4: Send messages to friends, family, and business associates.

Your employees can use chat programs to contact customers, for example, as they work on accounts, projects, reports, and other tasks. Chatting over the Internet is usually less expensive than long-distance phone calls and business trips to other states or countries.

File transfer

Transferring files over the Internet is a quick and easy method of acquiring updates, applications, documents, and other files. You can purchase and download a program, such as a game, a piece of shareware, accounting packages, utilities, and network management software. Many vendors supply free demos of their applications so that you can try it before you buy it. You also can download updated drivers and software for your computer or network.

In addition to downloading files from the Internet, you can upload files. Many companies use a special site for their remote employees to send files. You might upload a file to a technical support company, for example, or reports to universities, or documents to friends. File transfers over the Internet are faster and cheaper than transporting a floppy disk or using snail mail to send files.

Send presentations and reports to your customers, accounting information to a parent company or business partner, or publication files to your commercial printer over the Internet.

Conferences and meetings

Current technology enables people to hold meetings with colleagues and business associates. NetMeeting, a Windows application, is but one of these programs. Although conferencing software is similar to chat rooms, it also offers features that chat programs do not.

Some business meeting software, for example, enables the participants to engage in phone conversations at the same time; sometimes videoconferencing is also built in. Whiteboards are often used to take notes and organize ideas during a meeting; everyone can see the information on the whiteboard, add to it, and modify it.

Although conference and meeting software generally is used for business contacts, you easily could use it on your home network too.

Scheduling and calendaring

In addition to using a scheduling program on your local area network, you can make use of a Web-based calendar program that enables you to share your schedule with others over the Internet. You might want to schedule visits with your family and friends who are spread out over the country, for example.

Small Business Tip

You can share your calendar with colleagues to make business trips, meetings, deadlines, and even golf games easier to schedule.

Understanding Internet Connections

Most home users connect to the Internet with a dial-up modem, and in some cases, the modem is perfect for the job. You can use various speeds and types of modems to access the Internet, but the most common speed at this time is 56 Kbps. Instead of a modem, however, you can use other equipment that provides a fast, permanent connection to the Internet, such as DSL or cable modems, high-speed lines (T1, frame relay, fractional T1), and so on.

The type of connection you get depends on how much you use the Internet. If you and your family connect to get e-mail and do some surfing every day, a dial-up modem connection might be just fine. If you use the Internet many hours a day every day for work from your home or if your kids play online games, however, you may want to invest in a faster, more permanent connection.

Figure 16-5 shows a home network using one modem to attach to the Internet. All users can share the Internet connection, however, with the use of a piece of software. See the section "Sharing Internet Connections" later in this chapter.

You can connect to Internet services by using an analog phone line or a digital cable line. Traditional modems use phone lines, and DSL or cable modems and other equipment use high-speed digital lines.

Dial-up modems use a service through an ISP, a government agency, or some other service provider. Your phone line is attached to the dial-up modem; you dial your ISP and access the e-mail and/or Web server. When you disconnect from the ISP, you no longer receive mail or information from the Internet until you connect again.

Cable or DSL modems are not really modems but are called that out of convenience and familiarity with the word *modem*. Cable and DSL are also called broadband Internet connections. *Broadband* defines telecommunications that provide a variety of channels of data over a single wire. A dedicated line, such as a T1, is a special high-speed, or hard-wired, connection that is permanent. Any of these connections is always active, always ready. You can be working in your word processing program and hear the "you've got mail" sound at any time, because when mail is received at your ISP's e-mail server, it is sent directly to you over your permanent connection.

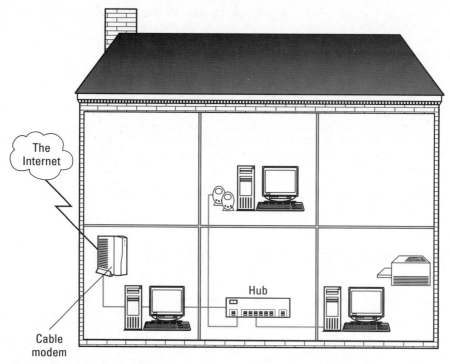

Figure 16-5: Whether you use a fast connection or a slower one, all network users can take advantage of the Internet.

Using phone lines

Modems use analog technology — transmission methods developed to transmit voice signals instead of digital signals. The phone lines in your home are analog lines built to carry voice transmissions, and perhaps other data, such as faxes. They also might carry your network transmissions on a phone line network.

Note   If you use a phone line for several services at the same time — such as home networking and an Internet connection — you are likely to notice a performance degradation.

Using phone lines for Internet access is more flexible than using cable modems or permanent lines. You can move the dial-up or DSL modems to other computers or rooms: All you need is a telephone line and a jack. Also, using a dial-up modem and phone line is much cheaper than using a cable modem or a dedicated line.

On the other side, however, a dial-up connection using a modem and a phone line is slower than a cable modem or dedicated connection. Generally, speeds are between 28 Kbps and 56 Kbps. Also, noise or interference over the lines can cut off transmissions unexpectedly. Finally, using the phone line for the Internet ties up your phone line unless you use a dedicated line for your modem.

Using cable and DSL modems

More and more homes are using cable or DSL modems. For a small monthly price, you can have high-speed connections to the Internet that enable you to download large files — like music, video, white papers, even entire books — in minutes. You also have a permanent connection via these modems, meaning you can send and receive e-mail anytime without having to dial up or connect to your ISP's server. In addition, both connection types leave you more vulnerable to viruses and worms because of their "always-on" configuration.

Local phone companies usually offer DSL connections, since DSL access is over standard copper lines. DSL connections receive up to 6.1 Mbps, so the technology is very fast indeed. However, not every area offers DSL, and you must be within a certain distance from your phone company's central office to use DSL. DSL lines are secure and offer low interference too. DSL is perfect for the power user, small businesses, and so on. The ordinary residential user isn't likely to need this much speed. The problem with DSL is its availability and expense.

Your local cable company can tell you more about a cable connection to the Internet. Connections are fast but not always consistent. For example, in the morning you might connect at 6 Mbps, and in the afternoon your connection might be 1.6 Mbps. Often, downstream cable speeds are from 10 Mbps to 30 Mbps for a distance of up to 30 miles. Upstream speeds might be 128 Kbps to 10 Mbps for the same distance. Cable television lines are usually coaxial.

Note   Speeds are measured in upstream and downstream. *Upstream*, or upload, is the speed at which information travels from your home to the destination; *downstream*, or download, is the speed at which information travels from the destination server to you. Download speeds are often faster because users download more often than upload.

Figure 16-6 illustrates upstream and downstream speeds from a home modem to an ISP attached to the Internet. Naturally, the speeds apply to the connection only as far as the ISP's Web or mail server is concerned. Generally, ISPs use higher-speed cables — such as T1 lines — to connect their servers to the Internet.

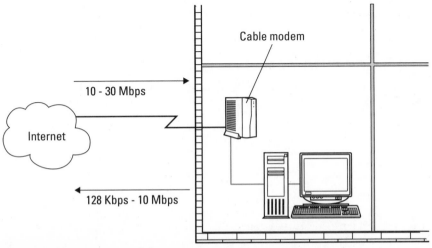

Figure 16-6: Upstream and downstream speeds are not the same for most technologies.

Speeds for cable lines are very fast, but you must remember that television signals also share the data path, plus everyone in your neighborhood shares the same cable. You have to consider not only how fast the line is, but also how fast the PC can handle the data inflow, how fast the PC-to-cable interface is, how fast the data travels on the TV cable, and how much traffic there will be during primary usage hours. For information, check with your cable TV provider.

Using high-speed lines

Digital lines transmit data at high speeds so that a link to the Internet enables users to perform multiple tasks simultaneously. For example, you can transfer large data files, have a videoconference, and perform other tasks all at the same time.

Generally, you lease a high-speed line from a local phone company, a long-distance service, or some other specialized company. Depending on the type of connection you get, you can transfer data from 56 Kbps to 45 Mbps.

Using dedicated lines, however, means that moving your computer isn't easy. You have to move and reconnect the cables too. Another problem with high-speed lines is that they are expensive. You must lease the lines and purchase the equipment for transferring data and often other equipment to help route messages, and you pay installation charges as well.

Small Business Tip

You may want to invest in a high-speed line for your small business if your employees spend enough time on the Internet to justify it. Keep a log for one month of all employees' time on the Internet just to see if a high-speed line is reasonable for your company.

Understanding Access Equipment

Whether you use a dial-up connection, attach to TV cables, or use other high-speed lines to access the Internet, you must have some sort of hardware attached to your computer. Modems generally come in two types: analog and digital. The common modem you use on your phone line is an analog modem. DSL and cable modems are digital and used with high-speed connection lines.

Using analog modems

Analog modems are becoming faster and faster with connections to the Internet and other online services. The 28.8 and 33.6 analog modems have become antiques in dial-up technology. A 28.8 modem transmits data at 28,800 bits per second (bps), and a 33.6 transmits at 33,600 bps.

Modem Standards

The ITU (International Telecommunications Union) defines standards for telecommunications that govern, in part, the definition of modem speeds and operations. The ITU also governs fax and digital modems.

For example, V-standards define speed, wiring, and error correction in modems and other telecommunications devices. V.32 bis is an ITU standard for 14,400 bps modems. V.33 is an ITU standard for 12,000 and 14,400 bps modems used over four-wire, leased circuits. V.34 defines a 28,800 bps modem over a dial-up line, with error correction and data compression techniques included. The V.90 standard used for 56 Kbps modems is now the most common standard.

The only analog modem speed you can buy these days is the 56 kilobits per second (Kbps). The speeds are not, however, truly 56 Kbps, because the FCC regulations prevent 56 Kbps support in the United States. Downloading speeds for a 56 Kbps modem are 53 Kbps, and uploading speeds are only 33 Kbps. Also, the actual speed depends on the phone line conditions and the current connection. A storm, for example, or interference from other sources, can slow connections through a phone line.

Using digital modems

A digital modem is a piece of hardware that transmits data in both directions, usually simultaneously, at high speeds. You use certain types of digital modems for the connection types you've got. If you have a DSL, for example, you use a DSL modem, which is a modem built specifically for use with that type of line.

Sometimes a digital modem is called a terminal adapter (TA) or router, but the process is still the same. A piece of hardware located at the end of the line—DSL, TV cable, ISDN, and such—transmits and translates the signal to and from the computer or server. When there's a digital modem on one end of the line, there must be a digital modem on the other end of the line for the two to communicate.

Note Integrated Services Digital Network (ISDN) is a telecommunications network that enables digital voice, video, and data transmission. ISDN was quite popular among small businesses until cable modems and DSL became more common and available. ISDN only offers 128 Kbps speeds for data transfer.

Figure 16-7 shows a cable modem connection between a home user, the ISP (in this case, the cable company), and the Internet. The cable modem in the home is connected, by coaxial cable, to the cable modem at the cable company's building. Note that multiple lines feed from the ISP to a larger Internet provider.

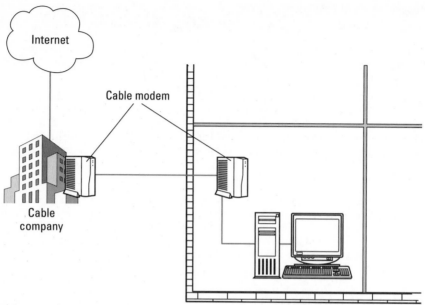

Figure 16-7: ISPs feed into larger ISPs, which feed into larger ISPs, and all together, these servers form the Internet.

Sharing Internet Connections

Dial-up modems are not shareable over a local area network under normal conditions. With the use of a third-party application, however, you can surf the Net and send and receive e-mail at the same time others on the network use the Internet connection. Various programs exist, often called *proxy servers*, which enable you to turn one phone line into multiple Internet connections.

Many people use cable modems or DSL modems in their home or small business for Internet connections instead of using dial-up modems. You can also use a software program or a hardware device, often called *firewall routers*, to share these modems.

Basically, these applications or devices enable all computers on a LAN to connect to the Internet, surf the Web, and send and receive e-mail simultaneously, using one Internet connection.

Tip   Some ISPs have policies against sharing an Internet connection. Check with your ISP for more information.

When using the proxy applications, you usually have to install TCP/IP to each computer on the LAN. Additionally, you install the proxy software on the host, or server, machine first; this is the computer that's attached directly to the dial-up or cable/DSL modem. Then you install the software on client or guest machines.

Network Address Translation (NAT)

Network Address Translation (NAT) is an Internet standard that enables a LAN to use one set of IP addresses for internal traffic and a second set of addresses for external traffic. NATs are a type of software application that lets multiple computers access the Internet. NATs are available for most Windows OSs and for many Mac OSs, although selection is limited for Macs.

The advantages of using NAT-enabled applications are as follows:

✦ Computers with NATs handle multiplayer Web gaming well.

✦ NATs are easier to set up than proxies.

✦ They can be expanded to handle many computers.

Disadvantages include the following:

✦ The computer running the NAT program must be running for other computers to access the Internet.

✦ Managing the access isn't as flexible as proxies.

✦ NATs don't support all applications, so adding services can be difficult.

If you use a hardware device, all computers connect to the device, through a hub or switch for example, so each computer is connected to the Internet all the time. Among the hardware devices previously mentioned for firewall use, many can be used for Internet sharing as well. A few more are described in this section.

Using software to share a connection

One of the most popular programs on the market is WinGate. WinGate has been in use for many years as a low-cost standard for Internet connection sharing, and with each new version, it improves. WinGate now offers an antivirus program, content filtering, and e-mail server, and a VPN solution for about $50.

WinGate supports dial-up connections, cable modems, satellite, DSL, T1, and so on. It also supports many Internet applications. WinGate includes a proxy server you can configure for various protocols, and it's also equipped with a firewall to protect your system from hackers. WinGate supports NAT. WinGate, by Deerfield.com, costs around $50 for a three-user version, $100 for six-user, and the more users you add, the higher the cost.

Microsoft has included ICS (Internet Connection Sharing) with Windows 2000 and XP. ICS enables the computers on the LAN to share an Internet connection. Any operating system can connect through ICS as long as the computer uses TCP/IP.

Tip

ICS may not work with some cable modems or other return network (telco) devices. (*Telcos* are connections that receive data through a NIC attached to a cable modem, and transmit data through a telephone line attached to a dial-up modem.) Check Microsoft if you're unsure.

ICS isn't a full-feature program; other programs offer more. For example, ICS doesn't support access controls or logging. For more information about ICS, see www.microsoft.com or www.practicallynetworked.com.

For the Macintosh, IPNetRouter by Sustainable Softworks is an easy way to share a dial-up, cable, or DSL modem Internet connection. IPNetRouter is a router and firewall and uses NAT and IP filtering. The cost of IPNetRouter is around $90.

WinProxy is another software program that enables you to share a high-speed Internet connection. WinProxy also supports dial-up modems, cable/DSL modems, satellite, T1 and T3, wireless, and other connections. WinProxy is also a firewall, enabling you to block access to sites, and it includes antivirus support. WinProxy is made by Blue Coat/Ositis and costs around $60 for a three-user version or $100 for a five-user version.

You can buy many other software programs to share an Internet connection, many of which are also firewalls or proxy servers. Some other products include SolidShare, as well as ezProxy from LavaSoftware.

Using hardware to share a connection

As previously mentioned, you can often use firewall routers to share an Internet connection. Just as you would connect the router to use for a firewall, you would connect the device to use for Internet sharing. You use the hardware router as a bridge between the modem (dial-up, cable, DSL, and so on) and the hub or switch you use to network your computers.

Some routers you use for sharing a connection are also Ethernet hubs or switches, which means you combine two functions into a single device. In this case, you connect the modem to the Ethernet router/hub/switch, and the computers connect to the router/hub/switch as well. See Chapter 9 for more information.

Linksys makes a cable/DSL modem four-port router you can use to connect your computers to one Internet connection. For about $50, you can get a 10/100 Ethernet router that also acts as a rudimentary firewall. NAT is also handled by the Linksys box.

Zoom makes an Internet Gateway for around $60. All computers on the network share one Internet connection through a DSL modem, a cable modem, or an analog (dial-up) modem using NAT. Computers share one Internet IP address while retaining their individual IP addresses. LAN connections are through 10/100 Ethernet. You can plug another hub into the gateway so that more computers are supported.

NETGEAR also makes a similar product, as do Asante, Black Box, and Hawking. You can also use wireless routers. Additionally, you can connect various operating systems to these routers with no problem in sharing the Internet connection.

Contracting a Service Provider

In today's market, you can find many providers of Internet services. Commercial online services, such as Prodigy and America Online, offer Internet access plus online shopping, groups, games, and file libraries. They even offer free browsers and e-mail programs for download.

Internet service providers, however, may provide more services for less than the commercial online services. An ISP provides you with a connection to the Internet, mailboxes, space on the server for a Web page or Web site, access to news servers, and more. Before you sign up for services with an ISP, however, you should consider a few things and understand that local ISPs are not always the best solution.

✦ Ask your friends which ISP they use and how satisfied they are with the service. Ask if the ISP is reliable, if the ISP has a lot of hardware problems, and if technical support is helpful.

✦ Find out prices. Ask whether there's a limit on connect time or if time and usage are unlimited. Ask if they include Web page space and any other perks.

✦ You also should consider how long the ISP has been in business. New ISPs pop up all the time, but are not always prepared to handle the job. Most new ISPs don't start with enough modems and connections, so they must upgrade within a few months. Others don't have a business plan and the business sinks after only a few months. Find an established ISP for your Internet connection.

✦ Local, regional, and national providers are available. Find out if there's a local access number for dial-up, or at least an 800 number that will cost less than long-distance connections. Also, your cable company provides ISP services, as does a phone company from whom you can get DSL services.

Working with Web Browsers and E-Mail

The Web browser and e-mail program you use on your computers in the network both should be programs with which you're comfortable. A *Web browser* is a program that enables you to view pages on the Internet in the special Hypertext Markup Language (HTML) format. A browser also enables you to control how the Web pages appear and how the graphic images look, and it enables you to jump from link to link while surfing the Web. An e-mail program might be a separate application or be connected to your browser. The e-mail program enables you to send and receive messages over the Internet.

You should use the same browser and e-mail programs on all computers on the network, if possible. Troubleshooting problems, upgrading versions, and maintaining the programs are easier for you if all the applications are the same brand and version. Also, compatibility issues are easier to deal with when you keep all the Internet programs the same on your computers.

If you're using Windows, Internet Explorer is built into the program. You may prefer to use Netscape or some other application. The program you choose depends on your preferences and will not affect sharing an Internet connection or account, as described earlier in this chapter.

Figure 16-8 illustrates Microsoft Internet Explorer. The Web browser enables you to view Web pages, navigate the Web easily, search for certain topics, and more.

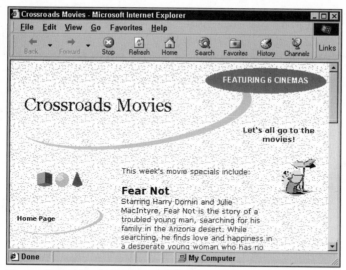

Figure 16-8: Use the Internet Explorer to surf the Net.

Internet Explorer and Outlook Express

All Windows operating systems ship with a Web browser and e-mail program—Internet Explorer and Outlook Express. Internet Explorer also includes a newsreader for viewing news-groups on the Internet and for reading messages.

Use Internet Explorer to browse the Web, save a list of favorite Web pages, download and upload files, and more. You can even browse pages offline with Internet Explorer.

HTML and Internet Technologies

With the Internet came an entirely new set of technologies built for easy-to-use file and data trans-fers and information exchange. HTML, TCP/IP, and hypertext are just a few of these technologies.

✦ **HTML** is a set of codes that creates the page formatting you see in a Web page; HTML is the standard for creating Web pages. HTML files are stored on a server, and people can read those files via a browser. Text, graphics, and links appear on screen as you see them because the Web browser interprets, or translates, the HTML codes for you.

✦ **Hypertext** is the text on the page that supplies the links. When you click on these links—represented as underlined text and, often, graphics on a Web page—you "jump" to another Web page. Using links, you can view information or images related to the original topic.

✦ **TCP/IP** is the protocol of the Internet. TCP/IP is supported by many hardware and soft-ware vendors, is compatible with many different computers, and is used worldwide on networks that are connected to the Internet.

Internet Explorer offers various preferences that you can change to suit your way of working. You can change home pages, security, connection information, and more. Figure 16-9 illustrates Internet Explorer's Internet Options dialog box from Windows XP. To open the dialog box from within the Internet Explorer, choose Tools ➪ Internet Options. Note that you also can change colors, fonts, and the language you use in your browser.

Figure 16-9: Internet Explorer enables you to set your preferences for working in the browser.

Outlook Express is an e-mail program you can use to send and receive mail, manage and sort messages, check your spelling, attach files, and more. You can read your messages while still attached to the Internet, or you can read and answer them offline if you use a telephone line and modem to connect to the Internet. If you use a permanent connection, such as a cable modem, your computer is always online. With a permanent connection, you can choose to have Outlook Express check your mail every 10 minutes, or every 30 minutes, and so on.

Create folders to organize your messages, and keep an address book that makes addressing your messages quick and easy. Figure 16-10 shows the Outlook Express Inbox. Note that there are only two window panes: a folder list and a message list. The message text pane is hidden (choose View ➪ Layout and deselect Show Preview Pane).

Caution The main reason to not show the message text in a preview pane is to protect your computer from viruses. When you select a message, the text it contains appears in your Show preview pane. If a worm or other virus has ridden the e-mail message to your computer, showing it in the preview pane is the same as opening the message and letting the worm loose.

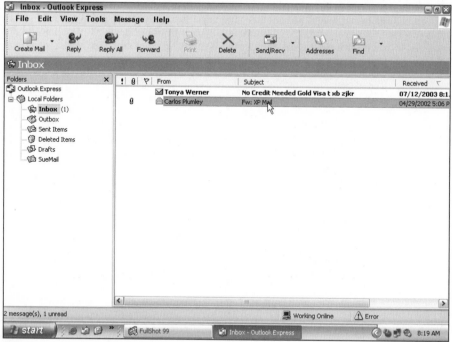

Figure 16-10: Use Outlook Express for sending and receiving messages over the Internet.

Cross-Reference   For more information concerning using e-mail, see Chapter 17.

Using Netscape Navigator and Netscape Mail

Netscape Navigator, a Web browser, performs the same tasks as Internet Explorer. Netscape enables high security and viewing of HTML formatting and provides context-sensitive help. Netscape Mail provides the tools for sending and receiving messages, organizing mail, sorting messages, and more.

Netscape 7.1 is compatible with Windows 98, Me, 2000, and XP; Mac OS X; and Red Hat Linux 7.0 and greater. In addition, the 7.1 browser suite of programs offers spam control, pop-up windows controls, image zoom, mail views, Palm sync, and developer tools as new features.

Configuring an Internet Browser and E-Mail Program

No matter what type of browser or e-mail program you use, you need to configure the program to work with your service provider. The ISP should provide you with the information you need to set up your program in Windows. Following is a description of the information you need.

You use a general Internet account to gain access to the ISP's server. If you use a dial-up modem, you need the ISP's access phone number that your modem dials to get onto the Internet. If you use a cable or DSL modem, a technician will likely come to set up your hardware.

No matter how you connect, you need an Internet Protocol (IP) address. The IP address is an identifier for the ISP's server. Often the IP address looks similar to this: 205.112.134.121. For more information about IP addresses, see Appendix B.

A subnet mask enables the computer in one segment of a network to see computers in another segment. The ISP uses a subnet mask — like 255.255.255.255 — to communicate with other segments on the Internet network. The ISP assigns a subnet mask for you to use.

Sometimes you need a default gateway address. The gateway is a physical device that connects two network segments. The gateway address looks like an IP address and subnet mask. An ISP assigns the gateway number you use in your configuration.

You also need at least one, and perhaps two, domain name system (DNS) names that describe the ISP's servers — such as iserver.net — or the IP address, such as 205.112.1.1. A name server on the Internet translates IP addresses into names, and vice versa. The ISP assigns the appropriate DNS server names you use to configure your connection.

When you use phone lines and a modem to connect, your ISP will tell you which interface type — such as Point-to-Point Protocol (PPP) or Serial Line Internet Protocol (SLIP) — it uses. These interface types are also protocols for communications used to run the IP protocol over telephone connections via a modem.

The ISP also assigns you a userid and a password. The userid is the username you enter to gain access to the ISP's server. You also need the password for access.

For an e-mail account, you need an e-mail username and password. These may be the same or different from your account username and password. Your ISP also assigns, or lets you choose, an e-mail address consisting of a username, the @ symbol, and the domain name of the service provider (splumley@onenetone.net, for example).

You also configure a point of presence (POP) e-mail host name, which is the server that holds the e-mail messages for you until you log on and get your messages. Similarly, you need a Simple Mail Transfer Protocol (SMTP) e-mail host name, which is the part of the system that sends the mail out to other e-mail servers on the Internet. Again, your ISP will give you the information and help you set up the account.

Legal Issues, Ethics, and Netiquette

Whenever you use an Internet service, you should consider issues relating to doing business and communicating with others. You and your family want to treat the information and contacts you make over the Internet with respect and care.

Legally, you want to remember that copyright and patent laws still exist, even over the Internet. Copying, sending, and otherwise transporting literature, book excerpts, music, video, and so on is protected by law. You want to be careful, too, in sending any such writings, music, or video to another country.

If you're selling goods over the Internet, be careful about exporting goods to other countries. Some items are restricted and you cannot export them; exporting other items requires that you have a license. It is, for example, illegal to send Phil Zimmerman's Pretty Good Privacy encryption program (that scrambles access codes so as to prevent unauthorized access to computerized information) to other countries.

You should honor the same good ethics over the Net as you would in any other personal or business dealings. Don't harass people with your e-mail. Don't behave immorally or dishonestly. Don't send obscenities through the system.

Netiquette, or Internet etiquette, is simply behaving politely and sensibly while online. Most often, good netiquette applies to e-mail and newsgroups, but sometimes it can pertain to Web sites. Don't send unsolicited e-mail to a list of users—known as spamming. Be careful when making statements that could be misconstrued in an e-mail. Remember, you can't read emotions, and so something said in jest may be taken seriously.

Using Mac Web browsers

You can purchase Mac Web browsers similar to Windows Web browsers. Microsoft Internet Explorer for the Mac is very similar to the IE for PC. Figure 16-11 illustrates the Microsoft Internet Explorer on the iMac, using Mac OS X.

In addition, you can purchase Netscape for the Mac. Netscape for the Mac is similar to Netscape for a PC. The tools, features, and controls are similar too. Netscape version 7.1, as described previously in this chapter, also works with the Mac OS X 10.1 or later. For more information about Netscape for the Mac, visit www.netscape.com.

Other browsers, such as Mozilla, exist for the Mac too. Mozilla is one of the early browsers that has continued to grow with the industry. For more information about Mozilla, go to www.mozilla.org.

Using Linux browsers

You can use Netscape Communicator for your browser in most Linux distributions. Netscape is a software suite that contains tools for Web browsing and e-mailing. The release for Linux includes a proprietary source code, so it's not covered under an open source, free license.

Mozilla for Linux uses the standard browsing tools. You can also download new looks for the software. Mozilla also lets you disable pop-up windows and display multiple Web pages at the same time, and it features spam controls.

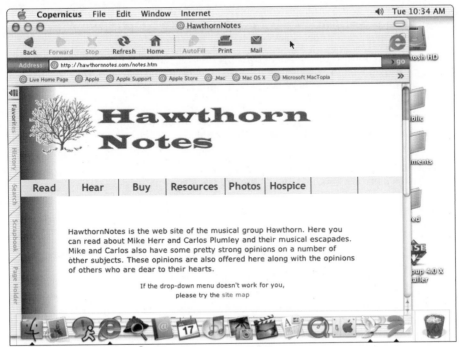

Figure 16-11: Macs can use Microsoft Internet Explorer.

HotJava is another Web browser for Linux. HotJava has a highly customizable user interface. You can download and execute applets from behind corporate firewalls. You can install new content and protocol handlers. HotJava includes proprietary source code that is not covered under an open source, free license.

Other browsers for Linux exist; plus, you can create your own code for browsers.

Applying Protection to Your Connections

You need protection against viruses and hackers if you plan to attach to the Internet. Viruses usually come in with e-mail messages, attachments to your e-mail, and so on. Read more about virus protection in Chapter 17.

Hackers, on the other hand, are the main threat from an Internet connection. A *hacker* is a person who attempts to access your computer from across the Internet. Hackers don't know who you are or what you're running on your computer. Hackers are not out to get you, in particular; they're usually just hacking away at systems to deface Web pages, forward spam or chat messages, remotely play with you to cause fear and paranoia, and so on. These days, most hacks are coming from worms.

A *worm* is a destructive software program that gains access to a computer or network via e-mail, the Web, or other method. Worms contain code that can damage data by deleting, modifying, or distributing the data in various ways.

Some software programs and hardware devices can limit the access hackers and worms have to your computer and therefore your network. Firewalls and proxies are two methods you can use to help prevent unauthorized access to your network.

✦ **Firewalls** block traffic on the network. A firewall can be either a software program or a hardware device. You must tell the firewall what traffic you want to block; in addition, a firewall cannot stop attacks in the traffic you allow into your network.

✦ A **proxy** (or **proxy server**) is software or hardware that separates a local network from outside networks. A proxy server usually caches all the pages accessed through the network. When a page is accessed that is not in the cache, the proxy server forwards a copy of that page using its own IP address, so as to protect the private network.

To make sure your network is protected, you should have either a firewall or proxy server and antivirus software installed on all computers on your network.

Cross-Reference For more information about antivirus software, see Chapter 17.

Make sure when you're looking at firewalls and proxy servers, you note two things:

✦ Can the program or device support various operating systems (if that's applicable to your situation)?

✦ Is the product for single use or for a network and all of the computers that are connected to the network?

Small Business Tip If you have an Internet connection in your business, you should distribute a list of rules regarding the use of the Internet and your employees. For example, users should not give out company passwords. You should maintain limits to sites they may visit, personal e-mails and chats, and so on. Protect yourself and your business first; worry about employees' feelings last.

Understanding and using firewalls

A firewall enforces control between two networks, for example, your private network and the Internet. Thus, a firewall blocks certain traffic and allows other traffic to pass. The emphasis with which the firewall blocks traffic depends on how you configure it. You use a firewall to keep sensitive or proprietary data on your network safe from hackers who have nothing better to do than try to hack into computers all day.

You can configure your firewall to protect against unauthenticated logins from the Internet, which prevents hackers from getting into your system. You might configure your firewall to block all traffic from the outside (including cookies, e-mails, and so on) but to let your network users communicate freely on the Internet.

Most firewalls enable you to audit access attempts and keep logs of those attempts. For example, if someone is continuously trying to access your system, the firewall can act like a phone tap and tracing tool.

Firewalls don't protect against viruses and worms. Viruses are encoded binary files that transfer over a large variety of networks and firewalls are not designed to protect against data-driven attacks—those that are mailed or copied and then executed, such as viruses, worms, and Trojan horses. See Chapter 17 for more information about virus protection.

Tip

For more information about firewalls, check out *Firewalls For Dummies* by Brian Komar, Ronald Beekelaar, and Joern Wettern (Wiley Publishing, Inc. 2003). This book is good for learning how to set up a firewall on your home or small-business network.

Choosing firewall products

Many firewall products exist, some software and others hardware. You need protection of some sort if you plan to use the Internet; but you especially need protection if you're using an always-on connection, such as a cable or DSL modem.

Generally, you'll find that firewall software products are personal firewalls, meaning they protect only the computer to which they're installed. Hardware products more often protect all of the computers connected to the device.

Software

One of the best firewall products is Norton Internet Security for Windows. This product protects your network from hackers, viruses, and many other privacy threats. For around $70, you get a suite of packages that include Norton AntiVirus, Norton Person Firewall, Norton Privacy Control, Norton Spam Alert, Ad Blocking, and Norton Parental Control.

Norton Internet Security for Windows protects your PC and network from viruses and hackers, keeps your personal information private, filters unwanted e-mail, protects your children from sites you do not want them to view, and blocks spam and pop-up ads when you're surfing the Web. The program works with Windows 98, Me, 2000, and XP.

For around $50, Broderbund's ZoneAlarm shields your system from viruses, hackers, cookies, and unwanted Internet ads. The program lets you track hackers, as well as perform other security checks and configurations. ZoneAlarm is available for Windows 98, Me, 2000, and XP.

BlackICE PC Protection is an easy-to-use software product that protects against hackers, Trojan horses, worms, and viruses. Internet Security Systems (ISS) manufactures BlackICE, and you can get it for around $40.

Hardware

Every major networking manufacturer makes some sort of hardware firewall device. Try to choose a brand with which you are familiar and perhaps even a brand that you already use with your network. Most hardware firewalls also provide you with multiple connections to your Internet provider.

Linksys, for example, makes the Instant Broadband EtherFast Cable/DSL Firewall Router. The router has a four-port switch that not only protects your connection to the Internet but also provides up to three other computers access to your Internet connection as well. You can configure the router to limit your network users' Internet access, such as time periods or certain URLs. More importantly, the router is also a firewall that protects your network from the Internet. The cost is about $75.

For around $130, NETGEAR has the FVS318, which is a cable/DSL firewall router that provides similar features as the previous router. The NETGEAR router, however, has eight switched ports. NETGEAR's router also allows other computers on the network to use one IP address assigned by the ISP. Also, the router provides virtual private network encrypting and decrypting technology, which enables you to connect to another private network via the Internet.

Windows XP's Internet Connection Firewall

If you're using Windows XP, the operating system contains a built-in firewall that is disabled by default. Before you enable the Internet Connection Firewall (ICF), you should understand that sometimes the ICF works well, but at other times, it can cause problems. For example, the ICF can prevent browsing through the Network Neighborhood and/or through the command NET VIEW. This is by design; the ICF closes ports by default for file sharing. See www.microsoft.com for information about opening ports. Other problems you might run into include the following: You might have trouble with remote administration, Internet programs might not work the way they're supposed to, playing games online might not work, and so on. In all fairness, any software firewall program might present these same problems.

The ICF is useful to protect a dial-up connection and for a LAN connection to a DSL or cable modem.

You can enable ICF for usage by following these steps:

1. Click Start ➪ Control Panel. The Control Panel window appears.

2. Double-click Network and Internet Connections.

3. Click Setup or change your home or small office network.

4. Choose the Your Computer Is Connected Directly to the Internet option.

To configure Internet Connection Firewall for a connection:

1. In the Control Panel, double-click Networking and Internet Connections.

2. Click Network Connections.

3. Right-click the connection on which you would like to enable ICF, and then click Properties.

4. On the Advanced tab, click the box to select the option to Protect My Computer or Network.

5. Click the Settings button to select programs, protocols, and services to be enabled for the ICF configuration.

NETGEAR provides other firewall hardware, such as the 11 Mbps cable/DSL ProSafe 802.11b Wireless-Ready Firewall. For around $110, you can use this firewall for the same type of security and protection of other similar devices. Using encryption, the four-port switched LAN port firewall enables multiple computers to attach to one IP address.

Understanding and using proxy servers

A proxy server is an application that is often used instead of router-based traffic controls, such as hardware firewalls. A proxy server separates a LAN from an Internet connection. When someone on the LAN requests a page from the Internet, the proxy server uses its own IP address to retrieve the page, thus protecting the computer on the LAN from hackers or other prying eyes.

An application proxy server must handle requests in some communication protocol, such as HTTP, FTP, Socks, and so on. For each protocol that is used, the appropriate proxy service must be enabled. Many proxies contain extra logging or support for user authentication. Proxy servers are application-specific. For each new protocol that the proxy must support, a new proxy must be developed.

You can develop or write your own proxy servers, or you can purchase proxy server software. Following are some of the more common and popular proxy servers. Often you'll see proxy servers that also contain firewalls, for extra protection.

Tip   Proxy servers can cause some difficulties in your network. For example, if your proxy server is down, you cannot establish a link to the Internet. For most home networks, a firewall will protect you and be easier to deal with.

✦ WinProxy 5, made by Blue Coat/Ositis, supports all Internet connections. It's easy to install and set up. WinProxy provides proxy service plus a firewall, spam blocker, and antivirus protection. WinProxy costs around $85.

✦ SpoonProxy enables a home network or small business to connect the entire LAN to the Internet on one connection. SpoonProxy works with analog modems, cable modems, and even T1 connections. The program costs around $20.

✦ You can purchase many other proxy servers as client/server software. For many you must purchase a license and software per machine, such as iPlanet Web Proxy Server. It filters Web content, distributes data like a router, and caches pages on demand. Plus this software boosts network performance. This type of proxy server is not what you need for a home network, even if you are using client/server. These proxy servers are more for large corporate networks.

Tip   For more information about basic security for home Internet users, see *Internet Privacy For Dummies* by John R. Levine, Ray Everett-Church, and Greg Stebben (Wiley Publishing, Inc. 2002).

Advanced Proxy Information

If you're knowledgeable about computers, networking, and proxy servers, you might be interested in some of the following programs and scripts you can use in addition to a firewall or to create a proxy server. You might be interested in the following, for instance, if you're running a Web server on your network.

Tcpr is a set of Perl scripts you can use in conjunction with a firewall. If you're running a Web server, for example, you can use Tcpr to forward `FTP` and `TELNET` commands across the firewall (see `ftp.alantec.com`—you must use an FTP client). Another similar package is Socks. Socks allows Gopher, FTP, and Telnet to be used through a firewall (see `ftp.nec.com` for more information).

You can use `IPFILTERD`, an IP address filtering daemon, to help build or strengthen your firewall. You can find out more through anonymous FTP at `coombs.anu.edu.au`. When you go to the FTP site, look through the list of commands for the `IPFILTERD` command. Click on the `IPFILTERD` command to learn more.

Protecting various operating systems

If your network is made up of various operating systems, be sure to check any firewall or proxy product you buy to see that it will operate for multiple systems. You might need to purchase a separate, personal firewall, for example, for your Macintosh. Alternatively, you can buy an 8-port firewall router into which you can connect all of your computers and protect them whether they are Mac, PCs, or Linux boxes. This section explains a bit about protecting the Macs and/or Linux computers on your network.

Macintosh

Norton Personal Firewall for Macintosh is similar to Norton Personal Firewall for the PC. The software keeps hackers out of your system, making your computer invisible on the Internet. You can control inbound and outbound connections, configure the software for users, intruder alerts, and view logs to see what has been occurring on your Macintosh when it's on the Internet. Norton Personal Firewall for Macintosh costs around $70.

Intego NetBarrier for Macs is another personal firewall for the Macintosh. The cost is around $60. NetBarrier protects all incoming and outgoing data, blocks hackers, detects wrong passwords, and keeps a log for all attempt that threaten security

Linux

In Linux, you can acquire various firewalls over the Internet. Some work well for beginners, and others are more complicated to configure and therefore more difficult to use. All firewalls protect your computer; the one you choose depends on the Linux distribution and the features you want from the firewall.

Check online to find out more about the firewall you're most interested in. Following are some names of firewalls you can use with Linux distributions: Firestarter, Limeware, and giFT.

Many Linux experts suggest creating your own iptables to make your own firewall. You can also get information online about this procedure. Creating iptables gives you experience in Linux, but if you're not the adventurous type, you might want to use a dedicated firewall distribution of Linux.

Using Linux as a firewall

A Linux computer is often configured as a firewall between your PC/Macintosh network and the Internet. You can download programs from the Internet that enable you to transform even an older, less powerful computer into a firewall. Check out www.linux-firewall-tools.com/linux for some ideas. As a firewall, the Linux computer doesn't need to perform any other tasks. You can use a 100 MHz, Pentium computer with 16MB of RAM and still have the best firewall protection, as long as you configure it correctly.

One Internet firewall/router for Linux is called SmoothWall. You can run SmoothWall on any Intel PC. Since the program was built using open source, it is free software and distributed under the GNU Public License.

The designer of SmoothWall created the program to be easy to manage with a Web browser; to support many existing network cards, modems, and other hardware plus many different connection methods; and to be installed by anyone, whether a home user or an IT technician. All you need on the SmoothWall computer is the box, an Internet connection, network interface cards (NICs), and cabling, and you're ready to connect your private network to the Internet safely.

Another software package called ClarkConnect enables you to transform a standard PC to a dedicated broadband gateway and server. A ClarkConnect system provides DNS services, antivirus protection, antispam tools, daily security audits, intrusion detection, and more.

Note A computer used solely as a proxy server or a firewall is often called a *gateway*. A gateway is an entry point into another network. A gateway computer has two network cards. One card is configured for the Internet, and the other is configured for the LAN. Computers and data on the LAN are completely safe from the Internet because the Internet connection and the LAN connection never cross or meet. Routers are also used as gateways.

Summary

In this chapter, you've learned about accessing the Internet from a network. Specifically, you have learned the following:

✦ Understanding Internet access and connections

✦ Understanding access equipment

✦ Sharing Internet connections

✦ Understanding Web browsers and e-mail programs

✦ Applying protection for your connections

In the next chapter, you learn more about using e-mail on the network.

✦   ✦   ✦

Using E-Mail

◆   ◆   ◆   ◆

In This Chapter

Understanding e-mail

Examining and using
e-mail programs for
various platforms

Securing from e-mail
hackers and viruses

◆   ◆   ◆   ◆

E-mail is not only all the rage, but it is also impossible to live and especially do business these days without e-mail. Nearly everyone has an e-mail address — friends, business associates, vendors, charities, even your kids' friends probably have e-mail accounts. Most often, you use e-mail over the Internet to contact people in other states or countries, as well as in your own hometown. With fast Internet connections in most homes today and with various software and hardware connection devices, every member of your household can have his or her own connection to the Internet and to an e-mail account.

Understanding E-Mail

Electronic mail (e-mail) is a perfect way to stay in touch with family, friends, and business associates, among others. You can send a message electronically, and the recipient can respond at any time that's convenient. You can send or receive e-mail in the middle of the night, middle of the day — anytime that's favorable for you.

E-mail can consist of memos, notes, letters, reports, or any other type of correspondence. You also can attach files to e-mail messages, in case you want to send a picture, story, spreadsheet, or other file type. Send a message to one person or to a hundred people. Forward a message you receive from your brother, for example, to your mom and to your sister, if you want.

Small Business Tip

Using e-mail at work promotes collaboration among your employees. Users can share ideas, solutions, files, and more when they can e-mail each other in the office.

You can save, print, reply to, or delete messages. Sort your messages to find one in particular. Change the layout and font of a message. Format messages to make them look nice. You can even add the look of stationery to your e-mail messages.

Using Internet e-mail

If you have an Internet account with an Internet service provider or if you have access to the Web, you can send and receive Internet e-mail. E-mail messages you send over the Internet can go anywhere around the world — to another country, another state, or across the street. Naturally, you must have the e-mail address of the person to whom you're e-mailing, although you might be able to find an e-mail address in the white or yellow pages in an online search engine.

E-mail programs — such as Outlook Express, Netscape Messenger, or Eudora — provide the interface you need to send Internet e-mail through your ISP or other service provider. Programs such as Hotmail and Juno provide a free e-mail service on the Web; you do have to view the "commercials," however, to get your mail service.

You'll need to configure your Internet e-mail. Each computer operating system is different, including each e-mail Windows configuration. Generally, you need a name, an e-mail address, a password, an incoming mail server, an outgoing mail server, and your mail server type (such as POP or IMAP). Your ISP will give you all of the information you need to set up your operating system for e-mail; plus, your ISP should offer free technical assistance if you should need it. If you have trouble, check with your program's documentation and with your ISP for technical support.

Using Web-based e-mail

Hotmail, Juno, and other Web-based e-mail enable you to check on your e-mail messages wherever you are. For example, if you visit your sister in another city, you can use her computer, go to the Web site, and retrieve your e-mail, answer it, and send a response. Many people have Web-based e-mail accounts because of this convenience.

Tip   Make sure that on any day you want to check your Web-based e-mail away from home, you close your Outlook Express or other e-mail program at home or at work. Otherwise, you won't receive copies of the messages later, at home.

Most ISPs enable you to receive your e-mail via a Web-based site. All you need to know is the name of the site, your username, and your password for e-mail. For example, say your ISP is HomeLinkRUs. You go to your Web browser and type **www. HomeLinkRUs.net**. Press Enter. Figure 17-1 illustrates the HomeLinkRUs site. On some sites, such as HomeLinkRUs, you see the Web mail link.

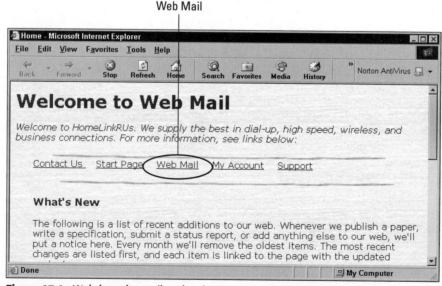

Figure 17-1: Web-based e-mail makes it easy to get mail anywhere, anytime.

Next, click the Web mail link and you see a login screen similar to the one shown in Figure 17-2.

Many ISPs do not have a Web mail link on their site or do not advertise that you can get your mail on their site; however, you might be able to retrieve your mail. Go to your computer's Web browser and type **mail.*ISPname*.net** (or **org**, or **com**). Do not type ***www*** or ***html:***. For example, if you type **mail.homelinkrus.net**, you see the resulting screen in Figure 17-3.

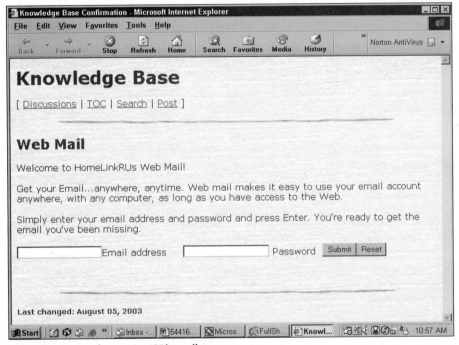

Figure 17-2: Log in to your ISP's mail server.

When you enter your username and password, you get a screen similar to the one shown in Figure 17-4, from which you can send and receive mail, change configuration, and perform other tasks.

Note   If you cannot access your e-mail in either of the described ways, call your Internet provider and ask how you can obtain Web-based e-mail.

If the members of your network are connected to the Internet and you each have a separate mailbox, you can e-mail the others on your network. Usually, an ISP provides multiple mailboxes with one Internet account. This way, everyone in the family can have their own e-mail address. Some ISPs provide one or two extra mailboxes for no additional charge; other ISPs charge for multiple mailboxes.

Figure 17-5 illustrates an Internet e-mail message from two separate e-mail servers. The reply is written above the original message.

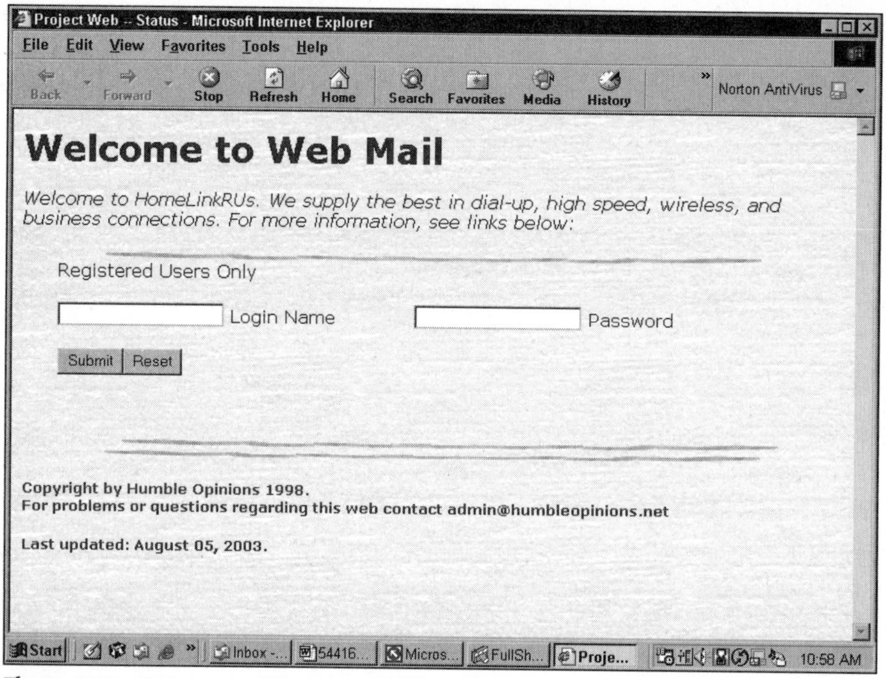

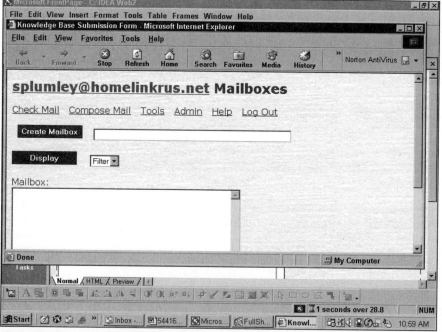

Figure 17-3: Get your mail from your ISP's mail server.

Figure 17-4: Send and receive e-mail from anywhere on the Web.

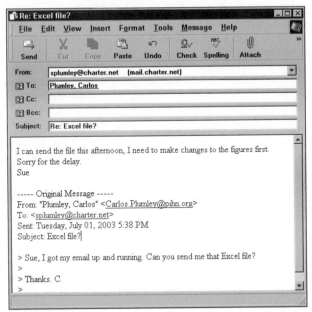

Figure 17-5: Internet e-mail keeps you in touch with the world.

Examining E-Mail Programs

Most e-mail programs operate in the same way — you have an inbox and an outbox, and you can delete items, create mail, send mail, and store addresses for easier access to your e-mail addresses — it's just the interface that changes. This section describes various available e-mail products for the Windows, Mac, and Linux programs.

Each person on your network can use a different e-mail program, if you like. It is a good idea to keep your e-mail applications (and your Web browsers) up-to-date with the latest versions. Requirements, recommendations, and information change so quickly on the Internet, you could wake up one day with an older e-mail program that cannot access the Internet. So no matter what type of program you use, keep it updated as much as possible.

Using Windows e-mail programs

Windows 98, Me, 2000, and XP all come with an e-mail program — Outlook Express — built into the operating system. Alternatively, you can use a third-party application, such as Netscape Mail or Mozilla. The one you choose depends on what you're used to and your preferences.

Outlook Express

Outlook Express is easily the most popular Windows e-mail program. One reason for its popularity, of course, is that it is built into every Windows operating system. Outlook Express is easy to use and easy to upgrade. You upgrade the program by going to www.microsoft.com and downloading the installation program.

Note Outlook is another e-mail program that is part of the Microsoft Office suite of products. You can use Outlook for e-mail on the Internet and for internal e-mail in your home or business. Outlook is a more comprehensive program than Outlook Express. Outlook contains more features, such as calendars and to-do lists.

The following information describes the Outlook Express program in some detail. Realize that all of the other applications discussed in the following pages are very similar to form and function; therefore, not all programs are described in such detail.

Using the Inbox

You can send and receive messages from the Inbox on any computer on the network. You can open messages you receive, and then print, reply, save, delete, and sort messages in the Inbox.

You can create folders, delete folders and messages, move and copy messages from folder to folder, and otherwise manipulate folders in the Inbox. The Inbox features and tools help you organize and manage your messages.

To open Outlook Express, double-click the icon on the desktop, or choose Start ⇨ (All) Programs ⇨ Outlook Express.

Figure 17-6 illustrates the Inbox in Outlook Express. Note that the Inbox comes with several Local folders: Inbox, Outbox, Sent Items, Deleted Items, and Drafts. Depending on your version of Windows, your folders may appear in a different order. There is also a folder in the figure called SueMail that was created by the user. Following is a description of the folders in the Outlook Express left window pane:

✦ **Local Folders** — This folder contains all folders, including those created by the user and by the program.

✦ **Inbox** — The Inbox stores all messages you receive. You can open and read, reply, print, and delete messages from this folder.

✦ **Outbox** — This folder contains all messages you write and send. To deliver messages, you can click Send/Recv (Send/Receive) on the toolbar or select Tools ⇨ Send and Receive.

✦ **Sent Items** — Sent Items contains a copy of all messages you send.

✦ **Deleted Items** — This folder holds all messages you delete until you empty the folder. To delete a message, select it in the right pane and then press the Delete key. To empty the Delete Items folder, right-click the folder and choose Empty 'Deleted Items' Folder from the quick menu.

✦ **Drafts** — This is a folder to which you can save mail that you're composing before you're ready to send it.

Changing views

You can change elements on the Inbox window to better view your messages and folders. You can change the way you view messages; you can hide or show the toolbar and status bar; and you can change layout, fonts, and various other options using the View menu.

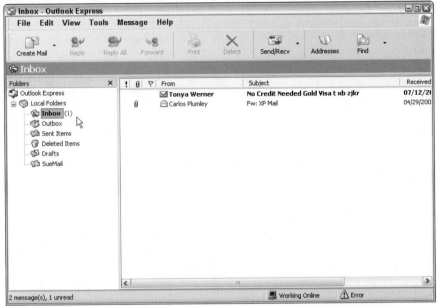

Figure 17-6: Use Outlook Express to send and receive e-mail on the network.

Adding new folders

You can create new folders at any time. To create a new folder, follow these steps:

1. Select File ⇨ New ⇨ Folder. The Create Folder dialog box appears.

2. Choose the folder you want as the parent folder, as shown in Figure 17-7.

3. Enter a name for the new folder and press Enter. The new folder appears in your list.

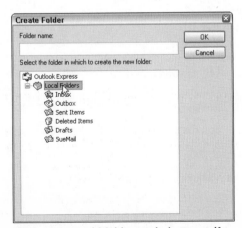

Figure 17-7: Add folders to help yourself organize your messages.

Renaming and deleting

You also can rename any folder, or delete it if you no longer need it. To rename a folder, select the folder, right-click it, and then choose Rename from the quick menu. Enter the new name and click OK.

To delete a folder, select the folder and then right-click it. Choose Delete from the quick menu. The folder is deleted without confirmation. Naturally, any file or folder you delete is still in the Deleted Items folder; to completely delete an item from your computer, you must empty the Deleted Items folder.

Setting options

In Outlook Express you can set various options, such a sound that plays when new mail arrives, the font to send messages in, various priorities for outgoing messages, and so on. To set options, choose Tools ➪ Options. Figure 17-8 shows the Options dialog box.

Figure 17-8: Set your mail preferences in the Options dialog box.

Following is a brief description of some options you can set:

✦ **General tab** — Use this tab to set options for new mail notification, deletion warnings and confirmations, profile default, and so on.

✦ **Read tab** — Options include the action the program should take when you delete an item, whether to use original text in a reply, and which font to use for replies.

✦ **Send tab** — Here you set options for items such as which font to use for new messages, requests for notification of delivery, priority of messages, and so on.

✦ **Spelling tab** — Options here include whether to check spelling before sending a message, as well as some items to ignore when checking spelling.

✦ **Security tab** — Options discuss virus protection as provided by Outlook Express, encryption, and digitally signing messages.

Sending and Receiving

When you open Outlook Express, you can immediately check to see if you have received any messages. You then can reply to those messages, if you want. You also can send new messages to anyone on the network.

To check for mail, click Send/Recv (Send/Receive) on the toolbar. Any new messages appear in the right pane of the Inbox.

To read a message, double-click it. Alternatively, you can choose File ⇨ Open. After you read a message, you can close it, delete it, reply to it, and even forward the message to someone else, if you want. Use either the menu or the toolbar buttons in the open message to perform these tasks. Toolbar buttons and menus are similar to the toolbar buttons and menus in other Windows products.

When you receive a message, you can reply to or forward that message immediately or later, whichever you want. All you do is click the Reply or Forward button, as appropriate. Replying to a message automatically addresses a message to the person who sent the original. It also includes the original message text in the reply, as shown in Figure 17-9.

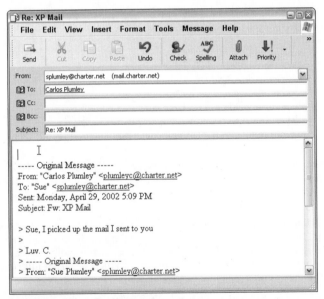

Figure 17-9: Reply to a message.

When you forward a message, you send a copy of the original text, along with any comments you want to add, to a third party. When you forward a message, you must type the address of the person to whom the message will be sent.

Sending new mail

You can send a new mail message at any time. Open Outlook Express, then click the Create Mail button or click Message ⇨ New Message. The New Message box appears. The dialog box displays toolbars for cutting, pasting, copying, and formatting messages. You can learn what each tool does by holding the mouse pointer over the tool, because a short ToolTip appears to indicate its purpose.

When you compose a new message, you type a name in the To box to designate the recipient. You also might send a Cc (carbon copy) to someone else on the network by entering a second name in the Cc box. You can send multiple copies by entering multiple names or addresses in the Cc text box; separate the names with semicolons. Optionally, you can add text to define the subject of the e-mail. Enter the message of the e-mail in the message text box.

If you want help with the recipient's name, click the To box. The Address Book appears, as shown in Figure 17-10. Note that the names of users on the network appear in the list box.

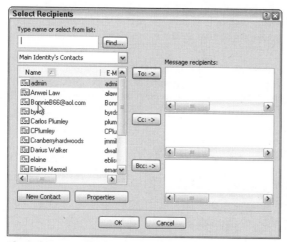

Figure 17-10: Use the Address Book for quick naming of recipients.

To choose a name, double-click it in the list. The name moves over to the To list. Click OK to return to your message. Complete your message, and then send it by clicking the Send button.

Netscape Mail

Netscape Mail is part of the Netscape suite of products, which include a Web browser, antivirus software, and more. Netscape Mail operates similarly to Outlook Express in that you'll see an Inbox, Outbox, Sent Items, and other folders. Sending and receiving mail is similar. In fact, nearly every feature is the same as Outlook Express except for a slightly different interface.

Netscape Mail version 7.1 also offers a free Netscape mail account, junk mail controls, a Palm sync, various mail views, a quick search, mail alerts, and other enhancements. You can purchase Netscape version 7.1 for less than $20. Go to www.netscape.com for more information.

Using Mac e-mail programs

In addition to using Microsoft Internet Explorer on the Macintosh, you can use various other e-mail programs, including Netscape 7.1, Eudora, Mozilla, and more. The type of program you use depends on your preferences.

Naturally, you must configure your e-mail, as with any e-mail program. Figure 17-11 shows the Mail Configuration dialog box on the Mac OS X. This mail program came with the Mac OS X as a default mail program.

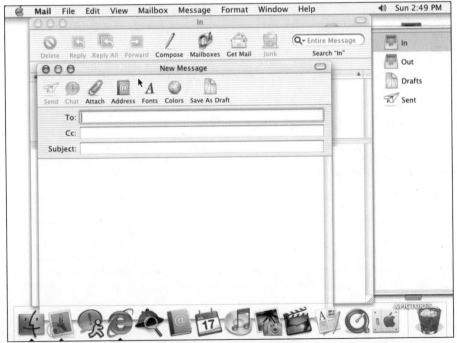

Figure 17-11: Set up the e-mail account on the Mac.

This Mac Mail includes instant messaging (see Chapter 18 for more information), a junk mail filter, and QuickTime to view movies. It also includes helpful organizational, searching, and cleanup features, and the mail program uses encryption for enhanced security.

Figure 17-12 shows the Inbox of the Mac Mail program with a New Message box open and ready to begin e-mailing.

Figure 17-12: Use the Mac Mail program to send e-mails.

Netscape makes a mail program for the Mac OS X in its 7.1 suite of programs. Netscape provides the tools for sending and receiving messages, organizing mail, sorting messages, and more. See the section "Using Windows' e-mail programs" earlier in the chapter for more information.

Mozilla and Eudora are other Mac e-mail programs you can use. Check www.mozilla.org for more information about the Mac version. Check www.eudora.com for more information about Eudora.

Tip   Eudora also has a version for Windows computers. See www.eudora.com for more information.

Using Linux e-mail programs

Netscape Mail, Eudora, and Mozilla all make versions that work with various distributions of Linux. Naturally, you can also write your own code to create your own e-mail program. Depending on your distribution, many e-mail client programs are available: Mutt, Pine, KMail, Aethera, and more.

Your best bet with Linux is to talk to others who are using the same distribution as you, get on the Internet to see what others are doing, and then experiment with various programs and procedures before you make up your mind.

Applying Security in E-Mail

E-mail is not as secure as many people would like to think. First, good hackers can usually find a way into your e-mail messages, if they want to. Second, after the mail is received, anyone with access to the receiving computer can read your e-mail. For these reasons, make sure you don't put anything into an e-mail that is extremely sensitive or private. Always expect someone besides the intended recipient to read it.

In addition, viruses, worms, and Trojan horses pose considerable threats to your computer, your data, and your network. Antivirus programs are important to anyone who is attached to the Internet.

Using digital IDs and encryption

That being said, there are precautions you can take to help to protect your e-mail from prying eyes. Most e-mail programs include at least two options for security: digital IDs (also called certificates) and encryption.

✦ A **digital ID** proves you are who you say you are when you send an e-mail. Digital IDs, or certificates, are made up of a public key, a private key, and a digital signature. When you digitally sign your e-mail, you add your digital signature plus a public key to the message.

When someone receives your e-mail message, he or she can verify your identity through the digital signature. Then the person replies to your message using the public key you originally sent the person. When you receive the return message, only you can read it because you have a private key that verifies that the person sending the e-mail is who he or she says.

✦ **Encryption** scrambles the actual message so that it cannot be intercepted and read anywhere between the two machines sending and receiving the e-mails. If you want to use encryption with your e-mail messages, you must use digital IDs in conjunction with encryption. So the people in your address book must have a digital ID; you use their public key to encrypt the messages. When the recipient gets the message, his or her private key decrypts it. And so it goes, back and forth, between the two of you.

Tip   Pretty Good Privacy (PGP) is a freeware program that uses public key authentication and encryption. PGP is a product of the PGP Corporation. Noncommercial U.S. citizens can obtain PGP from many Web sites, including `http://web.mit.edu/network/pgp.html`. MIT's Web site contains PGP for a variety of platforms. For more information about PGP, see Chapter 22.

Using virus protection

Virus protection is *most* important with your e-mail program. E-mails with attachments come into your computer and your network and can damage and even destroy data and hardware. You should definitely use a firewall to help screen out viruses (see Chapter 16), but you should also use an antivirus program on each computer attached to the network.

Generally, viruses come in on the Internet or via e-mail. A virus could come in on a floppy disk brought from work or from your child's school as well. So even if you don't have an Internet account, you should protect yourself from viruses.

You can choose from many antivirus programs. Rather than downloading a free copy an antivirus program, you would be much better served to purchase a copy of a program that is trusted and tested. Free antivirus programs do not usually let you update virus definitions to catch the latest threats. Plus, free programs are not as meticulous at scanning your computer and protecting it.

Viruses, worms, and Trojan horses

Viruses come in different permutations, and they are constantly changing. Some people use the terms virus, worm, and Trojan horse interchangeably, but they are not the same thing. These pests are designed to cause problems by people who know a lot about programming and have nothing better to do with their time.

✦ A **virus** is a software program, script, or macro that propagates itself by infecting other programs on the same computer. Viruses can destroy or damage a computer, data, or applications. Or a virus can just pop up an annoying window and do no damage. True viruses cannot spread to another computer without your help, such as through trading files using a floppy disk or via an e-mail attachment.

✦ A **worm** is a type of virus; it also propagates itself. A worm, however, can gain access to the computer and travel across networks from one computer to the next, traveling on file-sending and -receiving features. It causes damage not only to the computer and software but also to the network by deleting or modifying the data.

✦ A **Trojan horse** refers to a program you think you want, such as a free game, but it contains something harmful. For example, you start the free game but find it erases every file in the directory. A Trojan horse could alternatively contain a virus or a worm, which then spreads the damage.

Continued

Continued

For the purpose of the following discussion, the word virus will be used, but the information applies to worms and Trojan horses as well.

After a virus is created, it's usually distributed through shareware, pirated software, or e-mail. The virus infects one computer, starts destroying and damaging data, and then usually copies itself to other computers on the network.

Following are some interesting facts about viruses:

✦ Viruses can infect a computer even if files are just being copied. Viruses can open when you open an executable file (a program file with an .EXE extension, for example).

✦ Some viruses can modify their own code as they spread, making various similar variants.

✦ A virus can be memory- or non-memory-resident. If the virus is *memory-resident*, it attaches itself to the memory and then infects the computer. If it is *non-memory-resident*, that means you must run the virus program (like double-clicking on an e-mail attachment) in order for it to run.

✦ A stealth virus attaches itself to files and then attacks the computer; stealth viruses spread more quickly than other viruses.

✦ Viruses can remain on the computer even if the computer is formatted, for example, by infecting portions of the CMOS battery or master.

✦ Viruses usually attack EXE, COM, SYS, BIN, PIF, or any executable files. Viruses also like to infect data files like those from Word or Excel.

✦ Viruses can increase in size without your even knowing they're on your computer.

✦ Viruses can reboot the computer, delete files, change volume labels, cause hardware problems, disable ports, cause the system to hang or freeze, increase file size, display pictures, and perform a host of other tasks you may never attribute to a virus.

The best way to protect yourself against a virus is to install an antivirus program to all computers on the network and to keep the definitions updated. *Definitions* are fixes and identifiers for new viruses being found every day.

Norton AntiVirus is one of the best protections against threats, including viruses, worms, and Trojan horses. Symantec, the maker of Norton AntiVirus, even offers a Web site where you can learn about viruses and find fixes to help clean viruses from your computer — www.sarc.com. You can use this site and the fixes and information whether you buy the antivirus software or not.

Norton AntiVirus has many different versions and licenses. You can purchase the software to protect one machine — PC or Mac; you can purchase the software for a network with various licenses for your users; you can purchase different versions that include personal firewall and other similar applications.

Norton AntiVirus not only removes viruses, but also it can scan incoming and outgoing mail, detect and block threats from instant messaging attachments, and enable you to update your definitions daily. It has excellent technical help as well if you have problems with the software or with any virus. AntiVirus also has worm-blocking and script-blocking technologies to help you protect your computer and your network. Norton cleans files, quarantines those it can't clean, and even deletes infected files that are not appropriate to keep.

McAfee is another common and popular antivirus program. Like other products, McAfee offers a simple antivirus program or an entire suite of protection programs. McAfee does include versions for Windows, Mac, and Linux, which might be of interest to those who use Linux. The McAfee program offers similar features to Norton, and the cost of the two is about the same. It all depends on how many licenses you buy and what type of protection you want.

Other antivirus programs include Computer Associates' EZ Antivirus, OLP eTrust Antivirus, and Internet Security Systems' RealSecure.

Summary

In this chapter, you've learned how to set up e-mail on your local area network. You covered the following topics:

✦ Understanding e-mail

✦ Using the Inbox and other e-mail features

✦ Securing your computer and network e-mail

✦ Using various antivirus programs

In the next chapter, you learn about using chat programs.

✦   ✦   ✦

Using Chat Programs

Chat programs are popular for use over the Internet; however, they are also useful in your home network. You can send a message upstairs to tell the kids that dinner is ready, for example, or you can send a quick message to your spouse to say the phone is for him or her. Windows comes with a built-in chat program, but you can download several from the Internet as well.

Understanding Chat Programs

Chat programs enable you to talk to other people online, on the Internet, or on your own local area network. Chat programs involve two or more people in a conversation in real time. Real time describes something that is happening right now. A phone conversation is in real time, for example, but a message on the answering machine is not.

There are Web-based chat programs, Internet Rely Chat (IRC) programs, and instant messaging programs that you can use to chat over the Internet.

✦ Web-based chat involves a plug-in (mini-program) that lets you chat with someone from your Web browser.

✦ You install IRC programs to your computer; then when you're online, you can participate in discussion groups.

✦ Instant messaging lets you set up a list of people to check when you're online. If they are online too, you can send messages to them and they receive the message instantly.

Using Internet instant messaging programs

Many popular Internet applications for instant messaging exist, including AOL Instant Messenger, ICQ, iChat Pager, and so on. You install one of these programs on your computer, and then you can chat with anyone else who also has the program installed. Most chat programs require the same program on the other end of the chat; ICQ, for example, isn't compatible with iChat Pager. If you and a friend use the same program, however, you can chat over the Internet anytime you're both online.

Note   Some of these programs also have LAN options. Read the individual program's documentation or online help for more information.

Most of these programs start when you attach to the Internet. The program then operates in the background, waiting for you or one of your chat "buddies" to get online.

The manufacturer of the chat program assigns each person a code number (like a telephone number). When you set up the program, you enter your friend's numbers into the program. The program monitors the Internet and detects when your chat buddy's number appears online. The program notifies you that your buddy is online, and your buddy's program notifies him or her that you are online.

If you want, you can initiate a chat with your friend. You initiate a chat by sending a brief message asking if your friend would like to chat. Alternatively, your friend may send a message asking you to chat.

Some instant messaging programs, ICQ for example, let you talk to your friends, but you can also meet other people online with the same interests as you. Most other programs are the same or similar. Figure 18-1 shows the Chatter Bug site. You can choose to search for people by interest, location, or family, or you can do an advanced search by your own topics. If someone is online the same time you are, you can talk to them in an open discussion window in real time.

You can also use message boards with most chat programs. Message boards aren't instant; they are more like e-mail. You can read a message from someone and then reply to that message, or you can create a new thread (set of related messages) of your own. Figure 18-2 shows the Chatter Bug Chat message board.

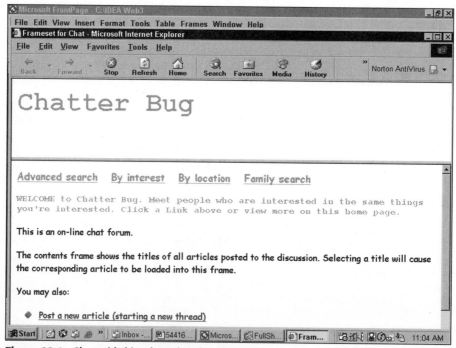

Figure 18-1: Chat with friends and make new ones.

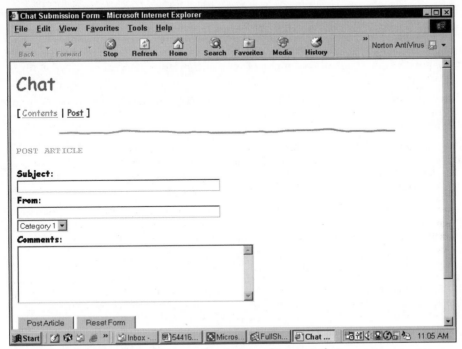

Figure 18-2: Message boards are another feature of Internet chat.

Yahoo, AOL, Delphi, MSN, and other Web sites have Web-based chats available for free. You must, however, register with the site to obtain admittance to these sites and chat rooms. You can choose a category of chat room to join, such as hobbies, computers, sports, art, and so on. Then you choose from various chat rooms in that category, based on how many people are in the chat room.

Caution   Most chat rooms and message boards are safe to join, but you should not reveal any personal information, such as your last name, phone number, or address. If you have children who participate in Internet chats, you should keep a close check on their chat friends; after all, anyone can pretend to be someone else online.

Note   Most IRCs, Web-based chats, and instant messaging programs have versions for the Macintosh as well as for Windows.

Using LAN instant messaging programs

In addition to Internet chat programs, LAN chat programs are available that you can use to communicate in real time with others on your LAN. You might wonder why you need to chat over the computer when you're in the same house as the other members of your network. LAN chats do not go out over the Internet; therefore, they are safer and more secure than Internet chats. Plus, consider the convenience of online chatting over the network.

Suppose that you're upstairs working and you answer the phone. It's for your spouse, who is working downstairs on the computer. Instead of running downstairs or yelling, you send a quick message. WinPopup is a chat program that is included with the Windows 95/98 operating system, but the Windows 2000 and XP operating systems do not include the program. You can, however, get a copy of the program from a shareware source, as described in the next section.

MacPopUp is a program that allows Windows users to send and receive messages from different operating systems, such as Mac OSs, Windows, Linux and UNIX OSs. MacPopUp is similar to WinPopup.

For instant messaging on your home network, you can use any of the free programs offered by MSN, AOL, ICQ, and other Web-based messaging services. When you want to use an instant messaging program for your home use, you'll still go over the Internet to connect. So you'll have to dial –up, or you can use a permanent connection, as with a cable modem.

When you want to communicate with another person in your household, or even a friend, you enter his or her assigned number. You can alternatively search for someone by e-mail address or name. You send a message, and the recipient can either accept or decline the message.

Then the other person can answer you. The conversation can go on and on.

You also can use a chat program to announce dinner, to ask someone to feed the cat or take out the garbage, or send a multitude of other requests. Additionally, you can hold longer conversations on a chat program. You might want to discuss a computer problem, an important decision about finances, or whether to let your kid borrow the car this weekend. Chat programs add to the convenience of working on computers and to being on the network.

Small Business Tip

LAN chat programs can help encourage office communications and collaboration. Users can quickly get answers to questions, query coworkers about contracts or invoices, and shoot ideas back and forth by using a chat program.

A variety of LAN chat programs are available. You can purchase some programs that supply special features, such as file transfer capabilities, programmable Away messages (messages the program sends automatically when you're away from the computer), and alarms for incoming messages. Other chat programs are shareware or freeware that offer basic services. You can use ICQ, Yahoo, MSN, or other programs that are free.

Looking at LAN-Only Chat Programs

If you don't have an Internet connection or you would prefer to not use an Internet messenger service, you can us a LAN-only chat program. Check www.shareware.com for shareware or freeware you can use on your home network. Some programs that are useful include LAN Spirit, RealPopup, LANMessage, InterChat, WinPopup Gold, Windows Communicator, and many more for Windows. For the Mac, you can try QuickPopup or SnapTalk. For Linux, try Vypress Messenger for Java. Most of these applications are free to try; many require a payment of $25 if you plan to use the application.

Using WinPopup Gold

The following information is about one of these programs — WinPopup Gold — but the instructions are similar to all of the LAN-only chat programs.

Installing WinPopup Gold

You can acquire WinPopup Gold from various places on the Internet. CNET's download.com is a great place for finding various shareware and freeware programs. After download, you open the folder containing the WinPopup installation program and double-click the icon. Installation takes only a few minutes. WinPopup Gold works on all versions of Windows, but it does not work on Macs and Linux machines.

To open WinPopup, you can put a shortcut on your desktop or you can go to Start ⇨ Programs ⇨ Smart Is On ⇨ WinPopup Gold and click WinPopup Gold. Figure 18-3 shows the WinPopup screen when you first open it.

Figure 18-3: WinPopup lets you send messages across your LAN.

Sending messages

To use WinPopup, you must start the program and leave it running. You can minimize the window so that it doesn't interfere with your work. You can put a shortcut for the program in your StartUp folder so it starts with Windows.

You can send a message to one user by entering the user's name or the computer name. You can also click the Who Is Connected button to choose from someone who is on the network. You can even go to a chat room on the LAN, if you prefer.

To send a message, follow these steps:

1. Open the WinPopup window.

2. Click Send Message.

3. Enter a name to send, and type your message, as shown in Figure 18-4. Click Send.

4. Click Read Messages. Any messages addressed to you appear in the window, as shown in Figure 18-5.

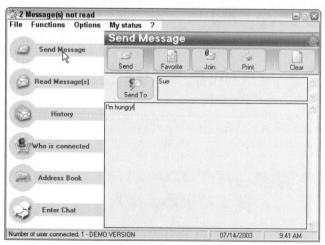

Figure 18-4: Create a message to send to network users.

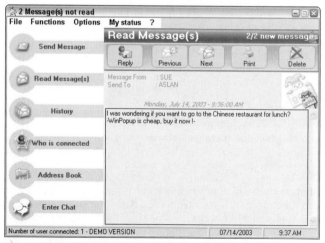

Figure 18-5: Message important information or just chat with those on your network.

Changing options

You also can change a few options in WinPopup. You can change whether or not to play a sound when a new message arrives, whether always to display the WinPopup window on top of all other windows, and whether to pop up the window when you receive a new message.

To change options, choose Options ⇨ Options. The WinPopup Gold Options dialog box appears. Click the button on the left — General, Messages, My Status, Advanced, or Network — to change the following options.

✦ **General** — Enables you to change your nickname.

✦ **Messages** — Enables you to choose to open WinPopup automatically, play sound, show confirmation messages, and so on.

✦ **My status** — Sends an auto response when you're away. You can enter any message you want.

✦ **Advanced** — Sets how WinPopup minimizes and other program visibility options.

✦ **Network** — Enables you to add a workgroup to your mailing list.

Figure 18-6 shows the Messages options in the WinPopup Gold Options dialog box.

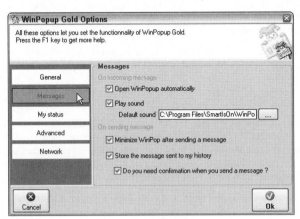

Figure 18-6: Set options for WinPopup.

You can also create an address book, find out who is connected to the network, and use various "skins" to change the look of WinPopup. (Skins are decorative colors and icons that change the look of the program but do not change the functionality.)

Other LAN chat programs

As previously mentioned, multiple LAN chat programs are available. You can download many programs as shareware from the Internet (the cost is usually $25 if you choose to keep the program), or you can purchase LAN instant messaging applications for $40 to $100. You can search the Internet for "LAN chat" and find multiple sources for various instant messaging programs.

You can use many available applications on your LAN. Some programs are chat programs; others are meant for sending messages only or for issuing warnings or cautions. You can find just about any type of program you want to use on your network on the Internet.

Tip   Most LAN chat programs don't work on the Internet.

Using RealPopup

RealPopup is a program similar to the older WinPopup that came with Windows 95/98. It is compatible with older versions of Windows and system messaging tools. RealPopup supports the HTML language, lets you set options for its use, and uses an internal network browser.

RealPopup is free and you can get it from CNET's download.com or downloads-zdnet.com.

Using Vypress Messenger

Vypress Messenger comes in a Windows version and a Linux version. You can use it to exchange instant messages over a TCP/IP network. Since Vypress Messenger is compatible with the Server Message Block (SMB) protocol, you can receive messages from other operating systems, such as Linux and the Mac, if they use the SMB protocol. You can also use the program with all of the Windows versions.

The program includes message filtering options, handles large quantities of messages, and can be used on the Internet as well as on your home or small-business network. You can try Vypress Messenger for free. If you like it, you pay $20 for the license.

Vypress Messenger for Java is specifically made for the Linux environment. This chat program is free. It works similarly to the Vypress Messenger for Windows, using TCP/IP to pass messages back and forth.

Using QuickPopup

QuickPopup is an instant messaging program for the Macintosh. Various versions of QuickPopup are available for the various versions of Mac operating systems. Similar to the other pop-up programs, QuickPopup appears when a message comes in. You can also set various options for sounds and warnings. QuickPopup enables you to communicate with another Mac or with a PC, which is handy if you have both computer types on your network.

You can let the program search for users who are attached to the network and have the QuickPopup program installed, or you can type the name of someone to send the message to. Figure 18-7 shows the QuickPopup screen with a message ready to send.

Figure 18-7: Use QuickPopup with the Mac.

QuickPopup is free to try and costs $25 if you decide to keep it. Again, you can download QuickPopup from CNET's `download.com`.

Using SnapTalk

SnapTalk is another chat program for the Macintosh. SnapTalk is nice because it automatically finds other users on the network and adds them to a list from which you can choose. It also notifies you when someone sends you a message, and you can set the program to speak incoming messages aloud. SnapTalk is free to try but costs $22 if you choose to use it.

Looking at Internet and LAN Chat Programs

If you're interested in chatting over the Internet, you need a little information about the instant messaging programs that are available. Some programs also enable chatting on a LAN. Following are a few of the more popular chat programs:

✦ **AOL Instant Messenger** is an instant program that enables you to send messages back and forth over America Online (AOL) and the Internet. The program is free. See http://www.aol.com for more information.

AOL Instant Messenger has a variation you can use with Linux; AOL Instant Messenger (AIM) version 1.1.112 has been tested on Red Hat Linux 6.0, SuSe Linux 6.4, and Mandrake Linux 7.0. Using AOL Instant Messenger with Linux means you can also communicate with Windows and Macs that use AOL Instant Messenger. This program is free and you can get it from www.zdnet.com.

✦ **ICQ** is an Internet program. ICQ lists your buddies who are currently online. See http://web.icq.com for more information. ICQ has versions for Windows and the Mac. ICQ also supports many languages, so you can connect to friends across the world.

✦ **Pagoo** is a pager service. The service costs $3.33 a month and provides a toll-free number for people to page you with a voice or text message to your desktop. See http://www.pagoo.com/ for more information.

✦ **Yahoo! Pager** for Internet Explorer or for Netscape is a chat program that alerts you when your buddies are on the Internet. The program also includes Yahoo! Mail Checker and sound alerts. Both Yahoo! Pager and Yahoo! Mail Checker are freeware. See http://pager.yahoo.com for more information.

✦ **MSN Messenger** is a program you can use to send messages to friends, use emoticons, share music and photos, page a mobile phone, and receive weather and news alerts. MSN Messenger is free for the download, and it's available for Windows and Macintosh. Go to http://messenger.msn.com.

✦ **Trillian** is freeware and it supports a variety of chat programs, including AIM, ICQ, MSN, and Yahoo Messenger. You can communicate with others on the network who don't use the same messenger as you do. Trillian also enables formatting user profiles, emotisounds, encrypted instant messaging, and more. Download Trillian from CNET's download.com.

✦ **NetMeeting**, available with all Windows operating systems, is a real-time collaboration and conferencing client you might use at home or in your small business. You can use NetMeeting for multipoint data conferencing, text chats, whiteboards, and file transfer.

NetMeeting provides a variety of communications to the Windows user. You can send text, audio, and video messages, and much more. Generally, NetMeeting is designed for business use. It is a program that promotes collaboration between colleagues, business partners, vendors, customers, and so on. Many large and small businesses use NetMeeting as a way of communicating across town or across the country.

For small businesses, you can use NetMeeting's data conferencing tools to share information with multiple users in real time. You can exchange graphics, draw on the electronic whiteboard, send text messages, record meeting notes, and more. If you have a sound card, microphone, and speakers, you can even talk to your colleagues over the Internet or your intranet. With a video capture card and camera, you can send and receive video images as well.

To open NetMeeting, click Start ⇨ All Programs (or Programs in Windows 98) ⇨ Accessories ⇨ Communications ⇨ NetMeeting. You must enter your personal information, define your modem (dial-up or cable, for example), and set up sound and audio information. Because there are so many features and you must configure NetMeeting specifically for your computer, this book does not cover setup and configuration. You can go to www.microsoft.com for more information or use the help within NetMeeting on your computer.

To use NetMeeting for a chat, follow these steps:

1. Open NetMeeting. Figure 18-8 shows the NetMeeting window.

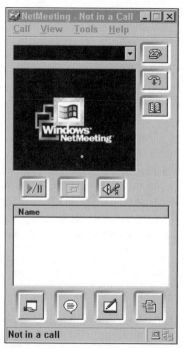

Figure 18-8: The NetMeeting box appears.

2. Click the Chat button or click Tools ⇨ Chat. The Chat window opens, as shown in Figure 18-9.

3. In the Message area, type your message.

4. Click Send To and click the person's name or click Everyone in Chat.

5. Click the Send Message button.

Figure 18-9: Chat with your friends.

Securing Chats

As with any communication over public airways, radio waves, or cables and wires, your chats with others are something you want to keep away from prying eyes. Internet chat applications transmit information between computers on the Internet. Chat clients provide you with the means to exchange dialog, URLs, and files. Many chat clients allow for the exchange of programs or executable code, as well; therefore, chat programs present risks to those who are chatting.

You can use any of several programs to secure chats; you can also take several precautions on your own.

✦ First, you should always be wary of exchanging files with someone you do not know, just as you would not open an e-mail attachment from someone you do not know.

✦ Second, when choosing a chat program, check for Secure Socket Layer (SSL) or Java-based code that ensures security. SSL is a protocol used to transmit private documents and data via encryption. Java is a programming language that allows for small programs, or applets, to be downloaded for use with special functions or features, such as security. Chat programs using SSL or Java are more likely to be secure than those not using these features.

✦ Programs such as MSN Messenger have security built into them to keep hackers from intruding on your chats, whereas ICQ uses ports on your computer that allow hackers easy access. The third thing you need to do is learn about the program you're using and find out if it's secure. If it's not secure, see if you can add another application for encryption to the original.

✦ One other thing you can do is use only chat programs that promise security, such as MSN Messenger. Following are some other programs that offer secure chats.

   • For about $30, you can buy KeptPrivate (www.keptprivate.com), a program that includes a secure Java-based chat program, as well as secure e-mail and secure Web mail.

   • Programs such as Secure Network Chat (SNC) are available for small and large businesses to use within their private network. SNC, for example, is designed to enable your employees to exchange text messages and files safely and securely. For more information, see www.secureaction.com/chat/.

Summary

In this chapter, you've learned about Internet and LAN chat programs, including the following:

✦ Instant messaging

✦ IRC

✦ Web-based chat

In the next chapter, you learn about setting up an intranet on your home network.

✦   ✦   ✦

Setting Up an Intranet

CHAPTER

19

You may want to add an *intranet* (a private Internet) to your home network for several reasons — it enables you to practice creating Web pages and publish your family's calendars and schedules, for example. If you get good enough at creating and managing your own intranet, you can take it to the Internet for fun and profit. An intranet is also invaluable to a small business; use the intranet for employees' handbooks, forms, instructions, memos, and more.

Understanding an Intranet

As you know, the Internet is a huge network of servers and other computers that can communicate, trade files, and otherwise share information. The Internet spans the world, using several specialized technologies, including TCP/IP, HTTP, and HTML. You might know these acronyms from their association with the Internet:

✦ **Transfer Control Protocol/Internet Protocol (TCP/IP)** is a set of communications protocols supported by various manufacturers and vendors. Corporations, universities, and other agencies use TCP/IP to communicate over the Internet. You use TCP/IP to communicate with your ISP's Web server, and from there, the Internet.

Tip   For information about setting up TCP/IP, see Appendix B.

✦ **Hypertext Markup Language (HTML)** is a format for documents used on the World Wide Web. HTML defines page formatting, including the font, images, colors, lines, and other elements on a Web page. HTML also includes hypertext links that enable you to jump from one Web page to another by clicking linked text or graphics.

✦ **Hypertext Transfer Protocol (HTTP)** is the protocol that transfers documents from a Web server to your own computer. HTTP in lowercase form — http — is often the first thing you type in an Internet address. HTTP indicates to the Web browser the protocol needed to locate a Web address.

These Internet technologies, plus others, are the same technologies you use to create an intranet in your home network.

Defining an intranet

An *intranet* is a private Internet, a network within your home network on which you publish documents to view with your Web browser. You use these Internet tools—HTTP, HTML, TCP/IP, Web browsers, and more—to create and use the intranet. An intranet might or might not be connected to the Internet.

An intranet is set up on a client/server basis; in other words, you need server software and client software. The client software is any Web browser installed on the computers. Server software organizes and manages the actual web pages so that browsers can connect.

So where do you get the web pages for your intranet? You create them yourself. You can create web pages in various ways. See the section "Creating Content for the Intranet" later in this chapter. Web spelled with the initial uppercase letter—Web—refers to the World Wide Web on the Internet. In all lowercase letters—*web*—the word refers to an intranet web, or network of documents.

Figure 19-1 shows a home page on a home network intranet. A home page is the default web page in your site. Usually a home page has several links to other important pages on the site, as well as an introduction of some sort. Note that the address in the toolbar is on the local hard drive and the title bar displays the "Working Offline" remark.

Small Business Tip   An intranet in your business can be useful for distributing company information, customer lists, newsletters, scheduling changes, meetings, memos, and more. Users can browse your intranet for all company and customer information.

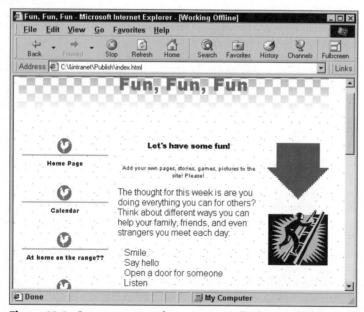

Figure 19-1: Set up your own home page to display anything you want.

Why an Intranet at Home?

You may use an intranet to display family schedules, stories, pictures, and more. The primary reason to use an intranet in your home, however, is to familiarize yourself and your family with the workings of a Web page, Web server, and other Internet technology.

Building your own intranet enables you to experiment with the process before taking your Web pages to the Internet, where you pay for time, Web server space, and mistakes. You might want to add a Web page to your ISP's server at some point. You can create a family page for the Internet by first testing it out on your home intranet.

If you're thinking about starting a small home business, you can use your intranet to try out your business Web site. Set up a home page and an index, create and test links to your pages, and otherwise carry out trials of your site before you place it on the Net.

You may want to start a larger Internet business. Instead of setting up your Web site, e-commerce (short for electronic commerce, which is a business that sells such things as books or computers on the Web) site, or iMall (a Web site containing multiple businesses) directly on the Web, you can set it up on your own intranet first. Experiment, test, and have your family contribute to and critique your site.

Advantages and disadvantages of an intranet

All technologies present advantages and disadvantages. You need to consider all the possibilities before deciding to add an intranet to your home network. If your goal is to learn about the technology, however, you should try at least a simple intranet.

Advantages

An intranet provides faster access to documents stored on the network. Additionally, instead of viewing a document in Word, you can view it in your Internet browser, such as Internet Explorer. Using a browser gives you certain advantages over using the program in which a document was created. For example, you can view animated graphics, movie clips, and sound clips in a browser.

All files on an intranet are displayed as documents in the browser. Users can scroll through text, use links to jump to related documents, print pages, and more. Instead of clicking through layer after layer of folders to get to a file, a user can click a link on the intranet and quickly open that file.

Figure 19-2 illustrates a page on the home intranet. Note the links on the left — Home Page, Calendar, At Home on the Range??, and Beach Week! Click a link to jump to a different page on the web site.

Intranets also can provide intricate search features that enable the user to find information about topics by using specific keywords or phrases. Consider Yahoo.com or Excite.com. Such Internet search engines and directories enable you to find the location of a variety of topics. Depending on the software you use to set up your intranet, you can have a search engine locate topics in your own documents. Microsoft FrontPage, for example, includes a program called Index Server, which works as a search engine.

Intranets are scalable, meaning that after you have created documents and set up an intranet on your home network, it's relatively easy to transfer your documents and knowledge to the Internet, because both use the same technologies and tools.

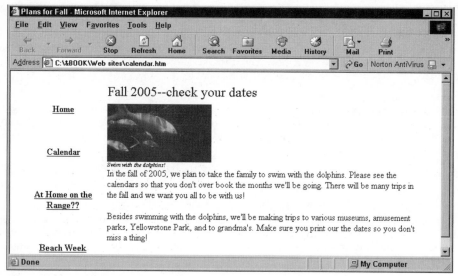

Figure 19-2: Let your family know what's happening in your family.

In a small business, you can publish many company documents on the intranet to make your work easier and your employees' work more efficient. You can publish sales presentations, training sessions, customer information, project schedules, a newsletter or brochure, the employee handbook, price lists, contact names, policies, procedures, and so on.

Disadvantages

Perhaps the largest disadvantage to setting up and running an intranet is the time it takes. You need to learn the technologies, create content, install and configure software, teach your family how to use the intranet, and so on. If you don't have the time or don't want to invest the time, then an intranet isn't for you. If, on the other hand, you want a hobby you can work on at your own pace and you want to learn the technology, then you should consider setting up an intranet.

Depending on how technical you want to get, an intranet can cost a considerable amount of money to set up. You can create an intranet with the equipment and software now on your network; alternatively, you can install a Windows 2000 Server, a Web server software package, and upgrade hardware to provide a fast and efficient intranet. You don't have to put a lot of money into it, but you can.

You'll probably need to spend a bit more money and time in setting up a company intranet than you would for an intranet for your home. You may need to set up a server specifically for the intranet, depending on how much you'll be using it. Setting up a server means that you need to upgrade your hardware as well.

Exploring three possibilities

You can put as much time, effort, and equipment into setting up an intranet as you want. You can set up a simple, easy, workgroup intranet using only the equipment already in your network. Alternatively, you can set up an elaborate network of linking documents and sites using a client/server arrangement. Following are three possibilities you might consider; each is explained in more detail later in this chapter:

✦ **Create a serverless intranet** — You can create a simple intranet on your network that displays anyone and everyone's web pages. All you need is a shared folder to which everyone has access. You don't need a Web server to create an intranet, although it does make it nicer.

✦ **Use Web server software on your Windows workgroup network** — This way, you can use one of your computers as a Web server, or if you already have a client/server network, you can add the Web server software to your server computer.

✦ **Use Windows 2000 Server or a Novell NetWare server on a client/server network to install Web server software that manages your intranet documents** — You might want to use this setup, for example, if you plan to move eventually to the Internet with your documents and web site.

Note

Gopher is a part of the TCP/IP protocol that provides a menu-based interface to files on an intranet or the Internet; Gopher is an older service but is still used in many places. File Transfer Protocol is another TCP/IP protocol. FTP enables the exchange of bulk information over an intranet or the Internet.

What Is a Web Server?

A web server can be hardware or software. As hardware, it is a powerful computer, with lots of disk space and RAM, on which you install web server software. Web server software manages intranet and Internet documents and applications. If you expand your intranet to the Internet, a Web server also can act as a Gopher and File Transfer Protocol (FTP) server.

Web servers also perform some specialized duties. You are unlikely to need these within your home network intranet; however, you may need these features in a company or corporate intranet. One of these features is the capability of processing HTML form data so that web sites can run search engines, guest books, and other fill-in documents. Another feature is the capability of using a server-side image map, which enables a user to view links to all pages on the site.

Do you need a Web server? No, not necessarily. You can create an intranet without a Web server for use in your home or on your small-business network. When you add more documents to the site, however, you may want to get a simple Web server. You can find freeware and shareware Web servers on the Internet.

If you plan to run a large corporate intranet or expand your intranet to the Internet, then yes, you need a Web server. You also need a client/server network, instead of a workgroup network.

Creating Content for the Intranet

Before you can see any documents on the intranet, you need to create your content — HTML pages for viewing in a browser. You may have seen many books or articles about formatting in HTML or writing the HTML code when designing your web pages. You can create HTML formatting in a text-based program, such as Notepad, WordPad, or any word processor that saves in text format.

Figure 19-3 shows a web page in WordPad with the HTML codes. To create a complex web page, you would have to learn more about HTML formatting. Using the code is great if you have complex design requirements for your web pages; however, you don't have to learn HTML in order to create a web page.

Figure 19-3: Using HTML code is complicated.

Many programs — word processing, desktop publishing, spreadsheet, and others — now have the capability of saving a document in HTML format. You create the page just the way you want it and then save it as a web page. Microsoft Publisher, Word for Windows, and Access are three programs you can use without purchasing and learning to use a separate program.

In addition, some programs supply web page creation wizards. Other programs offer a Save as HTML or Save as Web Page command on the File menu. Check the program's online help to see if it offers any assistance with creating web pages.

Tip   Some programs are built specifically for web page creation, such as Microsoft's FrontPage and Macromedia's Dreamweaver, among others. These programs are more difficult to learn and to use, but are well worth the time if you're interested. Check the Internet for other web page creation programs.

Using common programs for creating content

Whether you're using Office 97, Office 2000, or Office XP, whether you are in Word or some other program, you probably can find a way to save your documents for use on the intranet. Check to see if the program you're using saves documents for the Web. If you can find HTML as a file type in the Save As dialog box, then you can save your document as a web page.

Some programs offer even more help than saving as HTML. Web site wizards offer ready-made links, backgrounds, formatted text and designs, and more. Other programs offer web site previews and troubleshooters that can help you create an attractive, efficient web page.

Small Business Tip

If you plan to design web pages for the Internet or for a corporate intranet, you should read more about designing web page content. You want to design pages that load quickly and don't waste the user's time; you might want pages that offer special features as well. Learning about graphic file formats, fonts you can use on the Web, and good design can help you in your web site creation.

Many programs offer web design tools, including PowerPoint, Access, Corel WordPerfect Office 2000, Lotus WordPro, Lotus Approach, Lotus Freelance, Corel Presentations, and Corel Quattro Pro.

Using Microsoft Publisher

Microsoft Publisher offers many advantages for designing web pages. Publisher's Web Site Wizards supply a ready-made design with options for inserting links and pages, calendars, e-mail links, and more. Figure 19-4 shows a few of Publisher's Web Site Wizards. Choose a design you like from the options.

Publisher's wizards offer color schemes, various page topics (such as calendar, event, and story), sounds, animations, and so on. Figure 19-5 shows one of the wizards before it's been modified in any way. You can change graphic images, add animated art and music, and change the text to suit yourself. You also can add pages, navigation buttons, picture captions, logos, calendars, coupons, and more.

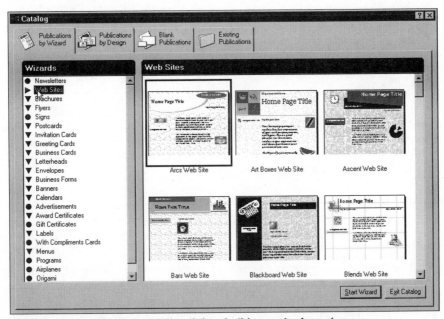

Figure 19-4: Start with a wizard and then build your site from there.

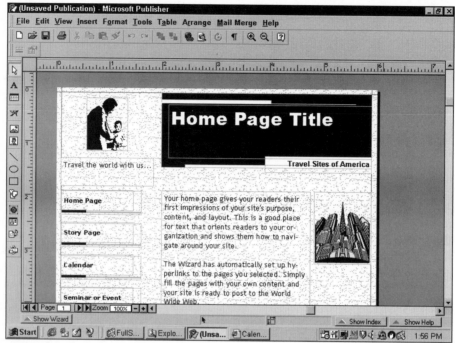

Figure 19-5: Modify the wizard text, graphics, and designs to fit your tastes and documents.

You also can create your own web document, without the use of a wizard, in Publisher. You can even take a document, such as a flyer or newsletter, and easily change it into a web page by saving it in HTML format. When you're finished with your web site in Publisher, you can save the document at a Web site, view web properties, and even publish to the Internet, with Publisher's help.

Small Business Tip

If you're planning on creating an intranet on your office network, you should use a program such as Publisher or FrontPage for web site creation. These programs offer professional-looking designs and wizards to help you create your site quickly and productively. Many HTML editors—programs that help you create web sites—also include built-in designs that you can use as a basis for your own web site.

Using Microsoft Word

All Word versions since Word 95 enable you to save a document in HTML format. You can create a document of any kind, format it, add graphics and images, and then save it to view on the Web. Naturally, some of your formatting may be lost in the transition, but most will survive.

Figure 19-6 shows the Word 2000 Save As dialog box with Web Page selected as the file type. After you save any document as HTML, you can view it through a Web browser.

Figure 19-7 shows a Word recipe list in the Internet Explorer. Because no unconventional formatting was used on the file, all formatting appears in the Web browser.

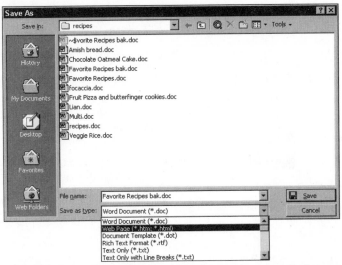

Figure 19-6: Save any document as HTML to view over the intranet.

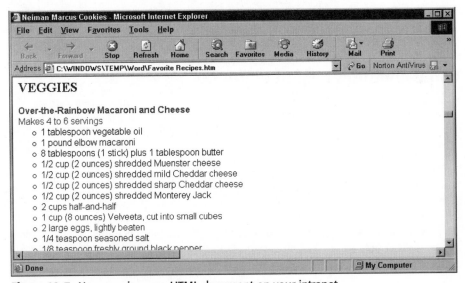

Figure 19-7: You can view any HTML document on your intranet.

Using FrontPage

Microsoft's FrontPage is a program for creating and managing web sites. The program is often included with the Microsoft Office Suite. You also can purchase the program separately. FrontPage includes tools that enable you to create and maintain a web site, manage hyperlinks, edit web pages, and more.

FrontPage consists of four components to help you construct and manage your intranet web: the Personal Web Server, the FrontPage Explorer, the Editor, and the To Do List. You can work with each component separately or together.

✦ The Personal Web Server is a tool for building a web site on a standalone computer. For example, you might want to work on your web pages as you travel with your notebook computer. You can transfer the web pages you create to your Web server at any time.

✦ The FrontPage Explorer enables you to create, manage, and maintain your web site. Use the FrontPage Explorer to view files on the site, work with your site in outline format, or view a graphical representation of the site.

✦ The FrontPage Editor is the tool you use to create and edit web pages in HTML format. The Editor is similar to a word processor, complete with a formatting toolbar, menus, status bar, and page layout features.

✦ The FrontPage To Do List is an organizational tool that enables you to generate and manage a list of tasks needed to complete your web site.

Using common design elements

When designing a web page, it's best if you concentrate first on the content — text and graphics. Make the text short and use interesting topics. Add small images and graphics (clip art, animated art, photographs, and so on) to attract attention. Large amounts of text might be too boring to read. Large images or graphics take too long to load onto the page, so try to keep them small.

You can create the page in any program, save it as HTML, and then view it often in your Web browser to see how it looks. Some elements may not look the same in the browser as they do in the original page. Experiment and have fun with designing the page.

Small Business Tip

When you design documents for your business intranet, consider using a template with your design elements. This way, all documents use the same colors, banners, type styles, and other components, so your web pages look consistent.

Helpful elements

You need to include some important items on each web page. First, add links. In Publisher, you can add links quite easily; some other programs, however, make it difficult. A *link*, or *hyperlink*, is a word (or phrase) or picture on which the user clicks to jump to another page. If you don't add links, you can view only one page in the browser. Read the program's online help to find out more about adding links.

A navigation bar or button is a graphic box or rectangle that is attached to a link, such as to a home page, calendar page, or other. Figure 19-8 shows a set of navigation buttons on the left side of the page; Home Page, Calendar, and At home on the range?? are links to other pages in the site.

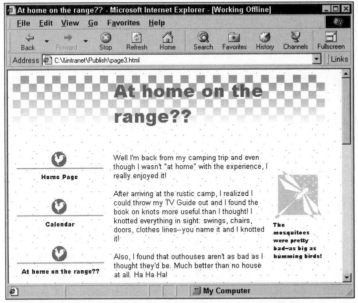

Figure 19-8: Add a navigation bar or button on each page so that the user can get around the site.

Make sure that you add the navigation buttons on each page of the site. You can add a Go Back button, Home button, or an entire set of buttons, as shown in Figure 19-8. Music is another good element to add to your pages. Consider animated clips and video as well. The elements you add depend on the program in which you're designing the page. Be careful when adding animation, audio, and video files, however; the file sizes can be too large to be practical.

Good design

You need to take into account some other design considerations when you're creating a web site. These issues make the page better looking and easier to read. Following are some things to consider:

✦ Be brief. Long paragraphs of text are difficult and tiring to read.

✦ Use several small graphics or images instead of one large one.

✦ Update the content frequently to keep everyone interested and excited about the intranet. Let everyone help with creating content.

✦ Try to use a heading or banner along the top of each page so that the user knows where he or she is in the site.

✦ Use plain fonts, for the most part. Fancy fonts are not always translated in the Web browser. You might need to experiment with different fonts.

✦ Don't use all uppercase letters; it's difficult to read in large blocks of text.

✦ Don't use too much bold or italic text; it's also difficult to read in large blocks of text.

✦ Don't use the Courier font; it's hard to read.

✦ You can add tables to a web page for easier presentation of information.

✦ Use Graphics Interchange Format (GIF) or Joint Photographic Experts Group (JPEG) as your image format.

Making the Preparations

No matter which method of creating an intranet you use, you need to perform some preparatory work. You need to create and share a folder for all intranet documents. You also need to create some content.

If you choose to use a Web server with your intranet, you also need to install and configure TCP/IP. If you create an intranet using no server, you don't need TCP/IP.

Creating content and a folder

Your first step is to create a folder in which to store all intranet documents. Locate the folder on a computer that everyone has access to over the network. If you plan to use Web server software, then save the intranet documents and folder on the computer that will be the Web server.

You can create your content at any time, but it might be more fun to begin by creating the content. You can discuss the content with your family and decide which topics will make up the intranet. Let each family member create a web page or two as well.

A web site is made up of multiple web pages. You can create many web pages and store them in the same folder. For organizational purposes, you should store all text, images, and web pages that belong to one web site in the same folder.

Tip   Programs like Publisher and PowerPoint enable you to create an entire web site easily, complete with multiple web pages, and linked together with hyperlinks and navigator buttons. See the program's online help for more information.

Sharing the folder

Make sure that you share the intranet folder so that everyone can access it. You can share the folder by selecting it in the Windows Explorer, for example. Right-click the folder to display the quick menu, and then choose Sharing.

You need to share the folder with full access so that users can add web pages to the folder if they want. For information about sharing, see Chapter 12.

Installing TCP/IP

You don't have to install TCP/IP if you're not going to use a Web server. You can view HTML files in your Web browser, and others on the network can view the web pages, without TCP/IP. You also can use links without TCP/IP. If you use a Web server, however, you must use TCP/IP.

Note   Because of its many advantages, TCP/IP is the preferred protocol for networking. Even the Mac comes with only TCP/IP installed. Windows 2000 and XP are built for TCP/IP, so if you're not using it, you should try to get used to it.

It's best if you remove any other protocol you might be using and then install TCP/IP. You need to do this on every computer in the network. Before you install TCP/IP, you need to understand the configuration. For complete information about installing and configuring TCP/IP, see Appendix B.

Tip   Appendix B suggests some addresses you can use for a private intranet network.

Creating a Workgroup Intranet without a Server

You can have an intranet on your workgroup network without buying any new equipment or software. If you have Windows on your computers and you have a network, you have everything you need to create an intranet.

Because you're not using a Web server, some people might say it isn't really an intranet. Nevertheless, it will familiarize you with the process of creating web pages and displaying them. Your family will be able to view web pages in a browser and get the experience of working with an intranet.

An intranet without a Web server cannot do everything a more equipped intranet can. You cannot have live discussions, for example, over the intranet. However, you can use NetMeeting or a chat program for that. See Chapter 18 for more information.

Also, if you expand your intranet later to include a Web server, you can keep the web pages you're creating now and use them in addition to your new content.

Small Business Tip   Consider using a Web server for any business intranet, even if you think it will be a small intranet. You'll be surprised at how many uses you find for the intranet and how fast it will grow. You are ahead if you start out with a Web server for your office intranet.

Looking at what you need

Using Windows to create an intranet is quick and easy. You don't really need any special talent, and you can have a lot of fun working with the documents and navigating your own intranet. Following are the items you need to build this kind of intranet:

✦ You need a working network, which you already should have in place. Whether your network uses phone lines, wireless connections, or traditional cabling isn't an issue, although if your network is slow, your intranet also will be slow. See Chapter 6 for information about network speed.

✦ Windows includes everything else you need. You can create content with Notepad or WordPad, if you want to try your hand at HTML. If, however, you have Word, Publisher, Excel, WordPerfect, or some other application, creating content is even easier.

✦ Finally, you must have an Internet browser for use with the intranet. You already might have Internet Explorer installed; alternatively, you can use another browser such as Netscape Navigator. Any Web browser works well with an intranet.

That's all you need to set it up!

Looking at the basic steps

The steps to setting up a serverless intranet are easy. Following is a complete set of steps to setting up this simple intranet:

1. Create the content and save all the documents in one folder.

2. Share the folder.

3. Install Internet Explorer (or another Web browser on each computer), if one isn't already installed.

4. Open the browser.

5. Choose View ➪ Toolbars ➪ Address Bar, if the address bar is not already showing.

6. Enter the path to any page in your web site. You can enter the name of the default page, called default.htm, home.htm, or index.htm, depending on the program with which you created your content. Figure 19-9 illustrates the index.html page of a web site created with Publisher.

Figure 19-9: Type in the path to a web page.

All you do now is click the links and scroll the pages.

You also can enter the path to your default page as your home page. This way, each time you click the Home button, the browser jumps back to the same page. To change your home page in the Internet Explorer, follow these steps:

1. Choose Tools ➪ Internet Options. The Internet Options dialog box appears.

2. In the General tab, enter the path to your default page in the Address text box of the Home Page section, as shown in Figure 19-10.

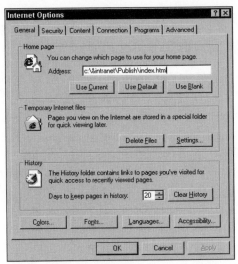

Figure 19-10: Enter the home page address (shown in Windows 98).

3. Click OK. In Internet Explorer, click the Home button anytime you want to go back to the home page.

Creating a Workgroup Intranet with a Server

You can create an intranet within your Windows workgroup network using a Web server. You can find some freeware and shareware Web servers on the Internet that work very well with your home intranet network.

You might want to use a Web server for many reasons. Some advantages are as follows:

✦ **A Web server stores and manages all the web pages and sites** — It provides access to the intranet or the Internet, manages access rights for remote users, enables publishing of file archives by creating links on other computers, and provides Gopher and FTP services.

✦ **A Web server enables you to view hot spots on the intranet** — A *hot spot* is a box that appears with the related URL. For example, you may have a photograph on the web page. When the user slides the mouse cursor around the photo, boxes containing URLs and related links appear. If the user clicks one of these links, the hot spot transfers him or her to the related web page.

✦ **Java applets are interactive programs that run on a web page** — Java is a programming language that enables embedded motion in a page, among other things, thus making a page more dynamic than static.

✦ **Play audio and video on pages with the click of a hyperlink** — Although you can add these elements to a static page, you can do so much more when you use a Web server.

✦ **Use non-Internet applications, such as Word or PowerPoint, to open and display a document within a web page** — Instead of jumping to a linked page to show a presentation in PowerPoint, for example, the user simply clicks a link and opens PowerPoint to show the presentation from the original page.

Looking at what you need

To set up an intranet with a Web server on your network, you need content, Web browsers on every computer, Web server software, and TCP/IP.

You set up the content as you do for any intranet. Save the content to one folder on the computer with the Web server software on it. Although the computer doesn't need anything more than extra space to hold the content, it may need more power, space, and memory for the Web server software. Check the program's documentation.

You also need to install and configure the TCP/IP protocol on all computers on the network. For information about TCP/IP, see Appendix B.

The Web server software is the last component. You might be able to acquire Web server software on the Internet that is freeware or shareware. You must choose software that is for a Windows workgroup network, however. Some Web server software must run under a network operating system (NOS), such as Windows 2000 Server or Novell NetWare.

Looking at Web servers and other utilities

Many shareware Web servers and other utilities that you can use in your intranet are available on the Internet. Each has its own special tools or features. You might want to try a shareware product first before paying a lot more for a Web server program; most shareware prices are between $20 and $100.

Tip   Search the Internet for "shareware," and then within the shareware site, search for "intranet server."

Each program includes instructions and help for installation and configuration. Check these sites for information about shareware and freeware: CNET's `download.com`, `www.zdnet.com`, and `tucows.com`. The following sections discuss some common Web servers you might choose.

Abyss Web Server

Abyss Web server is a personal web server you can use on your home network. It supports HTTP and Common Gateway Interface (CGI) scripts, and it includes access control, user management, file indexing, and more. Abyss is freeware, so you can't really lose. To download it, go to CNET's `download.com`.

Apache for Windows

Apache has long been a Web server for Unix and Linux but now there's an Apache for Windows. The Web server uses HTTP and is highly configurable, and you can even customize the server, if you know how. A bit more complicated than other Web servers, Apache offers database functions, an index for searches, and other features you can use on your intranet and on the Internet, should you ever decide to go on to the World Wide Web. See CNET's `download.com` for more information.

Hotline Connect Server

Hotline Connect Server is for the Macintosh, and it enables you to create an intranet on your home network. It's not quite a Web server because it requires specific client software; however, you can get many of the same intranet results from using Hotline. You can chat and share news and file distribution. You can use navigation tools, image file previews, and more.

Hotline Connect Server is freeware you can download from CNET's download.com.

Creating a Client/Server Intranet

If you use a client/server network in your home, you can set up an intranet using your file server as a Web server. A client/server network provides more power and flexibility for an intranet. You can authenticate your users, share files, and share web pages with them, all from one server. Users can print and save web documents, and use other network services in conjunction with the intranet.

You might want to invest your time and efforts in a Web server for your intranet for several reasons. Learning the technology is always a good justification. Another reason is to expand the intranet into the Internet at some point, if, for example, you plan to run your own web site on the Internet to sell products, advertise services, or otherwise make use of Internet connections.

Looking at what you need

Again, you need to create your content and save the content to the Web server. You also need to install TCP/IP on each computer, including the server. See Appendix B.

You install the Web server software on the file server. First, make sure that your file server has enough power, disk space, and memory to run the program. Also, depending on the amount of network and intranet traffic, you might want to invest in a dedicated Web server. If you plan to expand your intranet to the Internet, for example, a dedicated Web server also can house a proxy server to protect your LAN from Internet intruders.

Many Web servers exist for various operating systems. You should check with a vendor for your specific NOS. Windows 2000 Server includes a Web server with the operating system — Internet Information Services (IIS). Netscape Enterprise Web Server works well with Novell NetWare and is available with some later versions of the NOS.

In addition to the hardware and software, you must consider administration of the intranet. Working with a Web server requires more time and technical knowledge on your part. Naturally, Web server installation and configuration take some time and effort. Running the intranet on your home network shouldn't take too much time; however, if you use the intranet in a small business or expand to the Internet, your administration time is increased immensely.

Considering an Internet Web Server

You use a Web server to publish information in HTML format to either an intranet or the Internet. After you've worked with your local intranet, you might decide you want to publish your web site to the World Wide Web. You might want to publish to the Web to sell products or services, collect information, offer information on services or charities, or for dozens of other reasons.

You can publish, or place Web pages on the Internet, Web sites through your ISP or other service provider. Many providers supply free space for home users and sell space to businesses that want to put their sites on the Internet without the hassle of running their own Web servers.

If you use a service provider and purchase space on its Web server, you usually can publish any information you want. You might be subject to limitations of space or content. However, the service provider takes care of everything for you—running, maintaining, and troubleshooting the Web server. All you do is provide the content and keep it up-to-date.

If you want to run your Web site on your own Web server, however, you must consider many elements. First, you need a dedicated computer to connect to the Internet. This computer should have enough power to run your site so that users don't have huge wait times when pages are downloading. You also should invest in a T1, fractional T1, or frame relay connection to the Internet for faster service.

Next, you need to consider security. Install a proxy server or firewall on the Web server so that Internet intruders cannot infiltrate your server or the rest of your LAN. You also want to create your own search engines, FTP, and perhaps Gopher services for your Web server, depending on the services you offer. You need to consider how to deal with credit cards and security, if you run a shopping site of any kind.

Looking at Internet Information Services

You can use any of a variety of Web servers for your client/server intranet network. You should check with different vendors and find a Web server that's appropriate for your network operating system and your needs. If you're running Windows 2000 Server as your NOS, you have a built-in Web server—IIS.

IIS is typical of most Web servers in that it offers many technologies to manage and maintain your intranet. In addition, you can use IIS if you choose to expand your intranet to the Internet.

IIS provides World Wide Web services that enable you to publish your dynamic web pages to your intranet. You can add images, sounds, animations, videos, links, and non-HTML files to the network by using IIS.

A management program within the Internet Information Services enables you to configure access rights for Internet users, if you choose to take your web to the Internet. You also can publish Gopher and FTP services for use on the intranet or Internet.

Finally, IIS provides Open Database Connectivity (ODBC) drivers that enable you to use information from a compatible database in your intranet. You might not need this capability in your home intranet; if you start your own business Web site on the Internet, however, you will need to consider databases and their uses.

Using Linux as an Intranet Server

You can use a Linux computer as an intranet and/or Internet server. Linux has many available programs for making it into a Web server, depending on the distribution you use and the configuration you've chosen.

The Apache server is popular software that many Web sites use. Apache is available on Windows and/or Linux, as well as other operating systems. The software is HTTP-compliant and has powerful features for both an intranet and the Internet. Apache enables you to set up password-protected pages, use files like CGI scripts for setup, report errors, use an index for searching the Web, and perform many other tasks that are necessary for a Web server.

If you have a Linux computer on your home network, you'll need to research the operating system you're using to see what is available as Web server software.

Summary

In this chapter, you learned about creating an intranet for your home network. You learned about the following specific topics:

✦ Understanding and creating content for an intranet

✦ Creating a workgroup intranet both without and with a server

✦ Creating a client/server intranet

In the next chapter, you learn about working with applications over your home network.

✦   ✦   ✦

Working with Files, Folders, and Applications

In Part V, you learn about working with files, folders, and applications on a network. Chapter 20 explains various types of applications and how best to use each on your network. You also learn about client/server programs. Chapter 21 explains how best to store files on a network, how to back up files, and how to secure your data on a network.

Working with Applications

You are probably familiar with word processing programs, spreadsheet applications, Internet browsers, and other programs you can use on a standalone computer. You also can employ programs specifically made for network use and distribute the program's data in a variety of ways over the network. Applications used over a network can provide more versatility than when used on a standalone computer.

Understanding Local and Network Applications

Most programs you use in your home network are local applications. You also might use a few network applications. *Local applications* are installed on one computer; the program files are not shared. *Network applications* are those stored on one computer but shared over the network with the other computers.

Note   You can still share documents from locally installed applications. Say you and your spouse each have Word on a computer. If you both have shared your drive, or the folder in which the Word documents are stored, you can share the documents, add to them, delete from them, and so on, as long as only one person is using the document at a time.

Examples of local applications are a word processing program, a desktop publishing application, some games, or a spreadsheet program. Examples of network applications are a web server for your intranet, an accounting program for your small business, some games, or a program that enables you to share one modem and Internet account.

The types of programs you use depend on the tasks you want to perform. Whether the program is installed locally or on the network depends on how the program is built, its licensing, and its uses.

Using local applications

Many of the programs you use on your computer are meant to be used locally only. You install the program files directly on your computer. These programs supply a license for use on one computer only.

If you want to install the same program on another computer on the network, you must purchase another license and, usually, another copy of the software.

Figure 20-1 illustrates Excel, a program built for use on local computers. Although you can save your data files on any network computer and share those files, you shouldn't use the program over the network.

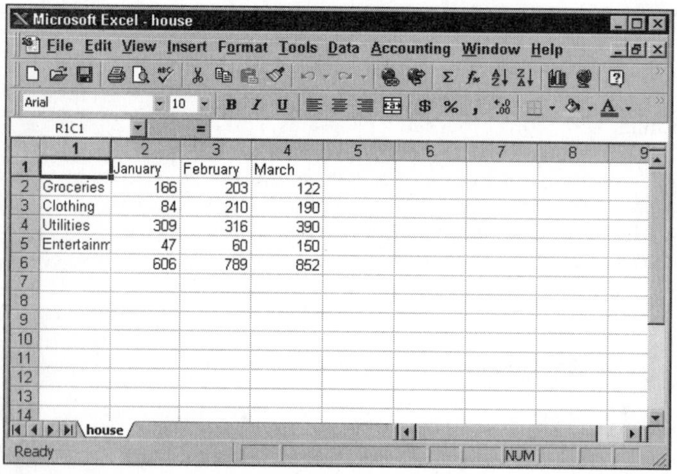

	1	2	3	4	5	6	7	8	9
1		January	February	March					
2	Groceries	166	203	122					
3	Clothing	84	210	190					
4	Utilities	309	316	390					
5	Entertainm	47	60	150					
6		606	789	852					
7									
8									
9									
10									
11									
12									
13									
14									

Figure 20-1: Use local programs on the computer on which they were installed.

Tip

With Excel, you can share workbooks over the network. Excel 2000 and later editions have a built-in feature that enables sharing a workbook with multiple users over a network at the same time. You can track changes so that you know what changes are and who has made the changes. You might want to use this feature if you have a small business, in particular. Often Excel is a commonly used program for small businesses.

A few other applications, such as accounting programs, specialized attorneys' programs, vertical applications, and so on, enable you to share documents over networks in this manner. Check the Help section of the application to see if it allows multiple people to use documents at the same time.

You can open some local applications over the network and run them; the speed and performance of the programs suffer, however. You cannot open other local applications over the network because of safeguards built into the program. Safeguards might protect your shared data or the application files, or even protect the software manufacturer from losing licensing money. Unless the application specifically says that you can use the software over the network, you should invest in multiple copies or licenses of the application.

Even though you cannot share a local application over the network, you can store and share your data files from any application on any other computer in the network. If you're using a workgroup network, you might store your data files — word processing documents, photographs, or spreadsheets, for example — on another computer that has more hard drive space than your computer. If you're working on a client/server network, you might store your data files on the server.

Following are some examples of local applications:

✦ Word processing

✦ Spreadsheet

✦ Database

✦ Painting or drawing

✦ Certain games

✦ Antivirus

✦ Desktop publishing

✦ Some accounting programs

Using network applications

Network applications are those that come in two parts—client and server. The server part of the application installs on a server computer, or, on a workgroup network, on a workstation that serves as a host. The client part of the software installs on the rest of the computers on the network. The client requests some service, and the server grants the request.

Figure 20-2 shows the Internet Explorer browser. The browser is a client program installed on a local computer. The server program is a Web server and might be installed on a computer on your network or on a computer on the Internet.

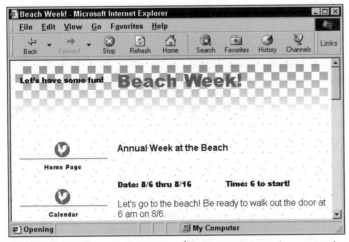

Figure 20-2: Client programs need a server program to carry out requests.

When you install a network application, you install the server part of the program on only one machine. You configure the software to take requests for services or add some security measures to filter requests, if you want. Then you install the client software. The program also carries specific licensing for server and client usage.

The data files for a client/server application are generally stored on the server, or host, computer and made available to one or all clients, depending on the program. A good example of a client/server application is a database management system, such as SQL (pronounced "sequel") Server or Oracle Server. The server contains all of the data in the database — for example, a price list of products or an inventory of equipment. Any user can use a client version of the database software to look up a specific product or piece of equipment by name, number, price, description, or other criterion.

Note   Most client/server applications let multiple people use documents at the same time. The server part of the program keeps track of the changes made and incorporates them into the information.

When the client makes a request for information, the database management system on the server searches the stored records. When the database management system locates the requested data, it displays the data on the client software for the user. You're not likely to use a database management system on your home network; however, you might use many types of client/server applications.

Following are some network applications you might use on your network:

✦ Web browser

✦ E-mail program

✦ Calendaring or scheduling

✦ Chat or newsreader

✦ Modem-sharing software

✦ Some games

✦ Some accounting programs

Advantages and Disadvantages of Using Network Applications

Network applications are great for providing services to your other network computers. If you need a service provided by a network application, you should go ahead and purchase that program. You must remember, however, that there are also certain disadvantages to using network applications.

Advantages of a network application include the following:

✦ One person can control the program's installation and configuration. Using a consistent interface and settings means that everyone sees the same thing every time they use the program. One user cannot make changes that might confuse other users.

✦ The server program files are located on one computer. Therefore, they're easy to update and available to everyone.

✦ Depending on the program, the user of the server machine might have control over who accesses the program and might be able to set limits. For example, some Web servers enable you to block certain Web sites from use.

Disadvantages of a network application include the following:

✦ If the machine on which the server program is installed is turned off, users cannot access the program. Similarly, if the computer crashes or has serious hardware problems, users cannot access the program until the server computer is fixed.

✦ A client/server application is subject to network use and traffic. If there is a lot of traffic, the program might operate slowly or be unavailable until traffic clears. Also, a heavily used client/server application slows down traffic for other network services.

✦ It takes a bit more time and effort for one person to install, maintain, and troubleshoot a client/server application than a local application. Hardware or software problems, security issues, corrupted files — all are multiplied by the number of program users.

Employing Application Types on Your Network

You already know the programs you can use locally — word processing, graphic programs, desktop publishing, database programs, and so on — and you know each of these programs has limits to licensing and network usage. Before you buy any application for network use, you also should understand any limits or consequences to using that program on your network.

Some network programs might raise compatibility issues, with either your current hardware or your software. Some might cause problems with sharing, permissions, or other security measures used within your network. The licensing on some programs may regulate its use on your network for one reason or another. Make sure that you find out about an application's limitations before purchasing it and installing it on the network.

In home networking, you might want to explore some common network applications. Depending on your uses of the network and your computer, you might use Internet applications, accounting programs, games, or other applications.

Using Microsoft Office on a network

Most of the Office applications — Word, Excel, Access, PowerPoint, and Publisher — are generally installed on the local computer instead of on the network. However, you can install one or all of these applications on a network server under certain circumstances. You need to use a true server — Windows 2000 Server, for example — and the appropriate network version of Office to do a network installation of Microsoft Office.

If you have the appropriate license to install Office on multiple client computers, you can choose to distribute the Office CD-ROM or disk to each user, or you can install Office from the server. Installing Office on the server calls for some special hardware and preparatory requirements.

Because of the expense of the network version of Office, it is unlikely you will use it with your home or even small-business network. It is more efficient and less expensive to use the Office products that come on a computer when you purchase them or to buy upgrades for stand-alone computers.

Using Internet applications

You probably already use Internet applications on your network. If you have a connection to the Internet, you also use a browser, e-mail and newsreader software, and perhaps an application for sharing your Internet connection.

You also probably already have the client programs you want to use. Internet Explorer and Outlook Express come with Windows, for example. Some people prefer Netscape Navigator and Mail as their browser/e-mail programs. There are also many other programs you can buy or acquire as shareware and freeware. Check the Internet for more ideas.

Caution You should be careful when installing any program on the network or on your computer, in case of incompatibility or some other problem. You should be extra careful, however, when using shareware and freeware. Many of these applications are very task-specific, so they also might be hardware-specific. If you're at all unsure about using a program, don't use it. Also, find out all you can about a program before installing it on your network.

The only server application you need when you attach to the Internet from your network is one to enable multiple users to share a modem and Internet account. This proxy server program, such as WinGate or WinProxy, acts as a server to organize and manage the network users when they want to use the modem. Of course, you could use a hardware router instead. For more information about sharing Internet connections, see Chapter 16.

Other applications you might use on the network, such as chat programs or messaging programs, might or might not use a client/server setup. For example, some programs don't use a server for sending messages across the network. All computers run a "client" version, each connecting and communicating with the other.

If you're using your Internet client applications to access an intranet, you might want to invest in a Web server for use with your home network. A Web server manages shared documents and enables clients to access information on the intranet network.

Adding a Web Server to a Small-Business Network

If you want to expand your business to the Internet, you can add a Web server application, with a firewall or proxy server, to manage your Web site. Web servers enable you to publish information, catalogs, schedules, and other information over the Internet.

Proxy servers and firewalls are server applications that enable an information exchange between your LAN and the Internet while maintaining security for your LAN and your users. Many proxy servers also enable control over users' access to the Internet. Both Netscape and Microsoft have a proxy server (software) you might want to check out. Norton, or Symantec, also has proxy server software that is quite popular and useful.

In addition to Web servers, you might want to install a merchant server or commerce server. These server applications enable you to gather user information and present an online store for Internet shoppers. Microsoft's Site Server and Microsoft's Commerce Server are two examples of programs that provide commercial Internet access and services. For more information, check with your Internet service provider about setting up an e-commerce site.

Cross-Reference For more information about sharing a modem and Internet connection, see Chapter 16. For more information about e-mail, see Chapter 17. For more information about intranets, see Chapter 19.

Using accounting applications

Most home network users are likely to use an accounting program that is a local application, instead of a network application. Programs such as Quicken or Microsoft Money are installed and used locally, although users can share data between computers with individual programs installed.

Network accounting applications are generally large, complex, and expensive. These programs — such as Solomon and Great Plains — consist of several server modules that handle payroll, accounts receivable, general ledger, cash manager, order processing, inventory, and other data for business use. Accounting programs used over a network share data files for use by multiple departments and for examination by supervisors.

Small Business Tip If you're not interested in investing thousands of dollars and months of your life in buying and learning a network accounting application, you might want to try QuickBooks/QuickPay, MAS90 or MAS200, or Peachtree accounting programs. These are fairly easy-to-operate, reliable, and less expensive programs than some business accounting programs you can buy.

Using groupware

Groupware is a network application that is most useful in business offices. Groupware products, or suites, usually include several programs, such as those for e-mail, scheduling, electronic meetings or chats, and so on. The products are built to encourage collaboration over the network.

One of the most useful and popular groupware products is Lotus Notes/Domino. Notes users can store a variety of documents in a shared folder, similar to an intranet. They also can send e-mail, share calendars, and use a bulletin board service for posting information and memos. Notes is a great program that offers many possibilities; it is also difficult to install and administer.

Components

Notes/Domino is one type of groupware, but several others exist. DCASoft's BrightSuite and Microsoft Exchange Server offer some groupware components, including e-mail, shared folders, and Internet mail. Groupware programs might or might not offer all the identifying components; but all components in a groupware suite offer both client and server software. Following is a brief description of each:

✦ **E-mail** is one of the major components of a groupware package. Users should be able to send and receive messages, attach files, and perform other tasks within the client e-mail program. A server e-mail application might be as simple as a post office or might offer other features, such as scheduled backups, permissions and rights, public folders, and so on.

✦ **Scheduling** enables users to create and share calendars over the network. The server application organizes and manages the calendar while users fill in their meetings, to do lists, appointments, and so on. With permissions, any user can access the scheduling program at any time to view anyone's appointments.

✦ **Conferencing** refers to electronic meetings over the network. With groupware, the network can be a local area network or the Internet. Real-time conferencing enables groups of people to get online at one time and discuss topics. In these types of conferences, only one person can enter a message at a time, so everyone has a turn without being interrupted.

✦ **Bulletin boards** are areas in which users can post messages, ideas, and replies to other members of the LAN. Users might want use bulletin boards to brainstorm ideas or simply to set a meeting.

✦ **Document management** is a method of organizing multiple documents for access by the members of the group. Each user can view other documents and contribute his or her own. Users also can copy, save, and search documents in the database. This works similarly to an intranet.

✦ **Workflow programs** send documents throughout the network to the people who need them. Think of workflow as a paper trail. The program sends the documents to their destination; after an action is taken on that document, it is forwarded to the next recipient.

Users of groupware

As previously mentioned, you probably won't use groupware on a home network; it works very well, however, with small to large office networks. Consider using groupware in situations where collaboration is the key, such as with public relations firms, and sales and advertisement businesses. Architects, doctors, lawyers, and many other professionals can use groupware to their advantage.

 Tip   If you have a home network, you can create your own groupware suite by using various technologies, such as chat programs, intranets, and so on. You get the same services and benefits without the administration headaches and expense of a groupware application.

Using vertical applications

A *vertical application* is one designed specifically for a particular business, such as businesses that deal with real estate sales, restaurant delivery systems, retail point of sale, theater seating, lumber inventory, print job estimates, and so on. Vertical accounting programs are common and standard in business today.

If you're running a business out of your home or small-business office, you may need to run a vertical application over your network. Some applications use client/server software, and others are installed locally on a computer.

Because of the problems a vertical application can cause, you need to ask the manufacturer or the programmer who wrote the program for you several questions before buying and installing the program on your network. Following are some questions to ask:

✦ Is the application written for a specific operating system? You want to make sure that the program is compatible with your version of Windows, Mac, or Linux. Also, if you upgrade your operating system, will future upgrades of the application follow suit, or are you stuck with one OS?

✦ Is it a client/server or a local installation? What are the hardware requirements? If it is client/server, what NOS is it written for?

✦ Can you share data? Can the data be stored on a computer other than the one containing the program? What permissions and rights are built into the program?

✦ Are there any compatibility issues with other programs or hardware? For example, if you upgrade your printer or print driver, or other hardware, will that cause a problem for the program? Are there any applications you're currently using that will conflict with the vertical application?

Using network games

Naturally, you're accustomed to using games on your computer. You probably started out with Windows Solitaire many years ago. The newest craze in games is playing with others over the Internet or over a local area network. Many games have been designed for multiple players and network use.

You can play multiplayer games over a LAN, via modem, and over the Internet. Internet games have really become popular over the last few years. Playing games on a LAN or on the Internet adds some extra requirements to your machine and network power. The Ethernet technologies have proven to be the fastest and most reliable for playing games. However, wireless technology is often used with LAN and Internet gaming.

Tip   Be careful to check any game you buy for network use to see what the minimum requirements are, such as memory, video, and network speed. Some multimedia games might not work over a slower-speed network, such as one with phone line or power line cabling. Check the required network protocol as well.

Games can be action-oriented, board games, card games, flight simulators, MUD (multi-user dimension/multi-user dungeon) games, role-playing games, sports, strategy, trivia, and puzzles. These classifications are also called the *genre* of the game.

You can play on various platforms, including Linux, Macintosh, PlayStation 2, Xbox, and online. You can play games using your browser, a browser plug-in, browser Java, e-mail, or Telnet, which is considered the client type. Some games are free, some cost to download, and others charge a subscription price per month. You can even buy CDs and/or DVDs with games on them; you pop in the CD and then play the game with multiple users online.

Note   Often many of the multiplayer games require you to download or install software, such as a video or sound enhancement program. Often the download begins without confirming that you want it. Always read carefully before starting any games or getting online to play games to make sure you know what is involved with downloads and extras.

Windows games

There are hundreds of thousands of Windows games available on the Internet, on CD, on DVD, everywhere you look. Many games are for standalone computers, but you can find many games for networked computers too.

You can play games with the computer or with friends over the Internet. Many sites advertise free games to play with friends, such as checkers, cards, backgammon, and other multiplayer games. www.zone.msn.com is one Internet site, sponsored by Microsoft, that enables you to download games, join into online and multiplayer games, buy CDs and DVDs to enhance games, and more. Other sites are games.yahoo.com, gamespyarcade.com, mpogd.com, multiplayer.com, and many more.

Microsoft has also created multiuser online games for the PocketPC with the use of DirectX. You can use the PocketPC games with wired and 802.11b wireless connections.

Mac and Linux games

Several of the aforementioned online multiplayer game sites include games for the Mac and Linux. The games not only work with multiple operating systems, but they also allow games to be played between multiple operating systems.

www.kidsdomain.com is an interesting site for multiplayer games for kids. The site recommends game sites that have been checked for safe and decent content and offers good advice for Macintosh users. gameranger.com and cyberjoueur.com are two additional online sites for games for the Mac.

You'll find fewer games for Linux than for the Mac and Windows; however, you can find games to play on Linux boxes. Loki Entertainment, for one, is currently releasing three new multiplayer games for the Linux environment. Additionally, you can play many online games with your Linux box. IGames Publishing and S2 Games make games for the Linux environment. Many games are along the same lines of Windows games as far as interface, action, and behavior are concerned. You can go to www.linuxgames.com for more information.

Console gaming on a network

Console gaming includes such devices as Xbox, GameCube, or PlayStation 2. These networkable gaming devices are processors through which you can play games. These devices require an input device called a *controller*, or you can use multiple controllers for multiple players. The output device for a gaming device such as this is your TV. Programs for these consoles come in the form of CDs, DVDs, or programs on the Internet. You can download games from specific sites for each device as well.

You don't usually need an IP address for the game processors, and you usually don't need an extra broadband-sharing device. You do need a broadband port that connects to the Internet, generally a cable or DSL modem, plus a network card, a hub or switch, and network cabling. If you use a firewall, you probably need to disable the firewall to play games with the game processor on the Internet. You can check the game processor's documentation for more information about security and firewalls.

Various games recommend different configurations and devices, but basically, the needs are the same for both the Xbox and PlayStation 2. Consult the Web site or the processor's documentation for more information.

One of the main pieces of the Xbox, GameCube or PlayStation 2 is the controller. The controller is a part of the hardware to which the triggers, analog buttons, directional pads, navigational buttons, peripheral expansion slots, cable, and often vibration feedback motors are attached for more reality when playing a game.

You often need to add on extras to your game processor to get more from it. The following sections describe more information about each gaming device.

Xbox

Microsoft makes the Xbox. You can buy Xbox starter kits for around $50, but as you get more interested in playing games, you'll probably want more equipment. An Xbox Live starter kit contains a headset and microphone (Xbox Communicator) that enables you to talk to teammates and opponents, a starter disc that you run on your Xbox video game system to update your Xbox dashboard, a subscription code for 12 months of service, and instruction manuals. Games cost between $20 and $60.

You can add on to your Xbox with more complex controllers, a DVD kit for DVD movie playback, a system link cable so you can connect two consoles for extra players, memory units for extra storage space, and more. Check www.xbox.com for more information.

Figure 20-3 shows how you would set up an Xbox on your home network. The Xbox is connected to your TV and to a switch, hub, or router on your home network. The switch is in turn connected to a cable or DSL modem, which is connected to the Internet. If you wanted to have multiple players in your home instead of connecting to the Internet, you can connect multiple controllers to the Xbox so everyone can play on the same TV.

Note   You also connect other game processors, such as a PlayStation 2, similarly to your network. For more information on a specific game, see the game's documentation or Web site.

PlayStation 2

Sony makes the PlayStation 2. PlayStation 2 uses a computer processor on which you can play games. The console, features, and games are similar to those of the Xbox. With PlayStation 2, you can get DVD video playback, Dolby Digital theater-quality sound, and more.

The PlayStation 2 has a built-in DVD player, interactive content, and a network adapter that you can use with a 56 Kbps modem or a 10/100 Ethernet connection. PlayStation 2 costs around $200, but then there are additional adapters and add-ons you can buy, such as the memory card, network adapter, headphones, and so on. Then you buy the games separately. Games cost between $40 and $60.

Nintendo

Nintendo's GameCube is another controller that provides control sticks, a rumble feature for special effects, and other features. The GameCube costs around $100. Games cost between $20 and $60.

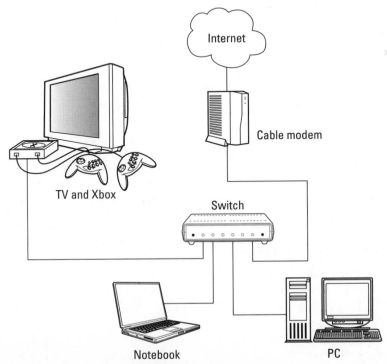

Figure 20-3: Connect the Xbox to your network.

You can use a wireless controller accessory that enables you to play from anywhere in the room. Other accessories include a 56 Kbps modem adapter and a broadband adapter. Another accessory is the GameCube Game Boy Advance cable, which enables you to connect the GameCube and the Game Boy Advance for more involved and complex games. See www.nintendo.com for more information.

Note   Each company that produces a gaming console also makes games for that console. There are other game publishers out there as well. www.sega.com is a good place to look for a variety of games for Xbox, PlayStation 2, and the GameCube. www.midway.com and www.sierra.com are two more publishers you can take a look at.

Examining Mac and Linux Network Applications

Similar to Windows, the Macintosh and Linux operating systems have their own applications for various uses. You can purchase word processing, spreadsheet, database, photo, drawing, accounting, and many more types of programs for both operating systems. Whether these programs are capable of networking is another question.

Many different operating systems exist for both the Mac and Linux. Mac's operating systems are similar, yet each system version is different enough to require new hardware and software. Linux, with its open source programming, opens the floodgates for multiple and varied distributions. Because there is so much variety in both operating systems, it is difficult to define specific software for each OS.

Following are some ideas of programs you can network, plus some places you can look on the Internet to locate more information about networking applications for the Mac and Linux.

Mac software

The Macintosh uses the Internet to enable you to share files, pictures, songs, documents, and more with friends and family. With a .Mac account, you can attach to the Internet, to the .Mac site, and share various documents with others. iPhoto and iCal are two programs you can use in such a way:

✦ **iPhoto** lets you import, organize, edit, and share digital photos. You can crop and touch up photos; you can e-mail photos, store images, and use the images in a variety of applications. iPhoto enables you to take pictures and create albums or slides for others to look at with their .Mac account.

✦ **iCal** enables you to keep track of your appointments, events, and such using one or multiple calendars. You can view calendars by day, week, or month, you can create a to-do list, you can send and receive e-mail and text messages, and more. In addition, you can publish your calendars online and share them with your family or friends. You can also subscribe to others' calendars.

iChat AV is a video chat program for the Macintosh. You can view people you're chatting with and hear them too. iChat works with any FireWire DV camera or Web cam, but Apple recommends using the program with iSight, a camera/microphone device you can purchase separately.

Other applications for the Macintosh are networkable. Many different operating system versions and different versions of applications exist, so you'll need to research the applications available for the Mac OS you're using.

Linux software

Linux is made for networking; therefore, many programs are available for Linux and networking, including databases, accounting, groupware, and more.

✦ Database applications enable you to manage large amounts of data so that multiple users can search the data. GNU SQL Server is available for Linux. SQL Server is a relational database management system for larger businesses. If you have a small business, you can use INFORMIX-SE, a database program that is relational and multiuser, but doesn't require a lot of administration. Other databases you might check into include MySQL, Oracle, and Shore.

✦ Accounting programs range from personal accounting, to small-business accounting, to corporation finances. CBB is a personal accounting program you can use to balance your checkbook. On the other end of the scale, SQL-Ledger Accounting is a multiuser accounting program you can use in your business.

✦ Groupware applications enable a team, or group of people, to share calendars, tasks, contacts, discussions, e-mail, and so on, over the network or Internet. A groupware application made by Axista called Xcolla works well for team collaboration across a network. Achievo and Amphora are two other groupware applications for Linux. Achievo is a Web-based project management application, whereas Amphora offers more basic office, intranet, and groupware functionality.

For more information about Linux software, visit `www.linuxsoftware.org`.

Summary

In this chapter, you learned about various networking applications, including the following:

✦ Internet applications

✦ Intranet applications

✦ Groupware

✦ Accounting programs

✦ Vertical software

✦ Network games

✦ Mac and Linux applications

In the next chapter, you learn about working with files and folders on a network.

✦   ✦   ✦

Working with Files and Folders

Y ou're familiar with working with files and folders on a standalone computer; handling network files and folders, however, is a bit different. You have more drives and storage areas to manage on the network. Also, backing up files is more than saving a few files to a CD; you can choose from a variety of backup options on the network. Finally, securing your confidential files and folders becomes more of a problem than just locking your office door.

Storing Files

If you're accustomed to storing files on your own computer, and you have enough space to continue to do that, that's fine. If, however, another computer on the network has more available disk space or a file storage device that you don't have, you can save your files over the network.

In the past, storing files was easy because they were smaller than they often are today. Word processing documents, spreadsheets, and most of the files saved took up less than a megabyte of space — 57K, 80K, and even 210K are small file sizes. You could store these files on a floppy disk, which holds 1.44MB.

With changing technologies and Internet access, though, file sizes are increasing. Graphic images, such as digital photographs, are usually 3,000K each. Applications you download from the Internet might be 15MB, 50MB, even 1 or 2GB each. Add to that the file compression programs that enable you to condense many files into one large executable file, and your file sizes quickly outgrow that 1.44MB floppy disk.

You need to consider file storage alternatives. With the use of a network, you have more choices than you have with a standalone computer.

 Tip   You should store your applications, for the most part, on each user's C: drive. You should store your data files separately from your application files. Older applications stored files within the program's folder; this method might cause a problem if you decide to delete that program from your hard disk. You could accidentally delete all of your data as well.

Most newer application installations place the data files in the My Documents folder by default. This folder or any other folder you create is fine for storing your data files.

Choosing a storage area

Whether you're using a client/server or a workgroup network, you want to make the best use of your resources. You should choose the computer with the most hard disk space as the main file storage area. Normally, on a client/server network, that computer is the server; however, if the server is overloaded with print, Internet, and other duties on the network, you might want to locate the storage area on another computer on the network.

Figure 21-1 illustrates the storage space on a home computer. This hard disk holds a total of 19GB; note that the status bar indicates the drive has 11.7GB of disk space free. Someone with limited space could save files to this networked computer; however, if you have a larger hard disk on the network, consider using that computer for file storage.

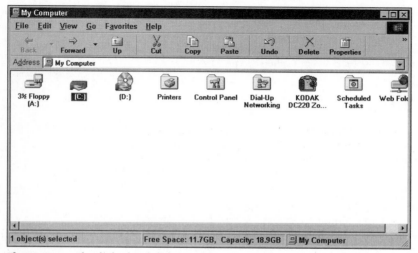

Figure 21-1: Check the hard disk space on all computers on the network to determine the one to use for file storage.

Computers today come with larger hard disks than ever before. You cannot easily find a new computer with a hard disk smaller than 20GB, and 80 to 120GB is becoming the norm. You can use a large disk such as this as a storage area for everyone on the network.

Small Business Tip

Consider buying large hard disks for each computer in your business network. You still may share a drive for storage of files, but users on a business network use more storage space than the normal home computer user. Using an 80GB hard disk in each computer in your business isn't at all impractical.

Partitioning a Large Disk

With such large hard disks common to new computers, you might consider partitioning the disk so that you can designate one area for network file storage. In *partitioning*, you divide your hard disk into sections. The operating system treats different partitions on the hard disk as if they were separate drives.

As an example, suppose that you have an 80GB hard disk. You can divide it into two or three partitions. If you divide it into two partitions, you might have a C: and a D: drive. Drive C: is the partition containing the operating system and one person's individual data files. Drive D: might be an extra partition for network file storage. You can make the partitions any size; you might make drive C: 40GB and drive D: 40GB, for example.

When you partition a drive, the partitions show up in programs such as the Windows Explorer as separate drives: C:, D:, E:, and so on. Your floppy drive remains drive A:, if applicable, and your CD-ROM drive becomes the last drive after the partitions, such as F: or G:.

Partitioning a drive does take some work. In the past, you had to use a utility called FDISK to wipe everything off of the partition, reassign partition names and sizes — such as drive C: as 40GB and drive D: as 40GB — and then reformat each partition on the hard drive. After formatting, you had to load the operating system and all your programs on drive C: again.

Today, several utility programs can help you partition a drive without reformatting it. These programs enable you to divide free disk space into a separate partition without affecting the operating system or your application files. Partition Magic is one such program. Acronis' PartitionExpert is another good partitioning program.

The advantages of using only one network hard disk for file storage are as follows:

✦ The other computers on the network can use smaller, less expensive hard drives.

✦ Backing up files is simpler.

✦ Finding and sharing files is easier for everyone concerned.

The disadvantages of using one network hard disk to store all files are as follows:

✦ The storage computer must always be on so that the files are available to everyone.

✦ If the storage computer's hard disk crashes, stored files are lost unless you have a good backup.

Small Business Tip

In a small business, the advantages of using a network drive for file storage far outweigh the disadvantages. First, the file storage computer will always be turned on in an office situation. Second, you should be backing up your files every day, so if the hard disk crashes, you still have a backup of files.

Next, your users easily can find shared files if they're stored on one computer hard disk instead of scattered around the network. Think of the time and aggravation you'll save.

File storage tips

When you share or store files on one computer's hard disk, you can get those files quickly and easily over the network. Following are some tips to make network file storage more beneficial to all:

✦ If you save all files on one hard disk on the network, map that drive to each computer for quicker and easier access. For information about mapping drives, see Chapter 13. Figure 21-2 shows mapped drives for quick and easy access to shared folders. Note that the mapped drives — C, D, and Accounting — are all located on Molly's computer.

Figure 21-2: Map a drive to the shared storage space for fast access.

✦ On the network drive, create a folder in which each user can save his or her files. You also might create folders for shared files that everyone uses and folders for backup files, in particular.

✦ When a folder contains information that is no longer current or necessary for the group, instead of deleting it or just leaving it in on the network drive, save that folder to a CD, Zip disk, tape drive, or other storage device, and then delete it from the network drive. This technique saves space and keeps the drive from becoming cluttered.

Note   Of course, you can use a variety of storage devices for saving files — tapes, CD-RW or CD-R discs (see the next Note for an explanation of the difference between these disc types), Zip disks, Jaz disks, and others. The reason your first choice for file storage might be a hard disk, however, is so that you can work with the file more efficiently. Working from a file stored on a hard disk is faster than working off of a Zip disk or other storage device. Of course, you always can copy the file from the storage device to your hard disk and then copy the revised file back to the storage disk when you're finished.

Backing Up Files

You hear a lot of talk about backing up your files, but you may think backing up is a process meant only for businesses. It's not. You should back up important files from your computer periodically, at least once a week, if not more often; the frequency depends on how much your data changes each day.

You should not back up your operating system, application files, or any other files you have on disk or CD-ROM. If you need to reload these, you can do so easily from the originals. Besides, backing up these files takes more time and storage space.

You should back up, however, any important data files and Registry files. Data files that you should back up include important letters, reports, spreadsheets, databases, drawings, accounting information, contact lists, pictures, music files, and so on. The Registry is the place in which Windows stores its system information, including all device information, user data, program settings, and more.

Backing up to the network or locally

You can back up important files to your local computer — to another folder, for example, or to a second hard disk, a CD-R, a Zip disk, or other storage device. Alternatively, you can back up to the network, or to another computer's hard disk, Zip disk, tape drive, or other storage device.

Note You can use a CD-R or a CD-RW as a storage device. A CD-R is a disk to which you write only once. You can leave the CD open so that you can write information at various times; however, once the CD is full, you cannot erase data and write to the CD again. A CD-RW is a disk you can use as another drive on your computer. You can copy files to it and delete files from it. CD-RWs are more expensive than CD-Rs. Choose the one that is right for your data. If files continually change, a CD-RW might be best. If you just want to keep your music files or photographs on a disk, a CD-R is perfect.

If you back up to your own computer's hard disk, you have no protection in case of a hard disk failure. If a virus attacks your system or your hard disk stops operating, all of your data — original and backup — will be gone.

You easily can back up to a CD drive, tape drive, Zip drive, or other device attached to your computer and know your data is safe if the hard disk should crash. These devices have their limits, however. A tape drive doesn't enable easy access to just one file or folder. Zip and Jaz drives are limited by the amount of information they can hold. CD disks are easy to use and easy to store; however, the quality of some CDs is always in question.

 Tip If you use a CD for a back up, make two backup CDs of the same data, just in case one CD goes bad.

Backing up to a computer on the network — whether it's another workstation or a server — affords many advantages to the user. Network backup is usually fast, depending on the speed of the connection. Space is most likely not an issue if you use one computer with a large hard disk. Restoring backed-up files to the original computer is also fast and easy, as long as there is a network connection.

Small Business Tip

If you back up your data files over the network, you save time and worry. Many small businesses use an extra hard disk or a tape drive for purposes of backing up files. Either will work; the important thing is to back up your data files every day. Consider the amount of time it will take to restore accounting, customer, and other files if even one hard disk crashes. Is the time involved worth the trouble of backing up your computers?

Backing up your files to a CD, Zip or Jaz drive, a tape drive, or some other device attached to a networked computer is not any better than backing up to an external device attached to your own local computer. You still have size limits, plus the backup must travel across the network, so speed becomes even a bigger issue. If you don't have a CD burner, Zip drive, or other device, however, using someone else's storage device is better than not backing up at all.

Figure 21-3 shows two shared storage devices the network users can use. When a user wants to back up multiple files in case of a hard disk crash, for example, he or she can back up to the CD-RW drive attached to one of the computers on the network. On the other hand, a user might just want to save a few files that will fit on a Zip disk. Because the Zip drive is also shared, anyone on the network can use this device as well.

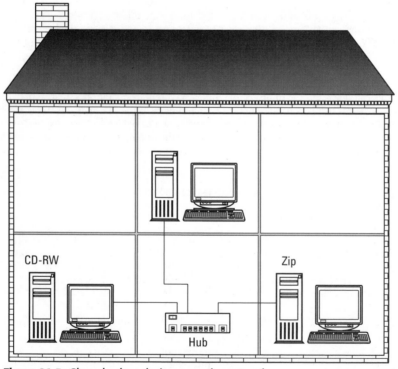

Figure 21-3: Share backup devices over the network.

The Importance of an Uninterruptible Power Supply

An *uninterruptible power supply* (UPS) is a useful tool for your computers, whether they're on a network or not. A UPS is a battery backup that attaches to your computer or multiple computers. The UPS kicks on in case of a power outage so that you can save the files you're working on and shut down your computer.

If the power goes out or if someone pulls the plug on your computer while you're working in a file, you lose all data since you last saved it. If you frequently save your work or if your work isn't critical, then you don't have to worry about a UPS. If you work on accounting files or other important data, you might want to get a UPS.

A UPS consists of a set of high-powered batteries. The purpose of a UPS is to supply power to the computer system in case power is interrupted or falls below an acceptable level. A UPS isn't a battery to run your computer until the power comes back on; most UPSs run for only 5 to 7 minutes. The idea is to give you enough time to shut down your computer or network in an orderly fashion.

If you're running a client/server network, you definitely should attach a UPS to your server. You could lose a lot of data if the server is cut off while multiple people are working on files and applications on the server. A UPS enables you to lock out clients and shut the server down safely. It's also a good idea to use a UPS on each workstation computer so that each user doesn't lose data or information in a power failure.

 Tip   Add surge protectors to your network if you do not use UPSs.a Each computer and modem should use a surge protector of some sort. Lightning, power surges, and brownouts can cause all sorts of trouble in your equipment. A surge protector does not take place of a UPS; however, a UPS does take the place of a surge protector.

Considering the files you should back up

Some files you should back up periodically, just to make your life easier in case of hard disk failure. Backing up these files is especially important for a server. Following are some files you should consider backing up:

✦ **Drivers and device software** — If you installed updated drivers — for your network card or sound card, for example — you should make backups of these. Also consider backing up CD-ROM drivers and printer drivers. Look for a folder named after your devices for the drivers matching the device; for example, look for a folder named Ethernet for network card drivers.

✦ **Configuration files, such as Config.sys, Autoexec.bat, System.ini, Win.ini, and Registry files** — These files are located on the root of your hard drive (C:, for example). Not many people use the config.sys and autoexec.bat anymore, but some do, especially if they're still using some DOS-based programs.

✦ **Any login scripts and password files for server use, as well as any user accounts or special initialization files for server use** — The location of these files depends on the network operating system (NOS); check the documentation of the NOS for more information.

✦ **All data** — Word processing documents, Web pages, accounting data, database files, spreadsheets, graphics and images, customer information, and so on. These files might be located in your My Documents folder, Program Files folder, or wherever you save your data files.

Using backup devices

If your network is small and your data is relatively noncritical, you probably will want to back up your files by copying them to a disk of some sort. On the other hand, if you're running your home business on your computer, and you don't want to lose all of your data, you might want to use a backup program and a tape or other device. The type of device you use depends on the amount of data you want to back up, the cost of the device and its media, and the difficulty of backing up.

Following are some devices you can consider for backing up files:

✦ Floppy disks are good for backing up small files. If your files are no larger than 1.44 to or 2.88MB, floppy disks are perfect, especially if you use a compression program such as PKZip or WinZip.

✦ CD-Rs, writable compact discs, are more affordable (about 18 cents each) than in the past and are a great way to save data. You must consider, however, that CD-Rs are read-only and you cannot overwrite the CD. CDs you can overwrite (CD-RWs) are more expensive than read-only CDs (a few dollars per disc). CDs usually hold 700MB of data.

✦ Zip drives are removable drives that are sometimes standard on computers, but more often than not, you must ask for a Zip drive to be added. A Zip cartridge holds 100MB or 250MG, and it's easy to use, transport, and store. Zip disks cost around $10 to $12 each. Other removable drives are available, such as SyQuest and Iomega Jaz drives. These drives furnish larger capacities than Zip drives.

✦ Tape drives are inexpensive and commonly used for backups. Sometimes tape backup programs are difficult to configure and to use. Also, make sure that the hardware is compatible with your computer.

✦ Additional hard disks are great for backing up data. You might use a disk on another computer in the network or add a hard disk to your computer. Share that disk with everyone so that backing up to one point on the computer is quick and easy.

Backing up the Registry

The Registry is the area of the Windows operating system that contains all configuration files for the computer user. The Registry lists, for example, user preferences, desktop colors, fonts, and program settings. If the Registry becomes corrupted, Windows might stop working completely.

If you make a backup of the Registry, on the other hand, you can get your configuration back quickly without losing anything. You should make regular backups of the Registry file. Anytime you add a program or you make changes to your setup, the Registry files change.

Tip Be extremely careful whenever you edit the Registry. A mistake in typing or an accidental keystroke can render your computer useless.

To make a backup of the Registry, follow these steps:

1. Choose Start ➪ Run. The Run dialog box appears, as shown in Figure 21-4.

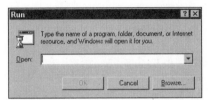

Figure 21-4: You can use the Run dialog box to run programs in Windows.

2. In the Open text box, type **REGEDIT** and press Enter. The Registry Editor dialog box appears (see Figure 21-5).

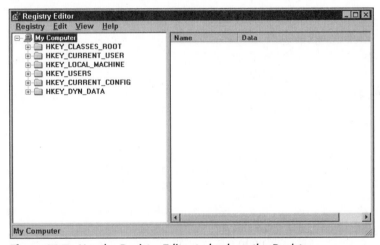

Figure 21-5: Use the Registry Editor to back up the Registry.

3. Choose Registry ➪ Export Registry File. The Export Registry File dialog box appears, as shown in Figure 21-6.

4. In the Save In drop-down list box, choose the drive to which you want to save the backup.

5. Double-click the folder to open it, and then locate the desired subfolder, if necessary.

6. In the File Name text box, enter a name for the backup copy of the Registry.

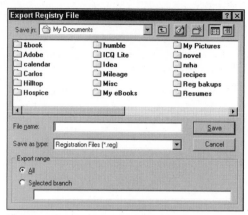

Figure 21-6: Save your Registry backup.

7. Leave the type of file as Registration Files (*.reg).

8. In Export Range, click All to save the entire Registry.

9. Click the Save button.

10. Choose Registry ⇨ Exit to close the Registry Editor.

If you ever need to restore the Registry, open the Registry Editor and choose Registry ⇨ Import Registry File. Choose the file you saved and then click the Open button.

Tip   You also can make a backup of the Registry by saving the User.dat and the System.dat files. These files are located in C:\Windows and contain all of the information in your Registry. Save the two files to a floppy disk, for example. If your Registry becomes corrupted, you can copy the files to the Windows directory to overwrite the corrupted files.

Tip   Windows creates a Registry backup for you each time you turn on Windows. To use one of these backups, start the computer in safe mode by pressing F8 when the computer is booting. Choose to start safe mode with a command prompt. At the prompt, type **scanreg /restore**. A list of the latest Registry backups appears. Choose the most recent backup and then reboot. If this backup doesn't work, it may be corrupted as well. Follow the same process to choose a different Registry backup in the list.

Using the Windows Backup program

The Windows Backup program is an application designed to back up your files on a scheduled basis. You can choose to back up every day, once a week, or on some other schedule. You can choose to back up only certain files or all your files. You also can choose to use a device such as a tape drive for backing up purposes.

The backup program also enables you to restore the backups in case of a problem with your original files.

Types of Data Backups

You might want to use a *copy backup*, which is simply copying your files to another disk or other device. Copying files works well when you don't update your data daily or when you need to back up only certain files periodically. A backup program, however, is good for backing up data such as accounting files, databases, or any file that changes daily or weekly.

If you use a backup program of some sort, you'll notice there are various types of backups you can use — *full*, *incremental*, and *differential*. Most backup applications give you the choice of how to set up your backup.

You generally start your backup strategy with a full backup. A *full backup* makes a complete copy of all selected files. You can use a full backup to restore all your files in case of a disaster.

You then can perform a full backup every day, or you can perform incremental or differential backups. An *incremental backup* backs up only the files that have changed since the last full backup. A *differential backup* backs up everything since the last full backup.

Incremental backups save time in backing up, but you use more media. You must save each incremental backup (on tape or disk), because the restore uses all the incremental backups. If your hard disk fails, for example, you restore the full backup and then you restore each incremental backup since you made the full backup.

Differential backups take longer to perform but they are easier to restore. Differential backups don't require as much media either.

No matter the method you use, you still must perform a full backup periodically. You might perform a full backup once a month, for example, and do incremental or differential backups in between.

You might prefer to perform a full backup every day or week or so, however, instead of using incremental and differential backups, depending on the amount of data you're backing up and how often it changes.

Consider this: How much work do you want to do to get back to where you were the day the disk crashed? With that in mind, decide how often to make backups.

The following steps outline backing up to a network drive. For information about backing up to a tape drive, see the Windows online help plus the documentation that comes with your tape drive. Different versions of Windows use slightly different backup programs; however, the steps are essentially the same. To use the Windows XP backup program, follow these steps:

1. Choose Start ➪ Programs ➪ Accessories ➪ System Tools ➪ Backup. The Microsoft Backup and Restore Wizard dialog box appears, as shown in Figure 21-7.

Note

If no backup device is attached to your computer, a dialog box appears, stating that the program cannot find the device. If you do not have a backup device, such as a tape drive, you still can use the backup program to back up your files to a network drive. Click No to close the dialog box and continue with the backup procedure.

Figure 21-7: The wizard guides you through the backup process.

2. Click Next. The second wizard dialog box appears, as shown in Figure 21-8.

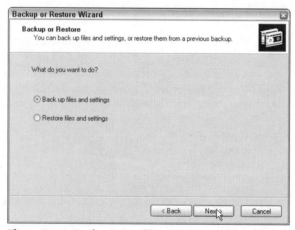

Figure 21-8: Back up your files.

3. Click Back Up Files and Settings, and then click Next. The third wizard dialog box appears, as shown in Figure 21-9.

4. Click Let Me Choose What to Back Up, and then click Next. The Items to Back Up dialog box appears, as shown in Figure 21-10.

Note

You can choose another option, if you want to back up, for example, your My Documents folder and some personal settings.

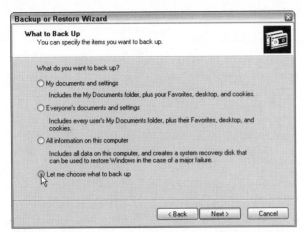

Figure 21-9: You can choose your own files or let Windows choose them for you.

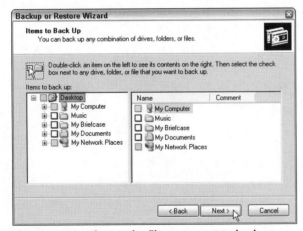

Figure 21-10: Choose the files you want to back up.

5. Open a folder by clicking the plus (+) sign beside it, as shown in Figure 21-11. Click in the check box to mark a folder for backup.

6. Click Next. The Backup Type, Destination, and Name dialog box appears, as shown in Figure 21-12.

7. Depending on the equipment attached to the computer, you can back up to a file, a floppy drive, a CD burner, a tape drive, and so on. You can click Browse to back up to a file on the network, as shown in Figure 21-13.

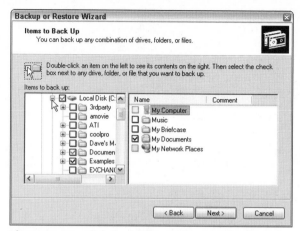

Figure 21-11: Click the folders you want to back up.

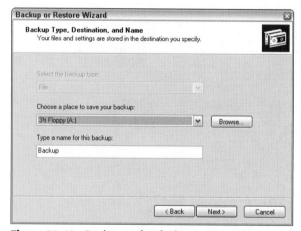

Figure 21-12: Designate the device.

8. Name the backup file. Click Next. The last wizard dialog box appears.

Tip

Name the backup for the date, such as 082203 or 090103, so you can easily find the backup file if you need to restore it.

9. You can click Finish to perform the backup immediately, or you can click the Advanced button to schedule the backup and choose the type of backup. Figure 21-14 shows the Type of Backup dialog box that results from choosing the Advanced button.

10. Click Next. Choose Verify Data after Backup.

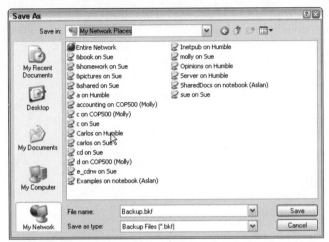

Figure 21-13: Back up to a network or shared drive.

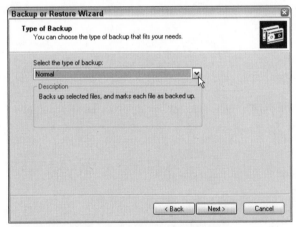

Figure 21-14: Choose a normal, differential, or other type of backup.

Note

A normal backup is the same as a full backup.

Note

You verify data after the backup to make sure the backup is usable. It takes a bit longer to perform a backup with verification than without it; however, it's a good idea to always verify data.

11. Click Next. You can choose whether to append or replace backups already on your media, depending on the media type. For instance, you can overwrite a tape but you cannot overwrite a CD-R.

12. Click Next. The When to Back Up, or scheduling, dialog box appears.

13. If you do not want to back up immediately, click Later and enter a name in the Job Name text box, as shown in Figure 21-15.

Figure 21-15: Name the job.

14. Click the Schedule button. The Schedule Job dialog box appears, as shown in Figure 21-16.

Figure 21-16: Schedule the job for late at night, for example.

15. Click OK and click Next. You might need to enter an administrative username and password, depending on the computer and the setup.

16. Click Finish.

The following steps guide you through creating a backup with Windows 98:

1. Choose Start ➪ Programs ➪ Accessories ➪ System Tools ➪ Backup. The Microsoft Backup Wizard dialog box appears.

2. Choose Create a New Backup Job and then click OK. The Backup Wizard dialog box appears.

3. Choose Back Up Selected Files, Folders, and Drives. If you choose the other option, Back Up My Computer, you'll be backing up application files as well as data files. Click Next. The second Backup Wizard dialog box appears.

4. If you put a check mark in the box beside a drive or folder, you're choosing the entire drive or folder. Click the plus sign to open a drive or folder.

5. Click the Next button. Another Backup Wizard dialog box appears. Choose to back up all selected files; if this is not the first time you've backed up, you can choose to back up only the new and changed files in the selected folders. The second backup option takes less time to complete.

6. Click the Next button. The next Backup Wizard dialog box appears. Enter the path to the folder in which you want to save the backup file. The backup file uses a .qic extension. You can name the file anything you want, but keep the .qic extension. The default filename is MyBackup.qic.

7. To save to the network, you can enter the path to the computer and folder, or you can use the browse dialog box. Beside the Path text box, click the Browse button. The Where to Back Up dialog box appears.

8. Click the arrow beside the Look In drop-down text box.

9. Choose the Network Neighborhood. Locate the computer and then the folder to which you want to back up. Click the Open button to return to the Backup Wizard dialog box.

10. Click Next. The next Backup Wizard dialog box appears.

11. Choose whether to compare the original files with the backup files and whether to compress.

Tip   It's a good idea to compare the original files with the backed up files. If the program catches a mistake or a problem, you can take the steps to correct it now instead of waiting until you really need the backup of your data.

12. Click Next. The last Backup Wizard dialog box appears. You need to choose a name for the backup job.

13. Click Start. The program backs up your files. It shows a progress report of the process. The status lists any errors.

14. A dialog box stating Operation Completed appears when the program is finished. Click OK.

15. Close the Microsoft Backup dialog box when your backup is complete.

Understanding the process of restoring backups

If you simply copy your files as a form of backing up, then restoring those files is no problem. You can overwrite current files with the backups, or you can copy files to a new hard disk, for example.

If you use a backup program to create backups, you need to restore the backup to get your files back in working order. You cannot simply copy the backups to a new hard disk; you must run a restore.

Tip   You should test your backups periodically to make sure that they're going to work. You don't want to take the time and trouble to back up, only to find that the backup is worthless when you really need it.

Following are some guidelines for restoring your backups.

✦ Before you start to restore your backups, write-protect the media so that you don't accidentally overwrite it. Write-protect means to disable the tape or disc from recording new data over the old. Different media use different write-protect methods; see the instructions that come with the media.

✦ If you have a hard disk failure, you need to reinstall the operating system and your applications on a new hard disk. Then you need to install the backup software before you restore your backup of files.

✦ Always restore your last full backup first. Then restore incremental or differential backups in order, from the earliest to the latest.

✦ After you restore your data, hold on to the backup media for a few days to make sure that everything is working, just in case you need to go back to the backup.

Restoring from the Microsoft Backup program

You can restore any backups you made with the Microsoft Backup program. These steps discuss restoring from a network drive. For information about restoring from a tape drive, see the online help plus the tape drive documentation.

To restore from Microsoft Backup in Windows XP, follow these steps:

1. Choose Start ➪ Programs ➪ Accessories ➪ System Tools ➪ Backup. The Wizard dialog box appears.

2. Click Next. The second Wizard dialog box appears.

3. Click Restore files and settings. Click Next.

4. The What to Restore Wizard dialog box appears, as shown in Figure 21-17.

5. In the left side of the window, select the files you want to restore. Click Next.

6. Click Finish to complete the restore.

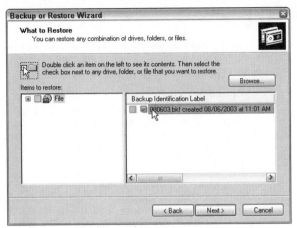

Figure 21-17: Restore a backup.

In Windows 98, follow these steps to restore a backup:

1. Open the Microsoft Backup program. In the Microsoft Backup Welcome dialog box, choose Restore Backed Up Files, and then click OK. The Restore Wizard appears.

2. In the first dialog box, choose the location to which you saved the backup file.

3. Click Next. Confirm the file location, time, and date of the last backup.

4. Click OK. The Restore Wizard displays the list of items to restore. As with marking folders for backup, add a check mark to the box preceding the folder you want to restore.

5. Click Next. The Restore Wizard dialog box displays the Where to Restore options. You can choose to restore to the original location, in which case the older files are overwritten. Alternatively, you can restore to another location that you specify in this dialog box.

6. Click Next. The Restore Wizard How to Restore dialog box appears. Choose whether to replace the original files.

7. Click the Start button. The Media Required dialog box appears, listing the network computer to which the backup file is saved. Click OK.

8. When the program is finished, it displays a dialog box telling you the operation is completed. Click OK.

9. View the Restore Progress dialog box to see if any errors appear. Click OK to close the dialog box if there are no problems.

10. Close the Microsoft Backup dialog box.

Backing Up Your Mac Files

Mac OS X does not come equipped with a backup program; however, you can back up any file by copying it to another location. The safest backup location is one other than your hard drive; for example, copy the files to a CD-R or CD-RW or to a network drive.

You can buy Dantz Retrospect 5.1 from Apple or other dealers. You download the program from the Internet and install to your computer. Retrospect 5.1 is a backup program designed for home use and for small business. Retrospect 5.1 enables you to run a backup program on one Macintosh plus two other networked computers. The other two computers can run a Mac OS, Windows, or Red Hat Linux. The price of Retrospect 5.1 is $100. Go to the store.apple.com for more information.

The site www.mac.com represents .Mac, which is a membership to various services and products expressly for the Macintosh computer. You can share files and photos, e-mail, use .Mac chat, publish online calendars so your friends know your schedule, and so on. .Mac also provides an online backup service. You can back up your files to the site using online backup software, plus you can use the .Mac's Virex antivirus software to protect your computer. You can also use other online services, such as Ahsay (www.ahsay.com). Search the Internet for "online Mac backup service" for others.

You can purchase a third-party backup program for the Mac, such as www.pure-mac.com's Drag'nBack 3.6 for $50 or Intego's Personal Backup V10.0 Mac for around $60. Drag'nBack is a shareware product; many others are available on the Internet.

Tip   For information about shareware for a variety of platforms, see www.tucows.com.

Backing Up a Linux Box

Linux backup programs are openly distributed and are thus easy to find. You'll need to locate your Linux distribution and find a utility (utils) for that specific operating system. If you search shareware sites, such as Tucows for example, you can find many backup utilities, including:

> ✦ **Afbackup**—For a client/server system that uses a GPL license
>
> ✦ **Burt 2.4.7**—A freeware backup and recovery tool
>
> ✦ **FlexBackup**—Another GPL licensed backup program
>
> ✦ **mtf**—A Linux reader for Microsoft Tape Format used by the NT system (open source)
>
> ✦ **scdbackup**—An open source program that is a simplified CD backup

Note   If you want more information about backing up a Linux box, see www.linux-backup.net.

Securing Files and Folders

The security you provide for your files and folders depends on the amount and type of data you use in your home network and the risks to that data. You might not worry about any of the files on your computer, for example, if you completely trust the others on the network to respect your files or if you have little to lose on your computer.

You might want to secure some of your files, for example, so that someone doesn't accidentally delete or damage your Windows operating system or your program files. You might want to incorporate some security into your network if a child on the network likes to experiment and explore files, if the network is open to people outside of the family, or if you save some confidential or sensitive files on your computer.

Looking at security risks

Risks come in many forms on a network. Naturally, the other members of the network can pose a threat to your data. Network intruders and hardware failures also can cause a problem for your data safety. Considering the risks to your data helps you decide how much protection you need.

Other members of the network might cause a problem with your files and folders — by accident or by intention. If others on the network can access your files and folders, they could inadvertently delete, move, or modify those files. Additionally, with access, any user can deliberately erase or alter files and folders on your computer.

Intruders into your network and your computer's contents include guests or visitors in your home and intruders from outside of the home. Your child's friends, for example, might use your network for playing games. While on the network, the child could also view or change any of your files to which he or she has access.

Intruders from outside of the home primarily consist of Internet users hacking into your system. Most hackers and crackers target business networks that use a Web server for advertising over the Internet. Unless you're using a Web server, you don't need to worry much about hackers.

However, you should consider the Internet intruder who sends a family member an e-mail message or meets someone in your house in a chat room. It's possible for children, in particular, to be duped by predatory adults over the Internet. A child then could give anyone information and files via the Internet.

Viruses are another threat to your system that preventive security measures can block. You can get viruses from files transferred over the Internet or from disks infected with the virus program. After a virus is transferred to one computer on the network, it can replicate itself quickly to the other computers on the network.

Small Business Tip

The security of your business files — payroll, customer or employee information, and so on — is important enough to make a real effort to protect your LAN. A disgruntled employee, an accident-prone partner, or a competitor can wreak havoc on your network. If any of these threats are real possibilities, consider using a network operating system to ensure the security of your LAN data.

Looking at security solutions

You can apply as much or as little security to your network as you feel is necessary. You can guard sensitive files or your entire computer; you can enforce safeguards to protect data and network users.

Tip

Naturally, you should protect the physical security of your network. If you have sensitive files on your computer that you want to protect, consider locking the door to the room in which your computer is located.

Protecting workgroup files and folders

To protect the files and folders on any computer on a workgroup network, you use the Share feature in Windows. With sharing, you can designate which folders, if any, you'll share with the other members of the network. You also can share folders with only specific users of the network, if you want.

Even though you cannot specify certain files as shared or not, you can place those files in folders and identify shared access to the folders. See Chapter 12 for more information about sharing your files and restricting access to folders.

Note   Windows 2000 and Windows XP, as well as Linux and some Mac operating systems, provide more security from hackers, intrusions, deletions, and so on. See the operating system's documentation for more information.

Protecting client/server files and folders

If you're using a client/server network, you have more control over file and folder access. You might choose to share only resources attached to the server. In this case, all files and folders on the client computers are safe from other network users.

If you use a network operating system (NOS) — such as Windows 2000 Server — you have even more control over the files, folders, and other resources. You can set permissions that enable only certain people to access any file or folder.

Most NOSs also have built-in logging features. These features create a log of information about each security event that appears on the network. If someone tries to log on to the network several times and fails, for example, these attempts are recorded in a log so that you can see when the logons took place and what username and ID were used.

Depending on your operating system, you can share files and folders on client computers as well as on the server computer. Again, using the Windows Share feature, you can control access to certain folders on any computer.

Cross-
Reference   See Chapter 4 for more information about network operating systems.

Protecting from the Internet

Use firewalls, proxy servers, or both to protect your network from unauthorized access via the Internet. Most proxy server software includes protection from hackers and other intruders from the Internet. If you're using a Web server on your network, you can install the firewall or proxy server on the server to protect your Web site.

A proxy server authenticates users from the Internet, protects data on the Web server, and otherwise controls Internet users' access to the LAN. A firewall hides the structure of your LAN from Internet users, rejects unknown protocols, and even checks e-mail headers to make sure that they are addressed to your network users.

Some proxy servers also can control your LAN users' access to the Internet. You can define the types of sites you don't want the users to access, and the proxy server takes over control.

Cross-
Reference   See Chapter 16 for information about proxy servers and firewalls.

Protecting from viruses

You should install an antivirus application on each computer on your network. You also should check all shareware, freeware, and other applications before installing them. Check the installation disks immediately on inserting them into the computer.

Similarly, you can check disks brought in from other sources — including programs, files, games, and so on. Make sure that you get periodic updates for your virus software so that you have the latest virus definitions installed on each computer.

It's especially important to scan files you receive over the Internet before using them on your computer. Many attached files and some downloaded files can be infected. Scanning a file before opening it can protect your computer and the network.

Tip   One of the most important preventive measures you can take in network security is backing up important files. If a virus does get through and attacks your computer, a backup might be the only way you can recover your files.

Summary

In this chapter, you learned about working with files and folders over the network. Specifically, you learned about the following topics:

✦ Storing files

✦ Backing up files and folders

✦ Securing files and folders

In the next chapter, you learn about using the Windows management tools, such as the System Policy Editor.

✦   ✦   ✦

Managing the Network

In Part VI, you learn how to perform tasks that help you control and monitor the network. Chapter 22 shows you how to view shared resources and monitor the network traffic for Windows, the Macintosh, and Linux. Chapter 23 explains how to set system policies to control the users and resources on the network. And Chapter 24 covers some tips for working with the Registry and the network.

Using Network Management Tools

You don't have to perform many management tasks on a peer-to-peer network. You might check shares or double-check file access on a computer; but for the most part, a peer-to-peer network runs itself. However, Windows does include a few management tools you may find useful. You can use these tools to see who's sharing which files, who's attached to which computer, and so on.

Understanding Network Management

Managing your network should be an easy job. If you're using a peer-to-peer network, all you really need to do is make sure that everyone on the network can access their files and the other network resources they need to accomplish computer tasks.

If you use a client/server network, you might have a few more management duties, but for a home network, you shouldn't have to do too much. Again, you need to make sure that everyone can access the resources they need. You also need to make sure that the server and network run smoothly.

As you add more applications, resources, and users to a network, you also add more network management duties. When you add Internet access, for example, you add the following management tasks:

✦ Configure Internet software, account information, and so on.

✦ Make sure that the modem, cable or DSL modem, or T1 or similar line works.

✦ Ensure that the connection to the Internet and the Internet service provider is working.

✦ Maintain the program on each computer, including the host or server.

✦ Troubleshoot problems with hardware and software having to do with the Internet connection.

✦ Keep the LAN and users secure with firewalls or proxy servers.

✦ Perform upgrades when necessary.

Think about other programs or hardware you might add to your network: printers, scanner, Zip or disk drives, CD or DVD-ROM drives, games and other software, more users, a server, routers, and so on. Each component adds to network traffic and problems. Each component you add multiplies your duties and responsibilities.

Using utilities or tools of some sort to help you manage, troubleshoot, and maintain the network saves time and effort on your part.

Note   You can view your system information at any time. System information includes hardware resources, the software environment (operating system and settings), and other components, such as the modem, the network, ports, devices, and so on. To view system information in Windows, choose Start ➪ Programs ➪ Accessories ➪ System Tools ➪ System Information. On a Macintosh, click the Apple menu ➪ About This Mac, and then click More Info.

General Tips for Managing the Network

Before you try diagnosing problems or managing your network with tools, you should follow a few general guidelines to make network management and troubleshooting easier.

First, keep a notebook log of everything about your network. You should include network maps, a list of each computer's contents and configuration settings, and other details that will help you quickly and easily find any information about your network as you need it. Following is a partial list of information you should log about your computers and your network:

✦ For every server and client on the network, list hardware, OS, software, manufacturer, model, serial number, monitor brand and specs, keyboard type, mouse type, motherboard, processor speed, RAM amount and type, size and type of hard disks, controllers, CMOS information, computer BIOS manufacturer and revision numbers, and so on.

✦ List each computer and pertinent information. Also note each username, password, and the programs most used by each individual on the computer and network.

✦ List protocols, clients, and address, if applicable.

✦ List networking hardware—network cards, cabling, connectors, hubs, and so on. Include brands, types, identification numbers, and any other information you need.

✦ List all drives, including sizes, brands, manufacturers, speeds, models, drivers, and so on—CD-ROM, Zip, Jaz, tape, and so on.

✦ List all peripherals: UPS, printers, modems, scanners, and other equipment. Give the manufacturer and model, and any specifications on memory, ports, cables, and so on for each peripheral.

✦ List the applications on each computer, plus the licensing and sharing designations.

Also, keep all documentation in one area and keep a list of contact names and numbers for help, tech support lines, and so on. Keeping this information handy and up-to-date will help you with optimizing your network and troubleshooting problem areas.

Next, add to that log any problems you have and how you fix them. If you run into a problem with your network once, you're likely run into it again at a later date. Having a log of those problems and solutions will help you later when the problem reoccurs.

Using Windows Monitoring Tools

Windows supplies Net Watcher in Windows 98 computers to monitor network connections. Windows 2000 uses a Network Monitor. In Windows XP, you can use Network Diagnostics to define and locate network problems. Each of these tools monitors the network, the computer, or traffic on the network in different ways. You can also use shareware, freeware, or purchased software to monitor activity on your network.

Note   The Windows 2000 Network Monitor is similar to the Net Watcher program in Windows 98; however, it has more features and performs more complex network management functions. For information on the Windows 2000 Network Monitor, see the Windows 2000 documentation.

Using Net Watcher for Windows 98

Net Watcher is an application you can use on a network to monitor shared resources. You can view each user attached to a computer, as well as the folders and files he or she is using. You also can disconnect a user, close a file, add a shared folder, and more.

You can view the shares on your own computer and on other computers if you have the password. You also can perform any task on a remote computer after you open the computer's window in Net Watcher.

Figure 22-1 shows the Net Watcher monitoring users on the network. The two users each have three shares open. Note that neither user has been connected to Hugh for very long, so no files are open at this time. You can see the folders, however, that the selected user has open.

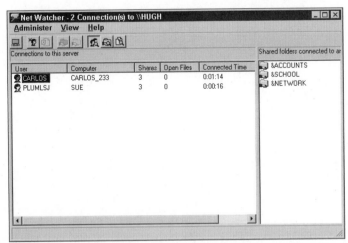

Figure 22-1: View shares, connection time, and more with Net Watcher.

Configuring the workstation for Net Watcher

Before you can run Net Watcher, you must enable remote administration on all workstations on the network. When enabling remote administration, you assign a password to each workstation. Be sure to use the same password on all workstations.

Enabling remote administration allows a user to create, change, and monitor shares on your computer. Windows enables you to assign a password to this permission so that only a person who knows the password can perform these tasks. The person who knows the password can monitor the workstations from any computer on the network.

To enable remote administration, follow these steps:

1. Choose Start ➪ Settings ➪ Control Panel. The Control Panel appears.

2. Double-click the Passwords icon in the Control Panel.

3. Choose the Remote Administration tab.

4. Check the box for Enable Remote Administration of This Server.

5. Enter the password in the Password text box, and then enter it again in the Confirm Password text box to confirm it. As you enter the password, Windows displays only asterisks, as shown in Figure 22-2.

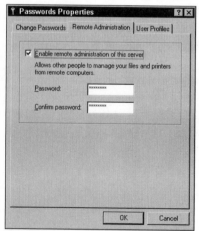

Figure 22-2: Enable remote administration.

6. Click OK. Repeat these steps on the other computers on the network.

In addition to enabling remote administration, you must enable file and print sharing, if you have not already done so. Open the Network icon in the Control Panel and then click the File and Print Sharing button. Make sure that both check boxes are checked.

Starting and quitting Net Watcher

When you start Net Watcher, any connections to your computer appear in the window. As new users or connections are made, the window reflects those connections as well. You also can refresh the view at any time to make sure that all connections are showing.

To start Net Watcher, choose Start ⇨ Programs ⇨ Accessories ⇨ System Tools ⇨ Net Watcher. The Net Watcher window appears. Figure 22-3 shows the Net Watcher window with the tools identified. Table 22-1 explains the tools.

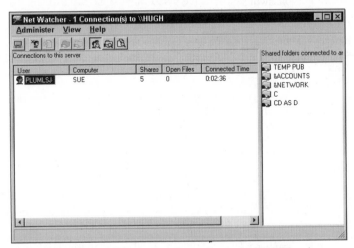

Figure 22-3: Net Watcher offers tools to help you view the network shares.

Table 22-1: Net Watcher Tools

Tool	Description
Select Server	Choose the computer you want to monitor. You must know the remote administration password.
Disconnect User	Disconnect any user from the selected share. The user loses all unsaved data.
Close File	Close any shared file, even while the user is connected. The user loses all unsaved data.
Add Share	Designate a folder or resource as shared.
Stop Sharing	Designate a folder or other resource as no longer shared.
Show Users	Display a view of connected users, their computers, the number of open shares and open files, the amount of time they've been connected, and the names of the shared folders. Refer to Figure 22-3 for the Show Users view.
Show Shared Folders	List the shared folders' paths, names, and access types. You also can view which computer is attached to each shared folder.
Show Files	List the open files, the share used, and the user connected to the file. You also can see the open mode, or access type, of the open file.

To close Net Watcher, choose Administer ➪ Exit; alternatively, click the Close (X) button.

Using Net Watcher

Net Watcher is easy to use; but you must be careful in performing some tasks. If you disconnect a user or close a file while it is in use, for example, the user loses all unsaved data.

Tip   If you must disconnect someone or close a file, give the user time to close the file before you complete the task. You might try using WinPopup Gold or another messaging program to broadcast your plans.

You can choose to change views in Net Watcher. You also can change the computer you're monitoring, disconnect users, close files, and add and change shares.

Note   If Net Watcher isn't installed, you can add it by using the Add/Remove Programs icon in the Control Panel. Net Watcher is listed as an Accessory.

Changing views

The default view in Net Watcher is Show Users. You can change the view easily to view shared folders or shared files. Viewing the files and folders in different ways presents different information about the shares.

To view shared folders, choose View ➪ By Shared Folders, or click the Shared Folders tool. Figure 22-4 illustrates the Shared Folders view. Note that you see the path and the share name as well as the access type of the share. If you select a shared folder, you can view the computers connected to the share in the right window pane. You also can view any shared printers in this view.

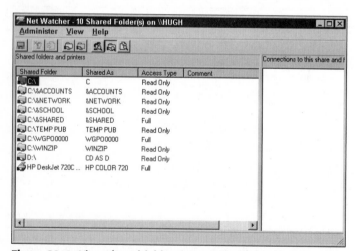

Figure 22-4: View shared folders in Net Watcher.

To view the open files of a computer, choose View ➪ by Open Files. Alternatively, click the Open Files tool. Figure 22-5 shows the Open Files view.

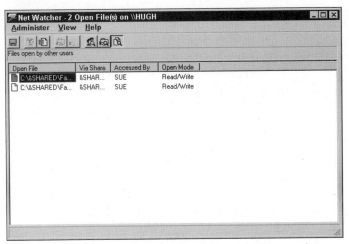

Figure 22-5: View open files and the person who is accessing the files.

Selecting a server

Net Watcher refers to any computer as a server, whether you're on a client/server network or not. The server, in this case, is the Net Watcher server software. You can view your own shared resources as well as other computers on the network, as long as you know the password set in the Remote Administration dialog box.

To select a server, follow these steps:

1. Open Net Watcher.

2. Choose Administer ➪ Select Server. The Select Server dialog box appears, as shown in Figure 22-6.

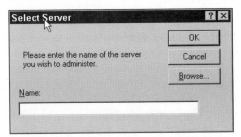

Figure 22-6: Select a server to monitor or administer.

3. Enter the server's name or use the Browse button to locate the computer.

4. Click OK. The Enter Network Password dialog box appears, as shown in Figure 22-7.

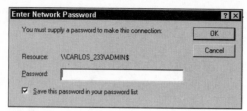

Figure 22-7: Use the password to access another computer's shares.

5. Click OK. The selected server's shares appear in the Net Watcher window, as shown in Figure 22-8.

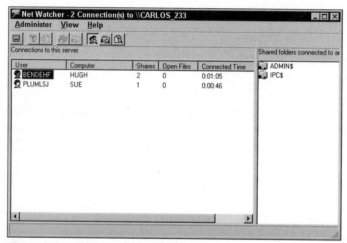

Figure 22-8: View shares on other computers.

Note

After you've accessed a server using the password, Windows adds it to your password list. You have to enter the password only once to access each server.

Disconnecting a user

You can disconnect a user from the server you're monitoring at any time. Before you disconnect the user, however, you should make sure that user has closed all open files from his or her computer.

You can disconnect a user only in Show Users view.

To disconnect a user, select the user and then choose Administer ⇨ Disconnect User. A warning dialog box appears. Click Yes to continue. Net Watcher doesn't warn the user when you disconnect him or her. When the user tries to access the computer, however, the drive is not available.

Closing a file

As with disconnecting a user, you must be careful when closing a file that is in use. You should warn a user before you close the file so that the user can save changes. If the user doesn't save changes, he or she will lose unsaved data.

To close a file, select the Show Files view. Select the open file and then choose Administer ⇨ Close File. A warning dialog box appears. Choose Yes to close the file. Again, Net Watcher doesn't warn the user.

Working with shared folders

You can share folders on any server computer to which you're attached with Net Watcher. You can open any drive and share any folder; the remote administration password gives you the permission you need to perform these tasks.

To share a folder, follow these steps:

1. Open Net Watcher and then open the computer you want to monitor.

2. Change to Shared Folders view.

3. Choose Administer ⇨ Add Shared Folder. The Enter Path dialog box appears.

4. Enter the path or use the Browse button to locate the folder on the server computer.

5. Click OK. The Share dialog box appears.

6. Choose Shared As and then enter the share name and access type.

7. Click OK to close the Share dialog box.

Preventive Maintenance to Optimize Your Network

The purpose of network "watchers" and system monitors is to locate problem areas on the network and try to alleviate traffic tie-ups and bottlenecks. Before you get to that point, however, you can lessen many problems by performing some preventive maintenance tasks.

Just like keeping a printer clean or the files on your hard disk orderly, keeping your network in top shape can help performance and efficiency. Periodic checks of equipment and configurations will contribute to optimum network performance.

Think about the following aspects of building and maintaining a network:

✦ Consider the quality of your networking hardware. If you use cheap network cards and second-rate cabling, your network performance suffers.

✦ If the cabling is out in the middle of the floor where people trample it and kids run toy cars over it constantly, you're putting your network connections at risk. Check the cabling periodically for damage.

✦ Periodically check all connectors, routers, hubs, and so on to make sure that connections are secure.

✦ Install and configure all programs — such as browsers, e-mail, and other shared applications — the same way so that maintenance and troubleshooting is easier.

✦ Use a UPS on each computer to prevent damage from power surges, brownouts, and power outages.

✦ Keep backups of your data, and from time to time, test the backups to make sure that they're reliable.

✦ Clean network printers regularly.

You also can stop sharing a folder by selecting the folder and then choosing Administer ⇨ Stop Sharing Folder.

You can view a shared folder's properties by selecting the folder and then choosing Administer ⇨ Shared Folder Properties.

Monitoring the network with Windows XP

Windows XP enables you to view your computer within the network connections but does not use a network monitor like Windows 98 or 2000 does. You can view the Local Area Connection status and you can use Network Diagnostics to view information about your computer and the network.

Note You can also get network monitoring tools for an Internet connection. These tools usually monitor ports for sites collecting personal information, watch the cookies saved on your computer, and so on. Many of these tools are free or very inexpensive.

Viewing the Local Area Connection status

With the Status dialog box, you can view the speed of your connection, the length of the connection, your IP address, the subnet mask, the default gateway, and other information. You can use this information to connect to the computer from another, for example, by identifying the IP address, or to help configure another computer with the correct gateway or subnet mask. To view the Local Area Connection status, follow these steps:

1. Click Start and Control Panel. The Control Panel appears.

2. Double-click Network Connections. The Network Connections dialog box appears.

3. Right-click Local Area Connection and click Status on the pop-up menu. The Local Area Connection dialog box appears, as shown in Figure 22-9.

Figure 22-9: View the status of the network connection.

4. Optionally, click Properties to change network settings.

5. Click the Support tab to view more information about the connection, as shown in Figure 22-10.

6. Click Close.

Figure 22-10: Quickly locate the
IP address and other configuration
information.

Using Network Diagnostics on Windows XP

Windows XP includes a Network Diagnostics program that tests your network connection for
different types of information. You can use the program to help diagnose a problem or to provide information to a tech support professional over the phone, for example.

Network Diagnostics enables you to set options for scanning your computer and the network
connections. You can choose to scan the following actions:

✦ **Ping** — Sends a basic command-line signal to another computer on the network to
make sure the network connections are working

✦ **Connect** — Attempts to connect to another computer on the network to make sure the
other computer is networkable

✦ **Show** — Displays certain information about your computer

✦ **Verbose** — Displays more advanced information about your computer

✦ **Save to Desktop** — Saves a file of information to your desktop for viewing later

You can also diagnose various categories in addition to the networking actions, including mail
or news service, computer and operating system information, modems, network clients, and
so on. You can save the options you checked so that the next time you use the Network
Diagnostics program, you use the same options.

To use Network Diagnostics, follow these steps:

1. Click Start ➪ Help and Support Center ➪ Use Tools to view your computer information
and diagnose problems. A list of tools appears in the window.

2. Click Network Diagnostics, as shown in Figure 22-11.

3. Set any scanning options. Save the options, if you want.

4. Click Scan your system. A resulting dialog box shows you the information.

5. Click the plus sign beside any category to view more information, as shown in
Figure 22-12.

6. Close the Help and Support Center.

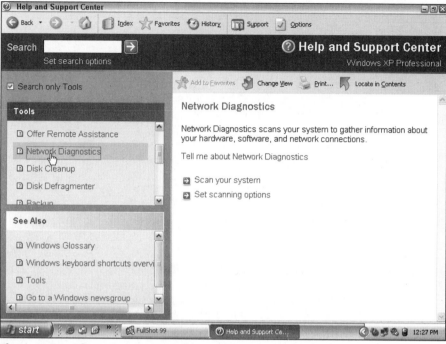

Figure 22-11: Diagnose your network connections.

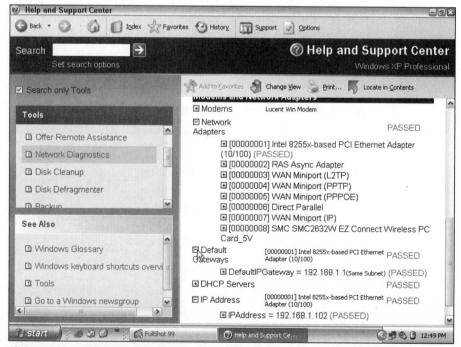

Figure 22-12: View the network diagnosis.

Looking at other network monitors

You can purchase network monitors for $10 to thousands of dollars, depending on what you need and want. For your home network, or even a small-business network, you do not need an expensive program to monitor your network. Generally, you can perform monitoring with the programs Windows supplies, or you can find some shareware to help you in your task.

✦ One such shareware program is Active Network Monitor. For around $30, you can gather information from every computer on the network.

✦ Another program, Essential NetTools, is freeware and contains many network tools for diagnosing and monitoring networks and connections. Essential NetTools uses commands such as PING, NETSTAT, TRACEROUTE, and so on to monitor the network.

You can monitor your own network using commands on your computer without these programs. For more information, see Appendix B.

Using System Monitor

You can use the System Monitor to view your computer's network or disk access in a graphical picture. The program enables you to monitor running processes, memory usage, dial-up access, and more. Most Windows operating systems automatically install the System Monitor.

Watching network traffic gives you an idea of where the bottlenecks are and the cause of some of the user's problems. You can use the System Monitor in Windows 2000 or Windows XP to see how network traffic affects your computer. If you have a client/server network, you can use the System Monitor to view each computer's connections and network traffic.

To use the System Monitor over the network, you need specific administrative permissions, user-level security, a remote service installed on your computer, and so on. If you plan to use the System Monitor over a client/server network, see the Windows 2000 Server documentation.

For your home or small-business network, you most likely won't need anything so complex and complicated.

Using the Windows 98 System Monitor

You can use the Windows 98 System Monitor to see how your computer works with others on the network. Basically, you connect to a specific computer and then watch the interaction between the two on the System Monitor. The monitor records system processor activity, such as the amount of data flowing between the two computers, memory used, details of open files and transactions, and so on.

To start the System Monitor, click Start ➪ Programs ➪ Accessories ➪ System Tools ➪ System Monitor. To exit the program, click File ➪ Exit.

Figure 22-13 shows the System Monitor on a Windows 98 computer. The peak shown in the Kernel Processor category shows heavy processor usage during that time. For more information about the System Monitor, consult the Windows 98 documentation.

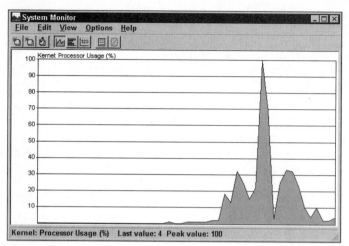

Figure 22-13: The System Monitor shows how your computer relates to the network.

Using the Windows XP System Monitor

The XP System Monitor is similar to the Windows 98 program. The System Monitor appears in a Microsoft Management Console, which is the underlying frame of all Windows 2000 and XP administrative tools. You use the System Monitor to measure processes that are most active, or that drain the majority of resources.

To start the Windows XP System Monitor, click Start ➪ Control Panel. Double-click Administrative Tools and double-click Performance. To exit the System Monitor, click File ➪ Exit.

Figure 22-14 illustrates the Windows XP System Monitor. You can see peaks in the graph that identify when another computer used this computer's resources.

Using third-party system monitors

You can find many third-party system monitors on the Internet. Some system monitors are targeted for viewing one computer's processes, others enable you to view the network and connections, and yet other monitors enable you to view activities over the Internet.

Internet spyware, or surveillance software, is an up-and-coming category of system monitors. This software monitors your spouse, children, or others' activity on the Internet. For example, if your daughter receives an e-mail from a friend, you receive the e-mail at the same time. Many programs can also record chats and log keystrokes.

✦ System Monitor by SoftPedia.com is a program for Windows 2000 and XP. System Monitor analyzes disk usage, memory, disk drives, and network adapters. You can scan the network for available computers and view and even manage remote computers. System Monitor is shareware with a cost of $99 if you plan to use it after trying it (www.softpedia.com).

✦ Big Brother by Quest Software is free and available for Linux and Windows. Big Brother enables you to monitor your system, your network, and the Web. You can monitor everyone in real time to see what each user is doing at any given moment (www.quest.com/bigbrother/).

✦ Symom by Moebius is a freeware program that monitors processes, services, bandwidth, applications, and so on and is available for Windows and Linux environments (www.symom.com).

✦ Spector Pro can record Web sites, e-mail, chats, and keystrokes so you can view the activities of anyone on your network who surfs the Internet. Spector Pro costs around $150. For more information, go to www.spectorsoft.com.

✦ Then there are anti-spyware programs, such as Cube'd Productions' System Monitor Detector. System Monitor Detector is shareware that helps you see if your system is being monitored by a program that records keystrokes, mouse movement, and so on (www.botspot.com).

✦ SpyCop costs around $20 and is another anti-spyware program. SpyCop is for Windows and blocks many programs that are designed to spy, infect, and otherwise harm your computer (www.spycop.com).

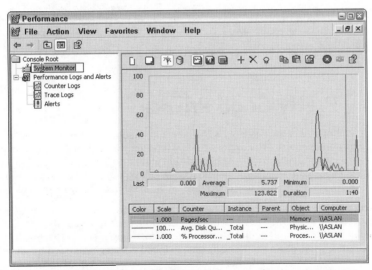

Figure 22-14: Processor peaks appear when another computer uses resources.

Optimizing the Network

You can take some steps to optimize a network that is sluggish. Sometimes, just adding some memory helps. At other times, however, you might have to add more hardware to keep the network running smoothly. You should weigh the benefits to the cost. Adding hardware isn't a cheap way to optimize your network, but you might not think the network is slow enough to warrant these measures.

✦ Most computers are at the least Pentium III and the newer ones are Pentium 4's and 5's. There are also Celeron processors, which are good for home and even small-business computers but are a bit limited in some areas, such as with some computer games and with heavy-duty accounting, graphics, or mathematics programs. Xeon is the most developed processor you can get now, and it's more in the range of a server processor because of its power, speed, and cost. Stick with Pentium to optimize network and computer efficiency.

✦ Add memory to your computers if you have less than 128MB; 256MB or more is better.

✦ Break up large files — video, music, data, and so on — to help reduce network traffic. If, for example, someone uses a lot of video files each day, try saving the files to a faster computer or to the user's computer instead of running the files over the network.

✦ Consider changing your network design. If you're using phone line networking and you want a faster transmission speed, consider going to 10Base-T. If you're using 10Base-T, consider changing to 100Base-T.

✦ If you're using multiple protocols — such as NetBEUI and IPX/SPX or TCP/IP and NetBEUI — consider changing over to just one protocol. This change could eliminate many bottlenecks and improve performance. Choose TCP/IP for the most flexibility and efficiency and remove the other, unused protocols from your computers. Extra protocols on a computer might slow the processing.

Understanding Pretty Good Privacy

Pretty Good Privacy, commonly known as PGP, is a utility that enables computers to exchange messages, secure files, and use network connections with privacy and strong authentication. PGP uses verification of individuals through authentication and encryption of data using keys. In addition to verifying those computers and users from whom you receive messages and files, PGP also stores the encrypted data on your computer, guaranteeing privacy from hackers.

PGP uses encryption and decryption keys to ensure privacy. The keys are a pair of mathematically related cryptographic keys. PGP uses a public key for the encryption. Public keys are published on many Internet sites and even on private servers, if you have a PGP or other secure program. You freely distribute your public key so it can be seen and used by all users.

A corresponding private key is used for decryption. The private key is unique; it remains on the individual user's PC. Private keys are securely protected. Private keys are located in a keystore, which is protected by many security measures. Anyone who attacks your computer needs the physical keystore to decrypt your files. With PGP, your server or computer generates a public key that it sends to others over the network, Internet, e-mail, and so on. Others use that public key to encrypt data and then send it back to you. You are the only one with the private key; therefore, you are the only one who can decrypt the files.

Some PGP programs are freeware, or you can pay for programs that offer similar and often more intricate features. PGP is a basic program you can use with Windows, Macs, and many Linux distributions. Generally, the freeware is for use by individuals as opposed to corporations. For more information about freeware, see www.pgpi.org.

PGP comes in the simplest of versions, such as GnuPG, for example. GnuPG (Privacy Guard) is a command-line utility that is a basic PGP utility for open source programming. GnuPG does not use the IDEA algorithm, which makes true PGP what it is. IDEA is a 128-bit encryption that is patented for use with PGP.

Many varied other PGP versions exist, some freeware, some shareware, and some commercial products. The most recent release of a commercial product is PGP version 8.0, for Macs and Windows users. You can purchase a single seat license for individual or small-business use for around $50. PGP 8 encrypts e-mail, files, instant messages, plus it enables you to manage your PGP keys. PGP 8 also encrypts data on your computer so that it cannot be hacked.

Note

There are other forms of encryption and protection over the Internet or on your own network. Certificates and digital signatures are two additional methods you can use to secure your data. For more information, see the sidebar "Certificates and Digital Signatures" or see www.articsoft.com.

Certificates and Digital Signatures

Public Key Infrastructure (PKI) is a security solution that provides digital security through authentication, data integrity, data confidentiality, and access control. The main question about your security structure is who should you trust? Certificates and digital signatures are a part of PKI that enable you not only to know who has access to your data but also to *control* who has access to your data.

A user who wants to take part in a specific PKI generates a public and private key pair; actually, a software program generates the keys and performs all of the encryption, decryption, signing, and so on, in the background. Anyone can get ahold of the public key, but only the original user and the certificate authorities (CAs) have access to the private key. The public key encrypts the data; the private key decrypts data. To someone who does not have the private key, the encrypted data is worthless.

With the private key, the sender puts a digital signature on data and files as a stamp of sorts, saying that data and signature is uniquely that user's.

Certificate authorities are the delivery and administration mechanism for certificates (also called digital certificates). The certificate is a file containing information identifying the sender and the public key. The CA is a trusted third party that verifies the information. So when you receive data using PKI, the CAs have verified that the data is from who it says it's from. Data not matching the appropriate certificates and digital signatures does not make it through the certificate authorities.

Monitoring on the Mac

Apple has created many system monitors for the Macintosh. Some, as with Windows system monitors, analyze on the computer; but many system monitors manage the network as well as the computer. Most of the network monitors you find are for the Mac OS X, although you can search the Internet and find monitors for earlier Mac operating systems. Many Mac monitors employ PGP.

✦ InterMapper is one of the most common and popular shareware programs. Made by Dartware, LLC, InterMapper shows you a graphical view of your computer network, including routers, servers, workstations, and so on. InterMapper includes an auto-discovery feature that locates your resources and creates the network map for you. It also uses various built-in network probes, such as ping and SNMP, to help you locate connection problems, track e-mails, and find failed network components (www.intermapper.com).

✦ AysMon (Are You Serving Monitor) is one system monitor that also analyzes the net-work. Not only can you monitor your Cable or DSL connection, you can also learn about other network services, such as login, disk space usage, and open network ports. AysMon is manufactured by Pepsan & Associates, Inc., and it is freeware. AysMon requires Mac OS X version 10.x or higher. You can get it from www.apple.com.

✦ Net Monitor, by Guy Meyer, is a shareware program for Mac OS X 10.1 or later. Net Monitor uses various graphs to display network information, such as network configura-tion, location, data throughput, and so on. For a single-user version, Net Monitor costs around $8 if you plan to continue using it after you try it out (www.macupdate.com).

✦ LoginManager is another application for the Macintosh that is also shareware. Made by Bright Light Software, LoginManager enables you to limit login time for each user, moni-tors disk usage for each user, and displays a basic login time accounting (www.zope.org).

✦ Granet (Graph Networking) is a freeware utility by Pepsan & Associates, Inc. Granet is a utility that displays the throughput of active computers on the network in a graph. Granet works with Ethernet, AirPort, and PPP (www.pepsan.com/granet/).

Considering Linux Network Monitoring

You can find many Linux network-monitoring utilities available on the Internet. Linux utilities are GNU General Public License, which means you can download and use the utilities for free. Make sure you match the utility with your distribution of Linux.

✦ InterMapper, as described in the previous section, also includes installers for Red Hat, Debian, Mandrake, and other Linux distributions. As a network monitor, InterMapper works well for Windows, Macs, and Linux (www.intermapper.com).

✦ Another monitoring utility is Iperf. Iperf measures bandwidth, data loss, and more in a Linux, Mac, or Windows environment. Iperf is copyrighted under the University of Illinois and is a GNU General Public License utility.

✦ nPULSE is a Web-based network monitor for Linux distributions. The utility monitors hundreds of sites on multiple ports. There have been problems with nPULSE and Red Hat and other distribution; make sure you read all the information you can before using any utility or application with your Linux distribution (`www.graal-npulse.com`).

✦ NetWatch, Cricket, and IPTraf are more examples of Linux-based network monitoring utilities (`www.linux.org`).

You'll need to do research on your distribution to see which monitor best suits your network.

Summary

In this chapter, you've learned about applications you can use to monitor a network. Specifically, the chapter covered the following:

✦ Windows Net Watcher, Local Area Connection status, and Network Diagnostics

✦ System Monitor

✦ Monitoring on Macs and Linux

In the next chapter, you learn about the System Policy Editor and how to control users on your LAN.

✦   ✦   ✦

Using Policies to Secure Windows

If someone on your network tends to experiment with the computer settings or change configurations that he or she shouldn't, you can limit that person's access to one or all computers. Suppose someone gets into your system, such as a friend or relative? You can protect the computers on your network from prying eyes. You can even prevent accidental deletions and changes, using policies for security in Windows.

Understanding Policies

The Windows operating system uses *policies* to control users, computers, and access to data. Policies are Windows' way of managing computers and users. User or group policies define limits and permissions for users, such as the user's desktop environment or Start menu options. Windows also uses local computer policies, which define application and security settings, permissions for folders and files, and so on.

Windows 98 enables you to use the System Policy Editor to manage policies for both users and computers. Windows 2000 and XP use a Group Policy Editor for similar configurations. Some of the policies you can edit and manage are as follows. (Some of these settings are available only in Windows 2000 and XP.)

- ✦ **Account policies** — Manage settings on passwords, such as password age, length, encryption, and so on; edit account lockout settings that govern if and when a user account is turned off; and set Kerberos policy, which is an authentication service that allows users and services to authenticate themselves and each other.

- ✦ **Local policies** — Configure settings for users rights, such as accessing the computer from the network, backing up files on the network, changing system time, creating shared objects, and so on; edit security options, like renaming accounts, auditing services, and controlling devices; and set audit policies, such as what services or activities are monitored.

- ✦ **Event log settings** — Set and manage configuration of the event log, such as the log size, how long the log is maintained, and so on. The event log contains information about applications, the system, and security.

Encryption, Authentication, and Cryptography

As you read and learn more about security with your computer and networks, you'll see more and more about encryption, authentication, and cryptography. *Cryptography* is actually a means of keeping communications private. There are many contributing elements to good cryptography, two of which include encryption and authentication:

✦ **Encryption** is a method of transforming data so that it is impossible to read without the exact decryption method, or key. Encryption is meant to ensure privacy in data transmission. With a key, decryption is possible; decryption transforms the encrypted data back to a readable form.

✦ **Authentication** is a method of ensuring you are who you say you are. You might sign your name to a contract, for example, thus authenticating yourself. Electronic authentication uses digital signatures or digital timestamps to authenticate data traveling over the Internet, a network, an intranet, and so on.

✦ **Restricted groups** — Defines who is a member of a restricted group, such as administrators or other security-sensitive groups.

✦ **System services** — Are mini-programs the operating system runs to perform activities to keep your computer working. Services work in the background, and they include such tasks as system processes, print spooling, and so on. System services policies enable a person to start, pause, or stop system services.

For your home network, you need worry only about local policies. You might want to keep a teenager or his friends from editing files on the server or renaming user accounts. In general, if your home network consists of adults, such as your spouse and grandmother, you don't have to worry about security from within.

In your small-business network, consider which computers need the most protection. For example, the server and the payroll and accounting computers most likely need the most protection. In these cases, you make sure security on these computers is tighter by applying more policies and fewer permissions.

Understanding the System Policy Editor

The System Policy Editor is a network administration program you can use with a client/server network and Windows 98. Using the System Policy Editor, you can configure settings that control individual users, individual computers, or groups of users. As administrator of the network, you can override any local settings a user might make, such as standard desktop settings, hardware configuration, and Windows environment settings.

The *administrator* is the person in charge of the network. Administrators troubleshoot connection problems, upgrade applications, set up networking hardware and software, and so on. They also have special permissions and access to computers on the network.

You can use the System Policy Editor on a Windows 98 or NT computer. The policies you set, however, apply only to other computers with the same operating system. In other words, a Windows 98 computer must create the policy files for other Windows 98 computers. Windows 2000 and XP, Macintosh, and Linux are not affected by the System Policy Editor.

Additionally, all computers must be on a client/server network run by a network operating system (NOS). You can place the policies on a server and set them to download onto individual computers as they log on. When a user logs on to the server, the server authenticates him or her, and then downloads the System Policy Editor file that controls the user's computer and settings. The System Policy Editor is a simple way to edit the Registry files on your computers. Registry files control all settings and the environment (display, colors, and other configurations) for the computer.

Note   You must be careful with the System Policy Editor; it's a powerful tool. Install it on only one computer on the network, and make sure that you restrict access to the System Policy Editor files. Before you create a system policy file, back up your Registry files. See Chapter 21 for information about backing up files and folders.

Changing user policies

Following are some policies you can control with the System Policy Editor:

✦ Keep users from changing the Control Panel settings.

✦ Prevent users from accessing applications and Windows features.

✦ Force users to use the same desktop environment.

✦ Control the menus a user can access.

✦ Hide the Start menu subfolders.

✦ Remove the Run command.

✦ Remove the Taskbar from the Settings menu you access from the Start menu.

✦ Hide all drives in the My Computer window.

✦ Hide all desktop items.

✦ Disable the Shutdown command.

✦ Prevent the user from viewing or using the Display, Network, Passwords, Printers, and System icons in the Control Panel.

✦ Restrict the user's use of wallpaper or color schemes.

✦ Disable the Registry Editor.

✦ Disable the MS-DOS prompt.

Most of these settings are to keep users from modifying settings on their own computer. Some of the restricted activities, such as changing the Registry, could be dangerous. Many of the settings you can apply, however, take the user's fun out of working with the computer and with Windows. You probably won't want to apply these restrictions to a home-networked computer.

You can make good use of the System Policy Editor when many users change settings and configurations on their computers continually and then ask you to put their computers back in working order. If you're spending a good deal of your time, for example, restoring settings in the Control Panel, removing applications that never should have been installed, deleting old MS-DOS programs, and so on, you can use the System Policy Editor. You might want to give your users the opportunity to configure their desktop — display, colors, screen saver, and so on — and then apply system policies that keep them from making any more changes.

Changing computer policies

As with user settings, the computer settings fall into two categories: network and system. Under network settings, the following list gives you an idea of some common controls you have in the System Policy Editor:

✦ Control the user's access to files and other resources.

✦ Use asterisks to hide a password as it's being typed in.

✦ Set multiple preferences for NetWare clients — such as setting a preferred server, supporting long filenames, hiding container and printer objects, hiding volumes, and so on.

✦ Disable file and printer sharing for Microsoft networks.

✦ Disable dial-in capabilities in Dial-Up Networking.

Under the system (or computer) settings, following are some of the more common controls:

✦ Enable/disable user profiles.

✦ Disable a Windows update.

✦ Override a local Web page.

Use computer controls when you have files that normal users, such as a secretary or receptionist, should not access. You can prevent these users from accessing files in a workgroup or on a client/server network.

Using the System Policy Editor

Using the System Policy Editor is a huge change in your network. If you have a peer-to-peer network, you must change to the client/server type and install a network operating system. When the network operating system is ready to go, you must install certain programs and services to enable the use of the System Policy Editor.

If you plan to use the System Policy Editor, make sure you have a full backup of all computers on the network plus the server. In addition, back up the Registry files before you make changes. For information about installing and using the System Policy Editor for Windows 98, see the documentation for that operating system.

Understanding Group Policies in Windows 2000 and XP

In Windows 2000 and Windows XP, an administrator uses *group policies* to control network resources and applications for users and computers. Group policies in a workgroup environment apply to the users of a specific computer or those accessing that computer over the network. Group policies in a client/server environment apply to users in the domain and their access to the server and its resources.

You must be an administrator of a computer to manage group policies for that computer. You can control group policies such as security settings, software installation, and administrative templates. Administrative templates govern policies contained in the Registry. For more information about the Registry, see Chapter 24.

 Note   Windows 2000 and XP use Microsoft Management Console (MMC), also called a snap-in, as a framework for administrative tools. If you are not familiar with MMC, see your Windows documentation for more information.

Using Group Policies

To open the Group Policies MMC, you must decide on which computer you want to work. If you want to apply policies to the local computer, you edit the Group Policy object on that computer. If you want to edit the policies on another computer, open the local Group Policy MMC and then browse to the networked computer. If you're working with a domain, a site, or an active directory on a server, see the documentation that came with Windows 2000 Server.

To use the Group Policy Editor, click Start ➪ Run and type **gpedit.msc** in the Open text box. Click OK.

Setting user policies

After you open the Group Policy Editor, you can choose to edit user policies or computer policies. To set user policies, follow these steps after opening the Group Policy MMC:

1. In the left pane, click the plus sign beside User Configuration. A list of settings you can configure appears.

2. Click the plus sign beside each setting to view all of the settings you can change, as shown in Figure 23-1. Notice the network connections setting is highlighted in the figure.

3. To change a setting, double-click the setting in the right pane. A related dialog box appears for you to configure the settings, as shown in Figure 23-2.

4. To close the Group Policy editor, click File ➪ Exit.

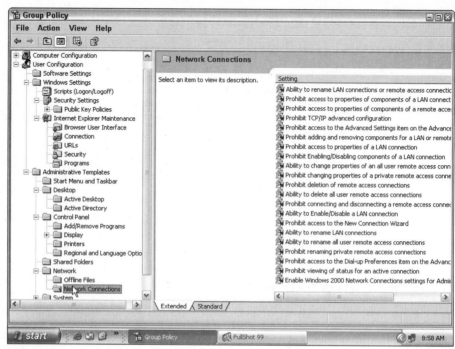

Figure 23-1: View the group policies.

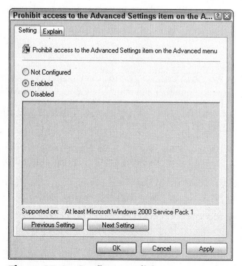

Figure 23-2: Configure policies.

Setting computer policies

In addition to setting user policies, you can also set computer policies in the Group Policy MMC. To set computer policies, follow these steps after opening the Group Policy MMC:

1. In the left pane of the MMC, click the plus signs beside Computer Configuration and all settings in the tree, as shown in Figure 23-3.

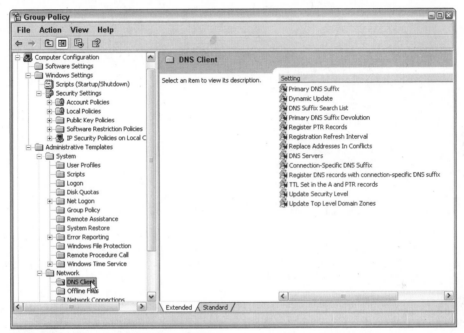

Figure 23-3: Examine computer policies.

2. Select a setting in the left pane to configure.

3. Double-click any setting in the right pane to edit. A dialog box that enables you to change the setting appears, as shown in Figure 23-4.

4. To exit the MMC, click File ➪ Exit.

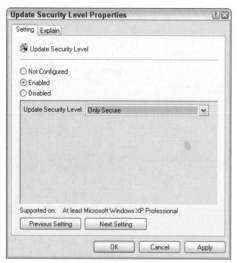

Figure 23-4: Edit computer policies.

Understanding Security Templates

You can use *security templates* in Windows 2000 and XP to create a security policy for your network. Security templates use the same security features as group policies, computer policies, and Registry protection; however, using a security template enables you to organize all policies in one area for easy administration.

Small Business Tip

Most home network users do not need to use security templates for their network. Security templates are more for business networks. You must consider the information on your network and how important it is to keep private. If your network is in healthcare, for example, you have patient's records that must be kept secure because of HIPAA (Health Insurance Portability and Accountability Act) regulations. In this case, security is extremely important. However, if you have a small business that makes signs for clients, the information on your computers is not likely to be as sensitive as other businesses.

After creating a security template, you can import the template to a local computer or to network. You save a template to an INF file, which is text-based. Because it's a text file, you can easily copy, paste, import, and otherwise manipulate the contents of the file.

You use the MMC to edit predefined security templates or to create your own. You need to understand the effects of an imported security template, and you should do extensive testing before applying a template to your entire network. If you want to work with security templates, see your Windows 2000 or Windows XP Professional documentation for more information. This section simply describes the templates and some of the changes you can make.

Understanding default security settings

Windows includes predefined security templates you can use. You can also create new templates; however, if you're just learning to configure security templates, you should stick with Windows' predefined templates to start. Predefined templates include using a highly secure environment, implementing a less secure environment, and securing the system root. One of the predefined templates enables you to reapply default settings.

Windows has default security settings. When you work with a security template, you are changing these default settings. Windows includes three basic levels of security for users: Users, Power Users, and Administrators groups:

✦ The **Users** group does not allow users to modify the operating system settings or use others' data.

✦ **Power Users** enables users to run Windows programs that are not certified (also referred to as legacy applications), which Users cannot do. Power Users may also modify computer settings.

✦ **Administrators** can perform computer maintenance and, therefore, have complete control over the system.

Tip

In a home networking situation, you can most likely let each computer's owner have Administrator status over his or her own computer. Even in a small-business network, many employees can have Administrator status. However, if you have young children at home or inexperienced users at home or work, then you should either create a new group with fewer permissions or keep these users in the Users group.

Using predefined templates

There are several predefined security templates you can use. Some you can use to make your network more secure but still workable; others can be more technical with more complex security features. These templates do not install default settings to a computer; these templates only modify default settings. You cannot use them on computers that do not already have default security settings, such as Windows 98, Me, or an operating system other than Windows 2000 or XP Professional.

Tip

When modifying a predefined template, you should save the modified template under a new name so that you do not permanently change the original template.

✦ The Default security (Setup Security.inf) applies to a specific computer and enables the user file permissions for the root of the drive. You use the default security template in case of a disaster, when installing Windows (Windows applies the default template), or when you want to reapply the security settings to a local computer. Never edit the Setup Security.inf, because it gives you the opportunity to reapply the default settings if need be. Never apply the Setup Security.inf to Group Policies; it could seriously degrade performance throughout the network. Apply the Setup Security.inf only to a local computer.

Tip

Don't use the default security settings to apply as a group policy; you'll lose any specific and individual settings, such as Administrator. Use the default security settings only on an individual computer.

✦ You might want to use the System Root security template (Rootsec.inf). This security template is used in Windows XP Professional only and specifies permissions for the root of the system drive. You can use this template if you need to reapply root directory permissions on a computer. Use this template if your root permissions are accidentally changed. This template does not apply to subdirectories (children) of the root; it applies only to the root drive of a single system.

✦ Another security template you might use is the Compatible (Compatws.inf) template. This template grants permissions to Administrators, Power Users, and Users, by default. You can use this template to improve security of the system by making sure that the appropriate users are members of each group. You can make changes to the templates to increase security with the least impact on applications.

Tip   You might want to relax permissions for users in your home network using the Compatws.inf while increasing security for administrators.

Note   Do not use the Compatws.inf for a domain controller. The Compatws.inf template is too secure for a domain controller but perfect for the administrator's computer or a payroll computer, for example.

IP Security and Public Key Policies

You can include most security attributes in a security template; however, you cannot include IP Security and public key policies.

✦ **IP Security (IPSec)** is a common means of integrity, authentication, and IP encryption through cryptographic security services. It uses encryption to establish the integrity of a datastream. In addition, IPSec ensures that the data is not tampered with during transit and provides confirmation about the datastream origin. IPSec encrypts packets of data that can be routed and switched on any network that supports IP traffic; therefore, the IP packet can travel the local area network, intranet, extranet, or Internet securely and transparently.

In addition, the end workstation and applications do not require any extra security software or other modification. There are federal regulations governing the exporting of IPSec encryption because IPSec is such a strong encryption.

✦ **Public key policies** use certificates to control authentication between domains and trusted domains, and in enterprise networks. You can use public key policy settings in group policies. In public key policy settings, a computer automatically submits certificate requests and installs the issued certificate. A *certificate* is a method of authentication between open networks, such as the Internet. The certificate secures a public key to the corresponding private key. Certificates are digitally signed, thus guaranteeing authenticity and higher security.

You do not need to use public key settings in your home or small-business network. If you do plan to join a larger network, such as a corporate or enterprise network, you might then want to consider the use of IPSec and public key policies.

✦ There are the Secure templates (Secure*.inf). These templates apply a bit less security than the High Security templates. The Secure templates define stronger password, lock-out, and audit settings without adversely affecting the application settings. The secure templates work best in a client/server environment. You must use Windows NT 4 or 2000 and a domain to apply some of these templates to a member machine. You must run LAN Manager in a workgroup using Windows 98 plus install DS Client Pack. For more information, see Windows 2000 or XP documentation.

✦ The High Security templates (Hisec*.inf) use security settings that have high levels of encryption and signing. You use the secure templates with domains in a corporate or enterprise setting. You most likely will not need this high security in your home or small-business network.

Using Security Configuration and Analysis

You can use Security Configuration and Analysis to check your network and system for security flaws. Security Configuration and Analysis is an administrative tool in Windows 2000 and Windows XP. You can use this tool to check your system and to make suggestions for ways to better secure your network.

You use the Security Configuration and Analysis tool to analyze your system and also make changes to templates. If you're going to make changes to templates, however, make sure you understand the consequences to the changes you are about to make by testing thoroughly before implementing those changes.

You open an empty Microsoft Management Console (MMC) in which to use administrative tools. After you create the MMC for Security Configuration and Analysis, you can save it to use again.

1. Open an MMC by clicking Start ➪ Run and typing **MMC** in the Open text box. Click OK. An empty MMC appears (see Figure 23-5).

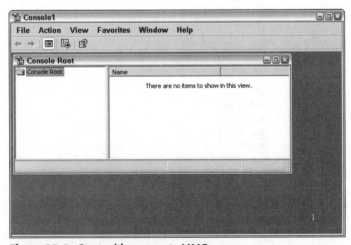

Figure 23-5: Start with an empty MMC.

2. Click File ➪ Add/Remove Snap-in. The Add/Remove Snap-in dialog box appears, as shown in Figure 23-6.

Figure 23-6: Add a snap-in.

3. Click Add. The Add Standalone Snap-in dialog box appears.

4. Locate Security Configuration and Analysis, as shown in Figure 23-7, and click Add.

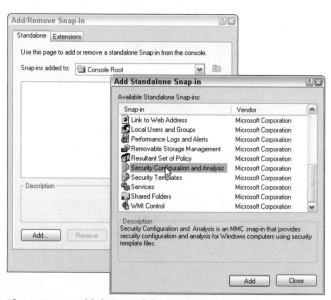

Figure 23-7: Add the Standalone Snap-in.

5. Click Close to close the Add Standalone Snap-in dialog box.

6. Click Security Configuration and Analysis in the Add/Remove Snap-in dialog box and click OK.

7. Click File ➪ Save As. The Save As dialog box appears.

8. Name the console and save it to the Administrative Tools folder. Make sure to retain the .msc extension.

9. Right-click Security Configuration and Analysis in the left pane of the console. Click Open Database.

10. In the Open Database dialog box, type a name, such as **sec2** or **secure2**, in the File Name text box. Click Open. The Import Template dialog box appears.

Note

You don't want to save any database under its original name, so by renaming with a number, such as 2, you effectively create a new database.

11. Click the template you want to import and click Open. You can import multiple databases to test and analyze.

12. To analyze the security configuration, right-click Security Configuration and Analysis and click Analyze Computer Now. The Perform Analysis dialog box appears.

13. Click OK to enable the error log to be saved in the default folder. The Security Configuration and Analysis analyzes your computer.

14. To view the analysis for each entry, click the plus sign in the left pane and view the policy in the right pane, as shown in Figure 23-8.

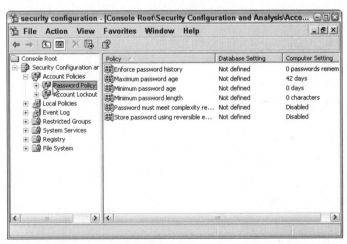

Figure 23-8: Review policies.

15. Save the console by clicking File ➪ Save.

16. To quit the console, click File ➪ Exit.

Note   If you want to edit the policy, you can do that from this console.

Summary

In this chapter, you learned about the setting policies to control users and computers on the network. Specifically, you learned about the following:

✦ Understanding the System Policy Editor

✦ Using the Group Policy Editor

✦ Using security configuration and analysis

In the next chapter, you learn about working with the Registry.

✦   ✦   ✦

Working with the Registry for Windows

The Registry controls your computer settings, the software, the hardware—everything. Be very careful when modifying Registry settings; you could render a device, an application, or your entire computer inoperative. Always make a backup of your Registry before making any changes, and always read editing instructions carefully.

Caution   You should be extremely careful when editing the Registry. Make sure you completely understand the Registry's components and how to edit them before you attempt to change entries. Always make a backup of the Registry before editing it.

Understanding the Registry

The *Registry* is a central database that contains information about the computer, hardware, software, user preferences, and rights. Each time you make a change to a display setting or install an application, for example, the change is recorded in the Registry. You might remember that in Windows 3.11, the initialization (INI) files recorded any changes to the operating system; the Registry takes the place of the INI files in newer versions of Windows.

The Registry presents a more structured environment than the old INI files for the complex makeup of Windows 98, 2000, and XP. Advantages of using the Registry include the following:

✦ All of the information about a user and the computer is stored in one place.

✦ Information about different users and configurations can be stored in the same database.

✦ Old INI files were text-based and therefore limited to a size of 64K; the Registry has no such space limits.

✦ Network-independent functions enable others to view the Registry over the network; for example, administrators can check a user's Registry when troubleshooting.

Changing the Configuration in the Control Panel

The Windows Control Panel offers icons and dialog boxes as a method of changing certain environmental options in the operating system. You can change the computer's date and time, for example, or the colors you use on the desktop.

Following are some of the settings you can change in the Control Panel:

- Desktop themes represent various colors and pictures you can use in Windows. When you choose a theme, an image appears on the desktop instead of a solid background, the desktop icons change to suit the scheme, and dialog box and menu colors change to match the scheme colors.

- Display enables you to set solid colors or wallpaper designs for the desktop; fonts and colors for menus, dialog boxes, title bars, and so on; icon properties; the screen area; and other options.

- Internet Properties offer various preferences you can set, including a home page address, connection options, and multiple choices for running your browser and e-mail program.

- The Keyboard icon enables you to adjust how the keyboard reacts to text entry, and it also defines languages you use in Windows.

- The Network icon enables you to add or remove network clients, adapters, services, and protocols.

When you use the Control Panel to make changes to your computer settings, those changes are recorded in the Registry. The Control Panel creates an easy-to-use interface to the Registry.

The Registry is a complex tool that you can use to change settings that describe how your computer runs. Other methods of changing these settings also exist — through the Control Panel, for example. It's better to modify the Registry by using the Control Panel whenever possible (rather than directly in the Registry), because if you make a mistake or there is an error in the Registry, your computer may stop functioning. The problem is that there are a lot of other configurations and settings besides those in the Control Panel. That's why you might need to use the Registry from time to time.

Always make a backup of the Registry before you make any changes to it. If you make a mistake, you can restore the backup to get you back to where you started. See the section "Backing Up the Registry Files" later in this chapter for more information.

Small Business Tip

Warn your users that changes to the Registry can disable their computers. Also, make sure that you have backups of the Registry files on all computers in your office. Even if you don't keep them updated regularly, an outdated backup is better than none at all. Note that you must back up the Registry files of each computer, because Windows creates the Registry particular to that computer's hardware and user information.

Defining the Registry database

The Registry is organized in keys, which describe specific information about the computer or user. For example, the HKEY_CURRENT_USER contains information describing the user's settings, preferences, favorites, and other data. The HKEY_LOCAL_MACHINE key contains information about the computer's configuration, hardware, software, and so on.

Each key contains subkeys, values, or both. The Registry Editor is a program you can use to view or edit Registry entries. Figure 24-1 illustrates the Registry keys, subkeys, and a value. Note that the keys and subkeys appear in the left window pane; values appear in the right window pane.

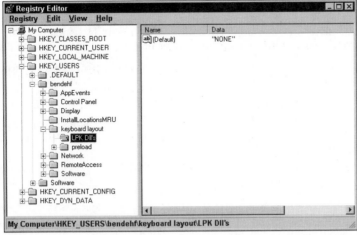

Figure 24-1: Keys and subkeys appear as folders in the Registry Editor.

Keys

Keys represent different types of configuration data. In each key is information that relates to that key. The Windows Registry has six keys; following is a description of each:

- ✦ **HKEY_CLASSES_ROOT** contains general information about Windows, such as the registered file types and their properties, Object Linking and Embedding components, and so on.

- ✦ **HKEY_CURRENT_USER** includes all settings for the default user.

- ✦ **HKEY_LOCAL_MACHINE** contains all information about the computer, such as installed hardware, the software configuration, drivers, and so on. The configurations in this key apply to any and all users logged on to the computer.

- ✦ **HKEY_USERS** contains settings specific to each user who logs on to the computer. These settings include desktop colors, applications installed by individual users, and so on.

- ✦ **HKEY_CURRENT_CONFIG** manages Plug and Play as well as other information about the current configuration of the computer. If multiple users exist, and each has a different computer configuration, those configurations are found in this key.

- ✦ **HKEY_DYN_DATA** (in Windows 98) reports the status of hardware devices in the Device Manager, a tab found in the System icon of the Control Panel.

Subkeys

Subkeys are folders, or subfolders, of keys. Each subkey contains more subkeys, or values. Some subkeys exist under multiple keys, which occurs because Windows stores a subkey under any and all keys to which it relates.

Following are explanations of the subkeys in each key:

✦ HKEY_CLASSES_ROOT

- The subkeys in this key affect file extensions, such as .bmp, .com, .doc, .tif, .gif, and so on. These subkeys define the file type associated with the extensions.

✦ HKEY_CURRENT_USER

- AppEvents deals with the sounds that play when something happens within the system, such as Windows starting up or an error occurring.

- Control Panel contains all the settings in the Control Panel, including network, date, time, and so on.

- Display lists screen resolution and other screen settings.

- InstallLocationsMRU lists the paths recently used for installing software. All these paths begin with A, B, D, or another letter representing a floppy drive, CD-ROM drive, Zip drive, or network path.

- Keyboard layout contains any special information about key assignments and dynamic library links (DLLs).

- Network contains drive definitions, network types, usernames as they appear in a login file, paths, and many of the recently accessed paths to networked computers. This key is discussed in more detail later in this chapter.

- RemoteAccess includes addresses, usernames, and other information related to Internet accounts or other networks to which you have access via phone line or dedicated line.

- Software includes subkey names for the drivers and programs on your computer. Some programs have no settings or defaults, and others have several. Settings might include a path to a network computer, default drivers, or other settings.

✦ HKEY_LOCAL_MACHINE

- Config contains the computer's configurations, including settings for the display and printers.

- Driver includes any special settings for hardware or software drivers.

- Enum manages the information for all installed hardware components, including the monitor, networking hardware, USB ports, and so on.

- Hardware contains settings for all ports on the computer, such as COM, LPT, and USB, if applicable.

- Network contains user login information, including username, password, and so on (if the computer is on a network, of course).

- Security names domains and other network information, if the network is installed.

- Software includes subkeys for all installed software and drivers, such as Office programs, modem drivers, and so on.

- System includes the information necessary for Windows to start up, such as error information, Plug and Play device addressing, the computer's name, and so on.

✦ HKEY_USERS

   • Default contains the common settings for the desktop, Start menu, programs, and so on, and each Username contains the settings specific to that user. Each user listed in this key contains the following subkeys (which are defined the same as those in HKEY_CURRENT_USER): AppEvents, Control Panel, InstallLocationsMRU, Keyboard layout, Network, RemoteAccess, and Software.

✦ HKEY_CURRENT_CONFIG

   • This key contains the following subkeys: Display, Enum, Software, and System (as defined in the HKEY_LOCAL_MACHINE key).

✦ HKEY_DYN_DATA

   • Config Manager manages the information for all installed hardware components, including the modem, ports, Plug and Play adapters, and so on.

   • PerfStats contains information about dial-up adapters.

Values

Values are the statements contained within a key or subkey. Values might name a file, a command, an error message, a path, a machine address, and so on. Figure 24-2 shows font values, stored in the HKEY_CURRENT_CONFIG key, and the Display subkey.

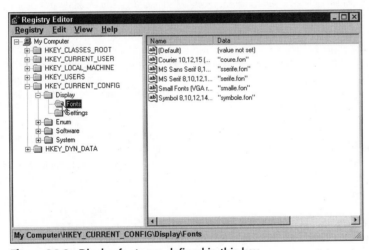

Figure 24-2: Display fonts are defined in this key.

Deciding when to modify the Registry

You should not modify the Registry directly unless it's absolutely necessary. Modifying the Registry could cause computer hardware, software, or even your entire computer to fail if you edit, move, or delete the wrong value.

It's best to modify the Registry automatically through the Control Panel, installation and setup programs, and various Windows utilities. You can change all settings and configurations within Windows without going to the Registry.

You do need to resort to editing the Registry, however, when you see recurring errors or Windows messages for which you cannot find a purpose. You might uninstall an application, for example, but every time you boot the computer, a message appears telling you Windows cannot find a file directly related to that program. Another example might be that you cannot uninstall a program through Windows, so you have to delete related entries in the Registry.

If you must modify the Registry, you should use the Registry Editor; however, save this method of editing the Registry as your last resort. In addition, before you edit the Registry, you must back up your Registry files in case you make a mistake and your computer crashes.

Backing Up the Registry Files

The Windows 98 Registry is completely contained in two files: user.dat and system.dat. Generally, these files are stored in the \Windows directory on the computer's hard disk. Windows 2000 and XP use only the ntuser.dat file to store information about each user who logs on to the computer. The ntuser.dat file is stored in \Documents and Settings in each individual's folder.

The user.dat file contains login names, settings for the Start menu, desktop colors and icons, and other information specific to the user. The user.dat file is automatically stored in the \Windows or the \Documents and Settings directory when you install Windows.

Small Business Tip

If you want to control a user's environment using Windows 98 — say, to keep the user from changing display settings, adding software, and so on — you can store the user.dat file on the server in a client/server network. Include with your permissions or rights a user profile that forces the user.dat file to load whenever the user logs on to the server. This way, each time the user logs on to the server, the default user settings load onto the computer and overwrite any changes the user may have made previously. For more information about user profiles, see the network operating system's documentation. The system.dat file must stay on the local computer; do not transfer it to a server drive.

In Windows 98, the system.dat file contains information about the hardware and software settings on the computer. This file includes all the necessary information to start Windows, load device drivers, and prepare the operating system to run the software. The system.dat file is located in the computer's \Windows directory as well.

In Windows 2000 and XP, many files take the place of the system.dat. You can alter many DAT and INI files through the Registry. These files contain the necessary data needed to start Windows, just as the system.dat file in Windows 98 does.

Backing up the Registry

You can back up the Registry by exporting it in a file to a folder on your computer, to another drive on the network, or to a CD or other backup media. Exporting the Registry takes only a few minutes and should be done each time you make major changes to your computer, such as adding hardware or installing a program. You definitely should back up the Registry files to each computer on your network; restoring the Registry is much faster and easier than losing all your data and then reinstalling Windows and all your applications.

System State Data

In addition to backing up the Registry, you should keep backups of other system files in Windows 2000 and XP. The SYSVOL folder, for example, is a shared folder on a Windows 2000 or 2003 server. The SYSVOL stores the domain's public files. The Active Directory, if you're using Windows server, is another important folder to back up. The Active Directory stores all the information about the network, such as user passwords, profiles, configurations, and so on, plus other pertinent information about the network.

For either Windows 2000 or XP, you should back up the system files. System files are the ones that enable Windows to load and run the operating system. There are other system files you should back up, including the Registry. You can use the Windows Backup program to perform a system state backup. For more information about the Windows Backup program, see Chapter 21.

You use the Registry Editor to back up the Registry, to import a Registry or Registry entry, and to edit the Registry. The Export feature in the Registry Editor, by default, saves the backup file to the My Documents folder. You can, and should, choose to back up the file to another media type, such as a tape, Zip disk, CD, or network drive. To back up the Registry, follow these steps:

1. Open the Registry Editor by clicking Start ⇨ Run. Type **regedit** in the Open text box and click OK.

2. Click File ⇨ Export. The Export Registry File dialog box appears.

3. In the File Name text box, enter a name, such as the date (091203).

4. Optionally, choose a folder in which to store the file.

5. Click Save. Windows returns to the Registry Editor when it is finished backing up the Registry.

Recovering the Registry

If your computer crashes or you find odd things happening to your desktop settings, passwords, or other configurations, you might have a corruption of the Registry. You first should try everything you can think of to fix the problems. Because those same symptoms often indicate a virus or worm, you should check your computer for a bug first. If you've tried everything you can think of and worse comes to worst, you can restore the Registry files and hope that alleviates the problems.

 Caution   Make sure you never replace a Windows Registry with the Registry of a different version of Windows. You could completely incapacitate your computer if you do.

Fixing a problem

Fixing a problem before restoring the Registry might take some detective work. You must decide if the problem is with the hardware, with a specific program, or with the operating system. If the problem is with a specific program, you can try reinstalling the program on top of the original; often, reinstalling corrects a corrupted file, and it usually doesn't harm your data files. Just to be safe, however, make a backup of your data before reinstalling the program.

Small Business Tip
Make sure each of your users knows the importance of writing down error messages before dismissing the dialog box. They also should write down exactly what they were doing when the error occurred. If you have this information to start with, detecting the problem will be much easier.

If you think the problem is with the operating system, check the Control Panel. If, for example, you're having trouble with your desktop settings, check the Display icon. If the trouble seems to be with the mouse, check the Mouse icon. The icons open Properties dialog boxes that contain settings, options, tests, and information about the device and its interaction with the operating system. Try to fix your problems here first.

If you think you have a hardware problem, use the Device Manager in My Computer Properties, or you can use the System icon in Windows 98 (Start ➪ Control Panel). The Device Manager lists hardware devices and notifies you if there is a hardware failure. Figure 24-3 illustrates the Device Manager. Note that you can display the specific device by clicking the plus sign next to the device category. Here, for example, the CD-ROM device is a Mitsumi CD-ROM.

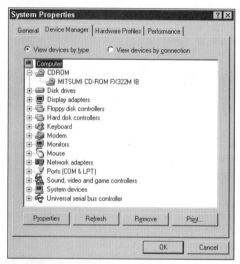

Figure 24-3: Look at your hardware devices in the Device Manager.

If there is a problem with any device listed in the Device Manager, Windows notifies you by displaying a red X or a yellow exclamation point through the device. If you see one of these indicators on a device, select the device and click the Properties button. In the device's Properties dialog box, you see the Device status area, which tells you if there is a problem and what the problem might be. Figure 24-4 shows the CD-ROM Properties dialog box. Note the Device status area.

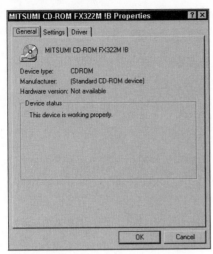

Figure 24-4: Check the status of the device.

For more troubleshooting techniques and ideas, see Appendix A.

Importing a Registry file

Before importing a Registry file, make sure you use the latest copy of your backed up Registry file and that the version of the operating system is correct.

If you exported your Registry files from the Registry Editor, you can recover them easily from that same program. Open the Registry Editor and choose Registry ⇨ Import Registry File. Choose the file you saved, and then click the Open button.

You can alternatively open the Windows Explorer and double-click the file with a .reg extension. Double-clicking the file automatically imports it into the Registry.

You can also export and import hives and keys to the Registry instead of the entire Registry. You might do this to change or reapply certain settings for hardware, software, or user settings.

Copying Programs and Registry Entries

If you need to copy a program from one computer to another, and you cannot locate the installation disks, you can copy the program files, plus Registry entries, to make the program work. This happens when, for instance, you're using an old program, you've lost the original installation disks or they've become damaged, or for some other reason you need to copy the program instead of install it.

1. The first step is to network the two computers together. You can use a crossover cable, a hub or switch, or wireless methods to network the computers.

2. Next, you copy the software program's folder; the folder might be in the root or it might be in the Program Files folder. The third step you take involves the Registry.

3. In the original computer's Registry, use the Edit ⇨ Find command to locate the name of the software you're copying. Alternatively, you can search in HKEY_LOCAL_MACHINE\SOFTWARE or HKEY_CURRENT_USER\SOFTWARE for the program's Registry folder.

4. Select the folder, click File ⇨ Export. Name the file by the program's name, so you can easily recognize it. There might be more than one folder relating to the program. Close the Registry when you're done.

5. Copy the REG files to the second computer. On the second computer, open the Registry Editor. Click File ⇨ Import. Select the REG file(s) and click Open. Windows automatically places the software folder in its rightful place in the Registry.

6. The last step in copying a program is to locate the executable file for the program on the second computer (usually an EXE or application file in the program's folder). You can make a shortcut on the desktop, if you like. Double-click the EXE file. As the program opens, it might ask for certain files it cannot find, most generally DLL files. Search for each file on the first computer, copy it to the location the second computer expects to find the file, and try opening the program again. You might not have to copy any DLL files; you might have to copy several.

When this step is complete, your copied program should work on the second machine.

Modifying the Registry

You can use several tools to modify the Registry. Each offers its own advantages and disadvantages. The Registry Editor is the easiest tool to use. The Registry Editor displays the keys, subkeys, and values in an easy-to-understand hierarchy. Also, the Registry Editor offers shortcuts and tools that help you edit the files.

Starting the Registry Editor

The Registry Editor appears in a window similar to the Windows Explorer. Two panes display the Registry information. In the left pane, you see the keys and subkeys; in the right pane, you see the values.

The file that opens the Registry Editor is the regedit.exe file, and it's located in the \Windows folder. To open the Registry editor, follow these steps:

1. Choose Start ⇨ Run. The Run dialog box appears.

2. In the Open text box, type **regedit**.

3. Click the OK button. The Registry Editor appears.

Figure 24-5 shows the Registry Editor as it appears in Windows 98 when you first start it. Note that the six Registry keys appear in the left pane.

In Windows 2000 and XP, only five keys appear; HKEY_DYN_DATA does not appear in later editions of Windows. In addition, the menu names are different. Instead of Registry, Windows XP uses File. Windows XP also adds Favorites to its menus, as shown in Figure 24-6.

Using Policies to Modify the Registry

As an alternative to using the Registry Editor, you can use the System Policy Editor in Windows 98 or the group policies in Windows and 2000 and XP to modify Registry values. Chapter 23 explains how to use policies to control and manage your users. Any changes you make with the System Policy Editor or group policy also affect the Registry.

The System Policy Editor and group policies present options in well-defined categories and easy-to-understand options, unlike the Registry Editor. Instead of entering cryptic values and searching through confusing keys, you can check boxes that represent options such as Hide Share Passwords with Asterisks, Disable Password Caching, Require Alphanumeric Windows Password, and Minimum Windows Password Length.

Almost all options in the Registry can be set somewhere else within Windows. Password options, for example, are set in the Passwords dialog box, Access Control is set in the Network dialog box, and so on.

Even though the System Policy Editor and Group Policies offer numerous choices and options for controlling the network, the Registry Editor is more adaptable, albeit more difficult to learn and to use.

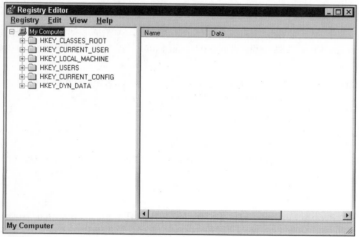

Figure 24-5: Use the Registry Editor to modify values.

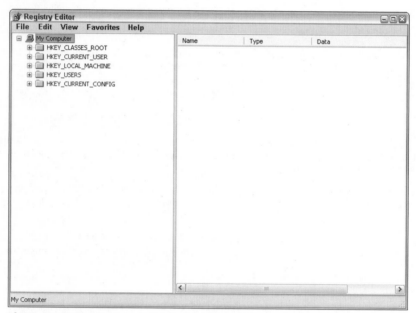

Figure 24-6: The Registry Editor in Windows XP looks similar to the one in Windows 98.

Using the menus

The menus offer commands that enable you to print, find values, import and export the files, and more. Following are descriptions of the menu commands. If you do not completely understand the effects changes to the Registry will make, do some testing on a seldom used computer before making global changes on the network.

Registry or File menu

The Registry (Windows 98) or File (Windows 2000, XP) menu contains the following commands:

Import/Export Registry File   Use these commands to back up and restore the entire Registry or parts of the Registry.

Load Hive (Windows XP and 2000)   Use this command to edit hives or move a hive from one system to another. The *hive* is a section of the Registry saved to a file on your computer.

Connect/Disconnect Network Registry   These commands enable you to edit the Registry of another computer on the network. To set this up, you need to install the Remote Registry service (in the Network dialog box), change your access control to User-level (also in the Network dialog box), be on a client/server network, and have permissions to make the changes over the network.

Print   Use this command to print the values in the right pane.

Exit   This command closes the Registry Editor.

Edit menu

The Edit menu contains the following commands:

Modify (Windows 98)   This command appears only when a value is selected. It enables you to modify the selected value.

New   This command enables you to create a new subkey or value within any Registry key.

Delete   Use this command to erase a value, subkey, or key. Be very careful when deleting keys; you can render your computer useless by deleting things from the Registry.

Rename   This command enables you to change the name of a key, subkey, or value. Be very careful when changing names; you can render your computer useless by changing names.

Copy Key Name   Use this command to create a copy of the key name without copying the subkeys and values.

Find   This command enables you to search for a keyword in the Registry. If you want to view the first appearance of Internet Explorer in any key, for example, you can use the Find command.

Find Next   Use this command to find each subsequent occurrence of the keyword you enter in the Find dialog box.

View menu

The View menu contains the following commands:

Status bar   Using this command shows or hides the Status bar, which contains helpful information, such as the path to a subkey, as shown in Figure 24-7. If you're buried deeply in subkeys, the Status bar can remind you of the key you're working in.

Split   This command enables you to change the dividing line between the window panes. Click the Split option to change the mouse tool into an arrow that can move the division line to the left or the right.

Refresh   This command redraws the screen. Use this command, for example, if you've added a new subkey and it's not showing up in the left window pane.

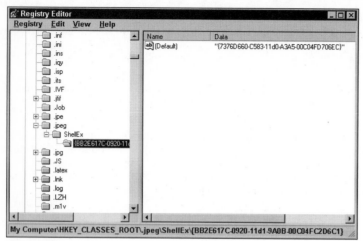

Figure 24-7: Use the Status bar to remind you of your location in the Registry.

Favorites menu

The Favorites menu appears only in Windows 2000 and XP. It contains the following commands:

> **Add to Favorites**   This command enables you to choose a Registry key or value that you often edit and make that value a favorite, for easier location. Favorites list at the end of the Favorite menu in the Registry Editor.

> **Remove Favorite**   Use this command to select and remove any favorite from your Favorites list.

Help menu

The Help menu contains the following commands:

> **Help Topics**   This command offers Content, Index, and Find features similar to other Windows Help.

> **About Registry Editor**   Issuing this command results in displaying the copyright information, the physical memory available, and the percentage of free system resources.

Displaying keys, subkeys, and values

The Registry Editor works similarly to the Windows Explorer. In the left pane are listed the Registry keys and subkeys. In the right pane are listed specific values relating to the keys.

To display a key's subkeys, click the plus sign or double-click the key folder. Subkeys also have plus signs you can click to display their contents. If a subkey doesn't have a plus sign, simply double-click the folder to display its contents.

Tip   The plus sign indicates that the key or subkey contains more subkeys, or folders. A minus sign indicates that all subkeys are displayed.

If you're searching for a specific value, such as a program name, username, address, or other value, you can use the Find command. To use the Find command, follow these steps:

1. In the Registry Editor, move to the top of the window so that you're sure you search the entire Registry.

2. Choose Edit ➪ Find. The Find dialog box appears, as shown in Figure 24-8.

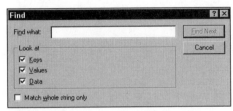

Figure 24-8: Use the Find dialog box.

3. Type the word in the Find What text box, and then click the Find Next button. The Searching the Registry dialog box appears.

4. When a match is found, the Registry opens to the key, subkey, and value matching the entry. Figure 24-9 shows the results of entering **wingate** in the Find What text box of the Find dialog box. Note the path to the key in the Status bar.

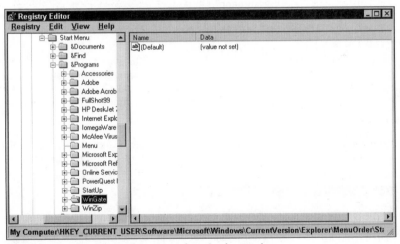

Figure 24-9: Find the program's values in the Registry.

5. To find the next occurrence of the key word in the Registry, press F3, or choose Edit ➪ Find Next.

Working with values

When you display values in the Registry, you see the values in the right pane of the window. The Name column displays the name of the value. The default value appears in every Registry entry. The actual value appears in the Data column.

Names use any of the following characters: a through z, 0 through 9, space, and underscore (_). Values cannot exceed 64K because the Registry limits the size of these files. Also, the total size of each subkey is restricted to 64K. You should use all lowercase characters to locate values.

Values can be text, binary, or DWORD data types:

✦ **Text** types refer to paths, usernames, program names, and so on. Text values are enclosed automatically within quotation marks. An empty text value appears as "". You don't have to enter the quotation marks when typing text data types.

✦ **Binary** data types consist of a sequence of hex bytes. *Hex* stands for hexadecimal, which is the base 16 numbering system. Hex numbering uses the digits 0 to 9, followed by the letters A to F, and is a convenient method of representing binary numbers. Binary represents the base 2 numbering system, using combinations of the digits 0 and 1 to represent all values. Binary numbers are easy for the computer to read. Hex is easier for us to read.

✦ **DWORD** is a data type that is a unique binary value consisting of both hexadecimals and decimals. A sample is 0x11100010 (0); the (0) contains the decimal representation, and the rest of the numbers represent the hex numbers. Basically, you can edit the DWORD data type by entering a value as either a hexadecimal or a decimal number and then indicating which it is. DWORD then enters both numbers, in code form, in the Registry.

After you display a key, subkey, and the value you want to work with, you can edit the value. Editing a text, binary, or DWORD value is different. Following are the instructions for editing a text value. Before you change binary or DWORD values, make sure that you have specific information about the changes and that you understand what the results will be.

Follow these steps to edit or modify a value in the Registry:

1. Double-click the value name, or select the value name and choose Edit ⇨ Modify to modify the value. The Edit String dialog box appears, as shown in Figure 24-10.

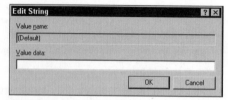

Figure 24-10: Edit a value.

2. If the Value data text box already contains a value, that text is highlighted. You can delete the text and enter your own value, or you can modify the existing data.

Applying a Path in the Registry

Just as an example, this sidebar explains how to edit an application path in the Registry. Application paths are contained in the following Registry key: HKEY_LOCAL_MACHINE\ SOFTWARE\Microsoft\Windows\CurrentVersion\App Paths.

An application is defined in this key as a subkey, such as Cchat.exe or EXCEL.EXE. Within this sub-key are two values: the Default and the Path. The Default value is set to the path and the name of the executable program file. For example, the Default value for Excel is "C:\Program Files\Microsoft Office\Office\EXCEL.EXE".

The Path value contains the path to the folders the application needs to run for the EXE file, for the DLL files, and so on. This value also might contain several paths separated by semicolons; the data path, for example, might be different from the program file path. The Path value for Excel is "C:\Program Files\Microsoft Office\Office" because this is the folder that contains files Excel shares with other Office products.

It is in this key that you would modify a path. You might, for example, choose to modify a path if you installed a second copy of the application in another folder on the computer.

Note   If you enter text data values, do not enter the quotation marks; the Registry automatically enters the quotation marks. If you enter them too, you end up with two sets of quotation marks, which causes an error.

   3. Click OK.

After you make any changes to the Registry, you should close the Registry Editor and then restart Windows.

Using the Registry to Modify Network Settings

Generally, you want to use the Network dialog box to modify settings for any computer. Those settings include protocols, bindings, services, clients, file and printer sharing, and adapter configurations. However, you might discover the need to change network data in the Registry.

The following examples of modifying the Registry might not apply to your network; however, there are many instances when editing the Registry is the only solution to some problems.

Note   Microsoft's online support site lists many networking and other types of problems. In the solutions to these problems, you often find directions to modify the Registry.

You need to install the network protocols, adapter, client, and services before any entries appear in the Registry.

Cross-Reference   For information about configuring the network in the Network dialog box, see Chapter 10. For information about solving network problems, see Appendix A.

Tip   Make Registry backups before you attempt any of the following procedures.

Limiting the use of network properties

You can limit a user's access to the Network dialog box (accessible via the Network icon in the Control Panel) through the Registry. You might want to restrict access, for example, if a teenager is constantly adding and removing protocols or services and thus disrupting his or her right to use the network.

Small Business Tip   Use this restriction in your small-business office if you want to keep your users from making changes to the Network properties.

To restrict access to the Network dialog box, follow these steps:

1. Open the Registry Editor.

2. Open the following key, as shown in Figure 24-11: HKEY_CURRENT_USER\Software\Microsoft\Windows\CurrentVersion\Policies\Network

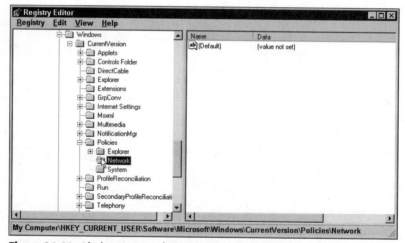

Figure 24-11: Limit access to the Network properties.

3. Double-click the name Default in the left column of the right pane. The Edit String dialog box appears.

4. Type the value **0x00000001** to disable access. If you choose to enable access again, follow Steps 1 to 3 and then enter the value of **0**.

5. Close the Registry to save the setting.

Limiting the use of passwords

If you want to keep your users from changing their passwords, for Windows and for the network, you can make a change to the Registry that accomplishes this goal. Restricting access means the user no longer can open and use the Passwords dialog box located in the Control Panel.

To restrict access to the Passwords dialog box, follow these steps:

1. Open the Registry Editor.

2. Open the following key:
   HKEY_CURRENT_USER\Software\Microsoft\Windows\CurrentVersion\Policies\System

3. Double-click the name Default in the left column of the right pane. The Edit String dialog box appears.

4. Type the value **0x00000001** to disable access. If you choose to enable access again, follow Steps 1 through 3 and then enter the value of **0**.

5. Close the Registry.

Changing Internet properties

As an example of a specific problem and solution for Registry editing, let's take a look at how to modify the Registry to enable you to change your home page address for the Internet Explorer. When you're working in the Internet Explorer, you can change the address to your home page from the default www.microsoft.com to any page on the Internet (or on an intranet) that you want (see Figure 24-12).

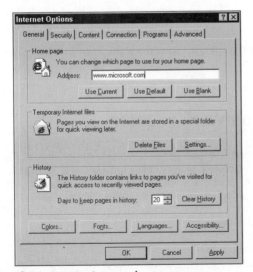

Figure 24-12: Set your home page.

Disabling Balloon Tips

Although this tip has nothing to do with networking and the Registry, it does offer some useful information. You can edit the Registry to rid yourself of those nasty balloon tips that pop up in Windows 2000 and XP.

1. Open the Registry Editor and go to the following key:

   HKEY_CURRENT_USR\Software\Microsoft\Windows\CurrentVersion\Explorer\Advanced

2. Right-click the right pane and create a new DWORD value.

3. Name the value: EnableBalloonTips.

4. Double-click the new entry and give it a hexadecimal value of 0. Exit the Registry Editor.

5. Log off of Windows and then log back on.

This disables all notification area balloon tips for the user. Unfortunately, you cannot disable balloon tips for specific programs using this tip.

If you've customized your version of the Internet Explorer, you might not be able to type in the Address box. Also, the Use Current, Use Default, and Use Blank buttons might be dimmed, so you cannot use them either. You can fix this problem by editing the Registry.

To enable yourself to enter a home page, follow these steps:

1. Open the Registry Editor.

2. Open the following key:

   HKEY_CURRENT_USER\Software\ Policies\Microsoft\Internet Explorer\Control Panel

3. Double-click the name HomePage in the left column of the right pane. The Edit String dialog box appears.

4. Type the value **0** and then close the Registry.

Adding IP addresses to a network adapter

If you're using TCP/IP as your network protocol, you can assign multiple IP addresses to your network card through the Registry. You might add multiple IP addresses to one card if, for example, you're connected to two different network segments (or sections of a network). One segment might use one IP address and another segment might use another. You can use the following settings in Windows 98; the settings are different in Windows 2000 and XP.

Cross-Reference   For more information about TCP/IP, see Appendix B.

To assign a second IP address to your network card, follow these steps:

1. Open the Registry Editor.

2. Open the following key: HKEY_LOCAL_MACHINE\System\CurrentControlSet\ Services\Class\NetTrans\

3. You see at least two subkeys, named 0000 and 0001, as shown in Figure 24-13. Select 0000 if the computer has only one network card.

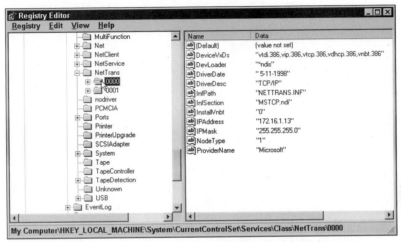

Figure 24-13: Locate the network adapter settings in the Registry.

4. In the IPAddress value, which contains the current IP address, insert a comma and the second IP address. Include no spaces and make sure that all numbers are inside of the quotation marks, such as "176.16.1.13,192.111.101.120". For more information about IP addresses you can use in your network, see Appendix B.

5. In the IPMask, which contains the subnet mask for the network, add the second mask, separated by a comma, with no spaces and within the quotation marks. For more information about assigning subnet masks, see Appendix B.

You can add multiple IP addresses in this manner. Each IP address must have a corresponding subnet mask.

Summary

In this chapter, you've learned about the Windows Registry and how it stores configuration information about your computer and its users. You've learned about the following information:

✦ Understanding the Registry

✦ Backing up the Registry files

✦ Modifying the Registry

✦ Using the Registry to modify network settings

In the next chapter, you learn about multimedia centers.

✦   ✦   ✦

Adding to Your Home Network

Part VII shows you the possibilities for adding to a home network. It explains the current technologies that are available for networking your appliances, lighting, security systems, and so on, as well as what the future holds. In this part, you also find information about multimedia devices to add to your computer and network to increase efficiency.

Understanding Multimedia

Multimedia is a term you hear quite often in relation to computer and software sales. The Internet, television sets, and even home automation designs spout forth acclamations of the great multimedia technologies you can own. Understanding what multimedia encompasses makes it easier to purchase the equipment you need.

Understanding Multimedia

Multimedia is extremely popular with more advanced sound, video, and DVD technologies on the market. In the not-too-distant past, all you needed to make a "multimedia" computer was a sound card and a CD-ROM drive. Today, the marketplace is overflowing with multimedia hardware and software.

The term *multimedia* includes any applications with sound and video enhancements. Some applications that take advantage of multimedia features include movies, music programs, educational software, and games. In order to use and enjoy DVDs, video animations, movies, and other multimedia, you need special cards and adapters in your computer.

A multimedia network is one that shares text, print, graphics, audio, digital, and full-motion data over a high-speed connection. In the home, you can create a multimedia network and share family photos, create your own music CDs, make videos of family and friends, make DVDs — and share them on the network. And your kids can play multimedia network games, both on the network and online.

Multimedia applications use video and audio features. Because of these elements, time relationships can be a problem when the audio or video gets out of synchronization. Multimedia data must adhere strictly to the boundaries on delay and delay variation. The elements of the video sequence must be delivered across the network in strict order to avoid jerkiness and flicker, and delivery must be constant. Video streams require large bandwidth that can be sustained for a length of time.

It's important to remember that whether you're using multimedia on a standalone computer or over a network, you need computers with enough power to supply the needs of multimedia applications. Multimedia often requires that computers use special hardware as well. In addition, multimedia causes your network traffic to increase and bandwidth to diminish. Depending on how much you do with multimedia, you might need to use faster computers, a faster network, and a faster Internet connection.

Looking at Multimedia Hardware

Multimedia applications demand a powerful and stable computer. You need a computer with enough processor power and RAM, as well as a fast CD or DVD drive, to make any multimedia application work efficiently. Thus, you cannot simply add RAM to a computer with a slow processor and expect it to perform well with your multimedia applications.

Following is a list of minimum requirements for using multimedia applications; naturally, you must check the device's or application's requirements to make sure that you have everything you need. For example, some programs may require a special sound card, a joystick, or other equipment.

Considering processors

You want to use a fast processor for your multimedia computer. Many types and many manufacturers of processors exist, including Intel and AMD.

The Intel Pentium III is a fast and efficient processor. Any Pentium III processor provides sufficient speed for most computer work and might work for some multimedia applications. However, multimedia requires more and more from your computer with each new game or program. You'll need at least a Pentium 4 for the most satisfying multimedia experience.

A Pentium 4 is designed for digital imaging, video, digital music, 3D gaming, and so on. Look for at least a 3.20 GHz processor. Many also add an advanced system bus to the processor, which gives you a boost in hyper-threading technology. This technology enables the processor to execute two threads in parallel, which simply means that the software runs more efficiently.

If you purchase a Pentium 4 processor with 3.06 GHz, you'll most likely get the 533 MHz system bus; if you go to a Pentium 4 3.20 GHz, you can get the 800 MHz system bus. The 800 MHz system bus is also available with lesser processors, such as the 2.40 GHz, 2.80 GHz, and so on. Any of these processors will work well for multimedia, considering, of course, the requirements of your hardware and software.

AMD's Athlon MP processors are designed for digital professionals. The features boost performance, and the processor works for end-to-end digital production and multimedia support. In addition, the AMD Opteron processor is designed to run 32-bit applications as well as transition to 64-bit technology. Generally, Opterons are targeted more to server/workstation multimedia; however, depending on what you're doing with your network and with multimedia, you might want to check an Opteron (www.amd.com).

Examining RAM and cache

RAM and cache are two types of temporary memory in your computer. Both significantly affect the way your computer runs multimedia applications. *Random access memory* (RAM) is the memory that applications, the operating system, and data use to keep information where it can easily be reached by the processor. RAM is faster to read and write than other kinds of storage; however, information stored in RAM stays there only as long as the computer is on. When you turn off the computer, RAM loses its data. *Cache* is another place for temporary storage. Naturally, the more RAM and cache a computer has, the faster it can process information, applications, games, and so on.

RAM

Most operating systems require at least 64MB and preferably 128MB RAM to operate efficiently. If you're running multimedia programs, or any processor-intense program (such as an accounting program), you should not settle for less than 256MB RAM. Check the requirements of the program to see if 512MB of RAM is suggested. If it is, the program will run more quickly and efficiently with more RAM.

Pay attention to the type of memory used in your computer. Synchronous Dynamic Random Access Memory (SDRAM) is the most common memory type. SDRAM supports burst access modes. *Burst access mode* is a method of transmitting data in which the data is collected first and then sent in one high-speed transmission instead of one character at a time. This process makes SDRAM faster than the other memory types.

In addition, Double Data Rate-SDRAM (DDR-SDRAM) is synchronous dynamic RAM. Theoretically, DDR-SDRAM improves memory clock speed by potentially doubling it.

Cache

Another component that affects the speed of the computer is the cache (pronounced "cash"). Cache is a special area of memory your computer uses on top of RAM. Cache helps boost the performance of the computer by making information even more available than that stored in RAM.

Similar to RAM, the cache remembers frequently accessed information — such as the latest command — and temporarily stores it. When you enter that command again, for example, the processor first goes to the cache. If the command is there, the processor can work more quickly than if it had to go to RAM or to the hard disk. Cache enhances the memory and performance of your computer.

There are two levels of cache in a computer, called, logically enough, level 1 (L1) and level 2 (L2) caches. Levels describe closeness and accessibility to the microprocessor. *L1 cache*, also known as internal cache, is a small amount of fast memory located on the same chip as the microprocessor. The *L2 cache* is a separate static RAM chip linked directly to the processor to make it react more quickly to processor requests.

Cache speeds vary depending on the processor speed. Generally, the speed of the L1 cache is the same as the processor speed; the speed of the L2 cache is half the processor speed. When the computer searches the cache, it goes first to L1, then to L2, and then to RAM. A computer with two levels of caching offers faster processing than a computer offering only one caching level.

Considering drives

You need a hard drive, floppy drive, and CD or DVD drive in your computer for multimedia applications. The floppy drive is often necessary for startup disks, some software, and file storage. The hard drive is important for storing large multimedia files, program files, and others. And the CD or DVD drive is most important because so many multimedia programs and so much multimedia content come on CD-ROM or DVD.

Tip   You might also want a CD-RW or DVD-RW or CD/DVD burner, to back up files such as pictures, videos, music, and so on.

✦ A CD-ROM drive should support — at the very least — a speed of 32×, and higher is better. Digital Versatile Disk (DVD-ROM) drives are just like CD-ROM drives except they have a higher capacity. A CD-ROM holds 640MB of data; a DVD-ROM holds 4.7GB of data. Therefore, DVD-ROMs are more expensive than CD-ROM drives. DVD-ROM drives can read a CD-ROM; however, a CD-ROM drive cannot read a DVD-ROM. If you want to run games or educational titles from a drive, then you should get a DVD drive.

Tip   Since a DVD drive can read CDs as well as DVDs, you should go ahead and pay the extra money for a DVD drive, especially if you want to use games on your computer.

✦ Make sure that your hard drive is an adequate size for storing huge multimedia files. Multimedia files — including sound, moving pictures, animations, and so on — can be 150MB or 350MB in size. At the least, your hard drive should have 20GB of space. If you can get a larger drive — 80 or 120GB — you'll be better off.

✦ The floppy drive is pretty standard in most PCs. A 1.44MB high-density floppy drive is all you need.

Exploring expansion slots

You also need a computer with the appropriate expansion slots for adding video and sound cards. When you purchase a multimedia application, make sure your computer has the slot and the cards necessary to run that application. Following are the common slots used in multimedia computers:

✦ **Peripheral Component Interface (PCI)** is the preferred bus slot for Pentium-class processors. PCI's 64-bit data bus increases the amount of data that can be transferred at one time. PCI uses all active paths to transmit data.

When using PCI devices, the first card you plug into your computer must be a PCI controller card. PCI is self-configuring, like Plug and Play, meaning the operating system usually recognizes PCI devices. In addition, you can attach up to 10 devices to a PCI bus.

PCI specifications define two card lengths: a full-size PCI is 312 millimeters long, and short PCIs range from 119 to 167 millimeters. Check your slots to see which you have before purchasing your card.

✦ **Accelerated Graphics Port (AGP)** is a technology built specifically for the demands of 3D graphical software. Many newer games and educational software, for example, use much more in the way of 3D graphics than previous programs; 3D graphics make the program appear more realistic — photos, scenery, and other images look more real. AGP also works for 2D software — like business, accounting, drawing programs, and so on.

AGP provide quick and smooth transfer of 3D images for gaming, three-dimensional video, and even sophisticated scientific/engineering graphics programs, such as AutoCad. An AGP card uses the computer's RAM to refresh the monitor image and to support the blending required for 3D image display. AGP offers high-speed data transfer, optimizes the use of memory, and minimizes the amount of memory necessary. AGP runs many times the bus speed of PCI cards.

AGP takes graphics off the PCI buses and gives them a bus all their own. AGP has some minimum requirements, such as SDRAM support and specific operating systems (Windows, in particular), and it works only with certain brands of adapter cards. Your computer must have an AGP slot or AGP graphics integrated on the motherboard, which is becoming more common all the time.

Windows Support for Multimedia

Windows supplies a wide variety of support for multimedia hardware. You can use DVD players, joysticks, digital audio speakers, and more with your multimedia applications and games. Following are some of the multimedia support features included with Windows:

✦ DVD-ROM and DVD-RAM devices, as well as DVD software and music CDs

✦ AGP for 3D support

✦ USB for adding serial devices to the computer

✦ WebTV support, including enhanced television, video playback, and support for hardware

✦ DirectX, a utility that supplies better 3D graphics and video playback than before Microsoft added DirectX

✦ **FireWire** is Apple's version of a high-performance serial bus, developed to make use of audio and video applications more effectively. FireWire is extremely fast; the data transfer rates are up to 400 Mbps. Use FireWire if you want to use your PC mainly for games; its power would be wasted for general or common use, such as word processing. You can connect up to 63 devices in a chain to a FireWire bus.

Scanning ports

Many peripheral devices attach to either a serial or parallel port. For speed, however, you might want to consider a universal serial bus (USB) port. A USB is a Plug and Play interface between a computer and add-on devices, such as audio players, joysticks, keyboards, scanners, printers, and so on. USB ports connect high-speed peripheral devices.

The USB port has an industry-standard connector that enables you to install a variety of devices; and because of the design of USB, you don't have to turn the computer off when installing new devices, as you would with other ports, and you don't need an additional adapter card. If you connect a modem to a port on your computer, for example, you have to turn the computer off and then on again so that the operating system can see you've added hardware. With USB, you don't have to turn it off.

Nearly all new computers come with six to eight USB ports now, and you can add more when you configure it. There are also USB hubs you can buy to extend the use of your USB devices. USB supports data speed rates of 12 Mbps, which accommodates MPEG video devices, data gloves, digitizers, and plug-in telephones.

Small Computer System Interface (SCSI) is another bus that enables PCs to communicate with peripherals, such as disk drives, CD and DVD drives, printers, scanners, and so on. SCSI (pronounced "skuzzy") allows for faster data transfer and more flexibility than previous interfaces. The latest SCSI is the Ultra-2, which is a 16-bit bus that can transfer data at up to 80 Mbps. SCSI also allow up to 15 devices to be connected to a single SCSI port. So rather than having a separate card for each device, a single host adapter can serve as an interface freeing up parallel and serial ports for other purposes.

Exploring monitors

The monitor you choose should display a good-quality image and match your video card for the best performance. See the section "Buying a video card" later in this chapter. You can buy a traditional monitor or a flat-panel LCD display if you prefer. Both are excellent displays; the cost is the separating factor.

Super Video Graphics Array (SVGA) is the most common screen specification today and can support a palette of up to 16 million colors. However, depending on the amount of video memory, some computers might display fewer of the colors. Also, the larger the diagonal screen measurement of an SVGA monitor, the more pixels it can display horizontally and vertically.

New specifications have improved upon higher resolutions as well as increased colors. Super Extended Graphics Array (SXGA) and Ultra Extended Graphics Array (UXGA) reference screens with 1,280×1,024 and 1,600×1,200 resolutions, respectively.

Use a 17-inch or larger monitor for multimedia, especially games. On a smaller monitor, it is too difficult to see the multimedia details and animations. If you do get a large monitor — say, a 17- or 21-inch — you should purchase a high-quality video card to match the image quality of the large screen display. Image quality is influenced by the connection between the monitor and the video card. A high-quality video card results in better image quality on screen.

Every object and character on the screen is made up of dots. The distance between the centers of the dots is called *dot pitch*. Dot pitch ranges from .25 to .52 mm. Look for a monitor with .26 mm dot pitch. Anything larger than .28 mm will look fuzzy or grainy.

Refresh rate describes how many times per second the image is refreshed, or redrawn, on the screen. The faster the refresh rate, the less flicker you see on-screen. The default refresh setting for most monitors is 60 Hz, but you should use 75 to 85 Hz to reduce flicker and eye strain. In addition to the monitor refresh rate, the video card must support that refresh rate. Make sure that the monitor and video card match, or you will see plenty of screen flicker.

Look for a monitor that is *noninterlaced*. Interlacing refers to how a monitor refreshes, or redraws, the screen. Interlacing monitors skip every other line during the redraw process, thus producing a flicker or jitter on the screen. Noninterlaced monitors scan every line and thus provide the best screen quality.

Considering CD drives

The CD drive might be the most important part of your multimedia computer. You use the CD drive to install applications; run applications; and record sounds, videos, and other multimedia.

Check access time on the CD drive. Access time describes how fast the drive can move data around. At the very least, a multimedia CD drive should be 48×; 52× is even better.

You can get a variety of CD drives, including drives with which you can record CDs as well as play CDs. You can create your own multimedia sounds, music, videos, and so on, and record them on your own CD.

Note   *Streaming* is a method for delivering video and audio data to your computer in a continuous flow. Streaming enables you to start viewing content as it's being downloaded or transmitted.

Networking CDs and Multimedia

You know you can share CD drives over the network for installing programs and so on. With multimedia, you might run into some speed problems. Even 48× CD drives depend on the computer's processor, hard disk speed, and graphics card to get the data from the CD to the computer screen. If your CD drive seems too slow to transfer multimedia files, other options are available.

For one thing, you can copy the CD to the server's hard disk, and then move data over the network. If you don't have a client/server network, you can copy the CD to your most powerful workstation. The computer reads the material more quickly from a hard drive than from a CD drive.

From the hard disk, the network routes the information before it's displayed on the user's screen. With multiple users accessing the data, the server has to be fast to display multimedia files correctly.

After info is transferred to the server, the problem becomes the type and quantity of data that the program contains. Networks are designed with data integrity as top priority; the server sends the requested data from the server through the network in small packets. When the correct packet arrives at the requesting computer, that computer sends back an OK to the server, and then the server sends the next packet.

The timing of sending the packets and receiving the packets isn't too important, as long as it all gets there eventually. The packets may not arrive at the destination in the order in which they were sent.

Multimedia applications with sound and video are time-sensitive. They require that a large amount of data be sent—in order. Data that's not sent in order briefly freezes the picture or produces sounds that aren't high quality. Too many pauses in the data or too many packets out of sequence can cause errors on the network and halt transmissions.

Multimedia files require huge amounts of bandwidth (wide pathways on which to travel)—but only periodically. In between bursts of multimedia, other networking processes take place, which can interrupt the flow of multimedia data. Each time the program requests more video or audio information from the multimedia program, it has to wait in line for other requests to be processed first. What you need to display multimedia data on a network is an unbroken stream of data from the server with a large bandwidth.

CD-ROM, CD-RW, and CD-R drives

Compact disc–read-only memory (CD-ROM) drives aren't used for storage of your files; rather, you use CD-ROMs for accessing music, program files, encyclopedias, games, and other files that you can use on your computer. Most software is distributed on CD-ROMs, so if you plan to install any software at all, you need a CD-ROM drive. You can buy external CD-ROM drives, as well; however, if you plan to buy an external CD drive, look into an external CD-RW. Prices are very inexpensive and the benefits are endless.

Compact disc–rewritable (CD-RW) or compact disc–recordable (CD-R) drives can record information onto a CD as well as read information. CD-RW drives can overwrite data on a CD so that you can use the CD over and over again. You must purchase special CD-RW discs for recording over, however; CD-RW discs are more expensive than CD-R discs — about twice as much. A CD-R drive can record to a particular CD only one time, because CD-R discs are made to record material only once.

Most CD-RW drives can use both media types. Discs created with a CD-R usually can be read by older CD-ROM drives, but CD-RW discs can be read only with newer MultiRead drives. Additionally, most CD-RWs can record in CD-R mode. In short, get the CD-RW drive. The added cost is usually minimal. Most CD-RW and CD-R drives can write at 24× speeds. Write speed doesn't affect playback; it just takes longer to record.

DVD drives

Digital versatile disk–read only memory (DVD-ROM) drives are just like CD-ROM drives, but they have a higher storage capacity. A CD-ROM holds 640MB of data; a DVD-ROM holds 4.7GB of data. DVD-ROM drives are more expensive than CD-ROM drives. DVD-ROM drives can read a CD-ROM; however, a CD-ROM drive cannot read a DVD-ROM.

In addition to DVD-ROM, DVD-RAM and DVD-R drives are available, which can read and write to the disc. DVD-RAM offers faster access and read/write times than CD-RW. DVD-R drives record to a DVD disc only one time, and the disc holds only 4.7GB of data. You can write to a DVD-RAM disc over and over; DVD-RAM discs hold 4.7 GB of data as well.

DVD-ROM drives can cost as little as $140; the cost for DVD-RAM drives ranges from $300 to $1,000 to even more for professional features. Manufacturers include Panasonic, Samsung, and Compaq, among others.

Buying a video card

You want to pay attention to your computer's video card, especially if you're interested in playing complex games, using encyclopedias, or running other sound- and graphics-intense applications. Many multimedia programs require more expensive and involved video cards than typical software does. Multimedia programs are any that take advantage of color, 3D graphics, music, and other sounds.

Common features

A common video card is fine, for example, when viewing your word processor documents or surfing the Internet. When you want to use multimedia applications, however, you need hardware that accommodates the special requirements of the software.

One feature you want to look for in graphics and video cards is *fast screen redraw*. Moving pictures, games, animations, and other multimedia applications feed information to the monitor very quickly. In order for the display to be smooth and without pauses, fast screen redraw is a necessity.

You also want smooth, full-screen video when playing any moving animations or pictures. A dedicated Moving Pictures Experts Group (MPEG) adapter card can supply this effect, as can DirectX and other technologies. The MPEG standard is for digital video and audio compression. MPEG cards support minimum communications, color, and sound standards.

 Note   DirectX is Microsoft's technology for offering enhanced video and graphics to Windows applications. DirectX makes an application, such as a game, accessible to a wide variety of hardware features. Some hardware may not be fully compatible with DirectX.

A computer with 3D video and graphics provides a more realistic look to your multimedia applications, and 3D accelerator graphics cards accelerate the display for better quality and speed. Also, 3D cards add functions such as texture enhancement, which makes the objects' surfaces look more real. The result of using 3D cards is a more realistic picture.

Finally, your graphics card needs to make multiplayer interaction over a network—LAN or Internet—fast, efficient, and realistic. The cards, therefore, must be able to integrate different mode connections and hardware technologies.

Requirements

You also should consider the video bus and video memory when looking at video cards. Bus, of course, refers to the type of slot the card fits into. Memory refers to video RAM, or the memory built into the card. Memory determines how fast the graphics appear on the screen.

As a minimum, 64MB of DDR (Double Data Rate) memory provides enough memory to play games, create drawings, and work with photographs, videos, and so on. For the best performance with new and intense games or with educational software such as encyclopedias, however, you should get 128MB of DDR memory.

Note

If you're playing specific games or have multimedia programs in mind, make sure that the video card is certified for those games, especially if the card is for 3D video. Otherwise, the program may not run or will cause problems with your computer. Check the program's documentation.

Also, check the following when buying a video card for multimedia applications:

✦ Check the video processor on the video card. The video card's processor handles incoming video-related data, just as the computer's processor handles digital data. You can alternatively purchase a video processor to use with your TV, PC, or multimedia entertainment center. A good video processor provides you with multiple video connections for your DVD player, digital camera, VCR, HDTV, or for a game console such as the PS2, GameCube, or Xbox.

✦ Check the RAM digital-to-analog converter (RAMDAC) for the video card. The RAMDAC is the electronic component that changes the digital video signal of the card to a signal the monitor can read. RAMDAC speed affects the speed of images appearing on the screen. The standard RAMDAC is 350 MHz, although some cards are faster. The faster the RAMDAC, the better.

✦ The speed at which normal programs use the video card is 2D. A speed of 3D, however, is important for games and other multimedia programs. Most cards combine 2D and 3D features, but make sure the one you purchase does too.

Buying a sound card

Like video cards, sound cards usually are targeted to games, encyclopedias, and other multimedia programs. The sound card plays the music and other sounds that some programs include. An encyclopedia, for example, might include the sound of a steam engine with a description of trains or a portion of a Bach concerto with Bach's biography. The sound card determines how good the sound quality is.

Types of sound cards

Sound cards generally are separated into two types: *FM synthesis* and *wavetable*. The difference between the two is how they synthesize music. Music files are usually small — the sounds of instruments playing the music aren't usually included in the files. The sound card must synthesize, or produce, the sounds of the instruments instead. Following are descriptions of each card type:

✦ **FM synthesis cards** generate the instruments, such as horns, piano, drums, and so on. The method used to generate the instruments sometimes produces sounds that are close to the instrument — and sometimes produces sounds that are nothing like the real instrument. This variation in quality depends on the manufacturer and the card quality.

✦ **Wavetable sound cards**, on the other hand, generate music by using actual instrument samples, so the instruments sound more real. If the card doesn't have the instrument needed, it uses the instrument that's closest in sound. Wavetable sound cards might cost a bit more, but they produce a better, more realistic sound.

Suggesting sound cards and speakers

Following are some things to keep in mind when you're buying a multimedia sound card:

✦ If you want to play graphic-intense games, you need to make sure you use speakers with a deep bass and high wattage to increase the excitement of the game. You also need to get a sound card that can handle that. Use a two-piece speaker system, which consists of two speakers plus a bass-rich subwoofer. Make sure the PCI sound card comes with a wavetable synthesizer and 3D sound.

✦ If you plan to watch DVD movies or listen to digital music, consider high-end, high-wattage multiple speakers with 3D sound. Again, make sure the PCI card has a wavetable synthesizer and 3D sound.

✦ To create professional sound files or music files, consider a high-end, high-wattage multiple speakers with 3D sound. Make sure the PCI card has a wavetable synthesizer and generates 64 or more voices.

Tip   When you get your new computer home and attach to the Internet, dial up the home page for your sound card manufacturer. Check to see if the manufacturer has an updated sound card driver you can download. The driver you get with a new computer is never the most up-to-date one, and a newer driver will always work better with multimedia programs.

Investigating speakers

If you have a sound card, you need speakers. You can buy cheap speakers that offer no sound quality, or very expensive speakers that rival your stereo speakers.

Following are some guidelines for buying speakers:

✦ Make sure that your speaker includes a subwoofer. A subwoofer enhances the sound, especially for games, educational software, and Internet uses.

✦ The speaker should have manual volume and balance controls in addition to software controls.

✦ Twenty watts is adequate power for most speaker usage, if the speakers are good quality.

Tips for Buying Sound Cards and Speakers

Whenever you purchase a sound card for multimedia, make sure you take advice from the game's or program's manufacturer. Requirements are not merely a suggestion; they tell you what is required for the game or other program to work well. For example, if the manufacturer requires Sound Blaster compatibility, make sure you purchase a fully Sound Blaster-compatible card.

Before you purchase a sound card, make sure your computer supports the sound card's software for audio CD-player programs, games, editing audio files, and so on.

64-voice cards reproduce the sounds of instruments and voices with great richness and realism. If you're using multimedia for gaming or music, you'll appreciate the higher number of simultaneous voices beneficial.

Use PCI cards instead of Industry Standard Architecture (ISA) cards. PCIs are faster and allow for wider streams of audio on your PC.

Use a wavetable synthesizer instead of an FM synthesis card for more realism and a better gaming or multimedia experience.

Before purchasing speakers, consider these tips:

✦ 3D sound technology is particularly impressive with three- or four-piece speaker sets.

✦ If you use a notebook, make sure your speakers operate with batteries, since there might not be outlets within reach when you're using your notebook.

✦ Headphones are an inexpensive option to speakers while still giving you a rich, realistic sound.

✦ If you can't get a subwoofer system, you can get speakers with bass boost to give you good sounds in music and games.

✦ If you already own a pair of speakers, getting a separate subwoofer will improve the range, depth, and realism of sounds for music and games.

 Note   Multimedia Personal Computer (MPC) is a specification for multimedia hardware — speakers, sound cards, video cards, CD drives, and so on — that ensures the hardware is compatible, reliable, and meets certain quality standards. MPC Level 3 is the latest version; however, realize that these latest standards were published in 1996. If any multimedia equipment states it's MPC-3–compliant, that's good.

Looking at network upgrades for multimedia

Multimedia applications can work on either a workgroup network or a client/server network. You can install the multimedia applications on a workstation or a server, although you should pick one of the most powerful computers you have on your network to run any applications, to connect to the Internet, and on which to store files.

Making upgrades to your network depends on the technology you already have. Before you do anything, test your multimedia computers on your current network to see if the speed is acceptable.

Tip You can share a fast CD-ROM drive, but it will run more slowly over the network.

If you don't use the network a lot for multimedia, or if the speed works well with your applications, you don't have to upgrade. If, on the other hand, you find some multimedia applications that don't work, you can speed up the network by changing technologies.

A phone line network, for example, running at 1 Mbps, will be too slow to show movies or to play some games over the network. Upgrading that network to Ethernet can make all the difference. Of course, you need to upgrade your network cards to 10/100 Mbps Ethernet, buy a 100 Mbps hub, and install CAT 5 UTP cabling. That can run into some money, but you'll see improvement in the speed, reliability, and efficiency of your entire network.

Tip You might also consider upgrading to wireless, but make sure you check game and application software in case there are limitations that include wireless.

Cross-Reference See Chapter 6 for more information about Ethernet technology and Chapter 7 for more information about wireless networking.

If you are currently using a 10 Mbps Ethernet network, you might want to upgrade to 100 Mbps (Fast Ethernet) for superior speed in multimedia applications, as well as in other facets of network performance. You should be using 10/100 Mbps Ethernet network cards and CAT 5 UTP cabling already, so all you need to purchase is a 100 Mbps hub to make the network complete. If you're not using 10/100 Mbps cards, buy those first and use them with the 10 Mbps hub until your budget enables you to buy the faster hub.

You also might consider replacing your NetBEUI or IPX/SPX protocol with the more efficient TCP/IP protocol. If you're using Ethernet or Fast Ethernet, TCP/IP can display a marked improvement over the others. See Appendix B for more information.

Troubleshooting Multimedia Devices

Anytime you add a new device or change an old device, such as a video card or sound card, you can cause your computer to stop working. Each device has its own settings; if you add another device that tries to take those settings, you have a *hardware conflict*. Hardware conflicts are more noticeable in Windows 98 computers than in Windows 2000 or XP computers because newer systems deal with conflicts automatically. You might, however, find a problem in any Windows, Mac, or Linux computer that deals with interrupt request (IRQ), direct memory access (DMA), or input/output (I/O) addresses.

Hardware lines carry a device's signal to the processor. When a device wants to communicate with the processor, it causes an *interrupt request* to gain the processor's attention. The *I/O* is the means by which data is transferred between the computer and its peripheral devices. *DMA* is a method of transferring information directly from a hard disk, for example, into memory by bypassing the processor.

Most PCs have 15 IRQs; some are assigned to specific devices, and others are free for cards and devices you install. Each computer is different, so the device might not have the same IRQ in one computer as it does in another. In addition, not all devices require an IRQ, IRQs cannot be shared by multiple devices, and the most common IRQ conflicts are between two COM ports.

I/O addresses refer to locations in a computer's memory map. Addresses are in hexadecimal format, which is a base 16 numbering system that uses the digits 0 through 9 followed by the letters A through F. Hexadecimal numbers represent the binary numbers computers use internally (they all fit into the 8-bit byte).

Direct memory access (DMA) channels might be an area for hardware conflicts. Plug and Play systems use DMAs. In Windows, you can make Plug and Play resource assignments under the specific device's Resource tab within the Device Manager (click Start ➪ Programs ➪ Control Panel, and then double-click System. Select the Device Manager and locate the hardware in question. View its properties. You can change setting for IRQs, I/Os, or DMAs, but make sure you understand the consequences of your actions and always write down the original addresses to change back to if necessary.

Considering Digital Cameras and Scanners

Although both scanners and digital cameras have been around a while, they've become the hottest new technological playthings for home users. With a scanner, you can convert any image from paper to a digital file that you can use in your computer. With a camera, you can capture images of your home, your family and friends, vacations, pets, and more.

Both of these tools are affordable and easy enough for any member of your family to use, and they provide exciting alternatives to images you get from other sources.

Examining digital cameras

Digital cameras are perfect for taking photographs that you can transfer easily to your computer and to your publications. The photos you take with the digital camera are similar to those you take with other cameras. The pictures are in color, but you can transfer them to black and white with the help of a photo manipulation program.

Digital cameras don't use film. When you take pictures with a digital camera, the image is stored on a memory card instead of on film. You can view and delete images on the memory card while it's still in the camera, and you can reuse the card time and again. The removable image card stores images and maintains those images until you delete the data or reformat the card. You also can purchase additional memory cards to use in your camera.

After you take the pictures, you transfer the images to the computer by using a serial port, a USB port, a card reader, or FireWire. Using a serial port is the least effective method, because it is so slow. Using a USB port is faster, but using a card reader is by far the most efficient method.

Your computer sees the card reader as another drive, as it would see a floppy disk, CD-ROM, or Zip drive. You simply open the drive and transfer the pictures you want. You remove the card from the camera and insert it into the card reader. The card reader is very small, about the size of a pack of poker cards, with two cables plugged into either side of the reader.

Card readers are available in both internal and external models. The cost ranges from $50 to $150. Manufacturers include Kodak, Actiontec, and Litronic.

Many cameras are on the market. You should look for a few key features when buying a digital camera. A zoom lens enables you to get close-ups and wide angles. You also want to check image quality, which depends on the resolution of the image. The image resolution, or the method of identifying how sharp and detailed the images are, varies between cameras. Low resolution, for example, is 640×480 (or 307,200 pixels per image)—but that is perfect for Web publishing, e-mail attachments, and other uses. On the other hand, high resolutions are 1,152×872 (or 1,004,544 pixels per image)—and you should use them only for printing photo-realistic enlargements.

Additionally, check to see that your camera includes the following:

✦ Automatic focus

✦ White balance (to adjust the colors to match the source of light)

✦ Autoexposure (to calculate the correct exposure for the scene)

✦ Autoflash (to flash automatically if there isn't enough light)

✦ Autoadvance (to prepare the camera for the next photo)

✦ Detachable or rotatable lens (helpful but not necessary)

✦ Glass lens instead of plastic

✦ Removable flash memory cards

You need some other equipment in addition to your camera. Make sure that the camera comes with the following:

✦ A cable to connect the camera to the computer's serial, parallel, USB, or FireWire port

✦ At least one memory card

✦ Batteries

✦ A memory card reader for fast transfer between camera and computer (optional)

Note Many digital camcorders also work as digital cameras, taking still photographs in addition to moving pictures. In addition, some digital cameras have a camcorder feature you can use to take short amounts of moving pictures.

Looking at scanners

A scanner is a tool for adding graphics, images, and photographs to your documents. You can scan photos, logos, line art, and even text to save as electronic files. Desktop scanning can be complicated and difficult.

Note Optical character recognition (OCR) is a means of using software to scan typewritten text and convert it to a file you can read and edit with a word processor. It's great for avoiding retyping text, whether you're scanning reports, records, letters, catalogs, or other documents.

Scanners transform analog data to digital data by converting light into the 0s and 1s that computers use to perform operations. The electronic scanner components, or eyes, record the reflected light off of the item scanned and report the information to the computer. The scanner divides a picture into pixels to build the image in digital form.

Flatbed scanners used to be the most common. You place the item being scanned on a glass plate, and then the scanning head moves beneath the item. In contrast, sheet-fed scanners move the page being scanned past the scanning head. Sheet-fed scanners are less exact than flatbeds because it's difficult to move a sheet of paper without distorting the image that's on it.

Many of today's scanners are included with a printer/copier/scanner, 3-in-1 device. This type of scanner makes scanning into your computer fast, easy, and efficient.

You need to check several criteria when buying a scanner to make sure that you're getting the right one. First, you want to check the size of the scanner or printer (called the footprint); some are very large and awkward. Second, make sure you get the right connection type, such as SCSI, parallel, USB, and so on.

Following are the other criteria to check:

✦ *Resolution* describes the number of pixels a scanner applies to an image. Resolution is measured by a grid, such as 300×300 pixels (or dots) per square inch. The higher the resolution, the better the image output and the more expensive the scanner.

✦ *Bit depth* describes the information a scanner records about the pixels it scans. Some scanners record only black and white (1-bit). To see grays or tones between the black and white, you need at least a 4-bit depth (16 tones) or an 8-bit depth (up to 256 tones). Color scanners are usually 25-bit or higher, which means they can capture more than 16 million different colors.

Tip

Most graphics software packages can manage nothing larger than 25-bit scans, so buying a scanner that offers 30- or 36-bit scans might not be necessary. The extra bits do, however, correct for "noise" (or distortions in the image) and produce better color images. Also, not all monitors can display a 25-bit image; most display only 8-bit images.

✦ *Dynamic range* measures how wide a range of tones the scanner can record. The range is from 0 (white) to 4 (black). Most color flatbeds tend to use a 2.4 dynamic range. Top-quality scanners might have 2.8 to 3.2.

✦ *Scanning area* describes the maximum size image the scanner will scan. Printer/scanner/copier, sheet-fed, and flatbed scanners are usually 8.5 by 14 inches.

✦ Make sure that you get a scanner driver disk with the scanner.

✦ You also should get some application software with the scanner. The program should provide image-editing features, such as those for adjusting brightness, contrast, color balance, and so on.

Getting the Best Scanned Output

When you're scanning images, always scan at the lowest resolution that will work. Extra resolution slows down the process and wastes disk space; also, quality may not be improved that much in the final product. If you're scanning a photograph for use in e-mail or for printing on your laser printer, for example, 250 dots per inch (dpi) should be fine.

Line art illustrations can be scanned at 1,200 dpi so that the lines will be smooth. You might scan at the higher resolution for duplication at a commercial print shop, for example. For color photographs that you will print on a color printer, scan at 300 or 600 dpi for best quality. Most laser and inkjet printers only go as high as 300 or 600 dpi, so don't waste extra resolution.

Images you convert to text, such as those scanned with an optical character recognition program, should be scanned at 300 dpi so that the computer can recognize more of the text characters.

If you plan to enlarge an image, you should increase the scanning resolution. When you enlarge images, the space increases between the pixels, or dots, and thus the image looks less detailed.

Looking at Multimedia Applications

You can find multimedia applications to edit photographs and video, manage multimedia files, record music, animate photographs, and more. Check out the Internet for multimedia applications, and make sure you look at freeware and shareware programs too.

In addition to Windows-based programs, many programs are available for multiple platforms. If you can write Linux code, for example, there are many multimedia applications available to help you. The Mac is also a well-known platform for creating your own multimedia.

Note

Shareware describes a program you can download from the Internet for free with the stipulation that you will pay a registration fee later or delete your copy. *Freeware* describes a program that is free for use and distribution. Many manufacturers also distribute *demonstration (demo) copies* of their software for free with the hope that you will later purchase the entire program. Some of these programs are full copies of the software; others are only pieces of the software that whet your appetite for more—for a fee, of course.

Working with photographs and images

If you like to take digital photographs of your family and friends or scan pictures for fun or for your business, you can use one of these applications to organize and display your digital image files.

✦ Adobe Photoshop enables you to edit photos, compile photo albums, and touch up, crop, and otherwise change photos to suit yourself. Photoshop costs around $600. In addition, Photoshop has the following features:

  • Manages images from scanners and digital cameras

  • Supports multiple users over a network

  • Supports a variety of graphics formats

  • Enables long filenames and path names

✦ Corel KPT Collection is a suite of products you can use to work with photos, edit them, distort them, and so on. This software costs around $90.

✦ Microsoft Picture It! is another photo-editing program you can use to organize and print photos fast. Picture It! costs around $50.

✦ ScanSoft's SuperGoo cost around $25 and enables you to stretch, warp, smear, and otherwise distort images.

✦ MGI PhotoSuite, Ulead Photo Impact, Corel Photobook, and Ulead Pick-a-Photo are all picture-editing tools you can try with your images.

Creating 3D animations and movies

You can subscribe to many Web sites that supply you with animations for your Web site or for other purposes. You can also create your own 3D animations and even more complex animations for playing on your PC, over the network, or on your own Web page by using a program for 3D animations.

✦ www.newcreations.net supplies click-here icons, zooming cars, animated musical notes, spinning cubes, spinning stars, and many more animations.

✦ www.3dlinks.com is another supplier of animations, and it also features an artist's gallery of animations where you can show your creations and view others'.

If you want to use shareware, there are many programs available for animations. Go to www.shareware.com for information on freeware and shareware programs.

✦ Animated Screen enables you to create 3D objects and manage their behavior, size, and appearance. You can mirror, rotate, change colors, and otherwise edit the objects.

✦ SWiSH is another shareware program that enables you to create Flash animations for a Web site. You can create shapes, text, buttons, and motion paths. You can also use over 150 premade animated effects, such as explosions, 3D spins, waves, and such.

✦ If you want to professionally produce movies and animations, Animation Master is a program that enables you to create characters by using image mapping and modeling for complex organic or mechanical objects. You can make scenery, characters, and various props. You can build libraries of characters and actions that you can reuse over and over. You make movies, design characters, enhance business presentations, and even create 3D storyboards. For information about Animation Master, go to www.hash.com.

✦ GenArts produces Sapphire plug-ins for Discreet Burn. Discreet manufactures a Linux-based background rendering software in which you can use the Sapphire plug-ins.

Other professional programs you can use for 3D animation include Strata's 3Dpro, SoftImage's XSI, and Curious Labs' Poser 5 for Mac OS X.

Exploring multimedia videos and video editors

When you create your own multimedia, you take digital photographs, record videos, and so on. If you want to retouch some photographs or add to your images and sounds, you can use a program to do that. A video editor lets you edit the film you take in ways that are similar to how a professional filmmaker might edit his or her films. You can add animation and subtitles, cut the frames differently so the focus is on another subject, and more. Many multimedia editors are available in both shareware and full versions.

You can start with taking a video yourself. Sony, Ricoh, Panasonic, and many others make digital video records you can connect to your computer and transfer the digital video for editing.

✦ Adobe has many professional video production products, such as Premiere Pro and Encore, for editing videos and DVDs.

DVStorm 2 by Canopus is a program that provides real-time editing of video in conjunction with Adobe video production software, such as Premiere Pro and Encore.

✦ 2d3 makes SteadyMove Pro, a plug-in that provides a range of features for stabilizing film and video footage.

Exploring music and sound editors

In addition to video, your multimedia work might be with music or other recorded sounds. You can find editors to enhance, modify, and otherwise edit the sounds you record or that have been recorded by others.

✦ Kazaa Media Desktop is a workgroup file sharing software application. Kazaa features the ability to search for and download music, playlists, software, video files, documents, and images. You can also use Kazaa to set up and manage music and video playlists.

✦ Morpheus is a file sharing program that is freeware. Morpheus includes enhanced privacy and security to protect your network. It also automatically scans downloaded files with antivirus software to make sure you are protected when downloading digital media, including music, audio, video, films, games, photos, software, and documents.

✦ iMesh is another workgroup file sharing program that enables you to find, download, share, and publish audio and video files, computer games, images, and other documents and files. It is another shareware program that is free for trial and then asks for a small fee if you buy the program.

Note   To locate any of the shareware mentioned here, go to www.shareware.com.

✦ Cakewalk Music Software offers Cakewalk Pro Audio for the serious musician. Cakewalk is a Musical Instrument Device Interface (MIDI) sequencer and digital audio workstation. You can record, edit, process, and mix multitrack audio projects. Cakewalk can record up to 128 tracks of digital audio with up to 256 real-time effects.

Depending on your interest in making music, you can spend anywhere from a couple of hundred dollars to thousands of dollars on this type of equipment.

Examining CD/DVD burning

If you have a CD-RW or a CD-R drive, you can create your own music, image, or text CDs. You might want to record some favorite tunes on a CD, for example, or store all your family photos on CD. Many applications can help you accomplish your goal.

Note   Be careful when recording other people's music. Most CDs and other recorded music are copyrighted and cannot be recorded legally.

Generally, a CD or DVD burner comes with its own software, such as Roxio's Easy CD Creator. You can also use Easy DVD Creator. These are very serviceable for both data and music. Other software choices include the following:

✦ Nero 6.0 Ultra Edition package includes Nero Burning ROM 6 for CD/DVD writing, Nero BackItUp for full backup control of your data, Wave Editor, Nero Soundtrax for multi-track audio editing and mixing, and much more. Nero is shareware made by Ahead Software. Nero Burning ROM 6 is an application that can write video and audio to CD-R and CD-RW discs. You can record images, music, and various other data. This software also includes Cover Editor, a tool for designing and printing CD covers.

✦ BurnQuick is another shareware program that enables you to burn data and audio files on CD. Other programs include JetAudio and MusicMatch Jukebox.

Working with Multiplayer Games

Gaming is one of the biggest pastimes for both teenagers and adults. Computers, the Internet, and home networking have made multiplayer games available to the general public, and the manufacturers of these games have made the games more realistic, exciting, and fun. Because of networking, you can play games that let you slay a dragon, solve a puzzle, save the world, and even create your own unique world in which others interact with you.

If you're playing games on your home network, you can play one-on-one or in groups; you can even play in teams. For the best gaming experience, you need high-speed connections between your computers, at least 100 Mbps if you're using Ethernet. Wireless works well for many games as well; however, you want to be sure to check the game's requirements.

To run multiplayer games, each computer needs to have a copy of the game installed. Check the game's documentation for information about configuring and playing the game. If you want to play over the Internet for multiplayer online games, you'll need a broadband connection, such as a DSL or cable modem.

Console gaming

Many video game systems can connect directly to your home network. If you want, you can connect multiple gaming systems, your PC, TVs, and such; up to 64 players can play a game simultaneously.

Consoles for gaming include Xbox, PlayStation2, and GameCube. For more information about console gaming, see Chapter 20.

 Tip People with home networks often host gaming parties on their local area networks so that the only competitors in the game are those you invite to your home. LAN gaming parties are great fun and perfect if you don't have a broadband connection to the Internet.

Xbox

Microsoft's Xbox is a powerful gaming console. You can connect the Xbox console to a TV and to the network, allowing multiple players to play games with people in other parts of the house.

Microsoft worked with many game manufacturers, including SEGA, LucasArts, and Capcom, to create games for the Xbox. Microsoft's Xbox uses a 733 MHz Intel Pentium III processor with custom 3D graphics processing by nVidia. There are 64 audio channels, 256 stereo voices, and the ability to encode Dolby digital audio in real time.

The Xbox costs around $200. You can only play games made for the Xbox. Games for Xbox include Soul Calibur II, NFL Fever 2004, Voodoo Vince, Buffy the Vampire Slayer, Halo, and RalliSport Challenge.

To set up an Xbox to your home network for multiple players, you need a System Link (explained in the next paragraph), an Ethernet hub, and one network cable for every console you connect. The game you choose must support System Link play. Many games support split-screen multiplayers by plugging two or more controllers into one Xbox. However, if you want to play with multiple Xbox consoles, you can do that as well.

You need one TV per Xbox. Check the game box to see how many players are supported. If a game has the System Link icon, it means you can connect it to other Xboxes to multiply the numbers of players who can play. You can use a System Link cable to connect the consoles to your TV; then connect the consoles from the Ethernet port on the back with the System Link cable.

To connect more than two Xbox consoles, use Ethernet cables and an Ethernet hub (prefer-ably 100 Mbps). Connect the consoles to the TVs and then connect the console to the hub through the Ethernet port using an Ethernet cable. Plug in the hub and follow the game instructions for multiplayer gaming.

PlayStation 2 (PS2)

PlayStation is another console you can use to play online multiplayer games. Some popular PlayStation 2 games include SOCOM: U.S. Navy Seals, Tony Hawk's Pro Skater, Midnight Club, and Amplitude.

With PlayStation, you must have a broadband connection to the Internet; a dial-up connec-tion will not work. To connect PlayStation 2 to the Internet, you need the PlayStation console, a memory card, and an Ethernet adapter made specifically for PlayStation. The Ethernet adapter fits directly on the back of the console. You then use an Ethernet cable to connect the PlayStation to the DSL or cable modem.

Cross-Reference

For more information about online gaming, see Chapter 20.

Online gaming

You can expand your local area network gaming to the Internet and play games with thousands of people around the world. Often, games you play at home on your local network can also be taken to the Internet to play with multiple people. You can thus join an online game or even host a game on your computer and invite others to play with you.

Some online games have communities in which you can set up challenges and compete for prizes. One of the newest online game types is called the Massively Multiplayer Online Game (MMOG). Some of the most popular MMOGs bring together over 300,000 players.

MMOGs are subscription-based games; generally you pay a monthly fee. Your characters con-tinue to live on, whether you're playing or not. The most popular MMOGs are fantasy role-playing with such games as Asheron's Call. In MMOGs, you and your friends can band together to conquer another community or storm a castle. MMOG games include spaceships, superheroes, knights, drag racing, historical figures, and many other characters and worlds.

Understanding high-performance gaming

Most online and multiplayer computer games have fast and furious action. Action is continuous. Game delays or slow-running games can really ruin the gaming experience. You need high performance in both the network and your computer.

Network performance relates to how fast the network connection is to both other gamers and the network server. Computer performance relates to how fast your computer is and how the computer is configured.

To improve game performance, follow this advice:

✦ Disable any programs that might take up your extra bandwidth, such as chat programs, messaging systems, and file sharing software.

✦ Don't download files while playing games, even from other computers on your LAN.

✦ Ask your Internet service provider how much bandwidth they provide and if the ISP can increase the bandwidth to your computer. Many ISPs will sell a larger Internet service subscription package that provides greater bandwidth.

✦ On your computer, check the minimum system requirements for the game. If your computer has only the minimum requirements, consider upgrading memory or processor, a new video card, and such.

✦ Anytime you install a game, use the full installation option; using all of the game's files often makes the game run faster than using some files off of the CD or DVD drive.

✦ Make sure you turn off any applications that run in the background while playing the game.

✦ Install any and all Windows updates, patches, DirectX drivers, or other performance- and security-enhancing features to your operating system.

✦ Make sure you have the latest updates for video and sound cards in your system.

✦ You can also adjust the video settings in the game itself. Screen resolution, color depth, and texture size can all affect game performance. Lower graphic settings might give you more power for playing online. Sound quality might also affect performance. Strike a balance between the very best and the very lowest settings so play is enhanced.

Creating games

You can also use different programs to create your own multiplayer games. Many of these programs are expensive and for professionals; however, you might want to look into them.

✦ Softimage XSI is a 3D program that enables you to create content and pipeline deployment needs. You use modeling and character animation tools in a dotXSI file format. Building the pipeline is done in C++ programming. (www.softimage.com)

✦ 3D Developer Studio Pro is a shareware program that adds 3D capabilities to any of these compilers: Microsoft Visual C++2, Microsoft Visual C, Borland C++ Builder 4, Borland Delphi 5, Visual Basic 6, and Visual Basic .NET. (www.tucows.com)

Managing Multimedia in Windows 98

Windows enables you to view streaming content—including audio, video, and other data used in multimedia applications. Windows also provides some controls to help you manage your multimedia devices, including audio, video, MIDI, CD music, and others.

In Windows 98, all multimedia controls are located in one dialog box—the Multimedia Properties dialog box. To open the Multimedia Properties dialog box, open the Control Panel and double-click the Multimedia icon. Figure 25-1 illustrates the Multimedia Properties dialog box.

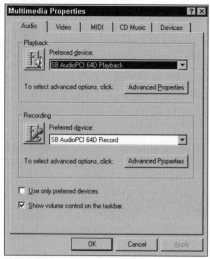

Figure 25-1: Windows offers some control for your multimedia devices.

Using the Audio tab

The Audio tab of the Multimedia Properties dialog box enables you to set options for audio playback and recording features. You should check with your hardware documentation to make sure of any special requirements before adjusting any options.

You can choose your preferred devices, if you have more than one playback or recording device attached to your computer. You also can fine-tune device performance.

Playback

Use Playback to set your preferred audio device. The drop-down list of devices describes any that are attached to your computer—a game device, your sound card, or voice recognition devices, for example. Your sound card should be listed as the preferred device as a default.

You can set other options for any selected device by clicking the Advanced Properties button in the applicable section of the Audio tab. Figure 25-2 shows the Advanced Audio Properties dialog box. In the Speakers tab, you indicate how your speakers are set up. You might have stereo speakers attached to your monitor or speakers sitting on stands beside your monitor. By choosing the speaker setup, you tell Windows how best to adjust the sound.

Figure 25-2: Identify your speaker setup.

The Performance tab offers options for you to set for hardware acceleration and rate conversion quality. You adjust these settings to manage how Windows plays sounds on your computer.

Hardware acceleration describes how fast you want to mix the sound coming from your multimedia applications. *Sound mixing* describes how various sounds work together to create the whole. If you play a music piece that has several different instruments on it, for example, the mix describes which instrument is the loudest, which sounds brighter, and so on.

In most cases, you should use full hardware acceleration. If, however, you notice that the sound is garbled or distorted, you can turn down the hardware acceleration. Figure 25-3 shows the Performance tab in the Advanced Audio Properties dialog box. To turn down the sound, click the hardware acceleration slider and drag it to the left.

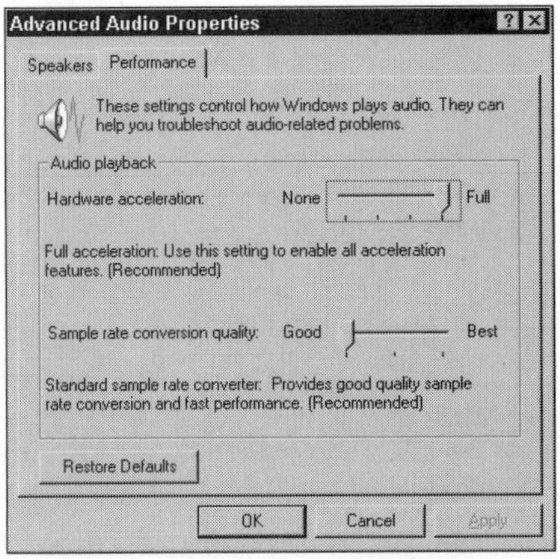

Figure 25-3: Adjust audio playback.

Rate conversion quality involves the processor's involvement in audio response time. This option indicates how much of your processor operation you want to dedicate to audio. For best results, choose Good. If, however, you find your processor is running slower and performance seems adversely affected, turn the rate conversion quality option down a bit.

If you click the icon in the Playback area of the Audio tab, the Volume Control dialog box appears, as shown in Figure 25-4. You can adjust the balance between the left and right speakers, as well as the volume, for any selected device.

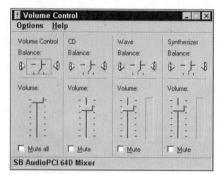

Figure 25-4: Control the balance between speakers when playing certain sounds and devices.

Recording

The Recording options are similar to the Playback options on the Audio tab. You can choose your preferred device and then set hardware acceleration and rate conversion quality for that device.

You also can display balance and volume controls for the recording devices. You have only two options here, though: the CD option and the microphone balance and volume option.

Setting video options

The Video tab of the Multimedia Properties dialog box enables you to choose the default size you want to use when viewing a video window. You can choose to view all videos at full screen, at 1/16th of the screen, at 1/4 of the screen, at 1/2 of the screen, or at twice the original size.

Working with MIDI options

The MIDI tab of the Multimedia Properties dialog box enables you to choose the instruments connected to your sound card, such as a keyboard or drum machine, and also enables you to add new instruments. If you don't have instruments connected to your computer, the MIDI tab displays your sound card but doesn't enable you to make changes.

You can add a new instrument by using the MIDI Instrument Installation Wizard. To initiate the wizard, click the Add New Instrument button in the MIDI tab. When you add an instrument, you define the port and sound card to which the instrument is attached.

Adjusting CD music

The CD Music tab of the Multimedia Properties dialog box enables you to set the default volume for the CD drive. If you have multiple CD drives, you can set each drive's volume separately.

Some CD drives enable you to use digital playback instead of analog. An analog device is slower than digital and uses older transmission methods. Digital represents values in the form of binary digits, which is the method computers use to communicate; therefore, digital signals are faster and more efficient. If you're not sure about your CD drive, check the documentation that came with the drive.

If your CD drive can use digital playback, you can enable Windows to use the digital playback instead of the analog playback. If the option is dimmed, it is not available for your CD player.

Looking at multimedia devices

The Devices tab of the Multimedia Properties dialog box enables you to view the properties for any multimedia device drivers attached to your computer. You can view audio, MIDI, mixer, joystick, and other control device drivers. To view the drivers in any category, click the plus sign to the left of the category.

To view the properties of any driver, select the driver and then click the Properties button. The properties for most device drivers are nearly the same. You can choose whether to use the features on the device or to turn off the features. You also can remove any device listed. Often, turning off the features helps in troubleshooting devices. If you find a driver is causing problems with a program or device, you can remove the driver and reinstall it.

If you want to prevent programs from using a device driver — suppose that you installed a third-party driver instead — you can choose the Do Not Map through This Device check box in the Properties dialog box.

Managing Multimedia in Windows 2000/XP

Windows 2000 and XP are more sophisticated than Windows 98 when it comes to multimedia. Windows versions based on NT are made to run complex programs, especially multimedia. DirectX is one of the features that is more complex with newer Windows versions, and DirectX directly affects sound, video, input, and other multimedia features.

In addition, both versions of Windows, and Windows 98, have many controls for multimedia in the Control Panel. You can change settings and configurations with the Game Controllers, Scanners and Cameras, Sounds and Audio Devices, and Speech features. Work with hardware configuration in the Multimedia Properties dialog box.

Tip　If you need to adjust configurations or correct errors in multimedia applications, you click Start ➪ All Programs ➪ Accessories ➪ System Tools ➪ System Information. Click Components and then Multimedia. You can edit the audio and video codecs in this area, if necessary. The Components category also includes information about CD and DVD-ROM, sound devices, displays, and other devices you use with multimedia. A *codec* is short for compression/decompression. It is an algorithm that reduces the number of bytes consumed by large files. To resolve some issues related to a codec, you should download the latest codec from either the media player manufacturer or from the developer of the type of video or audio file being played.

Diagnosing DirectX in Windows 2000/XP

All Windows operating systems depend heavily on DirectX for multiplayer games and other multimedia features. You can always use the DirectX Diagnostic Tool and the Multimedia and Games Troubleshooter to help you with problems you're having.

The tabs in the DirectX Diagnostic Tool gather information about certain areas of your system dealing with DirectX, including DirectX components and drivers. Following is a brief description of the DirectX Diagnostic Tool tabs:

✦ **System** — Lists the System Information for your computer, such as computer name, processor, memory, and the DirectX version you are currently using.

✦ **DirectX Files** — Lists all DLL, SYS, and other system files associated with DirectX, including the filename, size, date installed, and so on. If there is a problem with any file, it lists the problem in the Notes section of the tab.

✦ **Display** — Reports information on your display mode, the monitor driver, and DirectX features applying to the video. You can also test several features, such as DirectDraw, and view any problems in the Notes area of the tab.

✦ **Sound** — Lists the sound card, driver versions, acceleration mode, and a test for DirectSound. Also displays problems in the Notes area of the tab.

✦ **Music** — Lists the music ports, their types, whether they are input or output, and other information about sounds files. Also enables you to test various ports and reports any problems in the Notes area.

✦ **Input** — Lists all input devices, installed drivers, and problems found.

✦ **Network** — Lists all registered DirectPlay files and versions, enables a test of DirectPlay, and reports problems in the Notes area of the tab.

✦ **More Help** — Gives you information for testing other parts of the system that you might be having trouble with.

To view the DirectX Diagnostic Tool, follow these steps. The following steps are for XP; however, the steps for Windows 2000 are similar.

1. Click Start ⇨ All Programs in XP and Programs in 2000 ⇨ Accessories ⇨ System Tools ⇨ System Information. The System Information dialog box appears.

2. Click Tools ⇨ DirectX Diagnostic Tool. The DirectX Diagnostic Tool appears, as shown in Figure 25-5. The figure is taken in Windows XP.

3. Click the appropriate tab or click Next Page to view more information.

4. Click the Exit button to close DirectX Diagnostic Tool; then click the X to close System Information.

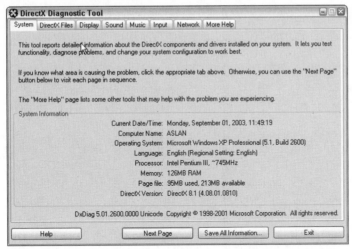

Figure 25-5: Use DirectX Diagnostic to keep your games running smoothly.

Working with other multimedia controls

In addition to checking the DirectX Diagnostic Tool when you have trouble in Windows 2000 or Windows XP, you can check the Control Panel for certain settings and information. To open the Control Panel, click Start ➪ Control Panel.

The Game Controllers icon in the Control Panel displays the installed game controllers on your computer. You can check properties and add or remove game controllers. You can also troubleshoot a controller causing a problem using this feature.

The Scanners and Cameras feature displays all imaging devices connected to your computer. You can also add or remove a camera or scanner. You can view properties and make changes to their configuration.

Use the Sounds and Devices icon to set volume, sounds, audio, voice, and hardware options for Windows. Figure 25-6 shows the Sounds and Audio Devices dialog box in Windows XP.

You can change the following settings on various tabs in the Sounds and Audio Devices dialog box:

✦ **Volume tab** — Set a device's volume, set it to mute, or add the volume icon to the taskbar. You can also set the speaker volume, type of speakers, and performance of audio playback.

✦ **Sounds tab** — Create sounds schemes — that is, program sounds for specific Windows events.

✦ **Audio tab** — Set the default sound playback device, sound recording device, and MIDI music playback device. Also set volume and other specific settings for each device.

✦ **Voice tab** — Control configuration of voice playback and voice recording. Test hardware through a diagnostic test.

✦ **Hardware tab** — View devices and their types, plus the manufacturer and device status. Troubleshoot problems or view properties of devices.

Figure 25-6: Check sounds, volume, audio, voice, and other settings with the Sounds and Audio Devices dialog box.

Finally, the Control Panel provides a Speech Properties dialog box in which you can control voice properties of your computer's default voice. You can select a voice, preview a voice, speed it up or slow it down.

Managing Multimedia in Linux and Macintosh

Managing multimedia in other operating systems is something you'll need to research in your specific system. Macintosh are famous for multimedia applications, whether you use a System 7 or an OS X. Linux can be a bit more difficult, depending on the popularity of your particular distribution.

For Macs, hundreds of multimedia applications are available, including video editing, DVD authoring, digital compositing, music editing and composition, and more. QuickTime Streaming Server is but one application you can use to supply streaming audio and video to your network. You can reflect live broadcast streams, manage concurrent connections, and monitor server activity with QuickTime.

Tip   FireWire is also available with the newer Mac operating systems. Make sure you do have the latest, updated FireWire software if you're using it with a multimedia device. FireWire benefits include fast real-time transfers and a higher-speed growth path. You can get FireWire products for digital video cameras, video decks, still-image cameras, and more. With the latest drivers and software, your FireWire can perform even better.

In general, if you're having trouble with your Macintosh multimedia hardware, go to www.apple.com and search under Support. You can download manuals for nearly every Macintosh application and hardware possible, join discussions of Mac users in support issues, get training, and even get professional advice for your problems.

For Linux computers, multimedia is beginning to take off. A lot of sites have advice and information on setting up multimedia with your Linux box. Depending on your Linux distribution, you can find utilities and instructions on how to set up music, video, DVDs and so on. If you're using Red Hat Linux, see www.linuxjournal.com.

X MultiMedia System (www.xmms.org) provides utilities, plug-ins, and programs you can use to enhance multimedia services on your Linux box. cgi.tripod.com offers hints and advice about specific multimedia configuration with Linux, such as recording sound with Linux, using NetMeeting with Linux, burning MP3s to CDs, and so on. Another site, www.yolinux.com, offers information about configuring multimedia for Linux as well.

Using Your TV with the Web

One result of the multimedia boon is the integration of the Internet with television. You can watch TV on your computer or surf the Internet with your TV. With cable modems and DSL modems, surfing the Internet with your TV is a fast as using your computer with the same broadband connection. Microsoft even has a system that enables you to pause your live TV, record two shows at the same time, and schedule recordings (see www.ultimatetv.com).

Considering WebTV

WebTV is a way you can connect to the Internet — without a computer. You can search for your favorite TV show, send and receive e-mail, use interactive links related to the programs you watch, and even display a picture within a picture to watch TV as you surf the Web. You can design a Web site, interact with a site, and chat with WebTV. The technology has grown and is offering more opportunities every day.

Most WebTVs offer access to around 95 percent of the Web sites. If you're new to computers and the Internet, need a quick connection to the Internet from your home, or are a nontechnical user, WebTV is perfect for you.

Several companies make WebTV–based receivers, including MSN, Mitsubishi, Philips Magnavox, and Sony. WebTV is a much less expensive solution than buying a computer, and Internet access and setup is easy.

WebTV, however, does have some problems. Following are a few of the drawbacks:

✦ Some users find WebTV to be slow. If you have a dial-up connection, you must contend with the modem speed, busy telephone lines, and servers and connections that make up the Web. If, however, you use a cable or DSL modem, speed won't be a problem.

✦ The quality of the display in the past has been a problem; however, if you use HDTV, you'll have no problem with viewing the Web on your TV.

✦ Video streaming speeds used to be slow; once again, however, if you use a cable or DSL modem, there should be no problems with streaming video and audio.

Adapting your TV

New technologies support many products for using your television as a computer, multimedia center, and Web browser. Set-top boxes are popular for enabling access to the Internet. A *set-top box* is a device that converts the television set so that it can receive some Internet services. The device attaches to your television set and enables you to connect to the Internet via your telephone cable service. The box usually includes a handheld remote, and sometimes a wireless keyboard.

A built-in modem attaches you to the Internet through an Internet service provider. Most set-top boxes include a Web browser, e-mail, and software for installation of the device drivers.

Summary

In this chapter, you learned about using multimedia with your computer and in your home. You've covered the following:

✦ Understanding multimedia

✦ Considering digital cameras and scanners

✦ Looking at multimedia hardware

✦ Looking at multimedia applications

✦ Playing online and multiplayer games

✦ Managing multimedia in Windows

✦ Playing online and multiplayer games

✦ Integrating your TV with the Web

In the next chapter, you learn about intelligent homes.

✦   ✦   ✦

Considering Smart Homes

I f you're considering networking your computers in your home, you also might want to consider networking your entire home. You can use a server computer, network cabling, and smart devices to automate your home. Automation includes security lights and alarms, coffee makers that start before you wake up, smart garage doors, lights that turn on as you walk through the house, and more. With new devices and technologies, you can automate your home as much or as little as you want.

Understanding the Smart Home

The world has gone digital. We use digital CDs and DVDs, digital modems, and other digital equipment to communicate. Many telephones are currently digital; there are even video telephones. Cable television systems have moved to digital. Digital Internet access has made the home much more intelligent by enabling you to research information, shop, pay your bills, perform banking chores, download files and music, send messages, and more.

Small Business Tip

Smart workplaces have been around longer than Smart homes. Automated assembly lines, security cameras, digital equipment to aid in communications, and so on have been in place for years. More products are available for businesses as well. If you're interested in automating your office, you can use many of the features discussed in this chapter and check out the Internet for automated office/business information.

A Smart home begins with digital communications, Internet access, and networking, but there is so much more. Smart homes, also called *intelligent homes* or *automated homes*, vary from simple motion detectors outside to a fully wired home with automatic heating and cooling, security cameras, whole-house video and audio, and more. You can add modifications to your current home to make it more convenient and comfortable, or you can build the house from the ground up, adding automated features as you go.

Today, kits, modules, and other technologies are available that can help you create the Smart home of your dreams. You can add features to your home little by little or all at once. You can spend as little or as much money as you want. You can hire someone to install the equipment for you, or you can install many of the Smart home devices yourself.

Exploring smart features

The benefits of using smart features in your home are many. Protect your home, your belongings, and your family with security features. Save energy and money by using environmental controls for lights, heat, air conditioning, and so on. Increase your enjoyment of the home by adding entertainment features and useful tools that do many chores for you.

Following are the most popular features you can find for creating your Smart home. Some manufacturers sell a kit that includes several features. Others sell their equipment in modules so that you can choose the ones you want; still others contract for the whole-house solution.

✦ Telephone systems include caller ID (with the number printed on a screen or read to you by a synthesized voice), voice mail, and intercom capabilities. You can computerize your phone system so that you can dial, speak, and even be seen over your computer. In addition to phone services within the home, service outside of the home includes cell phones and pagers that you can use to control your home while you're away from home. You can call your home from your cell phone to turn on the heat, lights, and answer the door, for example.

✦ Security systems are popular for protecting your home from intruders. Systems include sensors installed on the doors or windows, flashing lights, alarms, and even a telephone dialer that calls for outside help. You also can get sensors to monitor for fire, flooding, and other disasters.

✦ Motion detector lights and alarms are great for the outside of your house and property. Floodlights light up when they detect movement; a voice announcement, buzzers, or bells sound when movement occurs in the area. You can even add a feature to the system that automatically calls the police, fire station, or other emergency services.

✦ Security cameras positioned around the house, on the outside or the inside, help you keep an eye on your family and your property. Some systems enable you to view areas through your television; others enable you to view areas through additional equipment you install in the house.

✦ Lighting controls enable you to turn lights on or off in any part of the house from one room. With some systems, you can even turn your lights on from your car on your way up the driveway. Other controls enable you to call the house when you're away and thereby activate the lights. Some systems use lights to guide your path from the driveway to the house, up the walk, or in the house to guide you from room to room.

✦ Temperature or environmental controls for use with your HVAC (heating, ventilation, air conditioning) system enable you to set the heat or air conditioning to come on at certain times and to go off at other times. Sensors you set to specific temperatures regulate the heat and air conditioning as well. You can even telephone ahead and have the system turn on either the heat or the air conditioning for you before you get home.

✦ An intercom installed at the front door enables you to talk to your guests before you let them in the house. You can open the door from another part of the house. Some companies offer a remote unit with which you can answer the intercom from anywhere in the house.

Note

Some systems include a "virtual butler" that turns the porch lights on when someone comes to the front door. If you don't know the visitor, you can activate a voice message asking the visitor to wait while you come to the door. If you're not home, you can program the system to phone you at a predetermined number so that you can talk directly to the visitor, as if you were at home. Finally, if you cannot be reached by phone, the system asks the visitor to leave a message.

✦ Driveway sensors sound an alert in the home when a car pulls in. After the alert — a buzzer, voice announcement, or some other indicator — the lights automatically turn on to guide the visitor to the front door.

✦ Audio/video systems include a variety of features. You can wire your home throughout so that you can watch a movie or TV in any room, or install speakers in every room so that you can listen to your stereo no matter where you are. Audio/video systems enable you to check the Internet or security systems, or watch TV, depending on the remote button you push.

> **Note**
>
> Often, audio and video systems include a projector and screen, plus other equipment, to make the home into a theater. Home theaters often include surround sound speakers, a movie screen, automatic lighting controls, and even a device to close the window curtains when it's movie time. You also can find a home theater system that stops the movie when you leave the room and starts it again when you return.

✦ A mailbox alert signals you inside the home that the mail has been delivered.

✦ Surge protectors and battery backups are useful for the automated home during an electrical storm or power outage. Many systems include backup devices.

✦ Pool management equipment includes heating controls, water-level controls, and sensors for detecting intruders or small children in the pool area.

✦ Electronic fences formed by infrared beams protect your yard, pool, or any other area from pets and intruders. You can connect the fences to alarms that sound when the beams are broken.

✦ Automatic sprinklers turn on and off at preset times. Also, a rain sensor or freeze sensor prevents the sprinklers from wasting water during a rainstorm or freezing in winter.

✦ A built-in vacuum cleaner makes it easy to clean carpets, floors, furniture, draperies, and more in your home. The vacuum attaches to wall units distributed throughout the home. The exhaust air is vented outside, so you don't lose dust or other debris in the home. The vacuum is quieter than portable vacuum cleaners, powerful, and more healthful; mostly, however, the vacuum is convenient — no cords, no switches, and no heavy unit to carry around the house with you.

✦ Driveway gates that open only with specified security codes have become popular. They also might include an intercom for speaking to the visitor before you open the gates.

How does it work?

If you plan to add only small devices to your home to automate it, you might add modules that perform specific tasks, such as garage door openers, pool sensors, or a security camera. You can add multiple devices all over your home to make life easier for you.

You also can fully automate your home. Many systems use a central computer plus multiple controlling devices scattered around the home. You can purchase entire systems that include everything you need to automate the home; these systems include installation and configuration of the equipment, the computer, and the software that runs the equipment.

In some fully automated homes, a computer with special software acts as the control center of the automated devices. The software enables you to control security, lighting, temperature, and other smart devices connected to the system. It initiates and routes communications signals throughout your home as the conditions warrant.

A system such as this also includes numerous controlling devices placed throughout the house. You might have a keypad at the front door with a special code that unlocks the door, for example, or a remote control device that controls the stereo, television, and VCR. You might interface with the system through touch screens on any computer in the home, keypads, panic buttons, the television screen, or a handheld remote device.

In other automated homes, no computer is needed. Each device contains its own processor that makes smart decisions. A command runs through the system, and the appropriate device responds and completes the task. There is no need for a central unit to control some hardware.

Comprehending the Technologies

Whether you're using a few devices to automate common tasks around the house or you automate your entire home, various technologies are available. You're familiar with the cabling techniques and the ports for connecting devices to a computer network; the technologies used for home networking computers, however, aren't exactly the same as for automating a home. The communications protocols are also different from the ones used in home networking.

For more information about computer network cables, see Chapter 6.

Considering wiring

You can choose various wiring options for your Smart home. The type of wiring you select depends on the size of your home and the degree to which you want to automate. Also, specific products might require certain cabling and connections. As with networking computers, you must buy your hardware specific to the type of cabling or connections you use.

To wire your entire house for the Smart home, you need wiring that carries the load without the threat of overheating. Power lines, speaker wires, and so on are a concern because they create heat as well as draw power. You also need a connection that protects against interference from other nearby cabling or appliances with their own electric and magnetic fields.

With low-voltage lines that carry voice, data, and video, you don't have to worry about overheating as much. Data lines, however, do need enough bandwidth to carry the appropriate frequencies and signals for all your automated appliances and devices.

Many of the current Smart home products use Category 5 twisted-pair cabling, like you use in your Ethernet network. To create lines that carry the signal without losing strength in larger homes, you might have to reinforce the hardware. You should use four or eight twisted-pair wires when cabling your Smart home.

In addition, a Smart home might use dual- or quad-shielded coaxial cable. Coaxial cable enables you to have distributed audio and video usage. Often, the installer or builder of your home system will run the wiring through a central PVC (plastic) pipe to save time and to make the wiring neater and easier to get to for repairs.

The power lines in your home provide another wiring possibility. Some devices connect to transmitters and receivers that manage the various automated devices. If you plan to use power lines, you want to guarantee that these lines can handle the extra load. Have an electrician check your house wiring before buying any of the products that use your existing power lines.

Looking at Quality Cabling

You might be tempted to automate your home yourself by installing the cabling, devices, and software. You should make sure that you use quality cabling and do a first-rate job. Don't be tempted to extend your cable TV with inexpensive coaxial cable, for example, or buy the cheapest cable and connectors you can find to extend your telephone wires. When you buy cheap or deficient cabling and patch the job together, the equipment and the connection won't be reliable or durable.

Poorly grounded coaxial cable connectors can cause noise on the TV; signal leakage from wiring can result in garbled phone transmissions. Make sure that your cabling meets all standards and quality ratings.

Category 5 cables carry a bandwidth of up to 100 MHz, as contrasted with phone wiring that supports 3 KHz, or CAT 3 (TV) cable that supports 16 MHz. CAT 5 might cost more, but it's well worth it. This CAT 5 cabling is the very same you use when networking your computers.

The Telecommunications Industries Association (TIA) has formed standards for residential wiring for the United States. TIA-570-A introduces a grading system that's based on services the house will support. You need to make sure that you match these standards for a safe and efficient system in your home.

Grade 1 covers the generic cabling system for telecommunications services, such as telephone, satellite, cable TV, and so on. Grade 1 includes standards for data communications as well, to include twisted-pair cabling of CAT 3 or better; however, CAT 5 is recommended.

Grade 2 is a generic cabling system for multimedia telecommunications services. Grade 2 twisted-pair cabling states you should use CAT –5-quality cabling with one or two coaxial cables. You might use CAT 5 for the security systems, for example, and CAT 3 for your stereo/TV system.

Fiber-optic cabling is optional in Grade 2. Fiber-optic cabling uses pulses of light along specially manufactured optical fibers to transmit signals. Fiber-optic cable is lighter and smaller than traditional cabling, immune to electrical interference, and transmits signals more efficiently. You also can use fiber-optic cable for a computer network. Fiber-optic cabling is very difficult to work with; you should get professional help if you plan to install it in your home.

The standards include CAT 5 wire that uses at least four twisted pairs, and possibly eight twisted pairs, plus two quad-shielded coaxial cables for audio/video purposes. Twisted-pair cabling uses one wire to carry the signal and the other in the pair to ground the wire. Eight twisted pairs increase the number of signals that can be sent. Quad-shielded coaxial cables offer more protection because of the foil shields, and they offer transmissions at higher speeds than basic coax cable.

These standards are only recommended practices and are voluntary for builders and installers to follow. It benefits the homeowner to use these standards, so you should monitor all cabling in your home and make sure that it follows the standards.

Probably the most expensive, most dependable, and most efficient wiring being used today is fiber-optic. Fiber-optic consists of hollow cables that send data by pulses of light; data transmission is at the speed of light.

Wireless is another method by which you can create your Smart home. You can even combine wiring types — using some wireless, with CAT 5, with fiber.

No matter what type of wiring you use, consider installing all the wiring—for power, voice, audio, video, alarm messages, data from outside, and data within the walls—all at once through the home. If you're wiring a home as you build it, this shouldn't be a problem. If you're wiring an existing home, you might have more obstacles to overcome. You save money in the long run and are more likely to use cabling that works together if you do your wiring all at one time.

Examining communications protocols

Even though home automation products run across CAT 5 cable or use power line connections, they still must use a communications protocol. Three common protocols for home automation are X10, LonWorks, and CEBus. Bluetooth is another protocol that has recently been added to Smart home technology.

These are standards in communications protocols. Devices from multiple vendors can work with an X10, LonWorks, or CEBus network. Generally, you choose only one protocol to use throughout your home. All three protocols support lighting, heating, air conditioning, home security, and many other home automation products and features.

X10

X10 is a communications protocol that uses a power line carrier to control compatible devices. An X10 transmitter device sends low-voltage signals superimposed on the 110 VAC (volts alternating current) power lines. Any X10 receiver device connected to the household 110 VAC power lines receives the signal but responds only to signals carrying their own receiver address.

X10 usually works up to 100 feet from the transmitter. You can overcome this limitation, however, by plugging transmitters into several outlets to extend the distance. Receivers connect to televisions, garage doors, stereos, and other devices for remote-controlled automation.

Commonly, an X10 system uses one central transmitter that activates multiple receivers. No house rewiring is needed if your power lines are sufficient to carry the load. X10 transmitters and receivers plug into the wall or are hardwired into existing outlets or light switches.

X10 devices and kits are available, so you can automate a few devices or your entire home. For home kits, you can use your PC and software supplied by the vendor to control the automation in your home.

Note   X10 wireless communications are also available for audio/video signaling. Use X10 products with your security cameras and intercoms, for example.

X10 commonly is used for home automation because it's reliable and inexpensive. Also, many products from multiple vendors use the X10 protocol.

LonWorks

LonWorks is another protocol used in home and building automation. Although designed initially for commercial and industrial applications, LonWorks can address home control as well.

Small Business Tip   LonWorks offers multiple configurations for the workplace. If you're planning to automate your office, check into LonWorks devices first.

LonWorks works over a variety of cabling options, as the following list indicates:

✦ Twisted-pair cabling

✦ Power line

✦ Radio frequency

✦ Coaxial cable

✦ Fiber-optic cable

✦ Infrared technology

You can connect up to 32,000 devices to a LonWorks network. Smart control devices, called nodes, communicate with each other by using the LonWorks protocol. Each node has the intelligence to use the protocol to perform its own control functions. Nodes might be sensors, motion detectors, instruments, and so on.

CEBus

Consumer Electronics Bus (CEBus) is another communications protocol you can use with appliances, such as dryers and dishwashers, lighting, and other systems. CEBus is similar to LonWorks in that each device is capable of transmitting and receiving signals from other devices on the network. CEBus also is similar to X10 in that it works over your power lines so that you don't have to install new wiring.

CEBus is also capable of monitoring home usage of electrical, gas, and water utilities, providing you with information about your energy usage.

Bluetooth

Bluetooth wireless technology is used in many speech recognition devices for Smart homes. Recorders, microphones, and other devices that use Bluetooth can work up to a meter or so away from each other, and the devices are very inexpensive.

In this solution, a portable wireless device recognizes speech patterns and words because you program in a limited number of commands. You can use a telephone, headset, or other device to communicate with Bluetooth devices — appliances, for example.

Looking at the computer ports

The computer you use for home automation varies, depending on the system; however, you might be able to use a PC you already have in your home. You need to equip the computer to accommodate certain controls and hardware, however.

For most Smart home systems, you use a computer interface, such as X10 or RS-485 port. These interfaces aren't normally standard on most computers, but you can add a converter or expansion card to supply the port and slot you need. Other interfaces on a PC that you can use, depending on the product, include USB, Ethernet, and FireWire.

✦ X10 is inexpensive and easy to use. You can purchase an X10 converter that fits into an RS-232 port (which is a standard for serial connection on a PC). You can connect a mouse, printer, modem, or other device to an RS-232 port, for example.

The maximum number of devices you can use with X10 is 16. The length X10 can reach isn't really limited because it runs on the power lines in your home. As long as devices share one transformer (located in your home), you have no problem. The speed for X10 is only 360 bits per second. RS-485, on the other hand, supports a distance of 4,000 feet at a speed of 10 Mbps. You can connect 32 devices when using RS-485.

✦ The USB port has an industry-standard connector that enables you to install a variety of devices; USB ports are almost always standard on newer computers. FireWire is a bus developed to make more effective use of audio and video applications. FireWire is extremely fast; the data transfer rates are more than three times those of PCI.

You use FireWire for the quick transfer of video, audio, and other large amounts of data. USB can connect up to 127 devices, with 16 feet between devices. The maximum speed for USB is 12 Mbps. FireWire can support up to 64 devices for a maximum of 15 feet between devices. The speed, however, is 400 Mbps.

✦ Ethernet ports are used with CAT 5 cabling, in particular. Although not quite as fast as other technologies (unless you go Fast Ethernet at 100 Mbps), Ethernet is still an industry leader. Ethernet connects up to 1,024 devices for up to 1,600 feet. The maximum speed is 10 Mbps. Ethernet is fast and reliable, but the hardware is a bit difficult and expensive for some.

Integrating Today's Technology

Most homes already have power outlets and phone lines in all rooms, plus several rooms set up for audio and video entertainment. Somewhere, in most homes, is a video line from the outside, such as an antenna, cable TV, satellite TV, or other. You probably have other equipment—such as a DVD player or intercom system—that you are already using to modernize your home. There are many more products for automating and modernizing your home.

You can extend your power outlets, for example, with power strips that add surge protection and circuit breakers. To modernize your current telephones, you can extend voice transmissions with cordless technology. Today's 900 MHz models provide a longer range with clearer sound and more security from eavesdroppers.

Following in this section are discussions of some more specific products and technologies you can use to modernize your home.

Looking at security features

You can purchase as much or as little security as you want for your home. You might want to install motion detectors or floodlights, for example, or a fully automated system with panic buttons, security cameras, and other devices to protect your home and family.

Integrated security in a Smart home might include interior and exterior lighting, electrical outlets that turn off whenever you leave the house, phone service to the police and fire department, and more.

If you prefer to install smaller, less expensive devices to make your life easier and safer, however, you can find the exact device to perform just about any task you want.

Motion detectors and floodlights

You can find motion detectors of various types to install either outside or inside your home. Some detectors have alarms attached; others have floodlights attached. Following are some features to look for:

✦ A motion sensor that turns itself on at dusk to detect motion after dark.

✦ A device to turn on floodlights when it detects motion and then turn the lights off if there is no more motion for 5 or so minutes.

✦ A motion detector for inside the home that sets off an alarm. The alarm should sound both within the house and feed into the police or other monitoring station.

Alarms

You can purchase various alarm modules to warn of unauthorized movement inside and outside your home. Some modules are motion detectors, and others also can hear unusual sounds.

The Outdoor PIR Motion Detectors are motion detectors made by Optex. These detectors have wide- and long-range detection. You also can adjust the sensitivity settings to allow for pets. Optex also makes wireless detectors, infrared detectors, and detectors that trigger a voice when disturbed.

Video surveillance

You can purchase cameras of all kinds to install on the outside or the inside of your home. You can get small or large cameras, panning dome cameras, zoom lenses, four-way cameras, and recessed cameras.

Following are brief descriptions of various types of surveillance cameras, just to give you an idea of the variety available:

✦ Clock video camera that sits innocently on your nightstand has adjustable angle views. This camera-within-a-clock also works as a clock.

✦ Remote panning dome camera that pans 180 degrees by remote control.

✦ Miniature video camera that is the size of a postage stamp.

✦ Weatherproof outdoor video camera for protecting your front door.

✦ Recessed light camera that looks like a light fixture.

✦ Ball video camera that is enclosed in a weatherproof container (the ball rotates the camera in all directions).

✦ In-wall camera that's adjustable to any angle and connected to a door intercom system.

Personal assistance system

A personal assistance system includes a call button and a voice dialer that calls a friend or neighbor when you press the emergency button. A recorded message plays to notify the friend of the emergency.

Some personal assistance systems include alarm sirens and flashing house lights to make sure someone sees that you need help.

Examining appliances

Instead of the smart kitchen, you might want just a timer that turns your coffee pot on in the morning(or a refrigerator that does your shopping for you. There are appliances you can add to your kitchen to make it more convenient and efficient.

Makers of refrigerators are building in features that help you with your day by making shopping lists, attaching to the Internet, keeping an inventory of what is used, and otherwise saving you time and effort. Check out Bosch, Fisher & Paykel, Frigidaire, Jenn-Air, and GE for refrigerators and other appliances you can use in your Smart home.

Other appliances that are becoming smart include microwaves, dishwashers, ovens and stoves, and washers and dryers.

Using smart phones

One of the newest trends for the busy person is the smart phone. A smart phone takes multiple technologies (cell phone, faxes, pagers, PDAs, and so on) and integrates them into one product you can use to perform all your tasks.

Smart phones offer news and stock prices, tailored to your needs; they send and receive e-mail, let you shop online, and locate good restaurants in a new town. Many financial institutions enable you to do online banking via cell phone; you can navigate your road trip and get local weather forecasts and parking updates, all by phone.

Newer high-end cell phones are now the equivalent of a low-end PC with 100 MHz processor, flash memory, and color display with GUI. You can surf the Net, send e-mail, and complete your business without leaving the comfort of a phone in your ear.

Identifying home theater technology

Without actually building a home theater (with a film projector, large screen, and several viewing seats) you can use various products to enhance the audio and visual features of your home.

You can use terrestrial or satellite TV and video signals to feed into any TV in any room through one primary control box. Your home can be wired for surround sound with speakers in the rear, front, center, and side of the main TV/DVD yet buried unnoticeably in the walls. All rooms can be wired to a central music system that allows you to turn the system on and off, control volume, select sources, and more through one or many switches in the house.

If you do want to build your own home theater system, you need to consider room acoustics, the proper equipment, speaker placement, and equalization. There are many companies that can help you plan your home theater.

You can use plasma and flat screens for your TVs to present a neater, roomier home theater. With your drop-down screen and a projector, tap a theater button to activate the entire room: Close the blinds, dim the light, and the movie begins.

Handling messages

Whether you're recording messages for others or they're recording them for you, several devices are available that can automate the process. Some of these devices come as part of an entire Smart home kit; alternatively, you can purchase others separately to install as you need them.

A message recorder that works with Smart homes enables you to record and play back a message when certain events in the home take place. If the motion detector senses someone in your backyard, for example, you can have a message play that notifies you of the intrusion. These devices enable you to enter the messages and program them for specific events.

Looking into Internet access

Besides placing a PC in every room for work, Internet surfing, or controlling smart devices in your home, you can network the computers together to share files and printers, and even to monitor your child's access to the Internet.

In a Smart home, Internet access is wired into every room, enabling multiple users to surf the Net or retrieve e-mail at any one time throughout the home. ISDN, DSL, even cable modems no longer limit access to one specific location.

Automating plant and pet care

Naturally, the Smart home would be less than convenient if your plants and pets were left out of the equation. For example, several plant sitters are available that intermittently discharge water to over 30 plants located in the same area. Many companies offer pet feeders that will automatically feed and water your pets at preset times for several days at a time.

There are automatic pet doors and dog collar sensors that enable the dog or cat to come and go whenever he approaches the door. Of course, you can use invisible fences that prevent other animals from invading your property and keep your dogs and cats in your yard. There are automated cat litter box cleaning systems, bark controllers, and more for your animals in the automated home.

Using robots in home automation

Today's robots might be just the technology you want to help you automate your home. Robots have become common in the workplace, and it won't be long before they are common in the home as well.

You can use robots in a wireless Smart home to carry objects and to perform other menial tasks. They're inexpensive, but flexible in the home automation tasks they can perform. There are robots to water grass, and others to mow the grass. You can use a robot to vacuum the rug, or you can use a robot caddy on the golf course to carry your clubs. There are even robotic pets, such as dogs and small creatures called Furbies.

Exploring the Smart Home

You may be building a home and are prepared to add automation features as you build. On the other hand, you may want to automate your existing home. If you want to make your home a Smart home, you can have a professional install the cabling and controls for you, or you can do it yourself.

Questions to ask the home automation professional

The installer should ask you plenty of questions about what you want and where you want it. He or she should also be willing to spend a reasonable amount of time answering your questions about the system.

Before you buy a system, however, you need to ask the home automation professional, or installer, a few questions. Consider some of the following:

✦ Make sure that you ask for multiple references(and then check them thoroughly. Talk to at least four homeowners for whom the installer has worked in the past.

✦ Ask about the fee structure. Make sure that you understand when payment is due, whether payment is by the hour or per job (consulting, design, and installation, for example), and ask if the installer charges for adjustments made after the installation is complete.

✦ Ask about fees for maintaining, troubleshooting, and repairing the system. Find out whether there's 24-hour, 7-day-a-week service and whether there's an extra charge for weekends or evenings.

✦ Ask about payment plans.

✦ Make sure that the installer has liability insurance of at least $1 million.

✦ Find out if the installer trains you in the use of the system. If not, get suggestions for who can train you.

✦ Ask how long the entire job will take and find out how the system works, in detail.

✦ Get everything in writing.

Looking at home products

Smart homes can include simple, easy-to-install sensors or a complex, computerized central system of sensors and wiring. If you want to make your entire home smart, with integrated systems and fully compatible devices, you should use an installer to help you choose, install, and configure your system. There may be a company in your area that works with Smart homes; check the yellow pages and the Internet for more information.

Following are some of the available products you can use to bring the future to your home today.

Home Control Assistant

The Home Control Assistant (HCA) works with various devices to control lights and appliances through a Windows-based program. You can use HCA to turn on outside lights at dusk every day, heat the hot tub, turn on lights inside the house and turn them off again, turn on a coffee pot, and perform other chores automatically and at preset times.

HCA works with X10 and various interfaces, including USB ports, wireless, and serial power lines. HCA is a Windows-based program that works with PC switches and modules. The program uses Windows' features you're used to, such as wizards, dialog boxes, and the like. You can go to www.smarthome.com for more information.

Home Automation Systems, Inc.

SmartHome, from Home Automation Systems, Inc., includes multiple modules you can add to your home that use X10 technology. You can choose one or several of their products to install in your home, including an automatic pool water level control, outdoor speakers, automatic litter box for your cat, radio control projector clock, video modules, robo-dog alarm, and more.

SmartHome uses X10 devices. With X10 devices, you can plug your coffee maker into a module in the kitchen, and then enter commands from the bedroom, telling the coffee maker to turn itself on. You can add SmartHome to a new home or in parts to your current home.

You also can purchase the X10 software and system for Macs and PCs. The software enables you to enter your schedule and commands on the computer screen to control the appliances in your home.

SmartHome offers PC access software, dual X10 transmitters and receivers, Web-link software, a variety of automation controllers for various size systems and homes, LCD consoles, and touch screens for easy interfacing between your computer and your system. Visit www.smarthome.com for more information.

Home Director

Home Director uses high-speed wiring to centralize all connections in a new or remodeled home. Home Director is a fully integrated home networking system that connects subsystems, such as lighting, heating, and security systems. You can also use the system to connect multiple PCs, in-house video distribution, and Internet sharing.

Home Director connects video and CAT 5 cabling for networking and telephones, and all cabling is routed to one central location, the Network Connection Center, that enables you to link PCs throughout the home and to use a single VCR or DVD player to broadcast its signal throughout the home as well. Home Director includes phone systems, entertainment, computer networking, and security. For more information, see www.homedirector.com.

HomeStar system

Lucent Technologies makes the HomeStar system, which enables you to integrate the control of telephones, VCRs, cable televisions, home office equipment, security systems, and your heating and air-conditioning systems. HomeStar also supports work at home, video on demand, interactive video games, electronic shopping and banking, and child monitoring.

The HomeStar system also offers many services that integrate with their basic system. Caddx Networx System, a user-friendly alarm, covers burglary, fire, and medical emergencies. The alarm is compatible with X10 technology as well.

HomeStar also uses a built-in TiVo System and adds local programming to DirecTV, the Central Vacuum that enables you to plug a hose into various wall outlets throughout the house, and a whole-house audio system that you can use to listen to music anywhere in the home. You can even listen to different music in different parts of the house. For more information, see www.lucent.com.

X10's ActiveHome

ActiveHome uses the X10 protocol and devices to communicate to various pieces of equipment in your home, such as your garage door, television, radio, table lamps, HVAC system, coffee pot, sprinkler system, outside lights, and more. See www.x10.com for more information.

You use ActiveHome with your PC to supply better control over the system. ActiveHome comes in various kits. Kits include appliance modules, wall switches, motion sensors, lamp modules, or other devices to control your home. ActiveHome uses your existing power lines to lights and appliances. Plug and Play technology makes the program quick and easy to set up.

ActiveHome gives you PC control directly over your lights and appliances from the PC. You have remote control from any room in your house with a 6-in-1 remote to control your TV, VCR, cable, and stereo. You can also use PC automation by creating customized routines so that lights, TVs, a camera, and other equipment turn on and off while you're away from home. In addition, you can

✦ Add cameras: tiny nanny cams, wide-screen views, nightwatch, inside/outside cameras, and more.

✦ Use motion detectors, voice dialers, personal emergency alarms, keychain security remotes, robo-dogs, and other devices to ensure your security.

✦ Purchase appliance modules that work with fans, air conditioners, dehumidifiers, coffee pots, stereos, TVs, and other appliances in your home.

✦ Buy software to view your home cameras from the Web or from your PC. Use other software to view remote locations, check for emergencies at home, or to control your home automation software remotely.

✦ Add DVDs, VCRs, MP3 players, game hardware, speakers, remotes, and more for your home entertainment.

Note   www.home-automation.org is a good source for information and vendors of SmartHome technology.

Summary

In this chapter, you learned about some of the newest technologies used in Smart homes. The following was covered:

✦ Understanding the Smart home

✦ Comprehending the technologies

✦ Integrating today's technologies

✦ Exploring Smart home technology

In the appendix that follows this chapter, you learn how to troubleshoot your network when problems arise.

✦   ✦   ✦

APPENDIX

Troubleshooting Network Operations and Connections

Network problems can prevent you from completing your work, opening much needed files, backing up your data, printing, and performing other tasks on the computers attached to the network, even though you can continue to work on your own computer. After you become accustomed to a network, however, you will want to fix network problems as soon as they arise so that you can once again take advantage of the connections to other computers in your house or office.

Preventing Problems in Your Network

You can prevent many problems in your network if you plan a little before you set up the network. Always document everything, and keep all equipment information, documentation, instructions, and receipts. Also, buy quality networking hardware instead of the cheapest you can find; the better-quality equipment will last longer and work more efficiently.

You want to be careful when setting up your network, especially when handling a network card or other equipment that goes inside the computer. Oils from your fingers, for example, can ruin circuit boards. If possible, you also should get an uninterruptible power supply (UPS) to protect your network from power surges and other electrical problems.

Documenting network problems

As explained in Chapter 5, you should keep records of your hardware, cabling maps, and all documentation that comes with your computers and peripherals. Fill a notebook for each computer, including information such as processor speed, hard disk size, and RAM amount and type. List cabling type, network cards, and hubs. Keep the documentation that comes with CD drives, hard disks, sound cards, printers, and every other piece of equipment in your network.

You might never need the information, but you probably will. Say your hard disk crashes. You can check to see how old it is, whether there is a warranty, and what type of hard disk it is. Troubleshooting a problem with a computer or on the network begins with knowledge about the system. Following is a list of the things you should document for your network and other items you should save:

✦ The hardware for each computer, including processor type and speed, type and amount of RAM, type and size of hard disks and controllers, computer BIOS manufacturer, and revision numbers you've installed. Some of this information might be located in your computer documentation or on your invoice for the computer.

✦ Information about the monitor, keyboard, and mouse, plus any other hardware you added, such as speakers or joysticks.

✦ Operating system version number, plus any updates or patches.

✦ The manufacturer, driver, and model of each card; you can list the Web sites of the manufacturers as well.

✦ Details for each peripheral—printer, scanner, camera, UPS, and the like—such as manufacturer and model, drivers, and so on. Make sure that you know which driver you use for each peripheral.

✦ Application information, especially including licensing.

✦ IP addresses, subnet masks, and gateway if applicable, or any information about the protocol you're using.

✦ Cabling type and any external connections, such as phone lines for remote networking.

✦ Internet connection details, especially configuration information.

✦ Any information or instructions about kits you've installed.

Another important record to keep is your troubleshooting history. Whenever you encounter a problem with your equipment, write it down. Document the problem and the resolution to the problem. You never know when you might run into the same problem again.

Using preventive maintenance

If you're careful with your equipment when you install it, it should cause fewer problems as it gets more use. Also, keep cables out of the way of children and pets so that they don't constantly walk on or trip over it. Keep equipment, such as printers and computers, clean and free from dust, moisture, and animal hair. Cigarette smoke can ruin a computer, so be careful if you smoke.

Take care of your computers and peripherals to make them last longer and perform well.

Laying the cable

As discussed in Chapter 5, you should draw a map of your network and use it to identify cabling, layout, and the location of networking hardware. Use this map when you have problems with your network. You can save time and effort if you know which cable attaches to which computer.

In addition, you should be careful when laying the cable for your network. If you're using phone line or wireless cabling, you won't have any of the following problems. If you use traditional cabling, however, you can take a few precautions that will save time and money later.

Following are some guidelines for laying cable:

✦ Don't lay a network cable close (2 feet or less) to motors, fluorescent lights, or power lines.

✦ Use an electrician to help you pull wire behind walls and in ceilings so that you don't accidentally drill power lines.

✦ Don't drill through the studs in a framed wall when installing network cabling in the walls of your house.

✦ Don't kink the cable. Kinks in the cable can cause connection problems as well as ruin the cable.

✦ Don't use a staple gun or staples of any type to install cabling. You can nick the cable, which ruins it.

✦ If you use plastic or metal ties to hold several cables together, don't pull the ties too tightly. You might kink a cable and stop the connection.

✦ If you must cross a power line, cross it at a right angle only in order to get the least interference.

✦ Don't coil excess cabling when the cabling is in use. If, for example, you install the cable and have several feet left over, don't coil it up. Instead, lay the cable out as straight as possible. Coiling the cable can cause interference in the data transmissions.

Working with wireless

When setting up your wireless network, make sure you follow all guidelines as to distance and direction. These two factors make the difference in whether your wireless network works or not. If your wireless access point (WAP) is configured for 25 feet, it will not work at 100 feet. It may work at 50 feet but not reliably or consistently. If your WAPs or network cards say line of sight, they must be line of sight.

If you're having other connection problems and you're sure you've checked direction and distance, then next try uninstalling the network card software and reinstalling it. As with wired networks, often reinstalling the driver or even installing a newer driver will make the connection work for you.

If you're still having trouble connecting, check the configuration settings on both WAPs. Make sure all settings are exactly the same except for the name of the WAP — SSIDs should be the same, and Wired Equivalent Privacy (WEP) should be the same. Reconfigure if necessary. For more information, see Chapter 7.

Examining a UPS

An uninterruptible power supply protects the hardware when a power surge or power failure occurs. Suppose that someone trips over your computer's power cord and pulls it out of the wall. The UPS takes over until you can plug the computer in again. Your computer doesn't lose power, and you don't lose any data.

A UPS also protects your equipment from the following:

✦ **Spikes** are rapid, dramatic peaks in the voltage. Spikes are caused by lightning strikes or when the electricity is restored after a blackout.

✦ **Surges** are short-term increases in voltage. Surges can happen when, for example, a high-powered machine in the area is turned off; the extra voltage is dissipated through the power line, which causes the surge.

✦ **Noise** is electrical magnetic interference or radio frequency interference that happens because of electrical storms, electric motors, or microwave radiation.

✦ **Sags** are short-term decreases in the voltage level. A sag is caused by the startup demand of electrical appliances, for example.

✦ **Brownouts** are steady periods of lower voltage. Brownouts are caused when the electric company can't meet the demand at peak times, such as on a really hot day in the summer.

It is important to remember that a UPS is meant to carry the load for the electricity only during short periods of time — 5 to 10 minutes. If you have a blackout, you shouldn't use the UPS to continue work until the power comes back on; use the UPS to save and close all programs and then shut the computer down and turn it off. Repeat with other computers on the network. Often, after a blackout, an extensive power surge jump starts the power. You might want to leave your computers off and unplugged until the power is back in working order.

You may want a UPS for any of the following reasons:

✦ You don't want any of your equipment to burn up from a lightning strike.

✦ It would take too long to recover data if your power went out while you're working on the computer.

✦ You live in an area that has frequent power outages.

✦ Your computer is in close proximity to heavy current devices, such as elevators, welding equipment, high-power amplifiers, or industrial machinery.

✦ Your computer is close to fluorescent lighting, air conditioners, switched-mode power supplies (a heating unit, for example), and so on.

The battery life of your UPS depends on temperature and the number of discharges the UPS has experienced. The temperature of any computer room should be on the cool side, with circulating air; cooler temperatures are good for the UPS as well. A UPS is designed for long periods of continuous low charging with occasional minor discharges; however, deep discharges — such as running for five or more minutes at a time — drain the life from the battery.

UPS power is rated in watts; the more equipment you plug into your computer — printer, modem, scanner, and so on — the more power you need for your UPS. A UPS should be rated at 550 volt-amps (VA) or more. Don't use anything less.

Use one UPS for each server on the network. You also can attach a UPS to each computer, if you think you need the battery backup. You don't need to use a UPS on a game computer, for example, but you might want to use a UPS for the computer on which you perform accounting or work tasks.

Taking the First Steps to Diagnosing a Problem

As your first order of business, you want to figure out just where the problems with the network originate. You should rule out each computer by checking the system and devices. Don't begin your search at the most unlikely place; begin with the simple things first, such as connections and power cords.

Windows Protection Errors

Windows protection errors, or general protection faults (GPF), are most common in Windows 98. GPFs are less common in Windows 2000 and XP but still occur. Although they don't normally affect the network, they can be quite bothersome. They often lock, or freeze, your computer, and you must restart your computer to get back to work. Here are some possible causes for GPFs:

- ✦ The Plug and Play isn't working correctly with the computer's basic input/output system (BIOS). The BIOS is a set of instructions that enables the computer's hardware and operating system to communicate with applications and devices.

- ✦ The Registry is corrupted.

- ✦ You have a virus that's affecting the Win.com or Command.com file.

- ✦ Memory or a caching file is corrupted or damaged.

- ✦ The motherboard isn't working properly.

- ✦ Incorrect settings exist in the complementary metal-oxide semiconductor (CMOS). CMOS is an integrated circuit used for the processor and memory.

If you have one or two GPFs, you can reboot your computer and that may clear up the problem. If you continue to have several GPFs over several days, you can try the following methods to resolve it:

1. Start the computer in safe mode to see if the error occurs there. If you don't see the error, your problem is probably a device error — check cards, IRQs, Plug and Play, and so on in the Device Manager. If you do see the error, it may be a virus, or a CMOS or memory/caching problem.

2. Check your CMOS settings to make sure they're correct. See your computer's documentation for more information.

3. If you're using Novell Client 32 software, remove it and use Microsoft Client for Novell Networks.

4. Reinstall Windows. You should reinstall Windows directly over the top of your current Windows, without uninstalling Windows first. All of your data will remain intact, although you should always make a backup before undertaking a reinstallation. Reinstall the same version of Windows that is currently on your computer. Reinstalling should fix any corrupted or missing files. If it doesn't fix your problem, you might need to make a complete backup and then format your drive. Install Windows and all of your programs from scratch. This is a *huge* job, however, so first try everything you can to fix the Windows you have.

Using Microsoft System Information

You can use Windows tools and utilities to help you locate the problem as well. For example, you can view your system information at any time. System information includes hardware resources, the software environment, and other components, such as the modem, network, ports, devices, and so on.

Examining tools

To view system information, choose Start ➪ Programs ➪ Accessories ➪ System Tools ➪ System Information. Figure A-1 illustrates the Microsoft System Information dialog box in Windows 98. Windows 2000 and XP have a similar System Information dialog box.

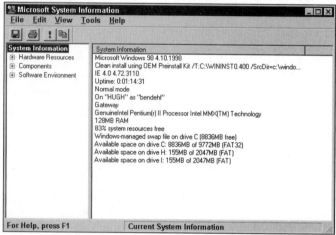

Figure A-1: Check for conflicts or problems in the System Information dialog box.

System Information lists general facts, system resources, and so on, but the dialog box can show you so much more. Following is a list of the tools included with the Microsoft System Information utility:

✦ **Windows Report Tool** creates a report you can send to Microsoft about the problem you're having. Microsoft technicians then can help you diagnose the problem. (Windows 98)

✦ **Update Wizard Uninstall** helps you uninstall various software packages. (Windows 98)

✦ **System File Checker** scans system files that might be corrupted and, with your permission, restores original files. (Windows 98)

✦ **Registry Checker** checks the Registry for errors and restores the latest backup, if necessary. (Windows 98)

✦ **Dr. Watson** is a program that runs in the background while you work in Windows. Dr. Watson records a log of system events. (All Windows versions)

✦ **System Configuration Utility** enables you to start your computer using various files so that you can diagnose startup problems. It also shows the config.sys, system.ini, autoexec.bat, and win.ini files and enables you to edit them, if you want. Finally, the System Configuration Utility displays a list of programs that load at startup. You can disable any file for startup to help you diagnose a problem (see Figure A-2). (Available in all Windows versions; Windows 2000 and XP make this option available during startup by pressing F8 or F2.)

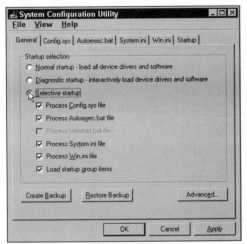

Figure A-2: Use the Configuration Utility to locate problems with starting up.

✦ **ScanDisk** scans your hard disks for errors, corruption, and other problems, and then fixes these problems, if you want. (Windows 98; available in Windows 2000 and XP through System Tools)

✦ **Version Conflict Manager** lists any files that are in conflict with your current operating system. (All Windows versions)

✦ **Net Diagnostics** scans the system for information about network hardware, software, and connections. (Windows 2000 and XP)

✦ **System Restore** enables you to restore the system to its original configuration or to a restore point. A *restore point* is a point in the life of the computer that you, or the computer, create, in which all system settings and performance are optimal. (Windows 2000 and XP)

✦ **File Signature Verification Utility** checks your system for files that are not digitally signed. By default, the operating system (OS) creates digitally signed, or secure, system files. If any system files are present that have not been signed, the File Signature Verification Utility can delete those files. (Windows 2000 and XP)

✦ **DirectX Diagnostic Tool** checks the DirectX information and drivers on the computer so you can diagnose problems with DirectX. DirectX components normally have to do with display, sound, music, and the network. (Windows 2000 and XP)

Start any of these tools by choosing the Tools menu in the Microsoft System Information window. These tools can help you diagnose and fix problems with an individual computer, and some tools help with network connections.

Looking at hardware resources

The Microsoft System Information window displays information about your hardware resources, including IRQ conflicts and sharing, I/O ranges, and memory allocations. Figure A-3 shows the IRQs and devices using each address. All Windows versions are similar in the Hardware Resources feature.

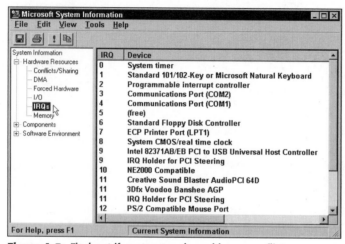

Figure A-3: Find out if your network card has a conflict.

To view the Hardware Resources, click the plus sign to the left of the entry in the left pane of the Microsoft System Information window, and then select any topic in the list. View the contents in the right window pane.

Looking at components

Your system components include multimedia, input, display, sound, infrared, modems, network, ports, and other devices. When you view information about any system component, you see the device name, description, CPU usage, data transfer rates, and other information pertinent to the device. You can even view a window containing details about the devices with which you have a problem.

Figure A-4 shows the Printing components. Note that each printer installed on the computer, even network printers, appears. You can view the version of the files, the date they were installed, and the language the printers use.

Under the Network component, you can view information about the adapter, protocol, and WinSock. WinSock is a DLL (or library) file that allows communication between TCP/IP and Windows.

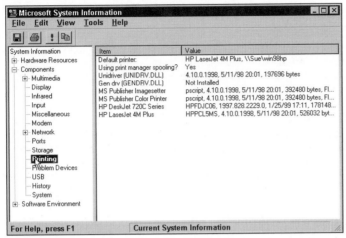

Figure A-4: View information about your system components.

Looking at the software environment

The *software environment* refers to device drivers and other software that runs hardware, such as 16- and 32-bit modules, files for starting applications, your startup programs, and OLE files that affect your Registry.

Figure A-5 shows the dynamic link library (DLL) files loaded in the computer. If you ever have a conflict of DLL files, find out if you have the latest version by checking here.

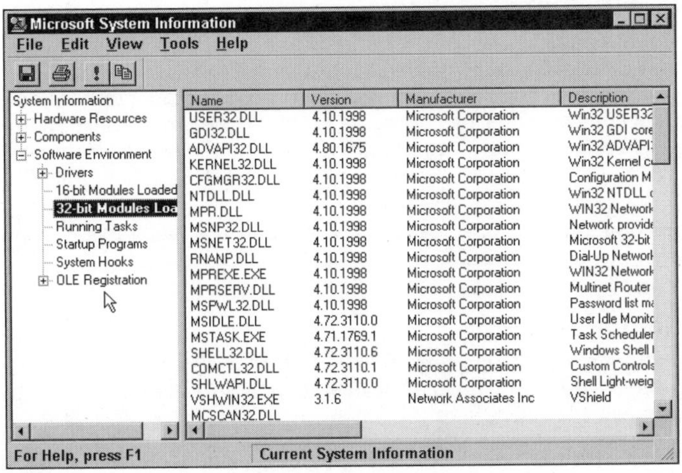

Figure A-5: Locate current versions of DLL files.

Tip   You can print any of the information in the System Information window. Choose File ⇨ Print.

The Software Environment category also offers information in Windows 2000 and XP about signed drivers, environment variables (system paths), mapped network connections, startup programs, and more. The Software Environment is a good place to check if you're concerned about virus entries, outdated drivers, and the like.

Looking at Internet Settings

Windows 2000 and XP add one more component to the System Information — Internet Settings. Internet settings list DLL file versions and locations, connection and proxy service information, security certificates information, plus security settings for various Internet and intranet sites. For example, your local intranet might be set to medium-low security, whereas Internet restricted sites are set at high security.

Finding problems

A network usually is made up of many different components, each of which can cause problems with connecting to other computers on the network. In addition, two or more components could fail at the same time, thus producing confusing symptoms that are difficult to diagnose.

Depending on the type of network you have, only three or four things can go wrong. If you have a client/server network, the server can experience a problem. Whether you use client/server or workgroup networking, you can have problems with a hub, the cabling, or a workstation computer. Your first step is to figure out which of these is causing the problem, and then narrow the field of possibilities.

Diagnosing trouble with one PC

Find out if the problem is with one PC, two, or the entire network. If the problem is with only one PC, you want to check for unplugged or broken cables, bad network cards, or other such hardware problems. If you can't see any problems, you can try plugging in another computer at that same spot. If the second computer has the same problem, then the cable or a hub is likely responsible. If the second computer doesn't have a problem, the first computer is the culprit.

Tip   If the PC is new or if you just added an adapter or other hardware, the problem probably involves the system's configuration. Double-check all configuration settings.

Having trouble with multiple PCs

If you're having trouble with multiple computers and all of the PCs were working before, then you probably have a problem with a hub or other device, such as a router or gateway, or the problem could be in a segment of cable. Check the patch cables on the hub as well.

If the entire network is having trouble, you might have a problem with your server or host computer. Depending on the network problem, the server computer might have crashed, lost its network card (either a driver was corrupted or the card went bad), received an error that's locking it up, or be busy in an involved operation.

Trying the simple solutions

Even though some of the following suggestions sound too easy or even ridiculous, you should check them first. Often the answer to a connection problem is a loose plug or a nicked cable. You can save a lot of time and trouble by checking the basics first.

Make a physical check of the machine, whether it's a computer, printer, hub, or another part of the network. If the network cards have ready lights, make sure they are all green. Also, check hub lights to make sure they are ready and functioning. Often, you can simply shut down the entire network—hubs, switches, server, and all workstations—then bring them up again slowly, and that will reset things back to normal. Try this first.

If you still have problems, turn the machine off and check the following items:

1. Check the power cables to be sure that every cord is firmly in its place.

2. Check the network cable and connectors from one end of the line to the other. Check to see that connectors are firmly joined and that cables have no nicks, cuts, or bends.

3. Check inside the computer case to make sure that the cables are not crimped, torn, loose, or split. Make sure the cables are plugged into the appropriate socket and the pins match. Cards should be well seated.

4. If all the physical connections seem to be working, restart the computer. As it boots, watch for any error messages and listen for beeps that indicate a problem. The computer's manual should include information about what each beep means.

If the problem still exists, you might try exchanging parts. If the keyboard doesn't seem to work, for example, switch it with another one in the house to see if the second keyboard works. If it does, the problem is with the keyboard. You can try exchanging many different parts: network cards, printer cables, and so on. If the network cards are not the same brand, you need to load the correct driver for the card you are trying out.

Investigating computer problems

If you're having trouble with your Windows computers, on the network or off, you can try several things to help you pin down the problem. First, try booting the computer in safe mode.

To boot in safe mode, press the F8 key during the Windows startup. Choose Safe Mode with Network from the menu that appears. You can choose different options from the menu to see if the problem resides in the network configuration, sound and video cards, and so on. Restart the computer each time you want to try a different menu option.

A common Windows problem is caused by Plug and Play hardware. If you have problems with booting, shutting down, or connecting to the network, it might be a Plug and Play problem with your network interface card. You can disable Plug and Play for that card and try it again. Disable Plug and Play in the Device Manager.

If a user is having trouble connecting to the network, check the user's logging-on process. Often, users cancel the logon dialog box in order to get to work more quickly. Another possibility is that someone else might have used the computer and entered a different name in the logon dialog box. Most users forget to check the username; they just type in the password and expect to log on to the network. It usually doesn't work.

Another simple thing to check is to see if the user has changed any network configurations, added any hardware or software, or had any problems with the computer lately. If you ask those questions first, you might get to the root of the problem more quickly.

Using the System Monitor

If you have network problems and you use a client/server network, you can use the System Monitor to help find the cause of the problems on a Windows 98 computer. If you don't use a client/server network, you can view one machine's use of system resources to help find the bottleneck in your system. The System Monitor enables you to monitor running processes, memory usage, dial-up access, and more.

In order to use the System Monitor over the network, you need the following:

✦ A client/server network using either NT Server or Novell NetWare server

✦ User-level security selected for each computer, which removes all network shares you set for a peer-to-peer workgroup

✦ The Remote Registry Service installed on each computer

✦ File and Printer Sharing enabled on each computer

Using the Network Troubleshooter

Windows XP has included a network troubleshooter that can help you determine problems with adapters, terminal services, modem sharing, even TCP/IP configuration. To use the Network Troubleshooter, right-click My Network Places and choose Properties. In the Network Connections dialog box, click Network Troubleshooter.

The Network Troubleshooter performs many tasks. It can perform tests on TCP/IP by performing the PING command and/or the NETVIEW command for you. The Network Troubleshooter can check your dial-up or Internet connection as well, automatically.

Note   If you use Windows 2000, you can use Windows Help to locate a variety of networking troubleshooters. One, in particular, is for TCP/IP networks; another is for users; another for hardware; and so on.

Examining the Network Hardware and Software

Network connection problems sometimes affect only one computer, but they often affect all computers on the network. When you have a problem, you can check a computer's network interface card, cabling, and then the network hub.

You also can check the protocols used on the network. TCP/IP configuration often causes connection problems as well. A problem with network speed might have to do with hardware and software. If you have problems with bottlenecks, you should check certain areas of the network.

When experiencing network connection problems, ask yourself the following questions to help diagnose the problem:

✦ Did the connection work before, or did it just recently stop working?

✦ If it just recently stopped working, what equipment or software have you added?

✦ Did something happen or change since it last worked?

If the connection never worked, you probably have configuration problems or a bad cable. If it recently stopped working and you added something new to the network, remove that added equipment and see if the situation improves. If nothing's changed and the connection quit working all of a sudden, check network cards, cabling, and hubs, in that order.

Tip   If you have a problem you cannot solve on your own, check the Microsoft Knowledge Base for help. The address is www.support.microsoft.com.

Exploring network card problems

If your computer won't connect to the network, you might have a problem with your network card. If the computer is new and you just added the card, check the IRQ (interrupt request) and DMA (direct memory access) addresses. Configuration might be the problem. If the card worked and then just stopped working, the card might need to be replaced.

Tip   The easiest and quickest troubleshooting solution for a network that is not connecting is to delete everything from the network properties dialog box—TCP/IP, client, services, and network adapter—reboot, and then install everything anew. This often refreshes corrupted software or settings and makes the network magically work.

Checking in the Device Manager

If you're having a connection problem, check to make sure that Windows sees your network interface card. If you see a red or yellow icon to the left of the NIC, then there's a problem with your card. Figure A-6 illustrates the Device Manager tab of the System Properties dialog box. To check the adapter card in the Device Manager, follow these steps:

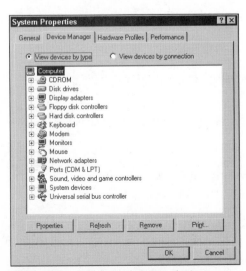

Figure A-6: Check your system devices.

1. Choose Start ⇨ Settings ⇨ Control Panel ⇨ System in Windows 98. In Windows 2000 and XP, right-click My Computer ⇨ Properties; click the Hardware tab and then Device Manager. The System Properties dialog box appears.

2. Choose the Device Manager tab in Windows 98, and choose the View devices by type option.

3. Click the plus (+) sign to the left of Network adapters.

4. Check to see if your adapter has a yellow exclamation point in a circle or a red x. The yellow exclamation point means the device isn't working properly; the red x means the device isn't working at all.

5. If your adapter card does display one of these icons, select the adapter and then click the Properties button. The adapter card's Properties dialog box appears, as shown in Figure A-7.

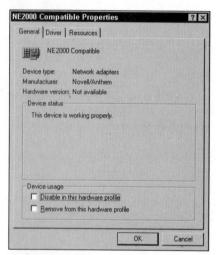

Figure A-7: Look at the adapter's properties.

6. In the General tab, view the Device status area for a definition of the problem.

7. Click OK to close the Properties dialog box.

8. Close the System Properties dialog box, and then close the Control Panel.

Note Some network cards, especially the Plug and Play cards, come with special software that you can use to configure the card. If you're having trouble with the IRQ or other addressing information, check to see if your card manufacturer supplied this software.

Checking network settings

You also should verify that all your settings in the Network dialog box are correct. To check your adapter settings, follow these steps:

1. Choose Start ⇨ Settings ⇨ Control Panel in Windows 98. The Control Panel window appears. In Windows 2000 or XP, right-click My Network Places ⇨ Properties.

2. Double-click the Network icon in Windows 98. In Windows 2000 or XP, right-click Local Area Connection and Properties. The Network (Windows 98) or the Local Area Connection Properties (Windows 2000 and XP) dialog box appears.

3. In the Configuration tab, select your network adapter card, as shown in Figure A-8 in Windows 98. In Windows 2000 or XP, click the Configure button.

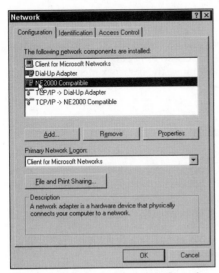

Figure A-8: Select your network card.

4. Click the Properties button in Windows 98 or the Resources tab in Windows 2000 or XP. The adapter's Properties dialog box appears.

5. Choose the Resources tab if you're using Windows 98, as shown in Figure A-9.

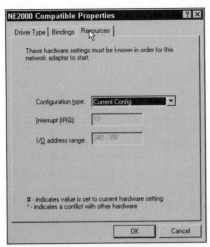

Figure A-9: Check the IRQ and I/O address range.

For more information about IRQs and I/O addresses, see Chapter 25.

6. Make sure the configuration is correct, and then click OK.

7. In the Configuration tab (Windows 98) or the General tab (Windows 2000 or XP), check to be sure you have the Client for Microsoft Networks installed.

8. Next, check the Identification tab of the Network dialog box in Windows 98, as shown in Figure A-10, to make sure that you're using the correct workgroup name and that your computer name is unique in the network. For Windows XP, you must right-click My Computer ⇨ Properties and choose the Computer Name tab. For Windows 2000, right-click My Computer ⇨ Properties and choose the Network Identification tab. The computer name and workgroup name are listed. You can change either by clicking the Properties button.

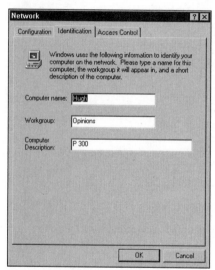

Figure A-10: Make sure you have the right workgroup name.

9. Click OK. Restart the computer if prompted.

If your power management is on, try turning it off. Sometimes power management features can cause network problems. In the Control Panel, double-click the Power Management icon. In Settings for Always On (Power Scheme area), choose Never for the following two items: Turn Off Monitor and Turn Off Hard Disks.

Looking at protocol problems

When two or more PCs have problems communicating with each other, you could have a protocol mismatch. Say that one PC cannot see others on the network. Check that PC's protocol settings and bindings. Compare the protocols listed in the Network dialog box of a working computer to the one that isn't connecting. Check all protocol properties as well.

For information about protocols, see Chapter 10 or Appendix B.

If you're having trouble with network connections, it could be the protocol. When running TCP/IP, configuration is usually the first thing you should check. Use PING, an MS-DOS prompt command you use to test TCP/IP configuration, to verify that the TCP/IP configuration is correct, that local computers are communicating with each other, and that remote computers are communicating. For more information, see Appendix B.

Use IPCONFIG to display the IP addresses, subnet masks, and default gateways for all network adapter cards on each computer. Make sure that the IP addresses are unique, that subnet masks match, and so on. IPCONFIG is a command you use to test IP addressing. For more information, see Appendix B.

Use NETSTAT to track down strange or unusual network problems. You can troubleshoot incoming and outgoing packet errors with this command. NETSTAT is an MS-DOS prompt command you use to test TCP/IP configuration. For more information, see Appendix B.

Use WINIPCFG, an MS-DOS prompt command you use to test TCP/IP configuration, if you're having trouble with your Dynamic Host Configuration Protocol (DHCP) lease. DHCP is a utility for assigning TCP/IP addresses to workstations automatically. Many DHCP servers provide networked computers with a lease that enables them to use the same number for a limited amount of time. You can use this command to release a lease when you stop using DHCP or renew a lease that you want to continue. For more information, see Appendix B.

See Appendix B for more information about troubleshooting techniques to use with a TCP/IP network.

Troubleshooting cabling problems

You might be using coax, twisted-pair, phone line, or power line cables for your network. *For reasons of safety, problems with your power line are best taken care of by an electrician.* Phone line problems may require a professional as well, although you can check some of the phone line yourself.

If you didn't install your own coax or twisted-pair cabling, you might want to call for help in checking the cabling. But you also can check some problems yourself.

For more information about coax and twisted-pair cables, see Chapter 6. For more information about phone and power line network cabling, see Chapter 8.

Looking at the phone line

You can check the phone wiring that connects the computer to the wall jack for nicks, crimps, and other problems. If you see an obvious problem, replace the wiring. You can buy a short length of phone wire, with the RJ-11 connectors attached, at a hardware store, discount department store, or any place that sells telephones.

If you don't see a problem but still think it might be the phone wiring, try trading the current wiring with another phone line wire to see if it works. You then can replace the bad wire if that will solve the problem.

Considering coaxial cable

Check all of the cable in the system for nicks or breaks first. Also check all the terminators to make sure that they are securely fastened to the cable and to the computers. Even if all looks okay, you still might have a break in the connection; it's difficult to tell with coaxial cabling.

You can try replacing the terminators and T-connectors, if you're comfortable with that. You also can try swapping out one cable with another too, unless your cabling goes into walls or under flooring.

You also can use a cable tester, if you have one. *Cable testers* are devices that test for loose connections, faulty cables, and other cabling problems. You can buy cable testers over the Internet and at some computer stores. Cable testers cost between $50 and $250.

Looking at twisted-pair cabling problems

Twisted-pair cabling usually displays a link light on the back of the computer, in the area of the network card port. As long as the link light is lit, the cable doesn't have a problem.

Again, check for physical problems with the cable: cuts, crimps, coiled cable, and so on. Check the connectors. If you have a cable tester, use it. If all else fails, you can call a cable professional to test the cabling for you and replace it as necessary.

Considering hub problems

If you have only one hub on your network and it fails, the entire network goes down. If you have multiple hubs on a network and one fails, only the segment serviced by that hub goes down. It's also possible that one port on a hub will fail — and that affects only one computer. That is a difficult situation to troubleshoot, because you usually start diagnosing the PC, network card, and cabling before you get to the hub.

If you think you have a cabling problem but find nothing wrong with the cable, change the hub port to see if that's the solution.

You also can remove one workstation at a time to see if the other computers work. If removing one workstation eliminates the problem, there's something wrong with that workstation's cable. Make sure that the cable length is acceptable.

Examining bottlenecks

If your network is slow and everyone's complaining about it, you probably have a bottleneck somewhere in the system. A bottleneck is usually one network component causing sluggish traffic flow. If all your networking hardware works well together, you won't have bottlenecks. If you do, you need to locate the problem and alleviate it.

Memory is always a prime suspect for a slow computer or network. A server, for example, or a workstation that carries most of the load could be a bottleneck on the network. When everyone accesses one computer, its processes slow down. Adding memory can improve the situation.

Applications often create a bottleneck if they're faulty or a little buggy. Make sure that you use the latest upgrades to any program installed on your computers. If you think a program is running slowly, check with the manufacturer to see if there is an available upgrade or a patch that solves the problem.

When anyone on the network transfers several large files — such as images, sound clips, or motion files — from one computer to another, that transfer can cause a log jam. You might save those files to a Zip disk or CD-RW to help ease a network traffic problem.

Investigating Peripheral Problems

Each peripheral in your computer can cause multiple problems by itself or in conjunction with other peripherals. If you have a problem you cannot solve, check the peripheral's documentation and the manufacturer's Web site for extra information.

Examining network printer problems

Often, simple things cause printer problems — such as an unplugged network cable or a problem with the application. Other problems can be more difficult to find. If you have trouble with your printer and you've tried all the following suggestions, you should check with the manufacturer for more specific information (refer to the printer documentation or the manufacturer's Web site for contact information).

General printer check

As with any network equipment, you want to physically check a printer that's giving you problems before you check anything else. Make sure that the printer is turned on and online, check the paper tray and path, and check all power cords and cables. Always try turning the printer off and then back on again to reinitialize it, in case some settings are corrupted. If your printer doesn't have an on/off switch, unplug the printer for 10 seconds or so and then plug it back in.

Next, run the printer's self-test to see if the problem is in the printer or elsewhere. If the printer passes, use Print Screen from an MS-DOS prompt to see if the computer can communicate with the printer. The easiest method of printing with the Print Screen button on your keyboard is to first go to the MS-DOS prompt, and then type **dir** so that you have something on the screen. Press the button on your keyboard labeled Print Screen to see if the directory on your screen prints. If this second test fails, replace the cable between the printer and the computer. If this second test is successful, check the application that is printing to the printer.

If the printer works from MS-DOS but not from Windows, you might have a Windows problem. Try removing the printer driver and then installing it again.

If the printer still won't print, check the server if there is one, or the computer to which the printer is installed locally. For example, if the printer's icon in the user's Print Folder is grayed, or dimmed, that means the printer is offline or turned off.

Next, have the user print another document — something simple from WordPad, for example. Check the print queue on the computer attached to the printer to see if the job is listed. If the job isn't listed, check to see if the network user who is trying to print is logged on to the network. Also check to see if the user has permission to print, if the printer is shared, and so on.

Network printer check

If the previous steps don't solve or address your printing problem, try these network printing troubleshooting steps.

Print to a local printer. If that works, print to a file and copy the file to the network printer. To do this, follow these steps:

1. Choose Start ⇨ Settings ⇨ Printers. The Printers window appears.

2. Right-click the printer's icon and then choose Properties. The printer's Properties dialog box appears.

3. Choose the Details tab, as shown in Figure A-11.

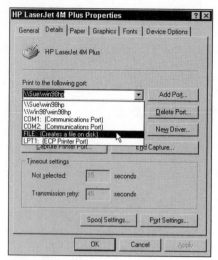

Figure A-11: Set to print to a file.

4. In Print to the Following Port, choose FILE: (Creates a file on disk).

5. Click OK to close the dialog box.

6. Print any file from any application. When prompted, enter a filename for the print job.

To print the file, open the MS-DOS window and, at the prompt, type the following:

```
copy <path\filename> <networkprinter> /b
```

For example, type **copy c:\docs\letter.prn \\Sue\win98hp /b**. The */b* makes the file a binary one, which means the entire file will print. If you don't use a */b*, only part of the file might print.

If this printing process works, the problem lies with the computer. If the printing process doesn't work, the problem is with the connection to the network printer.

You also can try capturing the printer port, as described in Chapter 15. Sometimes a captured printer works when a printer using a universal naming convention (UNC) connection won't.

Solving Spool32 errors

When you're printing to a network printer, you might receive a Spool32 error. Spool32.exe manages print spooling, which enables the computer to process a job more quickly and efficiently. Following are three samples of Spool32 errors:

```
SPOOL32 caused a Stack Fault in module Kernel32.dll at ...(address).
SPOOL32 caused an Invalid Page Fault in module Kernel32.dll at ...(address).
SPOOL32 caused a General Protection Fault in module Kernel32.dll at
...(address).
```

Your first step should be to make sure you have the most updated printer driver for your printer. Check the printer manufacturer's Web site (or call the manufacturer) to see if an updated version of the driver has been released. Often, manufacturers release another version of their printer driver when they find a coding error in the previous driver version. Replacing the driver not only clears the Spool32 error but also makes your printer run more efficiently.

An antivirus program, a terminate-and-stay-resident program (a DOS program that stays loaded in memory, such as calendars or calculators), or some other program could be blocking your printing. You can figure out what is blocking the printing by following these steps:

1. Disable the config.sys, autoexec.bat, winstart.bat, system.ini, and win.ini files all at the same time. You can do this by using System Information, as described in the section "Using Microsoft System Information," earlier in this chapter.

2. Restart the computer. Now print. If you still have problems, go to Step 3. If this takes care of the problem, complete your printing, and then go back to System Information and enable the files you disabled in Step 1.

Tip   You probably won't run into a Spool32 problem very often. If you do, however, you can find out which program is causing the problem by enabling only one of the files listed in Step 1, starting your computer, and printing. If the printing works, enable another file and try again. When one file blocks the printing, open the file in a text editor and see what programs it's loading. You can disable each program, one at a time, to find the cause of your Spool32 error.

3. Print directly to the printer by changing the spooling format from Enhanced Metafile (EMF) to RAW. You do this in the Details tab of the printer's Properties dialog box. In the Spool Settings dialog box, click Print Directly to the printer; in the Spool Data Format box, click RAW.

Looking at remote connection problems

As often as not, remote connection problems are the fault of the remote computer. Before you spend too much time on your end searching for the cause, check with the person running the remote modem and computer to see if he or she has a problem.

Printing and Dial-Up Networking

If you have trouble printing a remote page, such as a Web page or an intranet page, over a dial-up connection, you might be trying to print on a different subnet than your dial-up connection.

You can work around this problem by printing the page *while on* the Web or intranet. Next, quit the Dial-Up Networking connection. Choose Start ➪ Settings ➪ Printers. Right-click the network printer, and then click Use Printer Offline to remove the check from the check box.

Press F5 to refresh the printer's status and close the Printers folder. The Web page should print normally now.

Error 645 with Dial-Up Networking

An error 645 occurs when Dial-Up Networking cannot complete a connection. The error reads as follows: "Dial-Up Networking could not complete the connection to the server."

The problem generally occurs when the Require Encrypted Password option is enabled. To alleviate this problem, follow these steps:

1. Open My Computer.

2. Double-click Dial-Up Networking.

3. Right-click your connection icon and choose Properties.

4. Select the Server Types tab and then click the Require Encrypted Password check box to remove the check.

5. Click OK.

Problems opening Dial-Up Networking

Problems with your DLL files can result in the Dial-Up Networking folder disappearing, not opening, or appearing briefly before disappearing. Even reinstalling Windows doesn't help.

The problem could be caused by any of the following DLL files being missing or damaged:

✦ Wsock32.dll

✦ Wsock32n.dll

Note   Windows 98 doesn't have the Wsock32n.dll file unless you have upgraded from Windows 95 or you installed a program that also installed the file.

✦ Rnaui.dll

✦ Msvcrt20.dll

✦ Rasapi32.dll

✦ Rnaapp.exe

You can resolve the problem by following these steps:

1. Restart the computer, but when you see Starting Windows appear on-screen, press the F8 key.

2. From the menu, choose Safe Mode, Command Prompt Only.

3. Rename the Wsock32.dll, Wsock32n.dll, Rnaui.dll, Msvcrt20.dll, Rasapi32.dll, and Rnaapp.exe files (found in the Windows\System folder) to the same filenames but use a different extension, such as aaa or ccc. Wsock32.dll, for example, becomes Wsock32.aaa, and so on. Be careful not to use an extension often used in Windows, such as exe or com. If the files do not exist, skip this step.

4. Restart Windows.

5. Extract a new copy of the files from the original Windows CD-ROM. See online help for information on extracting files.

Decreasing logon time to ISPs

Often you see a long logon delay when you're dialing your ISP or other service provider. By default, Windows enables the software compression and log on to network options for Dial-Up Networking. It also binds NetBEUI, IPX/SPX, and TCP/IP to the dial-up adapter by default. By changing some of these options, you can speed up the logon process.

You can cut down the delay time in Windows 98 by doing the following:

1. Open My Computer.

2. Double-click Dial-Up Networking.

3. In the Dial-Up Networking window, select the connection. Right-click the connection and choose Properties.

4. In the Properties dialog box, choose Server Types. Figure A-12 shows the default options that are set.

5. Deselect Log on to the Network, NetBEUI, and IPX/SPX Compatible.

6. Click OK.

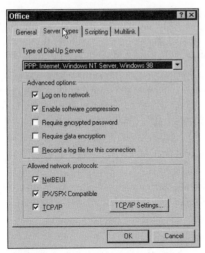

Figure A-12: Disable some default options.

Solving Specific Problems

You can experience some pretty specific problems on a network. The Internet is a wonderful source for finding solutions to networking problems. You also might try to contact the manufacturer of the products you're using or take a look at the Web site of the manufacturer or vendor for ideas. Following are some of the more common problems you may encounter.

✦ **Computer crashes randomly and inconsistently** — Insufficient RAM usually causes frequent and random computer crashes. You might want to check to see if the RAM chips are well seated first. If a chip is not well seated, remove and replace the RAM chip.

✦ **Conflicts with a card or other device** — If you have problems with installing a new adapter card or other device, check to see that the IRQ isn't already in use. IRQs are limited in number, and no two devices can share the same one. For more information, see Chapter 25.

✦ **Defective data, printing problems, monitor static** — Power problems generally are related to damaged computer components. Line noise, power surges, spikes, and blackouts can overheat your hardware or corrupt data. If you notice problems with your lights or other electrical equipment, you can assume your computer equipment also is affected by these power problems. A UPS and surge protector are your best defense. See the section "Examining a UPS," earlier in this chapter, for more information.

✦ **Net Watcher doesn't disconnect the user** — Sometimes Net Watcher doesn't disconnect a client user when you indicate you want the user disconnected. This is a minor glitch in the program. It disconnects the user, but when the user logs on to the network again, he or she can reconnect to the resource. If you don't want a user connected to a resource, you must change the password on the resource.

✦ **Sluggish system resources** — Your system resources — memory, processor speed, caching, and so on — might seem to decrease even though no programs are running. This situation happens when you start a program and then quit it before you let it start all the way. Stopping the program before it starts "leaks" memory and decreases system resources. Leaked memory consists of data that is stored in temporary RAM and takes up space until you turn off the computer. The only way to resolve this problem is to restart the computer. If you still have the problem, check carefully for viruses on your system. Viruses often work in the background to eat system resources.

✦ **Problems with the System Monitor** — If your System Monitor suddenly quits without notice as you view other computers on the network, it's probably because someone on the network pressed Ctrl+Alt+Delete. This action not only causes the networked computer to reboot or display the task list, but it also hangs the System Monitor.

Solving share problems

If you need to look at the network resources and their shares for the network, you can use the NET VIEW command. Use the command at the MS-DOS prompt if you're having trouble locating a shared resource. NET VIEW is great for finding the drives, folders, printers, and other names of resources.

To view shared resources, follow these steps:

1. Choose Start ➪ Programs ➪ MS-DOS Prompt for Windows 98 or Start ➪ (All) Programs ➪ Accessories ➪ Command Prompt for Windows 2000 or XP.

2. At the C prompt, type the following command:

    net view *computername*

    For example, type **net view \\sue**.

The command displays the share name for the drives, folders, printers, and other resources; the type of share; and any comments about the share. Figure A-13 shows the results of the command example in Step 2. Note that the folders, a Zip drive, and a printer are shared on the referenced computer.

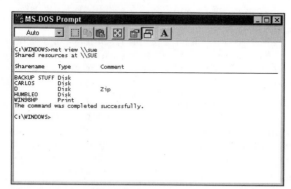

Figure A-13: Find out about the shared drives, folders, and other resources.

Missing the Network Logon dialog box

Sometimes the network logon dialog box disappears during logon. If the dialog box isn't there for the user to enter a username and password, the user cannot access the network resources. Any of several causes might be responsible; following are the more common reasons:

✦ AutoLogon in the Registry is a number other than 0.

✦ The network interface card is improperly configured.

✦ The Primary Network Logon field isn't set correctly.

To resolve the problem, check your Network dialog box first (choose Start ➪ Settings ➪ Control Panel ➪ Network icon) in Windows 98 or, for both Windows 2000 and XP, right-click My Network Places ➪ Properties then right-click Local Area Connection and choose Properties. Check to see if the network card configurations are correct. You should check to see that the card is bound to the correct protocol and that the IRQ and I/O addresses are correct. See Chapter 25 for more information. If you made any changes, restart your computer to see if the Network Logon dialog box comes up now.

Before you close the Network dialog box, check the Primary Network Logon in the Configuration tab, as shown in Figure A-14. The primary logon should be set to Client for Microsoft Networks. If it's been changed to a Windows Logon, the Network Logon dialog box will not appear. If you changed the primary network logon, restart the computer.

If neither of these configurations solves the problem, you need to change an entry in the Registry. The following entry will only be listed in your Registry if you're on a client/server network. Follow these steps:

1. Choose Start ➪ Run. The Run dialog box appears.

2. In the Open text box, enter **regedit** and then press Enter. The Registry Editor appears.

3. Locate the HKEY_LOCAL_MACHINE\Software\Microsoft\Windows\CurrentVersion\Network\Real Mode Net key.

4. Locate the AutoLogon entry. It should read AutoLogon=0. If it doesn't list 0, change the value to 0.

5. Close the Registry and restart the computer.

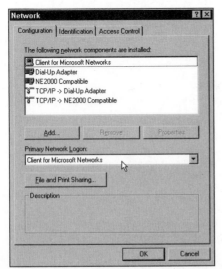

Figure A-14: Make sure that you're on the right network.

Troubleshooting with the System Configuration Utility

Windows 98 and XP have a program that helps you diagnose system configuration issues. The System Configuration utility is also called msconfig enables you to select check boxes that turn off certain settings so you can find out which settings are causing the problem. msconfig is especially useful in locating viruses in your system that could affect your computer and the entire network.

You can set your configuration preference for the following files in the System Configuration utility:

✦ System.ini

✦ Boot.ini

✦ Win.ini

✦ Programs that startup with the computer

✦ Environment and International settings (in Windows XP)

In XP, you must log on as an administrator to use msconfig. To start msconfig, follow these steps:

1. Click Start ➪ Run. The Run dialog box appears.

2. Type **msconfig** in the Open text box and click OK.

You can perform various tasks with msconfig. On the General tab, you can choose to start the computer with a diagnostic startup in which Windows loads only the basic devices and services, step-by-step, so you can determine if a device or service is causing your problem. When you use diagnostic startup, networking, Plug and Play, and other services are temporarily disabled.

You can alternatively use the Selective Startup option on the General tab. Deselect processing of the system.ini, boot.ini, win.ini, and so on to see if one of those files is causing a problem with Windows. When you use selective startup, deselect only one process or system at a time and then reboot. If you choose multiple services or systems to disable, you won't know which one is causing the problem.

You can stop individual files from loading on boot in the System.ini, Win.ini, or Boot.ini tabs. (The Boot.ini tab is available only in Windows XP.) Naturally, if you're unsure of what you're doing and you're not sure what these files do, you shouldn't edit the configurations; you could disable your computer.

A handy tool for locating viruses is the Startup tab of the System Configuration Utility. The Startup tab lists the programs, the program command and path, and the location of the files that open when you start up your computer. By deselecting a startup item, you can stop your computer from booting with that item. You can select the item again if and when you find the item was not causing a problem.

A virus might show up in the Startup tab of your computer. For example, Figure A-15 shows the `run=` command at the bottom of the list in the Startup tab. The `alexir.exe` and `instit.bat` are both leftover viruses. The antivirus quarantined the files, but the `run=` command in startup still searches for them when the computer boots. Deselecting the line in the Startup tab stops the operating system from looking for the virus files.

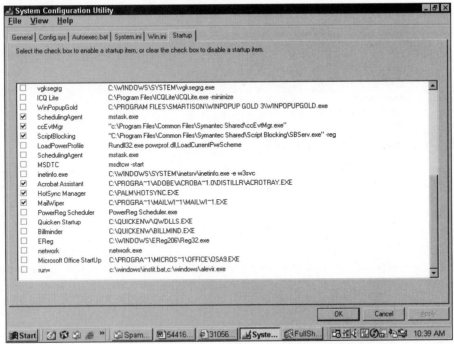

Figure A-15: Stop individual items from starting up with the operating system.

Troubleshooting Macs

There are many troubleshooting procedures to go through if you're using an AppleShare network — with all Mac computers. This book, however, is about using Macs with PCs, so this section is targeted to those networking problems you might have with your mixed network. If you have trouble with AppleShare or with your individual Mac computer, see the documentation or go to www.apple.com for more information.

You should use ping and other network troubleshooting tools just as you do with a PC to make sure the hardware connection is still viable. If the ping doesn't work, then check cables, network card, hubs or switches, and so on.

Next, verify that the Mac is correctly configured for TCP/IP. Many issues can cause problems with attaching to the network: A TCP/IP setting could accidentally change, a duplicate IP address could appear on the network, a system file or TCP/IP preference file might become corrupted.

In addition, you should check the following things on your Mac and network:

✦ Make sure network wires are strong and stable, or if wireless, make sure the network follows the wireless distance and direction guidelines.

✦ Swap out the network card with a working computer.

✦ Reset the PRAM (see your Apple documentation).

✦ Delete TCP/IP settings and reconfigure.

✦ Turn off non-MacOS extensions (consult your Apple documentation).

✦ Reinstall Open Transport.

✦ Reinstall the system software.

You can also check out some of these Wiley books for help and information about your Macintosh: *Mac OS X For Dummies, 2nd Edition; Mac OS Bible, Jaguar Edition;* and *Mac OS 9 For Dummies.*

Troubleshooting Linux

Linux comes in so many different flavors that it's hard to offer specific help. You can, however, purchase books, go to online forums, and check the Web for information troubleshooting your distribution. Following are some interesting sites that help you troubleshoot problems with Linux:

✦ `www.linuxquestions.org` for questions, forums, FAQs, a glossary, and more information about Linux.

✦ `http://www.ibiblio.org/pub/Linux/docs/` for documents that answer a variety of questions and troubleshoot problems with Linux.

✦ `www.cnet.com` is a good search engine for help with Linux, plus CNET offers advice and tips for Linux users.

✦ `www.linuxreinstall.com/debian.htm` offers troubleshooting information about the Debian distribution.

✦ `www.linuxreinstall.com/suse.htm` offers troubleshooting for the Suse distribution of Linux.

✦ `www.linux-mag.com` offers experts to answer your questions about Linux.

In addition, following are a couple of books you can purchase to help you with specific distributions of Linux. Wiley publishes the *Red Hat Linux 9 Bible* by Christopher Negus (2003) plus many other Linux titles, including *Red Hat Linux 9 For Dummies* by Jon "maddog" Hall and Paul G. Sery (2003), the WROX title *Beginning Red Hat Linux 9* by Sandip Bhattacharya et al. (2003), and *Linux For Dummies, 4th Edition* by Dee-Ann LeBlanc, Melanie Hoag, and Evan Blomquist (2002).

✦   ✦   ✦

IP Addressing

Transmission Control Protocol/Internet Protocol (TCP/IP) is an excellent protocol for using in a home or small-business network. Although it is difficult to configure, after you get the hang of it, you will be pleased with the results. TCP/IP is an efficient protocol that speeds up your network communications. Windows contains everything you need to install and configure TCP/IP on your network computers.

Understanding TCP/IP

TCP/IP is actually a set, or *suite*, of network protocols designed by the government's Advanced Research Projects Agency in the 1970s. Each of the protocols that are part of TCP/IP contributes to making it an efficient and fast communications language for the Internet and for local and wide area networks (LANs and WANs).

TCP/IP works with a variety of hardware and software products. You can use it on Unix computers, Macintoshes, and PCs using Windows, NetWare, OS/2, and more. Many manufacturers and vendors support TCP/IP because it is so widely used.

Note   The most common hardware connection for home or business TCP/IP networks is Ethernet. If you're using a phone line network or wireless, you need to check the documentation to make sure that they can use TCP/IP.

TCP/IP is especially useful today, because it enables local networks to plug into the Internet easily, corporate intranets to become virtual private networks (VPN) quickly, and VPNs to become extranets, thus linking the world together in a variety of ways. A *VPN* is a network you set up that uses the Internet as your communications base. The VPN, for example, might connect two or more corporate LANs across the country or across the world. An *extranet* is a corporate network that extends to the Internet so that vendors, manufacturers, and customers can access corporate data.

Note   Although most of the discussion in this appendix refers to TCP/IP and IP as it applies to the Internet, the topics also refer to the use of TCP/IP on a home or business network. The latter is just on a smaller scale.

Examining the basics

TCP/IP enables multiple computers to link together in a network. If your network uses TCP/IP, for example, you can link it to the Internet by using a router. A *router* is an intelligent device that connects network segments. Routers transmit network packets from one network to another.

The Internet is, in fact, one huge network of servers and computers attached to each other through a series of routers. They can communicate with each other because of the TCP/IP protocol. TCP/IP hides the routers, though, so all computers on the Internet seem like one big network.

IP

One TCP/IP protocol, in particular, enables network packets to move data between network segments and travel across routers — Internet Protocol (IP). IP is a routing protocol, meaning it directs datagrams from the source to the destination. *Datagrams* are packets of data that contain the source and destination addresses, as well as the data. Each datagram contains all the information it needs to find the target host, no matter which paths the other datagrams have taken.

IP chooses the path the packets take across routers and networks. IP regulates packet forwarding by tracking Internet addresses, recognizing incoming messages, and routing outgoing messages. Datagrams might arrive at the destination in any order, however, or they might not arrive at all.

TCP

Transmission Control Protocol (TCP) is a higher-level protocol than IP. It provides continuing connections between programs. TCP also makes IP datagrams smaller and faster.

TCP divides datagrams into smaller segments to fit the physical requirements of the servers on the network. It then uses IP to transmit the segments of data. IP doesn't guarantee the segments will arrive at the destination in the same order as they were sent.

TCP inserts a header into each segment that is used to track every segment from one port to the other. TCP guarantees that every byte sent arrives — and without duplication or loss. After the segments arrive at the target host, TCP checks for errors. If it finds any corrupted data, it discards that data and requests that the data be transmitted again.

UDP

User Datagram Protocol (UDP) is similar to TCP in that it divides some datagrams into segments and sends them over the network by using IP. UDP is, in fact, a primitive version of TCP. TCP performs error-checking tasks to make sure that the segments arrive without any faults or problems. UDP, on the other hand, doesn't guarantee that the datagrams will arrive intact or even at all.

UDP is used in many programs today. For example, UDP works with SNMP applications on the transport level of communications. SNMP, which is short for Simple Network Management Protocol, is a protocol that manages and monitors the network.

Miscellaneous TCP/IP protocols

Some of the other protocols in the TCP/IP suite include the following:

✦ Point-to-Point Protocol (PPP) enables connections between hosts and networks and the nodes (routers, bridges, and so on) in between.

✦ Simple Mail Transfer Protocol (SMTP) is for exchanging e-mail.

✦ File Transfer Protocol (FTP) is for transferring files. FTP enables one computer to transfer a file to another computer by using TCP.

✦ Server Message Block (SMB) enables a computer to use network resources as if they were local.

✦ Network File System (NFS) enables a computer to use files and peripherals as if they were local.

✦ Telnet is a terminal emulation protocol that enables you to connect to a remote service while in Windows.

✦ Address Resolution Protocol (ARP) translates 32-bit IP addresses into physical network addresses, such as 48-bit Ethernet addresses.

> **Note**
>
> An Ethernet address is also called a *MAC address* (MAC stands for Media Access Control). It's a number written as 12 hexadecimal digits — 0 through 9 and A through F — as in 0080001021ef. Alternatively, a MAC address might have six hexadecimal numbers separated by periods or colons, as in 0:80:0:2:21:ef. The MAC address is unique to each computer, but it does *not* identify the location of the computer, only the computer itself.

✦ Reverse Address Resolution Protocol (RARP) translates physical network addresses into IP addresses.

✦ Internet Control Message Protocol (ICMP) helps IP communicate error information about the IP transmissions.

✦ Internet Group Management Protocol (IGMP) enables IP datagrams to be broadcast to computers that belong to groups.

> **Note**
>
> Some of the TCP/IP protocols are also applications. FTP, Telnet, and SNMP, for example, are programs that you can use over the network because they're included with the TCP/IP suite.

Glimpsing the ISO/OSI model

International Organization for Standardization/Open Systems Interconnection (ISO/OSI) is a set of standards that defines network functionality. ISO/OSI sets standards for cabling, network interface cards (NICs), protocols, and so on.

TCP/IP's layered design works well with the ISO/OSI model to transmit network data efficiently and effectively. As the data moves from the network application (Layer 7) to the network card (Layer 2), one or more of the TCP/IP protocols accompanies it every step of the way.

The seven-layer model defines computer-to-computer communications. Following is a brief explanation of each layer:

✦ **Layer 1** — The physical layer defines the cabling.

✦ **Layer 2** — The data link layer controls the flow of data through the network cards.

✦ **Layer 3** — The network layer defines the protocols for data routing, to make sure that the data gets to the correct destination.

✦ **Layer 4** — The transport layer defines protocols for error checking and message formation.

- ✦ **Layer 5** — The session layer maintains the connection, or *session*, for as long as it takes to transmit the packets. The session layer also performs security and administration functions.

- ✦ **Layer 6** — The presentation layer identifies the way the data is formatted.

- ✦ **Layer 7** — The application layer defines how the applications interact with the network.

Exploring IP Addressing

IP addressing was standardized in 1981, with specifications that required each system attached to the Internet be assigned a unique, 32-bit address value. Systems include servers, routers, gateways, and other networking hardware. A router that attaches two network segments, for example, must have two unique IP addresses, one for each network interface.

Note   To ensure that IP addresses used on the Internet are unique, the Internet Network Information Center (InterNIC) must assign any address used on the Internet. InterNIC is the controlling agency for IP addresses and domain names.

Examining an IP address

An *IP address* identifies the computer or other node (router, printer, server, or other) on the network. Each IP address on a network must be unique.

An IP address is a binary number written in a series of four decimal digits, which is known as *dotted decimal*. Four period-delimited octets consisting of up to 12 numerals forms an IP address. For example, Microsoft's home page IP address is 207.46.131.137 and is a dotted decimal. The numbers represent decimal notations for each of the four bytes of the address; the address identifies the computer.

The IP address is really made up of two parts: the network number and the host number.

- ✦ The **network number** identifies the general location of the computer on the network, and the host number pins it down to the exact computer. In Microsoft's IP address, 207.46 is the network address.

- ✦ The **host number** is represented by 131.137. Each class of address uses a different manner of dividing the octets. Microsoft is a Class B network (see the following section).

The highest value in any octet is 255, because of the way the binary format translates to dotted decimal format.

Understanding address classes

IP addressing is divided into five categories, or *classes*. Three of the classes — Class A, Class B, and Class C — are in use today. The following list describes each of the classes:

- ✦ **Class A** is used for large networks. To identify a Class A network address, the first octet uses the numbers from 1 to 126. Class A networks have an 8-bit network prefix; therefore, they are currently referred to as /8s (pronounced "slash eights") or just "eights."

- ✦ **Class B** is mainly used for medium-sized networks, and the first octet values range from 128 to 191. Class B network addresses have a 16-bit network prefix; thus, they are referred to as /16s.

✦ **Class C** is reserved for smaller networks. To identify a Class C network, the values range from 192 to 233. Class C networks have a 24-bit network prefix, and so are referred to as /24s.

✦ **Class D** addresses aren't used for networks, because they're special multicast or broadcasting addresses.

✦ **Class E** addresses, with values higher than 233 in the first octet, are used only for experimental purposes.

All Class A addresses already have been taken by universities and corporations. Class B addresses are assigned to companies and institutions with a minimum of 4,000 hosts. If you apply for an Internet address, you will probably receive a Class C designation.

Each class defines its own 32-bit address boundaries. In Class C, the first three octets are for the network address; the last octet represents the host address. If you apply for an Internet address, the InterNIC will give you an address with the first three octets defined. You fill in the last octet with numbers ranging from 1 to 254. The numbers 0 and 255 are reserved. Each number you assign goes to one node on your network, so you can connect up to 254 nodes to the Internet.

Looking at the subnet mask

A *subnet mask* is part of the IP addressing system. A subnet mask creates subnetworks that enable a computer in one network segment to communicate with a computer in another segment of the network. The main reason for subnetting (or creating subnets on a network) is to divide a single Class A, B, or C network into smaller pieces.

The subnet mask is a 32-bit address that hides, or *masks,* part of the IP address so as to add to the number of computers added to the network. All networks must use a subnet mask, even if they don't connect to another network. If a network isn't divided into subnets, the default subnet mask is used. The default depends on the IP address class.

✦ Class A networks use a default subnet mask of 255.0.0.0.

✦ Class B uses a default subnet mask of 255.255.0.0.

✦ Class C uses a default subnet mask of 255.255.255.0.

Subnetting enables organizations to mix different network technologies across several physical segments. It also enables you to exceed the maximum number of hosts per segment, if you've used all your IP addresses.

Comprehending the gateway

The *gateway* is a bridge between two segments of a network. Messages travel between network segments through the gateway. A gateway is a combination of hardware and software; it creates a shared connection between, say, a LAN and a larger network.

Often, you use a gateway to bridge two networks that use different communications protocols. A gateway has its own processor and memory that it uses to convert protocols; converting protocols makes the gateway slower than a router or bridge. A gateway must have its own IP address.

Working with Domain Names

Every IP address on the Internet has a corresponding domain name, such as microsoft.com. Domain names make it easy to remember addresses, and you can use them in place of the IP address in the URL text box of your browser.

Regarding domain names

IP addresses are difficult to remember, so domain names also represent a computer on the Internet. Microsoft's domain name, for example, is www.microsoft.com. Domain names usually start with www, which stands for World Wide Web; however, www is not always included in an address. The letters *www* represent a route to a World Wide Web server. Other servers might use a different route, such as w2. If no route is listed, the address takes a default route as listed by the server.

Tip   Domain names are written from the least specific (top-level domain) to the most specific (host name). Each part is separated by a dot (.).

The second part of the domain name is the name of the organization, company, product, or another catchy word or phrase. Microsoft, for example, is perfect for the domain name of their Web site.

The third part of the domain name identifies the type of organization. The letters *com*, for example, stand for commercial. Following are other top-level domain identifiers and their meanings:

gov	Government
mil	Military
net	Network providers
org	Nonprofit organization
edu	Education

Other additions to the domain name include a country code, if the server is located outside of the United States. UK stands for United Kingdom, for example, and IT stands for Italy.

Domain names are listed in the Uniform Resource Locator (URL) to a site. The URL is the full address, or computer identifier, on the Web. URLs contain numerous slashes and dots that separate the parts of the address, similarly to the way you separate folders in a path.

Microsoft's complete URL is http://www.microsoft.com/. If you want a particular document on a site, you must use a longer URL, such as http://support.microsoft.com/support/index.html.

The letters *http* stand for Hypertext Transfer Protocol; this is the protocol your computer uses to attach to the server computer. HTTP defines the language the computers will use to transfer pages and hypertext (links). With most newer browsers, you don't have to type the http in the address, but it doesn't hurt to add it.

In the sample URL, no www is used, but the address of the server is identified as support.microsoft.com. The support between forward slashes represents a folder, or directory.

The HTML document is the one you view in that folder. There are no rules as to when to use `www` or `http`. The best practice is to copy the exact URL from literature or documentation about the Web site.

Understanding the domain name system

The *Domain Name System* (DNS) is a method of matching IP addresses with domain names. When you type a domain name in the URL address area of your browser, that query is transmitted to a DNS server. A DNS server maintains a database of domain names and IP addresses. The DNS server finds the IP address that matches the domain name and then sends your request on to that server. The process is called *name resolution*.

You might find a DNS server in a university or college, on a corporate LAN, or even on a smaller LAN. Most primary ISPs also have DNS servers. Local ISPs connect to larger, or secondary, ISPs, and those ISPs connect to much larger, primary ISPs that make up the Internet.

DNS, or name, servers are grouped into domains, which identify different levels of authority. At the top of this hierarchical structure is the root domain, or top-level domain, such as com, edu, org, and so on.

Within the top-level domains are second-level domains. Second-level domains contain hosts and *subdomains*. Going back to the microsoft.com example, `microsoft.com` is a second-level domain. A subdomain of `microsoft.com` might be `ftp.microsoft.com`. `support.microsoft.com` then would be a host name within the domain.

Each Domain Name Server has a specific area for which it stores addresses and domain names. Called the *zone of authority*, the Domain Name Server can resolve only addresses within its zone. If a Domain Name Server doesn't contain the IP address for the queried domain name, it forwards the query to another Domain Name Server.

Recognizing DHCP

Dynamic Host Configuration Protocol (DHCP) is a utility for assigning TCP/IP addresses to workstations automatically. DHCP servers are used mainly by corporations and large TCP/IP networks to configure their clients, although they are also used by some Internet service providers.

When a client accesses a TCP/IP network, the DHCP server assigns the client an IP address, a subnet mask, and a gateway, if needed. The DHCP server has a range of possible IP addresses from which to choose. Each time the client logs off of the network, the IP address goes back into a pool and might be assigned to another client logging on to the network. Letting the DHCP server configure clients when they attach to the network saves the administrator of a large IP network a lot of time and effort.

A DHCP server can grant a *lease* to a DHCP client. The lease provides one IP address for use by the client for up to 30 days. Each time the client logs on to the IP network, the lease is updated, so the lease doesn't run out unless the client doesn't log on within the 30 days of the lease. A lease is important for some networks, because to communicate with other corporate programs over the network, the client might need a stable IP address.

The DHCP protocol requires a client ID for each computer. By default, the DHCP server uses the client computer's MAC address.

DHCP works with Mac OS; Microsoft Windows 95, 98, NT, 2000, XP; Novell NetWare; Novell LAN Workplace for DOS (for attaching to a Unix workbox, or terminal); and Linux.

Why Use TCP/IP?

You can use TCP/IP to connect your LAN to the Internet or to create an intranet or simply to speed up your local area network. You might want to use TCP/IP because it's so compatible with many different hardware and software products, or simply because you want to experiment with it. In addition, most newer operating systems—Windows 98 Second Edition, 2000, and XP; Mac OS X 10; and Linux distributions—come with TCP/IP installed. Many OSs use only TCP/IP.

Although TCP/IP seems severe and awkward, it's really not that difficult to get the hang of it. You might start by configuring your computers for dialing up the Internet and then decide you want to try a TCP/IP network in your own home.

Cross-Reference   For information about intranets, see Chapter 19. For information about using the Internet, see Chapter 16. For instructions on setting up dial-up networking, see Appendix C.

Looking at advantages of TCP/IP

Using TCP/IP has many advantages. It's more efficient and faster than NetBEUI. Additionally, many hardware and software vendors support TCP/IP. You can use it with a variety of programs and products. If the computers on your network use different operating systems, such as Macintosh and PCs, TCP/IP enables those computers to communicate.

The following sections discuss some more advantages of using TCP/IP.

Intranet

Using TCP/IP, you can create a private internet (intranet) on your home network. Publish documents for your family to view on their Web browsers by using Internet technologies, including HTTP, HTML, and more.

Small Business Tip   If you create an intranet for your employees to contribute to and use, you can easily connect it to the Internet and extend its purpose to clients and vendors, as well.

Following are some other reasons to create an intranet on your home network:

✦ Create an intranet so that you can share family stories, pictures, and play games over the network.

✦ Familiarize yourself and your family with Internet technology and the use of TCP/IP, as well.

✦ If you're thinking about creating a Web page for the Internet, experiment with designs on your intranet before you publish to the Web.

✦ If you're thinking about starting a small home business, you can use your intranet to set up a home page and an index, create links to your pages, and test the site before you put it up on the Internet.

✦ If you're planning to start an Internet business, set up the e-commerce site on your intranet before taking it to the Web.

Internet

You need TCP/IP to connect to the Internet. Realize that there is a difference between installing TCP/IP on your network and installing it for dial-up networking use; these are two separate installations and uses for the protocol.

You install TCP/IP to use with the dial-up networking feature. This installation enables you to connect to the Internet by means of a modem. The TCP/IP communicates with Web servers on the Internet. If you install TCP/IP on your network, you use it to connect to the other computers on your LAN. One installation has nothing to do with the other. For more information, see the section "Installing and Configuring TCP/IP" later in this appendix.

Using TCP/IP to connect to the Internet provides you with all the Internet features and advantages, including e-mail, Web browsers, and file transfer. Also, TCP/IP includes various programs (which are also protocols) that you can use to access information on the Internet. If you have special needs for FTP or Telnet, for example, TCP/IP provides those programs for you to use.

If you plan to expand your network to the Internet someday, your knowledge and use of TCP/IP will help you tremendously. Knowing how to configure TCP/IP will make it easier for you to transfer your Web sites and pages to the Web and to configure clients and servers for the Internet. Having TCP/IP in place means less configuring when you move to the Internet.

Dial-Up Networking

You also can use TCP/IP to connect to your home or work computer. If you're on the road, for example, and want to call your home network to retrieve some information or your schedule, you can use Windows dial-up networking to accomplish this.

Note   You use TCP/IP in Terminal Services as well. Terminal Services is a method of communication between a remote computer and a server using Windows 2000 Server. For more information, see Appendix C.

If your work network uses TCP/IP, you can call in to that network from home or while you're on the road. Additionally, if your office network includes DHCP server, calling from a remote computer becomes even easier. The DHCP server configures your computer so that all you need to do is dial and connect.

Creating your own TCP/IP network

When setting up your own TCP/IP network, you need to choose IP addresses for your computers. Remember, each computer on the network needs a unique IP address. You also need to set a specific subnet mask for your network to use.

Several IP addresses are reserved for private use. Following are the three blocks reserved for IP addresses:

    10.0.0.0 to 10.255.255.255

    172.16.0.0 to 172.31.255.255

    192.168.0.0 to 192.168.255.255

For your home network, for example, you could use the following IP addresses for five computers on the network:

    172.16.0.1

    172.16.0.2

    172.16.0.3

    172.16.0.4

    172.16.0.5

Alternatively, you could use the following for your computers:

192.168.0.100

192.168.0.101

192.168.0.102

192.168.0.103

192.168.0.104

You can change numbers only in the last octet of the IP address for a home network or small-business network. If your corporate network is very large, you can make other changes to the IP addresses, as long as they are consistent.

In addition to IP addresses, you need a subnet mask. Use the same subnet mask for all computers on the network. The subnet mask 255.255.255.0 works very well.

Using Windows 98 LinkLocal

Windows 98 includes another method of configuring a TCP/IP network called LinkLocal. LinkLocal creates automatic private IP addressing. You can use LinkLocal if you have a network that doesn't use a DHCP server and if your computer is not a host computer on the Internet.

With LinkLocal, your Windows 98 computer can assign itself a private IP address without your intervention. LinkLocal IP addresses always begin with 169.254. Windows fills in the other two octets for you. LinkLocal uses a *block,* or *range,* of IP addresses, from which it assigns the addresses of computers on your network. Using LinkLocal makes administering the network much easier than filling in the TCP/IP information yourself.

Following are some rules and guidelines for using LinkLocal:

✦ LinkLocal does not work on your network unless all the computers are running Windows 98.

✦ If your computer is a desktop or tower, it can assign itself an automatic private IP address when it starts up — as long as no DHCP server is found and the computer does not have a valid DHCP lease.

✦ If you connect to a DHCP server later, the DHCP server-assigned IP address takes precedence over the automatic private IP address.

✦ If the computer is a laptop, it can assign itself an automatic private IP address as long as no DHCP server is present on the network.

✦ If your computer is using a DHCP service and that service fails for some reason, the computer assigns itself an automatic private IP address to use until the DHCP service is back up and working. It then surrenders the IP address to the DHCP server.

To enable LinkLocal, follow these steps:

1. Choose Start ➪ Settings ➪ Control Panel. The Control Panel window appears.

2. Double-click the Network icon. The Network dialog box appears, as shown in Figure B-1.

3. Select the TCP/IP Ethernet adapter and click the Properties button. The TCP/IP Properties dialog box appears. For information about installing protocols, see Chapter 10.

4. In the IP Address tab of the TCP/IP Properties dialog box, select the Obtain an IP Address Automatically option, as shown in Figure B-2.

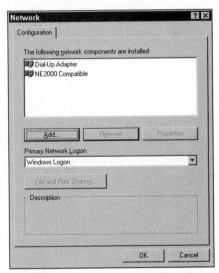

Figure B-1: Set the LAN TCP/IP in the Network dialog box.

5. Click OK to close the TCP/IP Properties dialog box.

6. Click OK again to close the Network dialog box. Windows prompts you to restart the computer.

When you start the computer again, it automatically assigns itself an IP address. You must repeat these steps with each computer on the network to complete the process. When you're finished, your network will be up and running using the TCP/IP protocol.

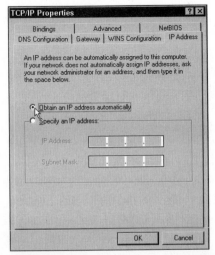

Figure B-2: Set the option to automatic IP addressing.

Web Servers and TCP/IP Addressing

Using private IP addresses doesn't affect your use of the Internet. You still can attach to the Internet by using your dial-up networking TCP/IP. You can add a Web page to your ISP's Web server, if you want. Your LAN IP addresses are separate from your Internet connection.

Adding a Web server to your network, however, might complicate matters a bit. (A *Web server* is a computer you attach to the Web so that you can display your own Web site.)

Generally, you install a special operating system (such as NT Server) and a Web server application (such as Internet Information Server) on the computer. You also should install a proxy server or firewall to keep Internet users from accessing your LAN through the server. Proxy servers and firewalls keep people from hacking into your LAN; they can also keep your LAN users from accessing certain Internet sites.

To attach your Web server to the Internet, you need an IP address and a domain name. That IP address applies only to your Web server, not to the rest of your network. You can keep your original IP addresses for your LAN, as long as you use a firewall or proxy server to separate them from the Web server and none of the computers using a private IP address try to get onto the Internet.

Installing and Configuring TCP/IP

You can install TCP/IP on your Windows computer without adding any other software or hardware. Windows 98, 2000, and XP come with Microsoft's TCP/IP protocol suite built in; all you need to do is configure it. It's important to note that you can install TCP/IP for two different purposes — LAN use or dial-up use.

For LAN use, install TCP/IP on the Network dialog box and bind that protocol to a network interface card, or adapter. Binding assigns the protocol to the device so that they can work together for communications over the network.

For Internet or remote access use, install TCP/IP through the Dial-Up Networking window. You install the protocol on a specific connection.

Cross-Reference See Chapter 10 for more information about using TCP/IP on the LAN. See Appendix C for information about using TCP/IP for remote access. If you want to use TCP/IP to connect to the Internet, see Chapter 16 for more information.

Using TCP/IP with Windows 98

When you install TCP/IP on a computer on the LAN, you enable it to communicate with other computers that use the same protocol. You must install TCP/IP on each computer on the network, use a unique IP address for each computer, and use the same subnet mask for each computer you configure.

Note You do not use this method of installation if you used LinkLocal to activate automatic private IP addressing.

You already may have installed a network client and adapter. If not, you can install those at this time. See Chapter 9 for more information.

If you have another protocol installed, such as NetBEUI or IPX/SPX, you should remove it before installing TCP/IP. Although you can have two or more protocols installed, such a setup slows down your system and makes the network less efficient.

Installing TCP/IP

When you install the protocol, it automatically binds to your network card. To install and configure TCP/IP for use on the LAN, follow these steps:

1. Choose Start ⇨ Settings ⇨ Control Panel. The Control Panel opens.

2. Double-click the Network icon. The Network dialog box appears.

3. Click the Add button. The Select Network Component Type dialog box appears, as shown in Figure B-3.

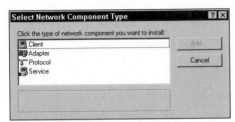

Figure B-3: Add a network component.

4. In the list of network components to add, select Protocol and then click the Add button. The Select Network Protocol dialog box appears, as shown in Figure B-4.

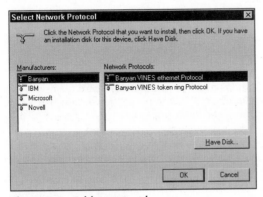

Figure B-4: Add a protocol.

5. In the Manufacturers list, select Microsoft.

6. In the Network Protocols list, select TCP/IP. Click OK. Windows returns to the Network dialog box, as shown in Figure B-5. Don't close the Network dialog box yet. Continue to the next set of steps.

Note When you install a network adapter card, Windows might install a dial-up adapter. A *dial-up adapter* is a device driver that is bound to the Client for Microsoft Networks and acts as an interface between the modem and your computer. You need the dial-up adapter if you plan to connect to another network over a phone line by using a modem. For more information about the dial-up adapter, see the section "Comprehending the dial-up adapter TCP/IP Settings" later in this appendix.

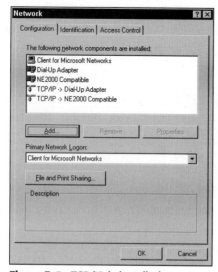

Figure B-5: TCP/IP is installed.

Configuring TCP/IP

You must configure the protocol before you can use it. To configure TCP/IP, follow these steps:

1. Select the TCP/IP protocol that is bound to your network card (as opposed to the TCP/IP bound to the dial-up adapter). Click the Properties button. The TCP/IP Properties dialog box appears, as shown in Figure B-6.

2. Select the option Specify an IP Address.

3. In the IP Address box, enter the address you're using—for example, 172.16.1.1.

4. In the Subnet Mask box, enter the four-octet number for the subnet, such as 255.255.255.0.

5. Click OK to close the dialog box.

6. Click OK to close the Network dialog box. When Windows prompts you to restart your computer, do so.

When the computer restarts, the TCP/IP is active. Make sure that you install TCP/IP on all computers on the network. Use a unique IP address for each computer but the same subnet mask.

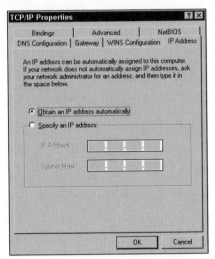

Figure B-6: Configure the IP address.

The TCP/IP Properties dialog box contains other tabs in addition to the IP Address tab. Each tab offers additional configurations for TCP/IP. For a home network, you don't need to configure the information on any of the other tabs; however, the following sections describe each tab so that you can understand more about TCP/IP configuration in Windows.

DNS Configuration tab

Use the DNS Configuration tab to enter a host and domain name for your network server on a client/server network. Many small networks use an Internet DNS server to resolve computer names. Most ISPs will maintain domain information for you, for a fee.

Alternatively, you can maintain your own DNS server with or without the use of the Internet. If you want to use your own DNS server on the Internet, you must file with the InterNIC for a domain name and IP address for at least two DNS servers.

If you set up your own DNS server on your local LAN, you can use only one server if you want. Microsoft recommends you use two DNS servers, however, so that one can act as a backup in case the other one fails.

Figure B-7 illustrates the DNS Configuration tab with a corporation's own DNS servers listed. Note that you can set a search order if you use more than one server as a domain naming service.

Gateway tab

The Gateway tab provides a space for you to enter the IP address of any gateway on your computer. The gateway acts like a bridge to connect two networks that use different protocols.

Figure B-8 shows the Gateway tab of the TCP/IP Properties dialog box.

WINS Configuration tab

Windows Internet Name Service (WINS) is another method of resolving computer names to IP addresses. WINS supplies a database that maintains IP addresses and NetBIOS computer names. *NetBIOS* is a protocol that contains commands for transmitting information from computer to computer. WINS must be installed on a server computer to perform name resolution.

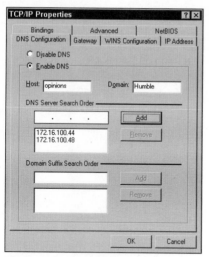

Figure B-7: Specify the DNS server addresses.

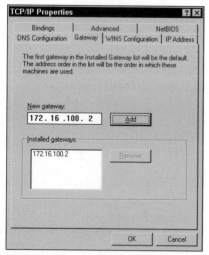

Figure B-8: Use this tab only if you have a gateway on your network.

WINS eliminates the need to broadcast computer names across the network when one computer is trying to connect to another. Instead, the request for a specific computer name goes to the WINS server. It resolves the name to an IP address and immediately sends the data to the target destination. WINS cuts traffic on a TCP/IP network.

> **Tip**
>
> If you have a few computers (10, 20, 40, or so), you don't need to set up a WINS server. Network traffic won't be affected much for so few computers. If your network consists of hundreds of computers on a TCP/IP network, however, WINS can help resolve the name/IP address issue quickly and efficiently.

Figure B-9 shows the WINS Configuration tab. After you enable WINS resolution, you enter the IP address of the WINS server.

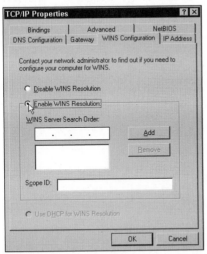

Figure B-9: Use WINS for name resolution.

Bindings tab
The Bindings tab shows which network client is bound to TCP/IP. If you're using a Microsoft network, TCP/IP is bound to the Client for Microsoft Networks, as shown in Figure B-10.

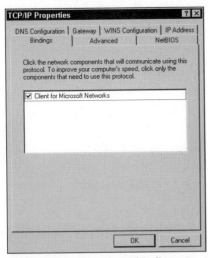

Figure B-10: Check your bindings.

Advanced tab
The Advanced tab contains any settings specific to the protocol. The TCP/IP protocol doesn't usually contain any advanced settings; however, other protocols do.

NetBIOS tab

When you use TCP/IP, Windows automatically configures support for using NetBIOS applications over the TCP/IP protocol. NetBIOS facilitates applications in transferring data over the network. This tab shows that NetBIOS is enabled for TCP/IP (see Figure B-11).

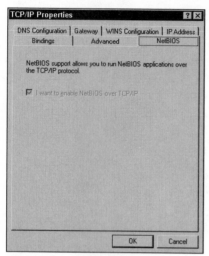

Figure B-11: NetBIOS support is always enabled for TCP/IP.

Using TCP/IP for Dial-Up Networking and Windows 98

When you want to use your modem to dial the Internet or to connect to a computer on another TCP/IP network, you configure TCP/IP for dial-up networking. The TCP/IP configuration takes place in the Dial-Up Networking window and is specific to the connection.

If you haven't created a connection for the Internet or remote office, see Appendix C for information about how to create connections.

To configure TCP/IP for dial-up networking, follow these steps:

1. Open My Computer.

2. Double-click the Dial-Up Networking icon. The Dial-Up Networking window appears, as shown in Figure B-12.

3. Right-click the connection you want to configure — in this case, Office — and then choose Properties from the pop-up menu. The connection's Properties dialog box appears, as shown in Figure B-13.

4. Choose the Server Types tab, shown in Figure B-14. Note that all three network protocols are selected by default.

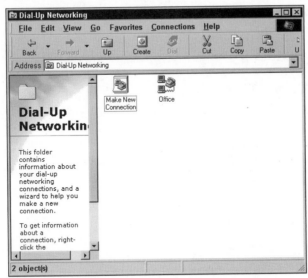

Figure B-12: Open the Dial-Up Networking window.

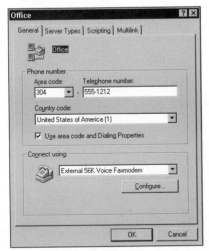

Figure B-13: Set the properties for the remote connection.

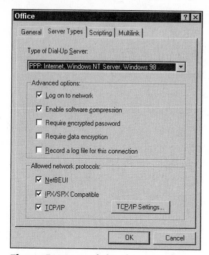

Figure B-14: Look for the protocols area.

 Tip   For information about the other options in the Server Types tab, see Appendix C.

5. In the Allowed network protocols area, make sure that TCP/IP is selected. Deselect any protocol you won't be using with this connection, such as NetBEUI and IPX/SPX.

6. Click the TCP/IP Settings button. The TCP/IP Settings dialog box appears, as shown in Figure B-15.

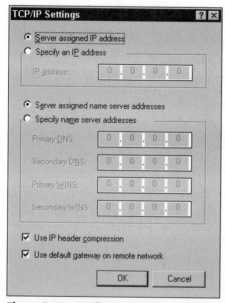

Figure B-15: Configure TCP/IP settings for dial-up networking.

7. Choose the options and enter the IP addresses for the connection, as explained in Table B-1.

8. Click OK to close the TCP/IP Settings dialog box. Click OK again to close the connection's Properties dialog box.

Table B-1: TCP/IP Settings for Dial-Up Networking

Setting	Description
Server assigned IP address	Use this option if you attach to a DHCP server.
Specify an IP address	Use this option if you want to specify a static IP address.
IP address	Enter the IP address of the computer to which the connection attaches.
Server assigned name server addresses	Choose this option if the server to which you're attaching assigns DNS server IP addresses.
Specify name server addresses	Choose this option if you want to enter the DNS or WINS server IP addresses manually.
Use IP header compression	Check this box if you want to compress the headers for your network packets sent to this computer. Using compression speeds up transmissions.
Use default gateway on remote network	Check this option if a gateway separates your computer from the computer to which you want to connect.

Comprehending the dial-up adapter TCP/IP settings

You are probably wondering why you didn't configure the TCP/IP for dial-up in the Network dialog box (in the Control Panel). The Network dialog box contains a dial-up adapter that is bound to TCP/IP and the Microsoft Client for Networks. As mentioned, the adapter is a device driver that enables your modem to attach to other computers via the telephone lines.

If you select the dial-up adapter in the Network dialog box and then click the Properties button, you'll see the warning dialog box shown in Figure B-16.

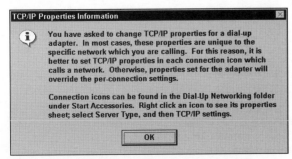

Figure B-16: Windows warns you away from the dial-up adapter TCP/IP settings.

The warning tells you that you should set TCP/IP configurations individually for each connection. If you set the TCP/IP settings in the Network dialog box under Dial-Up Adapter, those settings apply to *all* connections you create. In order to create different connections — say, for the Internet, for a work network, or for a home network — you configure TCP/IP for each connection in the Dial-Up Networking window.

Working with TCP/IP and Windows XP

Windows 2000 and XP install with the TCP/IP protocol. You can connect a new XP computer to a network, and the new computer figures out the protocol settings and joins the network without much configuration. You should, however, understand how to change configuration yourself, in case you need to change the network.

Cross-Reference For more information about setting up a network card, file and printer sharing, and other networking software, see Chapter 10.

To set up or edit TCP/IP in Windows XP, follow these steps:

1. Right-click My Network Places and click Properties from the pop-up menu. The Network Connections dialog box appears, as shown in Figure B-17. Your Network Connections dialog box might not display the same items in the figure.

2. Right-click the Local Area Connection and click Properties. The Local Area Connection Properties dialog box appears, as shown in Figure B-18.

Tip You can rename the Local Area Connection using the same pop-up menu if you prefer to call it Home, or Plumleys, or some other name more true to your personal network.

3. Click the Internet Protocol (TCP/IP) to select it, and click the Properties button. The Internet Protocol (TCP/IP) Properties dialog box appears, as shown in Figure B-19.

Figure B-17: Network Connections shows LAN connections, Internet connections, and dial-up connections.

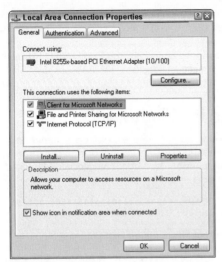

Figure B-18: Edit or add components to the network properties.

4. Click Use the Following IP Address. Enter the IP address, subnet mask, and default gateway you want to assign the computer in your network.

5. Optionally, assign a preferred DNS server and an alternate DNS server.

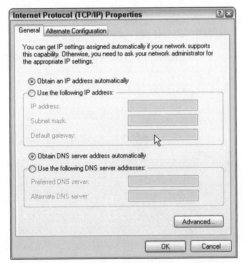

Figure B-19: Change TCP/IP address, subnet mask, or DNS server.

Tip You can click the Advanced button to assign additional IP, DNS, and WINS settings, if need be. On a small home or business network, you won't need to assign additional settings.

6. Click OK and then click OK again to close the Local Area Connection Properties dialog box. Reboot if prompted, although generally Windows XP does not need to be rebooted for TCP/IP configuration.

Using Dial-Up Networking in Windows XP

Windows XP uses a wizard to help you create and configure a dial-up connection. With the New Connection Wizard, you can set up a dial-up or LAN connection to the Internet or a dial-up or VPN connection to another location, connect to a home network, or connect to another computer using a direct cable or infrared port.

For a dial-up connection, use the Connect to the network at my workplace option. To create a dial-up network connection, follow these steps:

1. Click Start ⇨ Control Panel. The Control Panel dialog box appears.

2. Double-click Network Connections. The Network Connections dialog box appears.

3. In Network Tasks, click Create a New Connection. The New Connection Wizard dialog box appears.

4. Click Next. The second wizard dialog box appears, as shown in Figure B-20.

5. Click Connect to the Network at My Workplace; then click Next. The next wizard dialog box appears, as shown in Figure B-21.

6. Choose Dial-Up Connection and click Next. The next wizard dialog box appears.

7. Type a name for the connection, such as home, work, Tammy's, or some other easily recognizable name. Click Next. The next wizard dialog box appears.

8. Type the phone number. Add a 1 and the area code if necessary. Click Next. The final wizard dialog box appears.

9. Click Finish. The Connect dialog box appears, as shown in Figure B-22.

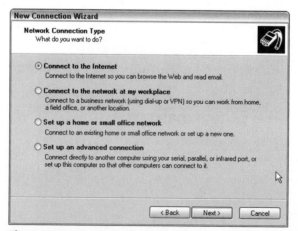

Figure B-20: Create a new connection.

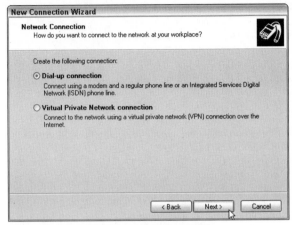

Figure B-21: Choose a dial-up connection.

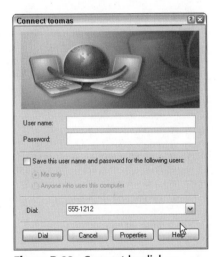

Figure B-22: Connect by dial-up.

10. Enter your username and password needed to connect to the dial-up connection. Click Dial to connect.

Using TCP/IP and the Macintosh

Macintosh OS X comes with TCP/IP installed by default. You can also change the TCP/IP settings, however, to fit into your network if necessary. In the Network Preferences dialog box, you can change settings for Ethernet, AirPort, an internal modem, AppleTalk, proxies, and other settings.

To edit TCP/IP settings, follow these steps:

1. Click the Apple ➪ System Preferences. The System Preferences dialog box appears, as shown in Figure B-23.

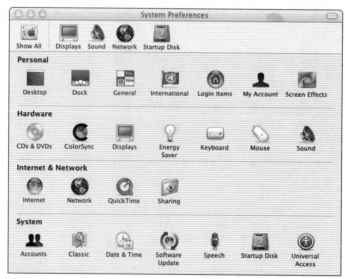

Figure B-23: Use System Preferences in the Mac to change Network settings.

2. Double-click the Network icon. The Network dialog box appears, as shown in Figure B-24.

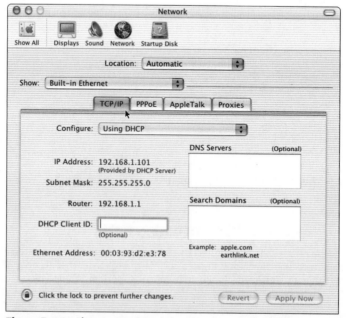

Figure B-24: Change TCP/IP settings in a Mac OS X system.

3. To change network settings, choose the port you want to change from the Show menu; choose the Built-in Ethernet port, for example.

4. Optionally, create a new location by clicking Location ⇨ New Location.

5. When finished with the dialog box, click Apply Now.

Creating a connection with the Mac

You can create a connection with the Mac OS X system easily by using the System Preferences and Network dialog boxes. To create a connection, follow these steps:

1. Click the Apple ⇨ System Preferences. The System Preferences dialog box appears.

2. Double-click the Network icon. The Network dialog box appears.

3. In Show, click Internal Modem. The dialog box changes to enable you to use TCP/IP, as shown in Figure B-25.

4. Alternatively, you can select Built-in Ethernet in the Show drop-down list, click the PPPoE tab, and configure PPPoE information, as shown in Figure B-26.

5. You can also, depending on what you select in the Show drop-down list, configure a proxy and adjust the modem settings in the same dialog box.

6. When finished, click Apply Now.

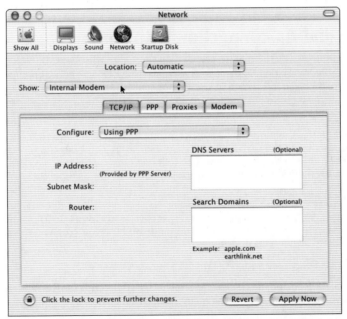

Figure B-25: Change TCP/IP settings for a dial-up connection.

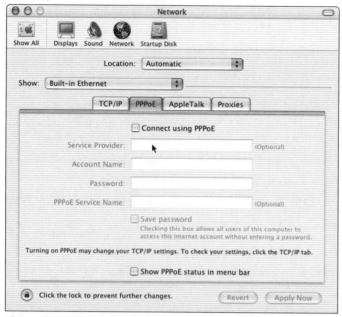

Figure B-26: Change PPPoE settings in a Mac OS X system.

Creating a dial-up connection with Linux

Linux machines are normally the dial-up server as opposed to the client. Because a Linux box is so basic and stable, many people use Linux as a base for FTP servers, Gopher servers, Web servers, and so on. If you're interested in using your Linux box as a dial-up server, there are a lot of sites you can go to on the Internet, such as `networking.earthweb.com` or `www.linux.com`.

As a dial-up client, your configuration varies according to your distribution. Configuration might be as simple as using the GNU/Linux PPP Configuration Utility or the Dial-Up Configuration Tool found in the Task menu. The following instructions are general, because each distribution, each package, and installation of a distribution is different.

1. Add a modem and make sure it is properly connected.

2. Load PPP as a module and compile it to the kernel. Many Linux distributions already have PPP compiled within the kernel; it depends on how you received the packages and which distribution you're using.

3. You next must determine which COM port your modem is on.

4. Install the dial-up script. You'll need to know the initial script for the modem you're calling, or you could use the default string, *atdt*.

5. Enter the phone number of the modem you're calling, along with your username and password, if required.

Troubleshooting TCP/IP

TCP/IP is difficult to configure if you don't understand the way it works. You might find that your most difficult problems with the protocol involve misconfiguration problems. Luckily, several TCP/IP diagnostic utilities are available that you can use to diagnose problems and — with some effort and luck — maybe fix yourself.

The first thing you should do if you have trouble connecting to a computer is check the TCP/IP configuration for that computer. Check the IP address, subnet mask, and any other settings of all computers involved with the problem. If the configuration seems okay, the next step is to try some diagnostic utilities.

Using ping

The PING command sends TCP/IP packets to the designated computer. If PING is successful, TCP/IP sends the packets back. Use PING to verify that the TCP/IP configuration is correct, that local computers are communicating with each other, and that remote computers are communicating.

Tip   PING your own computer first to make sure you have configured the TCP/IP correctly. If the PING doesn't return packets, you need to check your own configuration.

If the PING is successful, it means the TCP/IP stack is configured correctly on the local host, and your computer can reach others on the network. If you PING a remote network and the PING is successful, the connection between the two computers is working, hosts and gateways between the two computers are working, and the TCP/IP configuration on both computers is working.

You enter the PING command and then the computer name or IP address. Run PING from the MS-DOS prompt. To run PING, follow these steps:

1. In Windows 98, choose Start ➪ Programs ➪ MS-DOS Prompt. The MS-DOS window appears on screen.

   In Windows XP or 2000, click Start ➪ Run, and type Command in the Open text box and then click OK.

2. At the prompt, type **ping**, press the spacebar, and then type the name of the computer, as in this example: **ping sue**. Press Enter.

If the packets reach the destination, you see a response similar to the one in Figure B-27. Note that PING sends 32 bytes of data to the other computer. The replies indicate that 32 bytes of data were returned. PING also indicates the time it takes the packets to travel the network. At the end of the replies, the command lists statistics, including the number of packets sent, received, and lost, and the average time it took the packets to make a round trip.

If the PING was unsuccessful, the response might be that the host is unknown, the destination is unreachable, or the request timed out. This type of failure might indicate that your TCP/IP configuration is faulty, a name server is down, or your hardware — cable, network card, or hub — has a problem.

If the IP address of a remote computer PINGs successfully but the domain name doesn't, it means a Domain Name Server is down.

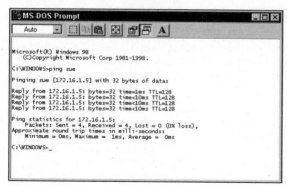

Figure B-27: A successful PING gets a reply.

If packets are lost or the PING is slow, check the network cabling on the system. A loose cable could be the problem.

If you PING your local host and all connections are working, but you still have trouble with a remote host — another network segment, a WAN, or an Internet server, for example — try using the TRACEROUTE command. If you can reach only a local host, the remote host might have problems. The problems also could be with a gateway or router connecting the two hosts.

> **Tip**   TRACEROUTE, or TRACE, maps the specific path traveled to a destination, including routers, gateways, and computers.

Using IPCONFIG

IPCONFIG, a utility included with TCP/IP, displays the IP address, subnet mask, and default gateway for all network adapter cards on your computer. IPCONFIG is handy for checking a computer's address quickly. It also can detect bad IP addresses or subnet masks.

To use IPCONFIG, type the command at the MS-DOS prompt. Figure B-28 illustrates the information from the IPCONFIG command. Note that the computer has two adapter cards, but only one is using the TCP/IP protocol.

> **Tip**   You can type IPCONFIG in lowercase or uppercase letters. MS-DOS doesn't recognize case changes.

IPCONFIG also includes a parameter, /all, that enables you to see more information about the computer. You type the following at the MS-DOS prompt:

```
ipconfig /all
```

Using the /all parameter displays the computer's name, any DNS servers, the type of network node, and other information about the WINS server, NetBIOS resolution, and even the MAC address of the adapter. Figure B-29 illustrates the results of the command.

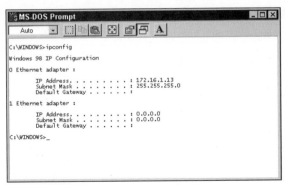

Figure B-28: List addressing information for a computer with IPCONFIG.

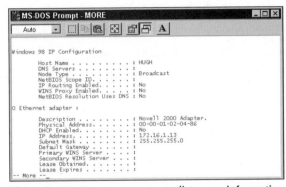

Figure B-29: Use a parameter to list more information about the computer.

Tip   Use the pipe (|) more command — ipconfig /all |more — to display one screen of information at a time. Press the Enter key to read the next screen of information.

Using NETSTAT

NETSTAT (network statistics) is useful for tracking down network problems. Use NETSTAT to troubleshoot incoming or outgoing packet errors or to verify the presence of needed routes.

If you type **netstat** at the MS-DOS prompt, you see the protocol used, the name and local address of the computer, and any connected computers and their current state, as shown in Figure B-30.

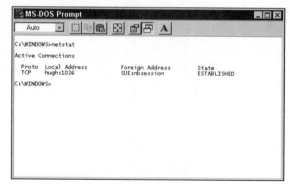

Figure B-30: Check network statistics.

The NETSTAT command includes various parameters that display information about the network connections. Table B-2 shows some of the commonly used parameters and their results.

Table B-2: NETSTAT Parameters

Type This Command	Results
Netstat -a	Displays all connections and listening ports
Netstat -e	Displays Ethernet statistics
Netstat -n	Displays addresses and numbers in numerical format
Netstat -s	Displays the statistics of TCP/IP protocols: TCP, UDP, and IP

Figure B-31 shows the results of the command using the -e parameter. The statistics list bytes sent and received, errors, and other details of the Ethernet statistics.

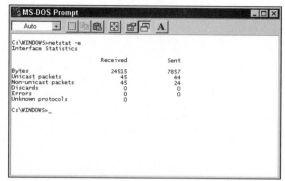

Figure B-31: View Ethernet statistics about your computer.

Using WINIPCFG

The WINIPCFG command yields the same results as the IPCONFIG command, but those results appear in a Windows dialog box instead of in the MS-DOS window. The WINIPCFG command includes several parameters. The most common is winipcfg /all. Using the /all parameter displays all of the information about your host and Ethernet adapter, including the host name, DNS server used, node type, adapter name and MAC address, IP address, and so on.

To use WINIPCFG, follow these steps:

1. Choose Start ⇨ Run. The Run dialog box appears. Click OK.

2. In the Open text box, type **winipcfg /all** and then press the Enter key. The IP Configuration dialog box appears. Click OK when you're finished.

Note   The IP Configuration dialog box enables you to renew or release DHCP leases if you're using a DHCP server.

✦   ✦   ✦

APPENDIX

Telecommuting

Telecommuting is an excellent way of working at home or on the road while communicating with an office network to keep up-to-date, exchange files, and print to the office printer, when necessary. You also can telecommute, or access remotely, other computers by using a dial-up connection and a modem. Windows supplies the software you need to connect to remote computers. You can also purchase software that enables you to remotely work on a computer. All you need is the modem and the connection.

Understanding Remote Access

Remote access refers to attaching to a network from another location and accessing resources from the remote computer. You might attach to your work computer from home, for example, in order to access a program or a file; or you might attach to your son's computer at college to copy a file or print your vacation schedule on his printer.

Many people work from home or bring their work home to complete. Using remote access, you can access files, programs, printers, and any other resource on your work computer and other computers on the network for which you have permissions. You can also transfer files between the remote computer and home or work.

Companies hire people to work from home part- or full-time then those workers use remote access to keep in touch with the office. By allowing workers to telecommute, companies save on office space, insurance, and time (less direct management), and spend less money on remote workers than office workers. In addition, remote workers save commuting time, set their own schedules, and have better morale than if they are stuck in an office all day.

Remote access also enables you to work from the road or another location. If you're in another city, for example, but have a modem, a phone line, and remote access, you can call your home computer or work computer to access your to-do list, your schedule, or any document that you have saved. Naturally, the remote computer must be turned on and available for you to access it.

Note You can use remote access for home use or for work; many people, however, use it to attach to an office computer. This appendix discusses several work situations, but you can apply any process, procedure, or information discussed to home use as well.

Examining types of remote access

Remote access can mean any of several processes. You might use remote node access to attach to another computer or network, for file transfer, as a gateway, or for software-controlled access. You probably will use remote node access or file transfer remote access.

✦ The most common method of remote access is when a computer connects to an office or corporate network. The remote computer user accesses any of the resources on the office network and then works as if he or she were actually in the office, sharing programs and files with coworkers.

The user can retrieve files, print on an office printer or local printer, log on to a server, get into shared calendars, and more. Remote access for the telecommuter sounds like a dream come true. The user can take breaks, play with the dog, and generally set his or her own schedule—as long as the work gets done, of course.

Working via remote access has disadvantages, however. Applications and large files do not transmit well over a remote access connection, sometimes the cost is prohibitive, and if the worker isn't focused on his or her work, the work may not get done in a timely manner. However, for the right company and the right workers, telecommuting can be the perfect arrangement.

✦ Another common method of remote access is file transfer. File transfer involves uploading a file to or downloading a file from the remote computer. You might send a file containing family pictures, a budget spreadsheet, or a letter to a family member. More likely, though, you will upload files to your work computer or download the information and research you need to complete a report.

✦ A gateway is a method of connecting to one computer to get to another. You might connect to the server at work, for example, in order to get to your workstation there.

✦ Software-controlled access is when you are permitted to attach to only one program remotely, such as accounting software.

Understanding Dial-up networking

Dial-up networking is a Windows feature that enables you to use your modem to call the Internet, your company's network, or some other remote network for the purpose of sharing resources, exchanging e-mail, and other network-specific tasks.

To use dial-up networking, you must install and configure it. Dial-up networking applies only to the connection. After making the connection, you use another program, such as a Web browser, to communicate with the remote computer.

To use dial-up networking, both your computer and the remote computer must have a modem, the connection needs to be configured, and both computers must be turned on. You also need to use the same protocol as the remote computer, such as TCP/IP.

Using pcANYWHERE

Symantec sells a popular remote access program called pcANYWHERE for about $100. Using pcANYWHERE, you can access another PC remotely, and through the connection, you can access a server or other remote node to transfer files or perform other network tasks. The other computer must also have pcANYWHERE installed and be turned on with pcANYWHERE running in host mode.

pcANYWHERE uses a Windows interface. You call using the program, the program authenticates you, and then you can perform file transfers or other tasks with pcANYWHERE running in the background. You can even train a remote computer user, troubleshoot problems on a remote computer, and perform programming tasks while connected to the remote computer. In short, you can do anything on the remote computer that you could do if you were in the same room as the computer.

pcANYWHERE includes many remote management tools that enable you to troubleshoot problems on the remote computer. You can edit the Registry, go to the command prompt, view logs, and so on. pcANYWHERE is perfect for computer consultants and their clients and for corporate help desks.

pcANYWHERE is also very secure. The program uses Public Key Infrastructure (PKI) and symmetric encryption; it can use up to 13 authentication types, mandatory passwords, and integrity checking. You're safe when you're online with pcANYWHERE.

pcANYWHERE requires a minimum of 64MB of RAM, 35MB of free disk space, and a Pentium processor, and it works with Windows 98, NT, 2000, and XP. For more information, see www.symantec.com/pcanywhere/.

Distinguishing the remote access user

Remote users may be telecommuters, home office users, or employees traveling on the road or otherwise away from the office. Remote users may be home users who dial up home from college, the office, a hotel room, or another location. There are as many reasons to access a network from a remote location as there are types of users who must access a remote computer.

Users might want to check e-mail, copy a file, or print a document at home or at the office for others to see. Other reasons to access a network remotely might be for research, for technical support, or for an online meeting or conference. Remote access enables you to communicate with others over the network without being in the same room or office.

Other advantages of telecommuting and remote access are tremendous. Besides easing highway congestion, lowering fuel usage, and saving wasted commuting time, remote access users can complete a job more efficiently and set their own schedules as they do it.

As a telecommuter, however, you must consider a few things. You want to make sure that you have the equipment you need and that you're using that equipment and the situation efficiently and considerately.

A telecommuter's needs

You need certain equipment in your home or remote office to enable you to work efficiently. Your company might supply the equipment you need, or you might have to purchase it yourself. Generally, you need the following items:

✦ A computer and modem

✦ Communications software

✦ A fast connection to the office

✦ A printer

✦ A business phone line

✦ Technical support for problems you encounter

✦ Backup media, such as Zip disks, a tape drive, or other

✦ Virus protection

✦ Perhaps a pager, cell phone, or handheld computer, or some combination of these

Tip   Keep a kit with you at all times that contains things such as an extra laptop battery, a spare phone cord, a list of support numbers, and so on. Make sure that you keep your laptop battery charged.

A telecommuter's duties

If you are working outside of the office, your first responsibility is to stay in touch with your coworkers to make sure that everyone is on the same page. You might need to telephone or send e-mail daily, for example, to discuss projects, procedures, or other factors affecting you and those who remain in the office.

Keep a regular schedule at home so that you're sure to get your work done. Get up in the morning and go to work by a specific time. Plan a lunchtime and a quitting time as well.

Create boundaries in your home for your work area. Your office space should be separate from entertainment, kids, pets, and other distractions.

Make sure that you understand how your company defines telecommuting and any guidelines they set for use of the equipment. Also, ask about insurance for the equipment, inquire about how upgrades and repairs are to be handled, and so on.

Using Terminal Services

Terminal Services (TS) is a feature offered by Windows 2000 Server that enables you to connect to your office computer or network. You must know the name and IP address of the server, the domain, your username, and of course, your password. In addition, the administrator of your network must set up permissions for you on the server and create client installation diskettes (usually two 1.44MB floppies) for you to install on your home computer.

You use a dial-up connection that you create with the TS client, and when you attach to the computer, you have control over applications, files, and printers for which you've been given permissions. If your company uses Windows 2000 Server and you think you would want to work from home, ask your network administrator about Terminal Services.

Exploring Virtual Private Networks

Virtual private networks (VPNs) are extremely popular with large and small businesses. You might find yourself using your company's VPN if you're working from home or on the road.

A *virtual private network* is a network between remote users and a company's private local area network; the connection between the two, however, is through a public network system, such as the Internet. A VPN provides safe and secure paths for the company and the user, even though the connection is public. VPNs also save the company money by applying existing technology; the company doesn't have to support or maintain the remote network.

You use Windows dial-up networking to connect to a virtual private network. As with any form of networking, you also must use a protocol to connect to the VPN. Remote protocols differ somewhat from other networking protocols. Probably, however, your company will use TCP/IP as the VPN protocol. For more information about TCP/IP, see Appendix B.

Note   The Internet also uses the TCP/IP protocol. If you install dial-up networking in Windows to use with your Internet connection, you will configure the TCP/IP protocol.

Other possible protocols you can use with VPNs include the following:

✦ **Serial Line Internet Protocol (SLIP)** is an older protocol that isn't used much anymore; however, you still might run into servers using SLIP.

✦ **Point-to-Point Protocol (PPP)** is often used with remote access because it enables computers to load other protocols — such as TCP/IP, NetBEUI, and so on — in addition to the PPP.

✦ **Point-to-Point Tunneling Protocol (PPTP)** enables you to have secure access to a virtual private network.

VPNs use encryption and other security mechanisms to ensure that the data cannot be intercepted. Secure VPNs should protect the network from Internet threats, be easy to manage, use appropriate logging, and perform well for those calling into the VPN. There are software and hardware solutions you can use for VPNs. For more information, talk to your system administrator at work.

Defining Modem Technologies

Modems you might use for remote access include analog and digital modems. *Analog modems* are devices designed to work on a telephone line, which transmits voice signals. *Digital modems* transmit in binary digits, so the speed greatly exceeds analog speeds.

A digital modem could be your cable modem or DSL modem. This type of technology generally works only one way; for example, you can use your cable modem to access the Internet, send and receive e-mail, and so on, but you cannot use your cable modem to dial up work and access files. For now, until technologies improve, you're stuck with analog modems.

You use Windows dial-up networking with analog modems and ISDN devices. ISDN devices are slower than cable modems and DSL, but they do carry voice and data, which means you could use an ISDN device to contact a work computer, if that computer also has an ISDN. ISDN is an older technology, however, and is falling out of use.

Identifying analog modems

Analog modems come in 28.8, 33.6, and 56 Kbps, but most likely, your modem is a 56 Kbps modem. Although you can use any of these for remote access, the slower the modem is, the slower your connection to the remote computer. If you're planning to access a small file and then disconnect, slower modems might work fine. If you want to work for very long on a remote computer, however, you'll that find the faster modems are best. Most newer modems use data compression, so the throughput can be faster.

Modems that run at 56 Kbps are very affordable and offer fast downloading and uploading speeds. All data communications devices upload and download at different speeds. Downloading speeds are always faster. More people download than upload, so most servers, lines, modems, and other technologies make sure that downloading speeds are fast. For a 56 Kbps modem, download speeds range as high as 53 Kbps and uploading speeds are usually around 33 Kbps. The actual speeds depend on the telephone lines and the connection.

Note   The FCC's regulations prevent us from using 56 Kbps in the United States, so you won't see any speeds above 53 Kbps or so.

Recognizing digital modems

Digital modems are becoming more common in small businesses and corporate offices because they're not as expensive as they have been in the past. One of the problems with digital lines is the fact they're not available in many rural areas. Prices and availability vary greatly from area to area. You might expect to pay a $100 for the modem, around $30 to $60 a month for the line, and perhaps 2 to 5 cents a minute for connection time. If, however, you work at home a lot, your company may want to install a digital line for you to use. If you have a digital line, you can work via a VPN to connect to your company.

Integrated Services Digital Network (ISDN) is a digital modem and data transmission line that supplies voice, video, audio, and data transmissions at high speeds. ISDN offers low noise and interference, security, and consistent service. Again, ISDN is not used as much as it once was.

The ISDN modem is actually a terminal adapter (TA), but using the term modem is common and accepted. One TA is located on your end of the ISDN line, and another TA is located on the other end (at the phone company). With ISDN, your data should transfer with speeds of up to 128 Kbps with uncompressed data. Generally, an ISDN line can be no longer than 18,000 feet, although you can install special equipment to extend the distance.

Understanding V Standards

V standards are a way of rating modems and other data communications. These standards apply to facsimile transmissions, modems, and local area networks. Manufacturers meet these standards to make their products compatible with other manufacturers' products.

The V.90 standard for a 56 Kbps modem is mature and stable. Often, when a standard needs an upgrade or has problems, a manufacturer upgrades the firmware in order to make the changes. *Firmware* is any software stored in the form of read-only memory (ROM) and is part of the modem's design. When a standard is well established, like V.90, manufacturers don't have to upgrade it very often.

Digital Subscriber Lines (DSL) are more expensive but much faster than ISDN lines. You connect two DSL modems to transmit the data at 160 Kbps. There are several types of DSL (sometimes represented as *x*DSL). Asymmetric DSL (ADSL) is the most commonly used xDSL line. ADSL transmits at speeds of up to 6 Mbps and is therefore somewhat expensive.

Cable modems are another broadband device that you can use in your home or small business. Cable modems quickly transfer data and are targeted more to homeowners than business owners.

Looking at communications lines

Each type of modem or other data communications equipment has specific line types it can use. Analog modems, for example, communicate over plain old telephone (POT) wiring. The speed of the communications depends on the line.

Generally, digital lines are leased from a phone or other telecommunications company, and they are nearly always dedicated lines. A company, for example, might install a digital line between two branch offices for faster communications than with a modem. The line is always there, ready to use when someone wants to connect.

ISDN provides two types of lines: Basic Rate Interface (BRI) and Primary Rate Interface (PRI). BRI is not quite as expensive as PRI and provides 128 Kbps speeds. PRI provides speeds of 1.536 Mbps, so it is considerably faster. Because of the expense, mainly larger corporations and government agencies use PRI.

Cable modems use the same coax cabling used for TVs. The cable company installs the cabling for you. DSL uses existing phone lines.

Frame relay, T1, Fractional T1, and T3 are other communications lines that are high in quality and quite expensive. The following briefly describes these technologies:

✦ Frame relay supports speeds of 56 Kbps, transmits voice and data, and has no distance limits. Frame relay's equipment, however, is expensive, and the voice transmission quality isn't the best.

✦ T1 is a high-quality communications line. Total speed is 1.544 Mbps, and a T1 line is reliable. Because of the expense, T1 is best for corporations connecting a large number of users.

✦ Fractional T1 is a part of a T1 line. The speed is less than that of a T1 line but better than ISDN and frame relay. Also, as your network builds, you can add Fractional T1 lines to increase speeds.

✦ T3 is a long-distance communications line that reaches speeds of over 44 Mbps. T3 is very expensive and is used almost exclusively by AT&T and the regional telephone operating companies.

Installing and Configuring a Modem

If you don't have a modem installed in your computer, you must install it before you can remotely access another network. You also can use a modem to connect to the Internet or another communications service, such as America Online. Most newer computers come with an interior modem already installed; however, if you must install a modem, purchase an exterior modem.

When using an exterior modem, you can easily reset the modem by turning it off and back on again. An interior modem requires you reboot the entire computer to reset the modem. Often you must reset a modem during configuration or connection.

Installing a modem

Generally, you can shut down your computer and restart it to get Windows to find a new piece of hardware. Make sure that the modem is turned on so that Windows can sense it. Windows automatically installs the modem software for you and is ready to go. Most external modems have a USB plug that makes immediate recognition easy.

If, however, you want to install the modem yourself, or change the drivers that Windows used for your modem, you can do that by using the Modem icon in the Control Panel.

To install a modem, follow these steps:

1. Open the Control Panel.

2. Double-click the Modems (Windows 98) or Phones and Modems (Windows XP) icon. The Modems Properties dialog box appears, as shown in Figure C-1.

Figure C-1: Install and configure a new modem in Windows XP.

3. Click the Modems tab in XP, and then click the Add button. In Windows 98, click the Add button on the General tab. The Install New Modem Wizard appears, as shown in Figure C-2.

4. It's easiest if you let Windows detect your modem. Turn the modem on, if it's an external modem, and then click the Next button.

   Windows searches for the modem using the serial (COM1 or COM2) port. When it finds the modem, it lists a driver type. Figure C-3 shows the modem that Windows 98 located. If Windows doesn't find a modem, it prompts you to select the modem from a list.

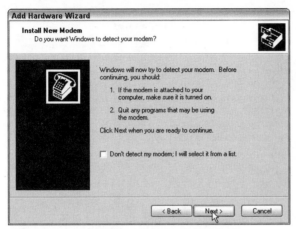

Figure C-2: Let Windows detect your modem.

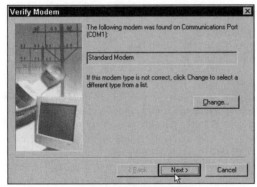

Figure C-3: You can change the modem type if Windows doesn't choose the right one.

5. If the modem type is right, click Next. If the modem type is not correct, click the Change button. The Install New Modem dialog box appears, as shown in Figure C-4.

6. Highlight the manufacturer of your modem from the list of manufacturers.

7. In the right window pane, highlight the model. If you don't see the modem in the list, click the Have Disk button and insert the disk containing the drivers that came with your modem.

8. Click OK. In the Verify Modem dialog box, click Next. Windows installs the modem.

9. When installation is complete, the last dialog box appears, telling you that the setup was successful. Click the Finish button.

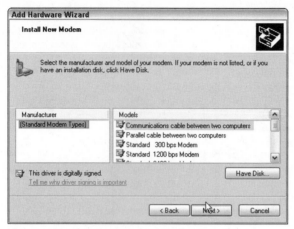

Figure C-4: Choose your modem from the lists.

Configuring a modem

You can set information about the modem, including the maximum speed, connection information, and other options, by using the modem's Properties dialog box.

Dialing properties

Dialing properties enable you to set your computer to dial using an area code, calling card, and other options that might be necessary for its use. Table C-1 explains the options in the dialing properties. Dialing properties in Windows 98 are similar to in Windows 2000 and XP; however, you might not find all of the properties in the same place in various versions of Windows. Consult your documentation for more information.

Table C-1: Modem Dialing Properties

Area	Option	Description
I am dialing from	New	If you dial multiple locations, such as the Internet, your office, and your home, enter a name for each one and configure them separately.
	Remove	Delete a location you no longer use.
	Country/region	Choose the country from which you're calling.
	Area code	Enter your area code.
	Area code rules	Set rules for dialing a 1 before the number.
When dialing from here	For local calls, dial	Enter a number to dial to get a local line, if applicable.
	For long distance calls, dial	Enter the number for long distance calls, if applicable.

Area	Option	Description
	To disable call waiting dial	Check this box if you have call waiting. You want to disable it while you're attached by modem so that you don't get kicked off when someone calls in.
	Dial using	Choose either tone or pulse dial, depending on your phone and service.
For long distance calls, use this calling card		Check the box to use a calling card.
	Calling Card button	Click to add multiple calling card numbers and set preferences for their use.

To set dialing properties in Windows 98, follow these steps:

1. In the Control Panel, double-click the Modems icon. The Modems Properties dialog box appears.

2. Select the modem in the list and then click the Dialing Properties button. The Dialing Properties dialog box appears, as shown in Figure C-5.

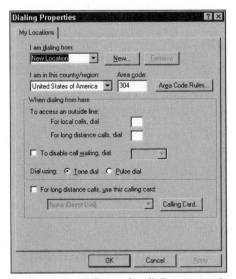

Figure C-5: Configure the dialing properties.

3. Set the dialing properties.

4. Click OK to return to the Modems Properties dialog box.

In Windows XP, follow these steps:

1. Click Start ⇨ Control Panel. The Control Panel dialog box opens.

2. Double-click the Phone and Modem Options icon. The Phone and Modem Options dialog box appears.

3. In the Dialing Rules tab, select the location and click Edit. Alternatively, click New to create a dialing connection.

4. The Edit properties dialog box appears, as shown in Figure C-6.

Figure C-6: Configure the dialing properties in XP.

5. Make changes to the dialing properties.

6. Click OK to close the dialog box, and click OK again.

Individual modem's properties

You can set modem properties for each modem installed in your computer. Modem properties include speed and other technical settings. Unless you understand the technical settings, leave them as they are. Otherwise, you could slow down the modem or render it useless.

In the modem's Properties dialog box, you can choose tabs in which to make changes. Not all modems have all the same number or even type of tabs; it depends on the operating system, modem, and modem software. Following is a description of each tab:

✦ **General tab (Windows 98)** — Set the speaker volume. The sound you hear after dialing is the modem negotiating with the modem on the other end of the line. Maximum speed sets the fastest speed the modem can go, depending on the speed of the communications line and of the other modem. Generally, you shouldn't check the option to connect only at a specific speed, because you limit the use and efficiency of your modem.

✦ **General tab (Windows XP)** — Description of the device, device status, and whether to enable or disable the device in this hardware profile.

✦ **Connection tab** — Use this tab to change the modem's default configuration only if you understand the settings. Other complex options include the Port Settings and Advanced buttons. You might want to set call preferences, however. Call preferences describe how to handle an unanswered call and idle connection, as shown in Figure C-7, from Windows 98.

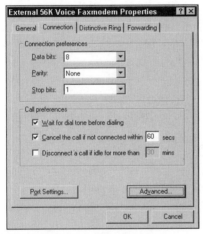

Figure C-7: Set call preferences.

✦ **Distinctive Ring tab** — If your telephone uses a service called distinctive ring, you can use this tab to assign numbers and rings to different services — data, fax, and voice. If you assign a specific ring to faxes, for example, when someone dials the number with a fax machine, the modem routes the fax to the fax program.

✦ **Forwarding tab** — If you use call forwarding on the phone line using the modem, you can activate it here. You use call forwarding when you are away from your computer but want to receive calls at another location.

✦ **Modem tab** — In 2000 or XP, set the speaker volume, the maximum port speed, and the dial control in this tab. You can also identify the modem's port.

✦ **Diagnostics tab** — Contains a Modem Information area that displays hardware information about the modem. This tab also contains a Query Modem button that sends communications to the modem to ensure it is working. Figure C-8 illustrates this tab in Windows XP after the Query Modem button was clicked.

✦ **Advanced tab** — Enables you to set initialization commands, port settings, or change default preferences for your modem. This tab contains advanced configurations.

✦ **Driver tab** — Describes the driver provider, version, date, and driver details. You can also update the driver for the modem in this tab.

✦ **Resources tab** — Lists the I/O range, memory, and IRQ information about the modem.

✦ **Power Management tab** — Sets power configurations for standby mode.

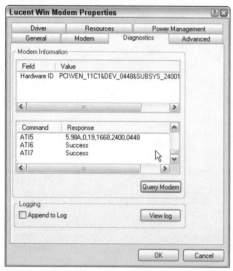

Figure C-8: Check to see if your modem is working correctly.

To set a modem's properties, follow these steps:

1. Open the Control Panel.

2. Double-click the Modems (Windows 98) or the Phone and Modem Options (Windows XP) icon. The properties dialog box appears.

3. In Windows XP, click the Modems tab. In Windows 98 or XP, select the modem, and then click the Properties button. The individual modem's Properties dialog box appears, as shown in Figure C-9.

4. Set any applicable properties, and then click the OK button.

Figure C-9: Set the modem's properties.

Installing and Configuring Dial-Up Networking

The dial-up networking feature in Windows is easy to install and configure. If you already have dial-up networking installed, you can skip to the configuring section that follows. Otherwise, install the feature and then configure it for remote access.

Before you can use dial-up networking successfully, you need to make sure that both computers — yours and the one on the other end attached to the network — have the following network components installed:

✦ Client for Microsoft Networks

✦ A common network protocol

✦ File and Printer Sharing services

✦ A valid computer name in the Identification tab of the Network dialog box.

Installing Dial-Up Networking

You can install the dial-up networking feature if it's not already installed in Windows 98. To check, open the My Computer window and look for the folder called Dial-Up Networking. If you don't see it, you must install it. When installing dial-up networking, you might be prompted to insert the Windows Installation CD. Windows 2000 and XP come with dial-up networking installed.

To install dial-up networking to Windows 98, follow these steps:

1. Choose Start ⇨ Settings ⇨ Add/Remove Programs. The Add/Remove Programs Properties dialog box appears.

2. Choose the Windows Setup tab.

3. Double-click Communications in the Components list. The Communications dialog box appears.

4. Check the check box to the left of the Dial-Up Networking component and then click OK.

5. In the Add/Remove Programs Properties dialog box, click OK to install the feature. If prompted to insert the Windows Installation CD, do so.

6. When Windows has finished installing the dial-up networking feature, it displays the Dial-Up Networking Setup dialog box. Click OK and restart your computer.

Creating a connection in Windows 98

To configure dial-up networking, you first must create a connection. You can create connections to Internet service providers, government agencies, your home network, and your office network, for example. Then, when you're ready to call, you simply open the connection and Windows takes over.

To create a remote access connection in Windows 98, follow these steps:

1. Open My Computer.

2. Double-click the Dial-Up Networking icon. The Dial-Up Networking window appears, as shown in Figure C-10.

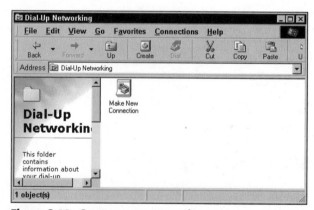

Figure C-10: Create a new connection.

3. Double-click the Make New Connection icon. The first dialog box of the Make New Connection Wizard appears, as shown in Figure C-11.

4. Accept the default name — My Connection — for the new connection, or type a name of your own.

Figure C-11: Configure the connection.

5. If you have more than one modem attached to your computer, select the modem from the Select a Device drop-down list.

 Tip

The Configure button displays the individual modem's Properties dialog box, which enables you to make any changes to the connection, speaker volume, maximum speed, or other property.

6. Click Next. The second wizard dialog box appears, as shown in Figure C-12.

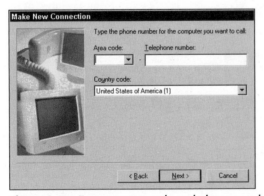

Figure C-12: Enter an area code and phone number.

7. Enter the area code and the telephone number of the computer you want to call. Make sure the country code is correct.

8. Click Next. The resulting wizard dialog box informs you that the connection has been created.

9. Click the Finish button to return to the Dial-Up Networking window. Figure C-13 illustrates the new connection icon.

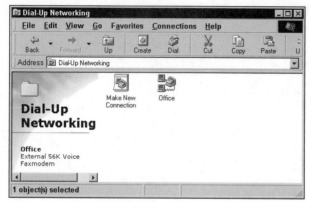

Figure C-13: Create connections for any computer you want to contact via modem.

Creating a connection in Windows 2000/XP

Windows 2000 and XP create a connection in a similar manner; however, the route to getting there is different from Windows 98. Follow these steps to create a connection in Windows 2000 or XP:

1. Open the Network Connections dialog box by right-clicking My Network Places and clicking Properties. The Network Connections dialog box appears, as shown in Figure C-14.

Figure C-14: Create a new network connection.

2. In Network Tasks, click Create a New Connection. The New Connection Wizard dialog box appears.

3. Click Next. The Network Connection Type dialog box appears, as shown in Figure C-15.

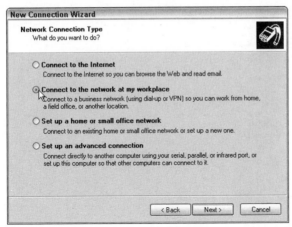

Figure C-15: Create a dial-up connection.

4. Click Connect to the Network at My Workplace. Click Next. The Network Connection dialog box appears.

5. Click Dial-up Connection. Click Next. The Connection Name dialog box appears.

Note You can create a VPN connection in this dialog box by clicking Virtual Private Network Connection instead of Dial-up Connection.

6. Type an identifying name in the Company Name text box and click Next. The Phone Number to Dial dialog box appears.

7. Type the number, with the 1 + area code if necessary, in the Phone Number text box. Click Next.

8. The final dialog box appears. Click Finish.

Configuring the connection

Before you can connect to a remote computer, you have to configure the connection to use the right server type, protocol, and so on. After configuring the connection, you can dial the remote computer and attach to the network.

The tabs of the connection's Properties dialog box enable you to change various connection settings. The following sections describe each tab. Some tabs will be different depending on the version of Windows you're using.

General tab

This tab contains the information you entered when you created the connection, including the area code, phone number, country, and modem information. Use this tab to modify any settings about the number and modem. You can set dialing rules in Windows XP on this tab as well.

Server Types tab

In this tab, you choose the dial-up server you're using, such as PPP, SLIP, or Windows NT. In Figure C-16, note that the PPP server includes an Internet server, a Windows NT server, or a Windows 98 server.

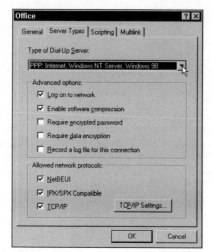

Figure C-16: Set server type, options, and protocols.

Also in the Server Types tab, you can choose from advanced options that enable you to log on to the network automatically, that enable software compression, and that perform other security-related tasks. The network protocols area of the tab is important. You want to make sure that you're using the appropriate protocol to communicate with the network to which you're attaching. Check the box next to the protocol your network uses. If you use TCP/IP, you need to configure it by clicking the TCP/IP Settings button. For more information, see Appendix B.

Note   Choosing a protocol in this dialog box sets the protocol only for your remote network. It doesn't affect your home network or the protocol you use on your home network.

Options tab

This tab contains a list of your dialing options, such as prompt for name and password, include Windows logon domain, and so on. You can use the check boxes to enable or disable any option temporarily. You can also set redialing attempts in the Options tab.

Security tab

You can set the security options in this tab of the dial-up connection's properties dialog box. Using the typical settings is usually recommended in Windows 2000 and XP. The security is tight in these Windows versions as is, and if you change a setting you're not familiar with, you might not be able to dial out at all.

You can also set a script and interactive logon in this tab in Windows 2000 and XP. See the "Scripting tab" section that follows for more information.

Scripting tab

The Scripting tab enables you to use a script, or mini-program, to log on to the remote network. You enter the name and path of the script file; Windows automatically initializes the file when you log on to the remote computer.

Understanding Script Files

Script files are mini-programs that automate logging on to another network, such as a remote network or the Internet. Generally included in a script file are the username and password. When you dial up another computer on a network, the script enters your username and password for you, so you don't have to type them. Script files also might include other information, such as special commands and parameters.

You create a script file in a text editor, such as Notepad. You must make sure that you follow exact directions as outlined in the Script.doc file in the C:\Windows directory. This file describes the basic structure of a script and the form it must take to work with dial-up networking. When you've finished creating the file, save it in the Accessories folder, using the .scp extension. The Accessories folder is located in the C:\Windows\Start Menu\Programs folder.

After you create the file, you must use the Dial-Up Scripting tool to allocate the file to the appropriate dial-up networking connection. To do this, open the Dial-Up Networking folder and select the connection. Choose File ⇨ Properties. In the Scripting tab of the connection's Properties dialog box, type the path and filename of the script file.

Networking tab

In Windows 2000 or XP, you use this tab to set the type of dial-up connection you plan to use, such as PPP, Windows, Internet, and so on. You can also configure, install, or uninstall TCP/IP, Microsoft client, and other services for networking in this tab.

Advanced tab

Use this tab for configuring information about the Internet firewall, if you're using one, and Internet Connection Sharing.

Multilink tab

You use this tab to set up multiple modems on your computer. Multilink is designed to work with ISDN modems. Don't use it for analog modems, because you might cause connection and port problems. This tab is only in Windows 98.

A multilink connection uses multiple modems for a single connection to the Internet or other network. You need two or more modems, one phone line for each modem, and your ISP or other computer network must support multilink and PPP connections.

To configure the connection, follow these steps:

1. In the Dial-Up Networking window, select the connection.

2. Choose File ⇨ Properties. The connection's Properties dialog box appears, with the General tab showing.

3. Choose the tab you want to modify. When you're finished, click OK to close the Properties dialog box.

Setting Up a Dial-Up Server in Windows 98

You can make any one of your home network computers a dial-up server for others to use. If you want to let your son call from college or your spouse call in from a business trip, for example, you can let a Windows 98 computer accept the call and enable the remote user to access the network.

Note   Windows 2000 uses Remote Access Service (RAS) instead of dial-up. By default, RAS is enabled, and therefore, Windows 2000 computers are dial-up servers. All you need is a modem and a telephone line. Windows XP can use either RAS services or VPN services as a dial-up server. For more information, see www.microsoft.com.

Installing the Dial-Up Server

You must install the Dial-Up Server service on the computer. You can install it at the same time you install dial-up networking, or you can install it later. To install the Dial-Up Server, follow these steps:

1. Open the Control Panel.

2. Double-click the Add/Remove Programs icon.

3. Select the Windows Setup tab.

4. Select Communications in the Components list. Click Details. The Communications dialog box appears.

5. Choose the Dial-Up Server.

6. Click OK to return to the Add/Remove Programs Properties dialog box. Click OK again to install the feature.

Enabling the server

Before you enable the server, make sure that you've specified the folders and drives you want to share over the remote network. For information about sharing drives and other resources, see Chapter 12.

To configure a computer to be the dial-up networking server, follow these steps:

1. Open My Computer.

2. Open the Dial-Up Networking folder.

3. Choose Connections ⇨ Dial-Up Server. The Dial-Up Server dialog box appears.

4. Select the Allow Caller Access option.

5. If you want to add password protection, click the Change Password button. Type the password you want to assign, and then confirm the password by typing it again.

6. You can add a comment or note in the Comment text box, if you want.

7. Click OK. The computer checks for the modem and notifies you if the modem is not turned on or is not working properly.

Enabling browsing on the server

You must enable browsing on the server computer if you want remote users to see the network and its resources. To enable browsing, follow these steps:

1. Open the Control Panel.

2. Double-click the Network icon. The Network dialog box appears.

3. In the list of components on the Configuration tab, select File and Printer Sharing for Microsoft Networks.

4. Click the Properties button. The File and Printer Sharing for Microsoft Networks Properties dialog box appears.

5. Select Browse Master in the Property list. In the Value list, select Enabled.

6. Click OK to return to the Network dialog box.

7. Click OK to close the dialog box. If you're prompted to restart your computer, do so.

Connecting to a remote server

To connect to a remote server, you need to know the server's phone number, the protocols it uses, the type of network (PPP, NT Server, Windows 98, and so on) it runs on, and the remote server's computer name.

After you install the modem and dial-up networking, and you create a connection, you can connect to the remote server. You can connect to a network using the dial-up networking connection as long as the other computer is on and you have permission to connect.

To connect to a network, follow these steps:

1. Open My Computer.

2. Double-click Dial-Up Networking.

 Tip You can create a shortcut for your desktop that will save steps when connecting to a remote network. Right-click the connection icon and then choose Create Shortcut.

3. Double-click the Connection icon. The Connect To dialog box appears.

4. Type the appropriate username and password. Click the Save Password check box so that you don't have to enter it every time you connect. When you do this, the password is stored in your Windows's PWL file, not in the dialog box.

5. Click the Connect button. Windows dials the number and connects to the network.

When Windows connects, a dialog box appears, stating that you're connected to the server. You can use the Network Neighborhood or Windows Explorer to view the network after you connect.

 Note The browse list in the Network Neighborhood might take a long time to appear, especially if the network is a large one.

> **Tip** Map network drives to make the connections faster and easier to get to. For information about drive mapping, see Chapter 13.

Working with a Macintosh Modem

Working with a modem in a Mac is similar to working with a modem in Windows. You can control the modem's sound and connection, change drivers, and so on in a Mac. There are many differences between Macintosh operating systems — such as System 7, System 8, Mac OS X, and so on — so you'll need to consult the documentation for your particular operating system. This section covers only Mac OS X.

Mac OS X works with the PPP (Point-to-Point Protocol) similarly to Windows computers. You use PPP to communicate between computers through the dial-up modem connection. If your Mac does not have an internal modem connected to it, you can use an external modem just as well.

Generally, the Network dialog box contains the information for you to create a dial-up connection to the Internet. You can also use the Network dialog box to configure a dial-up to any other computer with a modem. To set up your modem for use with a dial-up connection, follow these steps:

1. Click System Preferences. The System Preferences dialog box appears, as shown in Figure C-17.

2. Double-click the Network icon in the Internet & Network section of the dialog box. The Network dialog box appears, as shown in Figure C-18.

3. Click the Show down arrow and click Modem.

4. Click the PPP tab of the Modem dialog box. Figure C-19 shows the tab.

5. Add the account name, password, and telephone number you wish to call.

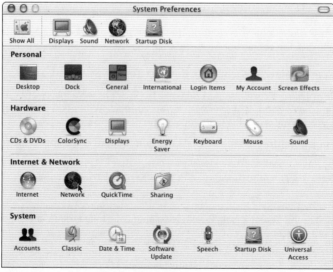

Figure C-17: Open System Preferences.

Figure C-18: Use the Network dialog box to set up the modem dialing properties.

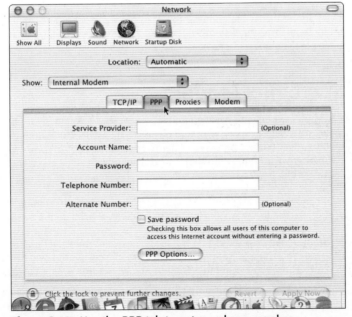

Figure C-19: Use the PPP tab to enter a phone number.

6. You can optionally click the Save password check box.

7. Click the PPP Options button. The Session Options dialog box appears, as shown in Figure C-20.

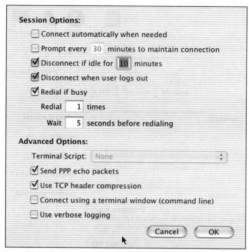

Figure C-20: Set any options for the modem and session.

8. Click OK and then close the System Preferences dialog box.

Tip   If you use a cell phone that is Bluetooth-enabled, you can pair the phone with your computer in the Bluetooth pane of System Preferences. Once you do that, you can use your Address Book to place outgoing phone calls.

Working with a Linux Modem

If you must buy a modem for your Linux box, choose an external modem as opposed to internal. External modems are easier to work with and easier to find drivers for, and they will most likely work with a Linux distribution. Internal modems are often built for Windows or have drivers meant for use only with Windows. Whether internal or external, avoid the modems advertised for Windows only.

Note   If all you can find are Plug and Play modems, you can likely deal with that through Linux. You can use a serial driver, use the isapnp program, or let the PnP BIOS do the configuring.

Hardware modems don't usually need a driver in Linux, although the serial port on which the modem resides does need a driver. Serial port drivers are either supplied as a Linux serial module or compiled into the kernel. You must also configure the IRQ and I/O for the port.

For more specific information about your modem and your Linux distribution, see these Web sites: www.tldp.org, new.linuxnow.com, www.extremetech.com, or any of hundreds of sites on the Internet.

✦   ✦   ✦

Glossary

2D The speed at which normal programs use the video or sound card.

3D In video and audio multimedia, this is a near-realistic sound or picture.

4-bit cable Available before 1992, 4-bit cables are parallel cables. Examples include the LapLink and InterLink cables.

/8s *See* Class A IP addresses.

/16s *See* Class B IP addresses.

/24s *See* Class C IP addresses.

10Base-2 An implementation of an Ethernet standard for coaxial cabling. The data transfer rate, or network speed, for 10Base-2 is 10 Mbps (megabits per second) over 185 meters. The 185 meters (around 600 feet) describes the maximum cable-segment length.

10Base-T An Ethernet standard topology for twisted-pair cabling. The data transfer rate is 10 Mbps over a distance of 100 meters (330 feet).

100Base-T Produces 100 Mbps throughput over twisted-pair cabling, usually Fast Ethernet. 100Base-T is built on the older Ethernet standards.

100Base-T4 Produces 100 Mbps throughput over twisted-pair wiring but uses four pairs of the wiring, thus making the network a lower quality than 100Base-TX, which uses only two pairs of the wiring.

100Base-TX Produces 100 Mbps throughput over twisted-pair wiring, usually Fast Ethernet. 100Base-TX is built on newer Ethernet standards, which means it is a faster technology than 100Base-T.

802 standards The IEEE 802 standards are set for networking, specifically LANs. Some standards identify wireless, others Ethernet, and so on.

1000Base-T Produces speeds of 1000 Mbps over twisted-pair wiring. Also called Gigabit Ethernet, this technology is normally used in corporations and businesses as a backbone (or foundation) of their networks.

1394 Also known as FireWire, this is a technology that has a bandwidth of up to 1000 Mbps. The bus is also hot swappable.

Accelerated Graphics Port *See* AGP.

accelerator card An adapter used in a computer to speed up graphics. An accelerator card is a type of video card.

access point A wireless-based device used to connect roaming wireless PC cards to a server, the Internet, or another wireless station. The access point provides mobility from a stationary connection.

access time How fast a drive can move data around.

adapter The software driver that makes a card work. The adapter driver is the program that enables a device to communicate with the computer and over the network. Examples of adapters are sound, video, and network cards.

address Can be an e-mail specification for a person, a specification for a Web page, or a number that identifies a computer on a network.

Address Book The Exchange post office maintains a list of all mailboxes for users on the network. This list is called the Address Book. Also, Outlook Express and other e-mail applications maintain their own versions of the Address Book. Some Address Books contain names, phone numbers, and other information; others contain e-mail addresses, Web page URLs, and so on.

Address Resolution Protocol *See* ARP.

administrator The person in charge of a network. Administrators troubleshoot connection problems, upgrade applications, set up networking hardware and software, and so on. They also have special permissions and access to computers on the network.

ADSL (Asymmetric Digital Subscriber Lines) A type of DSL line that provides access paths for 6 Mbps in one direction and around 640 Kbps in both directions simultaneously.

AGP (Accelerated Graphics Port) A new technology built specifically for the demands of 3D graphical software.

AirPort Apple's name for wireless adapters for the Macintosh.

alias A name given to a computer or person to replace long names or to keep your own name private. Used in chat rooms and computer gaming.

analog technology Transmission methods developed to transmit voice signals instead of digital signals. The phone lines in your home are analog lines built to carry voice transmissions and perhaps other data, such as faxes. They also might carry your network transmissions on a phone line network.

anonymous FTP (File Transfer Protocol) A method of transferring files between two Internet sites. FTP is a method of logging on to another Internet site for the main purpose of retrieving or sending files. When a user logs on to the FTP server, he or she can use the Anonymous account (which is like a guest account), meaning anyone can access those files.

antivirus software A program that detects and removes viruses from your computer. These programs search for suspicious activities on the system or characteristic patterns. Some antivirus programs compete with computer devices, hardware, and programs for network resources.

API (application program interface) A set of interface functions available for applications. API enables the Windows operating system to work with various programs.

AppleTalk The Macintosh network protocol.

applets Mini-programs included with software.

application layer One of the ISO/OSI layers. The application layer defines how the applications interact with the network.

application program interface *See* API.

ARP (Address Resolution Protocol) One of the TCP/IP protocols. ARP translates 32-bit IP addresses into physical network addresses, such as 48-bit Ethernet addresses.

Asymmetric Digital Subscriber Lines *See* ADSL.

authentication The process of checking a user and his or her password to make sure that the user has permission to access a client/server network.

backbone A main, high-speed cable from which transceiver cables are connected to computers, hubs, and other equipment. It's the main cable that connects everything together.

backup A copy of data, programs, or other information stored on floppy disks, Zip or Jaz disks, tapes, or, most commonly, CD-Rs and CD-RWs.

bandwidth A measurement of the amount of information or data that can pass through any given point on the network: cabling, server, network cards, and so on. The wider the bandwidth, the more data can pass through. With an Ethernet network, bandwidth is measured in megabits per second.

base station A Macintosh wireless access point.

basic input/output system *See* BIOS.

Basic Rate Interface *See* BRI.

batch file A text file that contains commands that are carried out automatically on startup. The commands are entered into the system, one at a time, just as if you had typed them in yourself. Batch files use a .BAT extension to identify themselves as batch files to the operating system.

baud rate A speed measurement for communication. Baud rate sometimes corresponds to the number of bits transmitted per second, but they are not always the same. At a baud rate of 300, the bits per second also might be 300; at higher baud rates, however, the number of bits transmitted per second is usually higher than the baud rate.

BBS *See* bulletin boards.

binary The base 2 numbering system, using combinations of the digits 0 and 1 to represent all values. Binary numbers are easy for the computer to read.

binding The process of assigning a protocol to the network card. Binding the protocol means the network card uses that particular language to communicate with other network cards on the network.

BIOS (basic input/output system) A set of routines that works with the hardware to support the transfer of data through components of the system, such as memory, hard disks, or the monitor.

bit The basic unit of information in the binary numbering system, represented by either 0 (for off) or 1 (for on). Computers read binary numbers, or strings of 0s and 1s.

bit depth Describes the information a scanner records about the pixels it scans. Some scanners record only black and white (1-bit). To see grays or tones between the black and white, you need at least a 4-bit depth (16 tones) or an 8-bit depth (up to 256 tones). Color scanners are usually 24-bit or higher, which means they can capture more than 16 million different colors.

bit rate The rate of data throughput for the medium (modem or other serial device), measured in bits per second.

bits per second (bps) A measurement of data transmission speed over a serial data link. A single character requires about 10 bits. For example, a 33.6 Kbps modem transfers 33,600 bits of data per second. Bits per second is a more accurate statement of modem capability than baud rate. *See also* baud rate.

blog Also called weblog, this is a Web page or group of pages usually run by one person, who updates the log daily, adding text, images, and other personal remarks about his or her life or emotions. A blog is a diary of sorts on the Internet, for all to see.

Bluetooth A wireless connection that works on short-range radio waves to enable communications between Bluetooth devices. A radio chip, placed in the computer, printer, telephone, handhelds, or other device, communicates with another Bluetooth radio chip.

BNC connector An end piece that connects two or three cables together. Cabling is coaxial.

boot disk A floppy disk that contains system files and enables a computer to boot, or start, when inserted into a computer's disk drive. You use a boot disk to diagnose system problems or to access a system when the computer cannot boot on its own. *See also* system disk.

boot sector The set of instructions your computer reads when it starts up.

bottleneck A place that slows the information moving from one computer to another. A bottleneck can be caused by a slow switch or hub, a slow NIC, a damaged cable, and so on.

box A computer's CPU, motherboard, hard drive, and the case are often called the "box." In Linux, in particular, a computer is often called a Linux box.

bps *See* bits per second.

BRI (Basic Rate Interface) BRI lines are a type of ISDN that enables a download speed of 64 Kbps.

bridge A network device that provides a communications path between two network segments to form one logical network. Generally, a bridge is used in larger or corporate networks.

broadband Also called wideband transmission, broadband refers to networking that provides multiple channels of data over a single wire; cable and DSL are two examples.

broadcast On a network, a message that is sent to everyone in the area. A server might send a broadcast regarding certain services that have become available, such as Internet access.

browser Software on a computer that enables the user to view Web pages on the Internet. A browser reads the HTML language and displays it in an attractive manner.

BTW (by the way) Used in chat programs and e-mail to represent the words *by the way*.

bulletin boards (BBS) Areas in which users can post messages, ideas, and replies to other members of the LAN. Users might want to brainstorm ideas, for example, or simply schedule a meeting.

burst access mode A method of transmitting data in which the data is collected first and then sent in one high-speed transmission instead of one character at a time.

bus An electronic corridor that sends signals from one part of the computer to another, such as from the processor to the memory. The bus sends signals in either 16 or 32 bits.

bus topology Connects each computer along a single length of cable, in a line. You can connect up to 30 users on this simple network. Installation is easy, and the network is relatively inexpensive.

byte A data measurement unit that is the equivalent of one character; a byte is made up of 8 bits of data, also known as an octet. Bits are grouped to form larger storage units, the most common of which is a byte. The word byte is a contraction of BinarY digiT Eight.

cable Any one of various types of wiring used for networking. Cabling must match the topology and protocol of the network.

cable (for television) This type of line is leased to you by your cable television company and provides high speed at an affordable price. Downstream (or downloading) cable speeds are from 10 Mbps to 30 Mbps for a distance of up to 30 miles. Upstream (or uploading) speeds might be 128 Kbps to 10 Mbps for the same distance. Cable television lines are usually coaxial.

cable modem A device, not actually a modem, that connects your PC to a cable television line instead of a phone line. The device enables you to have Internet access 24 hours a day. The connection is much faster than a dial-up modem.

cache Pronounced "cash," this is a special area of memory your computer uses on top of RAM memory. Cache helps boost the performance of the computer by making information even more available than that stored in RAM.

capture a printer port Capturing a printer port is similar to mapping a drive. You assign a network path to an LPT port to fool an application. Many MS-DOS applications and some 16-bit Windows programs print only to an LPT port. These programs cannot recognize a network path as written — \\Sue\\WinHP, for example.

CardBus A PC Card slot that is a 32-bit bus mastering slot. This slot is commonly the bottom slot on laptops that support it.

CAT 3 cable There are categories, or levels, of twisted-pair cabling. Each level describes the performance characteristics of wiring standards. Category 3 (CAT 3) is less expensive than CAT 5, and its transfer rate isn't as fast; in fact, you can hardly find CAT 3 in use anymore.

CAT 5 cable There are categories, or levels, of twisted-pair cabling. Each level describes the performance characteristics of wiring standards. Category 5 (CAT 5) is the best cable for any network — business or home. CAT 5 works equally well with 10Base-T or with 100Base-T.

CCITT (Comité Consultatif International de Téléphonique et Télégraphique) An organization that sets international telecommunications standards that govern, in part, the definition of modem speeds and operations. The new name for the CCITT is the International Telecommunications Union-Telecommunications Standards Section, or ITU-TSS.

CD-R (recordable) CD-Rs, writable compact discs, are more affordable than in the past and are a great way to save data. You must consider, however, that unless you get the right type of CD (CD-RW, as opposed to CD-R), you cannot overwrite the CD. CDs usually hold 650MB of data.

CD-ROM (compact disc–read-only memory) A high-capacity disc (around 650MB) containing data stored with laser optic technology instead of through magnetic means.

CD-RW CD-RW drives can overwrite data on a CD so that the CD can be used over and over again. You must purchase special CD-RW discs for recording over; CD-RW discs are more expensive than CD-R discs.

CEBus (Consumer Electronics Bus) A communications protocol you can use with appliances, such as dryers and dishwashers, lighting, and other systems. CEBus is similar to LonWorks in that each device is capable of transmitting and receiving signals from other devices on the network. CEBus is similar to X-10 in that it works over your power lines, so you don't have to install new wiring.

central processing unit (CPU) The part of the computer that controls devices, components, and so on. Also called a processor, the CPU is a printed circuit board that often includes slots for memory and device cards.

chat programs Programs that connect two or more people online at the same time. The conversation is held in real time.

CIFS (Common Internet File System) A protocol that runs over TCP/IP and enables users from different platforms, such as Linux and the Mac, to use Windows operating systems.

Class A IP addresses These addresses are used for large networks. To identify a Class A network address, the first octet uses the numbers from 1 to 126. Class A networks have an 8-bit network prefix; therefore, they are currently referred to as /8s (pronounced "slash eights") or just "eights."

Class B IP addresses These addresses are mainly used for medium-sized networks, and the first octet values range from 128 to 191. Class B network addresses have a 16-bit network prefix; thus, they are referred to as /16s.

Class C IP addresses These addresses are reserved for smaller networks. The values for a Class C range from 192 to 233. Class C networks have a 24-bit network prefix and are referred to as /24s.

Class D IP addresses These addresses aren't used for networks because they're special multicast or broadcasting addresses.

Class E IP addresses These addresses, with values higher than 233 in the first octet, are used only for experimental purposes.

client A computer that accesses shared network resources provided by a server. Also refers to one-half of a program installed on a workstation; the other half of the program is installed on a server. The two halves work together to provide data to the user. Also, the network client is the software that enables your computer to become a member of a network.

client application A program on a workstation that connects to another computer's resources. The client might access a server application, such as a database management system, or simply another workstation that contains a host application, such as an Internet access program.

client/server network A network in which one computer — called the server — shares its resources with all other computers — called clients.

CMOS (Complementary Metal-Oxide Semiconductor) An integrated circuit used in processors and for memory. CMOS devices operate at a high speed while using little power. In a PC, battery-backed CMOS memory stores operating parameters when the computer is switched off.

coaxial cabling A fast, expensive network cable. Coaxial (coax) cable consists of a plastic jacket surrounding a braided copper shield, plastic insulation, and a solid inner conductor. The cabling is generally free from external interference and supports greater distances, and it is also a secure transfer medium.

collision Happens when two computers or other networking devices send data at the same time to another computer, server, or device. When a collision occurs, the server or network device sends a request back to the original computer asking for the original data. It's best to avoid collisions because they take longer for services to be delivered over the network and they add more network traffic. Switches and routers are good solutions.

COM Refers to the serial port on a computer. Often the COM port attaches a mouse, modem, or keyboard to the computer. Computers usually have two COM ports: COM1 and COM2.

Comité Consultatif International de Téléphonique et Télégraphique *See* CCITT.

command.com The command interpreter, a system file, for your operating system—DOS, Windows 95/98, and so on. This file is a necessary startup file for a PC system.

communications server A server, or even a computer, that enables many computers to use its communications lines, such as a cable modem, shared T1 line, and so on, usually to connect to the Internet.

compact disc–read-only memory *See* CD-ROM.

concentrator A communications device that enables a shared transmission medium to accommodate more data sources than there is currently room for.

conferencing software Refers to electronic meetings over the network. With groupware, the network can be a LAN or the Internet. Real-time conferencing enables groups of people to get online at one time and discuss topics. In these types of conferences, only one person can enter a message at a time, so everyone has a turn without being interrupted.

configuration files The files that load your device drivers when your computer boots. Many programs also have their own configuration files that load your preferences in that particular program.

connectable Refers to a Bluetooth device that is in range so that it responds to another Bluetooth device.

controller An additional card, board, or other piece of equipment that receives information from the computer's processor and uses the instructions to manage additional hardware.

cookies Identifiers that are saved on your hard disk during your visits to various Web pages. Software on the Web sends the cookie to collect information—such as your name, e-mail address, site password, and so on—and then logs that information on your hard disk. The next time you visit that particular site, software from the site recalls the cookie so that it knows who you are.

CPU *See* central processing unit.

daemon A program that runs automatically to perform a task. A daemon, pronounced "demon," can control the flow of print jobs to a printer, for example.

data bits Describe the number of bits used to transmit a piece of information, usually 7 or 8.

database management system The server software contains all of the data in the database — for example, a price list of products or an inventory of equipment. Any user can use a client version of the database software to look up a specific product or piece of equipment by name, number, price, description, or other criterion. When the client makes a request for information, the database management system on the server searches the stored records. When it locates the requested data, it displays the data on the client software for the user.

datagrams Packets of data that contain the source and destination address, as well as data intended for its target host. Each datagram contains all the information it needs to find the target host, no matter which paths the other datagrams have taken.

data link layer One of the ISO/OSI layers. The data link layer controls the flow of data through the network cards.

DCC *See* Direct Cable Connection.

Debian Debian GNU/Linux is a popular distribution of Linux. Debian is free, and it includes over 8,000 software packages you can pick and choose from to install.

dedicated line A special high-speed, hard-wired (limited flexibility) connection that is permanent. The connection is always active and therefore always ready.

default gateway A physical device that connects two network segments. The gateway address looks like an IP address.

desktop The on-screen work area containing icons and menus in Windows. A desktop computer is one that sits on your desk or table, as opposed to standing on its end, as a tower computer does (which is often mistakenly referred to as a desktop).

device driver The software needed to make a hardware device — sound card, mouse, CD-ROM drive, and so on — work through the operating system.

DHCP (Dynamic Host Configuration Protocol) A utility for assigning TCP/IP addresses to workstations automatically.

Dial-Up Networking A Windows feature that enables you to use your modem to call the Internet, your company's network, or some other remote network for the purpose of sharing resources, exchanging e-mail, and performing other network-specific tasks.

differential backup This kind of backup backs up everything that has changed or been created since the last full backup of the selected files.

digital modem Also called a terminal adapter (TA) or router, this is a piece of hardware located at the end of the line — ISDN, DSL, TV cable, and so on — that transmits and translates the signal to and from the computer or server. When there's a digital modem on one end of the line, there must be a digital modem on the other end of the line for the two to communicate.

Digital Subscriber Line *See* DSL.

digital technology Digital lines transmit data at high speeds so that a link to the Internet enables users to perform multiple tasks simultaneously. You can transfer large data files, have videoconferences, and perform other tasks all at the same time, for example.

Digital Video Disc–Read Only Memory *See* DVD-ROM.

Direct Cable Connection (DCC) Sharing resources between two computers over just a cable, using no network card. Windows includes the software necessary to set up this slow, but effective, networking scheme.

direct memory access *See* DMA.

directory (folder) Folders in Windows are the same as directories in DOS. Use a directory to contain files for an application, data, the system files, and so on.

DirectX A library of codes in Windows that presents a standardized format for programming. DirectX makes an application, such as a game, accessible to a wide variety of hardware features. Some hardware might not be fully compatible with DirectX.

disk cache Part of the system's RAM that's reserved for the data being read from a disk, which allows for faster access. The memory is cleared each time the computer is turned off, so the data in the cache is only temporary.

distro A Linux distribution that is based on the Linux kernel, to which enhancements have been added.

DMA (direct memory access) A method of transferring information directly from a hard disk, for example, into memory by bypassing the processor.

DNS *See* Domain Name System.

docking station You use a docking station with a portable computer to attach additional equipment, such as speakers, CD-ROM, or keyboard, and to plug the portable into a network.

document management software Document management is a method of organizing multiple documents for access by the members of the group. Each user can view other documents and contribute her or his own. Users also can copy, save, and search documents in the database.

domain name IP addresses are difficult to remember, so domain names can also represent a computer on the Internet. Microsoft's domain name, for example, is www.microsoft.com. Domain names usually start with www, which stands for World Wide Web; however, www is not always included in an address. Some addresses route to a different server and therefore use different prefixes than www; other addresses use a generic routing, so if you don't use www, the link finds its way on its own.

Domain Name Server *See* Domain Name System.

Domain Name System (DNS) A method of matching IP addresses with domain names. When you type a domain name in the URL address area of your browser, that query is transmitted to a Domain Name Server. A Domain Name Server maintains a database of domain names and IP addresses. The Domain Name Server finds the IP address that matches the domain name and then sends your request on to that server. The process is called name resolution.

DOS (disk operating system) An operating system that loads from disk devices at startup. There are various versions of DOS: MS-DOS, IBM DOS, and so on.

dot pitch Every object and character on the screen is made up of dots. The distance between the centers of the dots is called dot pitch. Dot pitch ranges from 0.25 to 0.52 mm.

download A method of retrieving files from another computer, via the Internet or a network.

downstream Also called download, this is the speed at which information travels from the destination server to you. Downstream speeds are often faster than upstream, because users download more often than upload; bandwidths for downloading are therefore extended.

driver A set of software routines used to control input and output between the operating system and a device, such as a modem, network card, or other computer equipment.

DSL (Digital Subscriber Line) A digital technology that transmits data in both directions at once over copper lines (existing phone lines), just like the ones the ISDN service uses. DSL also transmits voice and video. Speeds for DSL are around 160 Kbps. DSL lines are secure and offer low interference.

DVD-RAM DVD-RAM offers faster access and read/write times than CD-RW. You can write to a DVD-RAM disc over and over; DVD-RAM discs hold 2.58GB of data.

DVD-ROM (Digital Video Disc–Read Only Memory) DVD-ROM drives are just like CD-ROM drives except that they have a higher capacity. A CD-ROM holds 640MB of data; a DVD-ROM holds 4.7GB of data.

Dynamic Host Configuration Protocol *See* DHCP.

ECP cable *See* Extended Capabilities Port cable.

EISA (Extended Industry Standard Architecture) A 32-bit extension to the ISA standard bus.

electronic mail (e-mail) Messages, memos, letters, and so on that are created in a computer and sent electronically via the Internet or another network. Delivery can be nearly instantaneous.

Ethernet A protocol and cabling scheme that transfers data at the rate of 10 Mbps. Ethernet can use the bus or the spanning tree topology connected with various cabling types.

Extended Capabilities Port (ECP) cable This cable, which is used with an ECP-enabled parallel port, enables data to transfer more quickly than standard cables. The ECP port must be enabled in the BIOS.

FAQ (frequently asked questions) Documents that list common questions and answers about certain topics. Many Internet sites include FAQs.

fax server A high-powered server on a client/server network that manages incoming and outgoing faxes. The fax service routes any received faxes to an individual, department, or workgroup on the network.

fiber-optic cabling A fiber-optic cable transmits data in pulses of light along specially manufactured optical fibers. Fiber-optic cable is lighter and smaller than traditional copper cables, and it's immune to electrical interference. Fiber-optic cable also offers better signal transmission. Unfortunately, fiber-optics is also extremely expensive. The cable is difficult to install and hard to repair; thus, maintenance is more difficult as well.

filename extension A three-letter abbreviation that follows a period in a filename—such as letter.doc or picture.pcx. Extensions identify the type of file—PCX is a picture file, and DOC is a document file from Word, for example.

file server A computer with a fast processor and a lot of storage space (in the gigabyte range) that is used to store files in a client/server network.

File Transfer Protocol (FTP) A TCP/IP protocol, FTP enables the exchange of bulk information over an intranet or the Internet.

firewall Firewalls can be either hardware or software. Hardware firewalls monitor bandwidth usage and network or connection activity. They also protect the LAN from security breaches, perhaps authenticate users, and monitor incoming and outgoing e-mail messages. Software, or application, firewalls control access to the LAN from Internet users, control LAN users' access to the Internet, and issue alerts for security breaches. A good firewall also logs all events and notifies the administrator of any problems.

FireWire A newer bus developed to make more effective use of audio and video applications. FireWire is extremely fast; the data transfer rates are more than three times that of PCI. FireWire is ideal if you want to use your PC mainly for games; its power would be wasted on general or common use, such as word processing. You can connect up to 63 devices in a chain to a FireWire bus.

flatbed scanner With a flatbed scanner, you place the item being scanned on a glass plate, and the scanning head moves beneath the item. *See also* sheetfed scanner.

flavor Linux is considered a flavor of Unix. Unix isn't one single operating system; it's actually dozens of OSs by different organizations and groups of people. Often, a distribution of Linux is also called a flavor.

FM synthesis FM synthesis sound cards generate the sounds of instruments — such as horns, piano, drums, and so on. The method used to generate the instrument sounds sometimes produces sounds that are close to that of the instrument — and sometimes produces sounds that are nothing like the real instrument.

fractional T1 A part of a T1 line, fractional T1's speed is less than T1 but better than ISDN and frame relay. Also, as your network grows, you can add fractional T1 lines to increase speeds.

frame relay Frame relay supports speeds of 56 Kbps, transmits voice and data, and has no distance limits. Frame relay's equipment, however, is expensive, and the voice transmission quality isn't the best.

FTP *See* File Transfer Protocol.

full access Sharing option that enables anyone to open, change, add, or remove files and folders.

full backup This type of backup makes a complete copy of all selected files, folders, and drives. You can use a full backup of your hard disk to restore all your files in case of a disaster.

game port The game control adapter. You usually connect a joystick, game pads, steering wheels, and the like to a game port.

gateway Hardware or software that acts as a translator between two different protocols; any device that provides access to another system.

gateway remote access A method of connecting to one computer to get to another. You might connect to the server at work, for example, in order to get to your workstation there.

GB *See* gigabyte.

Gbit *See* gigabit.

Gbps Gigabits per second. Measures how much data transfers per second.

GIF (Graphics Interchange Format) A graphics format commonly used for image files and especially suitable for images containing large areas of the same color. GIF is the format's extension. Not a good format for photographs.

gigabit (Gbit) A gigabit represents 1 billion bits.

gigabyte (GB) A gigabyte contains 1,073,741,824 bytes. Giga- is the prefix for one billion in the metric system. You generally see gigabytes when talking about hard-disk capacity.

GNU The Free Software Foundation's project to provide a freely distributable operating system, namely Linux. (GNU stands for "GNU's Not Unix.")

Gopher A part of the TCP/IP protocol that provides a menu-based interface to files on an intranet or the Internet; Gopher is an older service but is still used in many places.

Graphics Interchange Format *See* GIF.

groupware Collaborative networking software. Groupware products, or suites, usually include several programs, such as those for e-mail, scheduling, electronic meetings or chats, and so on. The products are built to encourage collaboration over the network.

HAN (home area network) A new acronym for a network set up in the home.

handheld device Extremely small computer devices that you can hold in the palm of your hand. Handhelds enable you to schedule your time, update your address book, take memos, and more. You also can synchronize the information on your handheld computer with the programs on your desktop computer to make sure that you don't miss an appointment or lose an address. Also called a personal digital assistant (PDA). *See* palmtop computer.

heating, ventilation, air conditioning *See* HVAC.

hex (hexidecimal) Hex stands for hexidecimal, which is the base 16 numbering system. Hex numbering uses the digits 0 to 9, followed by the letters A to F, and is a convenient method of representing binary numbers.

home area network *See* HAN.

HomePNA (Home Phoneline Networking Alliance) An incorporated, nonprofit association of industry-leading companies working together to ensure the adoption of a single, unified phone line networking industry standard for vendors and manufacturers.

host Any computer on a network that offers services to other computers.

host computer Same as host; a networked computer that enables other computer connected to it to use programs, access data, and so on.

HP JetAdmin HP JetAdmin is a tool for managing network printing. Larger corporations use JetAdmin to administer multiple printers and print queues.

HTML (Hypertext Markup Language) A set of codes that creates the page formatting you see in a Web page; HTML is the standard for creating Web pages.

HTTP (Hypertext Transfer Protocol) The protocol that transfers documents from a Web server to your own computer. *http*, in lowercase form, is often the first thing you type in before an Internet address. HTTP indicates to the Web browser the protocol needed to locate the Web address.

hub A networking device that enables attached devices to receive data transmitted over the network. Most networks need a hub to help modify transmission signals and to extend the network past two workstations.

HVAC (heating, ventilation, air conditioning) A common acronym for the environmental systems in your home.

hypertext The text on the page that supplies the links. When you click on these links — represented as underlined text, and often as graphics, on a Web page — you "jump" to another Web page. Using links, you can view information or images related to the original topic.

Hypertext Markup Language *See* HTML.

Hypertext Transfer Protocol *See* HTTP.

ICMP (Internet Control Message Protocol) One of the TCP/IP protocols. It helps IP communicate error information about the IP transmissions.

IDE (Integrated Device Electronics) A popular hard disk interface standard that provides only medium-to-fast data transfer rates.

IEEE (Institute of Electrical and Electronic Engineers) Networking cabling and other equipment have standards that are set by the IEEE to ensure interoperability of products and services from vendor to vendor.

IGMP (Internet Group Management Protocol) One of the TCP/IP protocols. It enables IP datagrams to be broadcast to computers that belong to groups.

incremental backup This type of backup backs up only the files that have changed since the last incremental or full backup.

Industry Standard Architecture *See* ISA.

infrared A method of wireless networking connection using high-frequency light waves instead of cabling to transmit data. With infrared, you must have a clear line of sight between the two computers, because the light waves cannot penetrate obstacles.

input/output *See* I/O port.

Institute of Electrical and Electronic Engineers *See* IEEE.

Integrated Device Electronics *See* IDE.

Integrated Services Digital Network *See* ISDN.

intelligent home (also SmartHome or smart home) Intelligent homes vary from those having simple motion detectors outside to those that are fully connected and fully wired with automatic heating and cooling, security cameras, whole-house video and audio, and more.

International Organization for Standardization/Open Systems Interconnect *See* ISO/OSI.

International Telecommunications Union-Telecommunications Standards Section *See* ITU-TSS.

Internet An internetwork of smaller networks that spans the entire world. Each smaller network contains servers that display information of various types on the Web (WWW, or World Wide Web). The Internet is a public network, available to all who have a computer with the appropriate software and a connection to the Internet.

Internet Control Message Protocol *See* ICMP.

Internet Group Management Protocol *See* IGMP.

Internet Protocol *See* IP.

Internet Relay Chat *See* IRC.

Internet service provider *See* ISP.

Internetwork Packet Exchange/Sequenced Packet Exchange *See* IPX/SPX.

InterNIC (Internet Network Information Center) To ensure that the IP addresses used on the Internet are unique, the InterNIC must assign any address used on the Internet. InterNIC is the controlling agency for IP addresses and domain names.

interrupt request *See* IRQ.

intranet A private Internet—that is, a network within your home network on which you publish documents to view with your Web browser. You use these Internet tools—HTTP, HTML, TCP/IP, Web browsers, and more—to create and use the intranet. An intranet may or may not be connected to the Internet.

I/O (input/output) port A port on the computer to which you can attach hardware, such as a joystick. The I/O is the means by which data is transferred between the computer and its peripheral devices.

IP (Internet Protocol) One of the TCP/IP protocols that provides routing services over multiple networks. IP enables network packets to move data between network segments and to travel across routers. IP is a routing protocol, meaning that it directs datagrams from the source to the destination.

IP address An identifier for the ISP's server. Often the IP address looks similar to this: 205.112.134.121.

IPCONFIG A utility included with TCP/IP that displays the IP address, subnet mask, and default gateway for all network adapter cards on your computer. IPCONFIG is handy for checking a computer's address quickly. It also can detect bad IP addresses or subnet masks.

IPX/SPX (Internetwork Packet Exchange/Sequenced Packet Exchange) A protocol frequently used with Novell NetWare networks, although you also can use it with Microsoft networks. IPX/SPX supports many of Windows's features, including NetBIOS, Windows sockets, and others.

IRC A popular method used on the Internet and in private networks to chat between computers and sometimes share applications.

IRQ (interrupt request) A hardware signal sent to the central processing unit. Each device must send an IRQ before the CPU can process the request for service. Hardware lines carry a device's signal to the processor. When a device wants to communicate with the processor, it causes an IRQ to gain the processor's attention.

ISA (Industry Standard Architecture) A 16-bit bus design.

ISDN (Integrated Services Digital Network) A digital service that transmits data, voice, and video. ISDN lines are copper, twisted-pair cabling that you can lease from your local phone company. ISDN supplies low noise, less interference, and good security. ISDN runs at speeds from 56 Kbps to 45 Mbps, depending on the cabling type.

ISO/OSI (International Organization for Standardization/Open Systems Interconnect) The ISO/OSI model is a set of standards that define network functionality. ISO/OSI sets standards for cabling, NICs, protocols, and so on.

ISP (Internet service provider) A company or service that provides access to the Internet for a monthly fee.

ITU-TSS (International Telecommunications Union-Telecommunications Standards Section) An organization that sets international telecommunications standards that govern, in part, the definition of modem speeds and operations; formerly known as the CCITT.

Java A programming language that enables embedded motion on a Web page, thus making the Web page more dynamic than static. Java programs you download from the Internet are usually safe from viruses or other harmful additions.

jitter The fluctuation of a data packet with respect to the standard clock cycle.

JPEG (Joint Photographic Experts Group) A file format for graphics. A good format to use on the Internet, because the graphic is compressed when saved in this format. Use JPEG for photographs, in particular.

jumpers Small switches that complete a circuit between two pins on an adapter card. When you adjust the jumpers, you can change the IRQ, base memory address, or I/O port address. Plug and Play cards don't have jumpers.

Kbps (kilobits per second) A measure of data transmission or network speed. 1Kbps is 1,024bps.

kernel The core of the operating system that interfaces directly with the hardware.

kilobits per second *See* Kbps.

kilobyte A kilobyte (K) contains 1,024 bytes. Your file sizes represented in the Windows Explorer, for example, are listed in kilobytes if the files are small. Kilo- is the prefix for 1,000 in the metric system.

L1 cache There are two levels of cache in a computer: L1 (level 1) and L2 (level 2). L1 cache, also known as internal cache, is a small amount of fast memory. *See also* L2 cache.

L2 cache The L2 cache is linked directly to the processor to make it react quicker to processor requests. All computers have L1 cache; not all computers have L2. *See also* L1 cache.

LAN (local area network) A set of computers and other equipment (printers, hubs, and so on) that communicate through local cabling using networking protocols. A LAN might refer to a workgroup or client/server network; it might cover computers in one room or office, in a building, or spanning several buildings.

laptop computer A portable computer with a flat screen and keyboard that fold together in one piece. Laptops are larger and heavier than notebooks. They are also older than notebook computers.

LAWN (local-area wireless network) A network that uses radio transmissions to communicate with other computers.

leased line Refers to a phone, ISDN, xDSL, frame relay, or other line that is rented for exclusive, 24-hours-a-day, 7-days-a-week use.

LED (light-emitting diode) A device that radiates light at a single frequency through plastic or glass.

legacy Refers to any pre-Windows software or hardware. Legacy cards, for example, don't support Plug and Play. Legacy software might be designed for Linux or Unix operating systems, even though it still works with Windows.

licensing These are issued by the manufacturer and state the legal uses of programs.

light-emitting diode *See* LED.

link (also called hyperlink) A phrase or picture that you click to jump to another page in a Web site.

LinkLocal Windows 98 includes another method of configuring a TCP/IP network called LinkLocal. LinkLocal creates automatic private IP addressing. You can use LinkLocal if you have a network that doesn't have a DHCP server and if your computer is not a host computer on the Internet.

Linux A free operating system that began in 1991. The Linux kernel runs on Intel and Alpha hardware. The program is in the general release and available under the GNU General Public License. There are hundreds of "flavors" of Linux available, including Mandrake, Red Hat, and many others.

local area network *See* LAN.

local printer Your local printer is attached directly to your computer with a parallel or serial cable or by means of wireless communications.

LocalTalk A protocol for networking Macintosh computers.

log on Logging on means you enter your username and password in a dialog box, and then Windows uses that information to authenticate you on the network. When you are authenticated, you gain access to the network resources for which you have access. Log in means the same as log on.

logical drive A logical drive isn't a physical drive in your computer; rather it is a partition on one drive that is given an arbitrary letter, such as E, F, G, and so on.

LonWorks A protocol used in home and building automation. You can connect up to 32,000 devices to a LonWorks network. Intelligent control devices, called nodes, communicate with each other by using the LonWorks protocol. Each node has the intelligence to use the protocol to perform its own control functions. Nodes might be sensors, motion detectors, instruments, and so on.

M *See* megabytes.

MAC (Media Access Control) address An Ethernet address also is called a MAC address. It's a number written as 12 hexadecimal digits — 0 through 9 and A through F — as in 0080001021ef. Alternatively, a MAC address might have six hexadecimal numbers separated by periods or colons, as in 0:80:0:2:21:ef. The MAC address is unique to each computer and does not identify the location of the computer, only the computer itself.

macro virus A macro virus travels in a Word document and is activated only when the document is opened in Word. If you don't open the document containing the macro, the macro isn't activated. You might catch a macro virus from an infected file on a floppy disk or attached to an e-mail message.

mail server A central point where the electronic mailboxes are stored. The server may be remote or central to the network.

map Network maps describe how a network is put together. Not only does the map show where the computers and peripherals are located, but it also tracks important information about wiring, networking hardware, and even software used throughout your system.

mapping a drive A method of reconnecting to a network drive and folder as a shortcut. You assign a drive letter — such as J, K, L, M, N, or other drive not currently in use — to represent the path to the resource.

MB *See* megabytes.

Mbps (megabits per second) A measure of data transmission or network speed equaling 1 million bits (or 1,000 kilobits) per second.

MCA (Micro Channel Architecture) A 32-bit expansion bus designed for multiprocessing. Expansion boards identify themselves, thus eliminating any conflicts created by manual configuration. Used only on IBM PS/2s.

meg *See* megabytes.

megabit A megabit (Mbit) equals 1,048,576 binary digits, or bits of data. In general, a megabit is the equivalent of 1 million bits.

megabits per second *See* Mbps.

megabytes (MB, M, or meg) A megabyte (MB) contains 1,048,576 bytes. Mega- is the prefix for 1 million in the metric system. It is used in representing file size, as well as computer memory and hard disk capacity.

megahertz *See* MHz.

mesh topology Represents a wide area network (WAN) used in large corporations, universities, and government agencies. Mesh uses multiple paths to connect multiple sites or buildings.

MHz (megahertz) One million cycles per second. A unit of measure for frequency.

Micro Channel Architecture *See* MCA.

microprocessor The processor chip in a computer. A microprocessor is miniaturized, whereas previous processors were built into integrated circuit boards with many large components.

Microsoft Client for NetWare Networks A client that's created by Microsoft to enable users to connect to a NetWare server over the network. As a NetWare client, Windows can share files, print, and use other resources on the server for which it has permissions.

Microsoft Exchange A mail program that supplies a universal inbox for e-mail. You can receive e-mail from a local network or the Internet, among others.

MIDI (Musical Instrument Digital Interface) A MIDI interface enables you to control synthesizers and other electronic instruments connected to the computer. MIDI is also a file type.

modem (MOdulate DEModulate) A device connected to the computer, either inside the box (internally) or externally, that enables the computer to communicate over telephone lines in analog waves with another modem and computer on the other end of the line.

motherboard The main circuit board on a computer. The motherboard includes the processor, RAM, support circuitry, and a bus controller.

Motion JPEG A variation of JPEG, this is a compression scheme for video files. *See also* JPEG.

Moving Picture Experts Group *See* MPEG.

MPC (Multimedia Personal Computer) A specification for multimedia hardware — speakers, sound cards, video cards, CD drives, and so on — that ensures the hardware is compatible, reliable, and meets certain quality standards.

MPEG (Moving Picture Experts Group) A graphics file format that enables video to be stored in compressed form.

MS-DOS–based application MS-DOS applications were built for the original MS-DOS operating system. Some MS-DOS programs can run in Windows and others cannot.

multimedia Includes any applications with sound and video enhancements. Some applications that take advantage of multimedia features are movies, music programs, education software, and games.

multimedia network A network that shares text, print, graphics, audio, digital, and full-motion data over a high-speed connection.

Multimedia Personal Computer *See* MPC.

multitasking The simultaneous execution of two or more programs in a Windows or OS/2 operating system.

multithreading A process by which Windows can multitask portions, or threads, of a program.

Musical Instrument Digital Interface *See* MIDI.

narrowband transmission One in which the data transfer is slow or has a small transfer rate.

NDIS (Network Driver Interface Specification) A set of functions that causes a request to be submitted to the operating system or causes a local action to be performed. Mainly, the NDIS enables protocol drivers to send and receive packets on the network.

NetBEUI (NetBIOS Extended User Interface) A Microsoft protocol you can use with any Windows program — most commonly used with Windows for Workgroups, Windows 95/98, and Windows NT, and very seldom used with Windows Me, 2000, and XP. NetBEUI is easy to set up, provides good performance, and is a fast protocol. NetBEUI uses very little memory and also provides good error detection over the network.

NetBIOS (Network Basic Input/Output System) A programming interface for developing client/server applications; NetBIOS also works with other protocols and various network types.

NetBIOS Extended User Interface *See* NetBEUI.

netiquette Netiquette, or Internet etiquette, is simply behaving politely and sensibly while online and in discourse with others, whether via e-mail, bulletin boards, or a chat program.

NETSTAT Short for network statistics, this is a command that is useful for tracking down network problems. Use NETSTAT to troubleshoot incoming or outgoing packet errors or to verify the presence of needed routes.

NetWare Novell's network operating system.

Net Watcher An application you can use on a network to monitor shared resources. You can view each user attached to a computer, as well as the folders and files they're using. You also can disconnect a user, close a file, add a shared folder, and more.

network A system that connects two or more computers plus peripherals (printers, CD-ROM drives, scanners, and so on) so that all computers can communicate and share resources with each other.

network adapter *See* network interface card.

network address Another way of referring to the IP address. The IP address is the address for a computer, printer, or other device on the network. *See also* IP.

network applications Network applications come in two parts: client and server. The server part of the application is installed on a server computer; on a workgroup network, it is installed on a workstation that serves as a host. The client part of the software installs on the rest of the computers on the network. The client requests some service, and the server grants the request.

Network Basic Input/Output System *See* NetBIOS.

network commands Windows includes several network commands you can use at the MS-DOS prompt. These commands enable you to view your current network connections, view any computer's shared resources, and even create permanent connections, or drive mappings.

Network Driver Interface Specification *See* NDIS.

Network File System *See* NFS.

network interface card (NIC) Also called a network card or a network adapter, this is A circuit board installed in your computer that uses specific software drivers to work with your computer and attaches to the network by means of a network cable or a wireless connection.

network layer One of the ISO/OSI layers. The network layer defines the protocols for data routing, to make sure the data gets to the correct destination.

network operating system (NOS) Designed specifically for a server, a NOS offers many features and tools that help you manage clients, applications, security, and other facets of the network.

network path A path that leads to a computer on the network, and then to a folder or file on that computer. For example, \\Sue\My Documents\My Pictures leads to the My Pictures folder on Sue's computer over the network. (The double backslashes tell the operating system to locate the following over the network instead of on the local computer.)

network printer A printer attached to a computer on the network; you access a network printer over the network.

network technology Refers to the type of wiring and hardware you use and the general speed of the network. Ethernet networks, for example, use Ethernet cards and hubs, and the speed is 10 Mbps. Phone line networks use phone line network cards, and the speed is between 56 Kbps and 1.5 Mbps.

newsgroup On the Internet, a group of individuals who post messages about a specific topic. Newsgroups use Usenet, a network of thousands of topics and posting sites.

NFS (Network File System) NFS enables a computer to use files and peripherals as if they were local.

NIC *See* network interface card.

node Any device connected to a network, such as a client, server, hub, printer, and so on.

noninterlacing Interlacing refers to how a monitor refreshes, or redraws, the screen. Interlacing monitors skip every other line during the redraw process, thus producing a flicker or jitter on the screen. Noninterlaced monitors scan every line, providing the best screen quality.

NOS *See* network operating system.

notebook computer A portable computer with a flat screen and keyboard that fold together to form one piece. Notebooks are smaller than laptops.

Novell NetWare A 32-bit operating system that runs on 386 and higher processors. NetWare works with a variety of client computers, including Windows, Macs, and Linux.

null modem A cable used to connect two computers. Data flows from one computer to the other, only in one direction at a time, so the two computers cannot try to send data to each other simultaneously. A null modem cable is an RS-232-C cable. A null modem cable connects the serial ports.

OCR (optical character recognition) A type of program that enables you to scan typewritten text and convert it to a file you can read and edit with a word processor.

octet A set of eight. With computers, octet refers to the 8 bits in 1 byte.

offline Refers to a device that is not ready to accept input, such as a printer or your modem.

online Working on a computer while it is connected to another computer, via a network, the Internet, and such.

open source A type of software freely distributed. The source code for the software, such as with Perl or Linux, is free to everyone so they can help develop the software and customize it.

Open Systems Interconnection *See* OSI model.

operating system (OS) The software that controls hardware resources and enables you to interact with the computer's applications. Windows XP, Macintosh System 8, 9, and OS X, and Slackware are operating systems.

optical character recognition *See* OCR.

OS *See* operating system.

OSI model (Open Systems Interconnection) A seven-layer model that establishes a standard set of protocols for interoperability between networked computers.

packet Data is sent over a network in packets, or blocks. Each packet not only contains a part of the data you want to send, but also contains the name of the sender and the receiver and some error-control information to help make sure the packet makes it to its destination in one piece.

palmtop computer Also called a handheld device, a palmtop computer is a PC or other electronic device that has many of the same features a computer has, but the palmtop fits in your hand. *See* handheld device.

parallel port An input/output port that manages information 8 bits at a time; parallel ports are often used for connecting printers to a computer as well. You generally can find a high-speed direct parallel cable at any computer store.

parameters In MS-DOS commands, parameters are additional information the command needs to continue or to complete the task. The parameter defines the object on which the command acts.

partitioning Refers to dividing your hard disk into sections. The operating system treats different partitions on the hard disk as if they were separate drives.

passkey An authentication method used with wireless access points. Generally, a passkey phrase is entered by the user; the phrase (words) generates an alphanumeric key that you enter into a second access point so that the two WAPs can communicate.

patch panel Patch panels contain 8, 12, or 24 jacks within a strip for easy connection to solid cables. You can attach the patch panel to the wall, insert the solid cables, and then insert the patch cables on the other side—leading to your hub—for safe and effective wiring of your network.

path Defines the complete location of a folder or file, such as C:\Windows\Program files. A network path begins with two backslashes, to identify the path as a network path, such as \\Sue\My Documents.

PC (personal computer) A microcomputer for use by an individual, as in an office or at home or school. Also, an IBM-compatible computer, as opposed to a Macintosh.

PC card A type of PCMCIA card. The card is smaller than normal adapter cards and works with portable computers to provide functionality for modems, sound, video, and other devices.

PC companion Similar to a notebook PC but costing considerably less, PC companions are lightweight devices that have an instant-on capability, and maintain keyboards that are large enough for touch typing. The PC companion enables users to send and receive e-mail and perform simple word processing, task management, scheduling, and so on.

PCI (Peripheral Component Interface bus) An Intel specification that defines a local bus that enables up to ten PCI-compliant expansion cards to be plugged in to the computer.

PCMCIA (Personal Computer Memory Card International Association) PCMCIA is a standard for portable computers. The PCMCIA card is usually about the size of a credit card. There are several versions, or types, of PCMCIA cards; the types define the thickness and uses of the card.

PDA (personal digital assistant) *See* handheld device.

peer-to-peer network A network in which all computers on the network have an equal rank; all share their resources—including files, folders, drives, printers, and so on—with all others on the network. *See also* workgroup network.

peripheral Any piece of equipment attached to a computer, such as a CD-ROM drive, tape drive, Zip or other drive, printer, scanner, digital camera, and so on.

Peripheral Component Interface bus *See* PCI.

permissions Similar to rights, permissions are characteristics given to users of a network to allow or prevent access to files and other resources on the network. *See* Rights.

personal computer *See* PC.

Personal Computer Memory Card International Association *See* PCMCIA.

personal digital assistant (PDA) *See* handheld device.

physical layer One of the ISO/OSI layers. The physical layer defines the cabling.

PING The PING command sends TCP/IP packets to the designated computer. If PING is successful, TCP/IP sends the packets back. Use PING to verify that the TCP/IP configuration is correct, that local computers are communicating with each other, and that remote computers are communicating with local computers.

Plug and Play A Windows specification that makes it easy to install adapter cards and other hardware. All you need to do is insert the hardware and turn Windows on. Windows automatically configures the IRQ, DMA, and other settings for the hardware.

PnP or P 'n' P *See* Plug and Play.

point of presence *See* POP.

Point-to-Point Protocol *See* PPP.

Point-to-Point Tunneling Protocol *See* PPTP.

POP (point of presence) The e-mail host name. The host is the server that holds the e-mail messages for you until you log on and get your messages.

port The device that enables data to transfer to and from a computer or other piece of equipment. A parallel port, for example, enables the computer to send printing data across a cable to the printer. A serial port enables information to travel to a modem or other device.

post A term for sending a message to a newsgroup or other service.

power line network In a power line network, you use electrical outlets in your home to attach computers for sharing files, printers, Internet accounts, and peripherals. It's important to note that the transmission speeds for power line networks are slow. Data transmission speeds are around 350 Kbps.

PPP (Point-to-Point Protocol) This protocol is often used with remote access, because it enables computers to load other protocols — such as TCP/IP, NetBEUI, and so on — in addition to the PPP.

PPTP (Point-to-Point Tunneling Protocol) A protocol that enables you to have secure access to a virtual private network.

presentation layer One of the ISO/OSI layers. The presentation layer identifies the way the data is formatted.

PRI (Primary Rate Interface) PRI lines are a type of ISDN line that are more expensive than BRI because of a higher bandwidth connection. PRI supplies speeds up to 1.5 Mbps.

print queue An area in which all print jobs for a specific printer wait to be printed. The print queue holds the jobs so that you can get on with your work in Windows. As the printer becomes available to print a job, the queue sends them along, one by one.

print server The server that manages the printing for all users on a network. It receives all requests for print jobs sent by the networked PCs, places the jobs in a queue to wait their turn, and then routes the job to available printers attached to the server.

program virus Viruses that attach themselves to executable files and load themselves into memory when you run the file. The file might be an EXE or COM file, but it also might be a SYS, DLL, BIN, or other file on your system. If you double-click an infected EXE file, such as an animation file you receive from a friend, the virus activates and spreads through your computer.

proprietary Describes a protocol or communications system that was developed by a company rather than one that follows established standards.

protocol Part of software is a language that the computers can use to communicate, called a protocol. Windows contains three such protocols from which you can choose.

proxy server These servers control what the user can and cannot access on the Internet. Proxy servers also might reduce user wait times by relieving bandwidth congestion, offer network security features, log events, and so on. Some proxy server software is installed on a dedicated computer that acts as a gateway and barrier between the LAN and the Internet.

QoS Short for quality of service. QoS is Microsoft's addition to Windows 2000 and XP, although it is used by other manufacturers, to enable a smoother flow of traffic on the network. An administrator can set higher and lower priorities on a network using the QoS settings.

quick logon This type of logon ignores any network drive connections you might have set so that you can get on the network and start working immediately.

radio frequency (RF) A method of wireless networking, radio frequency describes the number of times per second a radio wave vibrates (900 MHz, in this case). Radio signals penetrate light obstacles, such as thin walls.

radio frequency shielding Also called RF shielding, this is usually a thin piece of metal placed between a circuit board and other electronic equipment to help prevent interference with the circuit board.

RAM (random access memory) Temporary memory in a computer. The memory stores the data related to a task that the processor is currently dealing with.

RAMDAC (RAM digital-to-analog converter) In a video card, RAMDAC is the electronic component that changes the digital video signal of the card to a signal the monitor can read. RAMDAC speed affects the speed of images appearing on the screen. The standard RAMDAC is 135 MHz, although some cards are faster. The faster the RAMDAC, the better.

Random Access Memory *See* RAM.

RARP (Reverse Address Resolution Protocol) One of the TCP/IP protocols; it translates physical network addresses into IP addresses.

read-only access Sharing option that enables others to open and view folders, or open, view, and copy files; however, read-only access doesn't enable others to modify a file or delete anything.

read-only memory *See* ROM.

real time Describes an event or process that is currently taking place. A good example of real time is this: When you're talking on the telephone to someone, you're talking in real time. When you leave a message on someone's answering machine and that person hears the message later, that person is not hearing your message in real time.

Red Hat Linux A popular distribution of Linux.

refresh rate Describes how many times per second the image is refreshed, or redrawn, on the screen. The faster the refresh rate, the less flicker you see on screen. The default setting for most monitors is 60 Hz, but you should use 75 to 85 Hz to reduce flicker and eyestrain.

Registry The area of the Windows operating systems that contains all configuration files for the computer user. For example, the Registry lists user preferences, desktop colors, fonts, and program settings. If the Registry becomes corrupted, Windows might stop working altogether.

Registry keys The Registry is organized in keys, or folders, that describe specific information about the computer or user. The organization is a hierarchy: Six keys represent all configurations and settings. Contained within the keys are subkeys and values.

Registry subkeys Distinct categories represented by folders and found within Registry keys. Each subkey holds values that describe hardware, software, or other computer components.

remote A hardware device that enables a user to communicate with another computer or networked device; for example, there are remote sensors you can use with your SmartHome, there are routers you can use to remotely connect to another computer, and there are wireless remotes to connect your computers.

remote access Refers to the process of attaching to a network from another location and accessing resources from the remote computer.

remote administration Enabling remote administration allows a user to create, change, and monitor shares on your computer. Windows lets you assign a password to this permission so that only a person who knows the password can perform these tasks. The person who knows the password can monitor the workstations from any computer on the network.

remote file transfer Another common method of remote access is file transfer. File transfer involves uploading a file to or downloading a file from the remote computer.

remote node The most common method of remote access is when a computer connects to an office or corporate network. The remote computer user accesses any of the resources on the office network and works as if he or she were actually in the office, sharing programs and files with coworkers.

Remote Registry Service A network service that enables programs such as the System Policy Editor or System Monitor to change the Registry in a network computer

repeater A network device that boosts and amplifies an analog signal in the network.

repeater functions Refer to the retransmission of network packets when a collision or timing problem takes place.

resolution Describes the number of pixels a device such as a scanner or printer applies to an image. Resolution is measured by a grid, such as 300×300 pixels (or dots) per square inch. The higher the resolution, the better the image output and the more expensive the scanner.

resource Any item or component that can be shared with other computers on the network, including files, drives, folders, printers, CD-ROM drives, Zip drives, and tape drives, among others.

Reverse Address Resolution Protocol *See* RARP.

RF *See* radio frequency.

rights Characteristics given by a user or administrator on the network to prevent or allow access to files on the network. Common rights include all, execute, read-only, write, and so on.

ring topology A networking layout in which computers are connected by a closed loop, or ring. The ring topology uses a hub to redirect network packets.

RJ-11 A four-wire connector used to join a telephone line to a wall plate or a communication peripheral, such as a modem.

RJ-45 An eight-wire connector used to join twisted-pair networking cable.

ROM (read-only memory) A chip that permanently stores data, also called firmware.

router A network device that connects two or more network segments; a router then can choose the best way for network packets to travel the network to arrive quickly and efficiently at their destination.

RS-232 A serial connection port on a PC, used for connecting a mouse, printer, modem, or other device.

RS-232 cable This cable transmits data at about a 20 Kbps. A serial cable generally used for connecting a computer to a peripheral device, the RS-232 has a maximum cable limit of 15 meters, or about 50 feet. Used for Direct Cable Connection in Windows. *See also* Direct Cable Connection.

RS-485 RS-485 is a serial connection port that enables you to connect from 10 to 32 devices.

Samba A freeware software program that enables clients to access and use files with any operating system that uses SMB/CIFS. Users can use files, print, and share other resources. Samba is normally used on Linux computers, although Windows and Macintosh can also use Samba.

scheduling software A server application that organizes and manages the calendar while users fill in their meetings, to-do lists, appointments, and so on. Any user can access the scheduling program at any time to view anyone's appointments, with permissions.

script files Mini-programs that automate logging in to another network, such as a remote network or the Internet. Generally included in a script file is the username and password. When you dial up another computer on a network, the script enters your username and password, so you don't have to type them.

SCSI (Small Computer System Interface) A standard high-speed parallel interface used to connect the microprocessor to peripheral devices, such as drives and printers, or to connect computers together or to a LAN.

SDRAM (synchronous dynamic random access memory) SDRAM is currently the standard memory type. SDRAM supports burst access modes.

Secure Sockets Layer *See* SSL.

Serial Line Internet Protocol *See* SLIP.

serial port A serial port transmits data a bit more slowly than parallel ports, one bit at a time. Serial cables transmit data sequentially over only one pair of wires. Since parallel cables transmit data simultaneously over multiple lines, parallel is the faster of the two connection methods. A serial port is also a COM port.

server The computer on a network that provides services — such as file storage, print management, Internet access, and so on — to other computers on the network.

server application An application that acts as a host to client programs. The application might be installed on a server computer or on another workstation in a workgroup network. A database management application is an example of a server application.

Server Message Block *See* SMB.

session layer One of the ISO/OSI layers. The session layer maintains the connection, or session, for as long as it takes to transmit the packets. The session layer also performs security and administration functions.

share A resource that is designated as usable by two or more computers — a folder or printer, for example, can be considered a share.

share-level access control With a peer-to-peer network, you use share-level access control to enable all users to share files, folders, printers, and other resources on their computer. Each user sets his or her shares, adds passwords if desired, and so on.

shareware Programs you can try out before you buy. Usually, you can download the shareware, try it out, and then send the money to the manufacturer if you plan to use it.

sharing The process of several computers using a resource in a cooperative manner.

sheetfed scanner These scanners move the page being scanned past the scanning head. Sheetfed scanners are less exact than flatbeds, because it's difficult to move a sheet of paper without distorting the image that's on it.

shielded twisted-pair (STP) cable Cable with a foil shield and copper braid surrounding the pairs of wires. STP provides high-speed transmission for long distances.

Simple Mail Transfer Protocol *See* SMTP.

Simple Network Management Protocol *See* SNMP.

SLIP (Serial Line Internet Protocol) An older protocol that isn't used much anymore; however, you still might run into servers using SLIP.

Small Computer System Interface *See* SCSI.

SmartHome *See* intelligent home.

smart phone A smart phone takes multiple technologies — cell phone, faxes, pagers, PDAs, and so on — and integrates them into one product you can use to perform all your tasks.

SMB (Server Message Block) SMB enables a computer to use network resources as if they were local. SMB is more commonly used these days, since Macintosh and Linux make use of the protocol.

SMTP (Simple Mail Transfer Protocol) The e-mail host name. SMTP is the part of the system that sends the mail out to other e-mail servers on the Internet.

SNMP (Simple Network Management Protocol) A set of standards for communications with devices — such as routers, hubs, and switches — connected to a TCP/IP network. SNMP, a TCP/IP protocol, manages and monitors the network.

software-controlled access Refers to the situation in which you are permitted to attach to only one program, such as accounting software, remotely.

Sound Blaster The Sound Blaster sound card is a popular adapter made by Creative Labs. The card is compatible with a wide variety of hardware and software. The Sound Blaster is so compatible with other hardware that other sound cards advertise as being Sound Blaster-compatible.

spam Use of a mailing list on the Internet to broadcast unwanted e-mail to hundreds of users.

spool A temporary holding area for documents waiting to be printed.

spooler The print queue is the list of jobs waiting to be printed, but it is the print spooler (created from the acronym SPOOL — Simultaneous Peripheral Operation On Line) that receives, processes, and schedules the jobs in the queue. Each print job is saved to a separate file and printed in turn when the printer becomes free.

spread-spectrum radio frequencies An RF standard physical interface that can pass through heavier walls. Spread-spectrum signals are fairly secure against tampering from outside sources. Additionally, spread-spectrum products provide 1 to 2 Mbps data rates at a range from 50 feet to 1,000 feet, depending on the building construction, interference sources, and other factors.

SQL (Structured Query Language) Pronounced "sequel," SQL is a specialized programming language used in databases.

SSL (Secure Sockets Layer) A protocol designed to enable encrypted, authenticated communications across the Internet.

standalone A computer that is not connected to a network.

star topology Also called spanning tree, the star topology uses a hub as a central connecting device. Each computer is attached to the hub with its own cable, and signals are passed from station to station until the designated computer is found.

startup disk Also called emergency startup disk, this is a system disk with the files it needs to boot your computer to the MS-DOS prompt.

STP *See* shielded twisted-pair.

streaming Describes the constant flow of audio and video files so that they look like they're running in real time, without pauses, jitters, or other interference.

Structured Query Language *See* SQL.

subnet mask Enables the computer in one segment of a network to see computers in another segment. The ISP uses a subnet mask — such as 255.255.255.255 — to communicate with other segments on the Internet network.

subnetwork A smaller network connected to a larger and more powerful system by a bridge or router.

SuSE A popular distribution of Linux.

SVGA (Super VGA) SVGA monitors offer more colors and images and have replaced VGA as today's standard on new PCs.

switch In MS-DOS commands, a switch modifies the way the command performs the task. You separate a switch from the command with a space and a forward slash (/). Normally, switches are single letters or numbers that represent the modification.

switch box (also called a/b box) A set of circuits into which you plug two or more devices. A simple switch knob on the front of the box enables you to change back and forth between computers; other switch boxes automatically make the switches.

system.dat A file that contains information about the hardware and software settings on the computer. This file includes all the necessary information to start Windows, load device drivers, and prepare the operating system to run the software. The system.dat file is located in the computer's \Windows directory.

system disk A floppy disk that includes certain system files to enable it to boot your computer. Use a system disk when your hard disk crashes, for example.

System Monitor You can use the System Monitor to view your computer's network or disk access in a graphical manner. The program enables you to monitor running processes, memory usage, dial-up access, and more.

System Policy Editor A network administration program you can use with a client/server network. Using the System Policy Editor, you can configure settings that control individual users, individual computers, or groups of users.

T1 A high-quality, reliable communications line. Total speed is 1.544 Mbps. Because of the expense, however, T1 is best for corporations connecting a large number of users.

Tablet A small, thin PC that is portable, accepts hand-printed lettering, and can translate the lettering into typed data the computer can understand.

TAN (tiny area network) A small network, usually set up in the home.

TAPI (Telephony Application Programming Interface) TAPI provides the method programs needed to work with modems. All Windows communications programs communicate with TAPI, which then issues the appropriate commands to a modem.

T-connector A T-connector is also used with coaxial cable. T-connectors attach two thin Ethernet cables and provide a third connection for the network interface card.

TCP (Transmission Control Protocol) A higher-level protocol than IP, it provides continuing connections between programs. TCP also makes IP datagrams smaller and faster. TCP divides datagrams into smaller segments to fit the physical requirements of the servers on the network. It then uses IP to transmit the segments of data.

TCP/IP (Transmission Control Protocol/Internet Protocol) A network protocol used on the Internet and on local area networks. TCP/IP is a set of communications protocols supported by various manufacturers and vendors. Corporations, universities, and other agencies use TCP/IP to communicate over the Internet.

telecommuting Refers to using remote access to keep in touch with the office. You perform your work at home and send it in via the remote network connection.

Telephony Application Programming Interface *See* TAPI.

Telnet A terminal emulation protocol that enables you to connect to a remote service while in Windows, one of the TCP/IP protocols.

terabyte A terabyte represents 1,000 gigabytes.

terminal A device that enables you to send commands to a computer somewhere else. Terminals are simple, consisting of only a keyboard and monitor. Terminal emulation on your Windows computer displays a black screen on which you enter cryptic commands to connect to another computer.

terminator A component or device that is placed at each end of a cable to absorb free signals.

ThinNet Coaxial cabling is also called ThinNet or Thin Ethernet cabling, and it's used with 10Base-2.

thread A concurrent process that's part of a larger process or program.

throughput A measure of the data transfer rate through the network. Throughput is measured on the network as a whole.

tiny area network *See* TAN.

token ring This protocol uses the token topology and can transmit data at 16 Mbps and 100 Mbps. Token ring is usually used for larger networks. The networking hardware and wiring is expensive and complicated.

topology The arrangement of cables, networking hardware, and computers on a network, as opposed to network technology, which refers to the type of wiring, network card, and general speed of the network.

traceroute Also referred to as trace, this utility maps the specific path traveled to a destination, including routers, gateways, and computers.

traffic The flow of messages and data over the network. Data transmission usually is measured in kilobits per second or megabits per second. *See also* Kbps and Mbps.

Transmission Control Protocol *See* TCP.

Transmission Control Protocol/Internet Protocol *See* TCP/IP.

transport layer One of the ISO/OSI layers. The transport layer defines protocols for error checking and message formation.

Trojan horse Destructive programs that hacker programmers sometimes hide in normal software. These programs don't necessarily copy themselves or spread from machine to machine, but they can damage or encrypt your data just the same.

twisted-pair cabling Wiring used in networks. There are two types of twisted-pair cabling: unshielded twisted-pair (UTP) and shielded twisted-pair (STP). UTP has fast throughput and is less expensive than STP. STP provides a high degree of protection from external interference and enables the use of greater cable distances.

UCM *See* universal cable module.

UDP (User Datagram Protocol) One of the TCP/IP protocols, UDP divides datagrams into segments and sends them over the network by using IP. UDP doesn't guarantee the datagrams will arrive intact or even at all. UDP is only used with some programs, not all.

Uniform Resource Locator *See* URL.

uninterruptible power supply *See* UPS.

universal cable module (UCM) A parallel cable, the UCM supports connection of different types of parallel ports.

universal serial bus *See* USB.

unshielded twisted-pair (UTP) Unshielded twisted-pair cable contains two or more pairs of twisted copper wires; however, UTP is easier to install, costs less, limits signaling speeds, and has a shorter maximum cable-segment length than STP.

upload The act of sending a file to another computer on a network or over the Internet.

UPS (uninterruptible power supply) A useful tool for your computers, whether they're on a network or not. A UPS is a battery backup that attaches to your computer or multiple computers. The UPS kicks on in case of a power outage so that you can save the files you're working on and shut down your computer in an orderly fashion.

upstream speed Also called upload speed, this describes the speed at which information travels from your home to its destination.

URL (Uniform Resource Locator) The standard method of addressing on the Internet. A sample address might look like this: `http://www.microsoft.com`. The URL is the full address, or computer identifier, on the Web. URLs contain numerous slashes and periods (dots) that separate the parts of the address, similar to the way you separate folders in a path.

USB (universal serial bus) USB ports and cables connect high-speed peripheral devices. The USB port has an industry-standard connector that enables you to install a variety of devices. Because of the design of USB, you don't have to turn the computer off when installing new devices, as you do with other ports and cables.

Usenet A network of thousands of newsgroups on the Internet.

user.dat This file contains login names, settings for the Start menu, desktop colors and icons, and other information specific to the user. The user.dat file is automatically stored in the \Windows directory when you install Windows.

User Datagram Protocol *See* UDP.

user-level access control User-level access control enables the administrator of a client/server network to assign and manage shared resources.

username An individual's identification, in name or number format, used to gain access to the Internet or a network.

user profile When a user logs on to Windows, the operating system checks the Registry for the user's profile. The user profile contains information about the user's Windows settings and configurations.

UTP *See* unshielded twisted-pair.

V.32bis A CCITT standard for14,400 bps modems.

V.33 A CCITT standard for 12,000 and 14,400 bps modems used over four-wire, leased circuits.

V.34 A standard that defines a 28,800 bps modem over a dial-up line, with error correction and data compression techniques included. V.34 is a mature and stable standard.

V.90 A standard used for 56 Kbps modems.

vertical software A vertical application is one designed specifically for a particular business, such as real estate sales, restaurant delivery systems, retail point-of-sale, theater seating, lumber inventory, print job estimates, and so on. Vertical accounting programs are common and standard in business today.

videoconferencing A method of real-time communications in which both parties see and hear each other via the computer.

video RAM The memory built into a video card. Video RAM determines how fast graphics appear on the screen.

virtual private network (VPN) A network between remote users and a company's private local area network; the connection between the two, however, is through a public network system, such as the Internet. A VPN provides safe and secure paths for the company and user, even though the connection is public.

virus A computer program that can disrupt or destroy your files, file system, software, or hardware. A virus might display only a message, or it could erase or reformat your hard disk.

VPN *See* virtual private network.

V-standards Define speed, wiring, and error correction in modems and other telecommunications devices.

WAN (wide area network) A large or corporate network of computers connected over long distances, such as across town, states, or a country.

WAP (wireless access point) *See* access point.

WAV WAV stands for sound wave. WAV files contain digital sound and are very large.

wavetable Wavetable sound cards generate music by using actual instrument samples so that the instruments sound more real than with FM synthesis.

Web browser *See* browser.

Web server A Web server can be hardware or software. As hardware, it is a powerful computer, with lots of disk space and RAM, on which Web server software is installed. Web server software manages the intranet and Internet documents and applications. If you expand your intranet to the Internet, a Web server also can act as a Gopher and FTP server.

WFW *See* Windows for Workgroups.

wide area network *See* WAN.

wideband network Also known as a broadband network. A wideband signal refers to a signal capable of being distributed over a large area, and quickly.

WinCE *See* Windows CE.

Windows 2000 Professional The client version of the former NT 5 operating system. The server version is called Windows 2000 Server and Advanced Server. The interface is similar to other Windows operating systems, but the 2000 OS is much more automated than previous versions. It also uses many wizards to help in setup and configuration.

Windows 95/98 Operating systems employing a graphical user interface to enable the user to manipulate data and software programs. Windows 95 and 98 are similar in that they operate, network, and look very much alike. Both OSs enable the user to efficiently use the computer without using cryptic commands. Windows 98 is an upgrade to Windows 95, offering advanced features such as FAT32, AGP and USB support, and DVD and ACPI support.

Windows CE (WinCE) Windows CE is a handheld operating system, but it's moving into use with other portable computers. The WinCE operating system takes about 200K of space, and the file system is based on FAT16. WinCE is a miniaturized Windows environment. Windows CE programs include word processing, e-mail, limited Web browsing, and a few games. Pocket Internet Explorer includes JScript, Pocket Word supports color printing, and Pocket Outlook offers contact management.

Windows for Workgroups (WFW) Also known as Windows 3.11, Windows for Workgroups was the first networkable Windows program. Windows 3.11 computers created a useful workgroup network for small businesses.

Windows Internet Naming Service *See* WINS.

Windows Me A Windows operating system made for home users who are not computer-literate. Windows Me configures everything for you; all you have to do is start the computer and go to work. Windows Me does not network to more than five computers and does not recognize a server in your network.

Windows NT Server A 32-bit network operating system that supports multitasking, security logging, error tracking, and user accounts over a network.

Windows NT Workstation The client operating system paired with NT Server. NT looks similar to Windows 95/98, but it has many more networking tools and features added to the operating system. With NT Workstation, for example, you have more control over who can access your files and resources and how much access each individual or group has.

Windows XP Home Windows XP is built using the Windows 2000 engine so that the operating system is friendly, easy to operate, and more secure. Windows XP includes more file security and stability, the Internet Connection Firewall, easy-to-use wizards for configuration, and system restore and analysis capabilities. Windows XP Home is perfect for a small network — three to five computers; however, you cannot use Windows XP Home edition with a server or with a larger network. *See also* Windows XP Professional.

Windows XP Professional Windows XP Professional differs from Windows XP Home in several ways: Networking features are more flexible and you can easily build your network as it grows; remote access of your home computer via laptop or dial-up is more efficient; sharing resources — such as printers, scanners, and the like — is easier and more flexible with Professional edition; and security features are more involved and safer than with Windows XP Home edition. *See also* Windows XP Home for more detail about Windows XP in general.

Windows XP Tablet Built on Windows XP Professional, Windows XP Tablet edition is similar to other Windows XP operating systems. The differences are the Tablet edition offers a Windows Journaling feature, handwriting recognition, text input panel, sticky notes, voice recognition, and built-in stylus drivers.

WINS (Windows Internet Naming Service) WINS is another method of resolving computer names to IP addresses. WINS supplies a database that maintains IP addresses and NetBIOS (Network Input/Ouput System) computer names.

wireless Connections for network computers that do not use wire; instead, devices are attached to computers, and the computers are placed within line of sight of each other. Infrared and radio waves are two forms of wireless connections.

wireless access point (WAP) *See* access point.

workflow software Workflow programs send documents throughout the network to the people who need them. Think of workflow as a paper trail. The program sends the documents to their destination; after action is taken on that document, it is forwarded to the next recipient.

workgroup network Workgroup, or peer-to-peer, networking refers to a group of computers (from 2 to 50 or even more sometimes) that share all of their resources, including printers, CD drives, hard drives, files, and programs. Workgroup networking can be made more secure; for example, any computer on the network can stop sharing its resources at any time. However, most computers on a workgroup network share. *See also* peer-to-peer network.

workstation In networking, a personal computer attached to the network. Not the file server. Also called a client computer.

World Wide Web *See* WWW.

worm A virus program that contains code that can gain access to computers and networks once a computer on the network has become infected. Worms delete, modify, distribute, and otherwise manipulate data.

WWW (World Wide Web) As part of the Internet, a group of services and special-interest groups. WWW, or Web, browsers display pages created by these different groups. Browse the Web for information on just about anything: products, services, travel, entertainment, and more.

X-10 A communications protocol that uses a power line carrier to control compatible devices. An X-10 transmitter device sends low-voltage signals superimposed on the 110 VAC power lines. Any X-10 receiver device connected to the household 110 VAC power lines receives the signal, but only responds to signals carrying its own receiver address.

Zip drives Removable drives that are often found on computers these days. A Zip cartridge holds 100MB or 250MB, and it's easy to use, transport, and store.

Index

Continued

Continued

Continued

Continued

Continued